www.wadsworth.com

wadsworth.com is the World Wide Web site for Wadsworth and is your direct source to dozens of online resources.

At *wadsworth.com* you can find out about supplements, demonstration software, and student resources. You can also send email to many of our authors and preview new publications and exciting new technologies.

wadsworth.com
Changing the way the world learns®

Social Work and Social Welfare

An Introduction

Social Work and Social Welfare

AN INTRODUCTION
Fourth Edition

ROSALIE AMBROSINO
University of Texas at San Antonio

JOSEPH HEFFERNAN
Emeritus, University of Texas at Austin

GUY SHUTTLESWORTH
Emeritus, University of Texas at Austin

ROBERT AMBROSINO
University of Texas at Austin

BROOKS/COLE

THOMSON LEARNING

Australia • Canada • Mexico • Singapore • Spain • United Kingdom • United States

BROOKS/COLE
THOMSON LEARNING™

Social Work Executive Editor: Lisa Gebo
Assistant Editor: JoAnne von Zastrow
Editorial Assistant: Sheila Walsh
Marketing Manager: Caroline Concilla
Marketing Assistant: Jessica McFadden
Project Editor: Lisa Weber
Print Buyer: Mary Noel
Permissions Editor: Joohee Lee

Production Service: Penmarin Books
Photo Researcher: Connie Hathaway
Copy Editor: Laura Larson
Cover Designer: Yvo Riezebos
Cover Images: PhotoDisc
Cover Printer: RR Donnelley & Sons, Crawfordsville
Compositor: Parkwood Composition
Printer: RR Donnelley & Sons, Crawfordsville

Frontispiece: Visitors at the capitol mall in Washington, DC, view panels of the AIDS Memorial Quilt, made by friends and relatives of individuals who died from the disease. The quilt honors more than 83,000 persons and includes more than 40,000 panels, which cover 25 football fields when laid out.

For more information, contact
Wadsworth/Thomson Learning
10 Davis Drive
Belmont, CA 94002-3098
USA
http://www.wadsworth.com

International Headquarters
Thomson Learning
International Division
290 Harbor Drive, 2nd Floor
Stamford, CT 06902-7477
USA

UK/Europe/Middle East/South Africa
Thomson Learning
Berkshire House
168-173 High Holborn
London WC1V 7AA
United Kingdom

Asia
Thomson Learning
60 Albert Street, #15-01
Albert Complex
Singapore 189969

Canada
Nelson Thomson Learning
1120 Birchmount Road
Toronto, Ontario M1K 5G4
Canada

Library of Congress Cataloging-in-Publication Data

Social work and social welfare / Rosalie Ambrosino . . . [et al.].—4th ed.
  p. cm.
  Rev. ed. of: Social work and social welfare / Joseph Heffernan, Guy Shuttlesworth, Rosalie Ambrosino. 3rd ed. c1997.
  Includes bibliographical references and index.
  ISBN 0-534-52599-7
  1. Social service—United States. 2. Public welfare—United States. I. Ambrosino, Rosalie. II. Heffernan, W. Joseph, 1932– Social work and social welfare.

HV91 .H424 2000
361.3'2—dc21

00-043231

Contents in Brief

Contents

Chapter 3

The Systems/Ecological Perspective: Understanding Social Work and Social Welfare   52

Chapter 9

Mental Health, Substance Abuse, and Developmental Disabilities   220

Chapter 10

Health Care 276

Chapter 11

The Needs of Children, Youth, and Families   322

Chapter 17

International Social Work 517

Part Four

WHAT DOES THE FUTURE HOLD? 537

Chapter 18

The Future of Social Work and Social Welfare 539

Preface

The fourth edition of this book is written at a critical time not only for the United States but the entire world. As we begin the new millennium, the United States continues to grapple with long-time social policy issues. Domestic policy issues include health care, the increasing numbers of persons living in poverty, homelessness, mental health issues, child abuse, and school violence, all exacerbated by racism, sexism, and homophobia. Foreign policy issues are also of paramount importance, even more now that we are part of a global economy. Wars and other violations of human rights, famines and other natural disasters, and policies of other nations continually impact the United States on a daily basis, raising critical issues regarding how to balance our need to pay attention to our own citizens and our role in an increasingly complex world.

At the beginning of the 20th century, the roots of social work were just beginning to take hold. It was one of the most prolific eras for social and economic justice in the history of the social work profession. The settlement house movement was in full force. Social workers (mainly women) were making significant contributions to social welfare policy that affected the lives of immigrants, the poor, the homeless, delinquent youth, those without medical care, individuals in need of mental health services, and many others. It was a time of massive social and economic change. Social workers sought to bring order out of chaos, to connect private troubles to public causes, to help the disenfranchised create better lives for themselves. Most of all, it was a period of hope—hope for a better future for all of humanity.

This new century is also a period of hope. It is a critical time for social workers as they advocate for policies and programs they believe will most effectively address these issues and also provide services and support to those vulnerable populations most likely to be affected by rapidly changing social policies and programs. Just as social welfare needs are diverse, so is the social work profession. This book is about the many social welfare issues facing the United States today and the many roles that social work professionals play in responding to those issues.

Approaches to social welfare have changed over the decades; however, the needs to which the social work profession responds remain much the same. These needs remain, not because the social work profession has been ineffective but because as society advances, so do the ways that we address social needs. Thomas Merton has suggested that in a community of saints, sin needs to be redefined—so, too, with social needs and social responses. There is a rhythm of social responses to social welfare problems. At this time, poverty, homelessness, AIDS, substance abuse, child abuse and neglect, teen pregnancy, youth violence, and inadequacies of health care stand high on the social agenda. At other times, these problems are barely perceived as problems at all, while other problems demand the limelight and receive the bulk of public attention. It is our intent that this text will help students develop a frame of reference to understand social welfare and an approach to address social issues which will serve them well in times of commitment and retrenchment.

We have reworked large portions of this fourth edition to reflect changes in the social work profession as well as in the social welfare policy arena. In keeping with the current Council on Social Work Education Curriculum Policy Statement, the text takes a generalist practice perspective in addressing social welfare issues, within the context of the systems/ecological framework, the overarching framework used by generalist practitioners as they intervene to address social welfare needs at the individual, family, group, organization, community, and societal levels. The text also focuses on social justices issues, including the impact of racism, sexism, homophobia, and other types of oppression on individuals and the ways that the allocation of resources reinforce these forms of oppression and injustices. Because homelessness is increasingly a result of poverty and economic conditions, the section on homelessness has been expanded and moved from the chapter on mental health to the chapter on poverty

and income assistance. Additionally, because it is critical that social workers incorporate a worldview into their interventions wherever they practice, and because social workers are playing ever increasingly important roles internationally, a new chapter on international social work has been added.

We have also added a number of enhancements that we hope will help students and their instructors. The end of each chapter includes a list of key terms, as well as discussion questions that can be used in the classroom or individually to help students strengthen their critical thinking skills. Two new sections have also been added: a list of key words that can be used to locate specific journal articles on subjects of interest using *InfoTrac College Edition®*, and a list of Web sites that students and faculty can use to locate additional information about the topics in each chapter. The Web sites include those operated by state and federal government agencies and advocacy groups that provide demographic data about populations discussed in the text, available resources, and historical and state-of-the-art practices and policies.

This text is a collaborative work among four colleagues. Where consensus was possible, we sought it; where it was not possible, we sought to identify the diverse views that exist about the established wisdom of social work. Each of us contributed the perspectives of our own education in addition to social work: child development, education, human behavior and psychology in the case of Rosalie Ambrosino; political science and economics in the case of Joe Heffernan; sociology and history in the case of Guy Shuttlesworth; educational psychology, policy, and administration in the case of Robert Ambrosino. The text is interdisciplinary in this sense, but it is disciplined by the continuity and the certainty of unresolved social issues to which social work skills are relevant.

Four "referent" groups played an important role in strengthening this book: our families, our student and faculty colleagues in Austin, and our colleagues in the profession. We owe our gratitude to our families—Jean, Bob, Megan, Will A., Will C., Catie, Coleman, and James—for their support and understanding when the book took priority over them. We also thank our colleagues at the University of Texas School of Social Work for their critique and support: Dean Barbara White, Associate Dean Dorothy Van Soest, Yolanda Padilla, Janice Laakso, and Michele Ballan.

We also personally thank the diverse group of reviewers whose comments significantly contributed to the quality of this fourth edition:

Lend Frison, Iowa Western Community College
Denise Dedman, West Shore Community College
William Fuller, Angelo State University
Alfred Joseph, Miami University
William Boline, Governors State University
Debra Ingle, Kellogg Community College
Pat Lindsay, Minot State University
Stephen Marson, University of North Carolina at Pembroke
Barbara Shank, University of St. Thomas

We very much appreciate the thoughtful guidance they provided to us in making revisions from the third edition.

The referent group of greatest relevance has been our students. Their comments in classes over our collective 90 years of teaching helped shape our views of what they wanted and needed to know to become better social workers and citizens in our complex society.

The most rewarding part of teaching is watching our students begin to see connections between the many complex factors that shape social welfare issues and their differential effects on the diverse populations within the United States. We especially appreciate their critique of the third edition and their enthusiastic suggestions for changes. We have incorporated many of their ideas into the fourth edition.

Last but not least, we express our gratitude to our acquisition editor, Lisa Gebo, for her persistence and encouragement in the book preparation and publication. Also, a very special thanks to the production guidance and abilities—and the patience—of Lisa Weber of Wadsworth Publishing Company and to all those who helped with this publication along the way.

We hope that a number of you using this text will be persuaded, or have your choices reinforced, to join the social work profession. We urge those of you considering a career in social work to talk with your course instructors about the BSW degree. We also recommend that you visit social agencies and complete some volunteer experience in conjunction with your course. Most important, however, we hope this book in some way contributes to your social conscience no matter what career you choose and encourages you to recognize social work as a dynamic, challenging profession.

As we continue to struggle with the many social welfare issues that have existed in various forms for centuries, we urge you to look back on the early roots of social work—to remember the profession's significant contributions to making the world a better place to live. We urge you to build on the many accomplishments of the social work profession that took root at the turn of the last century and have continued to this day. We urge you to rekindle the flame of hope that burned so brightly in those early days of the profession. We urge you to seek to advance what the social work profession stands for in everything that you do. And finally, regardless of what profession you choose, we urge you to build bridges to the future that those who come behind you can cross—to continue to make the world a better place to live.

Rosalie Ambrosino
Joe Heffernan
Guy Shuttlesworth
Robert Ambrosino

Social Work and Social Welfare

An Introduction

one

Understanding Social Welfare and Social Work

Key Concepts and Perspectives

© David H. Wells/Corbis

The beginning part of this book introduces you to the nature of social welfare and social work: what social welfare encompasses and what social workers who function in social welfare settings do. Historical and theoretical contexts also are provided that can be used as a framework for understanding subsequent chapters.

In Chapter 1, "Social Welfare, Past and Present," we discuss the historical context of social welfare to help you understand how the past has shaped present-day social welfare problems and society's views toward people in need. We examine selected historical welfare policies that have influenced the structure and format of our contemporary social welfare institutions, and we explore the evolution of social welfare.

In Chapter 2, "Social Work and Other Helping Professions," we examine the relationships between social welfare as a broad system intended to maintain the well-being of individuals within a society and the profession of social work. We explore the diverse roles and functions of social work professionals, contrasting the profession of social work with other helping professions. We also examine ways that related professionals are used by social workers as resources in helping clients. We portray the social welfare system and the profession of social work as challenging and dynamic arenas for those of you interested in careers in one of the helping professions.

In Chapter 3, "The Systems/Ecological Perspective: Understanding Social Work and Social Welfare," we provide a theoretical framework that can be used to understand content presented in subsequent chapters. We introduce the social work profession's use of a systems/ecological perspective for viewing individuals within the broader context of their environment. We discuss this framework from a broad societal perspective, a family perspective, and an individual perspective to help you begin to see how the framework is applied by social work practitioners. We also introduce generalist social work practice and the strengths perspective to help you understand how these perspectives fit together within a systems/ecological context to form the comprehensive body of knowledge that social workers use in addressing social welfare issues at all levels of the environment.

In Chapter 4, "Diversity and Social Justice: The Impact of Race, Ethnicity, Class, Gender, and Sexual Orientation," we discuss the ways that racism, sexism, homophobia, and other forms of oppression and discrimination disenfranchise vulnerable groups in our society. We use specific examples to explore the long-range effects of social injustice experienced at the individual, group, organizational, community, and societal levels because of color, gender, class, and sexual orientation. We also address the roles of the social work profession in promoting social and economic justice and working toward eliminating oppression at all levels of the environment.

These chapters introduce you to the major concepts on which the profession of social work is based, and they lay the groundwork for content addressed in the remaining chapters. They are intended as an overview. Many of the ideas presented may be new to you, and we do not expect you immediately to understand in depth what they all mean or how they all fit together in the context of the social work profession. As you continue in this text and in your classwork, these ideas and concepts will become clearer to you. If you are majoring in social work, by the time you graduate they will be second nature; you will use them daily, probably without even realizing it.

As you read the chapters in Part Two, in which you will learn about the methods of intervention used by social workers, and Part Three, in which you will study fields of practice and populations with which social workers are involved, you will be considering the issues raised in these parts within the context of the broad perspective of social welfare, the nature of the social work profession, the systems/ecological framework, and the impact of oppression and social and economic injustice on at-risk populations.

1

SOCIAL WELFARE, PAST AND PRESENT

Public welfare in the United States has had a checkered past and faces an unpredictable future. With the ebb and flow of the economic cycle and the vacillation between liberal and conservative political stances, establishing a firmly embedded system of provisions for the needs of the poor, disenfranchised, people with physical and mental disabilities, and others at risk has historically been problematic. As we enter the new millennium, questions regarding social security, health care, income maintenance, education, housing, dependent children, and a plethora of related social concerns have neither a firm nor cohesive base in legislative policy. Proponents and adherents of various resolutions to these social issues continue to press hard for their causes. As in the past, those who lie on the margin must await the next "reform" to assess the consequences in order to determine whether their lives will be improved as a result of new policies designed to help them.

Today no consensus exists regarding the nature, focus, and development of social policy or the responsibility—if any—that the government has in developing programs to assist those in need. In the following discussion, we identify some of the more salient factors related to developing a comprehensive approach to social welfare in the United States. But first, a few basic questions are in order: What is social welfare? Who gets it? Who pays for it? Does it create dependency? Why is our social welfare system organized as it is? Social welfare in our society long has been a matter of dispute and controversy. Often the controversy surrounding the topic of social welfare results from a misunderstanding of the policies that govern social welfare as well as misinformation about people who are entitled to receive social welfare benefits. Clients who receive public assistance (commonly called "welfare") are viewed by many as too lazy to work and willing to live off the labor of others. Others identify them as victims of a rapidly changing society who lack necessary employment skills. Some view poverty, mental illness, unemployment, broken homes, lack of income in old age, and related problems as matters of personal failure or personal neglect. It is understandable, then, that people who hold divergent views would have different opinions about the nature and scope of social welfare programs and the people served by them.

Determining who is in need has always been a problem in our society. This is particularly true in relation to providing assistance for those who are poor but appear to be able to work. This concern has resulted in analyses that are often incorrect and ill founded. Does it seem reasonable to assume that individuals who are poor choose a life of poverty? Why, then, does the problem persist? Assessments that conclude that the poor have elected such a lifestyle, are lazy, or lack motivation to rise out of poverty often fail to consider how changing social systems contribute to outcomes that result in poverty for a substantial portion of the population. Frequently, a distinction is made between the deserving poor and the undeserving poor. Many individuals are more accepting of the needs of the aged, disabled, and chronically ill than those of seemingly able-bodied persons. In this chapter, we examine selected historical welfare policies that have influenced the structure and format of our contemporary social welfare institutions.

A Definition of Social Welfare and Its Relationship to Social Work

What is social welfare? Definitions invariably reflect the definer's knowledge and value base. A broad definition of what constitutes social welfare may well include all organized societal responses that promote the social well-being of a population. Education, health, rehabilitation, protective services for adults and children, public assistance, social insurance, services for persons with physical and mental disabilities, job training programs, marriage counseling, psychotherapy, pregnancy counseling, adop-

tion, and a myriad of related activities designed to promote social well-being would be included in such a definition. P. Nelson Reid (1995), in the *Encyclopedia of Social Work*, states:

> Social welfare . . . is perhaps best understood as an idea, that idea being one of a decent society that provides opportunities for work and human meaning, provides reasonable security from want and assault, promotes fairness and evaluation based on individual merit, and is economically productive and stable. The idea of social welfare is based on the assumption that human society can be organized and governed to produce and provide these things, and because it is feasible to do so, the society has a moral obligation to bring it to fruition. (p. 2206)

The term **social welfare,** then, is commonly used to refer to the full range of organized activities of public and voluntary agencies that seek to prevent, alleviate, or contribute to the solution of a selected set of social problems. The length and breadth of that list of social welfare problems depends on the perspective of the person compiling the list. Included items may reflect a conscious social choice, as well as other factors such as the background of the person compiling the list, the historical time that the list is developed, and the perceived economic resources available to meet the social welfare problems listed. Regardless of what exactly gets listed as a social welfare program, it is clear that there is no one social welfare program in the United States but, in fact, thousands.

Social work is the primary profession that works within the social welfare system and with those served by the system, although individuals from a variety of other professions are also involved. The roles of social work professionals and other helping professions in the social welfare system are discussed in Chapter 2.

THE VALUE BASE OF SOCIAL WORK

Any discussion of social welfare and the development of social welfare organizations would be incomplete without identifying the value context within which they occur. **Values** are assumptions, convictions, or beliefs about the way people should behave and the principles that should govern behavior. Since values are beliefs, they may vary with socialization experiences. Many values are dominant and supported by the majority of the population. For example, life is viewed as sacred; killing another person with malicious intent or wanton disregard for that person's life is viewed as a criminal offense by just about everybody. Other values are not so readily shared. For example, support of capital punishment is a value around which our society is divided.

The history of the development of social welfare reflects differences in values as they relate to social responsibility for making provisions for the needy. Values, however, are not the sole determinant of social policy. Availability of resources, coupled with economic, religious, and political influences, results in an evolving policy of social responsibility for the vulnerable members of a society. One dominant value that has guided the development of our social welfare system is humanitarianism, which is derived in large part from Judeo-Christian philosophy and teachings (Marson & MacLeod, 1996). The social application of humanitarianism, however, often is obscured by the resolve to find the most efficient and effective way to help those with unmet needs.

Our society also is influenced largely by the economic doctrine of **laissez-faire,** which stresses limited government involvement, individualism, and self-motivation. From this perspective, government welfare programs are viewed as a threat to those cherished and desirable ends. Problems of the poor and the disenfranchised are perceived as a matter of personal failure that would only be perpetuated by government welfare programs. Social responsibility for the vulnerable members of society, from the laissez-faire point of view, would be carried out through volunteerism aimed at encouraging those in need to become self-sufficient. From this perspective, work is considered the only justifiable means of self-maintenance, since it contributes to the productive effort of society.

Another values perspective maintains that we all are members of society and, by virtue of that membership, are entitled to share in its productive effort. This belief argues that people become poor or needy as a result of dysfunctional or rapidly changing social institutions. For example, the recent shift in the United States to a **brain-based economy** has resulted in layoffs, unemployment, and obsolescent jobs. Individuals do not cause these conditions; rather, they are swept along and victimized by them. Members of some ethnic groups may face barriers such as inferior educational resources, limited (and usually menial) job opportunities, poor housing, and inadequate health resources. An analysis from this perspective would not lay blame for these conditions on individual group members but would identify such reasons as institutional discrimination and oppression as causal factors.

When considering these value positions, the reader can readily understand that there are wide variations regarding societal responsibility for vulnerable members of our society. As you follow our discussion of the historical influences that have converged to shape our present social welfare structure, see whether you can identify the value positions that have contributed to the formulation of social policy.

Our English Heritage

In England, prior to the period of mercantilism, care for the poor was primarily a function of the church. By extending themselves through charitable efforts to those in need, parishioners fulfilled a required sacred function. The church's resources usually were sufficient to provide the relief that was made available to the poor. The feudal system itself provided a structure that met the needs of most of the population. The only significant government legislation that existed during this time was passed as a result of the so-called Black Death—bubonic plague—which began in 1348 and resulted in the death of approximately two-thirds of the English population within 2 years. In 1349, King Edward III mandated the Statute of Laborers Act, which made it mandatory that all able-bodied persons accept any type of employment within their parish. Furthermore, it laid the groundwork for residency requirements, which later became an intrinsic part of American social welfare legislation, by forbidding able-bodied persons from leaving their parish.

Some 150 years later, with the breakdown of the feudal system and the division of the church during the Reformation, organized religious efforts no longer could provide for the increasing numbers of poor. Without the church or the feudal manor to rely on in times of need, the poor were left on their own to survive. This often meant malnutrition, transience, poor health, broken families, and even death.

Many of the poor found their way into cities, where they were unwanted. Employment was always a problem, since most of the poor were illiterate, and their skills generally were related to agricultural activities. Many turned to begging. Local officials were pressed to find suitable solutions for the problem. As Europe struggled with the transition from an agricultural society to an industrial one, the numbers of dislodged persons increased. National practices differed, but in England, legislation originated in parishes throughout the country to deal with problems of the homeless, the poor, and dependent children.

Overseers were appointed by magistrates to assume responsibility for the poor residing in the various parishes. They assessed the needs of the poor and made judicious responses to those needs. The overseers' role was important, since usually their judgment alone determined the fate of the poor.

Analyses of the situation invariably led to the conclusion that problems were of an individual nature and most likely resulted from the economic transition. Unfortunately, legislation often had punitive overtones, which added to the burden of the poor and left them hopelessly entwined in impoverished conditions with little opportunity to find a way out. In response to these alarming conditions, the **Elizabethan Poor Law** (Elizabeth 43) was passed in 1601. This legislation is significant in that it attempted to codify earlier legislation and establish a national policy regarding the poor. The Elizabethan Poor Law established "categories" of assistance, a practice found in our current social welfare legislation.

The first of two categories was designed for individuals considered to be "worthy," since there was little doubt that their impoverishment was not a fraudulent attempt to secure assistance. These included the aged, the chronically ill, people with disabilities, and orphaned children. The worthy poor typically were placed in almshouses (poorhouses), where the physically able assisted individuals who were ill and had disabilities. This practice was referred to as **indoor relief,** since it provided services to the poor by placing them in institutions. In some instances, children were placed with families and often were required to work for their keep.

The second category included the able-bodied poor. Here, programs were less humane. Some of the able-bodied were placed in prisons, others were sent to workhouses, and many were indentured to local factories or farms as slave laborers. Unlike the worthy poor, the able-bodied poor were assumed to be malingerers or ne'er-do-wells who lacked the motivation to secure employment. The

treatment they received was designed to deter others, as well as to punish them for their transience and idleness.

The Elizabethan Poor Law was to be of crucial significance because it established the guiding philosophy of public assistance legislation in England until 1834 and in the United States until 1935. The important aspects of the law (Axinn & Levin, 1997, p. 10) in relation to U.S. policies toward the poor are the establishment of

- clear government responsibility for those in need,
- government authority to force people to work,
- government enforcement of family responsibility,
- responsibility to be exercised at the local level, and
- strict residence requirements.

The Elizabethan Poor Law was enacted less out of altruism and concern for the poor than as an orderly process of standardizing the way in which they were to be managed. It established a precedent for subsequent social legislation in the United Kingdom as well as the United States.

The Poor Law Reform Act of 1834 was passed as a reaction to concerns that the Poor Law of 1601 was not being implemented as intended and that liberalized supervision of the programs for the poor had served as a disincentive for work and had, in effect, created dependency on the program. The Poor Law Reform Act mandated that all forms of "outdoor" relief (assistance given to people in their homes) be abolished and that the full intention of the provisions of the Poor Law of 1601 be rigidly enforced. Furthermore, it established "the principle of least eligibility," which prescribed that no assistance be provided in an amount that rendered the recipient better off than the lowest-paid worker. This principle also served as a basic tenet of early American social welfare legislation and public welfare programs in existence today.

SPEENHAMLAND

Although the Poor Law remained the dominant legislation under which services to the poor were administered, attempts were made to create labor laws that would serve as an incentive for the poor to engage in employment. One such effort took the form of "minimum wage" legislation and was enacted in Speenhamland, England, in 1795. Motivated by a desire to induce large numbers of the poor to join the labor market, the Speenhamland Act provided for the payment of minimum wages to workers and their families. Wages were adjusted according to family size, thereby assuring minimally adequate income even for the largest of families. Employers were encouraged to pay minimum wages, and where this was not possible, the government made up the difference. It was anticipated that business would be stimulated to produce more commodities through the added incentives provided by the government subsidy, which in turn would create a need for more workers. However, the effect of the subsidy program was to drive wages down, and employers then turned to the government to make up the difference.

The Speenhamland Act was not designed specifically to be a social welfare reform measure, although it did have implications for the working poor, the unemployed, and the impoverished. In effect, it was an early form of a work incentive program. Although important symbolically, the Speenhamland Act had little impact. Ultimately rejected by employers, it proved expensive for the government and was never applied uniformly. It did establish the principle of government subsidy for private employers, a practice that is relatively widespread in our society today.

SOCIAL WELFARE IN COLONIAL AMERICA

Early American settlers brought a religious heritage that emphasized charity and the mutual interdependence of people. They also brought with them the heritage of the Elizabethan Poor Law. America, in the early days, was a land of vast natural resources, and settlers had to work hard to survive. When neighbors became needy through illness or death, church members usually were quick to respond. No formal government network for providing assistance existed on any significant basis. Later, as the population increased, many colonies passed laws requiring that immigrants demonstrate their ability to sustain themselves, or in the absence of such ability, sponsors were required to pledge their support for new arrivals. Transients were "warned out" and often returned to their place of residence (Federico, 1983, p. 98). In some instances, the homeless and unemployed were returned to England. Times were difficult, the Puritan work ethic was embedded deeply, and with little surplus to redistribute to those in need, assistance often was inadequate. The practice of posting names of habitual paupers at the town house was a routine procedure in many towns and villages.

Reliable estimates of the magnitude of public welfare in colonial America are difficult to obtain. One important fact was that the presence of the indentured servant system rekindled in this country a replica of feudal welfare. In the indentured system of the middle colonies and the slavery system of the southern colonies, there was a clear lack of freedom for the pauper class. Often overlooked, however, was the existence of a set of harsh laws—reasonably enforced up until the time of independence—that required masters to meet the basic survival needs of servants and slaves. (Almost half of all colonists came to the country as indentured servants.) Ironically, as the economy matured from plantation to artisan and became preindustrial in character, economic uncertainty also increased. Consequently, public relief was the largest expenditure in the public budgets of most major cities at the time of the American Revolution.

Concomitantly, the rigid restraint of the Poor Law philosophy was thoroughly consistent with the fact that the colonial economy was one of extreme scarcity. Colonial law stressed the provision of indoor relief, by which paupers could be conveniently segregated within almshouses and put to tasks that at least paid for their meager keep. The apprenticeship of children reflected a belief in family controls for children and stressed work and training for productive employment. Also, the deification of the work ethic and the belief that pauperism was a visible symbol of sin permitted a harsh response to those in need, as a means of saving their souls.

CHANGING PATTERNS AFTER THE REVOLUTION

Between the American Revolution and the Civil War, several broad patterns of welfare emerged, all of which were thoroughly consis-

tent with the basic tenets of the Elizabethan Poor Law. The American separation of church and state forced a severance of the connection between parish and local welfare office. Nevertheless, many states—most, in fact—retained a religious connection, with the requirement that at least one member of the welfare board must be a "licensed preacher." Local governments accepted grudgingly the role of welfare caretaker and adopted rigid residency requirements.

The most important shift in this period was from indoor to **outdoor relief.** Outdoor aid, with its reliance on in-kind aid and work relief projects, was most adaptable to the volatile economics of the first half of the 19th century. This led some to see early American welfare as principally an instrument for the regulation of the supply of labor. The contrary evidence, that it essentially is a fiscal choice, stems from the observation that the shift to outdoor relief occurred within places of both labor shortage and labor surplus.

Another significant movement before the Civil War was the shift away from public sector to private sector welfare, or voluntary welfare. The responsibility for welfare therefore was left to charitable institutions rather than remaining a public concern.

CARING FOR THE URBAN POOR

As the new nation grew, cities began to appear on the eastern seaboard. With immigrants arriving regularly, jobs often were difficult to find, and a large population of displaced poor began to emerge. Persons interested in those less fortunate sought avenues for meeting the needs of the poor. Although attaching the poor to subsistence-level employment usually was the goal, concern arose over assuring that basic needs were met until income could be derived through employment. Although almshouses often were used to care for the chronic poor, outdoor relief found increased acceptance as a suitable way of caring for the poor, including the practice of providing cash assistance to persons who remained in their own homes. Differing segments of the population found cause for alarm in the practices of both indoor and outdoor relief.

One of the earlier major organizations to seek solutions to problems of poverty was the New York Society for the Prevention of Pauperism, established in 1817. This society sought to identify and remedy the causes of poverty. Following the precedent established by Thomas Chalmers in England, the society divided the city into districts and assigned "friendly visitors" to each district to assess and respond to the needs of the poor (Axinn & Levin, 1997). Later, in 1843, the Association for Improving the Conditions of the Poor was established in New York City to coordinate relief efforts for the unemployed. One significant technique introduced by the association was the requirement that relief could not be disbursed until the individual's needs were assessed so that agencies providing relief could do so more effectively.

Perhaps the most effective relief organization for the poor was the Charity Organization Society (COS) in Buffalo, New York. A private organization modeled after London's COS, it was founded by wealthy citizens who embraced the work ethic yet had compassion for the deserving poor. The COS sought to add efficiency and economy to programs serving the poor, as well as to organize charities in an effort to prevent duplication of services and reduce dependency on charitable efforts. Like the Association for Improving Conditions of the Poor, which preceded it, the COS empha-

sized the necessity for assessing the poor's condition and added the dimension of engaging "friendly visitors" with clients in an effort to guide, rehabilitate, and assist them in preparing for self-sufficiency. The COS had little sympathy for chronic beggars, viewing them essentially as hopeless derelicts.

CARING FOR SPECIFIC POPULATIONS

During these early years, many other private charities emerged to address special problem areas, such as the Orphan's Home Movement, which gave institutional care to children left alone as the result of their parents' death. Other institutional services began to appear throughout the country to provide care for the deaf, blind, and mentally ill. These services largely were sponsored by state or local governments. A number of concerned citizens expressed grave concern regarding the treatment received by residents of these institutions. Dorothea Dix, a philanthropist and social reformer, traveled the United States observing the care given the "insane" and was appalled by horrid conditions and inhumane care. Dix sought to convince President Franklin Pierce to allocate federal and land grant monies for establishing federal institutions to care for the mentally ill. Her plea was blocked by Congress, which believed such matters to be the states' responsibility. Resources allocated for institutional care by states were limited. The results were poor conditions and limited treatment.

Toward the latter part of the nineteenth century, a number of states developed centralized agencies, following the precedent set by state boards of charities, agencies that had been organized in several states to oversee the activities of charitable institutions. State charity agencies sought to ensure a better quality of care for institutional inmates, as well as to seek greater efficiency and economy in the provision of poor relief. With the federal government assuming only limited responsibility for selected groups (veterans, for example), state agencies became the primary public resource for addressing the problems of the poor and debilitated (Leiby, 1978, pp. 130–131).

A new wave of immigrants from southern Europe entering the United States in the late 1800s and early 1900s further added to the burden of unemployment, homelessness, and poverty. Reacting to the problems experienced by immigrants in coping with the new culture, Jane Addams, a social worker, was instrumental in anchoring the settlement house movement as a resource for dealing with problems of assimilation and in preparing immigrants to live in a new society. Education was emphasized for adults and children alike. In Chicago, Hull House, established by Addams in 1869, sparked the initiative for similar movements in other cities. It also sought needed social reforms to improve the quality of life and opportunity structure for all new citizens. By addressing the problems of poor housing, low wages, child labor, and disease, Hull House and other settlement houses became major social action agencies.

We would be remiss if we did not point out the ideological conflict between the COS movement and the settlement house movement, as well as the contributions each made to contemporary social work practice. Proponents of Charity Organization Societies believed that urban poverty was rooted in moral and character deficiencies of the individual and that by helping poor people recognize and correct their flawed character, poverty could be abolished. The COS movement embraced social Darwinism as its theoretical underpinning for

helping (or not helping) the poor, labeling this process "scientific charity." The focus of COS workers was on client self-support or help provided by private sources, but only after a thorough investigation and determination of worthiness. The emphasis was on helping the poor find social and economic salvation through work (Axinn & Levin, 1997).

The settlement house movement was guided by a very different set of principles. Clients of settlement houses were viewed as able, normal individuals. No effort was made to separate the "worthy" poor from the "unworthy" poor. The emphasis was on the provision of neighborhood services and community development. The settlement house movement embraced a philosophy that combined the achievement of the individual with satisfying social relations and social responsibility. Settlement house workers took a holistic perspective of the person in society. The overall focus of the settlement house movement was on social reform (Axinn & Levin, 1997).

Both movements left an indelible mark on contemporary social work practice. The COS movement was the forerunner of clinical social work, with its focus on individuals and families, the use of scientific methods to determine need, and specialized training of social service providers. The settlement house movement was the forerunner of nonclinical social work, with a primary focus on individuals as part of their community, social needs assessment, community organizing, social reform and political action, understanding and appreciating the strengths of cultural diversity, and research on the community (Axinn & Levin, 1997).

The current debate in social work circles about whether nonclinical social work is indeed legitimate social work has its roots in the ideological differences inherent in these two early approaches to social welfare. Students should be aware of these differences, as they have a direct impact on how social welfare policy is formulated and carried out.

During the 1800s, more clearly defined parameters of public versus private welfare programs were established. Public welfare benefit programs relied on taxation for funding. Private welfare programs were funded through the voluntary contributions of individuals or philanthropic organizations. No clearly defined limits determined what types of benefits would be offered by either public or private (voluntary) agencies. As a result, services often overlapped. Public agencies were administered by government agencies at the local, state, or federal levels. Private agencies often had religious or philanthropic sponsorship or received contributions from citizens.

Following World War I, the nation entered a period of great social change and prosperity. The economy improved, and the nation experienced a great sense of euphoria. This mood ended abruptly in 1929 with the economic downturn that led to the Great Depression. In short order, conditions were grave. Businesses considered to be stable ceased their production, banks declared bankruptcy, and millions of workers lost their jobs. Although this nation had experienced recessions and depressions before, none was quite as devastating to Americans' economic security as the Great Depression.

THE NEW DEAL

Today, it is difficult for us to comprehend the effects the Great Depression had on Americans. Savings were lost as banks collapsed and businesses failed, and a large portion of the American population was left penniless, homeless, and without resources as unemployment increased. Jobs became scarce, and the unemployed had nowhere to turn. Organized charities quickly exhausted their limited resources. Pessimism and despair were rampant, and many experienced a sense of hopelessness. Unemployment insurance was nonexistent, and no federal guarantees existed for monies lost in bank failures. The economic disaster produced a state of chaos never experienced before on American soil. As conditions worsened, homes were lost through foreclosed mortgages.

State and local governments responded to the extent that resources permitted; however, many of the poor states lacked resources to provide even temporary relief. In the state of New York, an Emergency Relief Act was passed providing public employment, in-kind relief (food, clothing, and shelter), and limited cash benefits. This act later served as a model for federal relief programs.

Following the earlier constitutional interpretation of federal and state roles by President Pierce, subsequent administrations through the Hoover administration reinforced the position that federal involvement in relief programs was not mandatory but rather a matter that should be delegated to the states. Although sympathetic with those victimized by the Depression, President Herbert Hoover was convinced that the most effective solution to the Depression and its consequences was to offer incentives for business to regain its footing, expand, and provide jobs for the jobless.

The critical nature of the Depression was manifested in starvation, deprivation, and the suffering of millions of Americans and required an immediate response. It was under these conditions that Franklin Delano Roosevelt, the former governor of New York, was elected president in 1932.

One of President Roosevelt's first actions was to institute emergency legislation that

The Great Depression created immense hardship for millions of Americans.
© Corbis

provided assistance for the jobless and poor. This legislation marked the first time the federal government became engaged directly in providing relief. It also provided an interpretation of the health and welfare provisions of the Constitution that established a historical precedent. The result mandated the federal government to assume health and welfare responsibility for its citizens. The statement was clear: citizens were first and foremost citizens of the United States and, second, residents of specific states. This policy opened the door for later federal legislation in the areas of civil rights, fair employment practices, school busing, public assistance, and a variety of other social programs.

One of the first attempts to supply relief for depression victims was the Federal Emergency Relief Act (FERA). Modeled after the New York Emergency Relief Act, it provided food, clothing, and shelter allowances for the homeless and displaced. In a cooperative rela-

tionship with states, the federal government made monies available to states to administer the relief programs. States were responsible for establishing agencies for that purpose and also were required to contribute state funds, where possible, for the purpose of broadening the resource base available to those in need. This established the precedent for "matching grants," which later became an integral requirement for public assistance programs.

Additional federal emergency legislation was enacted to provide public employment for the unemployed. In 1935, the Works Progress Administration (WPA) was created to provide public service jobs. Although resisted by private contractors, the WPA ultimately employed approximately 8 million workers over the duration of the Depression. States and local governments identified needed projects and supplied necessary materials for laborers, who were paid by the WPA. Many public schools, streets, parks, post office buildings, state college buildings, and related public projects were constructed under the auspices of the WPA. It was anticipated that as the private business sector expanded, WPA workers would secure employment in the private sector.

Youth programs also were established. Perhaps the most noteworthy was the Civilian Conservation Corps (CCC), which was designed to protect natural resources and to improve and develop public recreational areas. Primarily a forest camp activity, the CCC provided young men between the ages of 17 and 23 with jobs, food, clothing, and shelter. Wages were nominal (around $25 per month), and the major portion of the wages ($20 per month) was conscripted and sent home to help support families. Many national parks were improved and developed by CCC labor. The National Youth Administration (NYA), also established under the WPA, gave work-study assistance to high school and college youth as an incentive to remain in school. In addition, the NYA provided part-time jobs for out-of-school students to learn job skills and increase their employability (Axinn & Levin, 1997).

Low-interest loans to farmers and small business operators also were extended through FERA programs as a means of enabling those activities to survive and become sources of employment for the jobless.

In retrospect, it is clear that the Depression legislation was designed to be temporary in nature and had as its main focus the creation of work activities that enabled individuals to earn their income rather than become objects of charity. It also was anticipated that the private economic business sector would prosper and emergency relief employment would no longer be needed.

The New Deal legislation offered a temporary solution to the crisis generated by the Great Depression. The jobless found jobs, the hungry were fed, and the homeless were given shelter. Perhaps of more importance, the nation felt the full impact of system changes. The issue of blaming poverty on idleness and laziness was put to rest, at least temporarily.

THE SOCIAL SECURITY ACT

The **Social Security Act** was passed by Congress and signed into law by President Roosevelt on August 4, 1935. This act remains the most significant piece of social legislation ever enacted in the United States. It also paved the way for greater federal involvement in health and welfare. The act reflected a realization that our economic system was subject to vacillations that would invariably leave many people without resources due to unemployment in an ever-shifting economic marketplace. It also acknowledged that older adults needed income security as an incentive to retire. This act was designed to be a permanent resource system administered by the federal government. Its provisions were outlined under three major categories (covered in more depth in Chapter 8): social insurance, public assistance, and health and welfare services.

Social Insurance

Social insurance, commonly referred to as **Social Security,** included two important benefit programs. The first (and most widely known) consisted of three categories: Old Age, Survivors, and Disability Insurance (OASDI; see Chapter 8). These programs were based on taxes deducted from employees' wages and matched by employer contributions. Eligibility was based on participation earned through employment. The second type of insurance program was unemployment insurance, with the funds contributed by employers. The purpose of the unemployment benefit program was to provide a source of income security for covered workers who had lost their jobs.

Benefits derived from these programs were considered to be a matter of right in that the recipients and their employers had paid "premiums" for the benefits they would receive. In many ways, social insurance was similar to private insurance, for which entitlement to benefits is directly related to beneficiary participation through contributions.

Public Assistance

Public assistance was based on "need" and was not established as a right earned through employment. This program was administered by states with monies made available by states and matched by the federal government (matching grants). Public assistance consisted of three categories: Old Age Assistance, Aid to Dependent Children, and Aid to the Blind. In 1955, the category of Aid to the Permanently and Totally Disabled was added. Benefits under each of these categories were invariably low and varied among the states according to each state's willingness to match federal funds. Eligibility requirements were rigid and rigorously enforced. Participation further was based on a "means" test that required applicants to demonstrate that they were hopelessly without resources. Recipients' private lives were opened to the scrutiny of welfare workers in an attempt to minimize fraud and to assure that benefit levels did not exceed budgeted needs. Perhaps the most controversial assistance program was Aid to Dependent Children (ADC). This program made limited funds available to mothers with dependent children where no man was present in the home. Since benefit levels were adjusted for

family size (to a maximum of four children), concern arose that promiscuity and illegitimacy would be rewarded by increasing benefits as the family size increased. Rigid cohabitation policies were instituted mandating that mothers guilty of cohabitation would lose their grant funds entirely. Since most ADC recipients were able-bodied, there was also concern that welfare payments were a disincentive for meeting their needs through gainful employment. In many ways, ADC recipients were treated as the "unworthy" poor of the time and, as a consequence, were often dealt with in a punitive manner.

Public assistance generally is referred to as *welfare* by the public. Since benefits are based on impoverishment and not earned through employment, participation in the program carries a stigma of personal imprudence, ineptness, or failure.

Health and Welfare Services

Programs authorized under **health and welfare services** provided for maternal and child care services, vocational rehabilitation, public health, and services for children with physical impairments. The provision of services was emphasized. Services authorized under this title are discussed more fully in later chapters.

In the ensuing years, amendments to the Social Security Act extended each of these titles and included more people in their coverage. Social insurance later added health insurance (Medicare), and a health assistance program (Medicaid) was instituted for public assistance recipients. The ADC assistance category was redefined as Aid to Families with Dependent Children (AFDC), and an AFDC–Unemployed Parent (AFDC-UP) provision was added so that states could assist families under limited circumstances when an employable unemployed male was in the home. Only a few states opted to implement the AFDC-UP provisions. As requirements for participation in these programs became less stringent in the 1960s and 1970s, welfare rolls increased dramatically.

SOCIAL WELFARE: THE POST–SOCIAL SECURITY ERA

Establishing well-focused comprehensive social welfare programs in the United States has been problematic because of differing values, economic upturns and downturns, and fluctuations in resources available to meet the needs of an expanding population. The period since passage of the Social Security Act has been tumultuous, with three major wars, a long-standing cold war, the fall of communism as a dominant world political force, periods of national economic well-being as well as recessions and depressions, and the emergence of a world or global economy. Unemployment in the United States has varied from 12% of the workforce in 1979 to less than 5% in 2000. The divorce rate has increased dramatically since the 1940s, single-parent families are more common, the population is growing older, affordable housing has become more difficult to find, and diseases have become more costly to treat. All of these factors affect how the government responds to social needs. In the following sections, we discuss some of the more significant social welfare programs that have occurred since the passage of the Social Security Act in 1935.

The Great Society Programs

Attempts to broaden the activities of government in securing the rights of citizens and pro-viding for personal, social, and economic development were introduced through social reform measures enacted during the Lyndon Johnson administration (1963–1968). The so-called **Great Society** legislation extended benefits of many existing programs and services designed to help the poor, the disabled, and the aged. The Social Security Act was amended to provide for health care benefits to the aged under the Health Insurance Program (Medicare) and to public assistance recipients through the Health Assistance Program (Medicaid). Several pieces of new legislation designed to meet needs not specifically addressed through existing resources were also passed. The Older Americans Act (1965) established a legal base for developing senior luncheon programs, health screening, transportation, meals-on-wheels programs, and recreational activities. The Civil Rights Act (1964) sought to end discrimination in employment and in the use of public business facilities. It also was targeted toward nondiscriminatory extension of credit. Education bills were passed that sought to rectify many of the educational disadvantages experienced by children of the poor.

Perhaps the most significant—and controversial—effort to achieve social reform came through the Economic Opportunities Act of 1964, also referred to as the War on Poverty. The objective of this act was to "eliminate poverty" through institutional change. Poverty was viewed traditionally as an individual matter, and its causes generally were thought to be the result of personal failure, the lack of motivation, or personal choice. War on Poverty program designers came to a different conclusion. They considered poverty to be the result of inadequate social institutions that failed to provide opportunities for all citizens. Traditional approaches to solving the problems of poverty were viewed as unsuccessful. Changing the status of the poor would come not through working with them on an individual basis but rather through modifying institutions that produced the problems in the first place. Hence, Economic Opportunities Act programs were structured to assure the poor a greater likelihood of success by creating opportunities for decision making and participation. Educational programs such as Head Start, Enable, and Catch-up sought to extend relevant learning experiences to educationally disadvantaged children. Community Action Agencies encouraged the poor to become more vocal in community affairs and to organize efforts for community betterment. Special employment incentives were generated to teach job skills. Youth job corps programs provided public service jobs contingent on remaining in school, thus assuring greater potential for employment on graduation. Job Corps centers taught teenage dropouts employment skills. Small-business loans were made to individuals with potential for developing businesses. Rural programs extended health and social services for the poor in rural areas.

In a nation that boasted the highest standard of living in the world, it was believed that the scourge of poverty could be eliminated forever. The euphemism of "War on Poverty" was selected to rally the population to a full-scale commitment to assure that the enemy, poverty, would be overcome. Social action advocates found the climate produced by the Economic Opportunities Act favorable for their efforts. It was a heyday for the expansion of social programs, with spending often outstripping planning. However, social legislation is invariably affected by the political climate. As government resources and attention were diverted to the Vietnam War, the domestic "war" was soon neglected and ultimately terminated.

Conservatism in the Mid-1960s and 1970s

The period from the mid-1960s through the mid-1970s was one of both domestic and foreign conflict. The antiestablishment movement in the United States was galvanized by the highly unpopular Vietnam War, rioting was occurring in the Watts section of Los Angeles and in Detroit, Martin Luther King was championing the cause of disenfranchised Americans, and inflation was depleting the buying power of those who were working.

In reaction to these disconcerting changes, many middle-class Americans initiated a wave of conservatism that led to an effort to dismantle many of the social programs enacted during the New Deal and expanded through the Great Society programs. The welfare "establishment" was viewed as costly, ineffective, and counterproductive. The conservatives maintained that the federal government was much too large and cumbersome and that many functions, including social welfare, could be assumed by the states. Although federal involvement in welfare had emerged largely because states had lacked sufficient resources to provide supports, conservatives were convinced that states and localities were better suited to determine policies and administer social programs. One result was the reorganization—and eventual termination—of the federal poverty program. Several popular programs, such as Head Start and job-training programs, were transferred to other government agencies. Under the Richard Nixon administration, a major welfare reform measure, the Family Assistance Program (FAP), was submitted for congressional approval as House Bill 1. Although never enacted into law, the reform would have eliminated the public assistance program and substituted in its place a proposal that was designed to provide incentives for recipients to work without losing all of the their government benefits. The level of defined need, $1,600 per year for a family of four, was far below benefit levels already in existence in the higher-paying states but higher than the benefits in over half the states.

The Family Assistance Act failed, but on a more positive note, public assistance programs for the aged, disabled, and blind were combined by the enactment of the Supplemental Security Income (SSI) Act in 1974. SSI increased benefit levels for millions of recipients. Since the AFDC category, which would have been abolished by the Family Assistance Act, failed to pass, AFDC continued to be funded and implemented under the federal-state arrangements already in effect.

Welfare Reform and the Late 1970s

The policymakers of the mid-1970s inherited a welfare system that had no positive constituency. Recipients, social workers, public officials, and tax-conscious groups agreed only on the inadequacy of the existing system. Each of the four constituencies had initiated a **welfare reform effort,** and each constituency had failed to achieve its reform, largely because of the others' opposition. Because of the political costs that had come to be associated with welfare reform efforts, no one was willing to champion a new welfare reform effort. The problems that had drawn such attention in earlier decades persisted. The rapidly expanding welfare costs in the years of Presidents Richard Nixon and Gerald Ford, in juxtaposition to the intractability of poverty, made welfare reform an urgent but unpleasant necessity.

Welfare reform continued to be an issue during President Jimmy Carter's administra-

tion, which proposed that $8.8 billion be appropriated to create up to 1.4 million public service jobs. It was expected that 2 million persons would hold such jobs in a given year, as they were processed through these jobs on their way to regular employment in the public or private sector. According to the proposal, most of these jobs would pay a minimum wage (projected to be $3.30 in 1980) and would be full-time, full-year jobs, thus yielding an annual income of $6,600.

In addition, a family would receive an income supplement geared to family size. The jobs would not be eligible for the earned income tax credit. A worker would always have an income incentive to move from the public job to regular employment in the public or private sector. Those eligible for such jobs would be adults—one per family—in the "expected to work" category of the second part of the program who could not find employment in the regular economy. Care was to be taken to assure that these jobs would not replace ordinary public jobs, thus removing the objections to the plan from the labor unions. However, Carter's proposal was not adopted, and debate about the most effective way to overhaul the welfare system continued.

Cutbacks in the Reagan-Bush Years

The 1980s were characterized by **"welfare devolution"**—relentless efforts to reduce and eliminate government social entitlement programs. Public expenditures for welfare were viewed as antithetical to economic progress. Mounting inflation was considered to be the result of federal domestic spending. The precarious state of the U.S. economy was considered the work of social progressives who had engineered welfare expansionism and, as a result, had caused the economy to falter. Many social support programs were either reduced dramatically or eliminated.

As part of his State of the Union message in 1982, President Reagan proposed his version of welfare reform. It went under the title "New Federalism." The centerpiece was a plan whereby the states would assume financial and administrative responsibility for food stamps and AFDC, while the federal government would assume responsibility for the Medicaid program. The program was dubbed the "Welfare Swap." The plan went through a number of variations before it was dropped by the administration as politically infeasible. The problem was that neither conservative governors nor liberal mayors liked the idea. Following his reelection in 1984, President Reagan began again to push for reshaping welfare responsibilities among the various layers of government. A presidential task force was appointed, and it was to issue its report after the congressional elections in 1986. That election resulted in a Democratic landslide, and the responsibility for welfare reform shifted from the White House to Capitol Hill.

President George Bush's administration continued to be influenced by a conservative view of welfare and welfare reform. With the winding down of the cold war, progressives held hopes that monies appropriated for defense spending could be directed toward domestic programs. Meanwhile, welfare costs continued to escalate. In 1988, the Democratic Congress passed the Family Support Act. It was hailed by proponents of welfare reform as the most significant piece of domestic legislation enacted since the Social Security Act in 1935. The Family Support Act mandated that states provide job opportunities and basic skills (JOBS) programs for most AFDC recipients (some, such as those with very young children or health problems, were exempted from participation).

The act also provided transitional benefits, including up to 12 months of Medicaid (health care) and child care after recipients found jobs to ease the transition from welfare to work without loss of income. The act also mandated that states provide AFDC-UP benefits for a limited time to those families with previously employed males unable to find employment. The act also required stronger enforcement of child support payments by absent parents. Parts of the act were not required to be implemented by states until 1992.

The Family Support Act failed to live up to its expectation as a major piece of welfare reform legislation. It took the federal government an inordinate amount of time to publish regulations governing the act. Funding for the act's programs was inadequate. Jobs that paid a living wage for former welfare recipients failed to materialize. Mobilizing the private sector to support the JOBS program proved more difficult than anticipated. In short, the program was doomed to failure before it even got off the ground.

The Clinton Years

By 1992, the political landscape of welfare reform had shifted again. The Democratic presidential candidate was a "New Democrat" who had been instrumental, as governor of Arkansas, in support of the Family Support Act of 1988. As a presidential candidate, Bill Clinton had sought a wider role for the states in the design of federal welfare programs. More significantly, as a "political centrist," he aimed to distance himself from "liberal Democratic reform" that had also been instrumental in the passage of the 1988 legislation.

As a candidate, Clinton promised to "end welfare as we know it," but he gave few specifics other than a vague endorsement of the principles of the 1988 legislation. The goal of the reform was to make welfare "a second chance, not a second choice." Employment readiness, parental responsibility, and state discretion were portrayed as the keystones of Clinton's reform agenda.

Welfare-to-work programs have been tried on numerous occasions without significant success in the past, but much greater pressure was behind this new welfare reform effort. Lawmakers at all levels of government and of both parties were now demanding that welfare recipients be required to take more responsibility for ending, or at least easing, their dependence on public support. The clamor for such change was being driven by a significant shift to the right in public mood and a much-increased effort to reduce the federal deficit. The General Accounting Office, a congressional agency that monitors federal programs, reported the number of unmarried mothers on welfare rose from 380,000 in 1976 to more than 1.5 million in 1992 (Demott, 1994). Charles Murray, in a report for the Heritage Foundation, a Republican think tank in Washington, DC, concluded that "the current welfare system bribes individuals into behavior—such as not marrying, and having children out of wedlock— which is self-defeating to the individual, a tragic handicap for children, and, because it contributes to every other social pathology, is increasingly a threat to society" ("Should the System Be Abolished?" 1994, p. 21). This view was not new; it had long been a theme of ultraconservative critics of welfare. What was compellingly different was that this view now represented mainstream thought.

The view that the welfare system had failed both those who financed it and those supported by it was shared by liberals who were long its strongest proponents. President Clinton's health and human services secretary, Donna Shalala, said more and more Americans were seeing "an unfairness" in the difference between "those who get up in the morning and go to work at entry-level jobs and those who stay on the welfare system" (Demott, 1994, p. 18). Mary Jo Bane, Shalala's assistant secretary for children and families, told *Nation's Business* that "the welfare system doesn't help recipients move into the labor market. It's in the wrong business. The welfare system is in the business of writing checks and filling out forms. It's not in the business of getting people to work" (Demott, 1994, p. 18).

The Clinton administration debated what would constitute genuine welfare reform. The critical choice was the White House's decision in 1994 to push for health care reform (discussed in Chapter 10) and then deal with welfare reform. This decision was based partially on the reasoning that many families received public assistance, or got off programs such as AFDC but then were forced to return to the AFDC rolls, because of health-related problems and the unavailability of adequate health care. The health care reform failed.

Following that failure, the Republicans won both houses of Congress in the 1994 national elections. They celebrated their electoral victory with the Contract with America. Many reform measures were introduced in the 104th congressional session by various coalitions and individual members of Congress. Nearly all would limit stays on welfare, restrict the right to welfare of unmarried mothers under the age of 18, and impose far more stringent work requirements. Perhaps most disturbing to members of the social work community were the efforts to end AFDC as a national government entitlement program and replace it with 51 different programs, one for each state and the District of Columbia.

Welfare reform legislation passed in 1996 did precisely that. Under the Personal Responsibility and Work Opportunity Act of 1996, each state was charged with administering various assistance programs, including AFDC, with a change in name to **Temporary Assistance for Needy Families** (TANF), at the direction of state legislatures with minimal federal guidelines and reciprocal federal funding. The thrust of the reform measures was to move recipients off the welfare roles and toward self-sufficiency by engaging in work, work-training, or education programs designed to enable them to develop skills essential for employment. However, many states implemented "work first" programs, moving recipients into jobs without training. Although such programs reduced the welfare rolls because the economy was strong, most recipients who moved off TANF entered "dead-end" minimum-wage jobs without health care benefits that do not allow for complete self-sufficiency. Time limits also were imposed (2 years) for recipients to engage in employment. Failure to do so can result in the termination of benefits. This approach presumes that mandatory work requirements will reduce, if not eliminate, dependence on welfare benefits.

The jury has yet to render a final verdict on the Personal Responsibility and Work Opportunity Act of 1996. While the precipitous decline in welfare caseloads has been touted by some as evidence that the legislation is working, others believe that it is the strong economy that has created these declines. Still others are fearful that the legislation is simply creating a larger underclass of working poor who are not adequately able to care for themselves and their families. The long-term impacts of this latest round of welfare reform are being studied by many entities, including the federal government and private groups such as foundations, think tanks, and universities. (The Welfare Information Network [http://www.welfareinfo.org] offers a comprehensive look at the latest information on the impact of the 1996 welfare reform legislation.)

Other controversial issues continued to be debated in 1999 and into the new millennium. Priorities include insuring the solvency of Social Security (social insurance) and whether it should be partly or fully privatized; health care—who should be covered and who should pay for it; and youth crime—prevention versus punishment. These issues are discussed more extensively in later chapters.

SUMMARY

Welfare, like all domestic policy, is in a constant state of evolution. We have preference for but not a knowledge of what it is evolving to. Always, policies and practice have emerged from a set of choices, national or state, governmental or voluntary, expanding or restrictive. Welfare in the United States will never be satisfactory to everyone. There will always be people who believe we have made the wrong choices. Sometimes those who disagree with choices made will be on the left and sometimes on the right. Welfare policy can never escape the contradictions in its dual goals: to respond compassionately to those in need but to structure the compassion in such a way that the natural tendencies of people to work, to save, and to care for their own are not eroded.

KEY TERMS

brain-based economy	health and welfare
Elizabethan Poor Law	services
Great Society	indoor relief

laissez-faire
outdoor relief
public assistance
social insurance
Social Security

Social Security Act
social welfare
values
welfare devolution

social welfare

Temporary Assistance for Needy Families (TANF)

welfare reform

DISCUSSION QUESTIONS

1. Identify the conditions that led to the enactment of the Elizabethan Poor Law.

2. Discuss the differences between indoor and outdoor relief. Give an example of each.

3. In what manner were the public assistance provisions of the Social Security Act different from those of the Economic Opportunity Act (War on Poverty)?

4. What effect did the passage of the Social Security Act have on the federal government's role in health and welfare?

5. In various forms, "workfare" has been attempted as a means of reducing welfare rolls. What is workfare? Why has it not been entirely effective in reducing welfare rolls?

6. Do you think that the political position (conservative, independent, liberal) should be a primary consideration in shaping social policy? Why?

INFOTRAC COLLEGE EDITION

To learn more about topics included in this chapter, enter the following search terms:

Elizabethan poor law

Family Support Act

Great Depression

Great Society

Hull House

New Deal

ON THE INTERNET

http://newdeal.feri.org/

http://www.roosevelt.edu/newdeal/

http://www.welfareinfo.org/

http://www.welfarewatch.org/

http://www.blpes.lse.ac.uk/

http://www.uic.edu/jaddams/hull/hull_house.html

http://tlc.ai.org/depressi.htm

REFERENCES

Axinn, J., & Levin, H. (1997). *Social welfare: A history of the American response to need* (8th ed.). New York: Harper & Row.

Demott, J. (1994). Welfare reform could work. *Nation's Business, 82*(18), 18–23.

Federico, R. D. (1983). *The social welfare institution* (4th ed.). Lexington, MA: Heath.

Leiby, J. (1978). *A history of social welfare and social work in the U.S.* New York: Columbia University Press.

Marson, S. M., & MacLeod, E. (1996). The first social worker. *New Social Worker, 3*(1), 11.

Reid, P. N. (1995). *Encyclopedia of social work* (Vol. 3, pp. 2206–2225). Washington, DC: NASW Press.

Should the system be abolished? Interview with Charles Murray. *Nation's Business, 82*(18), 21.

SUGGESTED FURTHER READINGS

Berkowitz, E. D. (1991). *America's welfare state: From Roosevelt to Reagan.* Baltimore: Johns Hopkins University Press.

Chatterjee, P. (1996). *Approaches to the welfare state.* Washington, DC: NASW Press.

Danziger, S., & Gottschalk, P. (1995). *America unequal.* Cambridge, MA: Harvard University Press.

Ehrenreich, J. H. (1985). *The altruistic imagination: A history of social work and social policy in the U.S.* Ithaca, NY: Cornell University Press.

Ellwood, D. (1988). *Poor support: Poverty in the American family.* New York: Basic Books.

Howell, J. T. (1973). *Hard living on Clay Street.* Garden City, NJ: Anchor.

Katz, M. B. (1986). *In the shadow of the poorhouse.* New York: Basic Books.

Kaus, M. (1992). *The end of equality.* New York: New Republic.

Mead, L. (1992). *The new politics of poverty.* New York: Basic Books.

Phillips, K. (1993). *Boiling point.* New York: Random House.

Rochefort, D. A. (1986). *American social welfare policy.* Boulder, CO: Westview.

Ryan, W. (1971). *Blaming the victim.* New York: Vintage.

Seccombe, K. (1999). *"So you think I drive a Cadillac?": Welfare recipients' perspectives on the system and its reform.* Boston: Allyn & Bacon.

Trattner, W. I. (1999). *From Poor Law to welfare state.* New York: Free Press.

Wilson, W. J. (1987). *The truly disadvantaged.* Chicago: University of Chicago Press.

SOCIAL WORK AND OTHER HELPING PROFESSIONS

Al Swanson has just completed his 5th year as placement coordinator for the Big Brothers/Big Sisters agency. He finds that his social work skills are very useful in matching boys and girls from single-parent families with community volunteers who will provide an additional positive adult role model for their "little brother" or "little sister." Juanita Gonzales, a social worker for the local battered women's shelter, assists abused women and their children in locating a safe haven and in developing coping skills that will enable them to live more productive lives free from threatening attacks. Jill Carlisle works as a social worker for the local Family Service Agency where she specializes in working with pregnant and parenting teens. Miguel Morales, a school social worker, focuses his efforts on working with families from at-risk environments, seeking to enable them to offer more positive support for each other and their school-age children. Andrea Salisby is a social worker employed by the local Community Council, where she assists in identifying needed services and developing resources to make them possible. Horace Washington, a medical social worker, assists patients and their families in coping with the effects of illness and in developing resources that provide support while individuals are in the hospital or convalescing. Lucille Brighton is a social worker for the State Department of Human Resources. She is based in a small rural town where she finds her generalist social work skills very helpful in dealing with a wide variety of problems and very few organized resources to deal with them. Across the world, Lucas Pike, a social worker with an international development organization, draws on similar generalist skills in helping refugees from a war-torn village begin the process of rebuilding their lives and their homes.

The cases just described represent only a few of the broad and diverse activities that encompass generalist social work practice. Social workers are employed by a wide variety of local, state, and federal agencies as professionals who engage individuals, families, groups, organizations, and communities in seeking solutions to unmet needs. In this book, our aim is to give you an understanding of the goals and objectives of generalist social work practice, the nature of the profession, and the types of needs that social workers help their clients address. Social work practice demands from its practitioners the utmost in intellect, creativity, skill, and knowledge. It is an exciting, challenging profession. Students who have the aptitude and desire to prepare for a career in the helping professions may find social work well suited to their needs and interests.

In this chapter, we examine the professional culture, activities, knowledge base, and skills incorporated into social work practice. But first, we examine why people have unresolved problems and why they need professional assistance in seeking solutions to them.

Why Do People Have Problems?

Social workers deal with problems that inhibit optimal functioning for individuals, families, groups, organizations, or communities. Poverty, marital conflict, parent-child relationship problems, delinquency, abuse and neglect, substance abuse, and mental/emotional stress are among the many problems that professional social workers help people address.

Why do individuals develop problems so great that outside assistance is needed? There is no simple answer. Obviously, no rational person plans to have debilitating problems. No child plans to spend a life in poverty, nor does an adolescent choose a life of mental illness. What newly married couple, much in love and looking forward to the future together, plans for marital disharmony, family violence, or divorce? Why, then, do these problems

emerge? Why do some individuals experience happy, satisfying marriages, whereas others move from marriage to marriage without finding satisfaction? Why are some people prosperous and readily move up the occupational and income ladders, whereas others remain deeply enmeshed in poverty? A matter of personal choice? Of course not! Problems of social functioning result from a mix of many factors. Briefly, we need to examine the factors that contribute to adaptation.

Genetics and Heredity

From the biological standpoint, people are born with many of the physiological characteristics of their ancestors. Some people have a tendency to be tall, others short; some are lean, others heavy; some are physically attractive, others less attractive; and so on. Undoubtedly, many people have greater intellectual potential than others; some are more agile, others less so. To a certain degree these characteristics affect adaptation and, indeed, opportunities throughout life. For example, regardless of desire or ability, it is extremely difficult for a 5-foot, 6-inch man to become a professional basketball player. Regardless of desire or skill, opportunity clearly is affected by physical characteristics. We encourage you to think of other examples in which genetic and/or hereditary factors might impose limitations on social behavior or opportunities.

Abnormal, or psychopathological, behavior is often linked to biochemical types of genetic disorders. **Psychobiological** approaches to behavioral dysfunctions focus on identifying anomalies in body chemistry and studying how environmental stress converges with those anomalies to produce maladaptive behavior. For example, conditions such as schizophrenia, depression, chronic anxiety, somatoform disorders, and others are often believed to be genetically linked.

Socialization

Whatever limits may be imposed by heredity, individuals develop as social beings through the process of **socialization.** Social behavior is learned behavior acquired through interacting with other human beings. Parents are the primary source of early socialization experiences. Family culture has a significant impact on the development of values, priorities, and role prescriptions. Families, of course, are not the only source of our social development. Neighbors, playmates, and acquaintances from school and other community institutions also play a part. Lower-income parents and wealthy ones may socialize their children in different ways, for example, because resources and problem-

solving opportunities vary so much. Thus, as children develop, their behaviors are shaped by the particular learning opportunities available to them. The thoughts people have and the mental attitudes they develop are as much a product of learning as are the skills they develop. Children who grow up in at-risk families often learn inappropriate techniques of problem solving.

Cultural Differences

Cultural differences may also serve to create behaviors that appear to be in conflict with broader societal norms and expectations. Traditional customs and behaviors may vary conversely with the majority group's requirements and create dissonance, which results in behavior that is interpreted as maladaptive or dysfunctional. The United States takes pride in and has been enriched by immigrants from around the world. It is expected that these immigrants will adapt and assimilate to the dominant culture, although trying to meet these expectations may be problematic for them. Language differences and cultural traits often result in stereotyping, categorizing individuals as "out-group" members, and imposing barriers to social opportunities.

Environmental Factors

Geography, climate, and resources all affect quality of life and opportunities available for satisfactory growth and development. These factors vary throughout the world. Added to this are the economic and political forces that largely determine the availability of opportunities and resources around which people seek to organize their lives. Smog-infested, polluted areas contribute to a variety of health problems. Unpredictable economic trends may result in job loss for certain segments of the population. Discrimination limits opportunities for career development and impedes adequate employment. The environment is a major element in the opportunity structure. It can serve as a stimulus for producing life's satisfactions or become a major source of the problems people experience.

The Opportunity Structure

Obviously, genetics and heredity, socialization and cultural differences, and environmental factors are important in understanding why people have problems. All of these factors shape an individual's **opportunity structure**—that is, the accessibility of opportunities for an individual within that individual's environment. For example, a person may have physical traits and characteristics that are valued by society, a strong educational background, a stable and supportive family, work-oriented values, and a desire to work yet have no job because of a recession or depression. In spite of suitable preparation, this person may remain unemployed for some time, with all the problems associated with lack of income. An individual may be born into a poor family, be abused as a child, lack encouragement or incentives from parents and teachers to complete school, and have limited social skills because of inadequate parenting. Even if jobs were plentiful, this person would be able to compete for only the lowest-paying positions, if at all.

Other illustrations relate to genetic endowment. Gender, race, and ethnicity often result in discrimination and unequal treatment in both job opportunities and the amount of remuneration a person will receive on the job. Women, African Americans, and Latinos, for example, are not afforded equal opportunity in the job market even when all other factors are equal.

SOCIAL WORK DEFINED

In the minds of many, **social workers** are often identified as "welfare" workers who are engaged in public assistance programs. Obviously, this is a false premise since social workers are involved in many different practice settings that offer a wide range of service. Social welfare literally means "social well-being." In the United States, it generally refers to the provision of institutional programs for the needy. The profession of **social work,** on the other hand, is one of the professions that is instrumental in administering planned change activities prescribed by our social welfare institutions.

We must keep in mind, too, that the opportunity structure consists not only of what is available in the environment but also of inner resources such as cognitive development and personality structure. Furthermore, many problems that individuals, families, groups, organizations, and communities experience result from the way society is organized and the limited choices that are available to some people.

Because social workers are actively involved in wide-ranging tasks, devising a specific, all-inclusive definition of social work is difficult. Unfortunately, this has resulted in definitions that are so general that they fail to relate appropriately all of the activities encompassed by the profession. For example, Box 2.1 lists some of the roles played by social workers today. The National Association of Social Workers (NASW) states that the primary mission of the profession is to enhance human well-being and help meet the basic needs of all people, with

Roles Played by Generalist Social Workers

Enabler: A social worker who provides encouragement, offers hope, helps clients identify and focus on goals, and enables clients to make choices that improve their functioning.

Mediator: A mediator helps resolve conflicts between client systems at one or more levels of the environment while playing a neutral role.

Integrator/coordinator: An integrator/coordinator helps bring together various components of a system into a unified whole to create positive change.

General manager: The general manager assumes administrative responsibility for a specific project, program, or agency.

Educator: The social worker whose main task is to convey information and knowledge to develop skills in an educator. This role can be played in many situations in addition to a formal classroom situation.

Analyst/evaluator: A social worker in this role gathers information to assess the effectiveness of work with clients or client systems and makes recommendations for change as needed.

Broker: A social worker who links client systems with existing resources is playing a broker role. It is also the social work profession's responsibility to work to ensure that those resources treat client systems in a humane and effective way.

Facilitator: A social worker facilitates change by bringing together groups of people and helping them use their own talents as well as other resources to create positive change.

Initiator: A social worker who calls attention to an unaddressed problem or need is playing an initiator role.

Negotiator: A social worker who advocates on behalf of a client system is playing a negotiator role. The social worker in this role is on the side of the client system.

Mobilizer: A social worker who assembles, energizes, and organizes new or existing groups plays a mobilizer role.

Advocate: A social worker who fights for the rights and dignity of people in need of help advocates for their cause.

Outreach worker: A social worker who identifies specific client systems and reaches out to provide assistance is an outreach worker.

Source: Adapted from K. Kirst-Ashman and G. Hull: *Generalist Practice with Organizations and Communities*, pp. 22–27. Chicago: Nelson-Hall, 1997.

particular attention to the needs and empowerment of people who are vulnerable, oppressed, and living in poverty (NASW, 1999, p. 1).

Social work is viewed as an activity that seeks to help individuals, families, organizations, groups, or communities engage resources that will alleviate human problems. Social work also is concerned with enabling clients to develop capacities and strengths that will improve their social functioning. As this definition indicates, social work is an active, "doing" profession that brings about positive change in problem situations through problem solving or prevention. The social work profession is also committed to effecting changes in societal values and policies that limit or prohibit the free and full participation of individuals. Social workers have a professional responsibility to work for changes in discriminatory or otherwise restrictive practices that limit opportunities and prevent maximum social functioning.

The Early Years

Professional social work developed slowly over the years as a result of efforts to refine and improve its knowledge and skill base. As discussed in Chapter 1, the early administration of relief to the needy was accomplished by a wide variety of individuals: overseers of the poor, friends and neighbors, church members, the clergy, philanthropists, and friendly visitors, among others. As early as 1814 in Scotland, the Reverend Thomas Chalmers expressed concern over wasteful and inefficient approaches used by relief programs and sought to encourage the development of a more humane and effective system for providing services and support. Chalmers emphasized the need for a more personalized involvement with the needy. He devised a system wherein his parish was divided into districts, with a deacon assigned to investigate each case to determine the causes of problems. If the resultant analysis indicated that self-sufficiency was not possible, an attempt was made to engage family, friends, neighbors,

or wealthy citizens to provide the necessary assistance for the needy. As a last resort, the congregation was asked to provide assistance (Trattner, 1999).

Later, in the United States, the Association for Improving the Conditions of the Poor (New York City) and the Charity Organization Society (Buffalo, New York City, and Philadelphia) used similar approaches when organizing activities to help the poor. The **Charity Organization Society (COS)** had a profound effect on establishing social work as a specialized practice. It promoted "scientific philanthropy," emphasizing that charity was more than almsgiving. Furthermore, the COS stressed the importance of individual assessment and a coordinated plan of service. The COS was the first relief organization to pay personnel to investigate requests for assistance and to refer eligible applicants to one or more existing agencies for intensive aid and supervision. Special emphasis was given to "following up" on the recipients of assistance, and efforts were made to secure someone to establish friendly relationships with them (Axinn & Levin, 1997).

Just as "friendly visiting" was encouraged, attention was also given to data collection and assessment. It was believed that a more structured, informed, and skillful approach would increase efficiency, discourage dependence on charity, lead to personal development and self-sufficiency, and reduce the practice of providing relief for chronic beggars.

The settlement house movement also emerged as a viable means for providing a variety of community-based services and advocacy for the poor and disenfranchised during the late 1800s. Perhaps the most noteworthy of the settlements was Hull House, established in Chicago in 1889 by Jane Addams, a pioneer social worker. The success of this venture was immediate, and the programs offered by Hull House captured the imagination of both philanthropic helpers and the needy. The settlements maintained a strong family focus, provided socialization experiences, and, through advocacy efforts, sought to influence the community to correct the dismal social conditions under which the poor were living.

This structured approach to managing charitable efforts quickly resulted in the need for trained workers. Mary Richmond, a major contributor to the COS movement (and considered by many to be the founder of the professional clinical social work movement), inaugurated the first training program for social workers at the New York School of Applied Philanthropy, the forerunner of schools of social work. Richmond also formulated the concept and base for **social casework,** a practice method designed to "develop personality through adjustments consciously effected, individual by individual, between [persons] and their environment" (Richmond, 1922, p. 9). She also maintained a keen interest in personality and family development and stressed the environmental influence within which interpersonal interactions transpired. Believing that environmental factors were significant contributors to personal as well as family dysfunctions, she maintained a strong interest in social reform that would promote a better quality of life for individuals (Axinn & Levin, 1997). Richmond was convinced that this task should be included in the social worker's sphere of responsibility. In her classic work *Social Diagnosis* (1917), she laid the framework for social casework practice. Under the impetus provided by Richmond, Jane Addams, and other early social work pioneers, a profession was born.

Schools of social work began to emerge along the eastern seaboard and in large cities

Jane Addams, one of the first social workers in the United States and the founder of Hull House in Chicago, advocated for social reforms to improve the lives of immigrants.
© Underwood & Underwood/Corbis

of the Midwest, emphasizing direct social work practice (casework). Many were influenced by newly developing psychological perspectives, most notably those of Sigmund Freud and Otto Rank. Schools adopting Freudian psychology were more prevalent and became identified as "diagnostic" schools. Schools incorporating Rankian theory were known as "functional" schools. Shaping of curriculum around psychological theories increased the scientific knowledge base for social work practice.

By the late 1920s, **social group work** had gained visibility as a method of social intervention, rather than "treatment" per se. Learning and social development were believed to be enhanced through structured group interactions. This technique soon became popular in settlement houses and in work with street gangs, organized recreational clubs, and residents of institutions. Social group work became well entrenched as a viable helping method and later was adopted as a social work method.

Community organization had its roots in the New York Society for the Prevention of Pauperism, the Association for Improving Conditions of the Poor, and the settlement house movement. It became prominent as a resource development method by the late 1930s. Dealing largely with community development and stressing the importance of citizen participation and environmental change, community organizers plied their skills in identifying unmet human needs and working toward the development of community resources to meet those needs. Skills in needs assessment, planning, public relations, organizing, influencing, and resource development were among the prerequisites for community organizers.

By the 1950s, social casework, group work, and community organization were all considered methods of social work practice. In 1955, the various associations established to promote and develop each separate method merged and became known as the **National Association of Social Workers (NASW).** NASW continues to serve as the main professional organization for social workers today, with over 100,000 members. It seeks to promote quality in practice, stimulates political participation and social action, maintains standards of eligibility for membership in the association, and publishes several journals, including *Social Work*. Each state has an NASW chapter with a designated headquarters, and local membership units are active in all major cities. Many college and uni-versity social work programs also have student units of NASW.

UNDERPINNINGS OF THE PROFESSION

Social work professional practice is based on values, ethics, a common body of knowledge that builds on a liberal arts base, and planned change. Each of these attributes is important to professional social workers. The **Council on Social Work Education (CSWE)** has incorporated these attributes into a curriculum policy statement and specific content areas that social work education programs must address at the bachelor's (BSW) and master's (MSW) levels. These specific areas are discussed later in the chapter.

Values

Social workers are committed to the dignity, worth, and value of all human beings, regardless of social class, race, color, creed, gender, or age. The value of human life transcends all other values, and the best interest of human beings merits a humane and helpful response from society. People with problems, regardless of the nature of those problems, are not to be judged, condemned, or demeaned. Social workers emphasize that nonjudgmental attitudes are essential for maintaining clients' dignity and privacy and that clients must be accepted as they are, with no strings attached. Furthermore, clients (or the **client system,** which may include more than one individual, such as a family or a group of adults with disabilities) have the right to autonomy—that is, the right to determine courses of action that will affect their lives. Likewise, groups and communities hold these fundamental rights.

NASW has established a code of ethics (see Box 2.2) for its members, and a strong professional culture has developed and is expressed through the state and national associations of social work practitioners.

Ethics

Ethics (that is, moral duty) is a product of values. Professional ethics, therefore, relates to the moral principles of practice. Social work

---

BOX 2.2

NASW Code of Ethics

Preamble

The primary mission of the social work profession is to enhance human well-being and help meet the basic human needs of all people, with particular attention to the needs and empowerment of people who are vulnerable, oppressed, and living in poverty. A historic and defining feature of social work is the profession's focus on individual well-being in a social context and the well-being of society. Fundamental to social work is attention to the environmental forces that create, contribute to, and address problems in living.

Social workers promote social justice and social change with and on behalf of clients. "Clients" is used inclusively to refer to individuals, families, groups, organizations, and communities. Social workers are sensitive to cultural and ethnic diversity and strive to end discrimination, oppression, poverty, and other forms of social injustice. These activities may be in the form of direct practice, community organizing, supervision, consultation, administration, advocacy, social and political action, policy development and implementation, education, and

research and evaluation. Social workers seek to enhance the capacity of people to address their own needs. Social workers also seek to promote the responsiveness of organizations, communities, and other social institutions to individuals' needs and social problems.

The mission of the social work profession is rooted in a set of core values. These core values, embraced by social workers throughout the profession's history, are the foundation of social work's unique purpose and perspective:

- service
- social justice
- dignity and worth of the person
- importance of human relationships
- integrity
- competence.

This constellation of core values reflects what is unique to the social work profession. Core values, and the principles that flow from them, must be balanced within the context and complexity of the human experience.

Source: National Association of Social Workers (1999). Used with permission

values provide the basis for the social worker's beliefs about individuals and society, while ethics defines the framework for what should be done in specific situations. Both value and ethical dilemmas and conflicts are common. Social workers, like their clients, have personal reference groups whose values may often conflict with those of others. For example, a client may belong to a religious group that forbids and censures the use of professional medical intervention in cases of illness. The social worker may strongly favor medical intervention in those cases. Noting the value differences, what is the social worker's moral (ethical) duty in such cases? How can the best interests of the client be served where value conflicts are present? Do clients have the right to self-determination in such cases? As you ponder these questions, ask yourself what you would do. You will discover that responses to these types of situations are seldom easily achieved.

Review the NASW ethics code summarized in Box 2.2 to see whether it helps you arrive at appropriate ethical behavior in assisting the client discussed in the preceding paragraph.

Liberal Arts Base

Social workers at all levels must have a strong liberal arts base on which to build as they gain additional knowledge about human behavior, social welfare policy, research, and practice. Courses in English composition and literature; foreign language; government, history, and economics; sociology and psychology; mathematics and science; and culture and the fine arts provide students with important connections to the past and a broad perspective on social and human conditions. These courses also strengthen critical thinking and problem-

solving skills and allow students to have a more holistic understanding of the world in which they live.

Knowledge that Builds on the Liberal Arts Base

Social work practice is derived from a common body of knowledge, which includes theories of human behavior as well as experiential knowledge related to practice. Research also is an integrally important contributor to understanding individual, family, group, organizational, and community behavior. Research also is a method of identifying more effective intervention techniques. Students of social work are expected to have an understanding of the life cycle, as well as personality development, social dysfunction, developmental processes, group dynamics, effects of discrimination, social policy formulation, research methods, and community environments. Schools of social work encourage students to become familiar with a wide range of social and behavioral science theories that serve as a basis for understanding how client systems adapt and cope with client needs, and how theory guides planned social intervention. This knowledge undergirds the social worker's practice competence.

Practice Skills

Social workers are familiar with techniques related to direct practice with individuals (casework) and groups (group work), as well as communities (community organization). Organizing, planning, and administration also are included as areas of focus for many social work practitioners. Research skills are essential for evaluating practice effectiveness, too.

Planned Change

Professional social work intervention is based on a process of planned change. Change is indicated when client systems present dysfunctional problems that go unresolved. **Planned change** is an orderly approach to addressing client needs and is based on assessment, knowledge of the client system's capacity for change, and focused intervention. The social worker functions as a change agent in this process. Planned change is characterized by purpose and a greater likelihood of predictable outcomes derived from the change effort. Box 2.3 presents a statement of the purpose of social work formulated by social workers.

These underpinnings of the profession (values, knowledge, practice skills, and planned change) are discussed in greater detail in later chapters.

SOCIAL WORK METHODS

Social workers are committed to the process of planned change. In their role, they become agents of change, who focus on improving the conditions that adversely affect the

---

BOX
2.3

The Purpose of Social Work

The profession of social work is committed to the enhancement of human well-being and to the alleviation of poverty and oppression. The social work profession receives its sanction from public and private auspices and is the primary profession in the provision of social services. Within its general scope of concern, professional social work is practiced in a wide variety of settings. It has four related purposes:

1. The promotion, restoration, maintenance, and enhancement of the functioning of individuals, families, groups, organizations and communities by helping them to accomplish tasks, prevent and alleviate stress, and use resources.

2. The planning, formulation, and implementation of social policies, services, resources, and programs needed to meet basic human needs and support the development of human capacities.

3. The pursuit of policies, services, resources, and programs through organizational or administrative advocacy and social or political action to empower groups at risk and to promote social and economic justice.

4. The development and testing of professional knowledge and skills related to these purposes.

Source: Council on Social Work Education: *Curriculum Policy Statement for Baccalaureate Programs in Social Work Education,* p. 2. Washington, DC: Author, 1999.

functioning of clients (or client systems). Change efforts may be geared toward assisting individuals, families, groups, organizations, or communities (or all five), and appropriate methods of intervention for achieving problem solutions are engaged. Practice methods incorporate social work values, principles, and techniques in

- helping people obtain resources,
- conducting counseling and psychotherapy with individuals or groups,
- helping communities or groups provide or improve social and health services, and
- participating in relevant legislative processes that affect the quality of life for all citizens.

A variety of social work practice methods exist. These are discussed briefly in the following sections and more extensively in Part Two.

Social Work with Individuals and Families

When the social worker's effort is focused on working directly with individuals or families, the process is called **direct practice** (casework). This type of method is geared toward helping individuals and families identify solutions to personal or other problems related to difficulty in social functioning. In many instances, problems related to social inadequacy, emotional conflict, interpersonal loss, social stress, or the lack of familiarity with resources create dysfunction for individuals. Practitioners are skilled in assessment and know how to intervene strategically in providing assistance for those problems. Direct practice is often considered to be therapeutic in nature.

Social Work with Groups (Group Work)

Group work techniques seek to enrich individuals' lives through planned group experiences. Group work stresses the value of self-development through structured interaction with other group members. This process is based on theories of group dynamics and encourages personal growth through active participation as a group member. Groups may be natural (already formed), such as street gangs, or formed purposefully at the group work setting, such as support groups. In either instance, the value of participation, democratic goal setting, freedom of expression, acceptance, and the development of positive attitudes through sharing is stressed. Group work generally is not considered therapeutic, and it should not be confused with group therapy, which also uses group processes. Group therapy is designed to be therapeutic in that it seeks to alter or diminish dysfunctional behavior through the dynamic use of group interaction. Members of therapeutic groups often share common emotionally distressing experiences (e.g., a group of recent divorcees) and through focused discussion develop options for more adaptive behaviors.

Community Organization

Social workers who practice at the community level use techniques of community organization to promote change. Recognizing that citizen awareness and support are vital to the development of resources in generating a more healthy and constructive environment for all citizens, community organizers work with established organizations within the community (such as Lions and Kiwanis Clubs, city governments, welfare organizations, the Junior League, political groups, social action groups, and other citizens' organizations) to gain support for needed services and to secure funding for their maintenance. Social workers who practice at this level are typically employed by city governments, planning agencies, councils of social agencies, or related community agencies.

Social Work Research

Although all social workers use research regularly, many social workers specialize in social work research. Research increases both the knowledge base of practice and the effectiveness of intervention. It also provides an empirical base on which more focused policy formulation may be designed. Social research is essential in the process of establishing a scientific framework for solving problems and refining social work practice methods. Evaluative research enables agencies as well as practitioners to gain a better understanding of the effectiveness of efforts designed to meet goals and objectives around which practice efforts are focused. Competent social work practitioners keep abreast of the professional research and use research findings in their practice.

Social Work Administration and Planning

Administration and planning is a social work method that seeks to maximize the effective use of agency resources in problem solving. Administrators must be skilled in organizing, planning, and employing management techniques, as well as knowledgeable about social

work practice. Many social agency administrators begin their careers as direct practitioners, subsequently become supervisors, and then move into administrative roles. Social planning also is seen as a social work role, which is discussed in Chapter 7.

PROFESSIONAL ISSUES IN SOCIAL WORK

By now, you have seen that social work is a multifaceted profession wherein social workers are employed in a variety of roles and settings. With economic and technological changes erupting at a rapid pace during the past century, the nature of problems experienced by the populace has mirrored the effects of those changes. At the same time, the knowledge base of the social and behavioral sciences has expanded and generated more insightful theories of human behavior.

However, in spite of the progress made over the past 100 years, the United States continues to have a substantial number of people who are poor and disenfranchised. Some have argued that the poor, oppressed, and disenfranchised have been abandoned (Specht & Courtney, 1994) by the social work profession in favor of the more esoteric practices of counseling and psychotherapy. Proponents of this belief argue that the profession, once identified as a bulwark and vanguard for the oppressed, has turned its back on community action in favor of a case by case approach. The debate over the proper role of the social work profession is not likely to end soon. We invite you to review the definition of social work and its history and consider the stance you deem most appropriate for the profession in the future.

THE SOCIAL AGENCY

The majority of social workers perform their professional functions through the auspices of a social agency. **Social agencies** are organizations that have been formed by communities to address social problems experienced by its citizens. Agencies may be public (funded by taxes), voluntary (funded through contributions), or, in increasing numbers, proprietary (profit-oriented). The typical social agency is headed by a board of directors of local citizens. It meets regularly to review the agency's activities and to establish policy that governs agency services. Many larger agencies have an administrator who has sole responsibility for supervising the agency's activities. In many smaller agencies, the administrator also may be involved in assisting clients with their needs.

Agencies are community resources that stand ready to assist in addressing needs that make day-by-day functioning difficult. Social workers are employed to carry out the agency's mission. Many agencies do not charge fees for the services they provide. In some instances, however, agencies employ a "sliding-fee scale" and adjust the fee to the client's ability to pay. All clients, regardless of their economic resources, are afforded the same quality of service.

Typically, agencies cooperate in meeting human needs. Referrals are often made when clients have needs that can be addressed more effectively by another agency. Interagency coordination is a helpful process, maximizing community resources to respond to unmet needs.

EDUCATION AND LEVELS OF SOCIAL WORK PRACTICE

Professional social workers are involved in assisting clients with a large variety of unmet needs. As a consequence, the nature and degree of skills necessary for addressing unmet needs vary with the complexities of the needs encountered. Recognizing that professional competence is a right clients have in seeking assistance, regardless of how difficult meeting their needs might be, the social work profession has developed three different levels of practice for meeting these divergent needs. The profession has also established the Council on Social Work Education (CSWE), which, through its division of standards and accreditation, serves as the accrediting body for professional educational programs at the bachelor's and master's levels.

Bachelor of Social Work (BSW)

The entry level for professional social work practice is the BSW degree. Social work practitioners entering practice at this level must complete the educational requirements for an undergraduate social work program accredited by the CSWE. Although professional social work educational programs offered by colleges and universities may vary, the CSWE mandates that each must build on a liberal arts base and provide basic education in human behavior and the social environment, social welfare policy and services, research, practice methods, social and economic justice, cultural diversity, populations at risk, and social work values and ethics as a minimum requirement for meeting accreditation standards. All students who graduate from an accredited BSW program must complete 400 clock hours of field experience in a social work or related setting under the supervision of a social work practitioner. Typical field placements include senior citizens' centers, battered women's shelters, child welfare agencies, residential treatment centers, juvenile and adult probation programs, public schools, health clinics, hospitals, industries, and mental health agencies.

The educational curriculum for baccalaureate-level practice is developed around the generalist method of practice. Typically, the generalist practitioner is knowledgeable about the systems/ecological approach (see Chapter 3 for a complete discussion) to practice and is skillful in needs assessment, interviewing, resource development, case management, use of community resources, establishment of intervention objectives with clients, and problem solving.

The CSWE (1999) *Curriculum Statement for Baccalaureate Degree Programs in Social Work Education* outlines the objectives that undergird social work practice at the BSW level:

1. Apply critical thinking skills within the context of professional social work practice.
2. Practice within the values and ethics of the social work profession and with an understanding of and respect for the positive value of diversity.
3. Demonstrate the professional use of self.
4. Understand the forms and mechanisms of oppression and discrimination and the strategies of change that advance social and economic justice.
5. Understand the history of the social work profession and its current structure and issues.
6. Apply the knowledge and skills of generalist social work to practice with systems of all sizes.

7. Apply knowledge of biopsychosocial variables that affect individual development and behavior, and use theoretical frameworks to understand the interactions among individuals and between individuals and social systems (that is, families, groups, and communities).
8. Analyze the impact of social policies on client systems, workers, and agencies.
9. Evaluate research studies and apply findings to practice, and, under supervision, evaluate their own practice intervention and those of relevant systems.
10. Use communications skills differentially with a variety of client populations, colleagues, and members of the community.
11. Use supervision appropriate to generalist practice.
12. Function within the structure of organizations and service delivery systems, and, under supervision, seek necessary organizational change. (p. 3)

Entry-level social workers are employed by agencies offering a wide spectrum of services. As generalist social workers, they may perform professional activities as eligibility workers for state human services departments; work with children and families as protective services (protecting children from abuse and neglect) workers; serve as youth or adult probation workers; work in institutional care agencies that provide services for children or adults, especially the aged; engage in school social work; act as program workers or planners for areawide agencies on aging; work in mental health outreach centers or institutions; serve as family assistance workers in industry; or perform their professional tasks in many other agencies providing human services. It is not uncommon for baccalaureate-level professionals with experience and demonstrated competence to be promoted to supervisory and administrative positions.

Social work professionals at the BSW level are eligible for full membership in NASW. The professional activities they perform in helping clients are challenging and rewarding. Many social workers prefer to practice at this level throughout their careers. For others, an advanced degree in social work is desirable and opens up areas of practice that are not typically in the domain of the BSW practitioner. For those who have completed their undergraduate social work education from an accredited college or university, advanced standing may be granted by the school of social work to which they apply. Although not all graduate schools accept advanced-standing students, the CSWE provides a listing of those that do. Advanced-standing students, when admitted to a graduate program, are able to shorten the time required to secure the master's degree without diluting the quality of their educational experience. Advanced practice in social work is predicated upon receiving the master's degree in social work (MSW).

Master of Social Work: Advanced Practice

One hundred thirty-five colleges and universities in the United States have accredited graduate schools of social work (CSWE, 2000). Students in these programs are engaged in an educational curriculum that is more specialized than the BSW curriculum. Depending on how the curriculum is organized, students may specialize in direct services (clinical social work), community organization, administration, planning, research, or a field of practice (child welfare, medical social work, mental health, social work with the elderly, or school

social work). All students master a common core of basic knowledge that builds on a liberal arts base, including human behavior and the social environment, social welfare policy and services, research, and practice methods related to their area of specialization. The 2-year master's degree program is balanced between classroom learning and field practice. Graduates seek employment in such specialized settings as Veterans Administration hospitals, family and children's service agencies, counseling centers, and related settings that require specialized professional education.

Doctorate in Social Work (DSW and Ph.D.)

Professional social workers interested in social work education, highly advanced clinical practice, research, planning, or administration often seek advanced study in the doctor of social work (DSW) or the doctor of philosophy in social work (Ph.D.) programs. A number of graduate schools of social work offer education at this level. Students admitted tend to be seasoned social work practitioners, although this is not a prerequisite for admission to all schools. Education at this level stresses research, advanced clinical practice, advanced theory, administration, and social welfare policy. Graduates usually seek employment on the faculty of schools of social work, in the administration of social welfare agencies, or, with increasing frequency, in private clinical practice.

SOCIAL WORK CAREERS

The number of employed social service workers grew rapidly from 95,000 in 1960 to well over 350,000 by 1999. While federal and state funding for some social welfare programs has declined, social work is still one of the fastest-growing professions. New positions are being created in addition to the vacancies created through attrition. Some fields of practice with a vast potential for growth are beginning to emerge. For example, the fields of health care, aging, and substance abuse are experiencing a great need for professional social workers.

Social work is an ideal profession for individuals interested in working with people and helping them address their needs. These broad interests are the heart of the social work profession. Positions in a wide variety of areas continue to attract social workers at all levels of practice, such as child welfare, health, corrections, developmental disabilities, family counseling, substance abuse, and public assistance programs.

Wages in social work usually are adequate, and increases are based on skill and experience. BSW-level workers typically earn less than the more specialized MSW degree workers. Entrance salaries may range from $18,000 to $30,000 per year, depending on experience, degree, location, and agency sponsorship. A few social workers earn upward of $75,000–$100,000 after extensive experience. Mobility often is a valuable asset to the social worker looking for an initial social work job. Rural areas often experience shortages of social workers, whereas some metropolitan areas tend to have a tighter employment market. Employment vacancies often are listed with college placement services, state employment commissions, professional associations, state agencies, or local newspapers.

In recent years, more social workers with advanced degrees in social work have engaged in **private practice.** Unlike more traditionally employed social workers, private practitioners must rely on fees from their clients to support their practice. Often, social workers spend most of their time employed by a social agency and see clients in private practice on a part-time basis. Others may devote full time to their practice. Generally, private practice focuses on clients in need of counseling or group therapy. Private practitioners are governed by the NASW Code of Ethics and the social work value base. They extend their services to clients who often would not seek assistance through traditional agency networks. Many private practitioners provide some services on a **pro bono** (no cost) basis to clients who could not otherwise afford them.

OTHER HELPING PROFESSIONALS

Social workers are not alone in assisting people who are experiencing problems. They often find that the unique skills of other helping professionals are beneficial in addressing needs that are beyond the scope of the social worker's skill and knowledge base or are otherwise inappropriate for social work intervention. Frequently, social workers are members of a collaborative effort with other professionals in assisting individuals, families, groups, or communities in finding solutions to troubling problems or in establishing prevention programs. For example, a school social worker, guidance counselor, clinical psychologist, and school nurse might combine their professional expertise in developing a program designed to prevent teenage pregnancy. Or, a social worker might work with a pastoral counselor and psychiatrist to help a former client with emotional problems become reestablished into community life. Although there are many instances in which professional teamwork enhances the opportunities of clients and furthers the opportunities for successful intervention, it is the social worker's responsibility to guard the integrity of the referral process when seeking the expertise of resources to whom they refer their clients.

In the following sections, we include a brief overview of the more prominent community professionals who practice in the area of human services.

Psychiatrists

Psychiatry is a specialized field of medical practice that focuses on mental and emotional dysfunction. Although psychiatrists typically treat clients experiencing some form of psychopathology, many help with other problems of social dysfunction and interpersonal relationships. For example, a psychiatrist may counsel couples experiencing marital discord, assist adolescents with problems in adaptation, use play therapy with children whose social development has been delayed, counsel individuals and couples who experience sexual problems, and so on. Unlike other professionals who assist with psychological and emotional problems as well as those of social dysfunction, psychiatrists can provide medications in cases where physiological symptoms indicate the need for them. Because psychiatrists are physicians (with a medical degree), they have at their disposal a wide array of medical interventions as well as their expertise in treating problems of a mental and emotional nature.

Psychiatrists practice in a variety of settings. Hospitals established for the treatment of the mentally ill constitute the most frequent employment sites. Many psychiatrists establish private practices, usually in major metropolitan areas. Others are either employed full-time or serve as treatment consultants in residential treatment centers, children's agencies, centers designed for the treatment of specialized problems such as family violence or alcohol or substance abuse, or suicide prevention centers. Some also assist other agencies that provide specialized services to the emotionally disturbed.

Like other helping professionals, psychiatrists are educated in various programs that emphasize different theoretical and methodological approaches to problem solving. Some embrace "insight therapies" such as those advanced by Sigmund Freud, Alfred Adler, Carl Jung, and Harry Stack Sullivan. In recent times, many psychiatrists have adopted learning theory approaches (behavior modification) as well as reality therapy, rational emotive therapy, transactional analysis, and related approaches. Psychiatrists typically are well educated within their specialty and constitute a significant and important resource for treating problems of the mentally ill and emotionally disturbed.

Psychologists

The American Psychological Association (APA) has identified 52 subspecialties in the field of **psychology** (APA, 2000). These include clinical, counseling, forensic, health, educational, school, industrial/organizational, sports, neuroscientific, experimental, and developmental psychology.

Without some awareness of the differences in specialty areas, it might be difficult to identify the appropriate resource for problem solving. Unlike psychiatrists, professional psychologists are not physicians. Those who engage in practice designed to assist with psychological and emotional problems generally are referred to as *clinical* or *counseling psychologists*. Like psychiatrists, psychologists are educated in universities and professional schools that emphasize a wide variety of theoretical and methodological approaches to practice. Again like psychiatrists, many have developed skills in psychotherapy and psychoanalysis. Others prefer methodological approaches that reflect a behavior modification, cognitive therapy, Gestalt therapy, or related practice modality. Psychologists treat clients with deep-rooted emotional conflict, inadequate personality development, interpersonal problems represented in marriage and family conflict, substance abuse, and various psychological and behavioral disorders. They typically use various forms of **psychometric instruments** (testing) in diagnosing a problem. These instruments are designed to provide information about clients and their functioning that often is not readily observable during a client interview. Tests also may be used as a basis for establishing a personality profile for clients and for providing insights into the client's abilities to handle stress and areas where the client is vulnerable. Tests, however, are only one of many sources of evidence needed to assess clients' problems.

Many psychologists are skilled in group therapy as well as individual practice. In recent years, group psychotherapy and group treatment have emerged as significant treatment techniques in helping clients with similar problems resolve those problems through the use of group dynamics and the skillful intervention of the group therapist.

Psychologists engaging in psychometry are often called on as consultants to test clients in social service agencies and educational institutions. This service is often very helpful in gaining better insights into clients and establishing appropriate treatment and intervention plans.

Sociologists

Sociologists focus on the study of society, its organization, and the phenomena arising out of the group relations of human beings. As such, professionals in this area contribute much to our awareness of human interaction, including the establishment of norms, values, social organization, patterns of behavior, and social institutions. Sociologists are skilled in research techniques and methodologies. Like other professionals, they may focus on a subspecialty such as the family, deviancy, industrial sociology, symbolic interaction, bureaucracy and related forms of social organization, and the sociology of knowledge and social problems.

The majority of sociologists are employed at institutions of higher education and related educational institutions, although a growing number are entering the field of clinical, or applied, sociology. Professionals engaging in clinical sociology seek to apply the knowledge and principles gleaned from sociological theory to identify or enrich the understanding of organizational or interactional relationships, with the goal of resolving problems. Sociologists using this approach may function as family counselors, group therapists, industrial consultants, problem analysts, or program planners. The contribution of sociology to the understanding of the impact of environment and group membership on behavior has proven immeasurable.

Pastoral Counselors

Perhaps no other single source of contact by persons experiencing problems is sought out more often than religious leaders. Priests, pastors, ministers, rabbis, and other persons in positions of spiritual leadership are called on readily by members of their congregations and others in trouble. Religious leaders are placed in a unique and valued position by the laity. As spiritual leaders, they are presumed to have an extraordinary understanding of human frailty and a special ability to communicate with spiritual powers. Just as congregations vary in size and sophistication, so do the educational background and experience of religious leaders as problem solvers. Many receive extensive theological education coupled with a specialty in counseling. Others become counselors by demand, with little academic and supervised practical instruction to do so. Still others are relatively uneducated and hold their positions by what they perceive as a unique calling from God. In most instances, they are committed to helping their parishioners find solutions to problems within the context of a particular religious belief system.

Professional **pastoral counselors** are most often educated at schools of theology offering specializations in counseling. Typically, these programs offer classroom theory and a practicum that utilizes various psychological approaches to intervention and problem solving. Many religious leaders complete their theological education and enter graduate schools in clinical or counseling psychology, social work, or guidance and counseling programs. Larger congregations frequently employ a pastoral counselor to supplement the overall pastoral ministry.

Pastoral counselors may assist parishioners with marriage and family problems, developmental problems, social problems, difficulties with interpersonal relationships, and a myriad of other problems. Individuals experiencing inner conflict with respect to spiritual problems are frequently given assistance and support by the pastoral counselor. Skilled practitioners also may form groups to work on specific problems. In addition, pastoral counselors are engaged in various educational activities designed either to enrich the awareness and understanding of the congregation or to prevent problems. Like other human service professionals, pastoral counselors must develop an awareness of the limits of their professional skills and make referrals, where necessary, to assure that the client's best interests are served.

Guidance Counselors

The majority of guidance counselors are educated in the same university units that train public school teachers and are certified by state education agencies. They are generally required to have classroom teaching experience before they are eligible for certification as guidance counselors. Guidance counselors specialize in assisting students with educationally related problems and in locating educational resources best suited to their individual interests. Students with behavioral problems, as well as those with academic difficulties, often are referred to the guidance counselor for assistance. Although guidance counselors focus on academically related concerns, they often become engaged in a therapeutic relationship with students who are experiencing adaptive or emotionally related problems. Guidance counselors also may assist the school psychologist in administering tests to students and, in smaller school systems, may assume primary responsibility for the testing program. They are called on to provide essential information to classroom teachers about student performance and, in collaboration with them, to develop an educational plan for students experiencing difficulty with their academic progression. Guidance counselors occasionally find themselves in the role of ombudsman as they seek to assist students and teachers or administrators in resolving conflicts in their interaction. They may work with the school social worker where truancy or family problems are related significantly to the student's academic performance. The guidance counselor's specialized awareness of educational processes and resource alternatives can be valuable to students needing information or an awareness of options available to them.

Guidance counselors are not all assigned to public school systems, however. Many are employed in correctional systems, where they help inmates assess attitudes and skills needed to obtain productive employment after release from prison. This type of intervention generally requires collaboration with other members of the correctional team—for example, with specialists in vocational education and/or related areas. Correctional counselors also often network with the inmates' families as well as community social service agencies. Experience has demonstrated that many prisoners have never had an adequate opportunity structure within which productive learning and job opportunities were available. The correctional counselor attempts to equip inmates with personal, social, and job-related skills that will enable them to use their time more creatively while in prison and to make a smoother, better-prepared transition back into society when discharged. Under most circumstances, each released inmate is assigned to a parole officer, who will continue to provide counseling and assistance with job opportunities and family-related problems.

Rehabilitation counseling is yet another form of guidance counseling. Most states have established agencies to help individuals with physical or mental disabilities in identifying competencies and securing academic or vocational training that will enable them to find employment. These counselors may also help clients get specialized medical treatment for enhancement of physical, mental, and social capacities. Rehabilitation counselors are, by the nature of their specialization, heavily involved in teamwork and networking with other human and vocational service workers in securing resources that will assist their clients in achieving their productive potential. If successful, the client's level of independence will increase along with greater self-esteem and employability.

Guidance counselors usually are required to have completed an advanced degree as well as specialized coursework. In general, required coursework does not prepare the counselor for psychotherapy or long-term counseling.

Employment Counselors

Professionals who focus on assisting clients in locating employment, assessing their skill levels, and enrolling them in educational courses designed to prepare them for skill development and ultimate employment often are identified as employment counselors. Their specialized knowledge of the employment market and unique skills in matching clients seeking work with the needs of employers are designed to improve the probabilities of securing job satisfaction as well as competence in job performance. Employment counselors are skilled at interpreting various tests used to determine a client's aptitude for various positions. Not only do they assist people needing a job or those who don't fit well in the positions they hold to find the most suitable employment, but they also are available to assist them with locating the essential supports to maintain involvement on the job. For example, the lack of reliable transportation or affordable child care could represent barriers for an individual who otherwise needs work. Locating and referring the client to an appropriate resource may resolve those problems and produce a more favorable arrangement for meeting job demands.

Employment counselors work with the business community in identifying employment needs and the skill requirements that will be necessary to provide optimum benefit for the business as well as the worker. Feedback and monitoring systems may be established as mechanisms for fine-tuning the job referral process.

Vocational education programs abound in the United States, providing instruction in a variety of areas: cosmetology, aircraft maintenance, welding, carpentry, computer technology, auto mechanics, heavy machine operations, office management, hotel administration, and many other specialty areas. Workers who are dissatisfied in their current jobs or whose jobs have disappeared because of changing technology, people reentering the job market, or new workers entering employment often find vocational education beneficial in learning and strengthening skills. Persons with disabilities also find vocational education an invaluable resource in adapting their abilities to marketable skills. Employment counselors typically are influential in helping clients use vocational educational programs that enhance development of job-related skills.

Nurses

In recent years, the role of nurses has changed dramatically. Traditionally viewed as "doctors' helpers" or as pseudoprofessionals whose primary responsibility was to see that the doctor's orders were dutifully carried out, contemporary nurses have emerged as professionals in their own right. Schools of nursing now focus on the psychosocial aspects of services to debilitated or hospitalized clients as well as mastery of the basic skills related to patient care. Nurses may specialize in a variety of areas such as pediatrics, gerontology, psychiatry and mental health, or oncology. The body of knowledge required to become a professional nurse today is far different than in past decades. Emphasis on the therapeutic use of relationships and psychosocial adaptation has enhanced the nurse's ability to engage the client in the healing process. Nurses are becoming much more involved in the mental health field. They serve in counseling roles ranging from handling stress-related illnesses to counseling with families of ill patients and collaborating with other specialists in seeking the best therapeutic treatment approaches for their clients. Many nurses are also administrators of mental health programs.

Professional nurses typically receive their education from colleges or universities that have accredited schools of nursing. They may opt to pursue the licensed vocational nurses (LVN) certification or a registered nurse (RN) degree. They must pass state board examinations to practice. Many pursue a bachelor's or a master's degree in nursing, and larger numbers are enrolling in Ph.D. programs. Other nurses At whatever level, nurses play a vital role in the delivery of physical care as well as human services.

Attorneys-at-Law

Lawyers are professionals who engage in both criminal and civil matters to assist individuals in securing their rights under the law. Most communities, large or small, have practicing attorneys. Law, like other professional areas, has many specialties. Many lawyers are employed by large corporations and deal with contracts and their interpretation, assessing legal specifications relative to business practices and providing legal expertise essential for corporate ventures. Others are in private practice, with many handling primarily civil matters such as lawsuits, divorces, property settlements, deeds, estate management, and wills. Lawyers are educated in graduate schools of law throughout the country. As professionals, they encounter a myriad of problems that have legal consequences. In some cases, such as that of divorce or child custody, the lawyer often becomes involved in a counseling role. Although many lawyers lack the appropriate educational background and expertise, clients often seek their assistance with emotional as well as legal problems. Lawyers also make referrals to appropriate agencies or other professionals when indicated.

Many communities have established legal aid clinics that specialize in offering legal counsel to the poor or near poor to address problems such as divorce, child custody, property settlements, and adequate defense in a court of law. Legal aid clinics are an invaluable resource for the poor. Many lawyers are employed as full-time legal counselors at the clinics, while others work part-time or volunteer their time. Legal aid clinics seek to promote justice for the poor as well as for those in better financial circumstances. Typically, law firms assign a portion of their staff time to pro bono ("for the public good") efforts, often representing indigent clients.

Lawyers constitute a valuable resource to the problem-solving process. Indeed, a number of social work students enter law school

after receiving their BSW degree. Matters that need legal attention often are a source of stress and are responsive to the skillful intervention of the legal profession.

THE NEED FOR PROFESSIONAL DIVERSITY

Although the brief discussion here of selected professions is by no means complete, it does encompass the primary disciplinary areas in the human service field. Social workers and others in the helping professions need to develop an awareness of the expertise available in their practice arena. Many problems require the attention of experts from diverse areas of practice to move toward resolution. It also is requisite that all professionals develop an awareness of their limitations as well as strengths, if clients are to maximize the benefits they receive from those assisting them in meeting their needs.

In our complex, highly technological society, the emergence of specialization is a necessity. With the explosion of knowledge and our understanding of human needs fostered by advances in technology, it would be impossible for any one person to master it all. Just as society is complex, so, we have learned, are human beings. Values vary, as do the many diverse groups with whom we hold an identity. Specialty areas have emerged in response to such diverse needs and to the understanding of the theoretical explanations of behavior. Life is a problem-solving process, and our ability to respond appropriately to life's problems involves not only our personality makeup but knowledge, awareness, resources, and sensitivities as well. Invariably, all of us will at times encounter problems for which there appear no ready solutions. Often, the friendly advice of a neighbor, spouse, or confidant is sufficient in providing the perspective that will lead to an acceptable solution. At other times, professional assistance is essential.

A question often raised relates to the likenesses and differences among the professions. What, for example, does a psychiatrist do with clients that is different from what a psychologist would do, or a social worker, or a pastoral counselor? And so on. All, for example, might engage in marital counseling or assist a family struggling with the behavioral problems of an adolescent. To an uninformed observer, the professional response to those problems may appear to be approximately the same. Clients see the professional for an hour or so per week, the content of the interaction consists primarily of verbal interaction, and generally the client is given specific tasks to work on until the next visit. The professionals may contact other social systems related to the client's functioning, such as the school or employment system. What, then, constitutes the difference?

In part, although not exclusively, the differences may lie in the theoretical perspective that the professional brings to bear on the problem. The specialized emphasis on individual psychodynamics as reflected in psychiatry and psychology often varies with social work's emphasis on the systems/ecological framework and the relationship between the person and the environment within which the person functions. Also, social work's mastery of and emphasis on using community resources are distinct from the typical approaches used in psychiatry and psychology.

Social work emphasizes a holistic approach that focuses on enhancing the strengths of the client. Recognizing that stress may be generated by the lack of resources as well as intrapsychic conflict, social workers also may help their clients with concrete resources, such as locating a job, adequate housing, health care services, child care, or other needed services. The various roles that the generalist social work practitioner plays, such as advocate, broker, enabler, case manager, and intervener, often are essential to creating an environment in which clients can move toward addressing their own needs.

Cooperation and respect among the helping professions are necessary if the optimum helping environment is to be attained. Social workers have clients who need psychiatric treatment or the special services provided by a clinical or counseling psychologist or pastoral counselor. Many clients are assisted by referrals to the employment counselor. Students experiencing difficulty adapting to school benefit from referrals to the school guidance counselor. Positive interaction and collaboration among these professionals enrich the service systems and increase the probability of securing a better quality of intervention for clients in need. Each profession has its own distinct professional culture, and an awareness of these varying cultures should promote more appropriate referrals.

THE BACCALAUREATE SOCIAL WORKER AND OTHER PROFESSIONS

Baccalaureate social workers (that is, those holding the BSW degree) typically function as generalist practitioners and hold a unique position in the professional community. Their attention to a great variety of human needs demands skills as counselors, resource finders, case managers, evaluators, advocates, brokers, enablers, and problem solvers. The BSW social worker's awareness of community resources and the ability to use them skillfully in the problem-solving process are particularly valuable in securing the needed assistance for clients. These social workers work in varied social service agencies and community settings.

In cases representing multiple problems, the BSW social worker may become engaged as a case manager, with a focus on securing referrals to appropriate resources. The social worker may also become involved in providing the necessary supports to ensure that the clients use the services. In this role, the BSW social worker would continue to monitor and coordinate the intervention effort, with all of the intervention system components cooperating.

The BSW social worker may serve as a vital link among community professionals. The knowledge related to individual, family, group, organizational, and community functioning within the context of the systems/ecological framework helps this social worker identify the appropriate referral resources, engage them, and become an essential component of the helping process.

SUMMARY

Social work is a complex profession. It relies on a strong value base and clearly defined code of ethics and the development of practice skills in direct practice, community organization, and research, as well as in administration and planning. All social work practice is based on knowledge of human behavior and social organizations. In this chapter, we discussed the profession's attributes and clarified

the definition of social work as a distinctive profession.

We also examined why people have problems. Problems stem from heredity and genetics, socialization, cultural differences, environmental factors, and deficiencies in the opportunity structure. The brief history of the development of social work included in this chapter should provide a basis for understanding factors that led to the profession's emergence and the need it fulfills in the community. We also briefly discussed the levels of social work education and career opportunities available for individuals interested in entering the helping professions. In subsequent chapters, we will explain each aspect of social work methodology in greater detail.

Other prominent community professionals seek to help clients with problems of adaptation. We attempted to identify similarities and differences among the professions. The need for interprofessional collaboration was examined in relation to obtaining the greatest expertise for clients in the intervention process.

KEY TERMS

Charity Organization
  Society (COS)
client system
community organization
competencies
Council on Social Work
  Education (CSWE)
direct practice
ethics
National Association of
  Social Workers
  (NASW)
opportunity structure
pastoral counselors
planned change

private practice
pro bono
psychiatry
psychobiology
psychology
psychometric
  instruments
social agencies
social casework
social group work
social work
social workers
socialization
sociologists

DISCUSSION QUESTIONS

1. What is meant by the term *opportunity structure*? What are the characteristics of the opportunity structure?

2. What are social work values? How do values
relate to ethics?

3. What constitutes direct practice? Community
organization? Research? Administration and
planning? How are they alike, and how are they
different?

4. Identify the major contributions of the Charity
Organization Society to social work practice.

5. What skills should the generalist-level (BSW)
social worker possess?

6. How important is a code of ethics for a profession? Why?

7. How does social work differ from other professions that also function in the human services
arena?

INFOTRAC
COLLEGE EDITION

To learn more about topics included in this chapter,
enter the following search terms:

community practice

direct practice

generalist practice

Hull House

settlement house

social Darwinism

ON THE INTERNET

http://www.naswdc.org/

http://www.cswe.org/

http://www.uic.edu/jaddams/hull/hull_house.html

http://gateways.unhny.org/

http://www.geocities.com/Athens/1058/index.html

REFERENCES

American Psychological Association. (2000). *Divisions of
the American Psychological Association.*
http://www.apa.org.

Axinn, J., & Levin, H. (1997). *Social welfare: A history
of the American response to need* (8th ed.). New
York: Harper-Collins.

Council on Social Work Education. (1999). *Curriculum
policy statement for baccalaureate degree programs
in social work education.* Washington, DC: Author.

Council on Social Work Education. (2000). *Statistics on
social work education in the United States: 1999.*
Washington, DC: Author.

Kirst-Ashman, K., & Hull, G. (1997). *Generalist
practice with organizations and communities.*
Chicago: Nelson-Hall.

National Association of Social Workers. (1999). *NASW
code of ethics.* Washington, DC: Author.

Richmond, M. (1917). *Social diagnosis.* New York:
Russell Sage Foundation.

Richmond, M. (1922). *What is social casework?* New
York: Russell Sage Foundation.

Specht, H., & Courtney, M. (1994). *Unfaithful angels.*
New York: Free Press.

Trattner, W. (1999). *From Poor Law to welfare state: A
history of social welfare in America.* New York:
Free Press.

SUGGESTED FURTHER READINGS

Dubois, B., & Miley, K. K. (1997). *Social work: An
empowering profession.* Boston: Allyn & Bacon.

Ginsberg, L. (1997). *Careers in social work.* Boston:
Allyn & Bacon.

Goldstein, H. (1990). The knowledge base of social
work practice: Theory, wisdom, analogue, or art?
Families in Society, 71, 32–43.

Grobman, B. (Ed.). (1999). *Days in the lives of social
workers: 50 professionals tell real-life stories*

from social work practice. Harrisburg, PA: White Hat.

Johnson, L. (1989). *Social work practice: A generalist approach.* Boston: Allyn & Bacon.

Lowenberg, F., & Dolgoff, R. (1988). *Ethical decisions for social work practice* (3rd ed.). Itasca, IL: Peacock.

Macarov, D. (1995). *Social welfare: Structure and practice.* Thousand Oaks, CA: Sage.

Zastrow, C. (1999). *Introduction to social welfare institutions* (7th ed.). New York: Wadsworth.

THE SYSTEMS/ECOLOGICAL PERSPECTIVE

Understanding Social Work and Social Welfare

Juan, a 12-year-old Mexican American male, is in the seventh grade in an urban school in California. His teachers are concerned about him and are recommending to Christina Herrera, the school social worker, that he be enrolled in the school's dropout prevention program. Recently, Juan has been socializing during school with a group of much older students who are members of a local gang. He has been skipping classes, not completing class assignments, fighting with other students, and arguing with his teachers when they confront him about his behavior. During the past 2 weeks, he has been caught smoking marijuana and pulling a knife on a classmate. Ms. Herrera has talked with both Juan and his mother. She has suggested that Juan participate in a school support group and has referred Juan and his mother to the local teen/parent outreach center for counseling as soon as a counseling slot is available. Juan's mother is very concerned about him. But she also has indicated to Ms. Herrera that she is under a great deal of stress and is angry that Juan is adding to it.

Juan lives in a one-bedroom apartment with his mother and his younger brother, who is 5 years old. Six months ago, Juan's parents divorced, and his father moved to a neighboring state 300 miles away. Juan always had a fairly close relationship with both his parents. Although he knew that they fought a lot and that his father drank and lost his job, he was surprised when his parents told him that they were getting a divorce.

When Juan's father moved out, his mother had to get an extra job to make ends meet. The family also had to move into a small apartment in another part of the city. Juan's mother's relatives and friends, all devout Catholics, were very much against the divorce and have not been at all supportive. When she is not working, Juan's mother spends much of her time crying or sleeping. At first, Juan tried hard to be supportive of his mother, cooking meals, cleaning the house, and taking care of his little brother. But at times he doesn't cook or clean exactly the way his mother wants him to. When his brother gets noisy, Juan gets in trouble for not keeping him quiet. Lately, Juan's mother has begun yelling at or hitting Juan when this happens. Because she was abused as a child, Juan's mother feels guilty when she gets so angry at Juan, but she cannot understand why he can't be more supportive when she is trying so hard to keep the family together.

Juan has felt abandoned by everyone since the divorce. His mother is usually angry at him, and his two longtime friends, who come from two-parent families, seem less friendly to him. When they do ask him to do things with them, he usually can't anyway because he has to take care of his younger brother or he doesn't have any money. Transportation is also a problem, since Juan's friends live across town in his former neighborhood. Although he used to do well in school, Juan has lost interest in his classes. He can't get used to the new school, and he doesn't know any of the teachers there. But he has several new friends who seem to accept him. They are older, and their interest in him makes him feel important. Juan is excited that they want him to be a member of their gang. As long as school is so boring, he can spend time with them during the day and still take care of his brother after school. But he is seriously considering running away from home and moving in with one of the gang members, who lives with his older brother. The friend's older brother recently got out of prison and has promised that Juan can make a lot of money as a drug runner for him.

Juan's case illustrates the many factors that influence how people react to what is going on in their lives. Juan's present situation is affected by his developmental needs as he enters adolescence; his relationships with his mother, father, younger brother, friends, and school personnel; his father's alcoholism and unemployment; his parents' divorce; the fact that his mother was abused as a child; his family's tenuous economic situation; the lack of positive social support available from relatives, friends, the workplace, the school, the church, and the neighborhood to Juan's family; the lack of programs available to divorced parents and teens in Juan's community; Juan's cultural and ethnic background; and community and societal attitudes about divorce, female-headed households, and intervention in family matters. From Juan's perspective, the family system, the economic system, the political system, the religious system, the education system, and the social welfare system have failed to meet his needs. Yet he is forced to interact continually with all of these individuals, groups, and social structures on a regular basis and depends on all of them in some way.

In this chapter, we explore frameworks used by social workers to understand social problems and issues faced by individuals and families in today's world. The **systems/ecological framework** is an umbrella framework used by generalist social work practitioners with bachelor of social work (BSW) degrees to understand both social welfare problems and individual needs and guide the various interventions social workers use when helping clients.

THE IMPACT OF THEORETICAL FRAMEWORKS ON INTERVENTION

All individuals perceive what is going on in their lives and in the world somewhat differently. For example, an argument between a parent and a teenager over almost any topic usually is perceived quite differently by the parent and the teenager. People view their environments and the forces that shape them differently depending on many things: biological factors, such as their own heredity and intelligence; personal life experiences, including their childhood; ethnicity and culture; and level and type of education. How people perceive their world determines to a large extent how involved they are in it and how they interact with it. For example, women who perceive themselves as unimportant and powerless may continue to let their partners beat them and may not be successful at stopping the abuse or being self-sufficient if they decide to leave the batterer. On the other hand, women who perceive that they have some control over their lives and feel better about themselves may enter a counseling program and get a job.

Professionals from different disciplines also view the world somewhat differently. A physicist, for example, is likely to have a different explanation about how the world began than a philosopher or a minister. A law enforcement officer and a social worker may disagree about how best to handle young teens who join gangs and harass the elderly. A physician may treat a patient who complains of headaches by meeting the patient's physical needs, whereas a psychologist may treat the person's emotional needs through individual counseling to ascertain how the individual can better cope. The way professionals who work with people perceive the world largely determines the type of intervention they use in helping people.

Worldview is an important aspect for social workers for two reasons. Not only do social workers continually have to be aware of their own worldviews and how they affect their choices of intervention in helping people, but they also must be aware of the worldviews of others. Some worldviews have more influence than others on world, national, state, and local policies and the ways our society at all levels is structured. One key to being an effective social worker is to understand those influences and how they have shaped current policies and systems and how those influences have affected at-risk and diverse populations. An important aspect of social work is to help people find their voices to advocate for themselves and to be allies for them when they cannot (Shriver, 1998, pp. 15–16).

Joe Shriver (1998), a social work educator, suggests the following criteria for analyzing worldviews, or ways of thinking:

- Does this perspective contribute to preserving and restoring human dignity?
- Does this perspective recognize the benefits of, and does it celebrate, human diversity?
- Does this perspective assist us in transforming ourselves and our society so that we welcome the voices, the strengths, the ways of knowing, the energies of us all?
- Does this perspective help us all (ourselves and the people with whom we work) to reach our fullest human potential?
- Does the perspective or theory reflect the participation and experiences of males and females, economically well-off and poor; white people and people of color; gay men, lesbians, bi-sexuals, and heterosexuals; old and young; temporarily able-bodied people and people with disabilities? (pp. 9–10)

Worldviews are sometimes called *paradigms* or *frameworks.* In our society many individuals are currently rethinking ways to view critical social issues such as poverty and health care. The profession of social work needs a framework that helps it understand how and why such views are changing and how to work for social change during this shift in viewpoints.

The Difference between Causal Relationships and Association

In the past, many professionals who dealt with human problems tended to look at those problems in terms of cause and effect. A **cause-and-effect relationship** suggests that if x causes y, then by eliminating x, we also eliminate y. For example, if we say that smoking is the sole cause of lung cancer, then eliminating smoking would mean eliminating lung cancer.

This limited worldview presents problems for many reasons. Let's use smoking as our example again. We know that smoking does not always cause lung cancer, and sometimes people who do not smoke get lung cancer. The relationship between smoking and developing lung cancer is also not always unidimensional. Other intervening variables or factors, such as living in a city with heavy pollution, also increase a person's chances of getting lung cancer. The chances of getting lung cancer are more than twice as great for a person who smokes and lives in a city with heavy smog than for someone who does neither. The causal relationship viewpoint is not usually appropriate when examining social welfare problems.

Juan's case definitely cannot be discussed in terms of a cause-and-effect relationship. Are the situations Juan is experiencing caused by the abuse his mother suffered as a child, by the divorce, by his father's drinking too much, by his mother's worries about money, by his use of marijuana, by his association with gang members, by the limited social support system available, or by discrimination because he and his family are Mexican American? It is unlikely that one of these factors caused Juan's present situation, but they all probably contributed to it in some way. In looking at factors related to social welfare problems, it is more appropriate to view them in **association** with the problem, meaning that all factors are connected to or relate to the problem, rather than saying that one isolated factor, or even several factors, directly causes a social problem.

The Need: A Conceptual Framework for Understanding Social Welfare Problems

The fact that there are obviously many factors associated with or that contribute to social welfare problems suggests the need for a broad theory or framework to understand them. First, it is useful to define *theory* and to discuss why theories are important. A **theory** is a way of clearly and logically organizing a set of facts or ideas.

All of us use theories in our daily lives. We are continually taking in facts, or information, from our environment and trying to order them in some way to make sense about what is going on around us. Although some of our theories may be relatively unimportant to everyone else, they are useful to us in being able to describe, understand, and predict our environment. Most important, theories are useful in helping us to change either the environment or the ways we relate to it. For example, a college student has a roommate who always turns up the compact disc player to full volume whenever the student gets a telephone call. Over the year that they have shared a room, the student has gathered a great deal of information about when this happens. She is now able to articulate a theory she has based on this information to describe the situation, to understand why it happens, and to be able to predict when her roommate will exhibit this behavior. Making sense of the facts in this situation has made it easier for her to deal with this trying behavior and try to change it. What theories might you suggest to understand why this roommate situation is occurring? A theory can be relatively insignificant, such as the one just described, or it can have major importance to many people.

A theory can be used to describe something, such as Juan's family situation; to explain or to understand something, such as why a family in crisis would exhibit some of the behaviors of Juan's family; to predict something, such as what behaviors another family in a similar situation might experience; or to change something, such as Juan's ability to get his needs met from his environment in a more healthy way.

The same set of facts can be ordered in different ways, depending on who is doing the ordering and the worldview of that person or group. If we think of facts as individual bricks and a theory as a way of ordering the bricks so that they make sense, we can visualize several different theories from the same set of facts, just as we can visualize a number of different structures built from the same set of bricks.

A good theory must have three attributes, if it is to be widely used. First, it must be **inclusive,** or able to explain consistently the same event in the same way. The more inclusive a theory is, the better able it is to explain facts in exactly the same way each time an event occurs. For example, if the person in the roommate situation could describe, explain, or predict the roommate's behavior exactly the same way every single time the telephone rang, she would have a highly inclusive theory.

A good theory must also be **generalizable,** which means that one must be able to transfer a general conclusion about what happens in one situation to other similar situations. Even though the person may be able to explain the facts about her roommate in a highly inclusive way, it is not likely that exactly the same situation would occur with all roommates in the same university, much less in the same city, the United States, or the world. The more a theory can be generalized beyond the single situation it is describing or explaining, the better it is as theory.

Finally, a good theory must be **testable,** which means that we must be able to measure it in some way to ensure that it is accurate and valid. This is the major reason that we have somewhat limited theory in understanding and predicting social welfare problems and human behavior. It is difficult to develop accurate ways of measuring what goes on inside people's minds, their attitudes, and their behaviors.

How do we measure, for example, behavior change such as child abuse, particularly when it most often happens behind closed doors? Can we give psychological tests to measure attitudes that would lead to abuse, or can we measure community factors such as unemployment to predict child abuse? Any time we try to measure human behavior or environmental influences, we have difficulty doing so. This does not mean that we should stop doing research or trying to develop higher-level theories. In fact, this is an exciting area of social work, and the problems merely point out the need to develop skilled social work practitioners and researchers who can devote more attention to the development of good social work theory.

Because social work draws its knowledge base from many disciplines, many theories are applicable to social work. These include psychological theories such as Freud's theory of psychoanalysis and its derivatives, economic and political theories, sociological theories such as Emile Durkheim's theory relating to suicide, and developmental theories such as Jean Piaget's. All of these theoretical perspectives are relevant to social work and an understanding of social welfare problems, but looking at only one limits understanding and, in turn, intervention. Thus, it is important to focus on a framework or perspective that allows us to view social problems and appropriate responses that incorporate a multitude of factors and a multitude of possible responses.

THE SYSTEMS/ECOLOGICAL FRAMEWORK

Social workers, more than any other group of professionals, have focused both on the individual and beyond the individual to the broader environment since the professional casework of the Charity Organization Societies and the settlement house reform movements of Jane Addams (Germain & Gitterman, 1995). Consider the definitions of *social work* discussed in Chapter 2. All focus on enhancing social functioning of the individual or in some way addressing the relationships, the interactions, and the interdependence between people and their environments. This perspective is exemplified by the many roles social workers play within the social welfare system. True generalists, they advocate for changing living conditions of the mentally ill and obtaining welfare reform legislation that enables the poor to succeed in obtaining employment and economic self-sufficiency; empower clients to advocate for themselves to reduce violence in their communities; lead groups of children who have experienced divorce; educate the community about parenting, AIDS, and child abuse; and provide individual, family, and group counseling to clients. The profession needs a broad framework that allows for identifying all of the diverse, complex factors associated with a social welfare problem or an individual problem; understanding how all of the factors interact to contribute to the situation; and determining an intervention strategy or strategies, which can range from intervention with a single individual to an entire society and can incorporate a variety of roles. Such a framework must account for individual differences, cultural diversity, and growth and change at the individual, family, group, organizational, community, and societal levels.

The generalist foundation of social work is based on a systems framework, which also incorporates an ecological perspective. We choose to use the term *systems/ecological framework* rather than *theory* because the systems/ecological perspective is much broader and more loosely constructed than a theory. This framework is most useful in understanding social welfare problems and situations and determining specific theories that are appropriate for intervention. Additionally, whereas various systems (see, for example, works by Talcott Parsons, Max Siporin, Allen Pincus, and Anne Minahan) and ecological approaches (see, for example, works by Uri Bronfenbrenner, James Garbarino, Carel Germain, Alex Gitterman, and Carol Meyer) have been extensively described in the literature, they have not been tested or delineated with enough specificity to be considered theories. A number of advocates of the systems/ecological framework, in fact, refer to it as a *metatheory,* or an umbrella framework that can be used as a base from which to incorporate additional theories.

A general systems framework has been discussed in the literature of many disciplines—medicine, biology, anthropology, psychology, economics, political science, sociology, and education—for many years, and it has been used somewhat differently in each discipline. Its principles, as well as similar principles associated with social systems, or systems associated with living things, have been incorporated into the social work literature since the beginning of social work. Mary Richmond, the social work pioneer discussed in Chapter 2, wrote in 1922, "The worker is no more occupied with abnormalities in the individual than in the environment, is no more able to neglect the one than the other" (pp. 98–99). Since then, many social work proponents (for example, Hearn, Pincus and Minahan, Siporin, Perlman, and Bartlett) have developed specific approaches or explored varying aspects of social work from within the boundaries of the systems/ecological framework.

More recently, other social work theorists such as Germain, Gitterman, and Meyer have advocated an ecological perspective, which incorporates many of the same concepts as the systems framework. It should be noted that some social work theorists (Meyer, 1983) clearly separate the systems perspective and the ecological perspective, considering them two distinct frameworks. These theorists view the systems framework as largely relating to the structure, or the systemic properties of cases, which helps us focus on how variables are related and to order systems within the environment according to complexity. In contrast, they view the ecological perspective as one that focuses more on *relationships* of person and environment, with greater emphasis on interactions and transactions than on structure. Others (Compton & Galaway, 1998) incorporate the very similar concepts of both and refer to one framework, the systems/ecological framework. This is the approach taken in this text. Rather than get confused over semantics, readers should focus on the broad definitions and principles of the various frameworks discussed and their commonalties rather than their differences. We emphasize these important points in understanding a systems/ecological perspective and its significant contributions to social work.

The Perspective of Systems Theory

Systems theory was first used to explain the functioning of the human body, which was seen as a major system that incorporated a number of smaller systems: the skeletal system, the muscular system, the endocrine system, the circulatory system, and so on. Medical practitioners, even ones in ancient Greece, realized that when one aspect of the human body failed to function effectively, it also affected the way that other systems within the body functioned and, in turn, affected the way the human body as a whole functioned. This led to further exploration of the relationships among subparts of living organisms. (For example, Lewis Thomas's *The Life of a Cell* clearly articulates the intricate interrelations among the many complex parts of a single cell that enable the cell to maintain itself and to reproduce.)

System

One early proponent of systems theory, Ludwig Von Bertalanffy (1968), defines a **system** as "a set of units with relationships among them" (p. 38). A system can also be defined as a whole, an entity composed of separate but interacting and interdependent parts. The early Greek physicians, for example, viewed the body as the larger system and the body's various smaller systems as interacting and interdependent parts. A family can be viewed as a system composed of separate but interdependent and interacting individual family members. From a global perspective, the world can be viewed as a system composed of separate but interdependent and interacting nations. One advantage of the systems/ecological framework is that it is a conceptual framework and can be applied in many different ways to many different situations.

Synergy

The contribution from biology to systems theory is the emphasis on the concept that the whole is greater than the sum of its parts; that is, when all of the smaller systems or subsystems of an organism function in tandem, they produce a larger system that is far more grand and significant than the combination of those smaller systems working independently. The larger system, when it functions optimally, is said to achieve **synergy,** or the combined energy from the smaller parts that is greater than the total if those parts functioned separately. Imagine for a moment that your instructor for this course gives you an exam on the chapters you have covered thus far in this text. Each student takes the exam separately, and scores of each student are listed. The lowest score is 50; the highest is 85. Now, suppose that your instructor decides to let the entire class take the exam together. Each person in the class now functions as part of the total group, together solving each exam question. As a class, your score on the exam is 100. Your class has demonstrated the concept of the whole being greater than the sum of its parts, or synergy.

Boundaries

An important aspect of any system is the concept of **boundary.** A system can be almost anything; but by its definition, it usually is given some sort of boundary, or point at which one system ends and another begins. The system's environment encompasses everything beyond this boundary. For example, the human body can be seen as a system, as discussed earlier, with the skin as a boundary and the various body subsystems as smaller components of the larger system. From a different perspective, the human mind can be seen as a system, with Freud's id, ego, and superego as components within that system that interact to form a whole greater than any of the three components alone: the human mind.

An individual can also be part of a larger system; for example, a family system might include one or two parents, a child, and the family dog. We might wish to expand the boundaries of the family system and include the grandparents and the aunts and uncles. We can establish larger systems, such as school systems, communities, cities, states, or nations, and focus on their interactions and interdependence with each other. We can also look at a political system, an economic system, a religious system, and a social welfare system and the ways that those broader systems interact with each other.

The important thing to remember when using a systems perspective is that the systems that we define and the boundaries that we give those systems are conceptual; that is, we can define them in whatever ways make the most sense in looking at the broad social welfare or the more narrow individual problem that we are addressing. For example, if we were to conceptualize Juan's family as a social system, we could include within its boundaries his mother, his younger brother, and Juan. We may also choose to include Juan's father as part of his family system (even though he is out of the home, he is still part of Juan's life, and his absence is a major emotional issue for Juan). We could also include grandparents or other extended family members, because although they are not actively involved either physically or emotionally in any supportive way with the family, they are a possible source of support since they have been very involved in the past (see Figure 3.1). If we were looking at another family system, however, we might well include a larger number of other members. The systems/ecological framework is a useful way to organize data to help understand a situation, and its flexibility allows us to define systems and their boundaries in a number of ways.

Open and Closed Systems

While we can draw boundaries wherever it seems appropriate when using a systems/ecological framework, it is also important that we be able to ascertain how permeable those boundaries are. Some systems have easily permeated boundaries between units (such as

people) in the system and those outside; we call those systems **open systems.** Some families exemplify open systems. Those are the families that readily incorporate others; when someone rings the doorbell at dinnertime, a plate is always added. A cousin or a friend may live with the family for a short or a long time period, and it is often difficult to tell exactly who is a family member and who is not. There are internal boundaries within systems as well.

Sometimes boundaries can be too open. For example, in some families members become overly involved in each others' lives. In other families parents do not set consistent limits for their children, and no clear boundaries are established between the parents and the children. Unclear boundaries within systems can lead to family problems, such as incest. But healthy open systems with clear boundaries are likely to achieve synergy because of their members' willingness to accept new energy from their interactions with the broader environment.

On the other hand, some families represent **closed systems;** they have extremely closed boundaries and are very tightly knit. They may have special traditions that are for family members only. Although they might get along well with each other, they are sometimes isolated and rarely incorporate other individuals into their system. Sometimes boundaries can be too closed. For example, an abusive husband may not allow his wife to go anywhere unless he goes along.

Before Juan's father began drinking heavily, his family was a fairly open system. Although his family did many activities together just as a family, they also socialized a great deal with friends and relatives. If Juan's friends were playing at his house, they were often invited to have dinner or to participate in family activities. When Juan's father's drinking increased, his family sys-

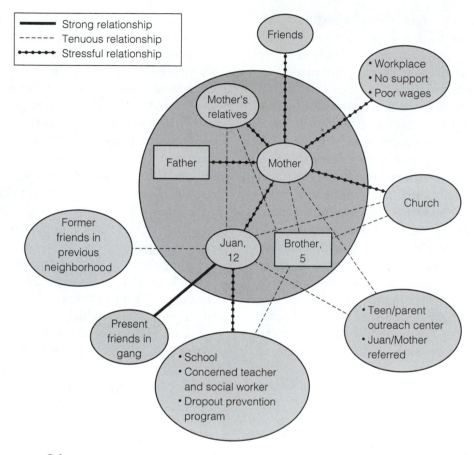

FIGURE 3.1

USING AN ECO-MAP TO UNDERSTAND JUAN'S FAMILY SITUATION

tem became more closed. Juan's mother tried to limit his father's drinking by limiting the family social activities. When relatives became more critical of his drinking, Juan's family stopped socializing with them to avoid being confronted about the problem. Because Juan's father lost his temper easily when he drank, Juan stopped inviting his friends over and began playing at their houses instead. The family became more isolated. The isolation continued, and the family system remained closed when Juan's father left and his parents divorced.

Organizations also may be open or closed systems. Some organizations welcome new members and readily expand their activities to meet new interests. Others are very closed and do not encourage new members, making those that try to enter the organization feel unwelcome and shunning new ideas. Communities and other social structures can also be viewed as open or closed. Juan's new school, for example, is a somewhat closed system, which has made his making friends and feeling as if he fits in difficult.

Usually, the more closed a system is, the less able it is to derive positive energy from other systems. Over time, closed systems tend to use up their own energy and to develop **entropy,** which means that they tend to lose their ability to function and can eventually stagnate and die. The more isolated Juan's family becomes, the less energy it takes in from the environment, the less energy there then is within the family system for family members, and the less able the family is to function. The family system becomes more and more lethargic and will eventually either change or die, with the family separating and members becoming part of other family systems. If, for example, Juan's mother were to become extremely abusive and Juan were to become involved in the gang and serious criminal activities, his brother might be placed in foster care and Juan in a correctional facility for youth.

Interactions and Interrelations

Boundaries and open and closed systems are *structural* aspects of systems. An additional feature of the systems/ecological framework is its emphasis on the *interactions* and *interrelations* between units rather than on the systems or subsystems themselves. This lends itself well to the need for focusing on associations among large numbers of factors rather than on cause-and-effect relationships between two factors. The interactions and interrelatedness between systems suggest constant motion, fluidity, and change. The relatedness and interactions also incorporate the concept that a change or movement in one part of the system, or in one system, will have an impact on the larger system, or other systems, as well. Imagine a room full of constantly moving Ping-Pong balls, each representing a system or a subsystem of a larger system. Hitting one Ping-Pong ball across the room will change the movement of the other balls. Similarly, a change in the economic system (for example, inflation) will result in changes in other systems: the educational system could be affected because fewer students could afford to go to college; the social welfare system could be affected because more people would have financial difficulties and need public assistance and social services; the criminal justice system could be affected because more persons might turn to crime; the political system could be affected because the dissatisfied populace might not reelect the party in office.

The results of interactions and interrelatedness between systems can also be seen when viewing Juan's family. Juan's father's drinking led to his job loss, which then resulted in an increased pattern of drinking. Both of these factors affected Juan's parents' relationships with each other, or the marital system; the parents' relationships with Juan and his younger brother, or the parent-child system; the communication patterns between the family as a system; and relationships between Juan's family system and other systems beyond the family, such as his father's workplace, his family's church, and Juan's school.

Such interactions and interrelatedness occur continually. There are usually constant flows of energy within and across systems. This creates natural tensions, which are viewed as healthy if communication is open, because the energy flow creates growth and change. Feedback among systems is an important part of the systems/ecological perspective, which emphasizes communication. It is important that social workers and others who work within and across various systems understand those systems' goals and communication patterns. In unhealthy systems, for example, the various members of the system may be communicating in certain ways and may have certain unspoken goals that maintain the system because its members are afraid to change the system or the system is in some way productive for them. In a family such as Juan's in which a parent is an alcoholic, the other parent or an older child may perpetuate the alcoholism and unconsciously try to keep the family system as it is because the nonalcoholic may see his or her role as one of caretaking—keeping the family together and protecting the younger children from the alcoholism. If the family system changes, the nonalcoholic parent or older child will no longer be able to maintain that role and thus may try to force the system back to the way it once was.

Steady State

Another important concept of the systems/ecological framework is that of **steady state,** in which systems are not static but are steadily moving. The concept of steady state means that the system is constantly adjusting to move toward its goal while maintaining a certain amount of order and stability, giving and receiving energy in fairly equal amounts to maintain equilibrium. A healthy system, then, may be viewed as one that is not in upheaval but is always ebbing and flowing to achieve both stability and growth. If Juan and his family receive counseling and other support from the broader environment, his family system should achieve equilibrium. The system will not stop changing but will move toward its goals in a less disruptive manner.

Equifinality

One last concept of the systems/ecological framework is that of **equifinality,** or the concept that the final state of a system can be achieved in many different ways. Because there are many ways to interpret a given situation, usually many options are possible for dealing with it. A number of alternatives can be considered, for example, when working with Juan and his family to help them function better as individuals and as a family unit. Options could include individual and family counseling, support or therapeutic groups for Juan and his mother, a child care program for his younger brother, increasing interactions between Juan and his father, enrollment in a chemical dependency program for Juan's father, enrollment in a job-training program for Juan's mother and/or father, involvement in positive recreational programs for Juan, and membership in a supportive church. Although not all of these options might be realistic for Juan and his family, various combinations of them could lead to the same positive results. The concept of equifinality is especially important to social workers because their role is to help clients determine what is best for them, and clients' choices are as diverse as the clients themselves.

Critiques of the Systems/Ecological Framework

One criticism of the systems/ecological framework in social work is that it encompasses the broad environment yet ignores the psychosocial and the intrapsychic aspects of the individual. Proponents of the systems/ecological framework argue, however, that the individual is perceived as a highly valued system itself and that **intrapsychic** aspects and psychosocial aspects, which incorporate the individual's capacity and motivation for change, are parts of any system involving individuals that cannot and should not be ignored. The framework's inclusiveness incorporates the biological, psychological, sociological, and cultural aspects of developing individuals and their interactions with the broader environment. In fact, the systems/ecological framework is often referred to as a biopsychosocial-cultural framework.

Another criticism of the systems/ecological framework is that, because it incorporates everything, it is too complicated, making it easy to miss important aspects of a situation. The ecological perspective articulated by social scientists Uri Bronfenbrenner and James Garbarino attempts to address this concern. Bronfenbrenner and Garbarino incorporate individual developmental aspects into the systems perspective of the broader environment, but they break the system into different levels, or layers of the environment. They suggest that for all individuals, both risks and opportunities exist at each of these environmental levels. Opportunities within the environment encourage an individual to meet needs and to develop as a healthy, well-functioning person. Risks are either direct threats to healthy development or the absence of opportunities that facilitate healthy individual development.

Levels of the Environment

Bronfenbrenner (1979) and Garbarino (1992) suggest that risks and opportunities can be found at all levels of the environment. They describe these levels as being like a series of Russian eggs, with a large egg cut in half that opens to reveal a smaller egg, which also opens to reveal a still smaller egg, which opens to reveal a still smaller egg (see Figure 3.2 and Table 3.1). They suggest that we consider the tiniest egg to be the **microsystem level,** which includes the individual and all persons and groups that incorporate the individual's day-to-day environment. The focus at this level would incorporate the individual's level of functioning, intellectual and emotional capacities, and motivation; the impact of life experiences; and the interactions and connections between that individual and others in the immediate environment. Also, the focus at this level would be on whether the relationships are positive or negative, whether the messages and regard for the individual are consistent across individuals and groups, and whether the individual is valued and respected. Juan's microsystem level, for example, includes all of his own personal characteristics, such as his biological makeup and intelligence; his culture and gender; as well as his interactions and connections with his mother, brother, father, teachers, and friends. His mother and his old friends, as well as the social worker, could be viewed as providing opportunity to Juan, while his new friends could be viewed as providing both opportunity through peer support and risk through drug use and skipping of school.

The next level of the system is termed the **mesosystem level.** A mesosystem involves the relationship between two microsystems that are linked by some person who exists in both microsystems. For example, because Juan is part of his family and his school, he provides the link between these two microsystems. The interactions in one microsystem influence the interactions of the others. For example, the conflicting messages to Juan from his school and family settings versus his peer setting had an impact on Juan and can be seen as environmental risks. While his mother and school personnel advocated against skipping school and experimenting with marijuana, his new peers encouraged him to become involved in these activities. His mother's involvement with the school social worker, however, can be viewed as a mesosystem opportunity for Juan.

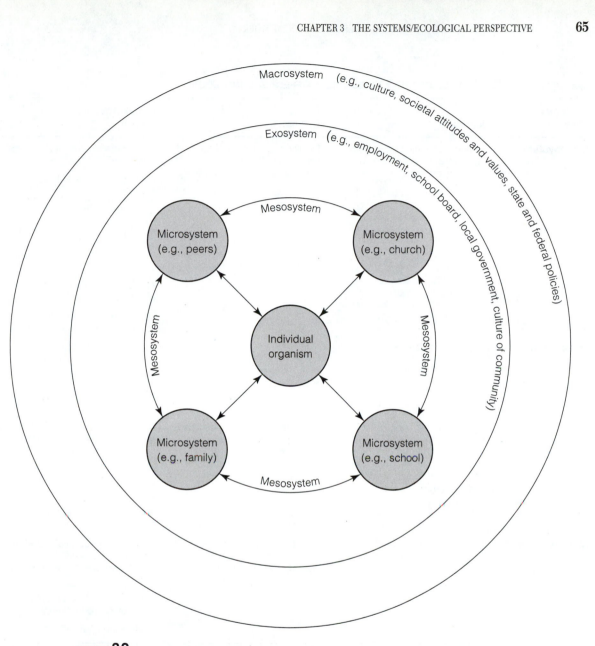

FIGURE **3.2**
THE LEVELS OF THE ECOLOGICAL SYSTEM

Source: Garbarino, James. _Children and Families in the Social Environment._ 2nd Edition. (New York: Aldine de Gruyter).
Copyright © 1992 Walter de Gruyter, Inc., New York.

The third level is the **exosystem level.** This level includes community-level factors that may not relate directly to the individual but affect the way the individual functions. This includes factors such as the workplace policies of the parents (if they cannot take sick

TABLE 3.1   **HOW LEVELS OF THE ENVIRONMENT AFFECT THE INDIVIDUAL**

Ecological Level	Definition	Examples	Issues Affecting Person
Microsystem	Situations in which the person has face-to-face contact with influential others	Family, school, workplace, peer group, church, or synagogue	Is the person regarded positively? Is the person accepted? Is the person reinforced for competent behavior? Is the person exposed to enough diversity in roles and relationships? Are the person's culture and ethnicity valued and positively affirmed? Is the person given an active role in reciprocal relationships?
Mesosystem	Relationships between microsystems; the connections between situations	Home-school, home-workplace, home-church/synagogue, school-neighborhood	Do settings respect each other? Are cultural factors respected between settings? Do settings present basic consistency in values?
Exosystem	Settings in which the person does not participate but in which significant decisions are made affecting the person or others who interact directly with the person	Place of employment of others in the person's microsystem, school board, local government, peer groups of others in the person's microsystem	Are decisions made with the interests of the person and the family in mind? How well do supports for families balance stresses for parents and children? Is diversity considered when decisions are made?
Macrosystem	"Blueprints" for defining and organizing the institutional life of the society	Ideology, social policy, shared assumptions about human nature, the "social contract"	Are some groups valued at the expense of others? Are some groups oppressed (e.g., sexism, racism)? Is there an individualistic or a collectivistic orientation? Is violence a norm?

leave when the child is sick, for example, this policy has an impact on the child), school board and community policies, community attitudes and values, and economic and social factors that exist within the neighborhood and

community. For Juan's family, exosystem risk factors include the lack of jobs that pay well for persons with his mother's skill level, the unavailability of affordable child care for Juan's younger brother, and community attitudes toward divorce, Mexican Americans, and single parenting. The teen/family outreach center provides an exosystem opportunity for Juan, if it is not too overloaded with other clients.

The final level is the **macrosystem level.** This level includes societal factors such as the cultural attitudes and values of the society (for example, attitudes toward women, people of color, the poor, and violence); the role of the media in addressing or promoting social problems (some suggest, for example, that the media promote violence and teen pregnancy); and federal legislation and other social policies that affect a given individual. Lack of governmental programs for single parents and potential school dropouts, societal attitudes toward divorce and single parents, discrimination toward Latinos, and the media's glamorization of gangs and violence all contribute to Juan's current life situation and can be viewed as environmental risks. But in spite of these risks, opportunities exist for Juan, such as democracy, freedom of religion, and education, that might not be found within other macrosystems.

Many advocates of the ecological framework as conceptualized by Bronfenbrenner and Garbarino agree that it is a derivation of systems theory and another way of defining boundaries of systems. They suggest that it is advantageous to use because it allows us to see the interdependence and interaction across levels from the microsystem level to the macrosystem level and also allows us to target intervention at a variety of levels to address social problems and individual needs. For example, we could provide individual counseling to Juan, counsel his family, and help him develop a new network of friends at the microlevel; work with Juan's mother, teachers, and peers to help them become more consistent in the messages they are conveying to Juan at the mesolevel; advocate for the establishment of a community program to assist teens who experience family problems and of low-cost child care for working parents at the exolevel; and lobby for legislation to develop national media programs that educate the public about gangs, drugs, and the working poor at the macrolevel.

Note that this framework is a guide to be used to understand how systems interact with and are shaped by the broader environment. It may not always be exactly clear at which level of the environment a factor fits, and some factors may fit at more than one level of the environment. For example, in Juan's situation, religion and the church can fit at all levels, depending on how they are conceptualized. If Juan has an individual relationship with a higher power/spiritual being, that relationship could be viewed as a microsystem relationship. Juan's interactions with individual members of his church—his priest, for example—could also be viewed as microsystem relationships. The church and Juan's family could be viewed as a mesosystem relationship, since Juan is part of both of these microsystems. The church can also be viewed at the exolevel of the environment, since the church's attitudes, values, and policies at the community level have a definite impact on how Juan and his family are perceived in the community, especially after the divorce. Likewise, the church plays a major role in shaping the norms, attitudes, and values about divorce and other issues at the societal level, and it can also be a macrolevel factor that shapes Juan's development. It is not as important to focus on where in the environment each factor fits as it is to focus on the interdependence and interactions between the different levels of the environment and how they influence and are influenced by the developing system being viewed (Garbarino, 1992).

Problems in Living

Social workers Carel Germain and Alex Gitterman (1995) incorporate the ecological perspective somewhat differently in their approach, adding still another important way of viewing individuals within their environments. They suggest that all persons have problems at some point in their lives, or what they term "problems in living." The first problem area they discuss includes those problems associated with life transitions—marriage, the birth of a first child, movement into middle age, movement of children out of the family, and so forth. They suggest that all individuals go through such transitions and that as a person moves from one life stage to another, transitional problems and needs develop that may require social work intervention. Juan's family, for example, is experiencing the transitions of divorce and a child moving into adolescence.

The second area Germain and Gitterman identify includes problems associated with tasks in using and influencing elements of the environment. Juan's mother has had difficulty locating affordable child care for her youngest son, and Juan is having difficulty adjusting to a new school setting. The limited social networks available to Juan and his family suggest the need for intervention in this area.

A final area of focus suggested by Germain and Gitterman is that of maladaptive interpersonal problems and needs in families and groups. Juan's family, for example, has developed some of the unproductive communication patterns typically found in families in which alcoholism is a problem. Although these patterns maintained the family as an intact unit for many years, they will continue to stifle individual and family growth unless they change. Germain and Gitterman reinforce the need to incorporate the transactional patterns between persons and their environment when planning any social work intervention.

In summary, a systems/ecological framework emphasizes that our lives are shaped by the choices we make, and that the environment shapes our choices, while our choices shape the way we interact with our environment. This continual interaction and cyclical perspective suggest that we cannot discuss the individual without focusing on the environment or the environment without considering the strong forces that individuals play in its formulation. The individual and the environment are continually adapting to each other. The social worker's primary role is to ensure that this adaptation is mutually supportive to both the individual and the environment.

The Utility of the Systems/Ecological Framework

The systems/ecological framework is intended to be used as a mechanism to order facts about social welfare problems or individual needs in such a way that appropriate theories can be identified to further explore the problems and needs or to determine interventions. Box 3.1 examines some ways the framework aids social workers. It is useful to think of this framework as a way to "map the territory" or gather and fit together pieces of a puzzle to understand a situation. When dealing with a problem such as poverty, for example, which is addressed in Chapter 8, many individuals may have unidimensional ways of explaining the problem—it is because people are lazy, for example, or the victims of their own circumstance. A systems/ecological perspective would identify many factors—a large, complex territory and a puzzle with many pieces. Individual factors, family factors, community factors, and societal

Value of the Systems/Ecological Framework for Social Work Practice

The systems/ecological perspective makes a number of valuable contributions as an organizing framework for social work practice.

1. The systems/ecological perspective allows one to deal with far more data than other models and to bring order to these large amounts of data from a variety of disciplines.
2. The concepts relating to systems are equally applicable to the wide range of clients served by social workers, including individuals, families, groups, organizations, communities, and society.
3. The systems/ecological framework allows for identifying the wide range of factors that have an impact on social welfare problems, their interrelationships, and the ways that a change in one factor affects other factors.
4. The systems/ecological framework shifts attention from characteristics of individuals or the environment to the transactions between systems and their communication patterns.
5. The systems/ecological framework views persons as actively involved with their environments, capable of adaptation and change.

6. The systems/ecological framework views systems as goal-oriented, supporting client self-determination and the client's participation in the change process.
7. If systems require constant transactions with each other to survive, the purpose of the social worker is to provide and maintain such opportunities for transactions for all populations and to work to reduce isolation of individuals and systems.
8. Social workers need to work to ensure that change and tension are not resisted in systems and to remove the notions that change and conflict are pathological.
9. Social workers need to be aware of the systems within which they work and how change within those systems affects the whole. This means that social workers must choose points of intervention with care.
10. Social workers are a social system and components of a social systems network.

Source: From *Social Work Processes* by B. Compton and B. Galaway. Copyright © 1998 Wadsworth Publishing Company; The Dorsey Press. By permission of Brooks/Cole Publishing Company, Pacific Grove, CA 93950, a division of Thomson Learning.

factors such as the impact of the economic system and of unemployment, racism, sexism, and so forth—all contribute to poverty in some way. Table 3.2 lists just some of the factors that

shape the interactions between individuals and their environments.

Once the territory is mapped out or all of the puzzle pieces (or as many as possible) are

TABLE 3.2   FACTORS THAT SHAPE INDIVIDUAL FUNCTIONING AND RELATIONSHIP WITH THE ENVIRONMENT

Personal Factors	Community Factors
Level of prenatal care received	Social class compared to rest of community
Intellectual capacity/ability	Ethnic/cultural/class diversity/attitudes and values
Emotional capacity/mental health	
Level of social functioning	Social roles available within community
Physical health	Community support
Age	Economic conditions
Ethnicity/culture	Employment opportunities
Motivation	Educational opportunities
Life stage/transitional period	Environmental stress
Crisis level	**Societal Factors**
Family Factors	Societal attitudes and values
Support systems/availability of significant others	Racism, sexism, poverty levels
Family patterns/structure/values	Supportive or lack of supportive legislation/programs/policies
Economic level/employment	Media role
Level of functioning/family crisis	

obtained, then the systems/ecological framework can also allow for further exploration of certain factors, parts of the terrain, or pieces of the puzzle. This perspective also allows for individualization and diversity, which also means that cultural and gender differences are readily accounted for (see Table 3.2). Once the larger picture is obtained, we can better ascertain where to focus; whether more information is needed and in what areas; and if intervention is required, at what level and within which system or systems within the environment. One or more additional theories or frameworks can then be used to obtain more information or to guide intervention. The advantage of the systems/ecological perspective is that we are less likely to miss a major aspect of a situation and thus intervene inappropriately.

The Utility of Other Theories and Frameworks

Other, more limiting theories and frameworks are used by social workers in their professional practice under the umbrella of the systems/ecological framework. Two useful types of frameworks include psychosocial frameworks and cognitive/behavioral frameworks (Turner & Younghusband, 1996). These and other frameworks commonly used by social workers are discussed in greater depth in Chapter 5.

Psychosocial Frameworks Psychosocial frameworks include psychoanalytic theory, ego psychology, and life-span development frameworks. These frameworks are often used to-

The systems/ecological framework helps social workers and their clients focus on both strengths and barriers at all levels of the environment that can be used to identify and understand client needs.

Jim Vecchione/Liaison Agency

gether and are not always viewed as mutually exclusive.

PSYCHOANALYTIC THEORY   Psychoanalytic theory, based largely on the works of Sigmund Freud, is built on the premise that children are born with biologically rooted functions, termed *drives,* that dictate individual functioning. These drives are primarily related to sexual expression and aggression. Psychoanalytic theory is also a stage or developmental framework, since its premise is that persons cope with different changes in biological, psychological, and social functioning at different stages of their lives. This framework focuses on both conscious and unconscious drives and on internal interactions within an individual among his or her id, ego, and superego. The focus on interaction between the individual and the broader environment is more limited than it is in many other theories, although psychoanalytic theory includes attention to the impact of life experiences, primarily during early childhood; on later functioning; and on the development of

internal defense mechanisms to cope with the environment, such as denial and rationalization. If Juan's situation were to be viewed from this framework, his sexual drives during preadolescence and the impact of his father leaving during this time would be major focal points.

This framework is complex and based largely on individual psychopathology, or emotional illness. If one uses this framework for persons who have problems, the suggested intervention is individual psychoanalysis to work through intrapsychic conflicts.

EGO PSYCHOLOGY AND LIFE-SPAN DEVELOPMENT FRAMEWORKS   Ego psychology stems from psychoanalytic theory but focuses mainly on the development of a strong ego as opposed to interactions among the id, ego, and superego. The ego psychology perspective also focuses more on the transactions between the person and environment and the impact of the environment in shaping the development of a healthy ego (Erikson, 1959). The impact of Juan's family situation during his childhood would be explored, and ways to help Juan feel better about himself and to increase his self-esteem would be major issues for intervention within this framework.

Both psychoanalytic and ego psychology are life-span development frameworks. These frameworks suggest that individuals interact with their environments in different ways to meet different needs at different points in the life cycle, and the ways that needs are met in previous stages shape individual functioning and later development. Like psychoanalytic theory, this approach strongly emphasizes ways that early life experiences shape later behavior. However, the emphasis is much more on the ways that the environment shapes the resolution of these issues. For example, using a life-span development framework developed by Erik Erikson, an individual addresses issues of basic trust versus basic mistrust during the 1st year of life. If an infant is placed in an environment where his or her basic needs (such as feeding or nurturing) are not met or are met inconsistently, the child does not develop a sense of trust. If trust is not developed later, the child has difficulty in other stages of life—for instance, in developing intimate relationships during young adulthood. Within this framework, Juan's developmental needs involve developing a sense of identity, primarily through peer relationships. Thus, for example, the gang members are filling a major developmental need for Juan that he does not feel can be met in other ways.

Although important and useful to social workers, these frameworks are more limiting than the systems/ecological framework. They place more emphasis on early life experiences than later experiences and less emphasis on interactions and transactions among broader levels of the environment and the impact on the individual. Finally, they suggest intervention primarily at the individual level.

Cognitive/Behavioral Frameworks   A second set of frameworks, cognitive/behavioral frameworks, place little emphasis on an individual's life experiences or biological aspects. Their premise is that environment, and not heredity, largely determines behavior. These frameworks focus primarily on the present and on shaping individual thinking and behavior within the person's immediate environment. The goal is to shape behavior, not to change personality. For example, Juan may have developed a series of self-messages that suggest he is not competent. These repeated messages have led to his poor schoolwork and his attempts to seek competence in other areas, such as drug use and illegal activities. If Juan is helped to change his self-messages to positive affirmations about himself, he will begin to see himself as competent and begin reengaging in school. The interventions within these frameworks are largely at the individual level, and there is much greater emphasis on the present and the environment. Cognitive/behavioral frameworks, however, are extremely useful to social workers. They can help individuals not only to understand ways that unproductive thought patterns shape behaviors but also to develop new thought patterns and behaviors that can lead to healthier functioning.

Political and Ideological Frameworks Social workers often use these frameworks, as well as other frameworks, in a variety of ways and often in tandem with each other. In a more political sense, people also may adhere to perspectives that are considered liberal, conservative, libertarian, or radical. Although people often label themselves as fitting in one category, their perspectives often fit more than one category, depending on the issue. Someone may be liberal when it comes to policies about child welfare and education and conservative about policies related to crime. Ideologies shape how people vote, their attitudes about social welfare programs and policies, and their beliefs about whether people are capable of change. The systems/ecological framework can help us understand how environment shapes the development of one's ideologies and political perspectives, as well as what might be likely to persuade someone to change a point of view. Understanding why someone holds a certain perspective is helpful for social workers not only in working with clients but also in engaging in community action and legislative and political advocacy.

Understanding a person's worldview as opposed to a more traditional approach based only on facts when addressing social welfare issues has gained increased attention in recent years. Many social workers adhere to a constructivist perspective (Franklin & Nurius, 1998), the idea that each individual constructs his or her own reality, based on perceptions and belief systems. Social workers with this perspective try to see the world from the person's perspective rather than their own, or employ a more global concept of reality. Since a social worker must also understand the person's interactions with the environment to understand his or her reality, one can see how this perspective is consistent with the systems/ecological framework.

Although the systems/ecological perspective can also be used when intervening with an individual or the broader environment, social workers almost always use it as the major framework for understanding a given situation/problem. However, once the problem is understood and the broad terrain is mapped out using this framework, other frameworks may be used for further assessment as well as intervention.

The Systems/Ecological Framework and Professional Practice

Because the generalist model of social work incorporates all different levels of the environment and the interactions and interdependence within and between levels, the systems/ecological framework is especially useful as an organizing framework for professional practice. Specifically, the framework

- allows the social worker to deal with large amounts of information from many different areas and to bring order to that information;
- includes concepts that are applicable to the full range of clients served by social workers, including individuals, couples, families, groups, organizations, communities, and broader societal systems;
- incorporates not only the structures of the social units involved but also the interrelatedness and interactions within and between units;
- shifts attention away from the characteristics of units to the transactions and interactions between them;
- views individuals as active participants in their environments, capable of change and adaptation, including shifting to new environments;
- incorporates the concept of client self-determination and recognizes that multiple approaches can be effective in facilitating change;
- focuses social workers on the need to provide and maintain continual transactions

between people and their environments for all populations and to monitor social systems heading for isolation;

- provides a constant reminder to social workers that change is healthy and necessary for systems to grow but that systems often resist change;

- places both the social worker and the agency within the client's environment; and

- reminds social workers that since a change at one level of the system creates changes at other levels, interventions must be thought through and chosen with care. (Compton & Galaway, 1998, pp. 130–131)

Applying the Systems/Ecological Framework: The Social Welfare System and Poverty

The systems/ecological framework is especially useful in understanding the complexities of large systems within our environment, such as the social welfare system. The social welfare system in place at any given moment is the product of the interactions and interrelatedness of historical, economic, and political forces. As a large system, it is constantly reshaped by changes in societal values and events beyond its boundaries. Changes in societal values, for example, result in increased public acceptance of programs for battered women and child care for children of working mothers. An economic recession results in extensive cutbacks in social welfare services.

The scope of social welfare systems in the United States is not as broad, comprehensive, and integrated as most social workers would like, nor is it as constrained and limited as some others would contend. In a sense, it is not a formal system at all but rather a collection of ad hoc programs developed in diverse

and special political circumstances. Thus, although we have programs for the aged, persons with physical disabilities, and dependent children, each program has its own political history and its own political constituency.

As a matter of practice, if not of principle, the target populations of social service agencies are those groups not adequately served by the primary social systems in our society (the economic system, the political system, the family system, the religious system, the health system, and the educational system). Typically, the social welfare system comes into play as a result of family breakdown, problems in income distribution, and institutional failure in the religious, education, health, and/or business sectors.

While each of us would probably give a somewhat different mission statement for an ideal social welfare system, at a minimum we would probably all agree that such a system should guarantee to each person a socially defined minimum standard of well-being. In meeting this standard, the social welfare system interacts with primary social systems within our society: the family system, the economic system, and the political system. Each of these primary systems has a principal function, as illustrated in Table 3.3. The social welfare system is most frequently perceived as a residual social system that comes into play when there is a failure in the primary system or when the primary system generates undesirable consequences (Johnson, Schwartz, & Tate, 1997).

The organized social welfare system, composed of numerous and varied social services and institutions, is designed to help individuals and groups attain satisfactory standards of life and health. This view implies recurrent failure in other social systems. It assumes that individuals sometimes need outside help in coping with a complex social order. Social welfare

TABLE 3.3   **SOCIAL SYSTEMS**

Systems	Functions
Primary	
Family	The primary personal care and mutual assistance system between parents and children, between adults and elderly
Political	The authoritative allocation of public social goals and values
Economic	The allocation and distribution of scarce resources to competing entities
Secondary	
Other goal-specific systems (i.e., education system, health care system, defense system)	The list and functions of secondary systems are dependent on individual choice. What would you include?
Social Welfare System	To respond to failure and/or dysfunction in primary and secondary systems

institutions that make up the social welfare system assist in time of crisis of the individual, but since recurrent and random crisis is the ordinary condition of social life, a structured set of social agencies must stand ready to respond to crises and failures—to overcome the crisis; to enhance problem-solving and coping skills of communities, groups, organizations, families, and individuals; and to empower these entities to create social change so that crisis is less frequent.

In this view, the social welfare system is seen as the structured set of responses developed to deal with the dysfunction of other systems. For example, the family system is intended to meet children's physical and emotional needs. But at times, the primary family system fails and is unable to serve this function. At that point, the social welfare system provides services, such as respite child care, foster care, and counseling. When the social welfare system functions to assist or replace the family in its child care roles, this exemplifies a social welfare system response to a pri-

mary system failure. A second example of a social welfare system response to a primary system dysfunction can be seen in relation to the economic system. We know that the economic system distributes income unevenly, leaving some people poor. Thus, we have generated an income security system to provide various types of income assistance to specific classes of persons in need.

Objectively speaking, an overview of American social welfare institutions and social work practice reveals an incredible range of public and voluntary agencies seeking to respond to social problems. For some areas of need, the response is well conceptualized and generous; for others the response is hasty and scanty; still other social needs invoke no response at all. A major problem with our social welfare system is that each need is usually treated as a separate issue, rather than an interactive and interdependent part of a larger issue. Seldom, for example, is attention given to how a response to need A is related to its impact on need B.

The federal welfare reform legislation enacted in 1996 serves as a good example. One of the highly publicized outcomes of the passage of this legislation has been the movement of increased numbers of former welfare recipients into jobs. In reality, most public assistance recipients receive benefits for only a short time, but they often have to move back and forth between welfare and work because they cannot make ends meet with the low-paying jobs they are forced to take because of their limited education and training. Thus, while increased numbers of recipients are now employed, the legislation has failed to address their other needs, such as child care, transportation, health care benefits, and affordable housing. As a result, many of these individuals are in worse circumstances then when they were receiving the public assistance benefits. These additional unmet needs are overloading local social service government agencies and the private sector, such as churches. Child advocates are also worried about the increased cases of spouse abuse, child abuse, substance abuse, homelessness, malnutrition, and other problems when the time limits for individuals unable to make it without public assistance end. The legislation unfortunately did not allow for allocation of additional resources to meet these needs.

Health care also exemplifies the interrelatedness between systems and social problems. In recent years, state legislators, concerned about the high costs of health care for the poor, reduced the funds allocated for health care rather than raise taxes. In doing so, they ignored the fact that state dollars are matched by federal dollars to provide health care for the poor. For every dollar that a state contributes, the federal government matches the amount with federal money. The reduction in dollars by the states limits the amount of federal money coming into the states, seriously reducing the number of clients that can be served by state public assistance health programs. No longer served by these health programs, the states' poor do not seek health care until they are desperate, and when they do, they come to local hospitals as indigent (nonpaying) patients. This means that local hospitals have to foot these bills, now higher than they might have been if care had been sought earlier. It also means that all of the higher costs in these states are footed by local taxpayers who all pay local taxes to support hospitals. Thus, what the legislators ultimately intended as a money-saving measure for their states' citizens has turned out to be far more costly in the long run.

The systems/ecological framework can be used to help understand issues at every level of the environment and across levels. The framework can also be used to determine types of intervention at all levels of the environment once the complex issues are understood.

THE GENERALIST MODEL

As we discussed in Chapter 2, the generalist model of social work practice taught at the BSW level suggests the use of multiple interventions in working with clients at the individual, family, group, organizational, community, or societal level. Generalist practice focuses on the interface between systems,

> with equal emphasis on the goals of social justice, humanizing systems, and improving the well-being of people. It uses a multilevel methodology that can be focused on varying levels of the environment, depending on the needs of the client system. Generalist practice incorporates a knowledge, value and skills base that is transferable between and among diverse contexts and locations. (Schatz, Jenkins, & Sheafor, 1990, p. 223)

The central theme of most generalist practice is the systems/ecological framework. Generalist practice is based on the idea that there needs to be congruency, or a positive fit between the person and his or her environment, and that the role of social work is to promote, strengthen, and restore—if necessary—that positive fit. **Person-environment fit** is the actual fit between the person's or group's needs, rights, goals, and capacities and the physical and social environment within which the person or group operates. The fit can be favorable, adequate, or unfavorable. When exchanges with the environment over time are inadequate, the individual's healthy development might be affected negatively, or the environment might be damaged (Germain & Gitterman, 1995, p. 817).

The Strengths Perspective

Generalist social work practice is directed toward identifying a system's strengths and using them to modify the environment with which that system interacts to increase the level of person-environment fit. Generalist practice requires social work knowledge and skills in working with individuals, families, groups, organizations, and communities, including advocacy, to empower individuals to change their environments. This focus views the client as the expert, most knowledgeable about his or her needs, with the social worker building on the strengths of individuals to facilitate their ability to change their environment, or their coping mechanisms in interacting with it. The generalist social work **strengths perspective** can be contrasted with what is commonly referred to as the "medical model," which focuses on the client as having some type of illness or weakness and the helper as the expert who determines and provides the treatment. Table 3.4 compares the generalist social work strengths perspective and the medical model.

All individuals have strengths, and they are much more likely to grow and change when their strengths, rather than their deficiencies,

TABLE 3.4   COMPARISON OF GENERALIST SOCIAL WORK STRENGTHS PERSPECTIVE AND MEDICAL MODEL

Generalist Practice/Strengths Perspective	Medical Model
Lack of goodness of fit between person and environment; needs not being met.	Problem with individual/weakness of individual; person is labeled as sick/deviant, given diagnosis.
Client and environment present strengths/opportunities and barriers/risks; building on strengths can motivate clients to change themselves/perceptions/ and/or their environment.	Client has problems/needs; sick clients need help in changing their world views to fit with the norm.
Client is expert about his/her life and needs; social worker is facilitator to help client discover needs and identify possible resources to get them met.	Helper is expert who diagnoses client and prescribes treatment; expert is in charge of treatment; client is expected to cooperate.
Client can be empowered to get needs met/use or learn new skills and resources.	Client needs expert helper to help change; needs to be dependent on experts for help.

Source: Adapted from *The Integration of Social Work Practice* by R. J. Parsons, J. D. Jorgensen, and S. H. Hernandez. Copyright © 1994 Brooks/Cole Publishing Company, Pacific Grove, CA 93950, a division of Thomson Learning. By permission of the publisher.

are emphasized. In his book *The Strengths Perspective in Social Work Practice,* Dennis Saleeby (1996), a social work educator at the University of Kansas, delineates six basic principles on which the strengths perspective is based:

- *Respecting clients' strengths*—Social work practice is guided first and foremost by a profound awareness of, and respect for, clients' positive attributes and abilities, talents and resources, desires and aspirations. . . .
- *Clients have many strengths*—Individuals and groups have vast, often untapped and frequently unappreciated reservoirs of physical, emotional, cognitive, interpersonal, social and spiritual energies, resources and competencies. . . .
- *Client motivation is based on fostering client strengths*—Individuals and groups are more likely to continue autonomous development and growth when it is funded by the coin of their capacities, knowledge, and skills. . . .
- *The social worker is a collaborator with the client*—The role of "expert" or "professional" may not provide the best vantage point from which to appreciate client strengths. . . .
- *Avoiding the victim mindset*—Emphasizing and orienting the work of helping around clients' strengths can help to avoid "blaming the victim". . . .
- *Any environment is full of resources*—In every environment there are individuals and institutions who have something to give, something that others may desperately need . . . and for the most part, they are untapped and unsolicited. (pp. 6–7)

Empowerment

Another key aspect of generalist social work practice is **empowerment,** the "process of increasing personal, interpersonal, or political power so individuals can take action to improve their life situation" (Gutierrez, 1990, p. 149).

Many of the individuals with whom social workers interact are members of at-risk populations who face barriers at all levels of the environment that often limit their functioning. Such individuals often lack the power and resources to change their environments, or they may be in situations where they perceive themselves as powerless, incompetent, and/or lacking in resources. Rather than "fixing" problems, which often reinforces such feelings, social workers help clients see that they can create change. People who are empowered can make changes at the individual, family, group, neighborhood, organizational, community, state, national, or international levels.

As Ms. Herrera continued to emphasize Juan's strengths, Juan realized that he had more power over his life than he had thought. He was able to talk with his mother and negotiate more time with friends. He also felt empowered to say no to his peers who were pressuring him to join the gang. Also, realizing that other teens were in situations similar to his, he became active in a school leadership program and a key member of a community group that helped establish a youth center.

Empowering clients like Juan gives them hope and helps them see that they have a sense of control over their lives. Empowerment leads to continual growth and change and increased feelings of competence.

Social and Economic Justice

The systems/ecological framework also is useful in applying the social work profession's commitment to the promotion of **social and economic justice,** which includes fairness and equity in regard to basic civil and human rights, protections, resources and opportunities, and social benefits. How resources are distributed at every level of the environment, who has access to those resources and opportunities, and how policies at all levels of society affect human development shape social work practice and types and levels of intervention. Juan and his family, because they were Mexican American, poor, and in a family situation involving divorce, faced social and economic injustice at all levels of the environment.

Social workers advocate for social and economic justice by working to expand individual access to resources and opportunities at all levels of the environment, including adequate education; food, clothing, and shelter; employment; health care; and participation in local, state, and national political processes. Social workers also have a commitment to alleviate social and economic injustice and its resulting oppression and discrimination. Some of the possible types of oppression that can result from social and economic injustice are shown in Table 3.5.

The Helping Process

The beginning generalist social work professional is seen as a "change agent" who can assist client systems in identifying needed change, developing strategies to make the change with those client systems, empowering and assisting client systems to implement those strategies, and monitoring and evaluating throughout the process to ensure that the desired change is taking place. Note that the term *client system* is used rather than *client* since social work intervention is often directed at a level of the environment beyond the individual. A **client system** can include individuals, families, groups, organizations, or communities, or larger social entities at which intervention is directed. BSW social workers are trained to use a generalist approach, which can be used to address individual needs that are a part of

TABLE 3.5	COMMON FORMS OF OPPRESSION	
Institutional	**Cultural**
Housing	Values/norms
Employment	Language
Education	Standards of behavior
Media	Holidays
Religion	Roles
Health services	Logic system
Government	Societal expressions
Legal services	The arts
Transportation	
Recreation	

Source: A. Condeluci, *Interdependence: The Route to Community* (Delray Beach, FL: St. Lucie, 1996), p. 18. Reprinted with permission of the publisher.

everyday life as well as to help larger client systems. No matter what level of the environment the social worker selects as an intervention point, the generalist approach can be a useful tool in bringing about planned change.

Although many variations can be used when delineating the stages of the helping process from a generalist social work perspective, all use the systems/ecological framework as a base. Miley, O'Melia, and DuBois (1998, p. 90) incorporate the framework with a strengths/empowerment perspective in their identification of three stages:

1. Dialogue
   a. Share and establish collaborative relationships with clients.
   b. Clarify client perspectives and social worker perspectives regarding strengths, challenges, and needs.
2. Discovery
   a. Search and explore resources and strengths clients may not know they have.

b. Assess and explore feelings and determine needs.

c. Develop plans and frame solutions.

3. Development

a. Strengthen and help clients get what they need.

b. Activate resources, including clients' personal resources.

c. Recognize success and reinforce strengths.

d. Build new resources and competencies.

Social work educators Compton and Galaway (1998, pp. 385–386) and others take a somewhat more traditional view, delineating what is referred to as a problem-solving approach, but suggest similar stages when working with client systems:

1. Contact or engagement

a. Develop a relationship with the client system.

b. Define the problem.

c. Identify preliminary goals.

d. Obtain as much information as possible to develop an intervention strategy.

2. Contract

a. Assess and evaluate the needs of the client system.

b. Formulate an action plan.

c. Determine what resources are needed for the plan to be successful.

3. Action

a. Carry out the plan.

b. Monitor and adjust it as needed.

c. Terminate.

d. Evaluate.

Note the similarities between these stages and those with a greater emphasis on the strengths and empowerment of the client system.

In moving through these stages with a client system, regardless of the specific model used, the social worker and the client address the following issues:

- Who has the power?
- What connections does the client have?
- What connections are working?
- What connections are not working?
- What connections are missing?
- Is this the way things should be? What would the client like to see changed?
- What connections can be used as resources to facilitate the change?
- What about the big picture? How do all the pieces of the system fit together? (Miley et al., 1998, p. 293)

As you can see from the phases and issues addressed, the systems/ecological framework is the organizing framework used, and intervention is from a generalist practice perspective, which incorporates the strengths of the client and the broader environment, empowerment, and the promotion of social and economic justice. A large part of generalist social work practice is often directed toward mediating between systems to strengthen their connections to each other.

After reviewing the phases of the helping process, it is easy to see the "goodness of fit" between this process and the systems/ecological framework and the many ways that the two are related. Ms. Herrera's involvement with Juan and his family can be used to demonstrate how this framework can be applied to understand or to intervene at various levels of the environment.

Applications with Juan and His Family

During the contact/engagement or dialogue phase of the helping process, Ms. Herrera, the school social worker, used all of the concepts of the systems/ecological framework. In developing an initial relationship with Juan and his mother, she used preliminary knowledge about areas such as 12-year-old boys and their developmental needs during this preadolescence stage, single-parent women and their special needs, the Mexican American culture, and ways that preadolescents and parents might view a professional from an authoritative organization such as a school. She empathized with Juan and his mother as she realized how they might view life from their day-to-day reality. As she continued to get to know Juan, Ms. Herrera allowed him to be the "expert," telling her what his life was like and what his needs were. She emphasized his strengths and helped him realize he had many on which to draw.

As Juan and Ms. Herrera began the contract or discovery phase, Ms. Herrera gathered information about Juan from his mother, his teachers, his friends, and others within his environment who could help them obtain as holistic a picture of Juan and his needs as possible. Ms. Herrera and Juan looked not only at the characteristics of Juan, his mother, his teachers, and his friends but also at their interactions with Juan and with each other. They focused not only on needs but also on strengths. They realized that both Juan and his mother were motivated to change and that his teachers were very committed to helping him. Ms. Herrera incorporated information she learned about Juan's family with her knowledge about the dynamics of a family in which substance abuse had been a problem, about long-term effects of child maltreatment on parents, about gangs and peer relationships when adolescents feel lonely and isolated, and about Juan's family's church, Juan's mother's

jobs, and the community and its attitudes toward Juan and his family. She was especially concerned about the lack of resources in the community and the lack of support for young adolescent males and single-parent mothers.

As she discovered more about Juan's situation, Ms. Herrera and Juan began to explore possible resources available to help Juan get his needs met. Ms. Herrera set up a meeting with Juan and his mother to clarify needs and to establish preliminary goals based on the information they had gathered. The three of them agreed that three initial needs were to reduce Juan's responsibility at home, to address his sense of loss over his father's leaving and anger because he had left, and to help Juan create a positive peer support group. They identified goals that focused on reducing the pressure from Juan's mother to take care of his brother and do so much at home, helping Juan deal with his feelings about the divorce, and helping him develop a positive peer support group. The three of them agreed that, although the initial referral related to Juan's school behavior and performance, these underlying needs were more critical and would, in fact, most likely improve his school performance if they were addressed.

After these three goals were identified, Juan and Ms. Herrera began meeting, sometimes separately and sometimes with his mother. They considered all possible options regarding how these goals might be met, listing potential resources available that might be helpful. Some resources, such as more financial help from Juan's father and Juan's mother quitting her job and going on public assistance, were rejected for various reasons. Finally, the three of them developed a contractual agreement that specified how Juan's needs would be addressed.

During the action or development phase, Ms. Herrera referred Juan's mother to the local human services agency, where she was able to qualify for low-income child care for her youngest child. Juan's mother also asked for information about a job-training program to upgrade her skills so that she could get a higher-paying job and be able to work one job instead of two. This would allow her to spend more time with Juan and his brother. With Ms. Herrera's help, Juan and his mother negotiated specific tasks Juan would do at home and agreed that he would have 2 hours after school every day to spend time with friends. They also agreed to rules regarding how he could spend his time with them. Juan and his mother also agreed that if Juan followed the rules and completed his chores, he could spend time weekly with his previous friends in his old neighborhood. In addition, Juan agreed to participate in a school support group for seventh-grade boys whose parents have experienced divorce. Ms. Herrera felt that this approach would help Juan not only work through some of his feelings about the divorce but also develop a new set of peers with whom he could become socially involved.

Juan and his mother also began counseling at the local teen/parent center, and the counselor and Ms. Herrera conferred regularly about his progress there. Ms. Herrera, while maintaining confidentiality about Juan's specific family issues, communicated with Juan's teachers, and they agreed to help Juan feel more accepted in his new school and to provide opportunities for him to get to know other students.

After 3 months, Juan's teachers reported that he was coming to class, participating in class discussions, handing in his homework, and no longer exhibiting behavior problems. His grades also improved significantly. Juan began

to feel more empowered, and he dropped his friends who were gang members and formed several solid friendships with his classmates at his new school. Two of his friends were from the support group. Although the group was terminated after 8 weeks, Ms. Herrera still met with Juan every 2 weeks or so to be sure that he was doing well. Juan spent a great deal of time in the group talking about the divorce and his feelings about his father. He visited his father twice and was looking forward to seeing him during his spring vacation. Juan and his mother, and sometimes his younger brother, also participated in family counseling sessions at the teen/parent center. Juan's mother developed a new set of friends and a support system through her youngest son's child care center, where there were also many other single parents. She enrolled in a computer-programming training course and was looking forward to the opportunity to upgrade her skills.

As the positive changes in one system occurred, they had a positive impact in other systems as well. The fact that Juan's mother was able to obtain child care, for example, reduced her stress and enabled her to interact more positively with Juan. Ms. Herrera's talking with Juan's teachers and helping them understand his needs for acceptance also enabled them to view Juan more positively. This, in turn, reduced some of the pressure on him, increased his self-esteem, and gave him the needed confidence to seek out new friendships and find more positive ways to gain acceptance. Juan became involved in a school leadership program and helped develop an outreach program for new students.

Although she felt that she was able to make a difference when helping Juan and his mother, Ms. Herrera was increasingly frustrated about the large number of students she had who were like Juan. She had referrals on her desk for 12 more students in similar situations. She decided that it would be a more productive use of her time to develop additional resources at other levels of the environment than to deal with each student on a case-by-case basis. Ms. Herrera contacted the head of the counseling center and a number of other individuals in the community who were also concerned. A group of 15 community representatives, including Juan as the teen representative from the school, began developing plans for a comprehensive program that would help teens and their families. The plan called for staff from the counseling center to come to the school weekly to lead additional support groups, for outreach efforts to be made to local businesses to locate adult mentors to work on a one-to-one basis with teens in need of additional adult support, and for the development of a teen center with after-school, evening, and weekend recreational programs. The group also decided to work with a state legislative group to advocate for additional funding for adolescent services and for single-parent families.

SUMMARY

Social welfare needs involve many complex and interrelated factors. These factors may be ordered in a number of ways to describe social welfare needs, to understand them, and to predict when they will occur and under what conditions. Because the needs are so complex and involve human behaviors and environmental influences that are difficult to measure, as well as a variety of disciplines, no one theory can be used to address all social welfare or human needs. However, the systems/ecological framework, which incorporates the concept that an

individual may be seen as part of a larger environment with whom he or she continually interacts and is an interdependent part of that environment, is useful in organizing information to determine what else is needed and to develop an appropriate intervention strategy. This framework incorporates factors at the individual, family, group, organizational, community, and societal levels and allows for a variety of interventions at one or more levels. The framework is also congruent with the generalist practice approach and its focus on client strengths, empowerment, and the promotion of social and economic justice.

KEY TERMS

association
boundary
cause-and-effect
   relationship
client system
closed systems
empowerment
entropy
equifinality
exosystem level
generalizable
inclusive
intrapsychic
macrosystem level

mesosystem level
microsystem level
open systems
person-environment fit
social and economic
   justice
steady state
strengths perspective
synergy
system
systems/ecological
   framework
testable
theory

DISCUSSION QUESTIONS

1. Why is it difficult to develop good theory to address social welfare needs?
2. Briefly identify the key components of the systems/ecological perspective. Compare and

contrast open and closed systems, and static and steady state systems.

3. Using a systems/ecological perspective, identify the systems that currently affect Juan's life.

4. Using the systems/ecological perspective as delineated by Bronfenbrenner and Garbarino, identify at least one strategy you might use if you were a social worker to help Juan and his family at each of the four levels of the environment: the microsystem, the mesosystem, the exosystem, and the macrosystem.

5. Identify at least four advantages of using the systems/ecological perspective to understand social welfare needs.

6. Briefly describe the helping process and its advantages to social workers within social welfare institutions. What type of intervention plan would you suggest if you were the school social worker assigned to work with Juan?

7. Show how the concepts of empowerment, client strengths, and social and economic justice are congruent with the systems/ecological framework.

INFOTRAC
COLLEGE EDITION

To learn more about topics included in this chapter, enter the following search terms:

economic justice

empowerment

microsystem

poverty

social justice

strengths perspective

worldview

ON THE INTERNET

http://www.jcpr.org/

http://www.clasp.org/

http://www.sc.edu/swan/

REFERENCES

Bronfenbrenner, U. (1979). *The ecology of human development.* Cambridge, MA: Harvard University Press.

Compton, B., & Galaway, B. (1998). *Social work processes* (6th ed.). Pacific Grove, CA: Brooks/Cole.

Condeluci, A. (1996). *Interdependence: The route to community.* Delray Beach, FL: St. Lucie.

Erikson, E. (1959). *Identity and the life cycle: Psychological issues.* Monograph no. 1. New York: International Universities Press.

Franklin, C., & Nurius, P. (Eds.). (1998). *Constructivism in practice: Methods and challenges.* N.p.: Families International.

Garbarino, J. (1992). *Children and families in the social environment.* New York: Aldine de Gruyter.

Germain, C., & Gitterman, A. (1995). Ecological perspective. In *Encyclopedia of social work* (Vol. 1, pp. 816–824). Washington, DC: NASW Press.

Gutierrez, L. M. (1990). Working with a woman of color. *Social Work, 35,* 135–153.

Johnson, L. C., Schwartz, C. L., & Tate, D. S. (1997). *Social welfare: A response to human need.* Boston: Allyn & Bacon.

Meyer, C. (1983). *Clinical social work in the eco-systems perspective.* New York: Columbia University Press.

Miley, K., O'Melia, M., & DuBois, B. (1998). *Generalist social work practice: An empowering approach.* Boston: Allyn & Bacon.

Parsons, R., Jorgensen, J., & Hernandez, S. (1994). *The integration of social work practice.* Pacific Grove, CA: Brooks/Cole.

Richmond, M. (1922). *What is social casework?* New York: Russell Sage Foundation.

Saleeby, D. (1996). *The strengths perspective in social work practice.* New York: Addison-Wesley.

Schatz, M., Jenkins, L., & Sheafor, B. (1990). Milford redefined: A model of initial and advanced generalist social work. *Journal of Education for Social Work, 26*(3), 217–231.

Shriver, J. (1998). *Human behavior and the social environment.* Boston: Allyn & Bacon.

Turner, F., & Younghusband, E. (Eds.). (1996). *Social work treatment: Interlocking theoretical approaches* (4th ed.). New York: Free Press.

Von Bertalanffy, L. (1968). *General system theory.* New York: Braziller.

SUGGESTED FURTHER READINGS

Anderson, R., Carter, I., & Lowe, G. (1999). *Human behavior in the social environment: A social systems approach.* New York: Aldine de Gruyter.

Bloom, M., & Germain, C. (1999). *Human behavior and the social environment: An ecological view.* New York: Columbia University Press.

Buckley, W. (Ed.). (1968). *Modern systems research for the behavioral scientist.* Hawthorne, NY: Aldine de Gruyter.

Council on Social Work Education. (1999). *Curriculum policy statement for the master's degree and baccalaureate degree programs in social work education.* New York: Author.

Day, P. (1999). *A new history of social welfare* (3rd ed.). Boston: Allyn & Bacon.

Germain, C., & Gitterman, A. (Eds.). (1996). *The life model of social work practice: Advances in theory and practice* (2nd ed.). New York: Columbia University Press.

Gutierrez, L., Parsons, R., & Cox, E. (1997). *Empowerment in social work practice: A sourcebook.* Pacific Grove, CA: Brooks/Cole.

Zastrow, C., & Kirst-Ashman, K. (1997). *Understanding human behavior in the social environment.* Chicago: Nelson-Hall.

DIVERSITY AND SOCIAL JUSTICE

The Impact of Race, Ethnicity, Class, Gender, and Sexual Orientation

Maureen Thompson and Josie Wiley have been lifelong friends. They grew up together in the same neighborhood, went to the same public schools, and even attended the same state college where they were roommates. While in college, they realized that their relationship had a sexual side to it as well. Both were very happy with their social as well as love life. Upon graduation, they moved to a small city where they became employed as stockbrokers in different companies. They rented an apartment in a high-rise building and were very pleased with their new environment. Both very spiritual, they joined a local congregation where they were soon asked to be Sunday school teachers. Both accepted the challenge of teaching young girls, were enthusiastic about their teaching, and soon found their small group growing in size. Life was good until a few parents complained to the minister of education, saying they were fearful that Maureen and Josie were lesbians and, if so, they did not want them teaching their children. The minister of education asked Maureen and Josie to come in for an interview, congratulated them on their dedication, and then related to them the complaints that he had received. Josie and Maureen readily acknowledged that they were lesbians, in love, and very happy with their relationship. The minister of education reluctantly asked them to resign to keep peace in the congregation, even though he acknowledged that he personally had no problems with their relationship. Devastated, they resigned and joined another congregation.

Situations such as those experienced by Maureen and Josie are not uncommon. Many individuals seek fulfillment and opportunities only to find that social barriers hamper their ability to achieve these goals. Maureen and

Josie represent only one case of millions of Americans who find that social and economic justice are not necessarily achieved through hard work, dedication, and quality performance. All too often, social mobility and opportunity are not equally available to all who seek to attain the American dream. Women, people of color, gays and lesbians, and other members of diverse groups have historically been denied opportunities in business, religious, political, and social life that white males have come to expect and take for granted. Under the subtle guise of institutional sexism, racism, and homophobia, the right to free and full participation in our social and economic institutions is denied to individuals who fail to meet dominant group criteria. In the case of Maureen and Josie, the unfounded fear that they would influence their young female charges into a life of lesbianism was sufficient justification for denying them the opportunity to continue in their roles. Stereotypes, once institutionalized, are difficult to overcome.

In this chapter, we will examine the characteristics of social inequality implicit in racism, classism, sexism, and gender preferences in more detail. The impact of social inequality is not always the same between people of color and women. It is somewhat ironic that white women, the targets of gender inequality, often discriminate against people of color. To understand better the differential effects of institutional racism, classism, and sexism, each is reviewed separately. Keep in mind that all lead to a life of second-class citizenship in our society. The ways that prejudice and discrimination are directed toward gays and lesbians are also discussed.

PREJUDICE AND DISCRIMINATION

Social inequality is generally considered to be a product of prejudice and discrimination. **Prejudice** is a value learned through the process of socialization. Once internalized, prejudices become an aspect of an individual's value system. People who are prejudiced rarely consider themselves to be so. Objects of prejudice are presumed to have behavioral characteristics that those who are prejudiced find objectionable. Through the process of negative stereotyping, women, people of color, poor people, gays and lesbians, and members of other diverse groups are presumed to hold behavioral traits that justify their exclusion from free and full participation in the social roles of society.

Stereotypes are beliefs that members of certain groups always or generally behave in specific ways. Hence, some in our society hold beliefs that women are not as astute at decision making as men; that African Americans are less intelligent and prone to idleness and crime; that Latinos prefer the slower pace of agrarian life; that gays and lesbians are persistent in encouraging heterosexuals to become homosexual. These are among the many negative stereotypes associated with each of these groups. On the other hand, positive stereotypes—that women are nurturing and supportive; that African

Americans gain strength from religion and their churches; and that Latinos place considerable value on their large, extended families—are just as liable to false presumptions as negative ones. The notion that white males are endowed with intellectual prowess and creative skills lacked by other groups is also an example of a positive stereotype.

To illustrate how prejudice affects decision making, consider the following paraphrases from the works of Sirkin (1994) in his article "Resisting Cultural Meltdown":

> A traditional Jewish family had an older daughter who had moved to Albuquerque, commenced dating her non-Jewish employer, and, in spite of long-standing Jewish traditions against intermarriage and strong family pressure not to do so, subsequently married her employer. As a consequence, her parents as well as her sisters discontinued contact with her. In effect, intermarriage tore this family apart. (p. 51)

In this situation, the older daughter violated strong in-group values and traditions that had become institutionalized and affirmed as a matter of faith and practice. There was little doubt that her husband was of impeccable character, a hard worker, an outstanding citizen, a man of faith, and a loving and caring husband. Those qualities from the family's perspective were necessary but not sufficient for their blessing and acceptance of the newlyweds. Indeed, from the parents' perspective, no non-Jewish male would have been acceptable as a marriage partner for their daughter. While most people hold deep respect for traditions and strongly held values, one can readily understand how prejudgment can ensue.

Like the family just described, dominant group members in society have long-standing values, attitudes, customs, and beliefs related to women, poor people, gays and lesbians, and

people of color. These beliefs often result in the erection of social barriers that preclude or limit members of these groups from living in a socially just society. Social distance is invariably a mirror of prejudice, just as discrimination serves as a vehicle to ensure social distance. Prejudice is the presumption, without the benefit of facts, that certain behaviors are characteristic of all members of a specific group. As a consequence, members of the dominant group may demean members of a minority group by assuming that assigned behaviors in fact are true, and by then relating to individual members of that group through the filter of prejudice.

Although the target of prejudice may vary, the paradox is that virtually no one is free from prejudice. For example, prejudice may not be directed toward gender, race, ethnicity, or creed—it may even be directed toward people who are themselves prejudiced.

Prejudice is a psychological construct that may result in discrimination. Although prejudice can exist without discrimination (and discrimination without prejudice, for that matter), they usually coexist (Pinderhughes, 1989). Prejudice fuels the fires and provides the justification for discrimination. If a person holds the false belief (an axiom for prejudice) that people of certain groups are less intelligent and incapable of equal participation or would threaten traditional practices, they may practice differential treatment (an axiom for discrimination), thereby placing the erroneously feared threat at some distance. Denying women, people of color, the poor, the elderly, gays and lesbians, and other social groups the right to equal social participation limits the opportunity structures through which the desired behavioral characteristics could be acquired. A vicious, self-perpetuating cycle is then set in motion. Discrimination is the action that maintains and supports prejudice. It involves "denying to members of minority groups equal access to employment opportunities, residential housing areas, membership in certain religious and social organizations, access to community services, and so on" (Zastrow & Kirst-Ashman, 1997, p. 205).

Although everyone has prejudices, the people most damaged by prejudice and discrimination are those who are not members of the dominant group. Those individuals who are members of the group that has the most power are the least likely to suffer from the repercussions of prejudice and discrimination. Over time, the impact of prejudice and discrimination becomes part of the very fabric of society, with members of both dominant and minority groups not always aware that what is taken for granted is discriminatory to some social groups.

Institutional discrimination is discrimination that occurs as the result of accepted beliefs and behaviors and is codified in societal roles and policies. It is thereby "intrinsic" to the mores of a society. Institutional discrimination is reinforced through the social practices of dominant group members, who may be oblivious to the effects of their actions. Access to housing in specific geographic areas and patterns of where ethnic groups have settled over time; the resulting ethnic composition of schools based on housing patterns; the location of freeways and storage units for dangerous chemicals; access to and participation in higher education; access to certain types and levels of employment; and pay differentials among white males, women, and people of color who are doing the same type of job are all examples of institutional discrimination. Institutionalized racism is based on a person's color, whereas institutionalized sexism results in the denial of rights or opportunities for participation on the basis of gender. In both instances, free and full participation is denied on the basis of group membership.

Members of the dominant societal group with prejudices against other groups have the power to use their prejudices against those groups. These prejudices coupled with power result in **oppression,** unjust uses of power against nondominant groups by the dominant group. This power restricts the actions of the nondominant groups and also allows the dominant group to exploit these groups to its advantage. Examples of oppression include the placement of tank farms and other dangerous environmental hazards in poor neighborhoods populated largely by people of color and restricted access of certain groups to educational and employment opportunities. Groups that experience prejudice, discrimination, and oppression from the dominant group are considered to be **populations at risk.** Because of their treatment, both historically and presently, members of at-risk populations are more likely to experience serious health and mental health problems, live shorter lives, and be victims of hate or other serious crimes.

SOCIAL AND ECONOMIC JUSTICE: WOMEN

In the book *The Compleat Chauvinist*, Edgar Bergman (1982), a physician in Maryland, raises the question, "What would our Neanderthal forefathers have thought of our succumbing to the outrageous myth of sexual equality?" (p. 185). In buttressing his antiegalitarian views, he refers to comments made by Marvin Harris, a professor of anthropology at Columbia University, who is quoted as saying:

> Feminists are wailing in the wind if they think they're going to abolish sexism by raising

consciousness. There is not a shred of evidence—historical or contemporary—to support the existence of a single society in which women controlled the political and economic lives of men.

Bergman offers a number of illustrations in defense of the position that men are clearly superior to women in decision making. To the detriment of social equality, Bergman's views and arguments are not new. Women have experienced social inequality throughout recorded history. Invariably, inequality was—and is—justified on the basis of the biological superiority of men, despite no evidence to support that premise.

In spite of advances made during the past several decades, women in our society experience discrimination. Sex-biased discrimination is more visible in the occupational market and economic areas than in other aspects of social participation. Although some progress has been made, many male-dominated job positions have remained difficult for qualified women to obtain. Positions such as pilots, military officers, and construction supervisors are still held primarily by males. Women tend to be concentrated in lower-paying, lower-status positions such as clerical workers, child care workers, receptionists, nurses, hairdressers, bank tellers, and cashiers. Men tend to be concentrated in higher-paying positions: lawyers, judges, engineers, accountants, college instructors, physicians, and dentists. Management and administrative positions at the upper levels also continue to be held mostly by men.

Income

From 1890 to 1997, the proportion of women in the labor force increased from 14.9% to just under 60% (U.S. Department of Commerce, 2000). This increase ushered in a number of conflicts and issues related to women's participation in the labor market. Chief among the issues was the concept of comparable worth.

Comparable worth is a concept often best understood by the phrase "equal pay for equal work." Much of the income disparity between men and women, however, is largely attributable to differences in occupational positions, which have changed little over the past decade. Income differences exist primarily because men are employed in positions of leadership or in technical fields, whereas women are disproportionately employed in the lower-paying clerical and service fields. Even when women hold positions similar to those of men, their income is less. Seniority or related factors do not always account for these differences, and employers generally concede that, for a given type of position, men get a higher income than do women. It is estimated that women earn approximately 72% of what employed males do (Dunn, 1996).

Notwithstanding traditional notions that incomes produced by women are less essential for family maintenance than those generated by men, the practice of channeling women into lower-level positions, with the resultant limited career choices and lower incomes, represents an institutionalized policy of sex-based discrimination. Although efforts recently have been made to provide equal employment opportunities for women, social roles continue to be gender typed and are passed down from generation to generation through the process of socialization.

It is interesting to note that women continue to be less well represented in business administration, engineering, law, medicine, and dentistry, while they are overrepresented in the fields of fine arts, social work, and nursing. When women are excluded or limited from participating in certain arenas of job opportunities, educational preparation programs are also affected because women are forced to make career (and consequently educational) choices on the basis of opportunities for employment and advancement.

Education

Ironically, men hold leadership positions in professions that predominantly employ women, such as public education and social work. A career-oriented woman entering the educational system usually has greater difficulty in securing promotion to an administrative position than a similarly qualified man. As a result, women are relegated to the lower-paying, less prestigious position of classroom teacher throughout their careers. Although nondiscrimination policies exist, qualified female educators who seek promotion to administration are confronted with the task of penetrating a gender-biased tradition of assigning men to those roles in the public school system. Evidence indicates that some changes are occurring in the numbers and percentages of women holding administrative positions. Opening the opportunity structure to accommodate all qualified professionals, regardless of gender, appears to be a slow, arduous process.

In 1995, women earned approximately 55% of the bachelor's and master's degrees awarded and 40% of academic doctoral degrees. During that year, women were awarded 42.6% of the law degrees earned, 38.8% of the medical doctor degrees, and 36.4% of the dental doctorates (U.S. Department of Commerce, 2000). Although larger numbers of women are now engaged in the educational process at both undergraduate and graduate levels, men continue to dominate the doctoral degree market in academic as well as professional schools.

Social Work

Historically, most social work professionals have been women. In 1997, nearly 70% of all social work practitioners were women (U.S. Department of Commerce, 2000). In a field that has championed equal rights for women (as well as one that is predominantly female), it is ironic that men often hold leadership roles. Men are represented disproportionately in administrative and managerial roles, and, as a group, receive higher salaries than women. To that extent, the social work profession—despite its advocacy of women's rights—reflects the tendency of other professions as well as the business community.

Religion

In organized religion, where women are more active participants, less than 5% are ordained to the clergy (U.S. Department of Commerce, 2000). Women hold primary leadership positions in churches in very few instances, and they are employed in higher levels of administration in religious associations even less often. Many religious groups base their male-biased pastoral leadership roles on the "holy writ," thereby effectively excluding women from appointments to significant leadership responsibilities in those bodies.

Politics

In 1995, only 47 of 435 U.S. representatives and 8 of 100 U.S. senators were women (U.S. Department of Commerce, 2000). Only 3 of the 50 governors were women. These figures reflect the subordinate role that women continue to play in the legislative process. Male bias is ever present in legislative debates in those areas where laws directly affect women. Some progress has been made at the state level (see Figure 4.1), where the percentage of women has been rising during the past 30 years.

INSTITUTIONAL SEXISM

The discussion and illustrations just presented indicate the strong gender bias in administrative and managerial positions. Women are treated differently in the professions and business. Their status as women negatively influences the opportunity to move into those prominent roles regardless of their competence or ability. In effect, women are discriminated against in the marketplace solely because they are women. This practice, called **sexism,** is a result of the values and practices embodied in our

---

Percentage of income a woman earned compared to a man in 1999: 76%[1]

Amount college-educated women earn each year compared to college-educated men: $11,900 less[2]

Amount average woman will lose during her entire career due to the gender wage gap: $523,000[2]

Total collective amount women lose annually in wages due to the gender wage gap: Over $1 billion[2]

Amount college-educated African American women earn each year compared to white, male, high school graduates: $400 less[2]

Percentage of income a college-educated Latina woman earns each year compared to a white, male, high school graduate: 57%[2]

Percentage of children under 6 living in families headed by single-parent mothers working full time that were below the poverty level in 1998: 27%[1]

Percentage of mothers with children under 2 who are working: 58%[4]

Percentage of working mothers giving birth each year who return to work within 6 months: 84%[4]

Percentage of senior management positions held by women: 3–5%[3]

Percentage of seats on corporate boards held by women in 1994: 6.9%[3]

Percentage of female senior managers in Fortune 1000 and Fortune 500 companies who are white: 95%[3]

[1]U.S. Department of Labor. (1997, 2000). *Facts on Working Women.* Available: http://www.dol.gov/.
[2]Equal Rights Advocates. (2000). *Pay Equity.* http://www. equalrights.org/Facts/.
[3]Equal Rights Advocates. (2000). *Why Women Still Need Affirmative Action.* http://www.equalrights.org/Facts/.
[4]*Catalyst,* Mothers' Day update on working moms (May 11, 1997).

FIGURE **4.1**

FACTS ABOUT WORKING WOMEN AND GENDER EQUITY

social institutions. Most children are taught by their parents that boys are to be aggressive and dominant and that girls are to be nurturing and submissive. Parents often model these attributes in family interaction, in which the father assumes the roles of rule maker, disciplinarian, and decision maker and the mother assumes responsibility for the nurturing roles of caring for the children and household. Even if parents try to raise their children in nonsexist ways, children still are exposed to sexist views in interactions outside their families and via the media.

Performance differences between men and women invariably reflect societal attitudes and values far more than any inherent physical or psychological variances in maleness or femaleness. In modern society, few roles exist that could not be performed by either men or women, although throughout the life cycle, gender role distinctions are made and differences are emphasized. These distinctions become entrenched in societal values, thus hindering women from "crossing over" into roles considered masculine. Hence, an aggressive, goal-oriented, intelligent woman may be viewed as masculine and censured for departing from prescribed female role behavior.

Societal values and practices continue to result in a gender-segregated division of labor. Although some progress has been made in identifying roles as "asexual" (neither male nor female), roles in general are gender typed. Women have great difficulty gaining access to roles identified as appropriate for men only. Gender differentiation also is observed in opportunities to secure credit, purchase homes, negotiate contracts, and obtain credit cards, in which men typically have the advantage.

In the past decade, the issue of sexual harassment has received considerable attention as a problem that women must contend with in the workplace.

Sexual harassment is a form of sex discrimination that violates Title VII of the Civil Rights Act of 1964. Unwelcome sexual advances, requests for sexual favors, and other verbal or physical conduct of a sexual nature constitutes sexual harassment when submission to or rejection of this conduct explicitly or implicitly affects an individual's employment, unreasonably interferes with an individual's work performance or creates an intimidating, hostile or offensive work environment. (U.S. Equal Employment Opportunity Commission, 2000)

Sexual harassment includes graphic comments about a person's body, sexually suggestive pictures or other objects in the workplace, or threats that failure to submit sexually will adversely affect a person's job or salary (Stover & Giles, 1987). A person may also file charges of sexual harassment if she or he is affected by the behaviors of others (for example, a boss and a coworker involved in a sexual relationship). It is highly likely that much sexually harassing behavior goes unreported by employees for fear of retaliation.

THE ABORTION DILEMMA

One of the more emotionally charged issues that epitomizes the conflict between feminist and traditional values is abortion. Abortion entails of three central concerns: (a) the legal issue, (b) the medical issue, and (c) the values issue.

The Legal Issue

The legal precedent for abortion was established in 1973 by the *Roe v. Wade* decision. In effect, the U.S. Supreme Court maintained that a woman has the constitutional right to seek an abortion, if she so desires. This decision defined abortion as a personal decision rather than one to be determined by government policy. Although the Court's interpretation was straightforward and clear, attempts were made to cut funds from family planning agencies that gave abortion counseling and references. The lack of acceptance of the Court's ruling did not, however, close the door on the controversy.

More recently, states have been delegated the power to determine abortion policy. A 1989 policy established by Florida's legislature imposed strict requirements on abortions, so that legal abortions could be performed only when a pregnancy resulted from rape or when the health of the mother would be in jeopardy, should the pregnancy continue. In 1990, Louisiana sought to pass similar legislation. In spite of *Roe v. Wade*, there is no uniform code that mandates "abortion on demand" across the states. It is estimated, however, that approximately 1.5 million abortions are performed in the United States each year.

The Medical Issue

From a medical perspective, abortion, during the first trimester of a pregnancy, is a relatively simple, uncomplicated procedure. Although any medical intervention entails risk, abortion is generally not considered a high-risk procedure, even during the second trimester. The majority of abortions are performed during the first trimester and very few during the last trimester.

Assessing women's psychological preparedness for an abortion can be difficult. Most abortion clinics require a psychological assessment and counseling as prerequisites for an abortion. Few studies have attempted to assess postabortion adaptation, and their results have, for the most part, provided limited insight.

Perhaps the most controversial medical abortion procedure, so-called partial-birth (third trimester) abortions, has been more heatedly debated by Congress because of the near-term development of the fetus and the more complicated medical processes involved. Theoretically, partial-birth procedures can only be pursued when the life of either the fetus or the pregnant female would be in jeopardy should the pregnancy be carried to full term.

The Values Issue

Perhaps the most emotionally charged aspect of abortion involves values. Members of the antiabortion (right-to-life) movement base their resistance to abortion on the conviction that life begins at conception. Consequently, they view abortion as murder. Members of pro-choice groups, on the other hand, argue that life begins at birth, and they further insist that a woman has the constitutionally granted right to decide whether she wishes to continue her pregnancy or terminate it. Antiabortion groups seek the government's protection of the life (and rights) of the fetus in the same sense that children and adults merit the protection of the law from injury or injustice.

Within each of the groups there is some variance of value positions. For example, while arguing that life begins at conception, some antiabortion groups take the position that abortion is acceptable and justified in instances of rape or when the mother's health would be jeopardized. Other antiabortion groups oppose abortion under any circumstance, arguing that taking the life of the fetus is not acceptable at any time.

Abortion is not solely a women's issue. However, only women become pregnant and have the legal right to decide whether a pregnancy will be carried to its full term or terminated. The law remains unusually silent concerning men's role in matters of conception and pregnancy. Fathers are referred to as "alleged fathers," and they have no legal right to affect a woman's decision to abort a pregnancy.

Recently, a number of states have enacted parental notification laws, requiring a physician treating a female under 18 to notify her parents prior to performing an abortion. Although most laws allow exceptions to be made by a court in some instances—for example, if the girl is being abused by her parents—the consequences of these laws are still being debated.

We have included this discussion to illustrate further the problem of differential treatment of women in our society. Social workers must be especially attuned to such treatment and to the views surrounding abortion. Although they may have personal views that would preclude their participation in abortion counseling, they have a professional responsibility to assure that referrals are made to protect the rights of the client. The National Association of Social Workers (NASW) clearly outlines the profession's position as follows:

> "The profession's position concerning abortion services is based on the principle of self-determination. Every individual (within the context of his or her own value system) must be free to participate or not participate in abortion services. Women should have the right to participate in or refrain from abortion counseling" (NASW, 1988, p. 3). . . . [I]n the event a woman chooses to consider an abortion, an array of services should be available to her. These include abortion counseling and referral, safe, surgical care, counseling concerning contraception, and provision of

the appropriate contraceptive technology. (Zastrow & Kirst-Ashman, 1997, p. 74)

While professional social workers may agree with the preceding statement, we must not conclude that all social workers support the pro-choice position. Social workers, like other professionals, vary greatly in their personal values, and this point is certainly true regarding the abortion controversy.

SOCIAL REFORM: THE FEMINIST MOVEMENT AND SOCIAL ACTION

Women have pursued equal social treatment since this nation's inception. Early leaders included Elizabeth Stanton (1815–1902), who petitioned for a property rights law for women in New York (1845); Lucretia Mott (1793–1880), who organized the first women's rights convention in New York; Susan B. Anthony (1820–1906), who helped to form the National Women's Suffrage Association in 1869; and Lucy Stone (1818–1893), who formed the National American Women's Suffrage Association. Carrie Catt (1859–1947), a political activist, founded the International Women's Suffrage Alliance and later, following World War I, the League of Women Voters, an organization that today wields significant political influence. Catt's efforts were largely responsible for the enactment of the Nineteenth Amendment to the Constitution, which extended voting rights to women in 1920 (Axinn & Levin, 1997).

In more recent times, women's groups have intensified their efforts to secure equal rights. The **Civil Rights Act** of 1964 addressed the problems of discrimination due to gender as well as race. A major attempt to secure women's rights was embodied in the **Equal Rights Amendment (ERA).** Bitterly opposed by organized labor, the John Birch Society, the Christian Crusade, and the Moral Majority, and over the protest of Senator Sam Ervin (D–North Carolina), who castigated the proposed amendment, the bill was passed by Congress in 1972 and remanded to the states for ratification. Pro-ERA forces, including the National Organization for Women (NOW), the League of Women Voters, and the National Women's Political Caucus, lobbied the states to seek ratification for the amendment. Anti-ERA spokespersons lobbied the states against ratification and argued that all women would be sent into combat, subjected to unisex public facilities, and required to secure jobs if the amendment passed. The Carter administration, favorable to passage of the ERA, had little influence on the states in encouraging its adoption. The Reagan administration opposed the measure. The unratified amendment died in June 1982.

Since that time, efforts to achieve gender equity have met with some success. Active efforts by NOW and related women's rights groups and public sentiment have coalesced to remove some of the barriers that historically had subjugated women in their pursuit of social equality. During the Clinton administration, a precedent has been set in naming both women and people of color to key roles in government offices.

Although the profession of social work has advocated for the abolition of societal barriers that deny equal treatment of women, it has not been in the forefront in providing leadership for the more significant feminist movements. During the 1960s, however, women's equality was established as a major priority for the profession. Both the NASW and the Council on Social Work Education (CSWE) initiated policies committing the profession to promotion of social and economic equality for women. Social workers are encouraged to advocate for women's rights and to treat all their clients equally.

SOCIAL AND ECONOMIC JUSTICE: SEXUAL ORIENTATION

Within the past decade, considerable attention has been directed to the prejudice and discrimination that characterize societal responses toward people who are gay, lesbian, bisexual, and transgendered. Transgendered individuals are born anatomically as one gender but have a psychological identity with the other. Transsexuals, whether or not they have had "sex change" surgery, are considered transgendered persons; note that this group is particularly oppressed, sometimes by gays and lesbians.

Although a person's sexual orientation is considered to be a personal and private matter not related to free and full participation in our society, such has not been the case for those who are not heterosexual. The intense negative emotional reaction to homosexuals, a result of fear and hatred, is a state of psychological conditioning termed **homophobia.** Acquired immunodeficiency syndrome (AIDS) has further promoted anxiety and fear toward homosexual relationships in spite of the fact that the fastest-growing groups of persons with AIDS are now heterosexual women and heterosexual people of color.

The rejection of homosexuality, with its accompanying prejudice and discrimination, has been bolstered by fundamentalist religions as well as the more traditional psychologies. For example, the Moral Majority and Christian Coalition movements argue strongly that homosexual practices are sinful and condemn homosexuals along with deviants, pornographers, and atheists. Irving Beiber (1962), a psychoanalyst, in his classic work titled *Homosexuality,* clearly describes traditional psychoanalysts' view that homosexuality is abnormal and that it can be cured through psychotherapy. These (and other) "authoritative" sources reinforce the biases and prejudices that have long existed in the general population.

Eighteen states currently have sodomy laws; 13 states have laws that make sodomy illegal for anyone, although the laws are usually enforced only for sodomy between homosexual couples, while 5 states have laws that make sodomy illegal only for homosexuals. Penalties range from $200 fines to 20 years' imprisonment. These are laws that are generally used to restrict (or punish) homosexual behavior. For example, some courts have used such legislation to justify removing children from the homes of gay and lesbian parents (American Civil Liberties Union, 2000).

While there have been recent efforts in many states to pass laws protecting the rights of persons who are not heterosexual, these attempts have not always been successful. Ten states have passed legislation to protect the rights of gays and lesbians in the workplace. Although 40 states have enacted legislation against hate crimes committed against individuals because of their race or ethnicity, only 21 states have legislation that includes sexual orientation (Anti-Defamation League, 2000). Hate crime legislation introduced in Texas after the tragic death of African American James Byrd, who was dragged behind a truck until his body became dismembered, failed because the proposed statute included protection because of one's sexual orientation.

Although experts disagree as to whether sexual orientation is determined by genetics or is a product of socialization, the general public continues to view homosexuality as a matter of choice. Some gays and lesbians have become more vocal and have sought legal redress for discriminatory practices, whereas others, fearing loss of jobs, intimidation, and harassment, have opted to remain "in the closet." In 1973, the American Psychiatric Association removed "functional homosexuality" from its list of behavior disorders, and as a result, mental health professionals no longer view homosexuality as a form of mental illness. However, a large segment of the public maintains the perspective that gay and lesbian relationships are a form of perversion and that social contact with homosexuals should be avoided.

Although some progress has been made in securing legal rights for members of the gay community, discrimination and prejudice continue to undergird public responses to them. Ambivalence surrounding this issue is best expressed by the "don't ask, don't tell" policy for members of the military enacted by the Clinton administration in the mid-1990s. Presumably this policy was designed to provide guarded protection to gay and lesbian military personnel (Lum, 2000).

Gays and lesbians have not been without advocates. One of the earlier groups to support the rights of gays and lesbians was the Chicago Society for Human Rights, established in 1924. In 1950, the Mattachine Society was founded to further rights for and acceptance of same-sex-oriented individuals. Currently, the Gay Liberation Front has established itself as a political organization promoting passage of legislation that would provide for nondiscriminatory practices against homosexuals, including recognition of same-sex marriages as well as adoption rights.

Stereotypical thinking based on erroneous information guides most heterosexuals'

Many individuals in the U.S. reacted strongly to the hate crime slaying of gay Wyoming student Matthew Shepard.

Evan Agostin/Liaison Agency

reactions to those with nonheterosexual orientations. Thus, individuals who are gay, lesbian, bisexual, or transgendered are often denied freedom of expression and access to the opportunity structure that is available for heterosexuals. In addition to these types of oppression, members of these groups are also subject to hate crimes committed against them. Antihomosexual hostility runs especially high in certain parts of the United States. The senseless slaying of a young gay college student in Wyoming in 1998 is reflective of the extent to which angry bigots will go in the expression of their derision for those whose sexual orientation differs from theirs.

Clearly, social work and related professions need to address more forcefully the prejudices and biases toward homosexuality as yet pervasive within the professions. In spite of the acknowledged reticence that exists, considerable progress has been made in the preparation of social workers for engaging clients who are gay, lesbian, bisexual, or transgendered. Accreditation standards for schools of social work require that course content address the needs of divergent populations, including gays and lesbians. Advocacy on behalf of the homosexual population directed toward the enforcement of antidiscrimination legislation has become a priority of the profession.

Unfortunately, until the fear and apprehensions concerning homosexual behavior are dispelled through public enlightenment, prejudice and discrimination will continue to remain barriers to social and economic justice for people who are gay, lesbian, bisexual, or transgendered.

SOCIAL AND ECONOMIC JUSTICE: CLASS

Too often when discussing social justice and equality, people ignore issues of class. Regardless of one's color, gender, or sexual orientation, persons in the lower ends of the economic structure in the United States also are treated differentially by the dominant group. The stratification of individuals and groups according to their social and economic assets and power is termed **class.** Discrimination toward members of a group because of their economic status is termed **classism.** Labeling persons who are poor as inferior gives justification to oppress this group.

Obviously, race, ethnicity, and gender play significant roles in determining the class to which one is likely to belong. Because of oppression experienced by these populations at risk, women and people of color are less likely to have access to superior educational opportunities, gainful employment that allows for upward mobility, adequate health care, and opportunities for their children that allow them to move into a higher economic class. Thus, members of these groups are likely to remain part of the lower class for multiple generations.

There is increasing debate in the United States about the impact of class on individual and social well-being. African American scholar William Julius Wilson and others write about what they call the **underclass,** "oppressed people who have not been able, due to barriers and obstacles in society, to escape poverty" (Johnson, Schwartz, & Tate, 1996, p. 59). As skill in technology becomes a necessity for successful employment, the numbers of individuals with limited access to education left out of the U.S. economic structure will grow significantly (Wilson, 1997). This growth will impact not only the poor but those in other classes as well. Murdock, Hogue, Michael, White, and Pecote (1997), for example, indicate that if Texas does not graduate at least 20,000 more college graduates annually, the average income of Texans in the year 2015 will be less than it was in 1991 because businesses are more likely to move to areas with educated workforces.

SOCIAL AND ECONOMIC JUSTICE: RACE AND ETHNICITY

Race and ethnicity are other personal attributes that often result in social and economic injustices. People distinguished by specific physical or cultural traits are often singled out for differential or unequal treatment. In the United States, the dominant racial group is Caucasian, and people of color, including African Americans, Mexican Americans, other Latinos, Asian Americans, Iranians, Native Americans, and Vietnamese, among others, are viewed by many members of the dominant (majority) group as having lower status.

The concept of race suggests that marked, distinct genetic differences are present. The term, in reality, is a social definition, since few genetic differences are found to exist among *Homo sapiens.* Race is commonly used to classify members of groups who have similar physical characteristics such as color or facial features. Behavioral traits are often attributed incorrectly to physical differences rather than to socialization experiences. In contrast to racial groups, ethnic groups tend to be classified by language differences or cultural patterns that vary from those of the dominant group. Both racial and ethnic groups are viewed as "different" by the dominant group, and prejudice and discrimination are often the result.

PLURALISM

Complete integration of all groups in society would result in the loss of racial or ethnic identity. Many people of color find this prospect objectionable. In recent years, ethnic and racial pride has been given considerable attention by groups of color. Although complete **assimilation** (the expectation that members of the nondominant group adopt the values and behaviors of the dominant group) theoretically would result in the erosion of racial and ethnic discrimination patterns, it probably will not occur. Many people argue that the contributions of our divergent ethnic and racial groups enrich our culture.

An alternative to assimilation is **cultural pluralism** (that is, cultural diversity), or the coexistence of various ethnic groups whose cultural differences are respected as equally valid. However, cultural pluralism is difficult to achieve within the matrix of prejudice, discrimination, and cultural differences. Recently, people of color have created and promoted cultural pride, yet less than equal coexistence continues to characterize their relationship with the dominant group.

Ironically, most immigrant populations have suffered the results of prejudice and discrimination as each new group settled in the United States—the Irish, Italians, Swedes, Germans, French, and others. The irony is, of course, that with the exception of Native Americans, all of us are descendants of immigrants. How quickly groups move from the role of the persecuted to that of persecutors. It is even more ironic that prejudices and dis-

crimination persist and become institutionalized by members of a society that values its Judeo-Christian heritage and provides equal constitutional rights and privileges for all.

Some progress has been made in opening up avenues for social and economic participation; however, members of nonmajority groups still must cope with differential treatment and limited opportunities. In the following discussion, we identify some of the issues and problems that confront racial and ethnic groups and examine antidiscrimination efforts designed to neutralize racial, cultural, and ethnic prejudices. As we discuss these groups, it is important to remember that although each group shares a common history and other characteristics, each group enjoys a rich diversity.

Social and Economic Justice: African Americans

All non-Caucasian racial and ethnic groups have experienced discrimination, but perhaps none more visibly than the African American population. Emerging from slavery, where they were considered chattel (property) and nonpersons, African Americans have continually found societally imposed constraints impeding their progress toward the achievement of social equality. During the "Jim Crow" days, for example, African Americans could not dine at public restaurants used by whites, could use only specially marked public restrooms and drinking fountains, had to ride in the rear of buses, were required to attend segregated schools, faced expectations of subservient behavior in the presence of whites, and could get only lower-paying domestic or manual labor jobs. Few could achieve justice before the law or gain acceptance as equals to even the lowest-class whites. Although the prescribed behaviors that characterized Jim

Crowism represented an extreme manifestation of discrimination, all nonwhite racial and ethnic groups have experienced social inequality in its subtler forms.

Today, the results of past and present discrimination are best reflected in the characteristics of African Americans, who represent about 13% of the total U.S. population. They earn only 60% as much income as whites, are unemployed in greater numbers than their white counterparts, and are three times more likely than whites to have incomes below the federal poverty line. Numerically, more whites receive public assistance than African Americans; however, African Americans are proportionally overrepresented on welfare rolls. Whites are more likely to complete high school than African Americans, and African Americans are underrepresented in the fields of law, medicine, dentistry, and business and overrepresented in occupations that require hard manual labor. These data reflect the differential opportunity structure available to the African American population in this country.

Social and Economic Justice: Latino Populations

Approximately 29 million people of Latino origin live in the United States, constituting 11% of the total population. Frequently referred to as "Hispanics," actually a term coined by Caucasians, the Latino population came to the United States from 26 nations. Latinos are the fastest-growing population group in the United States. By 2010, they are expected to become the majority group in some southwestern states and to comprise nearly 25% of the total U.S. population by 2050. The largest group are Mexican Americans (see Table 4.1).

People of Mexican descent constitute the second largest group of color in the United

TABLE 4.1 **HISPANIC/LATINO POPULATIONS**

Group	Percentage of Population
Mexican	60
Puerto Rican	12
Cuban	5
Other	23

Source: U.S. Bureau of the Census, *Census of Population, General Population Characteristics, United States,* CP-I-I (Washington, DC: Author, 1990).

States. Although most live in major urban areas of the West and Southwest, many continue to reside in rural areas. The Mexican American population is a diverse group. The urban population tends to be better educated, and the effects of acculturation are more visible among them. Those living in rural areas are more likely to be less acculturated, continue to use Spanish as a primary language, and work in lower-paying jobs often related to farming or ranching. The population of Mexicans and Mexican Americans in the United States is growing rapidly as "undocumented immigrants" continue to flow across the border into the southwestern states and California. Cultural pride is greatly emphasized and is best reflected in the retention of Spanish as a first language. Bilingual education programs have been designed in some public school systems to enable Mexican American children to progress educationally, although dropout rates continue to be much higher than for the dominant group population.

In general, people of Mexican ancestry have experienced the consequences of discrimination in that they hold lower-paying jobs, are underrepresented in politics, live in de facto segregated neighborhoods, and are viewed as being "different" by the dominant group. Upward mobility has been painfully slow in coming, although some progress has been made. Ethnic organizations such as La Raza and the League of United Latin American Citizens (LULAC) have sought to unite Spanish-speaking populations to promote favorable social change and to provide greater visibility to the issues and problems that impede the achievement of social equality.

Puerto Ricans and Cubans constitute the largest other Latino populations. Most of the Puerto Rican population in the United States resides in the metropolitan New York area or in eastern seaboard cities such as Newark, New Jersey, and New Haven, Connecticut. Cubans have settled primarily in the Miami area of Florida. The social and economic progress of these groups is similar to that of the Mexican American group. Housing is often inferior, jobs tend to be menial and lower paying, the school dropout rate is high, and access to services and support systems is difficult. Social progress has been considerably greater for the Cuban population due, in part, to the higher educational level of the first waves of Cuban immigrants to the United States.

As has been the case with newly migrated Mexicans, other Latinos came to the United States with the hopes of being able to achieve a higher-quality life, only to find that prejudice and discrimination presented barriers to achieving that dream. Cultural and language barriers continue to make them "different" and more visible targets for differential treatment.

Social and Economic Justice: Asian Americans

Asian American immigrants have cultural traits and physical characteristics that separate them from the dominant group but represent one of the most diverse ethnic groups within the United States, incorporating individuals of Chinese, Japanese, Korean, Indian, Vietnamese, and Pacific Islands descent. Although they represent less than 4% of the U.S. population, the number of Asian immigrants has increased in recent years. Chinese immigration dates back to the mid-19th century, and the Chinese represent the greatest percentage of Asian immigrants (see Table 4.2).

Japanese immigration began around the turn of the 20th century, the Korean population in the mid-20th century, and the Vietnamese in the 1960s and 1970s. The aggregate total of all Asian Americans in the United States is approximately 7.3 million people.

While all of the nationalities constituting the Asian American population have experienced differential treatment, many have been able to achieve a relatively high standard of living in spite of social barriers. The Chinese have been noted for their in-group living patterns; the "Chinatowns" in San Francisco, Los Angeles, New York, and other large cities encourage the preservation of the Chinese cul-

TABLE 4.2 ASIAN AMERICAN POPULATION BY NATIONALITY

Nationality	Percentage of Asian Americans
Chinese	22.6
Filipino	19.3
Japanese	11.6
Asian Indian	11.2
Korean	11.0
Vietnamese	8.4
Other	15.9

Source: U.S. Bureau of the Census, *Census of Population, General Population Characteristics, United States*, CP-I-I (Washington, DC: Author, 1990).

tural heritage. Prejudice and discrimination continue to be among the more significant obstacles for Asian Americans in achieving social and economic progress. Because of their physical characteristics, language, and cultural heritage, they continue to be viewed by many as "foreigners." The internment of the Japanese population in "holding" camps during World War II is one example of how Japanese citizens, many native born, were viewed as foreigners with presumptive allegiance to Japan rather than the United States. Ironically, German and Italian Americans were not treated in this manner even though Germany and Italy were, along with Japan, the Axis powers.

More recently, the Vietnamese have been the target of discrimination, as reflected in the difficulty they have experienced in securing housing, employment, and acceptance in American communities. In addition to physical characteristics, language barriers have intensified "differences," resulting in closed avenues for social and economic participation for this group.

Numbers of east Indian immigrants have increased in recent years because of political turmoil in their country as well as the demand in the United States for computer programmers and other technology workers. In spite of the fact that many are highly educated, they have also experienced discrimination.

Social and Economic Justice: Native Americans

Numerically the smallest group of color in the United States, Native Americans (American Indians) have over the years consistently been oppressed. Native Americans, who prior to colonialization were free to establish their villages and roam the countryside, lost all rights and privileges once conquered. Considered savages (less than human), most were relegated to reservations where they found oppressive limits on their behaviors and freedom of movement. The responsibility for overseeing these reservations was given to the Bureau of Indian Affairs, a federal governmental agency that more often was a barrier rather than a help. The fact that some Native American tribes have never lived on a reservation and lack access to programs designed for those Native Americans connected to a reservation creates a unique set of social justice issues (Dial & Eliades, 1996). The effects of differential treatment and limited opportunity are reflected in the limited average education for Native Americans age 25 or over, which is 9.6 years—the lowest of any ethnic group in the United States. Nearly one-third are illiterate, and only one out of five has a high school education.

Although they were the first "Americans," Native Americans seldom have been able to experience free and full involvement in society. Currently, large numbers continue to live on reservations, which further segregates them from interaction with the dominant group and limits their opportunity structure. Reservations represent the most overt form of purposeful discrimination. Although the status of Native Americans has improved somewhat in recent years (with higher levels of education and commercial development on the reservations), many barriers to free and full social participation remain.

Like other racial and ethnic groups, not all Native Americans share the same values and traditions. Lifestyles as well as opportunities vary among the approximately 300 tribes in the United States. Many Native Americans have migrated to urban centers in search of employment and better resources. The migration of Native Americans to urban areas has created

Valuing cultural traditions is an important part of one's identity. Too often, Native Americans and other groups have been given the message that they must reject their traditions to be accepted and viewed as successful. Fortunately, today many young people are learning to have pride in themselves and their heritage.

Jack Kurtz/Impact Visuals

identity problems for many; discriminated against, they don't always fit in well in city environments, yet because they have left their reservation, they also have difficulty being accepted if they return to their homeland (McLemore & Romo, 2000).

EFFORTS TO PRODUCE SOCIAL JUSTICE FOR RACIAL AND ETHNIC GROUPS

Bringing an end to institutional racism and discrimination is not an easy task. Long-standing prejudices that have lingered over many generations are difficult to extinguish, in spite of efforts to enlighten the public about the consequences of maintaining false beliefs and practices. Little progress was made in dismantling segregation until the government decreed it. Until President Harry Truman ordered the cessation of segregation in the armed forces in 1948, most government agencies supported separation of the races. Although racism and discrimination still exist

in the armed forces, its desegregation resulted in employment and educational opportunities for people of color inaccessible to them elsewhere in the United States.

School Desegregation

The catalyst for ending separate public school education was the Supreme Court decision *Brown v. Board of Education* in 1954, which mandated an end to segregation in public schools. Ruling that "separate was not equal," the Court ordered public schools integrated and opened to children of all races and ethnic groups. Because of de facto housing patterns, members of nonwhite racial and ethnic groups lived in common neighborhoods and their children attended neighborhood schools. To implement the Court's decision, busing became necessary. Many communities required students of color to be bused to schools in predominantly white neighborhoods, which resulted in strong resistance by the dominant white population. White citizens' councils emerged in the South and Midwest to resist school integration.

Many state governments questioned the constitutionality of the Court's decision and resisted taking appropriate action to hasten the integration process. "Evidence" was sought to support the position that integration of schools would have catastrophic effects on the educational achievement of all children of all races. In a 1962 report ("The Biology of the Race Problem"), Wesley C. George, a biologist commissioned by the governor of Alabama, attempted to offer scientific proof that blacks were innately inferior to whites and would not be able to compete with whites in the classroom. Other racist, white supremacist groups, such as the Ku Klux Klan, joined in efforts to prevent school integration.

In time, school busing became commonplace and school integration a technical reality. Universal public acceptance of desegregation through busing, however, was never achieved. In the 1980s and 1990s, movement to return to neighborhood schools, supported by the Reagan administration, was strong. Charles Murray's (1994) book *The Bell Curve* was a rallying point for many to urge the elimination of busing and a return to neighborhood schools. Although advocates for neighborhood schools have argued that these schools could be more culturally relevant to students and their families, in many instances schools in nonwhite neighborhoods have seen a significant loss of resources when busing has been eliminated.

Major Legislation

During the 1960s, significant progress was made in eliminating segregationist policies and controlling the effects of discrimination. President Johnson's Great Society programs sought to eradicate segregation entirely and to make discrimination an offense punishable under the law. In 1964, the **Civil Rights Act** was passed. This act, amended in 1965, sought to ban discrimination based on race, religion, color, or ethnicity in public facilities, government-operated programs, or employment. A similar act, passed in 1968, made illegal the practice of discrimination in advertising and the purchase or rental of residential property or its financing.

Under the new legal sanctions for desegregation, a groundswell of support mounted among disenfranchised people of color and sympathetic dominant group members. The Reverend Martin Luther King, Jr., and organized freedom marchers sought to raise the consciousness of society regarding the obscenities of segregationist policies. King's nonviolent movement provided great visibility to the injustices of discrimination and served to stimulate and influence policies for change. Other significant organizations, such as the Southern Christian Leadership Conference (SCLC), the National Urban League, the National Association for the Advancement of Colored People (NAACP), La Raza, and the League of United Latin American Citizens (LULAC), actively pursued social and economic justice for people of color during this period. As the new civil rights legislation was implemented, an air of hope prevailed that discrimination would soon become a matter of history. School busing facilitated public school integration, public facilities were opened to people of color, and the employment market became more accepting of minority applicants. Further advances were made under the influence of the Economic Opportunities Act of 1964. Neighborhoods were organized, and their residents registered to vote. This movement was furthered by the Voting Rights Act of 1965, which prohibited the imposition of voting qualification requirements based on race, color, age, or minority status. The impact of the civil rights movement was far-reaching in gaining ground in the struggle for full and equal participation by people of color in the social and economic areas of our society.

Erosion of Progress

The rapid pace of the change effort was short-lived. By the late 1970s, racial polarization had increased with a new wave of conservatism. Discussions about race focused, as they often do today, most often on whites and African Americans, ignoring other groups of color. Whites were much more prone to attribute the "lack of progress" among the African American population to African Americans themselves, rather than to discrimination, thus supporting the position that discrimination was no longer a problem for "motivated" African Americans. By the late 1970s, racial and ethnic issues were replaced by national defense, energy, and inflation as the top priorities for the white majority.

Affirmative action programs, which once mandated the selection of qualified members of oppressed groups for publicly operated business and education, have been downgraded and, in many instances, dismantled. The concept of affirmative action was derived from the civil rights acts of the 1960s and was, in part, an attempt to initiate actions that would equalize the social and economic playing field for all people and ultimately break the barriers of discrimination for those who had long been oppressed by established values, policies, and practices.

Compensatory justice, an underlying axiom for affirmative action directives, provided the impetus for eliminating institutionalized barriers to employment, education, and social parity in general. It required that women and people of color be hired or admitted to educational institutions and professional schools on an equal basis with that of white males. Public reaction to what was considered to be a "quota system" resulted in cries of "reverse discrimination." It is interesting to note that many of these cries have come from white women, the group that has benefited the most from affirmative action programs. Congress has been attentive to public outcries and is seriously pondering legislation that would remove the substantive force of affirmative action programs, if not abolish the programs altogether. The U.S. Supreme Court ruled in the late 1990s on a number of cases that reversed portions of affirmative action.

There is little doubt that affirmative action programs have opened up opportunities for the oppressed. Although "tokenism" has been a major concern, many women, African Americans, Latinos, and other members of nonmajority groups have been able to achieve higher educational status, secure jobs, and attain vertical mobility in the employment arena as a result of efforts to right historical wrongs. Critics of the downgrading of government efforts in the area of affirmative action argue that such actions will result in a return to past discriminatory practices. On the other hand, proponents of downgrading these programs feel that they have not been effective, and, in the final analysis, all populations will be better served if positions are awarded on competency and merit rather than arbitrarily mandated by social legislation.

The outlook for a well-articulated and implemented program to eliminate prejudice and discrimination as we begin a new millennium is not encouraging. The effort to creatively and forcefully address this issue has waned since the mid-1970s, and the topic of race continues to be a sensitive topic that many individuals at all levels of society choose to avoid. The current preoccupation with balancing the budget by scaling down government programs and services tends to overshadow concerted and focused efforts to dismantle the institutional barriers that result in differential treatment for groups of color.

Although efforts to achieve equality for oppressed groups continue, active government commitment has waned. The passage of welfare reform legislation in 1996 and the virtual abandonment of affirmative action programs reflect the general public's sentiment toward improving the opportunity structure for oppressed groups, thus serving to perpetuate the current power structure in place in the United States today.

Social Work and the Civil Rights Movement

Inherent in social work's identity is its commitment to social action directed toward the elimination of barriers that deny equal rights and full participation to all members of society. Since the early days, when social workers assisted in assimilating new immigrants into our culture and sought to improve social conditions for them, the profession has engaged the citizenry in working toward social equality and an equal opportunity structure. The National Association of Social Workers and the Council on Social Work Education have given high priority to incorporating content about vulnerable populations—including women; gays, lesbians, bisexuals, and transgendered persons; the poor; and people of color—into professional social work practice and social work education. Social work practitioners strive to be knowledgeable about racial and cultural backgrounds of their clients, including strengths and the impact of oppression, when

assisting them in achieving solutions to problems. Through social action, efforts are made to change community attitudes, policies, and practices that disadvantage members of at-risk populations. As advocates, social workers seek to modify rules and regulations that deny equal treatment to those assigned to an at-risk status. As organizers, they work with leaders from populations at risk in identifying priorities, gaining community support, and facilitating change through the democratic process.

Social workers are active in organized public efforts to abolish discriminatory practices. As citizens (as well as professionals), they support political candidates who are openly committed to working for social equality. They are involved in public education designed to dispel prejudice and to promote productive interaction among divergent racial and ethnic groups. In a public climate where the pursuit of social and economic equality has lessened, social workers have the responsibility to maintain a vigilant pursuit of equality.

Social workers should view the concept of **social justice** not as rhetorical verbiage but as a variable that is inherent as a mandate for the social work profession. In fact, since the profession's inception, social justice has been a basic axiom for practice. Social justice—that is, achieving a society in which all members have access to the same rights and privileges without regard to gender, race, ethnic affiliation, creed, age, sexual orientation, or physical and mental capacities—is essential for the establishment of a nondiscriminatory society. Only when that goal is achieved can social and economic equality prevail.

A fundamental avenue through which social justice is achieved is by empowering disenfranchised and oppressed individuals and groups. **Empowerment** is both a process and a goal, through which individuals and groups gain mastery over their lives, become active participants, and make decisions—that is, gain control over their lives and the environment in which they interact. Disempowered populations can only react to the norms and mandates of others, which can lead to the perpetuation of discriminatory practices.

SUMMARY

Few observers would deny that the United States has experienced a major sexual revolution during the past few decades. As part of the human rights movement, many advances have been made in reducing sexism in our society. Opportunities for economic and social participation of women are greater now than they have been before in the history of this country. Although there have been some reversals, such as the failure to ratify the ERA, societal pressures to assure equal treatment and opportunities for women continue.

Social inequality also has characterized the treatment of racial and ethnic groups, the poor, and homosexuals in the United States. Although some progress has been made toward more favorable treatment, full participation rights have not yet been achieved for these groups. Discrimination and differential treatment of women, people of color, the poor, and homosexuals continue to restrict their achievement of social and economic progress. Although past legislation has served as a catalyst for removing long-standing practices that denied equal rights, in recent years the conservative movement has lowered the priorities for attaining social equality for women and people of color. Even less attention has been given to social equality for homosexuals. Social work has a long tradition of promoting social equality, and the commitment of the profes-

sion to continue pressing for this will be greater as the societal thrust to do so declines.

Over the past decade, the euphemism "politically correct" has gained popularity among those who question the validity and viability of certain attitudes or practices that are directed toward oppressed or disenfranchised groups. Politically correct responses have become, for many, substitutes for "correct" responses. Unfortunately, the concept of political correctness invokes negativism for positive actions taken. For example, a person may behave in a certain manner because it is the politically correct thing to do—not necessarily the right (or decent) thing to do. In reality, many politically correct responses are socially responsible ones. It is quite possible for prejudiced persons to behave in a socially responsible manner even though their intentions are simply to be politically correct.

Unfortunately, some may use the guise of political correctness out of fear that a true and honest response may place them in jeopardy of losing an advantage they treasure. Social workers should not be overly concerned with being politically correct. The value base of the profession and commitment of social work practitioners to genuineness that is characteristic of socially responsible behavior should always be paramount when intervening with clients or serving as advocates on their behalf.

This chapter was not intended to provide an in-depth analysis of the parameters of oppressed groups in the United States. Rather, we designed the text to make you aware that prejudice, institutional discrimination, and oppression have long existed and that the targets of these practices continue to suffer the consequences of differential treatment and limited opportunity. Although advocacy groups have been able to bring about positive political changes and public attitudes have improved, much has yet to be accomplished to establish social equality for all groups in America. Prejudice and discrimination are the products of social interaction. As social constructs, they can be replaced by values that respect the dignity and worth of all human beings and result in a society that promotes equal treatment for all.

KEY TERMS

affirmative action
assimilation
Civil Rights Act
class
classism
comparable worth
cultural pluralism
empowerment
Equal Rights
   Amendment (ERA)
homophobia

institutional
   discrimination
oppression
populations at risk
prejudice
sexism
social inequality
social justice
stereotypes
underclass

DISCUSSION QUESTIONS

1. How do you explain the existence of prejudice and discrimination in a society whose values are based on Judeo-Christian ideology?

2. Discuss early efforts to eradicate discriminatory practices against women, people of color, and gays, lesbians, bisexuals, and transgendered individuals.

3. Why is it difficult to achieve social justice in a society characterized by cultural pluralism?

4. Assume you are a member of an oppressed group. What would your reaction be to the watering down of affirmative action programs? How would you react to so-called reverse discrimination?

5. Identify and explain social work's role in breaking down institutional barriers of discrimination.

6. How do you explain that some white women, who have historically experienced gender discrimination, discriminate against women of color?

INFOTRAC
COLLEGE EDITION

To learn more about topics included in this chapter, enter the following search terms:

affirmative action

civil rights movement

cultural divide

cultural diversity

egalitarianism

Equal Rights Amendment

feminism

gender equality

gender gap

institutional oppression

sexual orientation

social inequality

social justice

ON THE INTERNET

http://www.wmich.edu/politics/mlk/

http://www.cr.nps.gov/nr/travel/civilrights/

http://www.affirmativeaction.org/

http://hcl.chass.ncsu.edu/ganson/Burns18e/Docs/era.html

http://bostonreview.mit.edu/BR23.6/contents/html

http://eserver.org/feminism/

http://www.naswdc.org/

REFERENCES

American Civil Liberties Union. (2000). *State and local laws protecting lesbians and gay men against workplace discrimination.* Author: http://www.aclu.org

Anti-Defamation League. (2000). *Hate crimes laws.* Author: http://www.adl.org

Axinn, J., & Levin, H. (1997). *Social welfare: A history of the American response to need* (4th ed.). New York: Longman.

Beiber, I. (Ed.). (1962). *Homosexuality.* New York: Basic Books.

Bergman, E. (1982). *The compleat chauvinist.* New York: Macmillan.

Dial, A. L., & Eliades, D. K. (1996). *The only land I know: A history of the Lumbee Indians.* Syracuse, NY: Syracuse University Press.

Dunn, D. (1996). Gender in earnings. In P. J. Dubeck & K. Borman (Eds.), *Women and work: A handbook* (pp. 61–63). New York: Garland.

George, W. C. (1962). *The biology of the race problem.* Report prepared by Commission of the Governor of Alabama. Montgomery: State of Alabama.

Johnson, L., Schwartz, C., & Tate, D. (1996). *Social welfare: A response to human need.* Boston: Allyn & Bacon.

Lum, D. (2000). *Social work practice and people of color: A process-stage approach.* Belmont, CA: Brooks/Cole.

McLemore, S. D., & Romo, H. D. (2000). *Racial and ethnic relations in America* (6th ed.). Boston: Allyn & Bacon.

Murdock, S., Hogue, N., Michael, M., White, S., & Pecote, B. (1997). *The Texas challenge: Population change and the future of Texas.* College Station: Texas A & M University.

Murray, C. (1994). *The bell curve.* Washington, DC: New Republic.

Pinderhughes, E. (1989). *Understanding race, ethnicity and power: The key to efficacy in clinical practice.* New York: Free Press.

Sirkin, M. (1994, July/August). Resisting cultural meltdown. *Family Therapy Networker, 18*(4), 48–52.

Stover, P., & Gilles, Y. (1987). *Sexual harassment in the workplace: Conference report.* Detroit: Michigan Task Force on Sexual Harassment.

U.S. Department of Commerce. (2000). *Statistical abstract of the United States 1999.* Washington, DC: Bernan.

U.S. Equal Employment Opportunity Commission. (2000). *Sexual harassment.* Author: www.eeoc.gov

Wilson, W. J. (1997). *When work disappears: The world of the new urban poor.* New York: Vintage.

Women by the numbers. (1999, November). *American Association of Retired Persons Bulletin, 40,* 10.

Zastrow, C., & Kirst-Ashman, K. (1997). *Understanding human behavior and the social environment.* Chicago: Nelson-Hall.

SUGGESTED FURTHER READINGS

Abramovitz, M. (1988). *Regulating the lives of women.* Boston: South End.

Barker, R. L. (1999). *The social work dictionary.* Silver Spring, MD: National Association of Social Workers.

Chau, K. C. (1990). Social work practice: Towards a cross-cultural model. *Journal of Applied Social Sciences, 14*(2), 249–274.

Davis, L., & Proctor, E. (1995). *Race, gender & class: Guidelines for practice with individuals, families, and groups.* Boston: Allyn & Bacon.

DeVore, W., & Schlesinger, E. (1999). *Ethnic-sensitive social work practice* (5th ed.). Boston: Allyn & Bacon.

Ewalt, P., Freeman, E., Kirk, S. K., & Poole, D. (1996). *Multicultural issues in social work.* Washington, DC: NASW Press.

Knopp, L. (1990, May). Social consequences of homosexuality. *Geographical Magazine,* pp. 20–25.

Mallon, G. (Ed.). (1998). *Foundations of social work practice with lesbian and gay persons.* Binghampton, NY: Haworth.

Seift, C., & Levin, F. (1987). Empowerment: An emerging mental health technology. *Journal of Primary Prevention, 8,* 71–94.

Stout, K., & McPhail, B. (1998). *Confronting sexism and violence against women: A challenge for social work.* New York: Longman.

Winkelman, M. (1999). *Ethnic sensitivity in social work.* Dubuque, IA: Eddie Bowers.

two

SOCIAL WORK

Generalist Practice: Methods of Intervention

In this part of the book, you will be learning about methods of intervention used by generalist social workers. In Chapter 5, "Generalist Practice: Social Work with Individuals and Families," you will explore the most prevalent method in professional social work practice: intervention with individuals and families who are experiencing difficulties interacting within their environment. You will learn about theories and techniques used by social workers in assisting individuals and families to build on their strengths and identify strategies to meet their needs and improve their social functioning or the environment in which they function.

In Chapter 6, "Generalist Practice: Social Work with Groups and the Community," we examine methods used in working with clients in groups. Group work is an effective method of intervention that is receiving increased attention, both because of its effectiveness with many populations and because it is often seen as more cost-effective than working with clients individually. We review relevant theories related to working with groups and identify a variety of groups in which individuals interact. We also describe important factors to consider when social workers form groups, the importance of group process when working with groups, and different methods social workers use when working with groups. Because the exosystem—or community— level of the environment has such a major impact on individual and family functioning, one of the major ways that social workers can address client needs is by working within the community to develop or strengthen programs and policies, advocate for client needs, and empower community members to advocate for themselves and develop interventions that address their needs. In Chapter 6, we also explore the importance of the community in working with clients and various methods of community organization and community intervention commonly used by social workers to create individual and social change.

In Chapter 7, "Generalist Practice: Policy, Administration, and Research," we describe the relationships between social welfare policy and practice and approaches social workers can take to evaluate proposed and already-existing social welfare policies. We also look at the myriad of essential tasks used by social workers to bring together the resources, opportunities, roles, and objectives of social welfare agencies to meet human needs. We explore various administrative, leadership, and management strategies used by social workers to gather resources and opportunities to create and maintain efficient and effective social services agencies. As social welfare needs continue to grow, while at the same time resources to address these needs are reduced, managing social welfare programs efficiently and effectively and demonstrating that you have done so are increasingly critical for an agency's survival. Because sound practice and policy decisions should be based on research, this chapter also focuses on the interdependence of social work practice and research and the use of social research as an integral part of the problem-solving process. We discuss the vital role of research in policy and practice to continually buttress practice with data gained from research findings. This role is critical so that we can continue to develop new knowledge about ways to address social welfare issues and work with client systems more effectively and so that we can demonstrate our effectiveness in order to receive the resources necessary to address the many social welfare needs that exist today.

As you learn about the methods of intervention used by social work generalist practitioners in Part Two, ask yourself questions that draw from what you learned in Part One. For example, as *you read the chapter on individuals and families, ask yourself questions such as, How do past and present social welfare perspectives and policies shape the ways people view individuals and families today, the types of needs individuals and families might be likely to have as a result, and the methods of intervention that might be used in working with individuals and families to address these needs? How can the systems/ecological framework help us understand issues relating to individuals and families and the impact of the broader environment on their functioning? How might these issues be addressed using the methods of intervention discussed in this section of the book? What are the relationships among factors such as race and ethnicity, gender, age, and sexual orientation on individual and family functioning, and how would social workers consider these factors when working with individuals and families in practice settings?*

GENERALIST PRACTICE

Social Work with Individuals and Families

Until recently, Charles and Melinda were a hard-working, middle-income couple, both in their early 40s and married for over 20 years. Charles, a high school dropout, worked as a delivery person for a local office supply house, while Melinda worked as a nurse's aide at a local nursing home. Two children, Sean, 17, and Heather, 15, rounded out the family group. Both children were in high school, where Sean was a senior and Heather, a sophomore. While on the surface this family appeared happy and cohesive, underlying tensions had surfaced in recent years. Charles, who had always enjoyed a "night out with the guys," had begun drinking much more excessively, often not returning home at night. Melinda, feeling rejected, turned to Ed, an employee at the nursing home, for comfort and solace. Sean was arrested twice on drug-related charges, and the final trauma for the family came in learning that Heather was pregnant. What was once a finely tuned functional family had now emerged as one with multiple problems.

Melinda's coworkers were concerned over her apathy and apparent depression and suggested that she visit with Rachel, the nursing home social worker. Desperate for assistance, Melinda agreed to do so, finding Rachel to be a sensitive, caring, nonjudgmental listener. After several visits to help clarify the problems Melinda was experiencing, Rachel suggested that Melinda seek the services of a social worker from a family services agency. Trisha, the family services worker, met with Melinda and Charles and found that they were strongly committed to resolving family problems. They both supported any plan that would reduce stress and reengage the family members in mutually loving, supportive roles. Charles agreed to attend Alcoholics Anonymous meetings, and both Melinda and Charles agreed to marital counseling sessions. In a subsequent session with the entire family, Sean agreed to see the social worker at a local substance abuse clinic, while Heather was relieved to be able to discuss her needs with the social worker at the family services agency who worked with pregnant teens. Each family member felt it would be good for the entire family as a unit to meet regularly in family therapy at the agency as well.

As a result of these efforts, the family members were able to identify stress points in family interaction, develop functional coping skills, and be more open and mutually supportive of each other.

The society and world in which we live are characterized by rapid transition, change, and uncertainty. The technological revolution and globalization have contributed to sweeping modifications of lifestyles, increased mobility, and shifting values. As the capacity to create new products has grown, the shifting job market has required new skills and more adaptable employees. Relationships among individuals have become tenuous and short-lived. As a result, a sense of roots in the community is becoming increasingly difficult to achieve. Family life has been affected by social and job-related pressures and upward mobility. The pursuit of success has conflicted with long-cherished values regarding the sanctity of family-first goals. These changes, which began in the 1960s, have given rise to an emphasis on individuation and happiness as contrasted with strong family commitments. Broken families have become commonplace as marriages are being terminated with ever-increasing frequency.

Children with special needs, the illicit use of drugs by both adults and children, an increasing burden of caring for older adults, increased costs of housing and other necessities, and two-career marriages have created demands on individuals and families that often leave them disrupted, confused, tense, and frustrated.

These and many other social pressures generated by our rapidly changing society are experienced by virtually all of us at one time or another. It is neither an unusual response nor a sign of weakness for individuals and families in stressful situations to seek professional help with the hope of alleviating stress and its **dysfunctional** consequences. All of us have needed the steady guidance of a respected friend or professional at some time. When problems become increasingly stressful and self-help efforts fail to produce desired solutions, professional assistance may be needed. **Generalist** social work practice, as defined in Chapter 2, is a method of providing that assistance.

Generalist practice with individuals, families, and groups is the oldest social work practice method (traditionally referred to as *casework,* as noted in Chapter 2). As we indicated in Chapter 2, it had its formal developmental roots in the Charity Organization Society movement, when "scientific charity" was emphasized and the need for trained professional workers became a fundamental prerequisite to a more studied approach in working with client populations.

In this chapter, we identify the components and characteristics of generalist practice methods that are used with individuals and families. Generalist practice with groups and the community is explored in the following chapter. Be aware that the purpose of these chapters is to enable you to acquire a beginning-level acquaintance with the social work processes and methods as well as with the theories that undergird generalist practice. As you progress through the social work curriculum, more in-depth analyses of methods, processes, and theories will be examined.

GENERALIST PRACTICE: A DEFINITION

A social work generalist practitioner assists clients in a change process that focuses on producing a higher level of social functioning. Generalist practice is both a process and a method. As a process, it involves a more or less orderly sequence of progressive stages in engaging the client (or client system, such as a family) in activities and actions that promote the achievement of agreed-on goals. As a method, it entails the creative use of techniques and knowledge that guide intervention activities designed by the social work practitioner. Generalist practice also is an art that uses scientific knowledge about human behavior and the skillful use of relationships to enable the client to activate or develop interpersonal and, if necessary, community resources to achieve a more positive balance with his or her environment. Generalist social work practice seeks to improve, restore, maintain, or enhance the client's social functioning.

The key converging elements in social work practice are that it

- is an art—that is, it involves a skill that results from experience or training;
- involves the application of knowledge about human behavior;
- is based on client involvement in developing options designed to resolve problems;
- emphasizes the use of the client's resources (psychological and physical) as well as those extant in the community to meet client needs;
- is based on an orderly helping process;
- is based on planned change efforts; and
- focuses on solutions.

Although the basis for social work generalist practice with individuals and families was grounded in the philosophy and wisdom of early social work pioneers such as Mary Richmond, Gordon Hamilton, Helen Harris Perlman, Florence Hollis, and others, many changes in practice have occurred over the years. As greater knowledge of human development, ecology, economics, organizational behavior, stress management, social change, and more effective intervention techniques have emerged, social work practice with individuals and families has been enriched and offers a more scientifically buttressed model for intervention. The face-to-face relationship between the social worker and the client has maintained its integrity as a fundamental prerequisite for intervention, as has the emphasis on process (study, assessment, intervention objectives, intervention, evaluation, and follow-up). Democratic decision making and the belief in the dignity, worth, and value of the client system continue to undergird social work practice philosophy. The client's right to self-determination and confidentiality are fundamental practice values in the helping process. These values and practice principles form the fundamental concepts and interventive practice techniques that are identified with generalist practice with individuals and families.

PREPARATION FOR GENERALIST PRACTICE WITH INDIVIDUALS AND FAMILIES

Earlier in this chapter, we indicated that a requisite for generalist social work practice with individuals and families is an understanding of factors that affect human behavior. The practitioner not only must be armed with an understanding of personality theory and a knowledge of the life cycle but must also be able to assess the effects of the social systems context within which behavior occurs. Factors such as race, gender, ethnicity, religion, social class, sexual orientation, physical condition, occupation, family structure, health, age, income, and

educational achievement are among many of the contributing variables that converge to account for behavior within different social contexts. Practitioners obviously cannot master all knowledge related to behavior, but theories allow us to make guided assumptions about behavior from which we can make logical estimates of factors associated with the client's unmet needs. The generalist social work practitioner is able to arrive at probable causes of problems and to establish theoretically plausible interventions that will assist client systems in addressing needs.

THE GENERALIST PRACTICE PROCESS

The orderly process of social work generalist practice consists of social study, assessment, goal setting, contracting, intervention, and evaluation. Each step in this process is guided by the application of theory and knowledge of human behavior.

Social Study

The **social study** consists of obtaining relevant information about the client system and perceived needs. The client's perception of needs and problems, their antecedents, ways they are affecting life satisfaction and performance, attempts at life management, and outcome goals are important parts of the social study. The practitioner also obtains information regarding the client's ability to function in a variety of roles and collects data that enhance the practitioner's ability to initiate the process of making initial judgments about probable causes and potential actions that might lead to resolution. The social study responds to questions like these: Who is the client? What is the nature of the needs and problems as the client sees and experiences them? What has the client done to alleviate these needs and problems? How effective were the efforts? What other individuals or groups are affected by the needs and problems, and how is the client related to or associated with them? What are the client's strengths and weaknesses? How motivated is the client to work toward solutions to address these needs and problems (Dubois & Miley, 1998)?

Assessment

Assessment is the process of making tentative judgments about how the information derived from the social study affects the client system in its behaviors as well as in the meaning of those behaviors. As Dubois and Miley (1998) suggest, "the purpose of assessment is to understand the problem and determine how to reduce its impact" (p. 252). As such, assessment provides the basis for initiating and establishing intervention objectives and formally engaging the client system in the interventive process. It is at this stage of the generalist practice process that the perceived reality of client behaviors is filtered through the matrix of practice theory and a basic understanding of human behavior to arrive at potential sources of the problem(s).

Accurate assessment is the catalyst for establishing goals and objectives with the client and is an essential precursor for focused intervention. For that reason, assessment is a dynamic process that is modified and updated as the worker gains more insight, information, and experience in working with the client system, including estimates of how the client is using the helping process in addressing identified needs. In addition, a meaningful assessment always reflects the ethnic, gender, racial, and cultural context of the client system.

At the most rudimentary level, assessment seeks to answer such questions as, What factors are contributing to the client's unmet needs? What systems are involved? What is the effect of the client's behavior on interacting systems (and vice versa)? What is the potential for initiating a successful change effort?

Goal Setting

Goal setting is the process in which the client and practitioner ascertain intervention options that have the potential to address identified needs based on the client's abilities and capacities. Short- and long-term goals are developed after reviewing all options and determining which are most appropriate for the particular client, need, and situation.

The responsibility for goal setting evolves as a product of mutual exploration between the social worker and the client. Effective goal setting can serve as a therapeutic "jump-start" for the client as an initial commitment to engage in the change process. Goals always should be realistically achievable, organized around specific targets for change, and related to the client's capacity to engage in behaviors that will move in the direction of positive change. As a practical matter, the least emotionally charged goals should be addressed first since they are more likely to be achieved. As a consequence of successful achievement, the client's confidence is bolstered, and enthusiasm for the change effort is more likely to occur.

Contracting

In **contracting,** the practitioner and the client agree to work toward the identified intervention goals. To facilitate and clarify the commitment implied by the contract, the practitioner's role is identified explicitly, and the client agrees to perform tasks related to addressing identified needs and problems. The contract makes visible the agreement both parties have reached and serves as a framework from which they may periodically assess intervention progress. Contracts may be renegotiated or altered during the course of intervention, as more viable goals become apparent. Contracts also help maintain the focus of intervention.

Intervention

The focus of generalist practice **intervention** with individuals and families is derived from the social study and assessment and sanctioned by the contract between the practitioner and client. The implementation phase of intervention focuses on meeting established goals and may involve such activities as counseling, role playing, engaging other community resources, establishing support groups, developing resources, finding alternative-care resources, encouraging family involvement, offering play therapy, or employing related strategies. The goal of intervention is to assist the clients toward an acceptable resolution of problems and to address their unmet needs. The practitioner must skillfully involve the client throughout the intervention process by providing not only regular feedback and support but also an honest appraisal of the problem-solving efforts.

Evaluation

Clients are not likely to remain in the intervention process unless they feel some positive movement has been made toward meeting their needs. **Evaluation** is an ongoing process in which the practitioner and client review intervention activities and assess the impact on the client's problem situation. Both the practitioner and the client must intensively examine their behavior, with the goal of understanding the impact on intervention goals. What has changed? What has not changed? Why? How does the client view identified needs and problems at this time? Has social functioning improved? Become less functional? What is the overall level of progress? Are different interventions needed? Evaluation within this context becomes a self-, as well as a joint, assessment process. Based on the evaluation, intervention may continue along the same lines or be modified as implied by the evaluative process (Dubois & Miley, 1998).

THE SOCIAL WORKER–CLIENT RELATIONSHIP

The relationship between the social worker and the client (or client system) is the conduit through which assistance is extended by the social worker and received and acted on by the client. The principles and values underpinning the relationship are much more than a mere catechism to be learned by the social worker. They must be experienced by the client in interacting with the social worker. It is essential that the worker be genuine and approachable if the client is to feel enabled to share problems and to develop confidence and trust in the social worker and the helping process. As the client invests time and energy in the problem-solving process, trust (an underlying axiom for an effective helping relationship) will be established only if the relationship principles and values are a distinctive aspect of client–social worker interaction.

Social work practice principles are derived from the profession's value base and reflected in its code of ethics. Historically, professional social workers have been committed to the following principles as the basis for establishing a helping relationship with client systems:

- *Self-determination*—Social work practitioners respect their clients' rights to make choices that affect their lives. On occasion, those choices may not appear to be in the client's best interests; however, the role of the practitioner in such an instance would be to point out the potentially negative or dysfunctional aspects of the choices. Of course, this does not preclude or limit the practitioner's effort to assist the client in making more appropriate choices. However, it does indicate that exerting undue influence or belittling the client is unacceptable behavior in "bringing the client around" to more appropriate choices. Social work is based on a democratic process, in which self-determination is a fundamental part.

- *Confidentiality*—The client's right to privacy is guarded by the principle of confidentiality. It is based on the notion that information shared between the client and practitioner is privileged. The practitioner must not compromise the client by making public the content of information disclosed in the intervention process. Confidentiality assures that the client's feelings, attitudes, and statements expressed during intervention sessions will not be misused. This principle also commits the practitioner to using client information only for professional purposes in working with the client.

- *Individualization and acceptance*—Regardless of the nature of the client's problems, each client has the right to be treated as an individual with needs, desires, strengths, and weaknesses differ-

ent from those of anyone else. Acceptance is the ability to recognize the dignity and value inherent in all clients, in spite of the complex array of problems and needs that characterize their behavior.

- *Nonjudgmental attitude*—Recognizing that all human beings have strengths and weaknesses, experience difficult problems, make improper choices, become angry and frustrated, and often act inappropriately, the practitioner maintains a neutral attitude toward the client's behavior. To judge clients and their behaviors is to erect implicitly a barrier that may block communication with them. A social worker who is judgmental toward a client may be viewed by the client as just another person who may be making negative judgments about him or her. It is important to note that the social worker has the responsibility of confronting the client with inappropriate behaviors, even though the client should not be condemned because of them.

- *Freedom of expression*—The client's need to express feelings and emotions is encouraged. Often, pent-up emotions become disabling to the client and result in more problematic behaviors. The client should be encouraged to engage in free and unfettered self-expression within the safety of the social worker–client relationship.

THE DEVELOPMENT OF PRACTICE SKILLS

Social workers can develop competency in using the generalist practice method with individuals and families through study, role playing, and supervised practice. Since generalist practice involves the application of knowledge, it is an effective method of problem solving only if employed skillfully. As in other applied professions, skill is an "art" that is enriched and refined continually through controlled and thoughtful interaction with clients. Just as you might assume that the skill of a surgeon increases with time and experience, those same principles apply to the development of social work practice skills. We now examine some of the more significant skill areas that are essential for effective social work practice with individuals and families.

Conceptual Skills

The ability to understand the interrelationships of various dimensions of the client's life experiences and behaviors and to place them within an appropriate perspective provides a framework from which intervention goals may be established. Conceptual skills enable the worker to view the many incidents and interactions of the client not as discrete entities within themselves but as interacting parts of the client's behavioral repertoire. Without conceptual skills, social study data have little meaning, and assessment may become less accurate. Conceptual skills also involve an ability to place the client's needs within a theoretical framework and to arrive at appropriate intervention strategies directed toward addressing those needs.

Interviewing Skills

The interview is more than just a conversation with the client. It is a focused, goal-directed activity used to assist clients with their problems. Communication skills are essential in assuring that the interview will be productive. The practitioner must assume the responsibil-

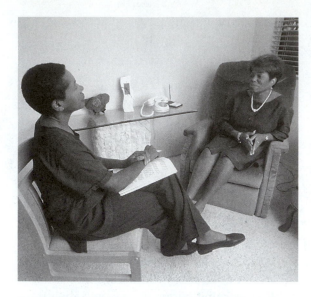

Generalist social workers practice in many settings. Here, a social worker in a family service center talks with an individual client to help her determine how to best meet her needs.

Spencer Grant/Liaison Agency

ity for maintaining the professional purposes of the interview. Sensitivity to both the client's statements and feelings is necessary. Putting the client at ease, asking questions that enable the client to share observations and experiences, and being a sensitive listener enhance the productivity of the interview. The social worker's sensitivity to the client's feelings and the ability to communicate an awareness of those feelings not only strengthen the helping relationship but also encourage and support the client. *Empathy,* or the ability to "put oneself in the client's shoes," is a benchmark quality of the helping relationship. Clients who feel that the social worker really understands their needs are able to feel more relaxed and hopeful that they will be able to work together to find ways to address their needs.

Not all interviews are conducted for the same purpose. Zastrow (1998) identifies three types of interviews that are used to facilitate the helping process in social work:

- *Informational interviews* are used primarily to obtain a client history that relates to the needs and problems currently experienced. The history-collecting process should not be concerned with all of the client's life experiences but with only selected information that may have an impact on current social functioning.
- The *diagnostic (assessment) interview* has a more clinical focus, in that it elicits responses that clarify the client's reactions to needs and problems and establishes some sequential ordering of events that enables the practitioner to make initial judgments about events that affect client behaviors.
- *Therapeutic interviews* are designed to help clients make changes in their life situations that will help them function more effectively. Not only are the client's feelings and emotions shared in these interviews, but problem-solving options are developed and efforts at change reviewed.

Recording

Maintaining case records that provide insightful information into the client's background (social study data), judgments about the nature of needs and problems (assessment), and client–social worker activity are essential in maintaining the focus of ongoing activities with the client. Practitioners typically carry a large caseload, with many clients over a long period of time. Properly maintained records enable the social worker to review the nature of the situation, objectives, and progress in each case before appointments with clients. In many instances, cases are transferred both inside and outside the agency, and the case record gives an up-to-date accounting of the client's problems and activities directed toward their resolution. Case records also are useful for research purposes. Properly maintained records strengthen the social work practice process. If viewed within this context, record keeping becomes less of an irrelevant chore and more of a vital tool for effective service delivery.

Beginning social workers should be informed that not all client systems are equally motivated to become engaged in a process designed to help them resolve problems. Even voluntary clients (that is, those who take the initial steps to seek help) are not always strongly committed, although all are motivated to some extent. Involuntary clients (those who are mandated to seek help, such as criminal offenders) may or may not be motivated to engage in the change effort. Workers must be aware that although they cannot motivate their clients (motivation comes from within), they may be able to provide the incentives that will result in the client's becoming motivated to work on problems.

PRACTICE THEORIES: INDIVIDUALS AND FAMILIES

Over the years, social workers have adopted a number of theoretical approaches used in their work with individuals and families. Some theories are used primarily to understand human behavior, while others are used primarily for intervention. Many practitioners use an eclectic approach; that is, they integrate aspects of several theories as a framework for understanding human behavior and for practice. Some find that a specific model is viable for one type of situation, whereas another may have greater utility in other situations. For example, a social worker may use behavior therapy with children and ego psychology with adults. The point is that many different approaches to social work practice are possible, each offering the practitioner a theoretical framework for intervention. In the following paragraphs, we include a brief synopsis of the theories often used by generalist practitioners.

Systems/Ecological Framework

This framework, discussed extensively in Chapter 3, is the overriding framework used by generalist practitioners to understand human behavior and how it is impacted by the environment, although it is also used as a practice model. Most other practice models can be incorporated within this broad framework. The systems/ecological framework is based on the observation that individuals and their environment are in a continual state of interaction and that problematic behavior is the result of disequilibrium between these entities (that is, the individual and the environment). Since people live in a constantly changing environment, adaptive skills are required to maintain coping abilities consonant with environmental demands. Adequate coping skills are predicated on the abilities of individuals, families, and groups both to integrate the consequences of environmental forces into their adaptive response repertoires and to influence (and change) those environmental factors involved in creating dysfunctional stress. The individual and the environment shape each other. Styles of coping with the demands of the environment emerge based on the person's perceptions of those demands and his or her capacity to respond.

The systems/ecological framework focuses the social worker's attention on the interacting systems within which the client system lives, as well as providing a theoretical framework for understanding the rationale related to the system's adaptive responses. As an assessment tool, this framework enables the social worker to identify both functional and dysfunctional responses to environmental demands and stresses. Once these have been identified, the social worker can focus on the processes of social work intervention and goal setting with the client system.

Ego Psychology

Often referred to as *psychosocial treatment theory*, **ego psychology** stresses the interplay between the individual's internal state and the external environment. The individual's developmental experiences, fears, hostilities, failures, successes, and feelings of love and acceptance all converge to form an estimate of self through which life experiences are filtered and responded to. A main feature of this theory deals with the individual's ability to cope with external pressures and to respond in such a way as to produce satisfaction and feelings of security and self-worth. Often, internal stress results from the inability to solve problems of a mental or physical nature. Inappropriate or underdeveloped coping skills aggravate and intensify the problems, thus causing the person to become apprehensive, insecure, unwilling to risk, anxious, or, in extreme cases, mentally ill.

Ego psychology is also concerned with environmental factors that affect the individual's adaptive abilities. Job loss, immobility, death, divorce, poverty, discrimination, and child management difficulties are among many potentially stressful conditions that may overextend coping capacities. Because stress is experienced individually, practitioners must give individualized consideration to the client and his or her specific situation. Knowledge of stress management, personality organization, and effective coping mechanisms is essential in the assessment process. Ego psychology is an "insight" therapy. Help comes to clients through developing an awareness of their unmet needs and problems and their reactions to them, and then learning to develop more adaptive coping skills.

Perhaps the key principle associated with using ego psychology as a treatment therapy is that of enabling the individual to develop more adaptive coping skills. The result should be the reduction of internal stress, more satisfactory role performance, and greater life satisfaction.

Problem-Solving Approach

One of the more widely used approaches in social work practice with individuals and families is identified as the **problem-solving approach.** This approach, developed by Perlman (1959), emphasizes that successful intervention is based on the motivation, capacity, and opportunity of the client systems for change. Recognizing that problems often immobilize the client, that the client's abilities then are neutralized or applied inappropriately, and that opportunities for problem solutions are not engaged, this approach stresses the need to "free up" the client system so that the client can work toward solving the problem. The problem-solving approach requires that the client do more than just identify and talk about problems, although both are necessary. The client must begin to move toward taking action (within his or her capacity to do so) to resolve or alleviate the discomfort produced by those problems. Often this requires that resources (the opportunity structure) be

tapped to achieve these goals. Generally, opportunity resources include those of the client, the client's family, and the agency involved in the helping process, although they may extend to other community resources.

Conceptually, the problem-solving approach is based on the premise that without *motivation* (or the will or desire to change), only limited progress can be made with the client. Motivation is often stymied as a result of stress experienced through dysfunctional or unresolved problems. Social workers often experience the client's doubts through statements such as "I know it will not do any good to try," "It has not worked out in the past," or "Nothing ever turns out right for me." In such instances, the social worker must provide inducements, such as encouragement, that will enable the client to risk taking steps toward problem resolution, with the social worker's assistance. As successful problem solving occurs, motivation is likely to increase.

In the problem-solving process, the social worker must be aware of other issues, too. *Capacity* addresses the limits (or ability) of the client to change and includes physical as well as psychological characteristics. For example, a client functioning at a sixth-grade level probably could not become an electrical engineer, but he or she could possibly attend a vocational training program and thereby develop skills that would enhance job opportunities.

Opportunity relates to possibilities within the environmental milieu in which the client interacts on a daily basis. As indicated in the preceding paragraph, a client might attend a vocational school if one is available within the client's locale. If the client had to travel 50 miles, however, transportation and finances might serve as deterrents, and the client thus might not have opportunity to participate. Optimal problem solving can be achieved only if the three components—motivation, capacity, and opportunity—are engaged in the process.

Cognitive-Behavioral Approaches

Cognitive-behavioral theories fall into the general category of behavioral intervention, which emphasizes the responsibility of the client to actively engage in behaviors that are designed to reduce or eliminate problems.

Behavior Modification Social learning theory undergirds behavior modification therapy. Based on the assumption that all behavior (adaptive as well as maladaptive) is learned, **behavior modification** is an "action" therapy (see Box 5.1). Developmental processes that contribute to the acquisition of positive human responses also are responsible for the development of inappropriate or dysfunctional ones. Since behavior is learned, it is possible to assist the client in discarding faulty behaviors and acquiring new and more appropriate response patterns. Recognizing that external events and internal processing result in specific behaviors, change is effected by modifying one's actions, which will result in changing thought patterns. Any attempt to change the internal process (that is, helping the client develop insight into the problem apart from directly addressing behavior changes) is considered largely ineffective.

Based on these general principles, the practitioner using behavior modification approaches intervention with the following organizing framework:

- In a social study, only information that is directly related to the current problem is essential for intervention, not past life experiences. Antecedent factors are pertinent, such as when the problem began, the circumstances that contribute to the problem behavior, and the client's efforts at problem resolution.
- Intervention must focus on specific problems, not the entire range of problems, that the client experiences. The practitioner assists clients in resolving each problem in an independent manner rather than treating them in total.
- Although the client's "feelings" are considered an important factor, the behavioral act is the target, not intrapsychic dynamics. The practitioner assists the client in developing specific techniques and learning more appropriate behavioral responses, as opposed to altering thought processes related to the problem and its effect. Thought processes are considered to be the results, not causes, of behaviors.

Behavior modification treats the objective, definable dimensions of human response patterns. To facilitate the intervention process, the practitioner and client must agree on the problem to be addressed, contract to work on that problem, agree on the responsibility each will assume in the change effort, specify goals and objectives, discuss the techniques to be employed, and commit themselves to the treatment effort. As with other therapies, monitoring and evaluation are important dimensions of the process. As more functional and acceptable behavior evolves, it is reinforced by more adaptive functioning. Dysfunctional responses are discarded as they become less functional and rewarding for the client.

Reality Therapy

Reality therapy is based on the assumption that individuals are responsible for their behavior. Maladaptive behavior is viewed as the

Behavior Modification

Shortly after Fred and Mary Chapman accepted 3-year-old Tonya into their home for foster care, their 6-year-old son, Frank, became enuretic. Neither Fred nor Mary could identify the reason(s) for Frank's bed-wetting behavior, since his last episode had been over 3 years back. In an effort to help Frank control this behavior, Fred and Mary reduced his liquid intake before bedtime, withheld privileges, and, in their frustration, scolded him—all to no avail.

The problem was discussed with the foster care social worker, who suggested that Frank's behavior may have resulted from Tonya's placement in their home—Frank felt displaced! Fred and Mary agreed that they had been overly solicitous of Tonya in their attempt to make her feel safe, wanted, and secure. Following the social worker's cue, they began spending more time with Frank alone and included him as an important family member in helping Tonya feel more secure. Within 2 weeks, Frank's enuretic episodes had ended.

Dramatic family changes such as the one described here can be very threatening to a child, as Frank's behavior demonstrated. His involuntary enuresis was a reflection of insecurity prompted by the arrival and attention given to Tonya. As a 6-year-old child, Frank lacked the insight and maturity to verbalize his feelings. As a consequence, regressive behavior took the form of enuresis. When his parents directed more attention to him and included him in planning for Tonya, his fears of displacement were abated and the consequent enuresis ceased.

product of an identity deficiency. Identity, a basic psychological need of all human beings, is successfully achieved through experiencing love and a sense of self-worth. Individuals who have been deprived of love fail to experience a sense of worth and, as a consequence, develop a poor self-concept. Change is effected by confronting clients with their irresponsible behaviors and encouraging them to accept responsibility for their behavior. It is assumed that clients cannot develop a sense of self-worth while engaging in irresponsible behaviors.

Since **self-concept** is a person's internal reaction to the perception of how others see him or her, the practitioner's role in establishing a warm, friendly, accepting relationship becomes an important factor in the intervention process. As with the case of behavior modification, the focus of intervention is on the client's actions, as opposed to feelings. Confrontation with inappropriate behaviors is emphasized, as is the rejection of rationalizations (excuses). Many practitioners elect reality therapy as an intervention framework because of its straightforward application and the more informal, relaxed role of the therapist.

Task-Centered Social Work

The **task-centered method,** which builds on the problem-solving approach, exemplifies a short-term therapeutic approach (Reid & Epstein, 1972). It stresses the selection and establishment of specific tasks to be worked on within a limited time. Although different models of intervention may be used (such as the ones previously discussed), the emphasis on setting brief time limits for problem solutions is an integral therapeutic ingredient. By "compacting" the agreed-on time limits to work on problems, the client must focus his or her attention and energy on the problem, and tasks for achieving resolution must be adopted quickly. The task-centered approach is an action model designed to engage the client quickly and meaningfully in identifying, confronting, and acting on problems.

Social Work Intervention with Families

Social workers have long recognized that the family unit provides physical and emotional support for its members and shapes their identity. As mentioned in Chapter 2, socialization of the young is a basic task of the family. When problems occur, all of the family members are affected. For example, when a father loses his job, the income available for food, clothing, shelter, and family recreation becomes limited, thus altering the family's daily patterns. The father may become depressed, which affects relationships with his wife and children. Or, a teenager may experience emotional problems, have difficulty with schoolwork, and in turn become resistant to completing home maintenance responsibilities. Again, all family members are affected by this problem. These (and, of course, a myriad of related problems) are problems with which we can all identify. We have experienced times in our family when disruption occurred, and we have witnessed the stress and tension that resulted.

Social workers often focus on the family as a unit of intervention. Recognizing that all members of a family are affected by the problems of any one member, intervention is focused on treating the family system. This approach recognizes that the attitudes and emotions of each family member are significant components in moving the family toward more healthy functioning. Family therapy (or intervention) does not preclude any individual member from specialized treatment. It is ideal, however, if all members agree to be included in the treatment process, since everyone in a family unit both contributes to and is affected by ongoing problems within the unit.

Other Approaches

In addition to the theoretical approaches already identified, social work practitioners may elect to use other approaches. *Rational emotive therapy* focuses on "self-talk" as a target for change. *Role therapy* examines both prescriptive and descriptive roles played by clients and identifies incongruities in role expectations as well as dysfunctional role behaviors. Its purpose is to guide the client toward more functional and appropriate role performance. Based on the perspective that clients know most about their problems and needs, **client-centered therapy** seeks to provide an accepting emotional climate in which clients can work out their own solutions with support and reflection from the therapist. **Feminist therapy,** which many also view as client centered, empowers individuals who have been members of an oppressed group to find their own voices and view themselves as equals as they make decisions about their lives. **Solution-focused therapy** takes a more cognitive-behavioral approach, often consisting of only several sessions, during which the therapist guides the client through a series of questions, such as "When does this problem you are talking about *not* occur?" "If you could wave a magic wand and make this problem go away during the night, when you woke up in the morning, how would things be different?" "On a scale of 1 to 10, how serious is this problem now for you?" and "What would it take for you to move from where you are on the scale now up one notch?" Clients are assigned "homework" between sessions and report back on their success the next session. It should be noted that, in spite of the fact that some of these approaches sound fairly simplistic, it takes a highly skilled practitioner to know when and how to use them.

Many other methods of intervention can be used in working with individuals and families. More advanced methods require additional training and are studied in MSW (master of social work) programs with a clinical specialization. Throughout their careers, social workers develop a deeper and more complete awareness of intervention theories. As new knowledge and understanding of human behavior evolves, social workers must remain vigilant and open to incorporating new theoretical concepts into practice modalities.

Practice Effectiveness

Like all professionals who are engaged with clients in efforts to strengthen their ability to function, social workers have a profound interest in assessing the effectiveness of their work. In social work practice with individuals and families, the concept of accountability relates to the social workers' ongoing monitoring, feedback, and evaluation of their efforts in assessing clients and client systems toward the resolution of issues and problems for which they sought professional help. Various methods have been developed (see Chapter 7) to provide an empirical framework for making this assessment. Not only is practice evaluation essential for viewing movement in cases, but it also provides a basis for reviewing the effectiveness of various techniques employed by the social worker to address specific problems, and an impetus for updating skills.

On the broader scene, social work researchers have been engaged continually in reviewing practice effectiveness using differing intervention modalities and found that outcomes may vary given the nature of the problem, the individuals or groups involved, and projected outcome goals. Issues related to the technique and/or personality of the worker in terms of positive outcomes are generally considered to be invalid. Like all professions, some social workers are more personable, highly skilled, engaging, and effective than others and provide good role models for all who desire to become helping professionals.

On the whole, research has been encouraging with respect to the effectiveness of social work practice with individuals and families. As techniques are refined through practice and as knowledge accrues through research, social workers should become even more effective in helping individuals and families meet their needs.

Supervision of Generalist Practitioners

Supervision is typically thought of as a management function—that of overseeing and assuring that employees are fulfilling the purpose and goals of an agency or organization. Although this function may be one of the responsibilities of social work supervisors, they must do much more through supervision. They provide enrichment to practitioners by helping them develop practice skills through periodic feedback and discussion of cases. Supervisors regulate the flow of cases assigned to social workers and use their unique skills through selective case assignment. They are at times an educator, a listener, an enabler, and a resource for identifying alternative techniques for addressing problems. In their management functions, supervisors present the need for resources to agency executives and maintain standards for excellence in the performance of the social workers they supervise. Supervisors play a vital role in helping an agency achieve its purposes.

SOCIAL WORK PRACTICE AND THE MSW SOCIAL WORKER

Most social workers work directly with individuals and families, although contemporary practice requires that the social worker become involved in other aspects of social work practice as well. MSW practitioners may specialize in community organization, social policy, research, social planning, or social administration as well as practice with individuals, families, and groups. At the master's level, **specialization** that builds on generalist practice knowledge and skills occurs. Many MSW workers are employed in highly clinical environments, such as psychiatric or family service settings, in criminal justice settings, at centers serving AIDS patients, or in related fields of practice requiring specialized knowledge and skill. Others may work at agencies such as a department of human resources, serving people with less specialized problems.

Competence in the use of all social work methods enhances the effectiveness of the social worker in helping client systems seek solutions to problems at all levels of the environment. As discussed in Chapter 2, private practice has increased in recent years; this kind of practice typically calls for competence in psychotherapeutic and intensive counseling skills. Practitioners continue to develop resources that will enable clients to achieve a more satisfactory level of adaptation regardless of the setting in which social work is practiced.

THE BSW SOCIAL WORKER IN PRACTICE WITH INDIVIDUALS AND FAMILIES

Education for social work at the BSW (bachelor of social work) level is geared toward enabling the student to become skilled in generalist social work practice. Guidelines for curricula content are established by the Council on Social Work Education, which also serves as the accrediting body for undergraduate social work programs.

As generalist social workers, practitioners at the baccalaureate level typically find employment in social agencies specializing in direct practice with individuals and families. An appreciation of the nature of client needs and problems in such settings is enhanced by a generalist background and focus. Direct practice with individuals and families does not always demand in-depth psychotherapeutic treatment. Although interviewing and assessment skills are always essential in establishing intervention goals, the BSW social worker need not be concerned with those skills required for intensive psychotherapy. It is important to remember that social work practice with individuals and families extends far beyond psychotherapeutic involvement. The case presented at the opening of this chapter is a good example. The BSW social worker could be involved as a case manager in helping identify needed resources for reducing stress and linking with other appropriate resources to ensure that needs were being addressed. His or her interviewing and counseling skills would be useful in providing an opportunity to identify needs and problems and explore resources necessary for resolving them. The skill of the BSW practitioner in articulating community resources in the problem-solving process also must not be underestimated. The knowledge of resources and the preparation of clients to use those resources are paramount in problem resolution.

BSW practitioners are employed in a variety of direct practice settings that provide services to individuals and families. Among the many opportunities are agencies such as state departments of human resources (or public welfare), mental health and substance abuse programs, programs that serve children and adults with disabilities, children's service agencies (child welfare and child care institutions), halfway houses, nursing homes and other long-term care facilities, areawide agencies on aging, agencies serving battered women, rape crisis centers, schools, and child care centers.

SUMMARY

Social work is a multifaceted profession requiring that its practitioners be familiar with theories of human behavior and social intervention. Social workers must also have knowledge of the logic of the social work process. Professional values serve as the basic underpinning for the relationship that social workers establish with their client systems. They are also the catalyst for promoting societal change designed for the enrichment of the lives of our populace. The goal of generalist social work practice with individuals and families is to empower client systems to take charge of their lives and to act on their environment in such a way as to produce positive change for themselves and those with whom they interact.

As we have suggested in this chapter, a social work practitioner must encompass far more than counseling skills to be an effective change agent. Generalist social workers engage a variety of social systems to facilitate positive change for their clients. This requires not only interpersonal skills but conceptual, planning, and evaluative ones as well. Social work practice, to become effective, requires the skillful application (an art) of scientific knowledge in the problem-solving process.

In this chapter, we have defined social work practice with individuals and families and have examined the components of the direct practice process, skills essential for practice, and theoretical models that serve to structure intervention. Social work practice with individuals and families has been identified as a direct services process that assists client systems through a therapeutic problem-solving process.

KEY TERMS

assessment	intervention
behavior modification	problem-solving
client-centered therapy	approach
contracting	reality therapy
dysfunctional	self-concept
ego psychology	social study
evaluation	solution-focused
feminist therapy	therapy
generalist	specialization
goal setting	task-centered method

DISCUSSION QUESTIONS

1. Define generalist social work practice. What components are essential in generalist practice intervention?

2. Identify the skills that are necessary to become a generalist practitioner. How do the skills used by generalist practitioners differ from those used by advanced specialist social workers?

3. Discuss the importance of theory in social work intervention.

4. Discuss the relationship between social work values and effective social work intervention.

5. Identify the components of the problem-solving process used in social work practice.

6. Review the vignette at the beginning of the chapter. Which practice approaches discussed in this chapter would be effective in working with the family members? How might the outcomes differ depending on the approach used?

7. Why is it important for social workers to evaluate their practice with clients?

INFOTRAC COLLEGE EDITION

To learn more about topics included in this chapter, enter the following search terms:

casework practice

case management

feminist models

social casework

social ecology

social ethics

social work profession

therapy

ON THE INTERNET

http://eserver.org/feminism/

http://homepages.together.net/~bieh/overview.htm

http://www.planet-therapy.com/

http://www.nyu.edu/socialwork/wwwrsw/

REFERENCES

Dubois, B., & Miley, K. K. (1998). *Social work: An empowering profession.* Boston: Allyn & Bacon.

Perlman, H. H. (1959). *Social casework: The problem solving process.* Chicago: University of Chicago Press.

Reid, W. J., & Epstein, L. (1972). *Task-centered casework.* New York: Columbia University Press.

Zastrow, C. (1998). *The practice of social work.* Pacific Grove, CA: Brooks/Cole.

SUGGESTED FURTHER READINGS

Blythe, B., Tripodi, T., & Briar, S. (1995). *Direct practice research in human service agencies.* New York: Columbia University Press.

Compton, B. R., & Galaway, B. (1998). *Social work processes.* Pacific Grove, CA: Brooks/Cole.

Dolgoff, R., & Feldstein, D. (1999). *Understanding social work.* Boston: Allyn & Bacon.

Goldstein, H. (1990). The knowledge base of social work: Theory, wisdom, analogue or art? *Families in Society, 71,* 32–43.

Hepworth, D. H., & Larsen, J. A. (1997). *Direct social work practice.* Pacific Grove, CA: Brooks/Cole.

Lowenberg, F., & Dolgoff, R. (1996). *Ethical decisions for social work practice* (3rd ed.). Itasca, IL: Peacock.

Murphy, B., & Dillon, C. (1998). *Interviewing in action: Process and practice.* Pacific Grove, CA: Brooks/Cole.

Paniagua, F. A. (1998). *Assessing and treating culturally diverse clients: A practical guide* (Vol. 4). Thousand Oaks, CA: Sage.

GENERALIST PRACTICE

Social Work with Groups and the Community

Harry, Charlie, John, Manuel, Frank, and Oscar were all teenagers who grew up in a lower-income area of a large city. Although they were not related, from very early in their lives they had played with each other, gone to school together, and now "hung out" together. None of them did very well in school, three were from single-parent families, two had fathers who were alcoholics, and one had a father in the state penitentiary.

Often considered to be a "gang," this small group had several brushes with the law for theft, fighting, and malicious mischief. Most of their hours after school were spent roaming the streets, often late into the night. Although on an individual basis each of the boys appeared to be somewhat compliant (if not shy), as a group they always represented a threat to be reckoned with. None of the boys had developed adaptable social skills, and they all had difficulty coping with peers who had.

Aaron Stein, a social worker at a nearby settlement house had, on occasion, discussed with his supervisor and the nearby high school the possibility of enrolling these boys in a socialization group at the agency. Initially, it was decided that Aaron would work with the six boys as a small group. Aaron met with the boys as a group (and later, individually), identified the group leader (Oscar), and was able to enlist Oscar's interest in settlement house activities. Aaron identified the strengths that each of these individuals brought to the group as well as the dynamics guiding their group activities. Using this knowledge and the strengths of each group member, he was able to assist group members in developing more adaptive social skills. As the group engaged in activities through the center, including a neighborhood cleanup project, a summer camping trip, and weekly group sessions during which they discussed a wide range of topics, the boys became motivated to achieve goals that were more socially productive and less threatening to the community.

Group work is a method of generalist social work practice that fosters personal development through the mechanism of group process. Many of the problems encountered by clients or client systems can be more effectively addressed and resolved through the group work process. As a generalist practitioner, the BSW social worker recognizes, first, the importance of groups in achieving intervention goals and, second, the utility of group methods in effective problem solving. In this chapter, we will examine social group work, as well as community work, as social work methods that assist individuals, groups, and communities in problem solving.

SOCIAL GROUPS: A DEFINITION

Social groups are formed for many purposes. The most common type is the **natural group,** in which members participate as a result of common interests, shared experiences, similar backgrounds and values, and personal satisfactions derived from interaction with other group members. A street gang or neighborhood group of individuals who hang out together is a natural group. Members of natural groups are further characterized by face-to-face interactions and share an emotional investment in the group. Natural groups are seldom formed purposefully to meet specific objectives. All of us are members of natural groups, and seldom is our membership in those groups the result of a planned effort to become involved. In natural groups, a leader often emerges without premeditation or election by group members but rather because one member possesses behavioral attributes or resources that are highly valued by the other group members. Like all groups, natural groups tend to be transitory, with old members exiting and new ones entering throughout the group's life cycle.

Other groups are formed purposefully for a specific reason. For example, apartment residents may organize to seek building repairs and better living conditions, or a church or synagogue may organize a softball team. Established agencies, such as the YMCA or YWCA, might organize recreational groups within the city. A common characteristic of each of these groups is that they are developed to fulfill a specific purpose.

Before attempting to understand the components and process of generalist practice with groups, it is helpful to have a basic understanding of what is meant by a **group.** Chess and Norlin (1996) define a group as a form of social organization whose members not only identify and interact with one another on a personal basis but also have a shared sense of the group as a social entity. The type of group with whom the generalist practitioner works is called a *primary group*—that is, a group in which there is face-to-face interaction with group members. Regardless of the reasons why a group is formed (that is, a natural or planned group), the group work method may be used to assist group members in achieving personal growth through the democratic process.

GOALS OF SOCIAL GROUP WORK

Group work is a process and an activity that seeks to stimulate and support more adaptive personal functioning and social skills of individuals through structured group interaction. The development of effective skills in communication, coping skills, and effective problem-solving techniques is the goal of the group work experience (Toseland & Rivas, 1998). Group work techniques can be used more effectively when goals and objectives are related to the needs of group members. Effective group work capitalizes on the dynamics of interaction among members of the group. Members are encouraged to participate in making decisions, questioning, sharing, and contributing their efforts toward the achievement of agreed-on goals and objectives.

GROUP FOCUS

Social workers engage in practice with groups to accomplish a variety of tasks. Generally, groups may be classified in terms of a specific purpose. Several of the more common types of groups are identified and discussed in Box 6.1.

Recreation Groups

The primary objective of **recreation groups** is to provide for participants' entertainment, enjoyment, and experience. Activities such as athletic games or table games are typical recreational outlets. Community centers, YMCAs and YWCAs, and settlement houses routinely provide this type of group activity, as do senior centers for older adults. Participation provides opportunities for shared interaction, interdependence, and social exchange.

Group recreational activities also provide constructive outlets for individuals in a monitored environment. Group workers must be sensitive to scheduling arrangements and willing to develop activities that are of interest to prospective participants.

Recreation Skill Groups

As differentiated from recreation groups, the purpose of **recreation skill groups** is to promote development of a skill within a recreational or enjoyment context. Ordinarily, a resource person with appropriate expertise teaches participants the essential skills necessary to develop greater competency in a craft, game, or sport. Tasks are emphasized, and instruction is provided by the resource person (for example, a coach).

Educational Groups

Educational groups are formed for the purpose of transmitting knowledge and enabling participants to acquire more complex skills. Although these groups may take on a classroom appearance, emphasis is given to group task assignments, and opportunities for interaction and idea exchange buttress didactic presentations. Educational groups vary in purpose, from learning to repair an automobile to learning the most effective ways to cope with a family member who has Alzheimer's disease. Group leaders usually are persons with professional expertise in the area of interest for which the group was formed.

Socialization Groups

From a more traditional perspective, **socialization groups** typify the purposes and goals of social group work in that they seek to

BOX
6.1

Illustrations of Different Types of Groups, Their Focus, and Membership

- **Recreation group**—A YWCA organizes and promotes dominos, cards (bridge, etc.), basketball, and volleyball groups for interested community residents of all ages.
- **Recreation-skill groups**—The extension division of a local community college offers courses in the manual arts, golf, swimming, volleyball, sewing, and pottery making for community residents who wish to develop skill in those areas. Task development is emphasized, and mutual interaction is encouraged in the learning process.
- **Educational groups**—A local family service agency offers a group of middle-aged adults opportunities to learn more about the aging process and how to cope with needs of their aged parents. At the same time, the agency sponsors a group on parenting skills for pregnant women and their husbands. In both groups, discussion is emphasized and group members are encouraged to identify their specific concerns for group reaction and discussion.
- **Socialization groups**—A halfway house serving delinquent adolescents develops a weekly group meeting for its residents. Discussion focuses on specific problems experienced by group members. Activities are introduced that require cooperative interaction among group members for successful completion (for example, yard maintenance,

household chores). Emphasis is given to democratic participation and personal decision making.
- **Self-help groups**—An Alcoholics Anonymous group is formed by individuals wanting to overcome an alcohol addiction. The purpose of the group is to provide support and reassurance to group members in dealing with alcohol-related problems, with the goal of helping members stay sober.
- **Therapeutic groups**—These groups may consist of individuals who have difficulty in dealing with emotional problems associated with divorce, interpersonal loss, alcohol- and drug-related problems, mental health problems, difficulties in parent-child relationships, or other areas in which dysfunctional behavior results. Typically, emotional problems are related significantly to the problems in day-to-day living being experienced by group members.
- **Encounter groups**—A group is organized by a local service agency to help young men and women who lack assertiveness, are self-deprecating, and feel inadequate. Members are encouraged to be self-expressive, learn to risk, gain insight into their own and others' feelings, provide mutual support, and establish meaningful relationships. A safe, nonjudgmental environment is essential for the successful participation of members.

stimulate behavior change, increase social skills and self-confidence, and encourage motivation (Euster, 1975, p. 220). The group focuses on helping participants develop socially acceptable behavior and behavioral competency. Personal decision making and self-determinism are emphasized as integral aspects of the group process. Typically, socialization groups may consist of runaway youth, predelinquents, or people with developmental disabilities (Toseland & Rivas, 1998). Leadership is provided by a social worker skilled in understanding group dynamics and knowledgeable about the problem area experienced by the participants.

Self-Help Groups

The underlying motivation for individuals who join **self-help groups** is to resolve a personal or social problem that they find perplexing, continually stressful, and unrelenting. Membership in self-help groups is usually a matter of choice, and the prospective group member may become aware of the group through acquaintances, friends, or related sources. In some instances, participation in self-help groups may be mandated. An abusive parent may be required by the court to participate in Parents Anonymous, or a person charged with driving while intoxicated may be required to participate in Alcoholics Anonymous meetings. It is common for members of the self-help groups to have "given up" on attempting to resolve the problem through their own efforts, counseling, or other traditional agency approaches.

As members of a self-help group, individuals are expected to make a strong personal commitment to the group, its members, and its goals. Self-help groups emphasize mutual aid and interdependence, personal involvement, face-to-face interaction, and an active role in responding to the needs of other group members. Typically, self-help groups elect their own convenor and mutually decide on the format for meetings. Ordinarily, professional group workers are not employed to assist the group with process or goal setting. Self-help groups may, however, invite professionals from a variety of areas to meet with them to share information about specific problems.

Self-help groups or support groups are formed for many different purposes: for recovery and growth, as in the case of Alcoholics Anonymous, Al-Anon, Narcotics Anonymous, or Overeaters Anonymous; advocacy, such as pro-life groups, women's liberation groups, or Mothers against Drunk Driving (MADD); or a combination of personal growth and advocacy, such as Parents without Partners or Parents Anonymous (Toseland & Rivas, 1998).

Self-help groups typically do not always seek professional leadership. Effective efforts to resolve problems are based on personal involvement and a willingness to assist fellow members in learning to cope and develop adaptive skills. Since members have experienced the same problem, they may be more empathetic, insightful, and able to respond with more understanding.

Therapeutic Groups

Therapeutic groups require skilled professional leadership. Group members typically have intensive personal or emotional problems that require the expertise of a well-trained professional, such as an MSW social worker, a clinical psychologist, or other professional counselor. Problems typically addressed in therapeutic groups range from interpersonal loss (death, divorce, abandonment), physically disabling injuries, terminal diseases, and marital or family conflict to psychopathology or other emotionally distressing dysfunctional behaviors. Consider the following case:

> Alice (age 35) recently became a widow when her husband, Carlos, was killed in an automobile accident. Alice has two children, Tina (age 6) and Sean (age 3). She had not worked outside the home since the birth of her children. As time passed since Carlo's death, Alice became more depressed, immobilized, and unable to care for her children. The local mental health outreach center arranged for Alice to be placed in a therapeutic group consisting of 10 people who were also experiencing interpersonal loss.

Monitoring group interaction and its effects on members is an essential requirement for the group leader. Various therapy approaches may be used to promote therapeutic interaction directed toward behavioral change. Therapeutic groups may also be supplemented by individual treatment.

Encounter Groups

A person may became involved in an **encounter group** oriented toward assisting individuals in developing more self-awareness and interpersonal skills. Such groups are characterized by a secure environment in which members can be openly expressive, develop a sense of trust, receive candid feedback, and develop sensitivity to their own and others' feelings and emotions. Assertiveness and confidence resulting from heightened self-acceptance and self-awareness promote more genuine relationships and enhance the quality of interpersonal communication. Encounter groups are identified by many different titles: T (training) groups, sensitivity groups, and personal growth groups.

EFFECTIVE GROUP DEVELOPMENT

The achievement of desired outcomes of the group process is dependent on several key considerations. Purposefulness is an essential characteristic for maximum effectiveness of the group work process. *Purposefulness* involves the establishment of specific goals and objectives and access to their achievement by the group. It provides the direction or intent for each group session and supplies a framework for monitoring and evaluating the group's progress.

Leadership is essential in helping the group maintain its focus and in encouraging maximum participation. The group worker may play an active or passive role in the group, depending on the needs of the group as it moves toward the established goals and objectives. The leader must be skilled in group processes and able to perform a variety of roles in supporting the accomplishment of tasks necessary to maintain group integrity and continuing progress. A wide range of role responses may be required of a group leader, such as director, policymaker, planner, expert, external group representative, facilitator, nurturer, disciplinarian, cheerleader, mediator, and scapegoat (Zastrow, 1998).

Effective leadership is essential for successfully achieving the group's purposes. The methods that a leader may use to accomplish group goals should be consistent with the values and purposes of social work practice. Although leaders of groups have diverse leadership styles, the style most compatible with social work encourages the empowerment of group members, helping members assume responsibility for the life of the group, including planning, developing skills and values, and making their own decisions about the group's goals and activities. The empowerment method fully embraces the principles of democratic process and encourages individual responsibility and risk sharing as products of group interaction and decision making. The success of group process and goal attainment is related to a large extent to effective group leadership. Needless to say, the group leader is accountable for group maintenance and the success (or failure) of the group in achieving its purposes.

The *selection of group members* is an important factor in achieving group cohesion. In composing groups, the group worker must accurately assess each individual's needs, capacity for social functioning, interests, and willingness to assume an active role as a group member. Although diversity of background and experience may enhance alternatives for achieving the group's purposes, homogeneous (similar) motives are essential to the formation of the group and identification as a group member. Members with few common interests often have more difficulty in becoming involved in group activities. Age, ethnicity, and/or gender may be critical factors, depending on the group's purposes and the activities designed to achieve those purposes. Individuals with severe emotional problems or behavior disorders may be disruptive to the group process; thus, careful consideration should be given to including them as group members. Members should have the ability to focus on group tasks. Systematic disruptive behavior is not only disconcerting but may lead to group disintegration. The type of group being formed (for example, recreational, educational) will determine the criteria for the selection of members. In all instances, selection should be based on the "principle of maximum profit" (individuals with specific needs that would be most likely to achieve the greatest benefit from the group). The assessment of individuals for group membership is enhanced by a personal interview prior to inclusion in the group.

The *size of a group* is to a large extent determined by its purposes. To determine in advance that 4, 6, or 15 members is the "ideal" size of a group has little validity. It is more effective to examine the goals and purposes of the proposed group when determining group size. If, for example, anonymity (or the ability to "lose" oneself) is a desirable end, a larger number of members may be indicated, thus assuring more limited interaction and group fragmentation (that is, the emergence of subgroups). Smaller groups, by definition, demand more intimate interaction, and group pressures typically are intensified. Absenteeism affects group process and task accomplishment more in small groups than large ones. Small groups may function more informally than larger ones, which usually require a structured format. The role of the group leader also varies with the size of the group. The democratic process can be achieved in both large and small groups, although it is more difficult in the former. The principles and techniques of social group work are effective with large and small groups alike.

The number of members selected for the group depends on the desired effect on its individual members, the needs of the members, and their capacity to participate and support group purposes. Generally, a small group may be composed of 4 to 9 members, whereas a large group may consist of 10 to 20 members.

THEORY FOR GROUP WORK PRACTICE

Social group work is a direct social work practice method requiring the social worker to be familiar with theories related to group behavior. Group theory provides a framework for promoting guided change through group interaction. The discipline of social psychology has contributed much to our understanding of group formation, roles, norms, values, group dynamics, and cohesion (Baron & Byrne, 1997). Early social group work pioneers also contributed valuable experiential and theoretical insights that added to the knowledge base from which an informed approach to working with groups can be employed (Toseland & Rivas, 1998).

Social group work can be distinguished as a professional social work method by the informed application of theory in helping groups achieve their objectives and goals. Since groups vary extensively in their composition, types, and purposes, the worker also must have a broad-based understanding of the life cycle, emotional reactions to stress, and maladaptive behavior. Group workers must have skill in working with the group and sensitivity in helping the group move toward achieving its goals.

SOCIAL GROUP WORK AS A PRACTICE

As we indicated previously, group work is directed toward the enrichment of an individual's life through a group existence. Although it is unlikely that group members derive equal benefit from the group experience, all can be expected to experience some measure of growth. Positive group work is a planned-change effort. Change is predicated on benefits derived from group process and interaction. The social worker is responsible for assuring that the principles governing social work practice are included in the process (National Association of Social Workers [NASW], 1999):

1. Assuring the dignity and worth of all members
2. Developing an articulated understanding of the group's purpose and the roles that group members agree to follow (for example, exercising confidentiality; treating each other with respect)
3. Assessing the problems and needs of individual group members and the group as a whole and offering support as needed
4. Helping the group develop its own identity, which reflects its unique character, relationships within the group, and needs
5. Facilitating the development of communication among group members, which permits the expression of feelings and emotions
6. Facilitating the planning and implementation of relevant group activities that promote constructive interaction, assessment of group process, and the advancement of the group's purpose
7. Preparing for termination

Each group also has its own life cycle, characterized by developmental stages. Within this context, the stages of a group's development often follow this pattern:

1. *Beginning*—basic orientation and getting acquainted; "honeymoon period"
2. *Norm development*—establishing ground rules for operation; beginning level of trust among members
3. *Conflict phase*—members asserting individual ideas; as members get to know each other better, the resulting conflict often leads to members questioning the group's purpose and suggesting that they leave the group or that the entire group disband
4. *Relationship phase*—replacing initial conflicts with acceptance of others; members working through the conflict and deepen-

ing their relationship with each other; sharing of leadership, tasks, and trust; appreciation for the group and a strong sense of group identity; flexibility, consensus, and decision making

5. *Termination*—ending of the group, with recognition of the loss that the group experience is ending, as well as personal growth

An awareness of these stages is helpful in monitoring the progress of the group as it moves toward greater cohesion and effectiveness. Dysfunctional "blocking" at any stage (the conflict phase), once identified, can be addressed and resolved by the group, and the developmental progress can continue. Allowed to continue unchecked, the unresolved blockage may result in group dissolution.

Both cyclical and progressive processes exist in groups. Although groups navigate through stages of development from beginning to end, they also come back to revisit or address certain basic process issues in a cyclical stage (Toseland & Rivas, 1998). Skill in working with groups is an important aspect of social work practice. The efficiency and effectiveness of the group work process may result in personal enhancement, skill development, and problem reduction.

GROUP WORK SETTINGS

Traditionally, social group work was practiced in recreational settings, such as the YWCA or YMCA, settlement houses, and community centers. With the growing popularity of group work, along with the redefinition of the scope of social work practice, group work has become a valuable practice method within most social service agencies. For example, a family service agency might form a group of prospective adoptive parents to orient them to the adoptive process. A treatment center might compose a group of adolescent substance abusers to assist them in learning to identify and eliminate using behaviors and to manage stress and interpersonal problems. A recreational center might sponsor athletic teams for middle school youth. Older adults living in a long-term care facility could constitute a "remotivation" group.

Working with groups not only promotes growth and change through the interaction of the members but also enables the agency and workers to serve a greater number of clients. Although some group members may need individual counseling in addition to the group experience, in most instances, the group activity is sufficient for personal change. When direct service with individuals is not provided by the agency offering the group, referrals are made to an appropriate agency, and a cooperative relationship between the service providers assures the client of maximum assistance with problems.

EVALUATION

Professional practice with individuals and groups must include an evaluative process. Evaluation is always focused on the extent to which the group is able to achieve its objectives. It may be an ongoing process as well as an assessment of the total group process, which comes at the termination of the group. In the former instance, the social worker continually "monitors" group behavior, to enable the group to focus on its goals. Monitoring also may help the group redefine its purpose and goals, should it become evident that the original ones are unachievable. Monitoring consists of a critical assessment of the group's output.

Evaluation includes an assessment of all activities and behaviors related to the group's performance. Factors such as group leadership, resources, attendance at sessions, changes in group structure, changes in dysfunctional behaviors, characteristics of group members, group norms, and agency support, among others, all are reviewed in relation to the achievement of personal and group goals and objectives. Evaluation has the potential of providing a basis for answering such questions as, What could have increased group productivity? What were the positive achievements of the group? What implications for change are suggested? Efficiency and better quality of service are likely when rigorous evaluative standards are maintained.

GROUP TERMINATION

Groups are terminated when the purposes for which they were established are achieved. Although many groups are initiated with a predetermined expiration period, termination usually is related to meeting group goals and personal goals of the members. Occasionally, a group is aborted when it becomes obvious that its goals are unattainable or when dysfunctional behavior of one or more group members continually disrupts the group's activities. However, most often conflict that occurs within the group is a typical part of group development, and how conflicts are addressed is an important contributor to individual and group growth and how well the group handles termination.

The worker must be sensitive to the needs of group members at the time of termination and assist them in phasing out their attach-

ment to the group. Often resistance to termination becomes highly emotional and vocal. Frustration, anger, withdrawal, and grief are among the more common reactions to the loss of the close ties that have developed among members throughout the life of the group. By helping the group assess its accomplishments and plan alternatives, the worker can help members develop a more adaptive transition.

SOCIAL WORK WITH COMMUNITIES

Social work with communities is a generalist practice method that enables individuals and groups to achieve a more desirable level of life satisfaction as well as more effective levels of adaptation. As presented in the following discussion, community social work may take a variety of forms. The following case vignette characterizes one type of situation that is commonly managed by the BSW practitioner:

Norma Carlson, a BSW social worker, has been working with Brenda Bostwick for several months. Brenda, age 16, is a single parent who aspired to complete her high school education in hopes that she could find a good job and better provide for her child. It was difficult for her to concentrate on her schoolwork because she often had to miss school to care for her baby. School officials had suspended her for absences on several occasions, and she was becoming more discouraged every day. With Brenda's consent, Norma visited with the school officials to engage them in working out an educational program for Brenda so that she would not fall behind in her studies. Norma also contacted a local child care center and helped Brenda arrange for her child to be cared for while she was in class. Norma was also successful in helping Brenda secure reduced-rate transportation with the local bus company, which agreed that Brenda should be supported in her determination to work toward her educational goals. Norma was assigned to work with other teen parents, and she realized that the community had no resources that worked specifically with teen parents. She helped organize a network of interested social workers and school officials. Together, network members secured reduced child care and transportation rates for all teen parents in the community so they could attend school regularly. Norma and other network members wrote a grant and received funding to establish a program to work exclusively with pregnant and parenting teens.

Successful social work intervention, as in the case of Brenda, often requires that the social worker engage community agencies and organizations in the process. It is doubtful whether Brenda, without Norma's knowledge and skill, could have made the arrangements that resulted in a positive solution to her need to complete her high school education. Clients are often unaware of available resources or the process through which successful solutions can be achieved. In some instances, they may not have the self-confidence to pursue alternatives that result in goal achievement. Also, needed resources may not be available in their communities. Social workers in direct practice find that work with the community often becomes an essential ingredient in the problem-solving process. In this section of the chapter, we discuss the concepts and principles of social work with the community.

What Is a Community?

Community is a descriptive term that has many meanings. Communities may be defined as groups of people who live within certain incorporated limits, such as Philadelphia, Pennsylvania; Boise, Idaho; or Mena, Arkansas. Or, others may speak of a "religious community," which refers to a group of people who share common religious values. A community may also be a subunit of a larger metropolitan area, such as Watts in Los Angeles or Shadyside in Pittsburgh. Members of an ethnic group who live in a specific geographic area are often referred to as a community. Illustrations are endless, and our purpose here is to identify the ambiguity of the concept. How, then, do we arrive at a usable definition that enables us to understand the focus of social work with communities? It is obvious from the preceding illustrations that communities vary considerably in organization, resources, values, and purpose. It is also obvious that a client may well be a member of several communities—for example, an incorporated city or town, a religious group, an ethnic group, and a well-defined neighborhood. Social workers need to be familiar with the community systems that serve as behavioral contexts for their clients. Keeping these definitional variations in mind, we will, for our purposes, consider **community** as a group of individuals who live in close proximity to one another, who share a common environment, including public and private resources, and who identify themselves with that community.

Social workers often feel overwhelmed by the concept of working with the community. Perhaps a different perspective could allay some of these fears: If we consider that the community consists of interacting individuals, then working with the community would consist of working with the individuals and groups who interact. The same basic skills needed to be able to work effectively with people are used in community practice.

Generalist social work practitioners engaged in community practice play many of the same professional roles played by those who work with individuals, families, and groups.

Many programs at the community level, such as Habitat for Humanity, bring together diverse groups of individuals to address the needs of community members.

Stone/Billy Hustace

Social work with the community may focus on a wide range of problems and issues. The case illustration with which we initiated this discussion is only one example. Social workers may serve as a **broker** with several agencies to obtain sources necessary for the achievement of treatment goals. In the broker role, the social worker helps clients plow through the maze of different agencies in locating resources that are most appropriate to problem resolution. In addition to the active role of negotiation with agencies, the social worker also gathers and transmits information between client systems and the broader environment (Kirst-Ashman & Hull, 1997).

At other times, the social worker in community practice may serve as an **enabler** in seeking to help people identify and clarify their problems (assessment) and in supporting and stimulating the group to unite in their efforts to secure change. For example, a group of tenants in a rat-infested apartment might be encouraged to unite and confront the owners or landlords with the problem and seek redress for those conditions. At other times, the social worker in community practice may function in the role of advocate for a client system in confronting unresponsive representatives of community institutions. In the advocate role, the social worker is clearly aligned with the client system in seeking to nudge unresponsive institutions to take action. A social worker may, for example, represent the client system in increasing police protection in high-risk neighborhoods. Finally, a social work community practitioner might serve as an activist who seeks change in institutional response patterns. For example, a social worker may serve as an activist in seeking changes in discriminatory hiring practices or in otherwise trying to secure the rights of disenfranchised groups (Kirst-Ashman & Hull, 1997).

As indicated earlier, generalist social work practitioners are constantly engaged in community practice as they work with various organizations to address specific needs of their clients or the populace in general. In Brenda's case, it was necessary for the social worker to engage the school system, a child care center, and the local transportation company to establish an effective solution for Brenda's dilemma and for teen parents in similar situations.

COMMUNITY PRACTICE APPROACHES

Social work with the community, like other methods of social work practice, is based on planned change and assumes familiarity, skill, and experience on the part of the social worker, including the basic social work skills of problem identification, data collection, assessment, analysis (or interpretation), and the development of planned intervention. Social workers who routinely practice with communities generally use a "social action, social planning, or community development" approach. The **social action** strategy was popularized by Saul Alinsky (1969) and was used extensively by oppressed groups in the 1960s "War on Poverty" programs. This approach stresses organization and group cohesion in confrontational approaches geared to modify or eliminate institutional power bases that negatively affect the group. For example, activists protesting a community transportation system's unwillingness to provide accessible transportation for people with disabilities chained themselves (and their wheelchairs, if they used them) to buses in one city to bring attention to their needs. **Social planning** emphasizes modification of institutional practices through the application of knowledge, values, and theory—a practical, rational approach to problem solving that assumes well-intentioned people will be responsive to sound arguments. Using the transportation

example, a social planner for the city would develop a systematic plan to be submitted to upper management and the city council detailing how to make services more accessible to persons with disabilities. The **community development** approach considers and respects the diversity of the population and uses those differences as strengths in achieving community betterment for all citizens. Again using the transportation example, diverse groups of citizens, including extensive representation by persons with disabilities, would work together with community agencies and officials to develop a plan for accessible transportation. Often citizens become polarized as an action group when "superordinate goals" are identified, requiring concerted community efforts for a satisfactory resolution.

Social workers with advanced degrees often specialize in community organization as a basic practice method as well as a field of practice. Social workers at this level may be employed by community councils, the United Way, community development centers, local administrators of state or federal programs such as child welfare or public assistance programs; as directors of agencies; or by a variety of related community organizations. A main objective of the community practitioner is to engage in planning and development that assures an adequate resource base and implementation structure that is directed toward improving the quality of life for populations in need as well as the citizenry in general. In their capacity as community planners, social workers often develop social policy proposals or provide their expertise to city councils, state and federal legislatures, and other policy-formulating groups (Netting, Kettner, & McMurtry, 1998).

As you are well aware, many negatives affect the quality of life in communities—

crime, substance abuse, discrimination, homelessness, and poverty. Social work has a long tradition and mandate to apply the knowledge, values, and skills in addressing negative forces and their impact on vulnerable populations, with the goal of instituting change efforts that move the community toward solving its own problems. Direct practice with communities is an integral practice role for generalists as well as specialized social workers. It is an essential, rewarding, and challenging activity that requires an awareness of theory, knowledge, and practice skills if intervention is to be successful.

SOCIAL WORK WITH GROUPS AND THE COMMUNITY

The baccalaureate (BSW) social worker develops beginning competency in working with groups and the community as part of the BSW educational program. Accredited BSW programs require coursework in both theory and practice in working with groups and in the community. Many opportunities exist for work with groups and the community at the BSW level. Agencies such as family service agencies, state departments of human services, hospitals, correctional centers, mental health agencies, programs that work with disabled persons, school social services, youth organizations, and a variety of related service delivery organizations use group and community practice methodologies. It should also be noted that social workers with MSW degrees are also often employed as community organization workers, sometimes specializing in that area as a field of practice. At this level, they may serve as administrators of state or federal programs, department heads in a city's human services division, or directors of agencies.

SUMMARY

Social work with groups and social work with the community are social work methods that promote the personal growth of individual members (group work) and enhance the capacity of the community to better serve the needs of its diverse members (community practice). Groups may be identified by their purpose: recreational, recreation skill, educational, socialization, encounter, self-help, and therapy. Community change efforts are facilitated through social action, social planning, and community development approaches. In all of these, members of the group or community establish goals and objectives, and the facilitator helps the members achieve their goals. Democratic decision making is important to the process. Monitoring and evaluation are major activities used to help the group and community achieve their goals and to enrich practice methods.

KEY TERMS

broker	natural group
community	recreation group
community	recreation skill group
development	self-help group
educational group	social action
enabler	social planning
encounter group	socialization group
group	therapeutic group
group work	

DISCUSSION QUESTIONS

1. Discuss the similarities and dissimilarities of natural and organized groups.

2. What are some of the primary considerations that the social worker must consider when forming groups?

3. Identify the differences between therapeutic groups and socialization groups.

4. Discuss the basic principles governing group work practices, and explain how those principles are related to successful social group work practice.

5. Review the definition of *community,* and discuss the characteristics identified in the definition in terms of their importance for community social work practice.

6. Identify and discuss the community practice approaches discussed in this chapter. Compare and contrast those approaches.

INFOTRAC
COLLEGE EDITION

To learn more about topics included in this chapter, enter the following search terms:

Alcoholics Anonymous

community organizing

community practice

group formation

group work intervention

group work method

self-help movement

settlement house

ON THE INTERNET

http://www.aa.org/econtent.html

http://www.communityleadership.org/

http://www.libertynet.org/kwru/

REFERENCES

Alinsky, S. (1969). *Reveille for radicals.* New York: Basic Books.

Baron, R. A., & Byrne, D. (1997). *Social psychology* (8th ed.). Boston: Allyn & Bacon.

Chess, W. A., & Norlin, J. M. (1996). *Human behavior and the social environment* (3rd ed.). Boston: Allyn & Bacon.

Garvin, C. D. *Contemporary group work* (3rd ed.). Boston: Allyn & Bacon.

Kirst-Ashman, K. K., & Hull, G. (1997). *Generalist practice with organizations and communities.* Chicago: Nelson-Hall.

National Association of Social Workers. (1999). *NASW Code of ethics.* Washington, DC: Author.

Netting, F. E., Kettner, P. M., & McMurtry, S. (1998). *Social work macro practice* (2nd ed.). New York: Longman.

Toseland, R., & Rivas, R. (1998). *An introduction to group work practice.* Boston: Allyn & Bacon.

Zastrow, C. (1998). *The practice of social work.* Pacific Grove, CA: Brooks/Cole.

SUGGESTED FURTHER READINGS

Cox, F. M., Erlich, J. L., Rothman, J., & Tropman, J. E. (Eds.). (1992). *Strategies of community organization: Macro practice* (4th ed.). Itasca, IL: Peacock.

Ewald, P., Freeman, E., & Poole, D. (Eds.). (1998). *Community building: Renewal, well-being, and shared responsibility.* Washington, DC: NASW Press.

Fellin, P. (1995). *The community social worker.* Itasca, IL: Peacock.

Kahn, S. (1994). *How people get power* (2nd ed.). Washington, DC: NASW Press.

Malekoff, A. (2000). *Group work with adolescents: Principles and practice.* New York: Guilford.

Martinez-Brawley, E. E. (2000). *Perspectives on the small community* (2nd ed.). Washington, DC: NASW Press.

Meenaghan, T., & Gibbons, W. E. (2000). *Generalist practice in larger systems.* Chicago: Lyceum.

Powell, T. (Ed.). (1990). *Working with self-help.* Washington, DC: NASW Press.

Tropman, J. (1997). *Successful community leadership: A skills guide for volunteers and professionals.* Washington, DC: NASW Press.

GENERALIST PRACTICE

Policy, Administration, and Research

Leticia Fontenot is an agency administrator for a state child protective services program. A licensed social worker, Leticia worked her way up through the agency ranks from a child abuse and neglect investigator to her present position. Daily, she is faced with a number of critical issues that impact children's lives throughout the state. Despite a number of prevention programs, rates of child maltreatment continue to rise. Staff caseloads are increasing, and turnover is alarmingly high.

A highly respected administrator within the agency, Leticia is convening a task force to develop strategies to address these issues before they result in the tragic deaths of children. The task force will propose recommendations for changes in agency administration, including staffing patterns and agency structure, as well as legislative initiatives that will garner more resources for the agency. As Leticia thinks about the problems, she realizes that a first step is to determine what research has been conducted that can help her and task force members better understand the issues. She then plans to conduct additional research to better understand trends in types of maltreatment reported and outcomes of those cases reported. Although Leticia no longer works directly with clients, her role as an agency administrator has a major impact on children and families in the state.

This chapter will address the roles of social workers in generalist practice at the exo- (community) and macro- (societal) levels of the environments, including policy, agency administration, and research. Sound social welfare policies and agency administration must be based on empirical research, and funding sources, including legislative bodies, are increasingly demanding agency accountability for any funding allocated. Additionally, because social welfare issues are complex and not always easily understood, agency administrators must have good data to support their recommendations for effective programs. Leticia, for example, knows that research supports the fact that in the long run preventive programs reduce the incidence of child maltreatment and result in healthier children and families. She also knows, however, that states often allocate limited funding to social welfare–related problems and that there isn't enough funding available even to fund staff to deal with serious crisis situations of child maltreatment, let alone prevention programs. One of the dilemmas faced by social agency administrators like Leticia is how to develop collaborative relationships with key policymakers and advocates within the state to support programs that will result in positive change for the children and families her agency serves.

Observations about the politics and administration of social welfare laws have a clear and direct relevance to planners, administrators, and policymakers. However, state and federal laws are often made without input from programs at the local level, where social worker and client interact directly. For most BSW students, graduation results in an entry-level job in direct practice—delivering social services in direct interaction with clients. It is the client with a presenting problem with whom the social worker interacts. It is the social worker at the local level who hears first what clients think and feel about these policies. Thus, the flow of information from client to policymaker and the heightened sensitivity of policymakers to clients' circumstances are best accomplished when social workers both appreciate and understand the opportunities and the limitations of the American policy-making process and when those in the policy stream have a knowledge of, and appreciation for, the tasks and limitations of the social worker.

POLICY PRACTICE

It has been said that some years ago a social worker testifying before Congress noted that when the president of the American Medical Association (AMA) speaks, he or she speaks on behalf of AMA members, fellow physicians. But when the president of the National Association of Social Workers speaks, he or she speaks for "our clients." If this testimony did, in fact, occur, the speaker was identifying one of the most fundamental faults of politics: the assumption that our side is the side of good and theirs of evil. For the most part, it is important to see the political process as a search for the common good, where most sides seek to do the right thing. Public policies have costs and benefits—some citizens have a gain; others, a loss. In politics we are concerned with the net benefit and net costs, as well as who wins and who pays. Public programs are intended to benefit society as a whole even though some citizens are made worse off or, at least, less well off than others.

Policies to eliminate poverty, provide high-quality affordable health care, or regulate abortion are controversial because responsible and decent citizens are in different circumstances and hold different values about what governments can and ought to do. What one person considers to be a good policy might be viewed as the tyrannical use of government by others. The most important lesson of politics in a democratic society is to respect the views of others.

Social workers also need to understand the policymaking processes so that they can intervene when policymakers have been ill informed or have acted capriciously. Only by understanding the range of choices that are economically efficient and politically feasible, while still being responsive to the underlying social problem, can social workers do this successfully. Proposed alternatives to a flawed policy must take into account that which is now available, as well as the values, both implicit and explicit, on which the alternatives are based. Social workers who are effective at not imposing their own values on the clients they directly serve often reject professionalism and use only their own values when judging social policies. It is easy, for example, to dismiss conservative economics as a pretext for securing the wealth of the very rich at the expense of the rest of society. The political and economic considerations that best explain distributions of wealth and income are far more complex then the rhetoric of the right or the left would suggest.

Approaches to the Study of Social Welfare

No single policy perspective is inherently superior. To understand and act intelligently about issues of social policy, we must ask a series of basic questions that fit within a basic framework. The central question is "What should I do to promote a better set of social welfare programs and policies?" This demands attention to the question "How and why have policies turned out as they are?" Yet other questions have to be addressed: "What would be a better set of programs and policies?" and "How do I know (or think) this set would be better?"

Three basic approaches are commonly used to seek answers to these interrelated questions. What should be done to change things requires a focus on the political process. How and how well things are done now demands an emphasis on evaluation of the current social welfare system. Finally, to discover the norms with which to judge the outputs of welfare services calls for a focus on values of a good society.

Studies of the dynamics of the policy process give specific attention to the economic, social, and political forces that shape the realistic options within the constraints of the political system. This *conceptual* framework is borrowed from political science, and economics are used to focus on the manner in which the input variables of the political process are transformed into the outputs of a formal set of social welfare institutions (Sabatier, 1999).

The *performance* perspective has a focus on the institutions of the social welfare system itself. Essentially descriptive studies are used so that the social worker is informed about the current shape of mental health institutions, foster care practice, adoption policies, and so on. One thought behind this approach is that the social worker can best help clients by knowing what the various social institutions do and how they do it. Also, to be effective at changing things, we need first to know something about the way things are now and how they got that way. How did rational persons acting in good faith place us in this position? We need to look at "observed outcomes" and their relationship to "expected outcomes" and not assume that they are the same. A fundamental purpose of evaluation in one sense is to measure the degree to which programs have attained their goals. Evaluative research measures the performance both qualitatively and quantitatively. The evaluative question asks what the observable consequences are that can reasonably be attributed to the introduction of a particular program. It is an effort basically to measure pre- and postprogram conditions and to isolate the programs' impacts on those differences.

The *normative* approach examines the social welfare system in a clearly nonneutral frame of reference. It seeks to ask essentially ethical questions about performance: What are the effects of social policy on the citizen and on the political system? In this broader approach, the effort is to make more explicit the central ethical and political dilemmas implicit in how a social welfare system ought to be structured.

GOALS OF THE WELFARE SYSTEM

Social policy experts Gilbert and Terrell (1998) assert that there is no broadly accepted, single definition of welfare policy. Rather, they view **social welfare policy** as "an 'explicit course of action' and focus on decisions and choices that help determine that course of action" (p. 2).

People who cooperate to pass a law typically have different goals. Members of legislative bodies who vote for a law may have no intent beyond repaying a past political favor. A federal Housing and Urban Development official may fund public housing projects as a means of correcting for imperfections in the low-cost housing market. A local community may seek the housing project because it will create jobs in the construction industry and/or provide an outlet for investment opportunities. Another purpose could be that locating public housing in a particular area might offset a pattern of residential segregation. Any complex law is the result of a compromise between many interested parties. The blunt political fact is that laws have many purposes—some manifest, some latent, some acknowledged, and some vehemently denied. In this frame of reference, to judge social welfare laws by the standards of intent is overly simplistic. Often the expressed intent, the manifest intent, and the latent intent are quite different.

The problem of separating the various components and consequences of domestic social welfare policy is difficult. Social welfare ends are promoted or retarded as a consequence of policy shifts throughout the whole of society, not only as a result of what is done by public welfare oriented programs. At the most general level, we can say that a society seeks to maximize societal benefits and minimize social costs.

Social goals do not exist in a political vacuum. In the American political system, a continuum of value systems (ranging from conservative to liberal) complement each other as social welfare organizations are shaped and transformed.[1] Overall, liberal values generally are more likely to be oriented toward having the government play a more dominant role in meeting social problems; promoting greater

---

[1] In popular discourse, the terms *liberal* and *conservative* are often used for their popular appeal rather than their descriptive merit. Nonetheless, they retain a certain utility as a shorthand expression for views about the way governments can use or abuse power in responding to social problems.

equality of opportunity if not of income or wealth; and having consumers, service providers, and program participants play more active roles in social decisions. Conservative values typically are more likely to be oriented toward using the power of the market place to prevent the occurrence of social problems; placing a greater reliance on family, church, neighborhood, and voluntary institutions to soften the consequence of societal or individual failure; and justifying the presence of inequality based on merit and inheritance. In either value context, or in a merged context, social institutions must be structured to yield well-thought-out programs of intervention.

Dimensions for Choice

Gilbert and Terrell (1998) believe that social welfare policies can be interpreted as choices among principles determining what benefits are offered, to whom they are offered, how they are delivered, and how they are financed. They express these dimensions of choice in the form of four questions:

1. What are the bases of social allocations?
2. What are the types of social provisions to be allocated?
3. How will these provisions be delivered?
4. What are the ways these provisions will be financed? (p. 55)

According to Gilbert and Terrell, the development and implementation of social welfare policies is influenced in important ways by the following: the range of available alternatives, the social values that support them, and the theories or assumptions that underlie them.

One of the most persistent questions in the design of social welfare programs is whether aid should be targeted to a specific population in need or provided in the same way for all. The social welfare planner typically finds that it makes sense to design unique welfare programs for well-defined categories of persons in need. For example, most would agree that the income security needs of the aged, the single parent, and the unemployed are quantitatively and qualitatively different. A specific strategy designed for one group might be totally undesirable for a second group. We may wish to encourage the aged to leave the labor force, but to encourage the younger unemployed to do all that can be done to find a job. One program for both would most likely not make sense.

Political difficulties, however, immediately arise. As a society, we clearly do not want to aid equally all those in need. Once a category of persons is separated out for purposes of planning, that group is subject to political speculation. Senior citizens, because of their organized political power, their specific historical conditions, and the beliefs we hold about individual responsibility, are almost certainly to be aided more generously than, say, a politically disenfranchised population such as unmarried mothers or recovering addicts, both of whom are often seen as more responsible for their conditions of need.

Stages of the Political Process and Social Work Roles

The process of choice in social welfare policy planning involves a series of iterative steps, and the social worker engaged in policy practice needs to accomplish different tasks at each step. Furthermore, distinct roles must be played if the political process is to have any chance to work. Some social workers need to function as advocates for a particular approach, while others are expected to provide public officials and high-level administrators with knowledgeable advice.

Suppose that a problem is identified as needing public attention. A course of action needs to be identified. Knowing, or agreeing, that government should act does not tell us what government should do and at what level. Is poverty better eliminated by job creation, social service, or government cash transfers? Presumably all, but at what mix? Strands of intervention need to be identified and their benefits and costs made known as far down the road as possible.

A course of action needs to be selected according to the dimensions of choice noted earlier, followed by a legislative process designed to implement that course of action.

Policy ideas are general statements of a linkage between a public problem and a social cause of the problem; *formulation* is the process that translates these broad policy ideas into specific proposals for action. Suppose, for example, long-term and persistent unemployment is seen as associated with worker characteristics, rather than general economic conditions or defects in the labor market system. The individuals who champion this perspective need to develop a specific action strategy. A job corps concept, for example, is one way of providing education and training to "hardcore" unemployed. Detailing how a job corps would work, who would be selected to participate, and where the centers will be located sets off political conflicts. The amount of detailing that goes into policy formulation varies from bill to bill, but in any formulation specific public actions are linked with specific targets.

Legislative legitimization of public policy is at the core of the policy cycle. Understanding what has happened and what can happen is crucial to influencing the policymaking process and its outcomes. At the same time, there is a desire that legislation be made to conform to the demands of the logical conditions for rationality and the normative conditions for a democratic rule. Too often these demands are in conflict with one another. The political feasibility of a policy formulation refers to the capacity of a formulated policy to attain a majority consensus. We all know of many policies that are technically efficient but politically unfeasible because they contain features unacceptable to a sufficient number of citizens with the capacity to block their passage.

An empirical examination of the origins of social welfare policy formulation reveals that who is included or excluded in the formulation stage fundamentally shapes the structure of the policy debate and resulting formulations presented to the legislature. Those involved in the formulation often do not (even within their own minds) have clear priorities or goals. Personal ambitions, crosscutting loyalties, and many other factors thus enter into the formulations presented. Finally, to the dismay of many, the success of certain proposed policies is often compromised by a lack of trust or respect between political decision makers and program experts.

Administration and the Delivery of Social Welfare Services

Social welfare policy does not begin or end with the passage of a law. Once the law is adopted and funded, it must be implemented, most often by administrators of social welfare agencies.

The social welfare agency is many things to many people. It is a place where people go for help when problems occur and a place society holds responsible for addressing specific problems. It is also a place of employment for some and a setting for voluntary action by others. With the multiple motives of multiple actors, there is no single purpose of the social agency but rather a myriad of purposes. Above all else, the major task of the social welfare agency's administrator is to bring resources, opportunities, and goals together in such a way that a variety of social missions are accomplished. Management activities are not the sole responsibility of agency administrators. All staff of the agency, the members of the board of directors, and the agency's clients play vital roles in the administrative process.

ADMINISTRATIVE STRATEGY

The administrative processes of an agency can be thought of first as a strategic task. **Strategy** is ongoing, dynamic thinking formulated to analyze problems and to establish specific objectives. This process may best be described as a cycle of administrative activity (see Figure 7.1). The parts of the cycle are as follows:

1. *Strategic formulation*—analysis of problems and of objectives with input from staff, community leaders, those with funding authority, clients served, and the media
2. *Planning and budgeting implementation*—development of specific budgets, resource budgets, fiscal budgets, and time budgets, and deployment of these resources
3. *Control and management*—direction of activities, which are constantly evaluated, establishing a feedback loop back to strategic formulation

To be effective, the cycle must involve feedback based on an analysis of data generated by those working directly with clients and community groups to enable a more precise problem formulation at the highest level of the organization. While it is typical to think of strategic formulation as the first phase of the administrative process, strategic formulation is

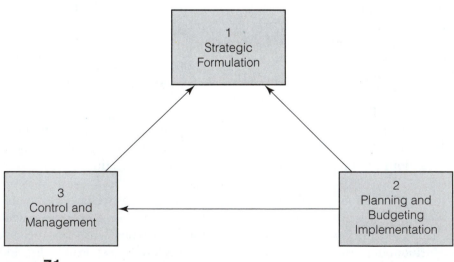

FIGURE **7.1**

THE ADMINISTRATIVE CYCLE

also the product of many previous administrative cycles.

APPLYING A SYSTEMS/ECOLOGICAL PERSPECTIVE

A key aspect of strategic planning is the recognition that the problems addressed lie far beyond the control of any given agency. As the board members, with the assistance of the executive director, contemplate these problems and the appropriate responses, they find that opportunities, risks, resources, and responsibilities interact and reverberate along the way. A systems/ecological perspective suggests that an agency's resources and its goals overlap and interact. Clearly, the goals specified influence the capacity to generate resources, just as the manner in which resources are obtained and the nature of those resources affect and change the agency's goals.

Netting, Kettner, and McMurtry (1998) propose a framework for analyzing human service organizations that involves the following tasks (see Table 7.1):

- Identify sources of cash and noncash revenues.
- Determine client population(s) and referral sources.
- Identify other important organizations in the agency's environment (for example, state and federal regulatory agencies, professional associations, labor unions, and accrediting bodies).
- Understand administration, management, and leadership style.
- Understand organizational and program structure.
- Assess the organization's programs and services.

TABLE 7.1	ORGANIZING PRINCIPLES OF SOCIAL AGENCIES	
Resource Base	**Some Examples**
Clients	Children, delinquents, workers with disabilities, retired persons
Fiscal base	Public, private, voluntary funds
Social work method	Direct practice, case management, advocacy
Human resources	Paid staff, volunteer staff, mixed staff
Mandate	Legislative mandate, United Way charter, license to practice

- Access personnel policies, procedures, and practices.
- Access adequacy of technical resources and systems such as budget management, facilities, equipment, and computers.

Each of these tasks involves responding to a series of questions designed to illuminate the key administrative, operational, and funding characteristics of the agency.

In administering any social agency, five essential elements must be considered: the agency, its clients, its product, its goals, and its staff. A specific agency has a set of social programs related to its service or product and its goals. The fit between the agency's product and its goals is one way the agency is judged. An essential administrative task is to achieve an optimal fit between the product and the goal. Similarly, the product and the staff must have some degree of congruence, if the agency is to operate efficiently. The staff members clearly need the training and competency to deliver the service effectively or to produce the product. Since social agencies tend to be labor-intensive organizations, assuring such staff readiness is a crucial aspect of administering an agency.

An outreach social worker provides food for a homeless man. Outreach vans offer food, clothing, blankets, and information about resources to the city's homeless. After developing trusting relationships with outreach social workers over time, many homeless ask them for help in accessing suggested resources.

AP Photo/Angela Rowlings

Weighing the Client's Best Interests

Social service agencies that represent clients with little or no political power have very special problems. Too much concern with the needs and desires of clients served can erode the economic and political support necessary for the very existence of the agency. But too little concern can result in exploitation of the clients the agency purports to serve.

Another concern faced by social service administrators is who makes what choices? Children, the mentally ill, persons with developmental disabilities, and others may not know what is in their best interest. Often, the agency is left to make such decisions. Both the complexity of the situation and the number of available options influence these decisions.

The professional social worker in the social service agency needs to steer between two dangers. Rigid adherence to the rules that govern the agency or the wishes of those who fund the agency can result in a subtle but debilitating form of tyranny. On the other hand, over-involvement of clients in decisions that affect the structure and nature of the services being offered can result in a limited agency perspective. Of course, the best course of action is to involve clients in a meaningful way while maintaining the integrity of the agency's overall decision-making process.

SOCIAL WELFARE AGENCIES: A HISTORICAL OVERVIEW

Since the early days of the United States, the responsibility for providing social welfare services has been split between government and the **private sector,** nongovernmental agencies that may be either nonprofit or profit oriented (see Table 7.2). The government was not expected—or able—to deal with the diverse circumstances associated with human needs. Sectarian, or church-related, groups generally administered private sector agencies at the local level. They provided the more intensely personal social services, such as those in orphanages, nursing homes, adoption agencies, and family counseling centers. Both the churches and professional social workers vigorously defended the notion that the government should stay out of the private social service sector.

Sometimes public and private agencies have been rivals, sometimes unwilling partners. The shape and structure of one at any point in time cannot be understood without reference to the other. The primacy of the voluntary effort in the 19th century was challenged by the social reform movement of the progressive era (1890 to 1920). The reform effort was split irrevocably following Woodrow Wilson's administration. State responsibility was for cash aid to the deserving poor, and the provision of social services was the responsibility of voluntary efforts. Following the Great Depression, government public assistance and social insurance programs replaced the previously provided cash aid function. The **voluntary sector** jealously guarded its independence from government.

The spirit of earlier cooperation resumed on a small scale in the 1950s, when voluntary agencies began to accept grants and contracts to deliver highly specific child welfare services. This relationship mushroomed in the mid-1960s, when Great Society programs funded "old" social work agencies to provide many of their "new" activities. During this time, public funds began to play the dominant role in the total budget for private voluntary agencies. Some social workers in the private sector raised questions about whether the heavy reliance on public dollars would affect the

TABLE 7.2   WELFARE RESPONSIBILITIES DATED ABOUT 1900

Public	Private Nonprofit
State	**Sectarian (Faith-based)**
Chronically mentally ill	Moral supervision
Prisoners	Orphan homes
Child welfare	**Nonsectarian**
Aged	Advocacy
Local	Settlement houses
Outdoor relief to widows and half-orphans	

autonomy and integrity of the private agency. Paradoxically, this period (1965 to 1980) saw the growth of advocacy organizations engaged in monitoring the performance of public actions and working to influence the quantity and quality of public funded social service expenditures. No doubt, these activities contributed to the significant rise in public spending for social services.

The Reagan administration eliminated much federal support for legal aid, social services, and organizing activities. The Bush administration, with its "Thousand Points of Light" programs, encouraged returning direct social service functions to private charity. The Clinton administration sought to separate its service strategy from the traditional New Deal approach of turning problems over to government. The Clinton administration and Congress had substantial disagreements over the role of the federal government in the provision of social services, but both administrations agreed there needed to be growth in the voluntary sector. In light of the restructuring of public responsibilities for welfare and state and federal welfare laws of the 1990s, both voluntary and for-profit social services expanded to match public withdrawals.

In campaigning for the 2000 presidential election, candidates from both major political parties pushed for a greater involvement of "faith-based" agencies in meeting human needs. They argued that private charity can and should meet the needs for service assistance that are being created by the curtailment of publicly funded social programs. We do not know how these arguments will turn out, but it appears that 21st-century social agencies will be different from 20th-century ones.

CONTEMPORARY STRUCTURE

Today, organized social service activities clearly are not limited to those provided directly by governments, by sectarian (faith-based) agencies, and by private nonprofit agencies. The private nonprofit sector of the social services system employs a majority of the social workers engaged in social work practice with individuals, groups, neighborhoods, and communities. The **private nonprofit social agency** is private in charter and organization but public in function. Neither the economic model of the private firm nor the public finance constructs of the public enterprises quite catches the essence of its operations. Private nonprofit agencies provide a host of services ranging from prenatal to bereavement programs to individuals, groups, neighborhoods, and communities. They also serve as an organizing entity and conduit for charitable funds and voluntary efforts, with tax dollars commingled and channeled to specific projects.

Three interdependent parts make up the social service portion of private nonprofit agencies. A specific agency can represent one or all three parts:

- Agencies that serve public and charitable purposes but serve principally for fund raising and planning, such as the United Way
- Advocacy organizations, which bring together a group of like-minded persons who seek to generate government funding or promote public understanding and support of a specific social problem area or a specific class of persons deemed to be in need, such as the aged or persons with disabilities (advocacy organizations are in essence political interest groups that attempt to garner support, including public spending, for their causes)
- Direct service agencies that deal with particular clients with specific or multiple problems of social functioning

Voluntary agencies are bounded on both sides—on one side by the private, profit-oriented approach of the free market, and on the other by a politically driven **public sector.** Governed by neither marketplace nor voting booth, voluntary agencies can be creative and innovative. But they are also vulnerable to their own excesses and to the expansionary drive of both profit and public enterprises. Thus, any agency may exist only briefly. Much like business firms, there are very few agencies that have existed for 100 years or more, a small number of agencies in their middle years, and a plethora of new agencies (those less than 10 years old).

A great deal of nostalgia persists about the voluntary approach with its emphasis on cooperation between private and community initiatives. Former President Reagan lauded the spirit of the free and vigorous voluntary way, in which communities, out of love, rebuilt the barn and cared for the victims of disaster in a warm, heartfelt, caring way. Conservatives listened to his message and feared the loss of a world that never was. Liberals listened to his message and recognized it for what it was—a historical inaccuracy. We cannot return to a voluntary way, not only because today the world is more complex but principally because the voluntary spirit, then as now, responded only to a small section of the total problem. The voluntary agency, in fact, has expanded as the public sector has expanded. Today, only a small segment of our social welfare problems is responded to by the voluntary sector.

It is likely that the 21st century will see an increasing number of mergers between private nonprofit agencies, more government funding contracted to both private nonprofit and private for-profit agencies, and greater emphasis on empirical accountability. These expectations call for administrators with solid social work knowledge, values, and skills.

RESEARCH

Clients cannot be helped, social welfare policy cannot be made, and agencies cannot be administered effectively without adequate research. Given the increased demand for accountability by those who fund social welfare programs, research plays an ever-increasing role in determining how resources are allocated. Even more important, social work as a profession is committed to empirical research to generate new knowledge and evaluate practice methods to ensure that client systems at all levels are understood and adequately served. Research is a required component of the BSW curriculum for these reasons.

Research, in its most general sense, refers to any disciplined strategy of inquiry. The term sometimes elicits an image of a white-coated individual in a sterile laboratory, but this conception is unduly restrictive for our purposes.

On the other hand, research is sometimes equated with the mere gathering of facts. For our purposes, this concept is too broad. Research within a profession such as social work has many manifestations, but in this chapter we focus on three reasonably specific types of research: (a) disciplinary research, (b) policy research, and (c) evaluative research.

All three types are scientific in that all depend on the scientific method. All three are objective in that the investigator is required to conform to established canons of logical reasoning and formal rules of evidence. Furthermore, all three are ethically neutral in that the investigator does not take sides on issues of moral or ethical significance. Each mode seeks to generate a proposition, or set of propositions, capable of falsification. Although similar in their demand for objectivity, each of the modes has its own specific purposes.

Disciplinary Research

Disciplinary research is the term used to distinguish investigations designed to expand the body of knowledge of a particular discipline. In general, that means to expand or modify the understanding of social, political, economic, and psychological processes so that social behavior can be explained. The intent is explanation for its own sake.

Disciplinary research begins with a paradigm or perspective that structures the research, the research goals, and the research methods used to analyze a particular topic. The paradigm directs the investigator as to where and how to seek evidence. Complex social behavior cannot be explained except in terms of a paradigm. The political scientist, the economist, and the sociologist each would describe, analyze, and explain identical phenomena in different ways. No single one is right and the others wrong; rather, each paradigm generalizes its own special insight into the problem at hand. The various perspectives have advantages and disadvantages. They allow researchers within a particular discipline to build on the work of others in their field. Social workers must make use of all these paradigms in their efforts to identify a pragmatic method of intervention. The desire to understand the intergenerational transmission of poverty and dependency can be used as an illustration. Investigators tend to agree that psychological immaturity, social isolation, and lack of economic alternatives produce multigenerational welfare. Investigators know that; they also know that when all three factors are present, the likelihood of multigenerational poverty becomes very large.

The social investigator is interested in providing an explanation of why something happened. The first step in this inquiry is to identify a dependent variable (that which we wish to explain) and show how it is related to one or more independent variables (those factors that produce changes in the dependent variable.) For example, as changes in economic and social circumstances (independent variables) occur, observable changes in employment opportunities (dependent variables) occur.

Careful selection of independent and dependent variables, careful use of both inductive and deductive reasoning, and precise application of the established rules of evidence are required to produce correct inferences about relationships. This is what is meant by an explanation.

The glue that holds together a disciplinary investigation is theory. A **theory** is a set of logically related, empirically verifiable generalizations that intend to explain relationships clearly. Since the process of theory building and research is cyclical and constitutes a single feedback loop, we can break into the process at any point.

A theory is derived from a set of generalizations. No one theory is right or wrong; some are more useful to understand and predict outcomes than others. The theory, in turn, sparks a **hypothesis,** which focuses attention on certain observations, which then yield more carefully phrased empirical generalizations (see Figure 7.2).

Sometimes the research process begins with observation. For example, the renowned 19th-century French sociologist Emile Durkheim (1897/1997) looked at crude data on suicides and found that suicide rates were lower for Catholics, married persons, and people in rural areas. The common feature of

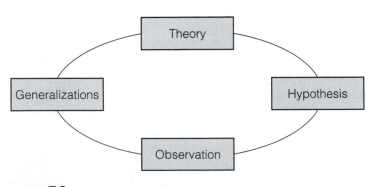

FIGURE **7.2**

THE INVESTIGATION PROCESS

these correlates was a sense of social involvement. This led him to articulate and link the theory of "anomie," or the sense of being without norms and standards, and suicide. Legions of scholars have deduced various hypotheses from Durkheim's groundbreaking work, which led to a number of empirical generalizations about the social consequences of anomie. These have been adopted into practice modes to reduce the sense of anomie via specific practice methods.

Policy Research

Policy planners and policy advocates discussed earlier in this chapter frequently use specific research methods to assist them in their efforts. A political decision maker desiring to resolve uncertainties before making a policy choice often seeks the aid of policy research. In deciding whether to expand substance abuse programs, for example, legislators will want to know more about the effectiveness of various types of intervention.

Policy research is a specialized form of inquiry whose purpose is the provision of reliable, valid, and relevant knowledge for public officials, agency managers, and others in the decision-making processes of government. It is used (or misused) at all levels of government and at all bureaucratic strata. Research studies employ techniques that vary from the simple collection and collation of available data to the design of sophisticated prediction models or social experiments.

Scientific research does not guide or control policy choices. History is replete with examples of public officials rejecting the advice of the research community. The rejection of research findings does not inevitably lead to negative results, nor does the acceptance of the recommendations of the research community

always yield the intended beneficial results. Deciding on the contribution to and limits of the research to public decision making is a complex topic (Weaver & Dickens, 1995). For example, if welfare benefits are to be raised and if eligibility standards are to be broadened, then there will be obvious consequences. There may be agreement about these consequences by those who have long studied the problem, but the value placed on each consequence can be enormously different. Reducing the policy uncertainty surrounding policy formulation and evaluating the consequences of policy implementation are central tasks of policy research. How a society uses the outcomes of policy research is a political issue. Politicians will often select the theory that best fits the ends or goals they seek. Just as expert medical testimony is used, and often misused, by both prosecution and defense attorneys in the same case, so, also, is social science used and misused for political gain.

Today, almost all graduate schools of social work have created concentrations of study designed to prepare the professional social worker to assist in the formulation and analysis of policy. Classes in advanced social work research are an integral part of such concentrations.

Problems arise in the design, execution, and interpretation of research for specific policy choices that are not encountered in disciplinary research. Policy analysis frequently is expected to produce specific kinds of information in a short time on a limited budget. Policy and disciplinary research differ in other ways as well. Both are governed by the canons of scientific methodology. Disciplinary research is structured to develop theoretically relevant explanations of social phenomena. But policy research is structured to identify, assess, and evaluate public strategies used to produce public ends. Policy research is both an art and a scientific process (Rubin & Babbie, 1997). Social workers are frequently called on to be both creative and scientific in conducting policy-relevant research studies.

The importance of policy-relevant research cannot be underestimated. All too often, social policies are formulated that have no empirical basis. Such policies are doomed to fail at some point because they do not reflect the realities of the situation(s) they address.

Evaluative Research

Policy evaluation is a specific kind of policy research used to assess the efficacy of a policy or set of policies or to measure the impact of a particular type of practice intervention. The typical starting point of **evaluative research** is to review the literature generally available. This task is made easier today due to search tools available via the Internet. Once the literature search has been conducted, the social worker can examine the information for common trends, unique differences and gaps, or unexplored areas. Few social problems are brand new, and an examination of how others deal with similar problems is a valuable way to use existing knowledge to evaluate practice and policy options. Sometimes the investigation is very specific, such as what happens to emergency room use when a particular payment method is introduced or which type of intervention works best with depressed adolescents. Sometimes it is very general, such as how applications for food stamps fluctuate with shifts in the economy. The social worker who serves as an adviser to policymakers needs to be alert to methods of dealing with such questions.

Evaluation, when competently done, measures the extent to which a program attains its goals. In evaluative research, the practitioner seeks to use the scientific method as the basic analytic tool in determining the program's impact. Because social work research rarely takes place in controlled laboratory conditions, specific research designs have been developed to maximize the likelihood of determining relevant results (Tutty, Rothery, & Grinnell, 1996). The principal task of the evaluator is not just to show success or failure but to indicate the range of certainty with which that judgment is made.

In addition to evaluating the effectiveness of social work programs, social workers also evaluate the effectiveness of their direct work with clients. **Single-subject designs** (Tripodi, 1994) are often used to evaluate the impact of interventions or policy changes on a single client or case. Such designs are typically used by social workers in clinical settings.

Identifying Goals   The evaluative process begins with an identification of the goals to be evaluated. This step seems obvious but in fact is a difficult task. Initially, there is the problem of ranking goals in order of importance and designed outcome. Second, the evaluator needs to identify and state clearly the goals that will be measured. Third, the evaluator considers the undesirable consequences of a particular policy action, program, or intervention. Social science methodology often is overwhelmed by attempts to measure too many goals at the same time. Thus, care in goal identification is a critical first step in devising a policy-relevant evaluation plan.

Formulating Operational Definitions   The second critical step is the selection of valid and reliable measures of positive and negative outcomes of the interventions, programs, or policy being evaluated. To be evaluated objectively, such outcomes must be defined in measurable terms; that is, operational definitions that define specific concepts and terms to be studied must be formulated. Once that is done, appropriate measures can be identified. A valid measure is one that measures what it is intended to measure. Reliable measures are measures that produce consistent results over time or between different observers. In social work programs, the evaluator has the responsibility of demonstrating that the "observed" changes are valid and reliable estimates of the impact of the intervention, policy action, or program. The test of success must stand up to criticism from the scientific and political communities. Thus, attention must be paid to the permanency of the impact, the reproducibility of the observation of success, and the reliability of the observation.

Demonstrating a Causal Connection It is insufficient to report that a favorable outcome occurred while an intervention, program, or policy was in place. The evaluator has to demonstrate that the outcome reasonably can be attributed to the intervention, policy action, or program and not to some other intervening factor. For example, if an intervention is developed to help children adjust to their parents' divorce, we need to be able to demonstrate that the children were better adjusted because of the intervention, not because of time spent with sympathetic teachers or relatives, or merely because the children grew older and the length of time since the divorce increased.

In the classical research design, the evaluator uses both theory and probability to increase the likelihood that the observed relationship is in fact a causal relationship. Theory is used to select the observations to be made. Theories thus guide observations and lead investigators closer to a realistic understanding of the relationship between observed outcome and the program or policy action. The real

understanding depends on the adequacy of the theory.

Second, social work researchers need to be keenly aware of chance as an alternate explanation for observed results. Fortunately, statistical tools are available that allow the researcher to calculate the probability that the observation would occur by chance rather than because of the intervention. Regardless of the level of sophistication of the researcher or the statistical tools available to analyze the results, the researcher cannot prove that A caused B. The best he or she can do is to conclude that there is a strong relationship between the two. Thus, social science evaluation can be used to help decision makers reject bad policy, but it cannot help them select with certainty the "best policy." Causal relationships that seem clear on the basis of logic are often difficult to test in the real world.

In this section, we have used the term *experimental* impact in a technical way but not strictly in regard to the rigorous rules of formal experimental design. Also, we have not tried to deal with the many complex problems associated with the choice of research methods— surveys, field observations, field experiments, classical laboratory experiments, intensive case studies, and single-subject designs. The important point here is that social workers need to back their beliefs about a program's success or failure with both theory and valid, reliable observations.

PRACTICE RESEARCH

The practitioner-researcher problem-solving process consists of four phases, or levels, of research activity. Each level of inquiry builds on the levels that precede it, as illustrated in Table 7.3.

TABLE **7.3** FORMS OF RESEARCH BY LEVEL OF RESEARCH AND INTENT OF INQUIRY

	INTENT OF INQUIRY			
LEVEL OF RESEARCH	Distinguish Concepts and Identify Significant Variables	Describe and Measure Interaction of Variables	Establish Logically Connected and Verifiable Causal Paths among Variables	Locate and Isolate Manageable Variables to Alter Outcome
Level 1: Exploratory	Case studies X			
Level 2: Descriptive	X	Cross-case comparisons and surveys X		
Level 3: Explanatory	X	X	Field experiments and statistical tests X	
Level 4: Perspective	X	X	X	Practice research X

Level 1: Exploratory

Level 1 research is undertaken to acquire familiarity with a topic. This may be necessary because the investigator is exploring either an old topic for the first time or a new interest or because the subject itself is new or unstudied. The purpose of level 1 research is to seek out the facts and develop a structure for thinking about the various aspects of the problem.

For example, suppose you are interested in the topic of domestic violence. As a student, you would want to know several things: How is domestic violence defined? How extensive is the problem? Is there an increase in the actual incidence of domestic violence, or is the

increase only apparent because of better reporting? Do any important subcategories of domestic violence need to be studied separately? You would want to examine the literature on the topic and check the figures being reported, interview social workers and volunteers working at crisis centers and other domestic violence programs, and perhaps talk with survivors and perpetrators of domestic violence.

You might find, for example, that low-income families are treated in public clinics, whereas other groups are treated in private settings such as physicians' offices; and that clinic doctors, for whatever reason, are more likely to report suspicious injuries. If such is the case, the relationship between socioeconomic status and domestic violence is apparent, but not necessarily real. You might find that class is linked to verbal skills, and verbal skills are inversely linked to domestic violence. This tells you that the real association between class and violence is only indicative of a more fundamental (yet harder to observe) association.

After the initial review of the literature, exploratory studies tend to become somewhat more focused. The purpose of exploratory study is to focus attention, to learn what the important questions are. Exploratory studies most typically are conducted to satisfy an initial curiosity or a desire for a better understanding or to lay groundwork for more careful inquiry.

In this first level of study, an effort is made to define the central concepts of inquiry. Returning to the example of domestic violence, as a researcher you would have considerable difficulty using the same conceptual definition for legal, educational, practice, and policy purposes. Also, investigators disagree on points such as whether to include emotional abuse in the concept of domestic violence.

Level 2: Descriptive

Inquiry at this level seeks to establish the presence or absence of empirical regularities in the problem area. How is socioeconomic class associated with domestic violence? Are shifts observed in the reports of domestic violence from one social class to the next? Is the observed change a reporting artifact, or does the actual rate of incidents shift? An evaluator's first general question is, Does the appearance of an association reflect a real association? Do people who differ from one another on social class lines differ from one another in

regard to the dependent variable—in this example, the incidence of domestic violence?

Level 3: Explanatory

Once a relationship has been established, the researcher seeks to show not only an empirical regularity but a causal connection. A causal connection requires a causal chain of events, such as the association between education and communication skills and domestic violence. A formal theory is stated that links educational attainment to communication skills and communication skills to domestic violence. If this were established, there would be an explanation of why family and educational levels are connected as well as what could change the situation. The practitioner cannot easily change educational level. But it is possible to provide instruction and information on communication skills and thus break the links between education and domestic violence.

Level 4: Perspective

The goal of practice research is the assessment and redirection of practice. Knowledge is gained not for its own sake but for direct use in social workers' day-to-day activities. Practice research has been criticized as being too subservient to theory yet insufficiently based in theory. Until recently, practice wisdom and social work research developed as separate spheres. Only a narrow overlap existed between research and practice. In recent years, social workers in practice have begun to expand that overlap, particularly with evaluative research. Many more practitioners, for example, are using assessment instruments, such as behavior inventories, at various points to evaluate the effectiveness of their interventions with clients (Rubin & Babbie, 1997).

The Status of Social Work in Shaping Social Welfare Policy and Agencies

The social work profession has shared key roles in the shaping of social welfare policy and agencies with a number of other groups, including politicians, economists, psychologists, educators, attorneys, and, increasingly, lobbyists for various constituent groups. To strengthen its relationship with these other entities and its role as a key shaper of social welfare policies and programs, the profession has continued to seek new ways to maintain credibility in an increasingly technological and politicized society. One way the profession has increased its status has been through state and national licensing and certification programs.

Social workers' status as professionals depends on the presence of two conditions:

1. A recognized body of knowledge that can be transmitted
2. A defined and legitimized (often certified) area of activity

Certification as a professional by the state serves both a general and a specific purpose. Its general purpose is to protect the public from unwarranted claims by individual purveyors of a service. Its specific purpose is to protect the intellectual property rights of a person trained and educated to perform the service. Technologies change rapidly and are often shared across professional boundaries. This aspect is conspicuous in generalist practice, where there is shared theoretical knowledge. In the field of mental health, for example, a member of the general public would have difficulty distinguishing between the modes of intervention of a psychiatric social worker, a clinical psychologist, and an educa-

tional counselor or a person certified to function as counselor in a specific area such as drug or alcohol abuse.

It is often difficult to discern whether the real political purpose behind the certification of a professional is to protect an unsuspecting public or to protect the practice rights of a politically powerful professional group. Each professional group seeks to enlarge its own domain of practice, and each professional group seeks to make more restrictive the rights to operate within that domain. Each professional group seeks to justify its expansive and protective stance with the ethic of client interest. Social work professionals are not exempted from this generalization.

Social workers have been and are the implementers of social welfare programs. The National Association of Social Workers (NASW), through special task forces of its members and paid professional staff, has taken policy positions on a number of critical social welfare issues. The organization has received numerous national, state, and local awards for its outstanding advocacy for social welfare policy on behalf of clients at all government levels. Eighty-two NASW policy statements passed by its delegates on affirmative action, women in the social work profession, cultural competency in the social work profession, persons with HIV, health care, family planning and abortion, child welfare, welfare reform, and other social welfare issues can be found in the NASW (1997) publication *Social Work Speaks,* currently in its fourth edition.

Although NASW and social workers at all levels have taken strong stands on many policy issues, social work is not as central to social welfare in the shaping of policies as it should be. As a professional group, economists have staked that principal claim as the persons with the technical facilities required for program design and evaluation. Social workers' very role as implementers has often led policymakers to see them as performing fairly bureaucratic local-level delivery roles with little say in promoting new policy directions and innovations. Increasingly, social workers are saying that their practice knowledge is highly relevant to policy development. A clear challenge for the future is to find ways to make the practice knowledge, the local-level knowledge about effective interventions, a central part of policy development.

There are signs of a new professional commitment to training in policy practice. The University of Tilburg in the Netherlands has established a new program in social policy and management, open to social workers of the European Community nations. The Department of Social Policy and Social Work at the University of Tampere, Finland, has a master's degree program in comparative social welfare that seeks to blend policy, management, and practice perspectives with policy perspectives across national lines. Using this approach, each nation does not have to start fresh to design policy initiatives but can adapt the perspective of another nation to its own unique needs.

The making of social welfare policy is the result of a political process. In the main, the social work literature has neglected a methodology for intervention in that process, relying instead on teaching policy development from a case or historical perspective. Traditionally, policy analysis has used frames of reference to answer questions about who is covered by the policy, what benefits are provided, the form of delivery, and the financial source (for example, Gilbert & Terrell, 1998). This approach is changing. Analyses of the dynamics of policy—legislative, judicial, and administrative processes—are finding their way into social work writings.

Hard choices are to be made in the next decade: Should state or national governments play the lead role in the delivery and funding of social welfare programs? Should unmarried mothers under 18 be eligible for direct income support? To what extent, if at all, should the right to a publicly supported abortion be abridged? To what extent can a cultural group deviate from the general standards of child welfare? These are tough questions, and they involve technical, political, and value considerations. Regardless of the auspices of the social agencies in which they work, social workers must maintain a strong professional presence in both the policy and practice arenas at community, state, and national levels.

CAREER OPPORTUNITIES IN POLICY, ADMINISTRATION, AND RESEARCH

An almost infinite number of career opportunities are available for social workers in the areas of policy, administration, and research. Social workers are employed as policy analysts by many state and local government agencies, including those that oversee programs that provide public assistance, services to abused and neglected children and their families, services for individuals and their families who have problems with substance abuse, and services that address the myriad of other social welfare problems discussed in this text. Policy analysts work with state and federal legislators to initiate legislation, provide interpretations regarding the impact of proposed legislation, and oversee the implementation of legislation once it is passed. These individuals play a key role in interpreting policy to direct service practitioners in their agencies. Policy analysts are also employed by social action agencies such as the Children's Defense Fund and the Child Welfare League of America. They provide their constituents and allies with information about the impact of existing and proposed policies. Social workers also are employed as policy advocates, working for activist organizations advocating for the needs of the constituent groups served by their organizations. Many social workers work in policy-related jobs in the offices of state and federal elected officials as well as congressional and state legislative committees in areas such as health and human services. A social worker in this role might draft bills, meet with advocates for and against various pieces of legislation, and attend countless meetings and legislative sessions relating to bills on topics such as homelessness, child care, welfare reform, hate crimes, health care, child abuse and neglect, domestic violence, long-term care and nursing homes, and criminal justice. An increasing number of social workers are being elected to local, state, and national office and are playing important roles in strengthening our social welfare system in a number of ways.

Other social workers serve as agency administrators for public, private nonprofit, and private for-profit organizations that address the wide range of issues discussed in this text. Social workers serve as branch or division administrators or commissioners for large state agencies, heads of local government agencies, and heads of private agencies of all sizes. Many social workers, frustrated with the lack of services available in an area in which they work or have an interest, have successfully begun their own agencies. One enterprising woman, for example, had difficulty getting already-existing agencies that served persons with AIDS, overwhelmed by the number of gay male clients served, to address the needs of the Mexican American women with AIDS

with whom she worked. She began a small outreach program to several women that has now grown into a nationally recognized program that serves a large number of Latino women and their families.

Social workers also are engaged in a variety of research-related jobs. State social welfare agencies; federal, state, and local governments; United Way and other agencies that distribute funds for human services programs; and local agencies, both public and private, employ social workers in research roles to determine the needs of their clients' and evaluate the success of their programs. The emphasis on outcome measures for social services provided at all levels of society has increased the demand for social work researchers. As new knowledge is generated that relates to biopsychosocial relationships between social problems, social workers' knowledge of the systems/ecological framework and their emphasis on an interdisciplinary approach make them excellent candidates for research positions.

SUMMARY

Policy, agency administration, and research are key components of generalist social work practice. Social workers involved in generalist practice with individuals, families, and groups must rely heavily on their colleagues involved at the exolevels and macrolevels of generalist practice to be effective and vice versa.

Social welfare policy determines the way resources are allocated and how they are delivered. Who becomes a client with need, how clients are served, and the likelihood that they will get their needs addressed are primarily the result of social welfare policies. How and which social service agencies are funded and what roles staff, including social workers, play in those agencies are also largely determined by social welfare policy. Social workers play critical roles in developing and shaping policy at all government levels. Increasingly, social workers are being elected to political office. Social work as a profession is gaining credibility in policy arenas at local, state, national, and international levels.

Policy has shaped the historical development and current status of social welfare agencies. The first social welfare agencies were private nonprofit agencies. The Depression began a move toward emphasis on public nonprofit agencies to provide a variety of services, including public assistance and child welfare. Since the 1980s under Republican presidential administrations, there has been a move toward privatization of social welfare services to for-profit agencies and increased emphasis on volunteerism. However, because many social services and volunteer efforts by private nonprofit and profit-oriented agencies are funded by various public entities, there has been a blurring of roles and responsibilities as partnerships and alliances have increased. At the beginning of the 21st century, public, private nonprofit, and even profit-oriented agencies are becoming more similar to one another, with administrators facing similar issues regardless of the type of agency they oversee. Social workers in administrative roles bring critical profession-based knowledge, values, and skills needed to be effective in dealing with increasingly complex funding, political, and service delivery situations.

The wide range of activities that constitute social work research are paramount to effective social welfare policy and agency administration. In this chapter, we reviewed the specific steps in the research process and showed how each step builds on previous ones. If this chapter has one message, it is that policy, administration, research, and practice are not separate spheres but interrelated domains, each fundamentally dependent on the other. All social workers need to be involved in evaluating their efforts and continuing to generate new knowledge that can be used to strengthen social welfare policies and services.

KEY TERMS

disciplinary research	private sector
evaluation	public sector
evaluative research	single-subject designs
hypothesis	social welfare policy
policy research	strategy
private nonprofit social agency	theory
	voluntary sector

DISCUSSION QUESTIONS

1. What are some of the factors that need to be considered when shaping the direction an agency takes in developing and implementing new programs?

2. How many social service agencies in your community are public? How many are voluntary? Are there ones for which you are not sure?

3. Discuss the differences between the public and the voluntary social service agencies in your community.

4. Which of the local agencies do you think ought to be voluntary and which ought to be public? Explain why for each one.

5. What principle of separation into public and voluntary would you use for social service agencies in the United States? What principle of separation appears to operate in practice?

6. What roles should the social work profession play in the development and administration of social welfare programs?

7. To what extent do you think the practice of social work research helps efforts to assist a client?

8. Can you think of an example in which the research process and the practice process actually reinforce one another?

9. Select a social work–related topic of interest to you. What are some research questions you might address at each of the four levels of research discussed in this chapter?

INFOTRAC COLLEGE EDITION

To learn more about topics included in this chapter, enter the following search terms:

nonprofit sector

policy evaluation

social policy analysis

social welfare policy

social work research

ON THE INTERNET

http://www.utexas.edu/research/cshr/

http://www.cfpa.org/

http://www.mdrc.org/

http://www.urban.org/

http://www.clasp.org/

http://danenet.wicip.org/snpo/

http://www.indeppsec.org/

REFERENCES

Durkheim, E. (1997). *Suicide: A study in sociology.* New York: Free Press. (Originally published 1897.)

Gilbert, N., & Terrell, P. (1998). *Dimensions of social welfare policy* (4th ed.). Boston: Allyn & Bacon.

National Association of Social Workers. (1997). *Social work speaks: NASW policy statements* (4th ed.). Washington, DC: Author.

Netting, F. E., Kettner, P., & McMurtry, S. (1998). *Social work macro practice* (2nd ed.). New York: Longman.

Rubin, A., & Babbie, E. (1997). *Research methods for social work* (3rd ed.). Belmont, CA: Wadsworth.

Sabatier, P. (1999). *Theories of the policy process.* Boulder, CO: Westview.

Tripodi, T. (1994). *A primer on single-subject design for clinical social workers.* Washington, DC: NASW Press.

Tutty, L., Rothery, M., & Grinnell, S. (1996). *Qualitative research for social workers.* Boston: Allyn & Bacon.

Weaver, K., & Dickens, W. (1995). *Looking before we leap: Social science and welfare reform.* Washington, DC: Brookings.

SUGGESTED FURTHER READINGS

Children's Defense Fund. (1992). *Childcare under the Family Support Act.* Washington, DC: Author.

Edwards, R., Yenkey, J., & Altpeter, M. (Eds.). (1998). *Skills for effective management of nonprofit organizations.* Washington, DC: NASW Press.

Ewalt, P., Freeman, E., Kirk, S., & Poole, D. (Eds.). (1997). *Social policy: Reform, research, and practice.* Washington, DC: NASW Press.

Flynn, J. (1992). *Social agency policy: Analysis and presentation for community practice.* Chicago: Nelson-Hall.

Ginsberg, L., & Keyes, P. (Eds.). (1995). *New management in human services* (2nd ed.). Washington, DC: NASW Press.

Haynes, K., Michelson, J., & Mikulski, B. (1999). *Affecting change: Social workers in the political arena.* (3rd ed.). Boston: Allyn & Bacon.

Heffernan, W. J. (1992). *Social welfare policy: A research and action strategy.* New York: Longman.

Janssen, B. (1998). *Becoming an effective policy advocate: From policy practice to social justice.* Pacific Grove, CA: Brooks/Cole.

Johnson, H., & Broder, D. (1996). *The system.* Boston: Little, Brown.

Kirk, S. (1999). *Social work research methods: Building knowledge for practice.* Washington, DC: NASW Press.

Meenaghan, T., & Kilty, K. (2000). *Policy analysis and research technology.* Chicago: Lyceum.

Perlmutter, F. (1990). *Changing hats: From social work practice to administration.* Washington, DC: NASW Press.

Specht, H. (1990). Social work and the popular psychotherapies. *Social Service Review* 64: 345–57.

Potocky-Tripodi, M., & Tripodi, T. (Eds.). (1999). *New directions for social work research and practice.* Washington, DC: NASW Press.

FIELDS OF PRACTICE AND POPULATIONS SERVED BY SOCIAL WORKERS

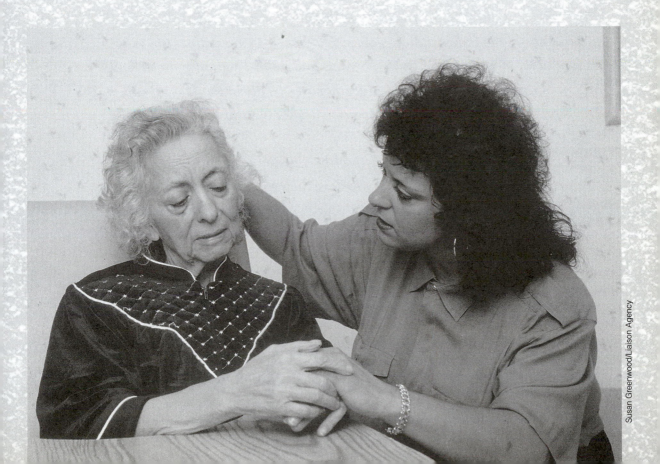

In this part of the book, you will explore many of the settings in which social workers practice and the special populations they serve. While not all settings and special populations can be presented in the limited space in this text, this section gives you an overview of the major social issues and populations that are the domain of the social welfare system and social work practitioners. Each chapter presents a broad systems/ecological perspective to help you understand the issues social work practitioners face in addressing the specific social issue or special population. You will also explore the specific roles and functions that social workers play in dealing with each field of practice and population served, so you will have an idea of what types of social work jobs are available in that field of practice and what the nature of those jobs entails.

In Chapter 8, "Income Assistance, Poverty, and Homelessness," we focus on how poverty is defined, why people are poor, who is poor in the United States, and what types of policies and programs exist to help reduce poverty levels in the United States. We also discuss the roles social workers play in the fight against poverty.

In Chapter 9, "Mental Health, Substance Abuse, and Developmental Disabilities," we explore definitional issues concerning mental health, mental illness, and developmental disabilities. We discuss historical and contemporary incidents that have shaped the way mental health problems are viewed and the types of mental health services available. We highlight several critical current mental health issues, including substance abuse and suicide. We also explore the many functions that social workers provide in this field of practice.

In Chapter 10, "Health Care," we offer an explanation of the present health care system in the United States, the problems it faces, and the types of health care policies and programs available. We also highlight a number of health issues, including increased costs of care, ethical decisions when balancing available technology with costs and needs, and AIDS. Health care is the fastest-growing area of employment for social workers today, and we also explore career opportunities for social workers in this setting.

Chapter 11, "The Needs of Children, Youth, and Families," gives an overview of the diverse types of families that exist today and the many issues even the healthiest of families face in our contemporary society. We also explore those factors found among healthy families, as well as those that place families more at risk to experience social problems. We focus on some of the issues families experience that may place individual family members at varying levels of risk, including divorce, alcoholism and other types of drug abuse, child abuse and neglect, and family violence. We also discuss issues more likely to be associated with at-risk adolescents, including teenage pregnancy, gang membership, and youth crime.

In Chapter 12, "Services to Children, Youth, and Families," we describe current policies and programs that attempt to prevent or alleviate the needs discussed in Chapter 11. We highlight the present service delivery focus on family preservation and other programs and policies whose goal is to keep families together. We also give you a chance to explore the diverse activities that social workers provide in serving children, youth, and families, including child protective services and school social work.

In Chapter 13, "Older Adulthood: Needs and Services," we discuss a special population that increasingly needs attention from the social welfare system and social work practitioners. We examine issues and needs that an older population creates for society, and we identify resources developed to provide physical and social support systems to meet their needs. Social work for the aged is a rapidly growing field, as more people fit this age category. Thus, you will also explore the types of activities in which social workers who assist this population are engaged.

In Chapter 14, "Criminal and Juvenile Justice," we discuss the nature of crime and the criminal justice system, including the roles of law enforcement, the courts, and the prison system. We have included a special section that gives you the opportunity to learn about the juvenile justice system and differences in treatment of adult and juvenile offenders. We also examine the roles that social workers play in providing services in the criminal justice system.

In Chapter 15, "Social Work in Rural Settings," we focus on an important segment of social work that is often not addressed. In this chapter, you will learn about important differences between rural and urban life and the implications for social workers who choose to practice in rural settings.

In Chapter 16, "Social Work in the Workplace," we explore a field of social work that is increasingly important as we consider changes in workplace demographics and the implications of those changes for employees and their families. We also discuss the importance of considering the impact of both the family setting and the work setting in understanding individual functioning and needs, and what social workers in the workplace do to help employees function better in the workplace and beyond.

In Chapter 17, "International Social Work," we discuss an exciting area of social work that has gained increased attention in recent years. We consider a number of global issues relating to economic development and social injustice and the many roles social workers can play in a variety of international settings.

As you learn about the fields of practice and populations with which social workers are involved in Part Three, ask yourself questions that draw from Parts One and Two. For example, as you read the chapter on poverty, ask yourself questions such as these: How do past and present social welfare perspectives and policies shape the ways people view poverty today and the ways poverty might be viewed in the future? What are the various roles the social work profession has played in addressing poverty? What types of social work intervention have been used to address clients who are affected by poverty? What types of intervention might be most effective in addressing client needs related to the issue? How can the systems/ecological framework help us in understanding issues relating to poverty, including who is more likely to be poor and why, the impact of poverty on individuals and families, and the impact of community, state, national, and international attitudes, policies, and programs that address—or fail to address—poverty? At what levels of the environment might it be most effective to intervene in reducing the numbers of individuals and families who are poor, and why? What are the relationships among factors such as race and ethnicity; gender, age, and sexual orientation; and living in poverty, and why?

CHAPTER 8

INCOME ASSISTANCE, POVERTY, AND HOMELESSNESS

Robert and Robin Warren, both aged 65, have just retired from very satisfying jobs. Their three grown children are well established with families and jobs. By any standard, the Warrens are well off, emotionally and physically. Financially, their retirement was planned around their employers' retirement plans and social insurance. Their annual retirement income amounts to just over $60,000. This, along with income derived from savings, means their retirement income is actually larger than their income during their working years. Neither Robert nor Robin thinks of their old-age benefits or their Medicare benefits as a form of welfare because, in their view, they paid for these through taxes while working. Robert wrote his congressional representative to complain about the health care reform package being proposed by Congress because he and his wife are already covered by a private plan, and both believed that such drastic changes would hurt them. In their working years, the social insurance system provided the Warrens with much-needed cash during brief periods of unemployment. Now the social insurance system has provided them with both security and income. While very happy with their income, both have worries about the future of Medicare funding, on which they are also dependent. While their children worry about the future of the Social Security program, the senior Warrens do not.

Mary Smith, widowed and aged 72, is also a recipient of social insurance. Her $684-a-month Social Security check provides 80% of her income. The remaining amount is from the invested income received from the sale of her home 6 years ago. She lives in a pleasant apartment, and with Medicare, she is covered for major illness and hospitalization. She is not covered for the more immediate threat of a long stay in a nursing home. Her investment income and Social Security payments would not be sufficient for the monthly fees, which run over $2,500.

Maria and Joe Saldana live in an inner-city area of a large city. Both in their early 30s, they have five children, ranging in age from 2 to 14. Joe works on construction projects and has received three promotions in 3 months. Maria worked in the housekeeping department at a local hotel when she could find child care for her younger children. When Joe's job picked up, she quit the hotel job. Joe and Maria have a combined annual income of $25,000—just over the poverty level for a family of seven. The rent for their two-bedroom house is $450 a month. Money spent for bus fare, utilities, and other necessities often leaves the Saldanas short on cash at the end of the month. Neither of the Saldanas works at a job that provides health insurance, which means that the family usually goes without medical care when someone is sick. Both of the Saldanas grew up living in poverty, and both quit school in junior high school to earn money to help their parents provide for their brothers and sisters. Although they have a strong value system and are hard workers, only recently have they found their hard work paying off. Before Joe found his construction job, he was unemployed for over a year when the local economy took a downturn and he was laid off. He and his family had to rely on Aid to Families with Dependent Children (AFDC) and food stamps to survive. During the transition from AFDC to full-time employment, the family retained eligibility for Medicaid and still qualifies for food stamps. They also qualify for Earned Income Tax Credit. They do not get this every month, but it is a major help in months when Joe's wages are down due to bad weather. Maria is thinking about going back to work, as her old job now pays 20% more than the minimum wage. Both think their income future is the best it has ever been, but they worry about recent legislative changes that have given states more options in addressing problems of unemployment and poverty. They are fearful that welfare as they knew it is no longer there in case the economy changes and they lose what they have.

Maria's sister, Alice, is not so well off. She is a single mother of three children and has not seen the father of her children since 6 months before her youngest child was born. For a while with AFDC (now Temporary Assistance to Needy Families, or TANF), food stamps, Medicaid, and subsidized public housing, Alice was better off than Maria. However, since changes in the state welfare program in 1998, her cash benefits and her food stamp benefits have declined by over 25%. Now she finds that her public housing assistance may also be threatened. Her monthly TANF allotment is scheduled to end in 3 months unless the current state law is changed or her caseworker grants her a rare exemption. Although Alice wants to work and dreams of becoming a nurse, she quit school at age 15 to support her younger siblings because her elderly parents were in poor health and unable to work much. Alice's limited job skills and her youngest son's serious health problems make finding a job that allows her to meet her financial needs, including affordable child care, difficult.

From the preceding stories, it looks as if the better off you are, the better the country's social welfare system helps you. Our social welfare system is structured to provide temporary help when income from work is disrupted. The social welfare system provides a tenuous safety net, but it is also structured to encourage quick reentry into the labor force, except for those who have left the labor force for retirement. The way the theory goes, gainful employment is supposed to keep people from a life of poverty and welfare dependence. In practice, it does not always work that way.

In this chapter, we look at the diverse thinking that has guided the U.S. poverty debate from colonial times to the present. As a society, we have been uncertain about the relative weights we wish to put on explanations of poverty linked to the person and explanations of poverty linked to the social and economic system. Even when we agree that individual responsibility needs to be enhanced, we debate between a strategy of deterrence and a strategy of compassion. The very goals of antipoverty programs are at the heart of the debate. To some the simple goal of the social welfare system is to help the truly needy but in a way that discourages dependency. To others the social welfare system should function to provide real opportunity to all citizens. Ideally, we would like to have a society with a guarantee against poverty but with the caveat that ensures that the family does all that it can to help itself.

MANY VIEWS ON POVERTY AND HOW TO HELP

Suppose that before you were born, you are given the following "opportunities":

- You are endowed with a native intelligence (whatever that is) above the normal range.
- Your parents are married, and they both love you and each other.
- One or both of your parents have a marketable job skill.

To be born with these three "opportunities," one is born to economic advantage. If one, two, or three of these opportunities are absent, you are at risk of being poor for part or all of your life. Antipoverty programs are designed to overcome or compensate for people who do not experience these "opportunities." In our society, your intellectual endowment, family, and employment opportunities influence most fundamentally your efforts to avoid not only poverty but also the stigma of being on welfare. In reality, social welfare policy can do little with respect to any of these three variables.

We do not know how much of one's intellectual endowment is genetic and how much is influenced by the environment. Furthermore, we do not know how much is immutable and how much is changeable. Few doubt, however, that verbal and mathematical skills are the strongest individual antipoverty weapons. *Poverty is concentrated among those who lack these skills.*

Intellectual endowment by itself, however, is not enough; it must be nurtured. In our society, nurturing has traditionally been the primary role of the family. If a child from birth to age 18 lives in a family in which the parent(s) enjoys continual employment in a job that pays enough for food, housing, and other necessities, the chances that the child will experience involuntary poverty at any time in his or her life are very low. Assuming one is paid at least a living wage, employment appears to be a strong deterrent to poverty at any time within one's life. Discussions about how to promote factors that are most likely to result in gainful employment, what type of safety net would be available for those not gainfully employed, and who should be supported by that net have become increasingly emotional in recent years.

Virtually no one is indifferent to poverty in the United States. However, very different ideas prevail about how to help the poorest in our society. The average citizen wants successful and efficient antipoverty programs, even if he or she is "against welfare." Some persons would like to transfer the public program responsibility to state governments, while others believe that federal leadership is both an economic and political necessity. Some prefer giving the poor cash; others want to restrict spending by providing aid as in-kind goods. Still others want to provide service and job training. Most people believe that a proper policy is some mix of cash, in-kind benefits, service, and training. Some want to limit the duration of federal assistance; others disparage that approach. Some are very concerned about the increases in nonmarital births. Some prefer a "tough love" approach that would limit direct assistance to very young single mothers. Others feel such an idea is out of touch with the real causes of poverty, dependency, and the rise of the number of births to unmarried women. Poverty and dependency are linked in the public mind. One thing is clear: the resolution of the poverty problem in a democratic society requires a healthy respect for those with distinct and different ideas about how best to conceptualize the problem.

Conceptualizations of Poverty

DiNitto (2000) defines five different approaches to the conceptualization of poverty in the United States: poverty as deprivation, poverty as inequality, poverty as culture, poverty as exploitation, and poverty as structure. Each of these conceptualizations is discussed further in the next sections.

Poverty as Deprivation   In this view, poverty is conceptualized as insufficiency in food, housing, clothing, medical care, and other items required to sustain a decent standard of living. This definition assumes that there is a standard of living (poverty level) below which individuals and families can be considered "deprived." Each year, the federal government computes the cash income (federal poverty income limit, or FPIL) required for individuals and families to satisfy minimum living needs. These figures are published every February in the *Federal Register,* a government document that includes federal proposed and final guidelines and regulations.

The 2000 FPIL for the 48 contiguous states and the District of Columbia is $8,350 for one person and $17,050 for a family of four ("The 2000 HHS Poverty Guidelines," 2000). Separate figures are also available for Alaska and Hawaii because the cost of living in these states is higher than that of the remaining states and the District of Columbia. Individuals with incomes less than $8,350 and families of four with incomes less than $17,050 are considered to be living in poverty. FPIL figures are adjusted annually to reflect changes in the **Consumer Price Index (CPI),** a figure used to adjust the prices of goods and services for inflation.

Poverty as Inequality in the Distribution of Income   In this view, some people perceive that they have less income than most Americans (relative deprivation) and believe they are entitled to more. One way to look at poverty as inequality in the United States is to measure the distribution of total personal income across various classes or groups of families. The most common method of achieving this is to divide American families into five groups, from the lowest one-fifth in personal income to the highest one-fifth. If each fifth of U.S. families received 20% of all family personal income, income equality would be achieved. The latest figures from the U.S. Bureau of the Census (2000) show this not to be the case. Rather, they indicate that the poorest fifth of U.S. families receive just over 4% of all family income. Conversely, the wealthiest fifth of U.S. families receive nearly 50% of all family income.

Poverty as Culture   In this view, poverty is seen as a way of life passed on from generation to generation. This conceptualization of poverty includes not only low income but also attitudes of hopelessness, indifference, alienation, apathy, and lack of incentives and self-respect. Proponents of this view would argue the futility of providing opportunities for upward mobility for the poor as they would be likely not to take advantage of them. This view of poverty is perhaps the most controversial as well as one that has generated the most debate among scholars and policymakers alike.

Poverty as Exploitation by the Ruling Class   In this view, more government assistance is seen as going to the middle and upper classes than to the poor. For example, the middle classes receive government assistance in the form of home mortgage loans and associated tax deductions. The wealthy receive government assistance through various income tax deductions, government contracts, and subsidies to business. Whatever this assistance, the middle classes and the rich receive more than their poor and near-poor counterparts in society. If this view of poverty prevailed, the only way to resolve it would be to radically restructure society to eliminate class differences.

Poverty as Structure   In this view, the continuation of poverty is fostered by institutional and structural discrimination. For example, poorer school districts typically receive fewer resources that can be used to purchase state-of-the-art technologies to support their educational programs than schools in wealthier districts. This results in the deepening of what has come to be known as the **digital divide,** or the gap between the technological competence of students enrolled in poor school districts compared to wealthy school districts.

Definitions of Poverty

Regardless of how poverty is conceptualized, the definition of poverty is elusive. **Poverty** generally means that a household income is inadequate as judged by a specific standard. The translation of this concept into practical terms produces ideological debate as well as technical problems. Even defining the term *household* for a census count is not simple. Is the unit to be composed of only the nuclear family, or do we count elders, boarders, roommates, foster children, and others who share the dwelling? Similarly, *income* is elusive. Should it include gifts or in-kind benefits provided by the employer or the government? What about goods and services traded in barter? What should the time frame be? How do we address the problem of wealth as opposed to income? Does volition enter into the notion? Should a Jesuit priest or Carmelite nun be considered poor? After all, they have vowed to be poor. What should the standard be? As each question is confronted, the problem of definition becomes more complex. As each question is given a specific answer, the numbers of persons considered poor changes. Several methods to define poverty are used today.

The Standard When the federal government began measuring poverty in the early 1960s, the continued existence of poor people in an "affluent society" was considered an anomaly. One idea favored by experts was to look at the distribution of income and make adjustments in terms of **relative poverty.** By this definition, after adjustments for family size are made, the lowest one-third, one-fourth, or one-fifth would be considered poor. One problem with this definition is that the proportion of the population of poor would remain constant, regardless of whether the economy worsened or improved or antipoverty

programs helped large numbers of individuals improve their standard of living.

Another way to measure poverty is to consider the relative income of the lowest income class. Measured in this way, our progress against poverty is not very good. After adjustments for family size, the lowest fifth's share continues to decrease, while the share of income to the richest fifth continues to increase (Citro & Michael, 1995).

A third way, the one used in the United States, is to measure poverty by the number of households with income below some fixed official standard. How the fixed standard is determined is one reason that different poverty rates are reported by various sources.

The Market Basket To counter this problem, public officials use a definition of poverty based on a **market basket concept.** Mollie Orshansky (1965) developed the market basket concept by some relatively simple calculations. She used a survey that determined the cost of a minimum adequate nutritional diet for families of different sizes. She used another survey to determine that families generally spend one-third of their income on food. Orshansky then multiplied the diet figure for a household of a given size by three, so that a family could purchase the minimum diet and still have twice that amount left over for housing and all other purchases. Since 1969, poverty thresholds based on this definition have been adjusted by taking into account the changes in the CPI. Poverty guidelines represent a simplification of poverty thresholds and are used by the federal government for administrative purposes to determine, among other things, who is eligible for federal poverty programs. The poverty guidelines for various-sized families for 1996 to 2000 are shown in Table 8.1.

TABLE 8.1	FEDERAL POVERTY GUIDELINES FOR DIFFERING FAMILY SIZES, 1996–2000				
Size of Family Unit	1996	1997	1998	1999	2000
1	$ 7,470	$ 7,890	$ 8,050	$ 8,240	$ 8,350
2	10,360	10,610	10,850	11,060	11,250
3	12,980	13,330	13,650	13,880	14,250
4	15,600	16,050	16,450	16,700	17,050
5	18,220	18,770	19,250	19,520	19,950
6	20,840	21,490	22,050	22,340	22,850
7	23,460	24,210	24,850	25,160	25,750
8	26,080	26,930	27,650	27,980	28,650

Note: Figures are for the 48 contiguous states and the District of Columbia. Separate figures are available for Alaska and Hawaii.

Source: U.S. Department of Health and Human Services (1999).

The "official measures" of poverty based on Orshansky's model used by the federal government count income from wages, salary, and self-employed income plus interest, dividends, and cash grants from the government. The measures do not estimate or consider the value of food stamps, Medicaid, or public housing subsidies. To count these benefits would lower the numbers of those considered poor. The calculation of the poverty line is made before taxes are paid or tax credits to be received are calculated. The wealth available to the household is counted for the real interest it produces, not for its purchasing potential. A *household* is defined as a group of not necessarily related individuals who share a domicile and share income and responsibilities for those in that domicile.

There is no economist's line in the sand that could account for the real dynamics of family incomes. It is nonetheless this line and the proportion of the population under this line that are used in calculating the proportion of the United States that is poor. Regardless of how poverty is measured, the important issues

to address are who is poor and why they are poor so that antipoverty programs can be developed that are relevant to these groups and their needs.

WHO ARE AMERICA'S POOR?

Many factors interact to determine who is poor in the United States. Four factors, however, predominate in affecting poverty demographics:

- Overall performance of the economy
- Composition of households within the nation (for example, more single-parent households headed by women) and their access to the economic system
- Levels of expenditure of social programs
- Types of programs implemented and the effectiveness of those programs.

The first factor significantly influences the others. If the free market economy cannot provide jobs that keep everyone above the poverty line, certain groups of individuals will be locked out of the opportunity structure that enables them to be self-sufficient.

Although most people's stereotype of a poor family in the United States is an African American single mother on welfare with three or more children living in an inner-city ghetto, the poor are a very diverse group. Most individuals on "welfare" in the United States are children, and many people who are poor live in two-parent families in which one or both parents work full-time, often with a second job. Table 8.1 shows, for example, that a single parent with one child who is employed in a minimum wage job at $5.15 per hour ($10,712 annually) would be living in poverty regardless of gender, ethnicity, or place of residence. See Box 8.1 for a description of one poor person's experience.

Table 8.2 reveals a great deal about who is poor in the United States. Overall, nearly 13% of all people are living in poverty. About one in 10 adults 65 years and older lives in poverty. Greater numbers of women live in poverty than men. This difference is particularly pronounced for the almost 30% of heads of households who are women. The poverty rates for African Americans (26.1%) and Latinos (25.6%) are some two-and-one-half times the rate for whites (10.5%). This pattern is even more dramatic when comparing the poverty rate of the nation's children under 18 years of age who live in poverty. Many individuals are surprised by the fact that one of every five children in the United States lives in poverty, when the country is portrayed as being so wealthy. This figure is nearly double for children who are African American (36.7%) and Latino (34.4%); in contrast, 15% of their white counterparts are growing up in poverty. The poverty rate for nonnaturalized citizens (22.2%) is nearly twice that for native-born individuals (12.1%). Interestingly, the poverty rate for naturalized citizens (11.0%) is slightly

	U.S. POVERTY RATES FOR SELECTED
TABLE 8.2	POPULATION GROUPS, 1998

Population Group	Percentage below Poverty
All persons	12.7
Children under 18	18.9
Persons 65 years and older	10.5
Female householder, no husband present	29.9
Gender	
Males	17.0
Females	22.6
Ethnicity (all persons)	
White	10.5
Black	26.1
Latino	25.6
Ethnicity (children under 18)	
White	15.1
Black	36.7
Latino	34.4
Nativity	
Native	12.1
Foreign born	18.0
Naturalized citizen	11.0
Not a citizen	22.2
Residence	
Inside metropolitan areas, inside central cities	18.5
Inside metropolitan areas, outside central cities	8.2
Outside metropolitan areas	15.9

Source: U.S. Bureau of the Census (1999).

lower than that of native-born persons. Poverty rates also vary considerably depending on where one lives. For example, the poverty rate for central cities of large metropolitan areas (18.5%) is more than double the rate for persons who live outside central cities of large

BOX
8.1

"So You Think I Drive a Cadillac?"

Terri Lynn is employed as a night cashier at a bowling alley across town. She continues to receive a partial welfare payment because the hours are sporadic and, at minimum wage, her income does not lift her above the eligibility of limits for aid. "But I wish I wasn't getting none of it," she told me. She's tried to get off welfare by taking computer classes at a for-profit business school in town. But after graduation, without experience, and without their help in finding employment, she could not find anyone to hire her. Instead, she found the job at the bowling alley and slowly works to pay off her tuition debts. Luckily for Terri Lynn, her mother or sister baby-sit her daughter for free, a savings of several hundred dollars per month. On her income and her small welfare grant, Terri Lynn would not be able to pay them or anyone else to take care of her child. She does not own a car, and neither does her mother or sister, so she relies on the bus to get to work. For Terri Lynn, transportation logistics are a nightmare. The bus ride takes over an hour and a half each way. Thus, between working and commuting, her daughter often spends 11 hours

a day with her childcare provider, in this case Terri Lynn's mother or sister. She is thankful she does not have to leave her with a stranger, and in an unfamiliar place, for such long periods of time. When she works late into the night and the bus has stopped running, she usually takes a taxi cab back to her mom's house, where her daughter is sleeping. The cab costs her $6.00, and cuts into a sizable portion of her minimum wage earnings. She cannot afford to take the cab all the way back to her own house on the other side of town.

> I leave here at 3:45, and get downtown at 4:15. Then I wait until 4:30 to catch the #7 bus. And then by the time I get there it's 5:05. And then I have to walk on down there, and I get there at 5:30 on the dot. But after work at 1:00 in the morning, I have to catch a cab because the bus has stopped running. So I catch a cab to my mom's house where she (daughter) is sleeping. I sleep there too, and then I get up real early so that we can catch the early bus back to my house so I can get her (daughter) ready for school. See, and by then I have to take her to school because

metropolitan areas (presumably in suburban neighborhoods).

Finally, many people assume that all poor people are on welfare. With increasingly limited access to education and the subsequent inability of those who are not well-educated to

obtain well-paying jobs, many individuals in the United States who fall below the poverty line work at least one and often two jobs. In 1998, the working poor constituted approximately 20% of families who fell below the poverty line (U.S. Bureau of the Census, 2000).

she'd done missed the school bus. After that I go back home and try to get some rest, and then, after school, I go back and pick her up. We take the bus back to my mom's house so she can watch her, and then I go to work again. So, I be running back and forth all day long.

Sometimes her brother is able to pick her up from work late at night, and take her and her daughter directly home, which makes their morning routine considerably easier. She told me, in no uncertain terms, that this assistance from her family was invaluable to her. Without it, she would not be able to work. Her daughter's father, in contrast, provides no emotional or financial support.

Terri Lynn has received welfare since her daughter was born 6 years ago. Is she "dependent" on the system? By traditional definitions of welfare dependency, yes. However, a cogent argument can be made that Terri Lynn's family provides at least as much assistance to her, if not more, than does the state. A closer look reveals a portrait of a hard-working young woman who is doing her best to improve the life condi-

tions for herself and her daughter. Yet, despite working hard, what are Terri Lynn's chances of beating poverty? Unless her income nearly doubles from her current minimum wage, her chances of pulling herself and her daughter out of poverty are slim at best. This is not because of her own laziness, personal inadequacy, or lack of family support, but because of structural features of the social system that snowball against poor women. Given the largely grim statistics of women's under-employment in general, what are the odds that a 24-year-old woman with a high school diploma, who is without reliable transportation, who needs childcare, and whose only work experience is in the service sector, will soon land the $8.00 to $10.00 per hour job needed to lift her out of poverty? Moreover, why does her daughter's father not contribute to her support? Can we really expect Terri Lynn, alone, to provide for all her daughter's emotional and financial needs without any help from the government?

Source: From Karen Seccombe, *So You Think I Drive a Cadillac?* Copyright © 1999 by Allyn & Bacon. Reprinted with permission.

Although significant sums of money have been spent on antipoverty programs in the United States since its inception, these expenditures have not been targeted at specific groups of the poor and increasingly meet only a small fraction of the total need. Therefore,

the number of poor people in this country has continued to rise, particularly for vulnerable populations such as people of color and female-headed households with children. Tracing how the needs of the poor have been addressed historically helps one see how we have arrived at the current provision of services and why these services are not working.

HISTORICAL CONTEXT OF AID FOR THE POOR

Structures and systems of aid for the needy are derived from the dominant social values of the historical period of time in which they are formulated. Social values change with the flow of history, and therefore attitudes toward and delivery of economic assistance to the poor also change with the flow of history. Following is a historical review of assistance to the needy in the United States, from early colonial times through the present. The reader will see that decisions about who should receive assistance, the type and amount of assistance to be provided, and the mechanism for providing that assistance are all affected by the dominant social values of the time.

Colonial America and Pre–Civil War Years: 1647–1860

In colonial America times were rough, life was austere, and there was not much money to go around. The social welfare response during this time was heavily influenced by the Poor Laws of Elizabethan England. The major focus was on controlling the poor, especially those who were unable to locate employment and who might cause disruption. The goal was to protect communities against strangers who threatened the stability of a society that was wary of new ways and different cultures. Strict residency requirements were enforced through such measures as "warning out" and "passing on" (Axinn & Levin, 1997, p. 21). Strangers who could not provide a reasonable

assurance of their financial independence and future contribution to the community were discouraged from membership in the community (warned out) and escorted out of town and told not to come back (passed on).

Poor residents of a community were classified as either "deserving"—orphaned children and adults who were "lame," blind, or unemployed through no fault of their own—or "nondeserving"—vagrants or drunkards considered to be lazy, shiftless, and unwilling to work. The nondeserving poor were often sent to a privately owned "workhouse," a publicly owned house of corrections, a poor farm, or an "almshouse" where care or "proper" punishment and hard labor could be more easily administered (Axinn & Levin, 1997, p. 19). "Indoor relief"—relief provided in a home other than one's own—was distinguished from "outdoor relief"—relief provided in an institutional setting such as a workhouse or an almshouse.

The apprenticeship of children was also a popular practice of the time. Unattached, neglected, or dependent children were often placed with persons willing to take responsibility for their care and who would educate and train them for some useful calling. Parents willing to accept responsibility for children were expected to recoup their expenses from the child's work. The apprenticeship of children reflected colonial society's concern with home life, work life, and the Christian life of the child (Axinn & Levin, 1997).

As noted earlier, the social welfare response of colonial America was heavily influenced by the Elizabethan welfare system, with its emphasis on local control of resources, individual and family responsibility, and the residency requirement of strict settlement. This response was also consistent with an important economic reality of colonial America: the fact that the colonial economy was one of extreme scarcity required that there be a minimum number of people who were unemployed.

The years between the American Revolution and the outbreak of the Civil War were characterized by major political, economic, and social changes. These changes were accompanied by rapid population growth, enormous geographic expansion, mechanization of farm and factory, and intense political and ideological struggles (Axinn & Levin, 1997). Between 1830 and 1860, consecutive waves of immigration resulted in over 5 million persons entering the United States, primarily from Ireland and Western Europe. Almost all of these immigrants entered and remained in the northern section of the country, where they congregated in large urban centers such as New York, Boston, and Baltimore.

Immigrants as a group were perceived as a threat to resident Americans. They were foreign and largely Catholic in a predominantly Protestant land. They were willing to take jobs at lower than generally accepted wages. Many arrived in need of immediate employment or emergency financial aid, thereby swelling the public assistance rolls and threatening to push an already precarious social welfare system over the edge.

The extensive industrialization and urbanization of this period led to many social welfare problems, the need for financial aid chief among them. The finding and holding of jobs became a necessity for maintaining family solvency. Extended family relationships became difficult to maintain because of the need for relocation and the necessity for adult family members to be away from the home for long hours at work. Increasingly, families were subject to forces beyond their control and a dependence on services provided from outside the family unit (Axinn & Levin, 1997).

The period 1776–1860 was a time of interesting contrasts. On one hand, there was an effort to address unemployment, the inequality of income distribution, and other social problems through a series of reform activities (the extension of suffrage, temperance, more effective poor relief, humane treatment of the insane, rehabilitation of criminals, child saving, and the abolition of slavery). On the other hand, most people continued to view economic need as a sign of individual failure. Public and private sources alike agreed that "the causes of poverty were to be found in individual character flaws and in organizations that encouraged and promoted dependency" (Axinn & Levin, 1997, p. 51). Overall, society's view of poverty and the plight of families in need changed little from that of the colonial period. Welfare legislation of the time continued to focus on individual and family responsibility. Local and state governments assumed the ultimate responsibility for the relief of individual suffering, but at the lowest possible cost to the taxpayer.

Post–Civil War Years to Early 1900s

The post–Civil War years and the first decade of the 1900s witnessed continued industrialization, heavy immigration, and migration from rural areas (particularly the South) into cities. At the same time, poverty problems intensified and the distinction between economic classes—primarily the "haves" and the "have nots"—became more pronounced. Government was generally reluctant to acknowledge social responsibility for poverty as well as to understand or appreciate being poor in the context of affluence. Large-scale immigration continued to pose a threat to wage standards as well as the employment of the existing native workforce.

In the immediate years following the Civil War, individual states focused their social welfare attention on wounded veterans and their families, widows and orphans of slain soldiers, and large numbers of freed African Americans. Sectarian and lay relief societies grew at a rapid rate, but competition among them was fierce, and they all struggled to meet the needs of their clientele. Efforts to address the problems of poverty fell far short of the goal, leaving those in the vanguard of these efforts frustrated at not being able to deal with poverty more effectively and efficiently.

Scientific knowledge was applied extensively to fuel advances on the industrial front. Numerous accomplishments were witnessed in such areas as agriculture, communication, and transportation. It was not long before private and public social welfare leaders turned to science and to the organization of scientific knowledge as a means to improve their efforts at eradicating poverty and pauperism.

The growing number of public institutions and the proliferation of private charitable societies resulted in the creation of State Boards of Charities, whose overall function was to protect the poor and the public. Fear in the private sector of being controlled by state bodies led to the establishment of Charity Organization Societies (COSs). This movement hoped to take leadership for charitable affairs from the hands of public officials (Dolgoff & Feldstein, 2000). The COS movement enjoyed strong support because of its emphasis on a "scientific approach" to poverty and pauperism. The movement embraced social Darwinism with its emphasis on evolution toward a more affluent society, combined with the openness of that society to individual achievement. Under this paradigm, personal wealth was not only a sign of individual fitness but a condition of moral superiority as well. The COS movement used the term *scientific charity* to describe its efforts to eradicate poverty and pauperism, and a system of services was developed that emphasized the individual and not the environment as the cause of the problem.

The settlement house movement also took root during the latter part of the 19th century, with the first settlement house (the Neighborhood Guild of New York City) established in 1887. One of the most famous settlement houses was established by social worker Jane Addams in Chicago in 1889. A modernized Hull House with expanded service offerings still exists today. Settlement houses emphasized neighborhood services and community development and served as a place where educated persons might live among poor immigrants and "bring about a sense of neighborliness that could lead to the making of good citizens" (Axinn & Levin, 1997, p. 107). The clientele and the neighborhoods served by settlement houses consisted of migrants and immigrants whose problems could be traced to making the transition from rural to urban living and from a known to an unknown culture. Unlike the COS movement, in which the individual was seen as the cause of his or her problems, the settlement house movement sought to connect private troubles to public causes such as poor working conditions, substandard living arrangements, crowding, health hazards, and the like. Social work as we know it today emerged from the intersection of the COS movement and the settlement house movement.

The early 1900s also saw the enactment of "mother's aid" and "mother's pension" laws by states, originally enacted to provide for the large numbers of widows raising children alone after their husbands had died due to the war or poor health. In addition, worker's compensation programs were developed to assist those injured on the job. The U.S. Children's Bureau was established in 1912 to investigate and improve the lives of children. Overall, the late 1800s to the early 1900s represent the liveliest period of social reform and political advocacy in the history of the social work profession, although there was still a lively debate as to what caused poverty—individuals or the society in which they lived.

The Great Depression, the New Deal, and Beyond: Late 1920s to 1940s

The 1920s, a decade of economic prosperity, was characterized by large-scale stock market speculation and out-of-control credit buying. The emphasis on acquiring consumer goods and the ready availability of credit resulted in a false sense of personal economic security. Spending outstripped the ability to save. Poverty was seen as something that could be conquered; in fact, the solution was thought to be "just around the corner." This euphoria abruptly ended with the stock market crash of October 24, 1929, and the ensuing Great Depression of the 1930s.

The Depression of the 1930s is considered to be one of the bleakest periods in U.S. history. In 1933, the worst year of the Depression, some 13 million people, or 25% of the civilian labor force, were unemployed. Economic ruin spread deep into the ranks of America's middle class. The stock market failed to sustain any kind of rally. Banks closed, industries failed, and farmers went into bankruptcy. Corporate profits, farm income, and wage earnings all declined. The U.S. economy came to a standstill. For the first time, the country came to believe that one could be poor and unemployed, not because of individual shortcomings but as a result of the mal-

functioning of society. American thought about social welfare changed dramatically. The "rugged individualism" characterized by early colonial times was replaced by an emerging federalism.

For the first time in U.S. history, large-scale federal intervention was required to get the country back on its feet. The New Deal programs of President Franklin D. Roosevelt epitomized this intervention. Massive aid was provided to the banking industry through the Federal Reserve banks, the Reconstruction Finance Corporation, and the U.S. Treasury to strengthen the system of private financial institutions. Private property was preserved through the Homeowners Loan Corporation that helped homeowners threatened with foreclosure to refinance their mortgages.

The New Deal package responded to the plight of farmers with legislation and administrative regulations designed to ease credit and raise commodity prices through restricting output. The Works Progress Administration (WPA) was established in 1935 to provide jobs for 8 million unemployed Americans in a wide range of public works projects across the country. The Civilian Conservation Corps (CCC) put thousands of unemployed youth to work on reforestation and flood and fire control projects. The Federal Emergency Relief Administration (FERA), headed by social worker Harry Hopkins, channeled half a billion dollars in relief money through state and local welfare agencies. This program also established a large-scale commodity food distribution program for the poor, which also assisted farmers because it allowed for the distribution of agricultural surpluses. In 1939, the predecessor to the current food stamp program began when public assistance recipients were allowed to purchase stamps that could be exchanged for food in grocery stores. The

FERA set a major precedent for a new fiscal relationship between the federal government and the states. It also marked a new interpretation of the federal government's responsibility for social welfare. In the 3 years of its existence, FERA spent in excess of $3 billion (Day, 2000).

The Social Security Act (Public Law 271) approved by President Roosevelt on August 15, 1935, constituted the major piece of social welfare legislation resulting from the Great Depression and the New Deal. This landmark legislation, considered to be the cornerstone of American social welfare policy (and still in evidence today although altered in many ways), served as demonstrable evidence of the federal government's concern for the social and economic well-being of the people of the United States.

The preamble to Public Law 271 articulates the federal government's newfound investment in the lives of the American people:

> An Act to provide for the general welfare by establishing a system of Federal old-age benefits, and by enabling the several States to make more adequate provision for aged persons, blind persons, dependent and crippled children, maternal and child welfare, public health, and the administration of their unemployment compensation laws. (U.S. 74th Congress, first session, Public Law 271)

The Social Security Act also established the Aid to Dependent Children program (later changed to **Aid to Families with Dependent Children**), a broader version of the earlier mother's pension programs intended to provide financial support to children of single, most often widowed mothers.

World War II brought prosperity to the United States in terms of full employment and rising incomes. Even for oppressed groups such as African Americans and women, the war resulted in increased opportunity for economic, educational, and social equality. Income redistribution during the World War II years benefited lowest income groups the most—the average increase in real income of families in the lower fifth of family income rankings was nearly 50% compared to only 18% for the highest fifth (Axinn & Levin, 1997). Social legislation of the time was focused primarily on the needs of communities disrupted by domestic war efforts (army camps and war plants) and the needs of families disrupted by the absence of fathers and mothers who joined the armed forces or went to work in a war-related industry. This legislation also provided funding for housing, child care, education, health, recreation, and transportation needs of families disrupted by the war. Interestingly, the typical postwar recession predicted by economists did not occur. As a result, people gained a renewed sense of confidence in the American economic system. The United States entered a period of economic prosperity and social complacency. Problems of the poor were either ignored or passed off as insignificant.

The Great Society, the War on Poverty, and Beyond: The 1950s, 1960s, and Early 1970s

Public welfare in the early 1950s expanded primarily through legislative changes that increased the number of potential program recipients, as well as formula changes that liberalized benefit payments. Despite the general well-being of the economy, public assistance rolls and the costs of maintaining these rolls continued to climb. For example, total public assistance payments in 1950 amounted to $2.5 billion. In 1960, such payments amounted to

$4 billion. Of additional concern was the dramatic increase in the number of single unmarried mothers with children receiving public assistance (nearly 3 million persons received government cash benefits in 1960 at a cost of more than $1 billion). In 1961, another half million clients were added to the public assistance rolls, raising total expenditures for these programs to $1.2 billion. By 1964, the number of public assistance recipients had reached 4 million, including 3 million children. Despite good economic times, high levels of poverty persisted, especially among rural families and persons of color. In 1964, ever cognizant of the economic problems of the poor and the growing strength of the civil rights movement, President Lyndon B. Johnson urged Congress to declare a "war on poverty":

> Declare war on a domestic enemy which threatens the strength of our Nation and the welfare of our people. . . . Today, for the first time in our history, we have the power to strike away the barriers to full participation in our society. . . . Having the power, we have the duty. (1964)

The Economic Opportunity Act of 1964 established American public policy in relation to the elimination of poverty:

> The United States can achieve its full economic and social potential as a nation only if every individual has the opportunity to contribute to the full extent of his capabilities and to participate in the workings of our society. It is therefore the policy of the United States to eliminate the paradox of poverty in the midst of plenty in the Nation by opening to everyone the opportunity for education, the opportunity for work, and the opportunity to live in decency and dignity. (U.S. 88th Congress, second session, Public Law 88-452, Section 2)

The Economic Opportunity Act provided for a series of youth programs aimed at giving young people and families, most often with limited income and of color, the education, skills, and experiences deemed necessary for success in mainstream society. Titles III and IV of the act provided for special programs to combat poverty in rural areas and for programs of employment and investment incentives in poverty areas. Title V of the act provided for short-term training and retraining courses aimed at reducing public assistance relief rolls. Title V also created an adult volunteer corps—Volunteers in Service to America (VISTA)—to help with the rehabilitation and improvement of delapidated inner-city areas and other impoverished areas of the United States. Title II of the act is considered by many as the most controversial provision of this landmark legislation. Title II created community action programs that provided for "the maximum feasible participation" of residents of the geographic areas covered by the program. The programs were administered by public or private, nonprofit community action organizations (Dolgoff & Feldstein, 2000).

The most popular programs funded by the Economic Opportunities Act of 1964 included:

- Head Start, a preparatory education program for preschool, low-income children;
- Upward Bound, an educational program aimed at preventing school dropouts and encouraging dropouts to return to school;
- child care centers;
- neighborhood recreation centers; and
- neighborhood health centers. (Axinn & Levin, 1997)

The attainment of jobs was at the core of the Economic Opportunities Act; job training, job placement, and counseling for a variety of psychological and social ills were viewed as essential to reducing the welfare rolls. The act reemphasized employment as an important American value.

The Economic Opportunities Act soon fell into disfavor, particularly among mayors of cities in the United States who were concerned over the federal funding of projects over which they had no control. The concept of "maximum feasible participation" gave poor and disadvantaged community members a new and powerful voice to express their dissatisfaction with their condition. In addition, programs funded under the act were often mismanaged, poorly conceptualized, or subject to fraudulent business practices. Social unrest was on the rise in the country because of the highly unpopular Vietnam War. Congress and the general public grew disenchanted with the War on Poverty, which to their way of thinking fell far short of achieving its stated goals.

Despite the significant investment of tax dollars on War on Poverty programs, the number of public assistance recipients and total expenditures for public assistance programs continued to climb. Congress responded by enacting amendments to the Social Security Act in 1967 that imposed a freeze on the number of children under 21 years of age who would be allowed to receive public assistance (cash) benefits because of absence of a parent from the home. The amendments also created the Work Incentive Program (WIN) that disqualified adults and out-of-school older children from receiving public assistance payments if they refused to accept employment or participate in work-training programs without good cause. By the end of the 1960s, the pendulum had swung yet another time to reflect a much more punitive and conservative approach to public welfare in the United States (DiNitto, 2000).

The United States, along with many other countries, entered into a period of economic stagnation in the 1970s, including the recession of 1975 and the world oil embargo of the early 1970s. Unemployment averaged over 5% throughout the first half of the decade, jumping to 8.3% during the recession of 1975. As a result, there was a general turning away from social welfare programs aimed at mitigating the inequalities of a capitalist economy (Axinn & Levin, 1997). Widespread disillusionment with the public welfare system ensued, underscored by the prevailing attitude that such programs encouraging dependency and discouraged self-determination. A period of retrenchment or "devolution" set in, characterized by the decline of public support and government expenditures for public social welfare programs. The pinnacle of welfare devolution came about with passage of the Personal Responsibility and Work Opportunity Budget Reconciliation Act of 1996 (Public Law 104-93), discussed in detail later in this chapter.

The 1980s: A Last-Ditch Effort to Reduce the Welfare Rolls

Economic stagnation continued throughout the 1980s. The unemployment rate in the United States reached an all-time high of 9.5% during the recession of 1982–1983. Consumer prices increased throughout the decade. Expenditures for public social welfare programs continued to rise. At the same time, a demand for restraint in governmental budgets grew in intensity. By the mid-1980s, the public had grown weary of government expenditures for cash assistance programs such as AFDC and nutritional assistance efforts such as the food stamp program. In addition, there was a growing concern among the public about the lifestyle of recipients, their commitment to family responsibility, and the viability of their communities (most recipients were divorced, separated, or never married mothers). It is important to note that this shift in attitude occurred at the same time that large numbers of women in the United States were joining the workforce. With the majority of mothers with young children working outside the home, increased resentment began to be directed at mothers on AFDC who were able to be at home with their children full-time. Architects of welfare reform began to focus on two primary issues: labor force participation and responsibility for the support of children.

The most significant social welfare legislation of the 1980s was the passage of the Family Support Act in 1988. Reflecting the negative attitude of the American public toward the poor, the act established more punitive measures for mothers who remained on public assistance and did not get jobs and also required that states establish paternity in a large proportion of AFDC (cash assistance) cases. Child support collections were assigned to the state to be applied against benefits. The Job Opportunities and Basic Skills (JOBS) training and education program was established to ensure compliance with the requirement that families avoid long-term welfare dependency through gainful employment. Those who were required to work under this program were subject to grant reductions (sanctions) if they refused to participate. However, there were delays in the release of final regulations for the JOBS program, coupled with inadequate funding levels for the program and the absence of jobs in the marketplace that paid a living wage. Not surprisingly, the programs of the Family Support Act met with little success in reducing the welfare rolls (Dolgoff & Feldstein, 2000).

The 1990s: An End to Welfare as We Knew It

The U.S. economy recovered toward the latter half of the 1990s, fueled by technology and the globalization of key markets. Cutting the federal budget deficit became a major goal of the Republican-dominated Congress. After gaining control of Congress in 1994, Republicans promised to carry out a new "Contract with America" that emphasized a balanced federal budget, reduced taxes, and decreases in social welfare expenditures. American social welfare policy once again shifted to an emphasis on personal and family responsibility for those in need.

After nearly half a century, the American view of the federal government as a positive necessity came to an abrupt end. Government at the federal level was seen as incapable of solving environmental problems, ending poverty and discrimination, and improving the quality of life for its citizens. For many, government was the problem. Welfare devolution was accelerated through legislation that called for revenue sharing, block grants, and a return to states of responsibility for many job training, education, community development, justice, and health programs (Dolgoff & Feldstein, 2000).

The most significant social welfare legislation enacted during the 1990s was the Personal Responsibility and Work Opportunity Budget Reconciliation Act (Public Law 104-93), signed into law by President Bill Clinton on August 22, 1996. The Social Security Act of 1935 established a "right to welfare" (entitlement) under conditions established by federal law; Public Law 104-93 ended that entitlement. The 1996 legislation featured deep cuts in basic programs for low-income children, families, the elderly, and persons with disabilities (nearly $55 billion over a 6-year period), as well as fundamental structural changes in the AFDC program.

The act converted the AFDC program to a block grant, the **Temporary Assistance to Needy Families (TANF)** block grant. Under this arrangement, states receive a fixed level of resources for income support and work programs based on what they spent on these programs in 1994, without regard to subsequent changes in the level of need in the state. Ironically, by using 1994 as the base funding year for the TANF grant, the federal government actually created the opportunity for large state surpluses in unexpended TANF block grant funds, as welfare rolls were substantially higher in 1994 than they were in 1996 and subsequent years.

The 1996 act did provide some additional "contingency funds" if need increased in the states, but it is widely believed that the contingency funds are insufficient to cover a sustained downturn in the economy. States may withdraw or divert substantial amounts of state resources (approximately $40 billion between 1997 and 2002) from basic income support and work programs for poor families with children from federal TANF block grant funds to other uses without such action affecting the level of federal block grant funds they receive.

The new legislation also allows states to deny aid to any poor family or category of poor families. In addition, with some exceptions, the legislation prohibits states from using block grant funding to provide aid to families that have received assistance for at least 5 years (the so-called federal "lifetime limit"), with a 20% hardship exemption. States were given authority to set time limits shorter than 5 years.

The bill also included an almost 20% reduction in food stamp program expenditures. These reductions affected all food stamp recipients, including the working poor, the elderly, and people with disabilities. The legislation includes a particularly harsh food stamp provision that affects poor unemployed individuals between the ages of 18 and 50 who are not raising children. Under the act, these individuals are generally limited to 3 months of food stamp benefits while unemployed in any 3-year period. Many of these individuals qualify for no other government benefits except food stamps, leaving them with an extremely limited safety net.

The legislation made most poor legal immigrants ineligible for almost all forms of assistance. Forty percent of the net savings in the act were achieved by denying a wide range of benefits to immigrants, including poor immigrant children and poor immigrants who are very old or who have become disabled after entering the United States and are no longer able to work. Immigrants in the United States illegally were already ineligible for most major means-tested entitlement benefits at the time the law was passed. Many states, in anticipation of the federal welfare reform legislation, applied for and were granted "welfare waivers" that allowed them to implement their own version of welfare reform. These waivers, which typically have a 5-year life cycle, allowed states even more flexibility in using federal funds for welfare reform.

Some of the initial provisions of the federal welfare reform law have been relaxed as a result of intense work by welfare advocates and a recognition by lawmakers that the provisions were actually creating the reverse of the intended effect. For example, in 1998, as part of the reenactment of the federal food stamp legislation, food stamp benefits were restored to the elderly, people with disabilities, and children of legal immigrants.

Although welfare caseloads throughout the country have dropped dramatically since the enactment of Public Law 104-193, the decrease in the percentage of people who are poor has lagged far behind those declines (see Table 8.3).

Over time, the AFDC program has shifted from one concerned with cash benefits (1935–1961), to one that provided a number of services to those who wanted the help to become self-sufficient (1962–1981), to one in which behavioral changes are being demanded as a condition of future assistance (1982–1996).

The real purchasing value of AFDC (now TANF) benefits has declined over the years because of inflation. The major changes between the two programs are summarized in Table 8.4.

An examination of state welfare reform initiatives reveals that states with the greatest caseload decline also have implemented the most aggressive or punitive welfare reform initiatives. One can't help but ask where all the women, children, and families have gone who once populated the U.S. welfare caseload.

TABLE 8.3   **TANF CASELOADS AND PERCENTAGE OF PERSONS LIVING IN POVERTY: COMPARISONS SINCE PASSAGE OF PUBLIC LAW 104-193**

State	TANF Caseload, August 1996	TANF Caseload, March 1999	Caseload Reduction (%)	1996 Poverty Rate (%)	1998 Poverty Rate (%)	Poverty Rate Reduction
Alabama	100,662	45,472	55	17.1	15.1	2.0
Alaska	35,544	25,393	29	7.7	9.1	1.4
Arizona	169,442	87,894	48	18.3	16.9	1.4
Arkansas	56,343	29,350	48	16.1	17.2	1.1
California	2,581,948	1,735,103	33	16.8	16.0	0.8
Colorado	95,788	35,469	63	9.7	8.7	1.0
Connecticut	159,246	83,458	48	10.7	9.0	1.7
Delaware	23,654	15,599	34	9.5	10.0	0.5*
District of Columbia	69,292	46,840	32	23.2	22.0	1.2
Florida	533,801	173,341	68	15.2	13.7	1.5
Georgia	330,302	130,210	61	13.5	14.0	0.5*
Hawaii	66,482	44,229	33	11.2	12.4	1.2
Idaho	21,780	4,365	80	13.2	13.8	0.6*
Illinois	642,644	344,320	46	12.3	10.6	1.7
Indiana	142,604	108,986	24	8.6	9.1	0.5*
Iowa	86,146	57,356	33	10.9	9.3	1.6
Kansas	63,783	32,532	49	11.0	9.6	1.4
Kentucky	172,193	93,444	46	15.9	14.7	2.2
Louisiana	228,115	100,577	56	20.1	17.7	2.4
Maine	53,873	35,313	34	11.2	10.2	1.0

(continued)

TABLE 8.3

TANF CASELOADS AND PERCENTAGE OF PERSONS LIVING IN POVERTY: COMPARISONS SINCE PASSAGE OF PUBLIC LAW 104-193 CONTINUED

State	TANF Caseload, August 1996	TANF Caseload, March 1999	Caseload Reduction (%)	1996 Poverty Rate (%)	1998 Poverty Rate (%)	Poverty Rate Reduction
Maryland	194,127	89,003	54	10.2	7.8	2.4
Massachusetts	226,030	123,933	45	10.6	10.4	0.2
Michigan	502,354	244,621	51	11.7	10.6	1.1
Minnesota	169,744	135,202	20	9.5	10.0	0.5*
Mississippi	123,828	33,853	73	22.1	17.1	5.0
Missouri	222,820	125,981	43	9.5	10.8	1.3*
Montana	29,130	14,079	52	16.2	16.1	0.1
Nebraska	38,592	32,228	16	9.9	11.1	1.2*
Nevada	34,261	18,308	47	9.6	10.8	1.2*
New Hampshire	22,937	15,416	33	5.9	9.4	3.5*
New Jersey	275,637	159,721	42	8.5	8.9	0.4*
New Mexico	99,661	77,896	22	25.4	20.8	4.6
New York	1,143,962	795,030	31	16.6	16.6	0.0
North Carolina	267,327	124,432	53	12.4	12.7	0.3*
North Dakota	13,146	8,227	37	11.5	14.4	2.9*
Ohio	549,312	258,773	53	12.1	11.1	1.0
Oklahoma	96,201	50,910	47	16.9	13.9	3.0
Oregon	78,419	44,563	43	11.5	13.3	1.8*
Pennsylvania	531,059	304,451	43	11.9	11.2	0.7
Rhode Island	56,560	49,897	12	10.8	12.2	1.4*
South Carolina	114,273	40,293	65	16.5	13.4	3.1
South Dakota	15,896	7,625	52	13.2	13.7	0.5*
Tennessee	254,818	147,137	42	15.7	13.9	1.8
Texas	649,018	288,525	56	17.0	15.9	1.1
Utah	39,073	28,909	26	8.1	8.9	0.8*
Vermont	24,331	17,585	28	11.5	9.6	1.9
Virginia	152,845	88,733	45	11.3	10.8	0.5
Washington	268,927	164,323	39	12.2	9.1	3.1
West Virginia	88,039	31,032	65	17.6	17.1	0.5
Wisconsin	148,888	27,140	82	8.7	8.5	0.2
Wyoming	11,398	1,621	86	12.1	12.1	0.0
U.S. total	12,241,489	6,889,315	44	13.8	13.0	0.8

Note: An asterisk next to a number in the Poverty Rate Reduction column denotes an *increase* in poverty rate since passage of Public Law 104-193.

Sources: U.S. Department of Health and Human Services (1999) and U.S. Bureau of the Census (1999).

TABLE 8.4   **SOME KEY DIFFERENCES: AFDC/EA/JOBS AND TANF**

	AFDC/EA/Jobs (Old Law)	TANF (New Law)
Federal funding	Unlimited for AFDC and EA. Capped entitlement for JOBS (federal share of AFDC and JOBS costs varied inversely with state per capita income)	Fixed grant, plus extra funding (for population growth/low federal spending per poor person, loan funds, contingency funds, bonuses for performance and reducing out-of-wedlock births), and (2 years only) welfare-to-work grant
State funding	Matching required for each federal dollar	States must spend 75% of "historic" level (100% for contingency funds) and must provide matching for contingency fund
Categories eligible	Children with one parent or with an incapacitated or unemployed second parent	Set by state
Income limits	Set by state	Set by state
Benefit levels	Set by state	Set by state
Entitlement	States required to aid all families eligible under state income standards	TANF expressly denies entitlement to individuals.
Work requirement	JOBS program had participation requirements, but participation did not require work.	By 2002, states must have 50% of their caseload in specified work activities.
Exemptions from work requirement	Parents (chiefly mothers) with child under 3 (under age 1, at state option)	None, but states may exempt single parents caring for child under 1
Work trigger	None	Work (as defined by state) required after maximum of 2 years of benefits
Time limit for benefits	None	5-year limit (20% hardship exceptions allowed)

There is no question that "work first" initiatives throughout the country have resulted in large numbers of former clients becoming employed. However, with some notable exceptions, most of these clients have only been able to find jobs that pay between $5.50 and $7.00 per hour, with little opportunity for advancement, and below the living wage needed to achieve self-sufficiency. Such jobs typically do not include employee benefits, particularly those related to health care. These jobs are also less likely to have flexible work arrangements that support the child care needs of former recipients, such as regular work schedules, schedules that do not include evening and weekend work, or schedules that allow for time off when children are sick or need heath checkups or for parent-teacher conferences.

The most recent round of welfare reform initiatives has done a good job of reducing the welfare roles in the United States, but to consider this a victory would be being short-sighted. Although many advocates for the poor agree that the previous "welfare system" created dependency for many recipients, most believe that the 1996 legislation will not reduce poverty in the long term because, like previous efforts, it fails to address issues of education and training in job skills that lead to employment at or above the living wage. In contrast, welfare reform advocates argue that local resources such as faith-based organizations, food banks, voluntary agencies, and the like should take up the slack in addressing the unmet needs of former welfare recipients. However, this private or voluntary infrastructure is simply not robust enough to accomplish the job. As a result, increasing numbers of former welfare recipients are becoming more deeply mired in poverty.

Although the White House and Congress herald their accomplishments in "ending welfare as we knew it," welfare rolls would not have decreased as significantly without a strong economy. The real test of these recent welfare reform policies will come when the economy takes a downturn, unemployment rises, and the private and faith-based infrastructure for helping people in need becomes totally saturated. The rush to dismantle the public welfare infrastructure in this country marks the disappearance of a safety net for those who need temporary assistance in difficult times.

CURRENT STRATEGIES FOR ADDRESSING POVERTY

Welfare policy requires an understanding of the relationship between market forces and the social welfare system. It is useful to think of poverty as those left behind after the market, social insurance, and welfare programs have "done their job."

A Strong Market and Family System

The first defense against poverty is a market and family system structured to provide full employment at wages sufficient to bring the worker and his or her family out of poverty. Within the family, work and child care are to be integrated in a way that children are cared for and jobs are done.

It is increasingly difficult for families to earn enough to pay for housing, food, and other necessities needed to maintain a minimum standard of living. In spite of the fact that regulations require workplaces to pay a minimum wage, this amount in many geographic areas falls far short of the amount needed to make a **living wage,** defined as three times the amount of money needed in a given location for fair market rent established by the U.S. Department of Housing and Urban Development (House the Homeless, 1999). Not only has affordable housing become increasingly difficult to obtain in the United States, but costs for child care, health care, and other basic necessities have become unaffordable for many families.

Social Insurance Programs

The second line of defense against poverty is a social insurance system that provides retirement income to supplement private pensions and savings of aged and disabled persons and their survivors. The social insurance system is structured for income security to all income classes, not just the poor. The most extensive social insurance program in the United States is **Old Age and Survivors Disability Insurance (OASDI),** commonly referred to as **social security.** This program is operated much like a private insurance program; employees and their employers contribute funding to federally operated trust funds. When retirement, disability, or death ends continued employment, members or their dependents draw income from the trust funds. Greater numbers of senior citizens and higher costs of living have raised questions about whether social security trust funds will be able to continue to provide adequately for those now paying into the system when they

While debates over what to do about the increasing number of individuals living in poverty continue to rage, those who are poor often face many barriers to escaping poverty, including substandard housing and unsafe living conditions; lack of job-training programs and jobs that pay above the minimum wage; and access to child care and health care.

Alan Weiner/Liaison Agency

need to draw income from the funds. Additionally, because social security provides a fixed income that is limited, even though there are provisions for periodic cost of living increases, many retired persons cannot afford to live just on this income, particularly with increased costs of housing and health care costs not covered by Medicare, the health care program for the elderly.

Another type of social insurance is **unemployment compensation,** a program that operates much like OASDI. The federal government requires employers to contribute to state-operated unemployment trust funds. These monies are used to provide assistance to certain groups of unemployed individuals. Persons who have been laid off involuntarily can apply for unemployment compensation. There are some problems with unemployment compensation. Benefits are not paid to persons who are fired, and employers sometimes fire rather than lay persons off so they will not qualify for benefits. Other individuals do not meet guidelines to qualify or live in

economically depressed areas and are unable to locate other jobs before benefit time periods run out.

Workers' compensation, another type of social insurance program, provides medical assistance and cash benefits to employees injured on the job or those who develop job-related illnesses. This program is not mandatory in all states, nor are all employers required to participate, although most employers provide some sort of workers' compensation program.

Public Assistance Programs

The third line of defense against poverty is a system of public assistance to those whose family system has fallen apart and to those who have limited or no wage income. Simply put, these people do not have enough money to maintain an adequate standard of living. These persons are helped by cash assistance (cash grants distinguished by category of need) programs such as Temporary Assistance for

Needy Families (TANF), discussed previously, general assistance, and Supplemental Security Income (SSI). These benefits are funded from general revenues (local, state, and federal) and are provided on the basis of the applicant's ability to prove need and fit into the category of persons targeted for help. The benefit amount is never enough to bring a person above the poverty line, only up to a standard that is established for the particular benefit program and the level of funds that a state is willing to put up to match federal funds for this purpose.

General assistance is a state and local public assistance initiative currently provided in 32 states. No federal funds are used to support general assistance programs. Such aid may be furnished to needy people or those with disabilities who are ineligible for federal categorical programs. Eligibility criteria and benefit levels vary by state and often within states. Payments are generally limited and for a short duration. Benefits range from cash payments to groceries and shelter.

Federal-state programs were enacted for old-age assistance and aid to the blind as part of the Social Security Act of 1935. Aid to the permanently and totally disabled was added in 1950. In 1974, the means-tested, federally administered **Supplemental Security Income (SSI)** replaced these state-administered programs. SSI provides minimum national monthly cash payments indexed to the CPI with uniform, nationwide eligibility requirements to needy aged, blind, and disabled people. People with disabilities have become the primary recipients of SSI, whose recipients are viewed as the "deserving poor." The average SSI benefit paid to eligible recipients in 1997 was $268.46 (*Social Security Bulletin Annual Statistical Supplement*, 1998).

In-Kind Benefits and Tax Credits

The final line of defense against poverty is a complex system of in-kind benefits and tax credits. The most significant is the **Earned Income Tax Credit (EITC)** program. From its passage in 1975 until its dramatic expansion in 1996, EITC has grown from a small program to one that will provide more Americans with more cash than any other public welfare program. It is estimated that by 2002, spending for this program will exceed $25 billion. Basically, EITC supplements the income for all working poor up to income just under $30,000. Taxpayers with one child can claim a credit of 34% of earnings, not to exceed $6,330. This amount of the credit is constant until $11,600 in earnings; after that, the amount is at a rate of 16% of earnings until it falls to zero at roughly $26,000. Since it is an earned income tax credit, those poor outside the labor force receive no benefit. The idea is to encourage work and to reduce the regressive impact of the Social Security tax.

Food stamps, subsidized housing, and Medicaid are other types of in-kind benefits designed to assist the poor. Administered and funded by the U.S. Department of Agriculture and states, food stamps are redeemable primarily at retail food stores for certain food items. Diapers, paper products such as toilet tissue, soap and shampoo, light bulbs, and other household necessities cannot be purchased with food stamps because of the historical connection of the food stamp program to the agricultural industry. The agricultural industry still strongly influences decisions made about the food stamp program. Paper food stamps have been replaced in most states by an on-line debit card. Other in-kind benefits, including subsidized housing and **Medicaid** (health care for the poor), are discussed elsewhere in this text.

Health care benefits through the workplace, vouchers given by some employers for child care, and employee retirement plans constitute other forms of in-kind benefits. However, many employers do not offer these benefits to those employed in lower-level jobs, making them inaccessible to many of the nation's poor.

Other Antipoverty Programs

Five types of programs exist to combat poverty that occurs despite our best efforts to prevent it through sound macroeconomic policies:

1. Cash support
2. Direct provision of basic necessities such as food, shelter, and medical care
3. Efforts to help the poor learn new behaviors to empower them to feel more in control of their own lives
4. Job training and job-searching help
5. Restructuring of existing institutions to produce a greater quality of economic opportunity

Our discussion about the historical context of aid for the poor in the United States shows that considerable efforts have been expended on behalf of the poor over the years in each of these five areas. Billions of state and federal dollars have been spent since the passage of the Social Security Act of 1935 to eradicate poverty in the United States and to ameliorate the negative effects of a market (capitalist) economy on those unable to reap the benefits of that economy.

Gilbert and Terrell (1998) argue that there are two basic political perspectives on American social welfare policy: the individualist perspective and the collective perspective. Unfortunately for the poor and the disadvantaged, the market economy favors the **individualist perspective.** This perspective holds that individual problems are the result of bad choices, personal dysfunction, and a culture of poverty. In essence, the "victims" are blamed for the situation they are in regardless of the fact that they had no choice in the matter, such as when children are born into poverty. The individualist perspective also supports markets with few or no government controls. The primary social policy agenda of the individualist perspective is to provide a minimum safety net for the poor.

The alternative to the individualist perspective is the **collective perspective.** This perspective holds that social problems reflect fundamental socioeconomic circumstances, barriers to access, and lack of opportunity. As Gilbert and Terrell (1998) point out, a collectivist's view of markets holds that "unregulated markets create risky economic cycles, unemployment, urban blight, poverty, and inequality" (p. 17). The primary social policy agenda of the collective perspective is to ensure full opportunity and economic security. As noted earlier, the market economy does not support the collective perspective.

Looking back some 65 years to the passage of the Social Security Act of 1935, one might ask what went wrong. Why, given the expenditure of billions of state and federal dollars, hasn't the problem of poverty been resolved in America? Where did all that money go? Why didn't the expenditures have the intended effects? A number of answers to these questions are possible. One is that money itself rarely solves a problem; there needs to be a carefully crafted and well-implemented plan as to how the money will be spent. We need to recognize that it takes time to solve serious problems that have deep roots and a long history. The United States needs to make investments in human capital and pay less attention to the immediate functioning of the marketplace. While many individuals may be able to survive at some minimum level in a healthy economy, ignoring human capital not only places those at or below the poverty line at considerable risk but makes it increasingly difficult for the United States to continue to compete in a global economy. Society must embrace the notion of social and economic justice, and that belief should be reflected in all of the social welfare programs provided to its citizens.

The United States has the necessary tools to solve contemporary social welfare problems. There is no "silver bullet" here; to the contrary, the solution is well within our reach if we are willing to embrace diversity, opportunity, and prosperity for all rather than aggregate them in the hands of a few. Social and economic justice are concepts that are easy to comprehend but difficult to achieve unless there is a commitment by all members of society to spread the wealth and power held by so few. Creating a just world is not about taking something away from one person or group and giving it to another. To the contrary, it is about sharing the wealth of society, however that is determined, with all members of society rather than a select few.

You might ask yourself how, then, do we get consensus or agreement on these issues? Most social welfare professionals agree that all five strategies noted earlier have their place in a comprehensive program to combat poverty in the United States. Most also acknowledge that all five strategies can be and have been misused, resulting in making things worse for the individual, for society, or both. The poverty debate in this country is not about the appropriate mix of strategies to address the problem. When all the rhetoric is cast aside, the debate is really about equality of opportunity and sharing the wealth. One thing is painfully clear: despite a long history of efforts to eradicate poverty in this country, poverty is still one of the most significant social problems. It is also at the core of the majority of other social problems in the United States today.

The New Millenium: 2000 and Beyond

State and federal welfare reform efforts continue to enjoy success in reducing the public assistance rolls throughout the United States. This success has been buoyed by a robust economy and a plentiful supply of low-paying service sector jobs. Large TANF block grant surpluses have been realized in many states as a result. Public antiwelfare sentiment in the United States continues to be strong and shows no sign of abating.

We have yet to see the long-term effects of welfare reform. The latest efforts at reform have swelled the ranks of the American **underclass** (Katz, 1997; Mink, 1998). Karger and Stoesz (1998) define the underclass as "the lowest socioeconomic group in society, characterized by chronic poverty; that is, its members are poor regardless of the economic circumstances of the society at large" (p. 486). These individuals are unable to rise above their situation even if the society in which they live enjoys a sustained level of prosperity such as that witnessed by the United States in the late 1990s. Consider, for example, the plight of millions of children who live in poverty in America today. About 14 million children currently live at or below the official poverty level in the United States. Child poverty is most prevalent among the very young (that is, those under the age of 6) and among populations at risk, such as African American and Latino youth. Nearly 11 million children in the United States have no health insurance coverage of any kind. The United States has the worst record among industrialized nations in reducing the poverty of children (Miringoff & Miringoff, 1999).

It is imperative that social workers and other groups continue to conduct sound research studies on the impact of welfare reform, the needs of the poor, and the types of programs that are successful at reducing poverty among specific groups (see Box 8.2). Policymakers need this information so that informed decisions can be made that are based on facts rather than emotion.

Thirty-five years ago, the United States was flush with the promise of solving the problem of poverty in the midst of prosperity. The nation has yet to find an effective solution to this problem. Public sentiment for resolving the problems associated with poverty in the United States has lessened considerably. At the same time, the poor and the near poor are faced with new challenges: a changing economy in which education is increasingly important to succeed and a lack of affordable housing, both of which have contributed to increases in the homeless population.

HOMELESSNESS

Increases in the numbers of persons living in poverty in the United States, coupled with substantial increases in the costs of housing, have resulted in large numbers of individuals and families who are homeless. According to the Stewart B. McKinney Act, 42 U.S.C. Section 11301, et seq. (1994), a person is considered **homeless** who

> lacks a fixed, regular, and adequate night-time residence; and . . . has a primary night time residency that is: (A) a supervised publicly or privately operated shelter designed to provide temporary living accommodations . . . (B) an institution that provides a temporary residence for individuals intended to be institutionalized, or (C) a public or private place not designed for, or ordinarily used as, a regular sleeping accommodation for human beings.

The term *homeless individual* does not include any individual imprisoned or otherwise detained because of an act of Congress or a state law.

Homelessness is not a recent phenomenon in the Untied States. During colonial times, individuals who were poor and had nowhere to live were housed in poorhouses (also called *almshouses*) and orphanages. The conditions within these institutions were, at best, dismal. Following the tradition of the English Poor Laws of 1601, colonial America had little tolerance for able-bodied men and women who were not gainfully employed (Axinn & Levin, 1997). Thus, the most meager of accommodations were provided for such individuals. This early tradition of treating homeless individuals as second-class citizens carried forward through the growth and development of this country to present times.

During the Great Depression, a nationwide census conducted by the National Committee on Care of Transient and Homeless suggested that some 1.2 million persons, or about 1% of the country's population, were homeless (National Coalition for the Homeless, 1999b). These people were not vagrants

BOX
8.2

The Fragile Families and Child Wellbeing Study

The Fragile Families and Child Wellbeing Study brings together three areas of great interest to policy makers and community leaders—nonmarital childbearing, welfare reform, and the role of fathers—in an innovative, integrated framework.* The study follows a new cohort of unwed parents and their children and provides previously unavailable information on questions such as:

*Sara McLanahan (Princeton University) and Irwin Garfinkel (Columbia University) are the principal investigators, and Jeanne Brooks-Gunn (Columbia) and Marta Tienda (Princeton) are co-investigators. Nancy Reichman is the project director, and Eleanor Cole Levinson is the assistant project director. Funding for the Fragile Families and Child Wellbeing Study comes from the National Institute of Child Health and Human Development (NIHCD) and from a consortium of national and local foundations, including the Ford Foundation, the Robert Wood Johnson Foundation, the William T. Grant Foundation, the Public Policy Institute of California, the California HealthCare Foundation, the Hogg Foundation, the St. David's Hospital Foundation in Austin, the Commonwealth Fund, the Fund for New Jersey, the Healthcare Foundation of New Jersey, the Foundation for Child Development, the Packard Foundation, the Kronkosky Charitable Foundation, and the A. L. Mailman Family Foundation.

- What are the conditions and capabilities of new unwed parents, especially fathers? How many of these men hold steady jobs? How many want to be involved in rearing their children?
- What is the nature of the relationship between unwed parents? How many couples are involved in stable, long-term relationships? How many expect to marry? How many experience high levels of conflict or domestic violence?
- What factors push new unwed parents together? What factors pull them apart? How do public policies affect parents' behaviors and living arrangements?
- What are the long-term consequences for parents, children, and society of new welfare regulations, stronger paternity establishment, and stricter child support enforcement?
- What roles do child care and healthcare policies play? How do these policies play out in different labor market environments?

and vagabonds, tramps, or thieves but responsible members of society who had lost their jobs and their homes as a result of the economic chaos in the country.

Two trends are largely responsible for the growth in the homeless population in the past 15 to 20 years: a growing shortage of affordable rental housing and a simultaneous in-

crease in poverty. Demographic groups who are more likely to experience poverty are also more likely to experience homelessness.

The classic stereotype of the homeless individual in America is a white male alcoholic who has lost his job and his family to his addiction and is forced to live on the streets. Other stereotypes include the belief that

Study Population and Research Design

Data are being collected in 21 cities across the United States. The total sample size will be 4,800 families, including 3,675 unwed couples and 1,125 married couples. The new data will be representative of nonmarital births in each of the 21 cities, and they will also be representative of all nonmarital births in U.S. cities with populations over 200,000. Response rates thus far have been excellent. We have interviewed over 90% of married mothers, married fathers, and unmarried mothers, and over 75% of unwed fathers. Follow-up interviews with both parents are scheduled for when the child is 12, 30, and 48 months old. Data on child health and development will be collected from the parents during each of the follow-up interviews, and in-home assessments of child well-being will be carried out at 48 months. Child well-being measures will overlap with those used in other national studies, including the Infant Health and Development Program, the Early Head Start Evaluation, the Teenage-Parent Demonstration Project, and the ECLS-Birth Cohort Study.

Content

The baseline questionnaires for mothers and fathers include sections on prenatal care; mother-father relationships; expectations about fathers' rights and responsibilities; attitudes toward marriage, parents' health; social support and extended kin; knowledge about local policies and community resources; and education, employment, and income. Follow-up interviews will gather additional information on access to and use of health care and child care services; experiences with local welfare and child support agencies; and parental conflict and domestic violence.

Source: From *Poverty Research News* (2000, March–April), p. 22. Evanston, IL: Joint Center for Poverty Research, Northwestern University/University of Chicago. Reprinted with permission.

---

homeless individuals have chosen homelessness as a lifestyle and have an aversion to working and following the rules of society. While some among the homeless might fit these categories, for the most part, homeless individuals have been forced to live on the streets because of a wide array of problems and issues.

Charactersitics of the Homeless

Homeless Youth   Homeless youth are individuals under the age of 18 who lack parental, foster, or institutional care. Sometimes, these individuals are referred to as "unaccompanied minors" or "unaccompanied youth." The homeless youth population is estimated to be approximately 300,000 young people each year (Institute for Health Policy Studies, 1995). An estimated 2.8 million youth living in U.S. households reported a runaway experience during the prior year (U.S. Department of Health and Human Services, 1995).

Causes of homelessness among youth fall into three interrelated categories: family problems, economic problems, and residential instability. Many homeless youth leave home after years of physical and sexual abuse, strained relationships, addiction of a family member, and parental neglect. Disruptive family conditions (their parents told them to leave or knew they were leaving and did not care) represent the principal reason that young people leave home (U.S. Department of Health and Human Services, 1995).

Some youth become homeless when their families suffer financial crises resulting from lack of affordable housing, limited employment opportunities, insufficient wages, no medical insurance, or inadequate welfare benefits. These youth become homeless with their families but are later separated from them by shelter, transitional housing, or child welfare policies (Shinn & Weitzman, 1996).

Residential instability also contributes to homelessness among youth. Roman and Wolfe (1995) report that a history of foster care is correlated with becoming homeless at an earlier age and remaining homeless for a longer period of time. Some youth living in residential or institutional placements become homeless upon discharge (Robertson, 1996).

Homeless youth face many challenges on the streets. Because of their age, homeless youth have few legal means by which they can earn enough money to meet basic needs. Homeless adolescents often suffer from severe anxiety and depression, poor health and nutrition, and low self-esteem (Robertson, 1989).

Homeless youth face difficulties attending school because of legal guardianship requirements, residency requirements, lack of proper records, and lack of transportation.

Homelessness among the Elderly   Burt and Cohen (1989) found that 31% of homeless persons were over age 45. Other studies have found proportions of homeless persons age 55 to 60 ranging from 2.5% to 19.4% (Institute of Medicine, 1988). Although the proportion of older persons among the homeless population has declined over the past two decades, their absolute number has grown (Cohen, 1996). Increased homelessness among elderly persons is largely the result of the declining availability of affordable housing and poverty among certain segments of the elderly. Of the 12.5 million in households identified as having the "worst case housing needs," 1.5 million were elderly people (U.S. Department of Housing and Urban Development, 1998). Thirty-seven percent of very low-income elderly people receive housing assistance.

Although elderly people have a lower poverty rate than the general population (10.5% compared to 13.3% for all people), they are more likely than the nonelderly to have incomes just over the poverty level threshold (U.S. Bureau of the Census, 1998a, 1998b). Elderly African American renters spend more than 30% of their income on housing (Gaberlavage & Sloan, 1997). With less income for other necessities such as food, medicine, and health care, the elderly population is particularly vulnerable to homelessness. In addition, overall economic growth will not alleviate the income and housing needs of elderly poor people, as continuing or returning to work, or gaining income through marriage, are often unlikely.

Once on the street, elderly homeless persons often find getting around difficult, and, distrusting the crowds at shelters and clinics, they are more likely to sleep on the street. Some studies show that homeless persons who are elderly are prone to victimization and more likely to be ignored by law enforcement (National Coalition for the Homeless, 1999a). Elderly homeless persons are also more likely to suffer from a variety of health problems, including chronic disease, functional disabilities, and high blood pressure, than are other homeless persons (Cohen, 1996).

To prevent elderly Americans from becoming homeless, we must provide enough low-income housing, income supports, and health care services to sustain independent living. For those who have already lost their homes, comprehensive outreach health and social services must be made available, as well as special assistance to access existing public assistance programs.

Women and Families Families with children represent the fastest-growing segment of the homeless population—approximately 40% of people who become homeless today represent this group (Shinn & Weitzman, 1996; U.S. Conference of Mayors, 1998). Families, single mothers, and children constitute the largest group of people who are homeless in rural areas (Vissing, 1996).

Stagnating wages and recent changes in welfare programs account for increasing poverty among families. The National Low Income Housing Coalition (1998) reports that in a median state, a minimum-wage worker would have to work 87 hours each week to afford a two-bedroom apartment that costs 30% of his or her income. Housing is rarely affordable for families leaving welfare for low wages, yet subsidized housing is so limited that fewer than one in four TANF families nationwide lives in public housing or receives a hous-

ing voucher to help them rent a private unit. Between 1995 and 1997, rents increased faster than income for the 20% of American households with the lowest incomes (U.S. Department of Housing and Urban Development, 1999). For most families leaving the welfare rolls, housing subsidies are not an option (Children's Defense Fund, 1998; National Coalition for the Homeless, 1997). Excessive waiting lists for public housing mean that families must remain in shelters or inadequate housing arrangements longer.

Homelessness impacts the health and well-being of all family members, particularly children. Compared with housed poor children, homeless children experience worse health; more development delays; more anxiety, depression, and behavioral problems; and lower educational achievement (Shinn & Weitzman, 1996). Moreover, large numbers of homeless children do not receive their proper immunizations and suffer from asthma and middle-ear infections at rates that are much higher than the national average (Redlener & Johnson, 1999).

Ethnicity About 50% of the homeless population today are African American, 32% are Caucasian, 12% are Hispanic, 4% are Native American, and 3% are Asian (U.S. Conference of Mayors, 1998). People experiencing homelessness in rural areas are more likely to be white, whereas homelessness among Native Americans and migrant workers is largely a rural phenomenon (U.S. Department of Agriculture, 1996). The effect of oppression and the subsequent lack of access to quality education, good jobs, and other opportunities is larger numbers of people of color living in poverty without informal or formal networks that can help provide affordable housing.

Survivors of Domestic Violence The homeless population in America also includes domestic violence survivors. In a recent study of homeless parents conducted in 10 U.S. cities, 22% indicated that they left their last residence because of domestic violence (Homes for the Homeless, 1998). Forty-six percent of the cities surveyed by the U.S. Conference of Mayors (1998) also identified domestic violence as a primary cause of homelessness. A 1990 Ford Foundation study found that 50% of homeless women and children were fleeing domestic abuse (Zorza, 1991).

States that have looked at domestic violence and welfare receipt report that between 50% and 60% of current recipients say they have experienced violence from a current or former male partner (Institute for Women's Policy Research, 1997). When a woman leaves an abusive relationship, she often has no place to go. Lack of affordable housing and long waiting lists for assisted housing mean that many women are forced to choose between abuse and homelessness. Shelters provide immediate safety to battered women and their children and help women gain control over their lives. The provision of safe emergency shelter is therefore a necessary first step in meeting the needs of women fleeing domestic violence.

Veterans   Forty percent of homeless men have served in the armed services, although veterans comprise only 34% of the general adult male population (National Coalition for Homeless Veterans, 1994). Homeless veterans are likely to be white, better educated, and previously or currently married than homeless nonveterans (Rosenheck et al., 1996). Female homeless veterans represent an estimated 1.6% of homeless veterans. They are more likely than male homeless veterans to be married and to suffer serious psychiatric illness but less likely to be employed and to suffer from addiction disorders.

People of color are overrepresented among homeless veterans, although some evidence indicates that veteran status reduces vulnerability to homelessness among African Americans (Rosenheck et al., 1996). The reduced risk of homelessness among African American veterans is most likely the result of educational and other benefits to which veterans are entitled.

Despite the overrepresentation of veterans in the homeless population, homelessness among veterans is not clearly related to combat military experience (Rosenheck et al., 1996). Contrary to popular belief, studies show that the veterans who are at greatest risk of homelessness are not Vietnam-era veterans but those who served during the late Vietnam and post-Vietnam era. It is suggested that these individuals may have increased rates of mental illness and addiction disorders, possibly due to recruitment patterns.

The U.S. Department of Veterans Affairs administers two special programs for homeless veterans: the Domiciliary Care for Homeless Veterans program and the Health Care for Homeless Veterans program. Both provide outreach, psychosocial assessments, referrals, residential treatment, and follow-up case management to homeless veterans. The U.S. Department of Veterans Affairs (1997) has initiated several new programs for homeless veterans and has expanded partnerships with public, private, and nonprofit organizations to increase the range of services for this group.

People with Mental Illness   Although many people become homeless because their mental illness impairs their ability to function, some individuals experience severe emotional problems *after* becoming homeless (see Chapter 9). Homeless people with mental disorders remain homeless for longer periods of time and have less contact with family and friends than those without mental disorders. They encounter more barriers to employment, tend to be in poorer physical health, and have more contact with the legal system than homeless people who do not suffer from a mental disorder. Approximately 20% to 25% of the single adult homeless population suffer from some form of severe and persistent mental illness (Koegel, 1996). However, only 5% of the estimated 4 million people who have a serious mental illness are homeless at any given point in time (Federal Task Force on Homelessness and Severe Mental Illness, 1992). Only 5% to 7% of homeless persons with mental illness require institutionalization—most can live in the community with the appropriate supportive housing options (Federal Task Force on Homelessness and Severe Mental Illness, 1992). When combined with supportive services, meaningful daily activity (including work), and access to therapy, appropriate housing can provide the framework necessary to end homelessness for persons with mental illness. Unfortunately, not enough community-based treatment services or appropriate, affordable housing is available to accommodate the number of people disabled by mental disorders in the United States.

Addiction Disorders   Untreated addictive disorders contribute to homelessness. The onset or exacerbation of an addictive disorder for persons with below–living wage incomes and just one step away from homelessness can plunge these individuals into residential instability. It should be noted that many homeless people with addictive disorders desire to overcome their addiction, but that the combination of being homeless and a service system ill equipped to respond to these circumstances essentially prevents their access to treatment services and recovery supports.

Surveys of homeless populations conducted during the 1980s found consistently high rates of addiction, particularly among single men. However, the results of those studies have recently been called into question because they used lifetime rather than current measures of addiction (Koegel, 1996). The frequently cited figure of about 65% is probably at least double the real rate for current addiction disorders among single adults who are homeless in a year. Thus, there is no generally accepted number with respect to the prevalence of addiction disorders among homeless adults. The destruction of single-room occupancy (SRO) housing is a major factor in the growth of homelessness, particularly among people suffering from addiction disorders (Koegel, 1996; Wright & Rubin, 1997).

Employment   Inadequate income and lack of affordable rental housing leave many people homeless. The U.S. Conference of Mayors (1998) survey of 30 American cities found that 22% of the urban homeless population were employed. The National Coalition for the Homeless (1997) reports that this figure is much higher in a number of cities not included in the mayors' survey.

Health Care and the Homeless   Poor health is closely associated with being homeless. The rates of both chronic and acute health problems are extremely high among the homeless population. Conditions requiring regular, uninterrupted treatment, such as tuberculosis, HIV/AIDS, diabetes, hypertension, addictive disorders, and mental disorders, are extremely difficult to treat or control among those without adequate housing.

Many homeless people have multiple health problems. They are also at greater risk of trauma resulting from muggings, beatings, and rape. Homelessness precludes good nutrition, good personal hygiene, and basic first aid. Some homeless people with mental disorders use drugs or alcohol to self-medicate, and those with addictive disorders are more at risk of contracting HIV and other communicable diseases.

People who are homeless are overwhelmingly uninsured and often lack access to the most basic health care services for their health care needs. A recent study reported that 675,000 people, including 400,000 children, lost their health insurance in 1997 as a result of federal welfare reform legislation (Families USA, 1999). Universal access to affordable, high-quality and comprehensive health care is essential in the fight to end homelessness. A universal health system could reduce the current homeless population as well as prevent future episodes of homelessness. It could also prevent unnecessary deaths on the streets and reduce the fiscal impact and social cost of communicable diseases and other illnesses.

HIV/AIDS and Homelessness   Studies show that the prevalence of HIV among homeless people is between 3% and 20%, with some groups having much higher burdens of disease (O'Connell, Lozier, & Gingles, 1997). Many homeless adolescents find that exchanging sex for food, clothing, and shelter is their only chance of survival on the streets. Thus, homeless youth are at greater risk of contracting AIDS or HIV-related illnesses. HIV prevalence studies conducted in four cities found a median HIV-positive rate of 2.3% for homeless persons under age 25 (Robertson, 1996).

HIV-infected homeless persons are believed to be sicker than their housed counterparts. For example, they tend to have higher rates and more advanced forms of tuberculosis and higher incidences of other opportunistic diseases. Homeless people with HIV face many barriers to optimal care. Injection drug use and lack of insurance have been shown to negatively affect health care utilization, level of medical care, and health status.

Homeless persons with HIV/AIDS need safe, affordable housing and supportive, appropriate health care. Emergency housing grants should be made available for persons with HIV-related illnesses who are about to lose their homes, and housing assistance should be arranged for those already on the streets. The federal government could play a key role by providing adequate funding for targeted housing and health programs as well as by enforcing antidiscrimination laws.

Rural Homelessness

Although homelessness is often assumed to be an urban phenomenon, many people experience homelessness in America's small towns and rural areas. Because there are far fewer shelters in rural areas, people experiencing homelessness in these areas are more likely to live in a car or camper or with relatives in overcrowded or substandard housing. Homeless people in rural areas are likely to be white, female, married, currently working, homeless for the first time, and homeless for a shorter period of time (U.S. Department of Agriculture, 1996). Other research shows that families, single mothers, and children make up the largest group of people who are homeless in rural areas (Vissing, 1996).

Rural homelessness, like urban homelessness, is the result of poverty and a lack of affordable housing. It is most prevalent in regions that are primarily agricultural; regions whose economies are based on declining extractive industries such as mining, timber, or fishing; and regions experiencing economic growth (Aron & Fitchen, 1996).

While housing costs are lower in rural areas, so are rural incomes, leading to high rent burdens similar to those found in urban areas. Homelessness in rural areas is often precipitated by a structural or physical housing problem jeopardizing safety—when families relocate to safer housing, the rent is often too much to handle, and they experience homelessness again.

Efforts to end rural homelessness are often hampered by isolation, lack of awareness, and lack of resources. Ending homelessness in rural areas requires jobs that pay a living wage, adequate income supports for those who cannot work, affordable housing, access to health care, and transportation.

Isolation   Homeless people increasingly detach from traditional social roles, such as being a family member or an employee. They reaffiliate with new groups of individuals who are in the same situation. As they reaffiliate, they become more comfortable with this new group because of the shared stigma and discrimination. As time goes on, the homeless become more isolated from others, more entrenched with other homeless persons, and lose touch with other social support systems that might help them in alleviating their situation, such as locating employment or housing.

Policies and Programs That Address Homelessness

The Stewart B. McKinney Homeless Assistance Act   In the early 1980s, the initial responses to homelessness were primarily local; homelessness was viewed by the Reagan administration as a problem that did not require federal intervention. In the years that

Homeless families represent the fastest-growing segment of the homeless population. Here a mother and her daughter who live in an old car share time together.
© David H. Wells/Corbis

followed, advocates from around the country demanded that the federal government acknowledge homelessness as a national problem requiring a national response. In late 1986, legislation containing emergency relief provisions for shelter, food, mobile health care, and transitional housing for homeless persons was introduced as the Urgent Relief for the Homeless Act. Following an intensive advocacy campaign, the legislation was passed by large bipartisan majorities in both houses of Congress in 1987. After the death of its chief Republican sponsor, Representative Stewart B. McKinney of Connecticut, the act was renamed the Stewart B. McKinney Homeless Assistance Act. The act was signed into law by President Ronald Reagan on July 22, 1987.

The McKinney Act originally consisted of 15 programs providing a range of services to homeless people, including emergency shelter, transitional housing, job training, primary health care, education, and some permanent housing. The McKinney Act has been amended four times. These amendments have, for the most part, expanded the scope and strengthened the provisions of the original legislation. However, McKinney programs have suffered setbacks in recent years. Although Congress authorized just over $1 billion in expenditures for McKinney Act programs in 1987 and 1988, a total of $712 million was appropriated for those years. Funding levels increased between 1988 and 1995; however, in fiscal year 1996, funding for McKinney programs was cut by a total of 27%. Several programs saw their funding eliminated entirely (Adult Education for the Homeless program, Homeless Veterans Reintegration Project, the Emergency Community Services Homeless Grant program, and Family Support Centers). Since 1996, funding has been partly restored to some of these programs, although few have surpassed their fiscal year 1995 funding levels.

While inadequate funding impedes the effectiveness of the McKinney programs, the act's greatest weakness is its focus on emergency measures—it responds to the symptoms of homelessness and not its causes. The McKinney Act remains landmark legislation for the homeless. However, after more than a decade of an emergency response to a long-term crisis, it is clear that only by addressing the causes of homelessness—lack of jobs that pay a living wage, inadequate benefits for those who cannot work, lack of affordable housing, and lack of access to health care—will homelessness be ended.

Other Programs

In addition to the programs authorized under the McKinney Act, 16 other national programs provide assistance to the homeless in some way. As with the McKinney programs, most of these programs concentrate on emergency assistance and do not address underlying causes.

Besides affordable housing for low-income families, other needs include increased employment, education, and job-training opportunities, allowing the homeless to accumulate assets, comprehensive physical and mental health services and substance abuse treatment, discharge planning for individuals from institutions, child care and education for homeless children, and public laws that prohibit the criminalization of sleeping and panhandling in public places (National Coalition for the Homeless, 1997).

A number of innovative programs to address problems of homelessness have been developed throughout the United States. Several programs use street outreach workers to link individuals with resources such as health care, immunizations, dental care, employment and job training, family planning, tuberculosis outreach, health education, substance abuse treatment, and housing assistance. Dade County, Florida, has established a trust fund that serves as a dedicated source of funding for programs for the homeless. This program is funded by a one-cent tax on all food and beverages sold in restaurants that have a liquor license. The fund is overseen by representatives of the civic, business, and religious communities; homeless service providers; former homeless persons; and homeless advocates. A number of child welfare service programs offer special transition programs to help youth in the foster care system make the transition to independent living. Some programs have established economic development and small business programs for the homeless, involving homeless clients in business efforts such as producing and selling artwork, newspapers, and other printed media; contracting out services such as housekeeping and home repair; and furniture refinishing and repair. One innovative program builds low-income housing and trains homeless and disenfranchised youth for jobs in the construction industry.

The common themes among these programs include an emphasis on community-based initiatives that include the homeless and homeless service providers in program design and development and empowerment. These efforts capitalize on the strengths perspective of social work by recognizing that homeless individuals have the desire, motivation, and skills to better their situation.

THE ROLES OF SOCIAL WORKERS IN THE FIGHT AGAINST POVERTY

Social work, more than any other profession, maintains a strong commitment to fighting poverty at all levels of the environment. Social workers provide direct services to individuals and families living in poverty; advocate for programs and policies that improve the lives of the poor and reduce poverty at the community, state, and federal levels; and develop and administer policies and programs that serve America's poor.

Some BSW graduates become public assistance workers in federal, state, and local human services agencies. They help individuals apply for TANF, food stamps, Medicaid,

and general assistance benefits. They also help individuals apply for social insurance programs such as Social Security and Medicare and oversee the provision of both public assistance and social insurance benefit programs.

Many public assistance programs have increased the roles of social workers in the fight against poverty by mandating that all TANF clients receiving employment services be assigned a case manager to help them obtain self-sufficiency. Using a generalist practice approach, these social workers assess client strengths and needs; work with clients to develop appropriate goals to achieve self-sufficiency; create appropriate service plans; assist clients in accessing needed resources; and terminate with their clients when the plans have been completed. Case managers also assist clients in developing skills in areas such as interviewing, assertiveness, and handling stress on the job; help them enroll in job-training and education programs; and help them locate appropriate resources such as transportation, housing, child care, health care, or family counseling.

Social workers are also employed by faith-based organizations such as the Salvation Army; housing programs; child development programs such as Head Start; teen pregnancy and parenting programs; school dropout prevention programs; settlement houses; and health clinics and hospitals in an effort to serve adults, children, youth, and families who live in poverty. Additionally, social workers work with federal, state, and local agencies and governments; state legislatures and the U.S. Congress; and advocacy organizations in developing, lobbying for, and administering antipoverty programs.

Social workers also work with the homeless in a variety of capacities. They are employed by urban housing authorities to work with individuals and families living in public housing to help break the cycle of poverty and homelessness. Because many individuals have difficulty making the transition from public housing to paying for housing themselves when they become employed and no longer meet income guidelines for public housing, social workers also link families with resources that can help them make this transition. Social workers also work as outreach workers to serve the homeless in many areas; in a number of cities roving workers provide services to homeless youth, helping them access health care, safe shelter, counseling, education, and employment. In some areas, programs for battered women have worked with programs that serve the homeless such as the Salvation Army to establish transitional living programs for women and their families to live until they can locate employment and save enough money to locate housing independently.

Social workers also are employed in advocacy and administrative roles in programs directed toward alleviating homelessness, such as Habitat for Humanity, an international program in which volunteers and future home owners work together to build low-income housing. In one city, a dropout recovery agency for young adults operates a highly successful construction program that trains individuals in a variety of construction jobs as they build affordable housing. In another, a social worker is the director of a private foundation that leverages funding from corporate and private donors to create affordable housing.

The values base of the social work profession mandates that social workers treat all clients, including those who live in poverty, with dignity and respect and work to empower them to be in charge of their own lives. Much of the debate in the years ahead will be about the place of faith-based organizations in supplementing publicly funded efforts to combat poverty and dependency.

SUMMARY

Welfare has always been a politically charged issue. As noted throughout this chapter, welfare involves contradictory views that different segments of society hold about poor and vulnerable people and how to prevent poverty. As the United States evolves with increasing technological sophistication requiring more highly educated workers, along with a slack labor market and constrained public spending, the issues of welfare in general will not disappear. As poverty continues to rise and affordable housing becomes increasingly scarce, the numbers of homeless men, women, and children will also increase. There are no easy answers; even more importantly, there are no correct answers, and that is why poverty is such a challenging and interesting problem.

KEY TERMS

Aid to Families with Dependent Children (AFDC)
collective perspective
Consumer Price Index (CPI)
digital divide
Disability Insurance (DI)
Earned Income Tax Credit (EITC)
general assistance
homeless
individualist perspective
living wage
market basket concept

Medicaid
Old Age Survivors and Disability Insurance (OASDI)
poverty
relative poverty
social security
Supplemental Security Income (SSI)
Temporary Assistance to Needy Families (TANF)
underclass
unemployment compensation
workers' compensation

DISCUSSION QUESTIONS

1. Do you believe that a preference for welfare keeps TANF recipients out of the workforce?

2. How does the changing shape of the American economy change the shape of American poverty?

3. To what degree is the number (or percentage) of poor people a good measure of a society's commitment to social welfare?

4. Which level of government, state or national, is best equipped to deal with poverty?

5. Identify at least five factors associated with homelessness. Suggest at least one possible intervention strategy for each factor.

INFOTRAC COLLEGE EDITION

To learn more about topics included in this chapter, enter the following search terms:

America's underclass

devolution

homeless children

homeless families

homeless women

income maintenance

public welfare

welfare reform

ON THE INTERNET

http://www.nami.org/

http://www.hcfa.org/

http://www.apa.org/

http://www.mentalhealth.gov/

http://samhsa.gov/

http://www.naswdc.org/

http://www.ddrcco.com/

http://nch.ari.net/

REFERENCES

Aron, L., & Fitchen, J. (1996). Rural homelessness: A synopsis. In J. Baumohl (Ed.), *Homelessness in America*. Washington, DC: National Coalition for the Homeless.

Axinn, J., & Levin, H. (1997). *Social welfare: A history of the American response to need* (4th ed.). New York: Longman.

Burt, M., & Cohen, B. (1999). *America's homeless: Numbers, characteristics, and programs that serve them*. Washington, DC: Urban Institute.

Children's Defense Fund & National Coalition for the Homeless. (1998). *Welfare to what: Early findings on family hardship and well-being*. Washington, DC: National Coalition for the Homeless.

Citro, C. F., & Michael, R. T. (Eds.). (1995). *Measuring poverty: A new approach*. Washington, DC: National Academy Press.

Cohen, C. (1996). *The aging homeless*. Brooklyn, NY: SUNY Health Science Center.

Day, P. (2000). *A new history of social welfare* (3rd ed.). Boston: Allyn & Bacon.

DiNitto, D. M. (2000). *Social welfare: Politics and public policy* (5th ed.). Boston: Allyn & Bacon.

Dolgoff, R., & Feldstein, D. (2000). *Understanding social welfare* (5th ed.). Boston: Allyn & Bacon.

Families USA. (1999). *Losing health insurance: The unintended consequences of welfare reform*. Washington, DC: Author.

Federal Task Force on Homelessness and Severe Mental Illness. (1992). *Outcasts on Main Street: A report of the Federal Task Force on Homelessness and Severe Mental Illness*. Delmar, NY: National Resource Center on Homelessness and Mental Illness.

Gaberlavage, G., & Sloan, K. (1997). *Progress in the housing of older Americans, 1997*. Washington, DC: American Association of Retired Persons.

Gilbert, N., & Terrell, P. (1998). *Dimensions of social welfare policy* (4th ed.). Boston: Allyn & Bacon.

Homes for the Homeless. (1998). *Ten cities 1997–1998: A snapshot of family homelessness across America.* New York: Homes for the Homeless and the Institute for Children and Poverty.

House the Homeless, Inc. (1999). *Wages as a barrier to housing.* Austin, TX: Author.

Institute for Health Policy Studies. (1995). *Street youth at risk for AIDS.* San Francisco: University of California.

Institute of Medicine. (1988). *Homelessness, health, and human needs.* Washington, DC: National Academy Press.

Institute for Women's Policy Research. (1997, April). Domestic violence and welfare receipt. *JWPR Welfare Reform Network News, 4.*

Johnson, L. B. (1964, March 16). *Message on poverty.* Washington, DC: U.S. Government Printing Office.

Karger, J., & Stoesz, D. (1998). *American social welfare policy: A pluralistic approach* (3rd ed.). New York: Longman.

Katz, M. B. (1997). *Improving poor people: The welfare state, the "underclass," and urban schools as history.* Princeton, NJ: Princeton University Press.

Koegel, P. (1996). The causes of homelessness. In National Coalition for the Homeless (Ed.), *Homelessness in America: Unabated and increasing.* Washington, DC: National Coalition for the Homeless.

Mink, G. (1997). *Welfare's end.* Ithaca, NY: Cornell University Press.

Miringoff, M., & Miringoff, M. L. (1999). *The social health of the nation: How America is really doing.* New York: Oxford University Press.

National Coalition for the Homeless. (Ed.). (1997). *Homelessness in America: Unabated and increasing.* Washington, DC: Author.

National Coalition for the Homeless. (1999a). Homelessness among elderly persons. *NCH Fact Sheet, 15.* Washington, DC: Author.

National Coalition for the Homeless. (1999b). How many people experience homelessness? *NCH Fact Sheet, 2.* Washington, DC: Author.

National Coalition for Homeless Veterans. (1994). *Providing reasonable estimates of homeless veterans in America on any given night in May, 1994.* Washington, DC: Author.

National Low Income Housing Coalition. (1998). *Out of reach: Rental housing at what cost?* Washington, DC: Author.

O'Connell, J., Lozier, J., & Gingles, K. (1997). *Increased demand and decreased capacity: Challenges to the McKinney Act's health care for the homeless program.* Nashville, TN: National Health Care for the Homeless Council.

Orshansky, M. (1965, January). Counting the poor. *Social Security Bulletin,* pp. 3–29.

Poverty Research News. (2000, March-April). The Fragile Families and Child Well-being Study. Chicago: Joint Center for Poverty Research, Northwestern University/University of Chicago, p. 22.

Redlener, I., & Johnson, D. (1999). *Still in crisis: The health status of New York's homeless children.* New York: Children's Health Fund.

Robertson, M. (1989). *Homeless youth in Hollywood: Patterns of alcohol use.* Berkeley, CA: Alcohol Research Group.

Robertson, M. (1996). *Homeless youth on their own.* Berkeley, CA: Alcohol Research Group.

Roman, N., & Wolfe, P. (1995). *Web of failure: The relationship between foster care and homelessness.* Washington, DC: National Alliance to End Homelessness.

Rosenheck, R., et al. (1996). Homeless veterans. In National Coalition for the Homeless (Ed.), *Homelessness in America: Unabated and increasing.* Washington, DC: National Coalition for the Homeless.

Secombe, K. (1999). *So you think I drive a Cadillac? Welfare recipients' perspectives on the system and its reform.* Boston: Allyn & Bacon.

Shinn, M., & Weitzman, B. (1996). Homeless families are different. In National Coalition for the Homeless (Ed.), *Homelessness in America: Unabated and increasing.* Washington, DC: National Coalition for the Homeless.

Social Security Bulletin. (1998). *Annual statistical supplement, 61*(2). Available: http://www.ssa.gov/policy/pubs/ssb/v61n2y1998/index.html.

The 2000 HHS poverty guidelines. (2000, February 15). *Federal Register, 65*(31), 7555–7557.

U.S. Bureau of the Census. (1998a). *Poverty 1998.* Available: http://www.census.gov/poverty/poverty98/pv98state.html.

U.S. Bureau of the Census. (1998b). *Poverty in the United States: 1997.* Washington, DC: U.S. Bureau of the Census, Income Statistics Branch.

U.S. Bureau of the Census. (1999). *Statistical abstract of the United States.* Washington, DC: Author.

U.S. Bureau of the Census. (2000). *Statistical abstract of the United States.* Washington, DC: Author.

U.S. Conference of Mayors. (1998). *A status report on hunger and homelessness in America's cities: 1998.* Washington, DC: Author.

U.S. Department of Agriculture. (1996). *Rural homelessness: Focusing on the needs of the rural homeless.* Washington, DC: U.S. Department of Agriculture, Rural Housing Service.

U.S. Department of Health and Human Services. (1995). *Youth with runaway, throwaway, and homeless experiences: Prevalence of drug use and other at-risk behaviors.* Silver Spring, MD: National Clearinghouse on Families and Youth.

U.S. Department of Health and Human Services. (1999). *U.S. welfare caseloads information.* Available: http://www.acf.dhhs.gov/news/tables.htm.

U.S. Department of Health and Human Services, Administration for Children and Families. (1999). *Change in welfare caseloads since enactment of new welfare law.* Available: http://www.acf.dhhs.gov/news/stats/aug-sept.htm.

U.S. Department of Housing and Urban Development. (1998). *Rental housing assistance: The crisis continues: 1997 Report to Congress on worst-case housing needs.* Rockville, MD: HUD User.

U.S. Department of Housing and Urban Development. (1999). *Waiting in vain: An update on America's housing crisis.* Rockville, MD: HUD User.

U.S. Department of Veterans Affairs. (1997). *Heading home: Breaking the cycle of homelessness among America's veterans: A post-summit action report and resource directory.* Washington, DC: Author.

Vissing, Y. (1996). *Out of sight, out of mind: Homeless children and families in small town America.* Lexington: University of Kentucky Press.

Wright, J., & Rubin, B. (1997). Is homelessness a housing problem? In *Understanding homelessness: New policy and research perspectives.* Washington, DC: Fannie Mae Foundation.

Zorza, J. (1991). Women battering: A major cause of homelessness. *Clearinghouse Review, 25*(4).

SUGGESTED FURTHER READINGS

Anderson, L. P., Sundet, P. A., & Harrington, I. (2000). *The social welfare system in the United States: A social worker's guide to public benefits programs.* Boston: Allyn & Bacon.

Anonymous. (1994). Dethroning the welfare queen: The rhetoric of reform. *Harvard Law Review, 107*(8), 2013–2030.

Bane, M. J., & Ellwood, D. (1994). *Welfare realities.* Cambridge, MA: Harvard University Press.

Berrick, J. D. (1995). *Faces of poverty: Portraits of women and children on welfare.* New York: Oxford University Press.

Danziger, S., & Gottschalk, P. (1995). *America unequal.* Cambridge, MA: Harvard University Press.

Danziger, S., Sandefur, G., & Weinberg, D. (Eds.). (1995). *Confronting poverty.* Cambridge, MA: Harvard University Press.

Dash, L. (1996). *Rosa Lee: A mother and her family in urban America.* New York: Plume.

Edelman, P. B. (1993). Toward a comprehensive antipoverty strategy. *Georgetown Law Journal, 81*(5), 1697–1755.

Edin, K., Lein, L., & Nelson, T. (1997). *Making ends meet: How single mothers survive welfare and low-wage work.* New York: Russell Sage Foundation.

Garfinkel, I. (1992). *Assuring child support.* New York: Russell Sage Foundation.

Handler, J. (1995). *The poverty of welfare reform.* New Haven, CT: Yale University Press.

Gueron, J. M. (1993). Welfare and poverty: The elements of reform. *Yale Law & Policy Review, 11*(1), 113–125.

Haveman, R. H. (1994). Transfers, taxes, and welfare reform. *National Tax Journal, 47*(2), 417–434.

Kingston, E. R., & Schulz, J. H. (Eds.). (1997). *Social security in the 21st century.* New York: Oxford University Press.

Mead, L. M. (1992). *The new politics of poverty.* New York: Basic Books.

Moffitt, R. (1993). Welfare reform: An economist's perspective. *Yale Law & Policy Review 11*(1), 126–146.

National Association of Counties. (1999). *The face of homelessness.* Washington, DC: Author.

Robbins, G., & Nelson, F. (1996). *Looking for a place to be: A report on AIDS housing in America.* Seattle: AIDS Housing of Washington.

Sachs, M. L. (1994). The prospects for ending welfare as we know it. *Stanford Law & Policy Review, 5*(2), 99–114.

Shelter Partnership, Inc. (1997). A report on housing for persons living with HIV/AIDS in the city and the county of Los Angeles. Los Angeles: Los Angeles City Housing Department.

Zucchino, D. (1997). *Myth of the welfare queen.* New York: Scribner.

MENTAL HEALTH, SUBSTANCE ABUSE, AND DEVELOPMENTAL DISABILITIES

Twenty-four-year-old Joanna Barclay currently lives in a halfway house in the inner-city area of a large northern city. She has lived there for 3 months, after being released from her 14th stay at a state mental hospital since the age of 16. Joanna and her roommates earn money for food and part of the rent by working for an industrial cleaning company. They are supervised by a social worker from the local mental health outreach center, who meets with them as a group twice a week and is available on an on-call basis whenever they need support. Joanna, with her social worker's help, is planning to enroll in a job-training program next month and to move into her own apartment with one of the other residents of the halfway house within the next 6 months. She is excited about the opportunity to live on her own.

Joanna enjoyed a relatively stable childhood, growing up in a rural area of the South with her middle-class parents and four brothers. During junior high school, she began to experience severe headaches and what she terms "anxiety attacks." Her parents took her to several doctors, but no physical reasons could be found for these problems. At about age 15, Joanna's behavior changed from calm and stable to erratic, ranging from screaming rages to long periods of crying to fun-loving, carefree behavior. She began experimenting with drugs, ran away from home a number of times, and got into several physical altercations with other girls at school. Her family had difficulty coping with her behavior. After one serious incident when Joanna threatened her mother and her younger brother with a knife, she was hospitalized in a local private psychiatric hospital for 30 days. She was placed on medication to help stabilize her erratic behavior, and she and her family received therapy. After her release from the hospital, Joanna functioned better for several months. But she soon reported feeling overwhelmed and pressured and told her family she "could not stop the frightening thoughts that kept running through her head." Her psychiatrist wanted to rehospitalize her, but her family's insurance benefits had been exhausted during her first hospitalization, and Joanna did not want to admit herself to the state mental hospital nearby.

After continual arguments with her family and school personnel and several minor run-ins with the law, Joanna quit school and moved with a boyfriend to California, where she held a series of temporary jobs. When the boyfriend left her because he could not handle her mood swings, her behavior became even more erratic. Finally, after she was found asleep in a dumpster and unable to remember who or where she was, the police picked her up and took her to the state hospital. During the next 6 years, Joanna repeated a pattern of briefly holding a menial job for a short time, losing the job, living on the streets, entering the state hospital, and being released in a more stable condition. When Joanna was released from her last hospital stay, the local mental health center in Joanna's area finally had space available at the halfway house where she currently is living.

The mental health needs of people throughout the world are receiving increased attention. The World Health Organization has determined that mental disorders account for 4 of the 10 leading causes of disability in established market economies worldwide (see Figure 9.1 and Table 9.1). The National Commission on Mental Health estimates that 15% of the U.S. population at any given time is in need of mental health services and that 25% of the population suffers from some type of emotional problem. Major depression is the leading cause of mental disability in the United States, with more than 19 million people over 18 years of age experiencing this illness at any given time. Depression alone, which also increases the likelihood of

1. Heart disease
2. Major depression
3. Cardiovascular disease
4. Alcohol use
5. Road traffic accidents
6. Lung and UR cancers
7. Dementia and degenerative diseases
8. Osteoarthritis
9. Diabetes
10. Pulmonary disease

FIGURE 9.1

LEADING SOURCES OF DISEASE BURDEN* IN ESTABLISHED MARKET ECONOMIES, INCLUDING THE UNITED STATES, IN 1990

*Measured in lost years of healthy life due to premature death or disability

Source: From National Institute of Mental Health (2000): http://www.nimh.nih.gov.

TABLE 9.1 **DISEASE BURDEN* BY SELECTED ILLNESS CATEGORIES IN ESTABLISHED WORLD MARKET ECONOMIES IN 1990**

Condition	Percentage
All cardiovascular conditions	18.6
All malignant diseases (cancer)	15.0
All mental illness, including suicide	14.4
All alcohol and drug use	6.2
All respiratory conditions	4.8
All infectious and parasitic diseases	1.5

*Measured in lost years of healthy life due to premature death or disability

Source: From National Institute of Mental Health (2000): http://www.nimh.nih.gov.

serious health problems, including heart attacks, strokes, diabetes, and cancer, costs the United States more than $30 billion each year (National Institute of Mental Health, 1999).

But mental health services in the United States are available to only one out of every eight individuals who need them and to far fewer individuals worldwide. Because of increases in individual stress, financial pressures, divorce and marital problems, and work-related pressures, it can be expected that most individuals will experience emotional problems at some point in their lives.

Emotional problems are highly correlated with substance abuse, a related field of practice in which large numbers of social workers are employed. The systems/ecological framework can be used to understand the relationships among environmental factors at all levels that contribute to emotional problems and substance abuse. Problems with one area, such as mental illness, do not automatically mean problems with substance abuse. But researchers from the U.S. Department of Health and Human Services (1994a) found that 30% of adults who had been assessed as having a mental disorder also had a substance abuse problem during their lives. Moreover, these same researchers found that more than half of adults with drug abuse disorders had one or more mental disorders.

Additionally, many individuals in the United States have some type of developmental disability, either physical or mental. Often, individuals with physical developmental disabilities abuse alcohol or other drugs as a way to cope with their disabilities. Some types of developmental disabilities are a result of drug abuse by mothers during pregnancy. The relationship between developmental disabilities and substance abuse is dramatized by recent legislation that prohibits the discrimination of persons with disabilities and includes both substance abusers and persons with emotional problems in its definition of disability.

In this chapter, we focus on mental health and mental illness, the abuse of alcohol and other drugs, and developmental disabilities. Students should keep in mind that the three problems do not always overlap and that different histories, policies, and issues surround each area. However, there are also many similarities, particularly in relation to the stigma, oppression, and discrimination experienced by each group. Social workers can play many important roles at all levels of the environment in working with individuals, families, and communities experiencing these problems. Key roles include recognizing the strengths of individuals, families, cultural groups, and communities and empowering them to use their strengths to develop a healthier environment in which to live.

MENTAL HEALTH

How do we determine who needs mental health services and who should receive them? The stigma placed on individuals with mental health problems and the stereotypes about the services provided them cause many individuals with mental health problems to avoid seeking services. People think of mental health services and those who receive them as portrayed in popular movies and books, such as the classic novel *One Flew over the Cuckoo's Nest* (Kesey, 1962) and the film *Silence of the Lambs* (1991). For this reason, many communities are passing zoning or other ordinances to prevent moving individuals with mental health problems into their areas.

The rights of persons with mental health problems also are receiving increased attention. Should these individuals be forced to be hospitalized, receive electric shock treatments, or get drug therapy against their wishes? Or, like Joanna, when they so desperately need treatment that is not available due to scarce resources, do they have a right to demand services, especially if it means that they will be less likely to need more intensive services, such as institutionalization, in the future? Does some-

one who is currently in an institution but could function in a less restrictive environment have the right to demand such a placement?

What about protections for those in our society who may encounter people with serious mental health problems? Some express concern about the accountability of those with serious mental health problems and what should happen when such individuals become dangerous to themselves or others? This issue was exemplified by several recent court cases. In *United States v. Kaczynski,* the "Unabomber" case, Ted Kaczynski was found to have "diminished capacity" and received a less punitive sentence as a result. In contrast, a young adult who killed a number of women over a period of several years was diagnosed by several psychiatrists as having severe psychological problems, was sentenced to death in a Florida court, and executed. And a retarded young adult who aided in a murder at the age of 17—when his mental age was about 6—recently was put to death, also in Florida. Similar executions have occurred in Texas and other states. Are such individuals less accountable to society for their actions because of diminished mental capacity? Who is responsible for looking after these individuals to ensure that they do not harm themselves or others? What legal protections should be guaranteed?

Current studies also show a strong relationship between mental health problems and physical health problems. When persons do not get help for their mental health problems, they are much more likely to become physically ill. For example, researchers found that 50% of persons coming to company physicians with health-related problems were experiencing mental health problems. A study of over 40,000 persons in Hawaii found that those who received short-term mental health services for a specific psychological problem experienced a 35% to 38% drop in subsequent medical costs. The high costs of health care could be reduced if more attention were given to the mental health needs of individuals.

Mental health problems, if left untreated, also disrupt families and increase the financial costs to taxpayers, as well as decrease productivity at the workplace. It is difficult to obtain accurate data on actual expenditures for mental health services and other related costs to individuals with mental health problems, as well as the costs to their families, workplaces, and communities. The National Alliance for the Mentally Ill (1999) places the total price tag of mental illness in the United States at $81 billion a year, including direct costs (hospitalizations and medications) and indirect costs (lost wages, family caregiving, and losses due to suicide). These costs do not include expenditures for most outpatient psychiatric or preventive care.

Over half of the individuals providing mental health services today are social workers, and about 65% of social workers are employed in mental health–related jobs. They work in state mental hospitals, private psychiatric treatment facilities, community outreach facilities, child guidance clinics and family service agencies, emergency hotlines, crisis centers, and private offices. The provision of mental health services is a rapidly growing area that offers many critical roles for social workers.

Mental Health or Mental Illness: Definitions

Societies have always developed their own systems for labeling acceptable and unacceptable behavior. What is tolerated in one society may be unacceptable in another. For each society, there is a continuum, with certain definitely unacceptable behaviors at one end and definitely acceptable and appropriate ones at the other. Typically, the behaviors at either end of the continuum are almost uniformly agreed on by most members of that society. But the behaviors in the middle of the continuum are often the subject of extensive debate and disagreement. For example, although murder would be considered a definitely unacceptable behavior by most, where on the continuum would continually talking to oneself fall or being convinced that you were King Tut? Some societies tolerate little deviance from acceptable behavior. For example, for a brief period during colonial times in Salem, Massachusetts, some persons whose behavior was considered "deviant" were labeled as witches possessed by the devil, and they were tortured and burned at the stake. Later research (Mechanic, 1999) suggested that many of these individuals had severe psychological problems, and others were women in nontraditional roles who refused to give them up. In other societies, those whose behavior deviates from the norm are given special roles and, in some instances, elevated to status positions. For example, in many Native American tribes, nonconforming individuals often became shamans, or medicine men, assuming high-status positions within the tribes.

Historically, those labeled as mentally ill or retarded often have been isolated or punished. In colonial times, individuals with mental illness frequently were locked in attics or cellars or warehoused in "lunatic" asylums. Today, our society is still ambivalent about how such individuals should be regarded. Attempts at integrating emotionally disturbed and mentally disabled individuals into classrooms and communities are often met with much resistance. David Mechanic (1999), a prominent social policy analyst in the mental health field, argues that the stigma attached to the labels the mentally ill and disabled are given is far more damaging to them than the extent of their problems. He believes that definitions of mental illness are made at varying levels in the social structure. Early informal definitions are made in groups within which the person operates, usually family members or coworkers. Such definitions depend on the norms of the particular group and what is tolerated, as well as on the position the person occupies within the group. A boss's behavior, for example, may be defined as outside the group norms much less quickly than a file clerk's. Definitions of this type also depend on whether the other members of the group can empathize—that is, whether they can fit that behavior into their own frames of reference. For example, a person who continually carries on an imaginary conversation with his mother while on the job is more likely to be tolerated if the group is aware that the mother recently died and the son is still grieving her death. But if there is no apparent context for the behavior or if the behavior persists, such individuals are likely to be labeled as strange or odd (Mechanic, 1999).

Definitions of so-called abnormal behaviors typically are based on visible symptoms, such as talking to people who are not present, rather than the severity of the actual problems.

Anytime you attempt to define a condition based on invisible factors, such as what is going on inside an individual's mind, specific definitions are difficult to achieve. Only those who in some way enter the mental health system are likely to be specifically defined as having some type of emotional problem. The mental health system, in spite of its problems, is likely to accept—at least for short periods of time—almost all individuals who seek its services, including the unwanted, the aged, the indigent, the lonely, and those with nowhere else to go. At times, this practice results in overestimates of the number of individuals defined as having emotional problems and underestimates of those who should enter the system.

Categorizing Mental Illness

Formal definitions of mental illness traditionally have followed the **medical model,** which considers those with emotional problems as sick and thus not responsible for their behavior. This model also assumes that sick people are entitled to be helped and that help or treatment should be guided by the medical profession in medical settings or settings such as psychiatric facilities directed by medical professionals. The medical model conceptualizes mental illness as severe emotional problems caused by brain dysfunction or intrapsychic causes, with little attention to systems or environmental influences. (See Chapter 3 for a comparison of the medical model and the systems/ecological perspective.) Traditionally, mental illness also has been viewed from a genetic or physiological perspective as a disease of the mind or a disturbance in the functioning of the individual.

The American Psychiatric Association has attempted to monitor the categorization and definition of various types of emotional disorders through a classification system termed the ***Diagnostic and Statistical Manual of Mental Disorders (DSM).*** This classification system is currently in its fourth revision and referred to informally as the *DSM-IV.* It uses a multiaxial system for evaluation, which focuses on the psychological, biological, and social aspects of an individual's functioning. The system incorporates information from five axes in diagnosing an individual. Axes I and II incorporate all of the mental disorders, such as schizophrenic and psychotic disorders. Axis III incorporates physical disorders and conditions. Axes IV and V rate the severity of the psychosocial stressors that have contributed to the development or the maintenance of the disorder and the highest level of adaptive functioning that the individual has maintained during the previous year (Williams, 1995).

Some social work professionals believe that the *DSM* classification system is consistent with a systems/ecological perspective in assessing an individual, allowing a focus on either organic factors or environmental factors, or both, that affect an individual's condition. They believe that the *DSM* allows for the incorporation of the individual's strengths as well as problems when completing an assessment. This classification system has been used increasingly in recent years for third-party insurance reimbursement when mental health services are provided (Williams & Spitzer, 1995).

Although many social workers find the *DSM-IV* helpful, its use by social workers and other professionals to label conditions of clients to obtain third-party insurance reimbursements has raised questions about whether such labels really are beneficial in improving services. Critics argue that such a diagnostic process may actually be more detrimental to clients, because labels such as "schizophrenia" or "conduct disorder" can negatively affect clients and the way others treat them, particularly if such labels included in clients' records are obtained and misused. More recent criticism of the *DSM* by social workers focuses on its reduced emphasis on environmental factors that affect a person's mental health and increased attention to disorders and deficits, more consistent with the medical model. Herb Kutchins and Stuart Kirk (1997), in their recent book *Making Us Crazy: DSM: The Psychiatric Bible and the Creation of Mental Disorders,* suggest that decisions surrounding what is considered a mental disorder are significantly shaped by societal prejudices and special interests. They note, for example, that the *DSM* included homosexuality as a mental disorder until 1973. These authors also point out the manual's lack of sensitivity to cultural factors that may shape a person's behavior.

The National Association of Social Workers (Karls & Wandrei, 1994) has published an alternative classification system, the person-in-environment system (PIE) that provides a more holistic approach based on the systems/ecological framework. Like the *DSM*, this system can also be used to describe, classify, and code the emotional, mental, and social problems experienced by adults. The PIE system assesses clients according to four major factors:

- Social functioning (social role in which each problem is identified: type of problem, severity of problem, duration of problem, and the client's ability to cope with the problem)
- Environmental problems (social system in which each problem is identified, specific type of problem within each social system, severity of the problem, duration of the problem)

- Mental health problems (clinical syndrome and personality and developmental disorders)
- Physical health problems (diseases diagnosed by a physician and other health problems reported by the client and others)

A major difference between the PIE and the *DSM* is that the PIE system focuses primarily on the importance of the interrelationship of the person and the environment. The PIE system also "seeks to balance problems and strengths; it delineates problems pertinent to both the person and the environment and qualifies them according to their duration, severity, and the client's ability to solve or cope with them" (Karls & Wandrei, 1994, p. 3). The PIE cannot be used as a basis for securing third-party payment as the *DSM* can.

Mental Health: A Matter of Viewpoint

The traditional view of mental health and mental illness is that they exist at opposite ends of a continuum. Others, like psychiatrist Thomas Szasz (1998), suggest that mental health and emotional problems are issues that defy specific boundaries. Szasz objects to labeling the mentally ill and argues that there is no such thing as mental illness. He agrees that there are illnesses due to neurological impairment, but he believes that such illnesses are brain diseases rather than mental illnesses. Although he acknowledges the existence of emotional problems, Szasz contends that labeling nonorganic emotional problems implies a deviation from some clearly specified norm. He feels that such labeling not only stigmatizes individuals but may cause them to actually assume those behaviors.

Szasz argues that instead of talking about definitions of mental illness, we should talk about problems of living—an individual's struggle with the problem of how to live in our world. He and others believe that positive mental health is promoted by our competence in dealing with our environment and our confidence of being able, when necessary, to cause desired effects. Szasz advocates a systems/ecological perspective for viewing mental health. Within his framework, problems in living can be viewed as being due to biological/physiological, economic, political, psychological, or sociological constraints. Promoting positive interactions between individuals and their environments is viewed as congruent with the promotion of optimal mental health and social functioning for individuals. Szasz (1998), a longtime activist in the mental health arena, proposes a classification system with the following categories of mental health problems:

- Personal disabilities, such as depression, fears, inadequacy, and excessive anxiety
- Antisocial acts, such as violent and criminal behaviors
- Deterioration of the brain, such as Alzheimer's disease, alcoholism, and brain damage

Many mental health experts prefer this system and its emphasis on healthy functioning to a system that emphasizes mental illness. This system assumes that at some point all individuals have difficulties in negotiating their complex environments. Mental health services are viewed as available to and needed by all individuals at some time during their lives rather than as something to be avoided. Szasz's perspective is much more consistent with the systems/ecological perspective and the PIE classification system than the medical model and the *DSM-IV*.

The Development of Mental Health Problems

There is considerable debate on how mental health problems occur. It is difficult, if not impossible, to say that one specific factor caused a mental health problem. More than likely, mental health problems are the result of a variety of factors. Research suggests a number of possible explanations

Heredity, Biological, and Genetic Factors

Recent research has determined significant relationships between biological factors and many mental health disorders. For example, modern brain imaging technologies indicate that in depression, neural circuits responsible for the regulation of moods, thinking, sleep, appetite, and behavior do not function properly, and critical neurotransmitters (chemicals used by nerve cells to communicate) are imbalanced. Genetics research indicates that vulnerability to mental disorders such as depression results from the influence of multiple genes acting together with environmental factors (National Institute of Mental Health, 1999). Research also suggests that schizophrenia, like heart disease and diabetes, results from the complex interaction of genetic, biological, developmental, and environmental factors. Mental illnesses are increasingly viewed as chemical imbalances of the brain. "Just as diabetes is a disorder of the pancreas, mental illnesses are brain disorders that often result in a diminished capacity for coping with the ordinary demands of life" (National Alliance for the Mentally Ill, 1999, p. 3).

Current research suggests that genetic factors alone do not cause mental health disorders but that some individuals are predisposed to certain problems through heredity, and under certain environmental conditions, this predis-position is triggered, resulting in the emotional problem. A variation of this position is that, due to genetic traits or physiological characteristics, some individuals are biologically less capable of coping with environmental stress.

Psychosocial Developmental Factors

This perspective, based on the work of developmental theorist Erik Erikson and others, suggests that mental health problems result from environmental experiences during childhood. Research shows that individuals who experience severe trauma during childhood—such as physical or sexual abuse, separation from a close family member, or alcoholism or drug abuse among family members—are much more likely to experience mental health problems later in life. Posttraumatic stress disorder, common among combat veterans, is also often experienced by survivors of child sexual and physical abuse and individuals who have witnessed violent attacks on others, particularly family members. Recent research indicates that exposure to such trauma also changes a person's brain chemistry, suggesting an interactive effect between physiological and developmental factors.

Social Learning

The social learning perspective suggests that mental health problems are the result of learned behaviors. Such behaviors may be learned by observing parents or other role models or used as survival mechanisms to cope with difficult life experiences.

Social Stress

This perspective, based on the work of Thomas Szasz (1998), focuses on the relationship between environmental stress and mental health, suggesting that individuals who are under greater stress—including the poor, people of color, and women—are more likely to experience mental health problems.

Societal Reactions and Labeling   This perspective suggests that society creates individuals with mental health problems through a societal reaction process. By establishing social norms and treating as deviant those who do not subscribe to the norms, a society identifies individuals with mental health problems. Additionally, individuals identified or labeled as somehow different will assume the role prescribed to them; that is, individuals labeled as having mental health problems will behave as they would be expected to if they had the problem. Individuals labeled as having mental health problems, even though they do not behave any differently from those without problems, may also be perceived as behaving differently because of how they are labeled (see Box 9.1).

Collective Mobilization   This perspective suggests that mental health problems are "as much the product of social expectations, social stigma, and exclusion from opportunities as they are a direct function of mental or physical impairments" (Mechanic, 1999, p. 85). Organizations representing persons with mental disabilities have mobilized to advocate for their inclusion in educational opportunities, employment, and access to social participation. These collective mobilization efforts have changed social definitions and viewpoints toward these groups, which in turn have changed individual behavior (Mechanic, 1999).

Systems/Ecological Perspective   This perspective suggests that mental health problems

---

BOX 9.1

Does Labeling Shape Our Expectations of How People Will Function?

The identification of individuals with mental health problems and the ways those problems are defined are hotly debated issues among mental health professionals. A number of years ago, psychologist David Rosenhan and his associates conducted a study that exemplifies this concern. Rosenhan (1973) and his seven colleagues went separately to the admissions offices of 12 psychiatric hospitals in five different states, all claiming that they were hearing voices. In every instance, they were admitted to the hospitals as patients. Immediately upon admission, they all assumed normal behavior. At least one of the researchers did not try to hide his role as a researcher—he sat on the ward and took copious notes on legal pads of all of the events going on around him.

In spite of the fact that the researchers all behaved completely normally while hospitalized, hospital professionals were unable to distinguish them from other patients. In a number of instances, however, the other patients were able to determine that they were not mentally ill. Rosenhan and his associates remained at the hospitals as patients from 7 to 52 days, with an average stay of 19 days, before they were discharged. The diagnosis at discharge for each of them was "schizophrenia in remission" (Rosenhan, 1973).

are the result of a variety of factors that interact in a complex fashion and vary according to the uniqueness of the individual and the environment within which he or she interacts. Current research on brain chemistry elevates the importance of physiological factors but also lends support to the systems/ecological perspective. Although environment cannot completely control whether a person develops an emotional disorder, it can certainly exacerbate the problem or, in some instances, facilitate an individual's ability to cope more effectively. Within the systems/ecological framework, for example, many factors that shape a person's self-concept, competence, and behaviors can be addressed, such as the person's biological characteristics; ethnicity; gender; place within the broader environment, including family, peer groups, and the neighborhood and community in which the person functions; and cultural and societal expectations.

The Systems/Ecological Perspective on Mental Health Issues

A systems/ecological perspective allows us to focus on all of the factors within an individual's past and present environment, as well as the individual's physiological characteristics, in addressing mental health problems. For example, a person may be predisposed biologically to experience mental health problems, may have suffered as a child from sexual abuse, may have had a parent who also experienced mental health problems, and currently may be in an extremely stressful living situation (for example, experiencing an unhappy marriage, a stressful job, or financial problems). If we know which factors are most important, we are much more likely to be able to intervene successfully in alleviating the problems. This focus on both the individual and the individual's environment allows the social worker and the client to "map out" the critical factors most likely to account for the problems and then to develop an intervention plan that specifically addresses those factors.

How and when an individual's emotional problems are identified and defined depend on a number of factors:

1. the visibility, recognizability, or persistence of inappropriate/deviant behaviors and symptoms;
2. the extent to which the person perceives the symptoms as serious;
3. the extent to which the symptoms disrupt family, work, and other activities;
4. the frequency of the appearance of the signs and symptoms, or their persistence;
5. the tolerance threshold of those who are exposed to and evaluate the signs and symptoms;
6. the information available to, the knowledge of, and the cultural assumptions and understandings of the evaluator;
7. the degree to which processes that distort reality are present;
8. the presence of needs within the family/environment that conflict with the recognition of problems or the assumption of the sick role;
9. the possibility that competing interpretations can be assigned to the behaviors/signs once they are recognized;
10. the availability of treatment/intervention resources, their physical proximity and psychological and monetary costs of money, time, and effort as well as costs of stigmatization and humiliation. (Mechanic, 1999, p. 114)

TYPES OF MENTAL HEALTH PROBLEMS

Although there is still extensive stigma toward those with mental disorders, increased openness by many persons with various diagnoses has created greater public awareness about them. The most common types of mental disorders are major depression, bipolar disorder (also referred to as manic depression), schizophrenia, anxiety disorders, attention deficit hyperactivity disorder, and autism. (Attention deficit hyperactivity disorder and autism are discussed later in the chapter in the section on developmental disabilities.)

Depression

Depression is the leading cause of disability worldwide, with many persons incapacitated for weeks or months if left untreated. Recent breakthroughs in effective medication have allowed large numbers of persons to lead completely typical lives. However, many people do not realize how debilitating depression can be and make fun of those who cannot function without medication. Depression is more than having a few bad days or sad moments; it is an overwhelming feeling of incapacitation that often results in not being able to get out of bed and go to work or school and being generally incapacitated. Symptoms include a persistent sad mood, loss of interest in activities once enjoyed, significant change in appetite and weight, changes in sleeping patterns, physical slowness or agitation, loss of energy, feelings of worthlessness, difficulty thinking or concentrating, and recurrent thoughts of death or suicide.

Nearly twice as many women (12%) as men (7%) are affected by depression each year, leading some researchers to suggest a relationship between hormonal imbalance and neurotransmitters of the brain. This argument is bolstered by the fact that most women diagnosed with depression are of childbearing age. Many women, as many as 50% to 90%, suffer postpartum depression after the birth of a child. Such depression has been linked to the abrupt hormonal changes that take place after childbirth. With better clinical skills and increased attention given to mental health issues in children and adolescents, more young people are also being diagnosed with depression. Recent estimates suggest that 2.5% of children and 8.5% of adolescents have severe and persistent depression.

Approximately 80% of individuals experiencing depression respond positively to treatment. Although new types of medication have helped many individuals with depression, a preferred method of treatment includes a holistic approach, incorporating counseling with an emphasis on cognitive/behavioral approaches to change negative thought patterns that often accompany depression, a healthy diet, exercise, and medication. Biofeedback and learning to monitor how one's body reacts to stress have also been found to be successful for some individuals experiencing depression. Electroconvulsive therapy, producing a seizure in the brain, has been extremely successful in improving severe depression in many individuals, but this procedure remains highly controversial because of its short-term and long-term side effects.

Bipolar Disorder

About 2.3 million people in the United States suffer from manic-depressive illness or bipolar disorder. Persons with bipolar disorder experience episodes of major depression as well as episodes of mania—

> periods of abnormally and persistently elevated mood or irritability often accompanied by overly-inflated self-esteem, decreased need for sleep, increased talkativeness, racing thoughts, distractibility, increased goal-directed activity or physical agitation, and excessive involvement in pleasurable activities that have a high potential for painful consequences. (National Institute of Mental Health, 1999, p. 2)

A combination of medications and holistic approaches to care have been successful in treating many individuals who experience bipolar disorder.

Schizophrenia

More than 2 million adults in the United States are affected by schizophrenia, the most chronic and disabling of the mental disorders. Increasingly thought to be a chemical disorder, this disorder usually appears in women in their 20s or early 30s and in men in their late teens or early 20s. Schizophrenia results in an impaired ability to manage emotions, interact with others, and think clearly, with symptoms that include hallucinations, delusions, disordered thinking, and social withdrawal. Although medication has helped large numbers of persons with schizophrenia, this disease is particularly debilitating and often results in periodic hospitalizations.

Only 20% of individuals with schizophrenia recover fully. More than half of individuals with schizophrenia receive inadequate care. They may spend time in a mental hospital where they are put on medication and then released; however, without appropriate community mental health facilities and outreach, many run out of medication or experience undesirable side effects and stop taking their medication. The stigma toward persons with schizophrenia results in many becoming homeless and at risk for serious safety and health problems. Approximately 10% of persons diagnosed with schizophrenia eventually commit suicide. The National Institute of Mental Health recommends antipsychotic medication; additional medication for the depression, anxiety, or hostility that often accompanies the illness; electroconvulsive therapy in some instances with appropriate monitoring; individual and family therapy; vocational rehabilitation; and assertive intervention in communities to accept and provide adequately for persons with this disorder.

Anxiety Disorders

More than 16 million adults in the United States suffer from anxiety disorders, which include panic disorder, obsessive-compulsive disorder, posttraumatic stress disorder, social phobia, and generalized anxiety disorder. Panic disorder includes feelings of extreme fear and anxiety that strike for no apparent reason, resulting in an overpowering shortness of breath, feelings of being out of control, and other intense physical symptoms. Obsessive-compulsive disorder includes repetitive, intrusive thoughts or behaviors, such as washing one's hands or checking to see whether lights are turned off when leaving a room. Posttraumatic stress disorder is a reaction to previously experienced terrifying trauma that results in frightening memories or intense body reactions. Generalized anxiety disorder results in excessive worry over everyday events and decisions. Phobias include fear of specific or generalized objects or events. Anxiety disorders may occur because of a chemical imbalance in the brain, experiencing emotional trauma, or a learned response to specific situations. Anxiety disorders are increasingly treatable with medication and therapy. Cognitive behavioral and desensitization therapies have been found to be especially effective in treating anxiety disorders.

Suicide

Suicide is a serious mental health problem in the United States, which has a higher suicide rate than many other Western countries. In 1997, approximately 31,000 people committed suicide in the United States. In this country that year, suicide was the eighth leading cause of death; homicide ranked 13th (American Association of Suicidology, 1999). People who suffer from manic-depressive illness, schizophrenia, and other mental health disorders are much more likely to make suicide attempts than others. There is also a strong relationship between substance abuse and suicide. Research indicates that 90% of people who commit suicide have some type of diagnosable mental or substance abuse disorder. Alterations in neurotransmitters such as serotonin are not only associated with depression, impulsive disorders, and substance abuse but also suicide (National Institute of Mental Health, 1999).

Determining which groups are most at risk to commit suicide is complex. Risk factors associated with suicide vary by ethnicity, gender, and age and often occur in combination. The highest rate of suicide in the United States is found in white males over age 85. The suicide rate for children and adolescents has increased significantly in recent years. In 1996, the most recent year for which statistics are available, suicide was the third leading cause of death among 15- to 24-year-olds and the fourth leading cause for children 10 to 14. The suicide rate is highest for white males and lowest for African American females. Men are more than four times as likely to commit suicide because they choose more lethal methods, although women are more likely to make a suicide attempt.

Attempts at suicide are also increasing; in 1997, over 750,000 people in the United States made suicide attempts. It is estimated that over 5 million living Americans have tried to kill themselves at some point in their lifetime

(American Association of Suicidology, 1999). The greatest risk factors associated with suicide attempts for adults are depression, alcohol abuse, cocaine use, and separation or divorce; while risk factors for youth include depression, alcohol or other drug use, and aggressive or disruptive behaviors. Other risk factors include a prior suicide attempt, family history of mental or substance abuse disorder or suicide, family violence, firearms in the home, incarceration, and exposure to the suicidal behavior of others, including family, peers, and the media in news or fiction stories (National Institute of Mental Health, 1999).

While the majority of persons contemplate suicide at some point in their lives, persons who make suicide attempts are likely to have experienced one or more significant losses in their lives—the loss of a parent, sibling, spouse, close friend, good health, or a job. They feel helpless and hopeless and are experiencing so much pain that they do not see any options other than ending their pain. Loneliness and isolation, coupled with lack of a stable support system, are other significant factors associated with persons who attempt suicide (Ivanoff & Reidel, 1995).

Persons at risk to attempt suicide also often abuse alcohol and other drugs as a means of reducing their pain. But because alcohol and some other types of drugs are depressants, these substances tend to make a depressed person more depressed, as well as impairing the person's ability to think rationally. Poor health, particularly among the elderly, who may not see any hope of getting better and may not want to be an emotional or financial burden to anyone, also contributes to suicide among this population. Other risk factors include having made previous attempts, changing from a depressed, hopeless perspective to suddenly seeming to get better, and giving possessions away.

Most suicide threats are not just attempts to get attention but outcries for help. Suicide threats by any person should be taken seriously. In such situations, persons should not be left alone, and immediate mental health intervention should be sought. Although much discussion has taken place about the relationship between increased access to firearms and increases in homicide rates, it is interesting to note that 58% of suicides are committed with firearms and that firearms are used to commit suicide far more often than to commit homicide.

Because the reasons that people make suicide attempts are complex and variable, multiple prevention efforts are needed. Community- and school-based prevention programs that focus on stress reduction, coping skills, substance abuse, and early identification and treatment of emotional problems, as well as limiting access to firearms, are suggested prevention strategies (National Institute of Mental Health, 1999).

Homelessness

Although homelessness was discussed in Chapter 8, it is important to note the relationship between homelessness and mental health and substance abuse problems. The release of the mentally ill, developmentally disabled, and chemically dependent from institutional care and the lack of community services have resulted in a significant increase in homelessness in the United States. The stresses of being homeless increase a person's risk to become mentally ill or chemically dependent. Approximately 30% of the homeless are mentally ill, and about 15% of homeless women and 45% of homeless men have serious problems with alcoholism or drug abuse (Burt, 1992; Koroloff & Anderson, 1989).

Many homeless persons have some type of mental health problem that contributes to their being homeless. In contrast, many individuals who are homeless, because of the stress of survival and the stigma associated with being homeless, develop mental health problems *after* they become homeless. In one study, researchers who tracked individuals released from a state hospital in a large Ohio metropolitan area for a 6-month period after their release found that 36% became homeless during this period. Of that group, approximately 75% were chronically mentally ill, and 15% were both mentally ill and substance abusers (Burt, 1992). Sosin (1989) compared homeless persons with very poor but not homeless persons. He found that 23.4% of the homeless persons studied had symptoms of alcoholism compared to 15% of never homeless persons, and 20% of the homeless had previous mental hospitalizations compared to 8.7% among the never homeless. But of those who were homeless and had been hospitalized in mental hospitals, over one-third had been hospitalized for the first time after they were homeless.

Many homeless mentally ill have serious cognitive disturbances, like Joanna (at the beginning of this chapter), and are out of touch with reality, unaware of where they are going or where they have been. Their most frequent contacts with community resources are with the police and emergency psychiatric facilities. Typically, they remain on the streets, extremely vulnerable, until they are unable to function and are rehospitalized. For many, their lives become a pattern of homelessness and hospitalization (Liebow, 1993).

ALCOHOLISM AND CHEMICAL DEPENDENCY

Problems of alcoholism and chemical dependency can be related not only to the area of mental health but also to developmental disabilities, child and family issues, poverty, criminal justice, and the workplace. Vulnerable populations, including women, the elderly, people of color, and gays and lesbians, are also at greater risk to experience serious problems with alcoholism and chemical dependency than other groups.

Alcohol abuse and alcoholism were until recently considered to be moral issues. The general societal perception was that persons drank too much because they were weak, and they could stop drinking if they wanted to. While many people still hold this view, during the 1940s and 1950s attention began to focus instead on the concept that alcoholism is a disease and must be treated as one might treat a person with diabetes or another chronic illness. The common contemporary view considers alcoholism as a chronic condition, meaning it is treatable but incurable; progressive, meaning it becomes worse if the drinking does not stop; and fatal, since if it is untreated, death can result.

Although debate continues on whether alcoholism should be viewed as an individual disease, a family or societal disease, or an individual, family, or societal problem, there are some advantages to conceptualizing alcoholism using the disease model. First, persons and their families are more likely to accept the alcoholism and become involved in an intervention program if they view the alcoholism as a disease rather than as a moral weakness or a social problem. Second, conceptualizing alcoholism as a disease also allows for coverage for treatment and hospitalization by insurance companies and public health care programs. Because of recent legislation in many states, the serious abuse of other drugs also can be treated as a disease. But because use of drugs other than alcohol more often involves illegal and/or counterculture activities, there has been much more reluctance to consider the abuse of drugs other than alcohol as a disease.

Alcoholism and the abuse of other drugs are denied as problems affecting them by many substance abusers and their families, who define a substance abuser in many ways— as someone who takes one more drink or drug than they or their family member takes; as someone who only drinks excessive amounts of hard liquor and not beer or wine as they do; as someone who uses more dangerous drugs and not marijuana, which they use; or as someone who drinks and uses every morning or every day and not only evenings or weekends, as they do. More recent definitions of alcoholism and chemical dependency focus on the personal implications of the drinking or drug use rather than the amount or frequency.

Alcoholism has been defined as any use of alcohol that results or interferes with personal life—including school, jobs, family, friends, health, or the law—or spiritual life (Royce & Scratchley, 1996). Definitions of drug abuse are similar. Although the abuse of alcohol is considered more socially acceptable than the abuse of other drugs, it is increasingly difficult to separate the two. It is important to call attention to the fact that alcohol is still the most widely misused drug and that it, too, has serious individual and societal costs. But 80% of persons under age 20 and 60% of persons under age 40 abuse more than one substance. Current research on addiction also shows that many individuals treated for one type of **substance abuse** stop using that substance and "cross-addict" to another drug. Thus, persons in the field of chemical dependency often refer to the substance a person has abused as his or her "drug of choice" and to those who abuse more than one drug as "polyaddicts."

Other professionals view chemical dependency as a problem of **addiction,** which can be defined as a "physical and/or psychological dependence upon mood changing substances, including, but not limited to, alcohol, drugs, pills, food, sex, or money" (Parkside Medical Services Corporation, 1988, p. 4). This conceptualization would support a treatment focus on eliminating addictive behaviors in all areas of a person's life, including food, work, and relationships as well as drugs.

Commonly Abused Substances

Alcohol, the oldest and most commonly abused substance in the world, is most often viewed as a depressant, although it can also be a stimulant, and, for some individuals, a hallucinogen. Nearly half of people over age 12 in the United States use alcohol. Of the 10 to 15 million persons in the United States who are considered alcoholics or problem drinkers, it is estimated that 4.5 million are adolescents. The leading cause of death for U.S. teens 15 to 24 is alcohol-related auto accidents. Medical problems stemming from alcohol abuse include neurological, cardiological, and respiratory problems; liver disease; damage to the gastrointestinal system, pancreas, and kidneys; malnutrition; suppression of the immune system; and psychological problems.

Other **depressants** include sedatives, such as sleeping pills, tranquilizers, and pain killers. Women and persons who have experienced or are experiencing chronic pain are two

groups more at risk to abuse depressants than other groups.

Narcotics such as opium and its derivatives, morphine and heroin, are also highly addictive. Legally, cocaine is considered a narcotic, but it often acts more like a stimulant, creating a high in its users. Although recreational use of cocaine declined in the late 1980s and early 1990s, its use increased again in the mid-1990s, particularly among adolescents. Cocaine is the most powerful central nervous system stimulant known. Crack, the smokable, rapidly reacting form of cocaine, has become extremely popular in recent years because of its lower cost, easy availability, and highly addictive nature. Use of crack and cocaine not only often results in high rates of addiction but also delusional and paranoid behavior, acute toxic psychosis, cardiovascular problems including strokes and heart attacks, depression, neurological problems, lung problems including respiratory failure, increased injury from accidents, increases in aggressive and violent behavior, and risks of hepatitis, HIV infection, and endocarditis (heart inflammation) (Phoenix House, 1999). Crack use also has resulted in high increases in crime, overdoses, prostitution, AIDS, and homelessness. Publicity has also focused on "crack" babies, who are born addicted and at risk to die during the 1st year of their lives or to survive with serious physical and emotional problems.

Heroin, which in the past was more likely to be used by individuals living in poverty in inner-city areas, has more recently become a drug of choice among middle-class youth and is currently the most commonly abused of all narcotics. A morphine derivative, heroin use affects the autonomic nervous system and often causes increased euphoria, which results in dangerous and often violent behaviors; life-threatening cardiological and respiratory problems; hepatitis, AIDS, and other infections; and addiction. Most habitual users are incapable of clear thought, holding a job, or maintaining relationships (Phoenix House, 1999).

Stimulants often abused also include caffeine—legal but not nearly as safe as once thought; nicotine found in tobacco, which is highly addictive and results in many serious health problems, including lung cancer and emphysema; and amphetamines such as speed.

Illicit drugs also include the **hallucinogens,** such as LSD, and marijuana, the most commonly used. One group of substances that is abused and often overlooked is inhalants. Use of inhalants is especially prevalent among Latino youth and often results in retardation or death. A wide variety of inhalants are used, including petroleum products such as gasoline, freon, aerosol products, paint, glue, and typewriter correction fluid. Amyl nitrate and butyl nitrate, commonly called "poppers," are also inhalants. Inhalant use can result in irresponsible, dangerous behavior; permanent brain damage; respiratory and cardiological problems; and sudden death (Phoenix House, 1999).

Marijuana is by far the world's most commonly used illegal drug. Although, like alcohol, many do not consider its use to be dangerous, marijuana's effects last for several days after its use. The drug inhibits the ability to learn and retain information and also results in respiratory and hormonal problems. Impairment of judgment and perception also results in increased accidents and violence; casual sex, sexually transmitted diseases, and pregnancy. In addition to its addictive nature, another concern is marijuana's use as a "gateway" drug. One study found that teens who used marijuana were 85 times more likely to use cocaine than those who did not use pot and that of those who used marijuana before they turned

15, 60% later went on to use cocaine (Phoenix House, 1999).

Social and Economic Costs of Substance Abuse

Substance abuse has been termed the most serious public health problem in the United States (New York State Office of Alcoholism and Substance Abuse Services, 1999). More deaths and disabilities occur each year from substance abuse than any other cause. But the problem extends much farther. The number of abused and neglected children in the United States in the last 10 years has more than doubled due to substance abuse. Eighty percent of children entering foster care come from families where substance abuse is a significant placement factor (New York State Office of Alcoholism and Substance Abuse Services, 1999).

While it is difficult to estimate the number of individuals who are dependent on alcohol or other drugs, current estimates suggest that 36 to 43 million persons in the United States, or 15% to 18% of the population, will become dependent on at least one drug during their lifetime (Royce & Scratchley, 1996). The majority of media attention is devoted to the use of drugs other than alcohol, primarily cocaine, crack, and heroin. Although it is difficult to obtain accurate numbers, recent national studies suggest that there are almost 10 million regular users of cocaine and that 25 million Americans have tried cocaine at least once.

Alcohol remains the most common drug of choice for most substance abusers in the United States. It is estimated that there are 15 million alcoholics in the United States and that 50 million Americans are affected directly by alcohol abuse by a family member. The common image of an alcoholic is an older male, unkempt, unemployed, living on the streets, derelict. In reality, only 3% of alcoholics can be characterized this way. About 45% of alcoholics hold professional or managerial positions, 25% are white-collar workers, and 30% are manual laborers. Physicians, air traffic controllers, airline pilots, law enforcement officers, attorneys, and members of the clergy all have high rates of alcoholism (Royce & Scratchley, 1996).

Children who grow up where substance abuse is a problem are also at risk of becoming substance abusers. Studies have found that 25% of males and 10% of females who grow up in families in which their parents abused either alcohol or other drugs become substance abusers themselves. Even those who do not develop substance abuse problems themselves often develop other addictive behaviors or experience emotional problems. Although fewer women repeat the pattern of substance abuse, they are much more likely to select a mate who is a substance abuser. Royce and Scratchley (1996) surveyed alcohol-related literature and journals, which reported that alcohol was involved in over half of child abuse and neglect cases, 40% of forcible rapes, 80% of spouse abuse cases, 8% of homicides, and 90% of incest situations.

As substance abuse becomes more widespread, the implications are becoming more obvious, more costly, and of greater concern. Costs include not only intervention for the substance abuser but also lost productivity, motor vehicle losses from accidents, and property losses from violent crimes. But cost estimates typically do not include personal costs such as physical and emotional injury and loss of life. The economic costs of alcoholism and alcohol abuse in the United States in 1999 were estimated at $313.6 billion (U.S. Substance Abuse and Mental Health Services Administration).

At-Risk Populations and Substance Abuse

Although substance abuse can affect anyone, some groups of people are more at risk than others. These groups include adolescents, the elderly, people of color, women, and children.

Adolescents   While alcohol abuse and chemical dependency are widespread among all age groups, their increased use among adolescents has caused concern. Recent studies show that approximately 25% of 10th graders and 33% of high school seniors reported drinking five or more drinks on at least one occasion within 2 weeks of the survey. Almost 11% of all teens between 12 and 17 reported using drugs at least once in the past month, almost twice the figure reported during the previous survey. The most alarming finding from the study, however, is the fact that reported use of tobacco, alcohol, and other drugs has increased 150% in the past 5 years (New York State Office of Alcoholism and Substance Abuse Services, 1999).

Whereas the death rate for other age groups has decreased, the death rate for adolescents has increased significantly in recent years, with most deaths due to traffic accidents and suicides in which alcohol or other drug abuse was a factor. Use of alcohol and other drugs by adolescents is often viewed as a way to be an adult—a "rite of passage" from childhood to adulthood—and part of the risk-taking behavior common among adolescents. Researchers who conducted a study in 1992 found a decrease in the numbers of individuals in the United States who believe that using drugs is not harmful for all age groups, but particularly for adolescents. Only 54% of 12- to 17-year-olds believed that a high risk was associated with trying cocaine once or twice (U.S. Department of Health and Human Services, 1994b).

But heavy substance abuse and addiction among adolescents is more often found among those experiencing other problems, such as survivors of childhood sexual abuse, gay and lesbian teens experiencing discrimination and oppression, and individuals experiencing depression. These adolescents turn to drinking and drugging to deaden their pain, as a form of self-medication so they will feel better or as a way to relate more comfortably to peers.

The Elderly   Substance abuse, particularly alcoholism, among the elderly is also a problem. This age group, like adolescents and young adults, also has a high death rate due to alcoholism, primarily because of chronic alcohol-related diseases such as cirrhosis of the liver, digestive diseases, and hepatitis. Factors associated with substance abuse among members of this group include loneliness and isolation and use of substances as coping mechanisms to deaden the pain they are experiencing because of physical or emotional problems in their present or past.

People of Color   Some ethnic groups are more at risk to abuse alcohol and drugs and to experience serious problems because of the abuse. African Americans, for example, are three times as likely to die as a result of alcoholism than whites, even though their actual rates of alcohol use are less than for whites, because of the interactive effects of oppression on access to healthy food and health care. The situation is similar for Latinos (Johnson, 1995).

Native Americans have the highest incidence of alcoholism of any ethnic group in the United States. They also have high rates of alcohol-related homicide, suicide, and serious car accidents. It has been estimated that as many as 50% of Native American children are born with either fetal alcohol syndrome or fetal alcohol effect, medical diagnoses of conditions at birth that usually result in serious developmental disabilities caused by the mother's consumption of alcohol during pregnancy.

Members of marginalized groups who are outside the mainstream of society are more at risk to abuse substances because they are more likely to be unemployed and living in poverty. Regardless of ethnicity, many individuals turn to alcohol and other drugs as coping mechanisms to overcome feelings of despair and hopelessness and discrimination. Additionally, in some communities drug pushers can easily tempt children, often from impoverished families, to become drug runners so that they can make large amounts of money quickly. While often still too young to realize the consequences of using drugs, they begin experimenting with the drugs they are delivering and become addicted themselves. The heightened risk of some ethnic groups for suffering the personal, emotional, and economic consequences of substance abuse raises a number of issues about our society, since nonmembers of these groups are most often those who oversee large-scale production and sale of drugs and reap the economic profits.

To be effective, interventions for people of color must be culturally relevant and sensitive. For example, while participation in Alcoholics Anonymous groups may be highly effective for some individuals, if group membership is largely white, people of color may not feel comfortable participating. Additionally, some cultures are reluctant to share any personal information outside of their families. Many Asians, for example, have been socialized to believe that personal problems they experience, like substance abuse, bring shame to their families and should not be discussed with people outside the family. From a macroperspective, opportunity and access to economic success are important ways to reduce substance abuse.

Women   Recent estimates suggest that one-third of all alcoholics in the United States are women and that 6 million women are addicted to drugs other than alcohol, with the largest increases among younger women. Women who abuse substances have different issues than men (Lex, 1994). They are more likely to abuse legal drugs, such as tranquilizers and sedatives, than male abusers. They are more likely to become addicted to multiple drugs and use drugs in isolation rather than with others. They are also more likely to have another family member who is a substance abuser and to have experienced rape, incest, or other sexual assault.

Women are much less likely to seek treatment than men, even though they experience more health problems related to their substance abuse and their lives are often more disrupted (Burman & Allen-Meares, 1991). Female substance abusers experience greater stigma than males. Researchers in one study found that 23% of women received opposition from friends and family when entering substance abuse treatment programs compared to 2% of men (Royce & Scratchley, 1996). Women are also less likely to have support from family members during treatment. Other studies show that in families in which alcoholism is a problem for male spouses, women remain in the relationship in 90% of situations. In families in which alcoholism is a problem for female spouses, however, men remain in the relationship only 10% of the time. Substance abuse has also resulted in increases in AIDS, prostitution, and homelessness among women.

Few substance abuse intervention programs are designed specifically for women, who face different issues than men. Women are more likely to experience depression and to abuse substances as a way to cope with the depression. They are also more likely to have been sexually abused, and repressed memories of sexual abuse often surface when women have been sober for a period of time. Recovery programs for women must include a recognition of client strengths, the impact of oppression on women and the financial disadvantages they face, the need for job skills, and the need for women to set healthy boundaries in and to establish positive and healthy relationships (Nelson-Zlupko, Kaufman, & Morrison Dove, 1995). Women also often need assistance with child care, transportation, support in parenting, housing, education, and employment as they recover from substance abuse (Finkelstein, 1994).

Children

Alcoholism and chemical dependency have serious impacts on children (see additional discussion in Chapters 11 and 12 and also Box 9.2). Increased attention has been given recently to the large numbers of infants born addicted or impaired because of their mothers' addiction or misuse of alcohol or other drugs during pregnancy. Five thousand infants born each year to addicted mothers in the United States have fetal alcohol syndrome, now the third leading cause of birth defects associated with mental retardation. Thousands more babies born to mothers who abused alcohol or other drugs during their pregnancies have other less serious disabilities.

Child welfare advocates suggest that the United States has not yet begun to experience the long-term effects of having such a large number of children born to women who are drug addicts. A recent report released by the

National Center on Addiction and Substance Abuse at Columbia University, *No Safe Haven: Parents of Substance-Abusing Parents* (Reid, Macchetto, & Foster, 1999), found that 7 out of 10 cases of child abuse and neglect are substance abuse related and that children whose parents are substance abusers are three times more likely to be abused and more than four times more likely to be neglected than children with non-substance-abusing parents.

Other Factors Associated with Substance Abuse

Reasons that substance abuse occurs are similar to the reasons that emotional problems occur among individuals. New research suggests that genetic factors may be associated with substance abuse. These include hereditary connections. Some researchers believe that substances are metabolized or broken down differently for some individuals, resulting in an inability of the body to eliminate some chemicals that then not only build up in the body but also serve as stimulants for even greater use when the addictive substance is used again.

Other researchers suggest that for some individuals, substance abuse is a form of self-medication or a way for them to attempt to regulate their emotions or the pain that they are experiencing. For example, persons who have been sexually abused, have experienced a significant personal loss or series of losses, or are depressed may use alcohol or other drugs to moderate their moods or try to deaden the pain they are experiencing. Other substance abuse experts suggest that persons use drugs to experience excitement, fit in with peers, alleviate pressure, or improve their performance along one or more dimensions; others see it as behavior learned from family members.

Intervention for Substance Abusers and Their Families

Early efforts to eliminate problems of alcoholism and substance abuse were aimed at moral rehabilitation, prohibition, and temperance. The most significant breakthrough in the alcohol field came in 1935 with the establishment of **Alcoholics Anonymous (AA),** a self-help group for alcoholics. AA was begun by Bill W., a New York stockbroker, and Dr. Bob, a physician, who discovered they could maintain sobriety by supporting one another and following a formal program of gradual recovery, which has since been incorporated into the 12 steps of AA. AA continued to grow in numbers and in popularity, and intervention efforts were developed that shifted attention from the moral concept of alcoholism to the disease concept. The formation of education and advocacy groups such as the National Council on Alcoholism in 1944 also aided in drawing increased attention to alcoholics' problems.

But needed federal attention to the problem of alcoholism did not occur until 1970, when Senator Harold Hughes of Iowa (a recovering alcoholic at the time of his election) advocated for the passage of the Comprehensive Alcohol Abuse and Alcoholism Prevention, Treatment, and Rehabilitation Act. This act provided financial assistance to states and communities to establish treatment, education, research, and training programs and established the National Institute on Alcohol Abuse and Alcoholism. The act also provided for the withdrawal of federal funding from any hospital that refused to treat alcoholics.

Much has been learned about intervention approaches, and programs have expanded significantly since the passage of the act. Although early intervention models focused on

BOX
9.2

A Young Adult's Story

Three years of drinking pushed a seemingly outgoing, good student to the depths of depression and despair. This is her story:

I began ninth grade excited about starting high school. I was like most other teenagers—I wanted to make good grades and be accepted by my teachers and peers. The peers I sought out were popular, cheerleaders, and on the student council, and they seemed to know everyone. I liked being included in their parties and other activities.

My mom asked me questions about my friends and the rules their parents had for them, but she usually let me go with them if I was waiting for her when she picked me up. At games and the other teen hangouts there was lots of drinking and it looked like people drinking were having a good time. One night I stayed over at a friend's house and we went to a party. When I was offered a beer I drank it. When the alcohol hit my body, I found I wanted more. That night I drank seven beers. I was 14 years old.

After that, I drank almost every weekend. I drank to be accepted, escape day-to-day pressures of my home and school life, and forget the pain from some experiences I had while growing up. When I drank, I usually laughed and clowned around a lot. People told me how much fun I was and what a great sense of humor I had. I felt relaxed and accepted when I drank.

I continued to drink on weekends, and my activities with my friends usually cen-

tered around sneaking beer or other alcohol from our parents' pantries or having older friends buy it for us. We drank it at games, parties, or at each other's houses after the parents were asleep. Soon we went to the mall to meet older guys. We had no sense of risk. Our parents dropped us at the mall, then we hopped in some guy's car to go to a party where everyone was drunk. Then we were dropped back at the mall in time for our parents to pick us up. We sprayed ourselves with perfume, chewed gum, and somehow managed to hide our drinking from our parents most of the time. I often felt guilty about my drinking and worried about what my parents would do if they found out, but I also enjoyed it. I felt grown up, and my friends enjoyed telling me how hilarious I had been with all of my antics. Boys paid a lot of attention to me and I discovered that it was much easier to relate to them when I had been drinking.

I became more popular and was elected to the student council. I rationalized that drinking even helped my grades, since the few times I decided that I was drinking too much and stopped for a week or two, I became depressed and my grades went down. I became more involved in school activities, got a part-time job at the mall, and partied even more. When my parents confronted me with their suspicions about my drinking, I either managed to convince them that everyone else was drinking except me or to tell them that I had a little bit now and then, but didn't every teenager?

During my junior year I made the dance team. I thought all my feelings of insecurity and my drive to fit in would be over, and that I could slow my drinking. To my surprise, being on the dance team meant even more pressure. I had to maintain my popularity, be more involved in school activities, and work even harder to be sure that I wasn't surpassed by the many girls who I thought were almost all smarter, prettier, and had more personality than I did. Soon I was drinking in the locker room in the morning before dance practice "just to wake me up and help me stretch better," in the parking lot or the bathroom after lunch "just to make it through the afternoon," or at my job "just to make it until closing," and always on the weekends.

I still could hide my drinking from teachers and my parents. I sat in the back of the classroom, answered questions, and did my homework and handed it in on time. I always gave my parents a plausible explanation what I would be doing when I went out and I was lucky enough to be where I said I would be when they checked up on me. When I didn't drink a lot, I came home at or before my curfew. When I did drink a lot, I stayed overnight at friends' homes. I began blacking out at parties and waking up at a friend's house and not remembering how I got there. I rode with drivers who were drunk and I would drive when I was drunk too. I also

began to get involved with a lot of guys who I never would have gotten involved with if I had been sober. I got really scared about getting pregnant, since I knew someone could take advantage of me during my blackouts.

At that point my drinking wasn't fun anymore, but I couldn't stop. In fact, I began drinking more and more. It was nothing for me to drink 16 to 17 cans of beer all by myself in one night. All of my friends could still drink and enjoy it but it started getting me in trouble. My grades went down and I started skipping school. I became edgy and worried about everything. I started having fights with my friends and my family over little things. The drinking was controlling me. The more I drank, the worse I felt, and the worse I felt, the more I needed to drink to ease my pain. What had started out to be fun was now completely out of my control.

During the summer my parents suspected something was really wrong. I started seeing a psychologist, and both she and my parents tried to convince me that my drinking was a problem and that I was using it to escape the pain I had about some of the things that had happened in my life. I got angry at them and refused to see the psychologist. I began to rebel more and more. One night a party I was at turned into a brawl. I got knocked out when I tried to break up a fight. I left with a friend and a guy I barely knew. I woke up the next morning in the guy's apartment, and couldn't remember what had happened. Driving home I was still so drunk that I had to stop and get out of the car to read the street signs, and I was only a half mile from home. I told my parents we'd stayed up all night talking at my girlfriend's house and I slept the whole next day.

Gradually I stopped caring what everyone thought of me and trying to hide my drinking from my parents. Finally one weekend I stayed out all night when I had a midnight curfew. When I came home and got grounded, I ran away and stayed with a friend for 3 days, mostly drinking. When my friend went to work, I got a six-pack of beer and drank it alone. When I came home my parents grounded me for a month and took away my car. They told me I had to see the psychologist. I was going to leave home for good, but I knew that I had reached a dead end and that my life was out of control. I didn't care about myself, my parents, or anything any more. Life had no purpose.

When I was confronted with my drinking again, I decided to enter a treatment program. I was tired of fighting, and at that time I thought that anything, even treatment, would be better than living at home and being nagged about my behavior. I now realize that entering treatment was the most important risk I have ever taken. The 6 weeks that I spent there were some of the hardest days of my life, but they were also some of the best. I was able to get rid of some of the pain, hurt, and anger that I had stored up for so many years. I learned new ways to communicate, share my feelings, and how to have fun while I was sober instead of drunk. I realized not only had I hurt myself, but also my family and other people who cared about me. My whole family took part in my treatment and we all grew together. They began going to Alanon while I went to Alcoholics Anonymous.

After I got out of treatment, I continued to attend AA regularly. I had found a place where I fit in. AA members understood how I felt and where I was coming from. Each day got better for me. I became more content and gained self-confidence. I also found the peace I had never had before. I got in touch with myself and met many wonderful people in the process. Today, I am a recovering alcoholic and have now been sober for 2 years. Finding sobriety at 17 has meant a whole new world for me. I have fallen in love with a wonderful person who understands my need for sobriety, and we are building our life together. My family and I enjoy being together. I am a college sophomore and plan to attend graduate school and work with children. I have goals and a sense of purpose I didn't have before. Although life is still difficult, I have learned to take things as they come, one day at a time. I am grateful that I had the courage to change myself.

Source: Journal entry by an anonymous student, University of Texas at Austin, 1991.

Substance abuse has long-term implications for family members without effective intervention. Here, a social worker focuses on building a trusting relationship with one of the children she counsels in a substance abuse treatment program for mothers and their children.

© Steve Chenn/Corbis

inpatient hospitalization and participation in Alcoholics Anonymous, research has shown that these programs are not effective with all substance abusers. Different types of clients require different intervention approaches. Some clients are so entrenched in their substance abuse that they require hospitalization, often undergoing detoxification before they can effectively begin treatment. Most hospitalization programs range in length from 30 to 60 days, although many substance abuse professionals argue that 30 days is not long enough for those receiving treatment to recover enough to stay sober after being released from the hospital.

In fact, in spite of the fact that some persons cannot achieve initial sobriety without being hospitalized so they can be removed from their daily environment in which they are used to abusing their drug of choice; insurance companies are increasingly refusing to pay for even short-term inpatient treatment. Proponents of outpatient and partial hospitalization programs argue that clients should be made to deal with the pressures of day-to-day living while receiving support from the program, rather than being placed in a sheltered therapeutic environment away from the previous pressures and individuals with whom they abused substances. Whether treatment is in- or outpatient, treatment programs usually include community-based self-help groups such as Alcoholics Anonymous or Narcotics Anonymous (NA). Individuals released from treatment programs are usually encouraged to continue attending NA or AA meetings, as well as aftercare programs, usually held evenings and weekends for periods of time up to 1 year after leaving the more intensive intervention program.

A family systems model is viewed by many addiction specialists as the most effective way to treat substance abuse, since family members reinforce, often unconsciously, the abuser's drug use and learn individual patterns of coping that often result in intergenerational substance abuse in families (Black, 1987). As a result, many chemical dependence programs in which social workers are employed incorporate a family systems model and also provide psychoeducational experiences for other family members in addition to the client. These experiences involve educational and therapy sessions with other clients and their families as well as individual, group, and family therapy.

Some chemical dependence programs focus on a more cognitive/behavioral approach, particularly with adolescents and persons in the criminal justice system. These approaches focus on consequences for abusing substances and other inappropriate behaviors and on reinforcers for appropriate actions. Many juvenile and adult corrections programs, including jails and prisons, include substance abuse treatment. But services are often limited in both duration and numbers served, in spite of the large numbers of inmates who are incarcerated because of substance abuse–related crimes. Without treatment, these individuals are likely to be incarcerated again, often for more serious crimes. Agencies that serve clients with a wide range of problems are incorporating special programs targeted at substance abuse. Many child protective services agencies that work with abusive and neglectful parents indicate that recent increases in reports of child maltreatment are related to substance abuse. In response, these agencies have developed substance abuse treatment programs for their clients. Such programs also incorporate information on parenting and the impact of substance abuse on children.

Few inpatient or residential programs exist for women with children that also provide care for the children. Those that do emphasize modeling of parenting skills, working through communication problems and other family dynamics, and providing a safe, supportive environment for both the mothers and their children with others in similar circumstances so they do not need to go through the added stress of reuniting with their children when the treatment is over. Increasingly, substance abuse programs also address the needs of clients who have other emotional problems in addition to substance abuse (**dual diagnosis**). Often, an individual will go through treatment for chemical dependence and, after maintaining sobriety for an extensive period of time, return to the mental health system for additional help in dealing with other emotional problems such as depression or family-of-origin issues, including sexual abuse.

DEVELOPMENTAL DISABILITIES

Generally, the term **developmental disability** refers to developmental problems, such as mental retardation or cerebral palsy, that developed before adulthood. Although in the past these persons were often referred to as "mentally retarded" or "mentally handicapped," today the terms *developmentally disabled* or *physically challenged* are preferred because they are viewed as less negative. But because individuals with developmental disabilities may have specific preferences about such terms, it is best to ask the person how he or she wants to be addressed (see Box 9.3).

In 1984, Congress passed the Developmental Disabilities Assistance and Bill of Rights Act (PL 98-527), which defined developmental disability as follows:

BOX
9.3

The Me in the Mirror

Do you know what people with disabilities want? Nothing special, nothing unusual. We want to be able to attend our neighborhood school, to use the public library, to go to the movies, to get on a bus to go shopping downtown or to visit friends and family across town or across the country. We want to be able to get into our neighborhood polling place to vote with everyone else on election day. We want to be able to get married. We want to be able to work. We want to be able to provide for our children. We want high quality, affordable medical care.* We want to be seen as real people, as part of society, not someone to be hidden away, or pitied, or given charity. We reject media portrayals that show us as evil, or pitiful, or super-cripples. We just want to be seen as what we are—regular people.

There are 49 million of us. Our disabilities vary. We cut across all designations of race, religion, politics, income, sexual orientation—you name it—whatever labels we use to describe and divide people, some people in each of those groups are disabled. I have read that most people will at some point in their lives experience a temporary or permanent disability and that virtually all families will be touched by the disability of one or more of its members. This makes me ask, what could be more *normal* than disability?

*Do you have time for another horror story? This highlights the kind of attitude that leads to discrimination. My family doctor recommended that I see a gynecologist and gave me a doctor's name. I called to check accessibility and the receptionist told me that I probably could get in okay with the wheelchair but she really didn't think it was a good idea for me in a wheelchair to sit in a waiting room full of pregnant women. What did she think? That they'd look at me and give birth to monsters?

Source: From "The Me in the Mirror" by Connie Panzzarino in The Disability Rights Activist: Why Disability Rights? at http://www.disrights.org/dr-whydr.html. April 10, 1996. Reprinted with permission of Adrienne Rubin Barhydt.

A severe, chronic disability of a person which
(a) is attributable to a mental or physical impairment or combination of mental and physical impairments;
(b) is manifested before the person attains age twenty-two;
(c) is likely to continue indefinitely;
(d) results in substantial functional limitations in three or more of the following areas of major life activity: (i) self-care, (ii) receptive and expressive language, (iii) learning, (iv) mobility, (v) self-direction, (vi) capacity for independent living, and (vii) economic self-sufficiency; and
(e) reflects the person's need for a combination and sequence of special, interdisciplinary, or generic care, treatment, or other services which are of lifelong or extended duration and are individually planned and coordinated. (PL 98-527, Title V, 1984)

This definition was expanded on in the **Americans with Disabilities Act (ADA),** passed in 1990, to include persons with AIDS, substance abusers, and individuals with mental disorders.

Although over 75% of those classified as having developmental disabilities are mentally impaired, other individuals also may be so classified due to cerebral palsy; epilepsy; autism; spina bifida; or speech, hearing, vision, or orthopedic disabilities. Other individuals may have learning disabilities, such as dyslexia (a reading disability in which symbols are perceived differently than they are) or attention deficit disorder (an inability to pay attention to an activity for a reasonable amount of time that may also include hyperactivity). Of those individuals classified as mentally disabled, 75% are only mildly disabled and can be educated to function fairly independently or with some supervision, 20% are moderately disabled, and only 5% are profoundly disabled and need constant care and supervision.

Increased attention has also been given to early identification of children with developmental delays to try to prevent more serious disabilities in later life. **Developmental delay** is the

slowed or impaired development of a child under 5 years old who is at risk of having a developmental disability because of the presence of one or more of the following:

- Chromosomal conditions associated with mental retardation;
- Congenital syndromes and conditions associated with delay in development;
- Metabolic disorders;
- Prenatal and perinatal infections and significant medical problems;
- Low birth weight infants weighing less than 1200 grams;
- Postnatal acquired problems known to result in significant developmental delays;
- A child less than 5 years old delayed in development in one or more of the fol-

lowing areas: communication, self-help, social-emotional, motor skills, sensory development or cognition;
- A child less than 3 years old who lives with one or both parents who have a developmental disability. (Developmental Disabilities Center, 2000, p. 1)

Factors Associated with Developmental Disabilities

The types of disabilities vary as much as the factors associated with them, and researchers still are uncertain why some types of disabilities occur. But a number of factors are associated with developmental disabilities based on current knowledge and research:

- *Hereditary and fetal development factors:* Factors such as metabolic disorders, brain malfunctions, or chromosomal abnormalities can result in disabilities such as Tay-Sachs disease and Down syndrome. Fragile X syndrome, a genetic disorder, is the leading cause of mental retardation. (ARC, 1999)
- *Prenatal factors:* Chemical and alcohol addiction, radiation, infections such as rubella (a form of measles), syphilis, and HIV, or exposure to environmental contaminants during pregnancy can result in disabilities, as can fetal malnutrition if mothers do not receive adequate prenatal care. Smoking also increases the risk of developmental delays, including mental retardation. (ARC, 1999)
- *Perinatal factors:* Premature birth, trauma at birth, and infections transmitted during birth, such as herpes, can result in developmental disabilities.
- *Postnatal factors:* Postnatal infections such as meningitis, trauma due to accidents or child abuse, lack of oxygen during illness or

an accident, and nutritional deficiencies can result in developmental disabilities. Environmental factors, such as lead poisoning, parents with severe emotional problems, or parental deprivation, also are important factors that can lead to developmental disabilities. Children who do not receive appropriate nurturing, especially during their early years, are often developmentally delayed, and if intervention does not occur soon enough, mental retardation, learning disabilities, or other types of problems can result and may be permanent.

Specific causes of developmental disabilities often cannot be identified. Many parents who give birth to children with such problems often spend a great deal of time—sometimes their entire lives—blaming themselves because their children have disabilities. Research has enabled the early identification of many types of disabilities, such as phenylketonuria (PKU), which results in retardation. A simple test at birth can allow for immediate treatment, which has virtually eliminated this problem in most Western countries. More attention needs to be given to understanding how and why such disabilities occur.

Legislation and Programs for Persons with Developmental Disabilities

Early efforts to improve conditions for the developmentally disabled focused primarily on institutionalization, usually in separate large state schools for the retarded, the blind, and the deaf. In the 1950s, parent advocates formed the Association for Retarded Children, which later became the Association for Retarded Citizens (ARC). This group has been instrumental in advocating for national and state legislation and improved conditions for the developmentally disabled. Additional attention to the needs of the disabled came during President John F. Kennedy's administration. Kennedy's developmentally disabled sister, Rosemary, received extensive publicity. Kennedy established the Presidential Panel on Mental Retardation during his term, which called for additional research and the development of a system that provided continuity in caring for the disabled. The Community Mental Health Centers Act, passed in 1963, included funding for research and facilities for this population.

The Americans with Disabilities Act

In 1986, the National Council on the Handicapped published its report, *Toward Independence*, which provided a comprehensive national approach to addressing problems of persons with disabilities. The Americans with Disabilities Act (ADA) (PL 101-336) passed both the House and Senate with little opposition and was quickly signed by President George Bush. Prior to the passage of the ADA, almost anyone could discriminate against a person with a disability. A major problem for many persons who experience mental illness or developmental disability has been the denial of basic rights that others take for granted. The ADA bans discrimination based on disabilities among private employers with a workforce of more than 15 persons, public accommodations, public services, transportation, and telecommunications. The act also extends protections included in the 1964 Civil Rights Act to an estimated 43 million people with physical and mental disabilities to include heart disease, diabetes, emotional illnesses, drug addiction, alcoholism, and persons with AIDS. The act requires public places—including nongovernment entities such as restaurants, hotels and motels, business places, and other facilities used by the general

Advocates for persons with disabilities still have to fight for accessibility in spite of legislation such as the Americans with Disabilities Act.

Stone/Robert E. Daemmrich

public—to provide reasonable accommodations to persons with disabilities, in terms of both service and employment. The act mandates the elimination of discrimination and establishes standards and mechanisms for enforcement.

The ADA significantly changed the way that persons with disabilities have been treated historically. Since the Elizabethan Poor Laws, persons with disabilities have been viewed as in need of public assistance, and definitions of who is disabled have been used primarily for determining eligibility for public assistance. The ADA empowers persons with disabilities to be less stigmatized by removing the numer-

ous barriers that have historically often forced them to remain isolated. Under the ADA, individuals with disabilities can insist on reasonable accommodations, as can their family members. For example, a mother of a child with a disability cannot be passed over for a job because the employer is worried that she will need to spend additional time with the child and miss extensive work time (Orlin, 1995).

As a result of the act, states and local communities have had to establish special transportation systems, place elevators and ramps in buildings, and install special telephones for persons with hearing impairments as well as for those in wheelchairs. Still more needs to be done, and additional education is also needed. One disabilities advocate, for example, gives the following report about her trip to check out accessibility at a large mall, which the mall manager claimed met ADA guidelines:

> There were numerous parking spaces for people with disabilities. However, they were in an area of the parking lot which was poorly lighted, and the closest entrance, some distance away, had heavy doors that could only be used by someone on crutches or in a wheelchair if someone came along to open them for you. There also was an elevator to go from the first to the second floor; however, it was located on the opposite side of the mall from this entrance. The one restroom that had been remodeled to meet ADA guidelines was not close to either this entrance or the elevator. The telephone that had been installed was in still another direction from all of the other facilities. The elevator and restrooms were marked in Braille, but the signs were made so poorly that it was impossible to distinguish the markings from each other. The manager had not considered the implications of these upgrades and has agreed to make changes so they are more accessible to persons with disabilities. (Barrera, 1995, p. 6)

The ADA also advocated for supported employment of individuals with disabilities, including employment for wages and benefits in workplaces that integrate both persons with and without disabilities and continuous on-the-job training to reinforce job skills. Community-based programs in many areas have obtained successful employment for clients with disabilities in recycling centers, mail centers, offices, food service settings, and landscaping and park programs. One program has successfully placed its clients as child care aides in centers that mainstream children with disabilities, giving them a chance not only to work but also to be successful role models for the children (Rapp, Shera, & Kisthardt, 1993).

The ADA has many implications for social service providers and social workers. Services must be accessible, and individuals cannot be denied participation in a program based on their disability, nor can they be required to participate in a program because of their disability (Orlin, 1995).

Researchers interviewing clients with disabilities who participated in social services programs found that social services providers often played a significant role in disempowering clients with developmental disabilities rather than empowering them to meet their own needs. For example, gainful employment and housing were identified by clients as their major needs if they were to live in a community setting rather than an institution (deinstitutionalization will be discussed later in this chapter). Yet 70% of clients interviewed said that the biggest obstacle they faced regarding employment was discouragement from their social service providers regarding seeking jobs (Rapp et al., 1993).

Social workers should ensure that clients have access to individuals who can meet their needs; for example, clients with hearing problems need social workers who can sign or interpreters to help them communicate. Additionally, social service agencies need to provide employment opportunities for persons with disabilities (and not just in agencies that work with persons with disabilities). Jobs can be structured with special equipment and accommodations such as part-time work and job-sharing. Table 9.2 suggests appropriate employment interventions for individuals with developmental disabilities, based on the systems/ecological framework, at levels of the environment ranging from the individual to the community. Successful programs for persons with disabilities require consistent advocacy and community support if people with disabilities are to receive the services they need.

Other Legislation

The quality of life for those who are mentally or developmentally impaired increasingly rests on the fate of federal and state legislation and funding, which decreased markedly since the 1980s. The previous pattern of categorical funding for mental health programs tied to specific client groups has been replaced by block grants to states that give each state considerable latitude in how it spends its funds. This change means that it is up to advocacy groups representing these constituents to try to ensure that resources are allocated to these groups.

In 1998, Congress passed several pieces of legislation aimed at providing services to individuals with disabilities. The Rehabilitation Act provides funding for education and rehabilitative services for persons with disabilities. The Assistive Technology Act offers resources for adaptive technology to assist persons with disabilities in leading more typical lives, and the Crime Victims with Disabilities Awareness Act provides specific services for persons with

TABLE 9.2	SAMPLE EMPLOYMENT INTERVENTIONS AT MULTIPLE LEVELS FOR PEOPLE WITH SEVERE MENTAL ILLNESS

Level	Sample Interventions
Individual	Career counseling
	Volunteer work opportunities
	Job placement
	Supported work
Group	Fairweather Lodge
	Job clubs
	Consumer-owned and consumer-operated businesses
	Consumer self-help groups
Organization	Make employment the number one agency priority
	Include considerations of work in all case reviews
	Set rewards for staff who get the most people employed
	Convert day treatment program to prevocational program
	Provide vocationally oriented staff training
	Put aside agency funds for transportation and clothing for work
Service system	Assign vocational rehabilitation counselors to treatment teams
	Increase funding for supported work programs
	Liberalize vocational rehabilitation eligibility criteria
	Include vocational content in core discipline degree programs
Community	Public educational campaign to reduce stigma in employment (for example, media exposure to consumer achievement)
	Chamber of commerce—initiated jobs program for clients

Source: C. Rapp, W. Shera, and W. Kisthardt, (1993), "Research Strategies for Consumer Empowerment of People with Severe Mental Illness," *Social Work*, 38(6), 731. Copyright 1993, National Association of Social Workers, Inc.

disabilities who are the victims of crime. Legislation that will be proposed by advocates in the first decade of the new millennium includes protection against discrimination in seeking housing, consumer protections in Medicaid managed care, adding persons with disabilities to the federal Hate Crimes Prevention Act, and funding and regulation of attendant services for persons with disabilities needing someone to assist them with daily care.

The United States has both the technology and the capacity to support persons with mental health problems and developmental disabilities in community-based settings. With adaptive equipment and facilities, and in some instances a personal care attendant, many persons with disabilities can function well in their own homes or a residential apartment-like facility with some assistance. Many can drive themselves to and from a workplace or use public transportation if it is disability-accessible, allowing them to hold jobs and make a living. However, people with disabilities remain one of the most discriminated-against groups in U.S. society. They are often left out when funding is allocated and programs are established. Many people with disabilities can contribute far more to society than they are allowed. But substantial and continuing resources will be required to help them reach their full potential.

CHANGING VIEWS TOWARD MENTAL HEALTH PROBLEMS, SUBSTANCE ABUSE, AND DEVELOPMENTAL DISABILITIES

As mentioned earlier in this chapter, the treatment of individuals with mental health problems has undergone considerable change.

Historically, the fate of the mentally ill depended on their family. In most cases, individuals remained at home and were at the mercy of family members. Although in some instances individuals were treated humanely, many mentally ill and retarded persons were chained in attics and cellars, and sometimes they were killed. When there were no family members to provide for them, they were often transported to the next town and abandoned. Later, almshouses were established (see Chapter 1). Some mentally ill or developmentally disabled individuals were placed in jails if they were deemed too dangerous for the almshouse. Most alcoholics also were jailed, and their family members, unable to care for themselves, were sent to almshouses.

The Pennsylvania colony's hospital, established in 1751 for the sick poor and "the reception and care of lunatics," was the first hospital in the United States that provided care for the mentally ill, although treatment of mentally ill patients was little better than it had been in jails and almshouses. Individuals deemed mentally ill were assigned to hospital cellars and placed in bolted cells, where they were watched over by attendants carrying whips, which were used freely. Sightseers paid admission fees on Sundays to watch the cellar activities.

From Inhumane to Moral Treatment

During the late 1700s, people throughout the world began to seek better approaches to address the needs of the mentally ill. What mental health historians describe as the first of four revolutions in caring for the mentally ill actually began in France rather than the United States, with a shift from inhumane to moral treatment. Phillippe Pinel, director of two hospitals in Paris, ordered "striking off the chains" of the patients in 1793, first at the Bicetre Hospital for the Insane in Paris. Pinel advocated for the establishment of a philosophy of **moral treatment,** which included offering patients hope, guidance, and support, and treatment with respect in small, family-like institutions.

The moral treatment movement soon spread to America. Benjamin Rush, a signer of the Declaration of Independence, wrote the first American text on psychiatry, advocating that the mentally ill had a moral right to humane treatment. But it was not until the 1840s, through the efforts of Dorothea Dix, a schoolteacher, that the mentally ill in the United States actually began to receive more humane treatment (see Chapter 1). Dix became aware of the plight of the mentally ill as a Sunday school teacher for a group of patients in a Massachusetts hospital. Appalled by what she saw, Dix gave speeches, wrote newspaper articles, and met with government officials to bring attention to the inhumane and abusive treatment she observed in the many facilities she visited. As a result of her efforts, a bill was introduced in Congress to use the proceeds from the sale of western land to purchase land for use in caring for the mentally ill. This bill was vetoed by President Franklin Pierce, setting a precedent for the federal government's refusal to be involved in state social services programs that remained unchanged until the New Deal era (see Chapter 8).

Refusing to give up, Dix turned her efforts to the individual states. By 1900, 32 states had established state mental hospitals. But Dix and other advocates for the humane treatment of the mentally ill soon had additional cause for concern. What began in many hospitals as humane treatment changed as hospitals became overused and overcrowded, admitting all who could not be cared for elsewhere. State insane asylums became warehouses, commonly described as snake pits.

Dix and her group of reformers demanded that strict guidelines be established for the treatment of mental hospital patients. Again, states responded, and expanding facilities adopted detailed and often burdensome operating procedures. Although abuse and neglect of patients decreased dramatically, the guidelines left little room for innovation, and until the 1960s, patients in state mental hospitals received little more than custodial care. In the years immediately following the Dix reform, nearly half of patients who had been admitted were released, often only to make room for new admissions and to alleviate overcrowding. Once the overcrowding stabilized somewhat, however, long stays in mental hospitals became the norm, with annual discharge rates falling to as low as 5%. While these state institutions had been intended to house a transitory patient population, the absence of effective treatment technologies forced the retention of many patients until their deaths. The desire for single state facilities to house large populations of mentally ill patients resulted in their location in rural areas, where land was less expensive, expansion of facilities possible, and the safety of the community protected. Thus, the state mental hospital became—and, in many instances, still is—the "principal industry" in the area where it is located.

Although much less attention was given to the developmentally disabled, institutionalization became prevalent for this group as well. During the 1850s, many states established state training schools for the retarded, which housed people who ranged from profoundly to mildly retarded. Many individuals who were retarded were also often mistakenly labeled as mentally ill and were placed in state hospitals for the mentally ill as well.

More Reforms Needed

In spite of the efforts of Dorothea Dix and others, overcrowded conditions and neglect of the mentally ill and developmentally disabled continued to exist in many state facilities. Facilities continued to be overcrowded, with large numbers of immigrant residents. While the staff could provide moral treatment, love, and respect to some residents, it was difficult for many to transfer this philosophy to foreigners. Also it was increasingly hard to get competent medical staff willing to work in state mental institutions. Graduates from medical school often were repelled by the foreigners, alcoholics, and severely disturbed individuals who populated the institutions.

A second effort to reform conditions in state mental hospitals was undertaken in the early 1900s by Clifford Beers, a Yale graduate from a wealthy family who had been hospitalized in a Connecticut mental hospital for 3 years. Beers almost immediately suffered a relapse after his release and was hospitalized for a second time. During this stay, he began to formulate plans for more effective treatment of the mentally ill. He kept careful notes of the maltreatment he received from physicians and the well-intended but ineffective care he received from caretakers. After his release in 1908, Beers wrote a book, *A Mind That Found Itself*, which exposed the horrendous conditions in mental hospitals. This book led to the formation of state mental health advocacy organizations, such as the Connecticut Society for Mental Health. Later, state organizations formed the National Association for Mental Hygiene, which became a lobbying force for the continual reform of state hospitals and the development of alternative systems of care.

The Introduction of Psychoanalysis

What has been described as the second revolution in the mental health field occurred in the early 1900s with the writings of Sigmund Freud and the introduction of **psychoanalysis** in the United States. Professional mental health workers trained in Freud's techniques attempted to gain cooperation and insight through verbal or nonverbal communication with patients, seeing them at regular intervals over long periods of time.

The first social workers hired to work in state mental hospitals actually were hired before Freud's teachings were introduced into the United States. Their primary role was to provide therapy to clients, but it was based on a limited knowledge about what the therapy should entail. As psychoanalysis gained popularity in the United States, psychiatric social workers, like others working with the mentally ill, were quick to adopt a system of therapy that was reportedly much more effective than the often haphazard treatment they were using. In 1905, Massachusetts General Hospital in Boston and Bellevue Hospital in New York City hired psychiatric social workers to provide therapy to patients. But because of staff shortages and the large numbers of patients, few patients actually received psychotherapy, which requires highly trained therapists, fairly verbal patients who speak the same language as the therapist, and long hours of treatment to be effective. Psychotherapy as a treatment approach for dealing with mental health problems was more likely to be used in outpatient facilities, either private practices established by psychiatrists or child guidance centers, which were established in the United States in the 1920s and focused primarily on promoting healthy relationships among middle-class children and their parents.

The Shift to Community Mental Health Programs

The third revolution in mental health, a shift in the care of individuals with mental health problems and developmental disabilities from institutions to local communities, began in the 1940s and continues today. Public interest in mental health issues and treatment of the mentally ill was stimulated by the onset of World War II. The military draft brought mental health problems to the attention of Congress. Military statistics showed that 12% of all men drafted into the Armed Forces were rejected for psychiatric reasons. Of the total number rejected for any reason, 40% were rejected for psychiatric reasons (Felix, 1967). Serious questions began to be raised about the magnitude of mental health problems within the entire U.S. population.

Initial Postwar Developments

After the war ended, state hospitals, which had been neglected during the war, again began to receive attention. Albert Deutsch (1949) wrote a series of exposes on state mental hospitals, later published as *Shame of the States*. This stimulated a series of similar books, one of which was made into a film, *The Snake Pit*. The attention resulted in widespread public outcry and created a climate for reform. In 1946, Congress passed the National Mental Health Act, which enabled states to establish community mental health programs aimed at preventing and treating mental health problems. The act also provided for the establishment of research and educational programs and mandated that each state establish a single state entity to receive and allocate federal funds provided for by the act.

In 1949, Congress created the **National Institute of Mental Health (NIMH),** the first federal entity to address mental health concerns. In 1955, with impetus from a working coalition of leadership from the National Institute of Mental Health and the **National Association of Mental Health (NAMH),** university medical schools and schools of social work, and organizations of former mental patients and their families, the National Mental Health Study Act was passed. This act signified the belief among both mental health professionals and government officials that large custodial institutions could not deal effectively with mental illness. The act authorized an appropriation to the Joint Commission on Mental Illness and Health to study and make recommendations in the area of mental health policy. The commission published a series of documents in the late 1950s and early 1960s calling for major reform. Commission reports called for a substantial increase in mental health expenditures to be used for comprehensive community mental health facilities, increased recruitment and training programs for staff, and long-term mental health research. The commission also called for an expansion of treatment programs for the acutely mentally ill in all facilities while limiting the numbers of patients at each hospital to no more than a thousand inpatients.

The commission also recommended a major emphasis on community programs, including preventive, outpatient treatment, and aftercare services that could reduce the numbers of institutionalized patients and allow for their successful treatment within their local communities. The group also recommended that the states play a smaller role in providing services and that the federal role be increased in addressing mental health needs. At this time, President Kennedy also made mental health issues a high priority and strongly supported the efforts of the commission, becoming the first U.S. president to address mental health concerns publicly. Furthermore, the public was beginning to see the effectiveness of **psychotropic drugs** in the treatment of the mentally ill and consequently was becoming more receptive to the idea of community care.

Community Mental Health Initiatives

Congress passed the Mentally Retarded Facilities and Community Mental Health Center Construction Act in 1963. This act provided major funding to build community mental health centers and community facilities for the developmentally disabled. The act mandated that centers built with federal funds be located in areas accessible to the populations they serve and that they provide the following basic service components: inpatient services, outpatient services, partial hospitalization (day, night, or weekend care) emergency services, consultation, and educational services. By 1980 there were over 700 community mental health centers in the United States partially funded with federal funds.

The intent of the community mental health care legislation was to replace the custodial care provided within large-scale institutions with therapeutic care within a community. Emphasis was to be placed on **deinstitutionalization,** or keeping individuals from placement in hospitals whenever possible, and on a **least restrictive environment,** or providing a setting as much like one for nondisabled individuals as possible. The Presidential Commission on Mental

Health (1978) defined the purpose of providing a least restrictive environment as "maintaining the greatest degree of freedom, self determination, autonomy, dignity, and integrity of body, mind, and spirit for the individual while he or she participates in treatment or receives services" (p. 44). Such programs were not only deemed cost-effective, because many individuals could work at paid jobs and live in situations requiring less expense than in an institution, but also were seen as increasing individual self-esteem and feelings of contributing to society.

The community health center legislation, coupled with the use of psychotropic drugs, significantly reduced the numbers of individuals in mental institutions. In 1955, 77.4% of all patients received inpatient services; 22.6% received outpatient services. By 1980, the numbers virtually had reversed themselves, with only 28% receiving inpatient services and 72% outpatient services (Mechanic, 1999). Emphasis on treatment had shifted from custodial care, shock treatment, or long-term psychotherapy to short-term treatment, group therapy, helping individuals cope with their environments, and drug treatment. The number of outpatient clients seen at community mental health centers continues to increase. Client caseloads in community mental health centers rose by more than one-third between 1990 and 1995 (NASW, 1995).

Legal Rights of Clients and Consumer Advocacy

Mental health and developmental disabilities professionals have identified clients' rights as the fourth and current revolution in the mental health/disabilities arena. The legal advocacy movement, begun in the 1960s, was part of the civil rights movement of the 1960s. It received further impetus in 1971 in the landmark case *Whyatt v. Sticknesy,* in which a federal judge ruled that "extraordinary or potentially hazardous modes of treatment" (Lin, 1995, p. 1706) used with patients in state mental hospitals in Alabama must be restricted. In a landmark 1975 decision, the U.S. Supreme Court ruled that being mentally ill and in need of treatment was not sufficient grounds for involuntary confinement.

The increased number of options available to individuals with developmental disabilities and mental health problems, including placement in less restrictive facilities, new counseling techniques, and drug treatment has resulted in the emergence of a number of important legal issues that require serious deliberation. On one hand, do individuals have the right to refuse treatment? On the other hand, if treatment technology or knowledge about more appropriate types of treatment exists but such treatment is not available, do individuals have the right to demand treatment? In some states, class action lawsuits have been brought on behalf of persons in institutions demanding that they be placed in less restrictive settings where they can receive treatment unavailable to them in the institutions.

The National Association of Mental Health and other advocacy organizations have forced the court system to establish a series of patients'/clients' rights, which include the right to treatment, the right to privacy and dignity, and the right to the least restrictive condition necessary to achieve the purpose of commitment (see Box 9.4 for the NASW's Mental Health Bill of Rights). The courts also have determined that persons cannot be deemed incompetent to manage their affairs; to hold professional, occupational, or vehicular licenses; to marry and obtain divorces; to register to vote; or to make wills solely because of admission or commitment to a hospital.

BOX
9.4

Mental Health Bill of Rights Project: Principles for the Provision of Mental

Our commitment is to provide quality mental health and substance abuse services to all individuals without regard to race, color, religion, national origin, gender, age, sexual orientation, or disabilities.

Right to Know

Benefits   Individuals have the right to be provided information from the purchasing entity (such as employer or union or public purchaser) and the insurance/third party payer describing the nature and extent of their mental health and substance abuse treatment benefits. This information should include details on procedures to obtain access to services, on utilization management procedures, and on appeal rights. The information should be presented clearly in writing with language that the individual can understand.

Professional Expertise   Individuals have the right to receive full information from the potential treating professional about that professional's knowledge, skills, preparation, experience, and credentials. Individuals have the right to be informed about the options available for treatment interventions and the effectiveness of the recommended treatment.

Contractual Limitations   Individuals have the right to be informed by the treating professional of any arrangements, restrictions, and/or covenants established between third party payer and the treating professional that could interfere with or influence treatment recommendations. Individuals have the right to be informed of the nature of information that may be disclosed for the purposes of paying benefits.

Appeals and Grievances   Individuals have the right to receive information about the methods they can use to submit complaints or grievances regarding provision of care by the treating professional to that profession's regulatory board and to the professional association. Individuals have the right to be provided information about the procedures they can use to appeal benefit utilization decisions to the third party payer systems, to the employer or purchasing entity, and to external regulatory entities.

Confidentiality

Individuals have the right to be guaranteed the protection of the confidentiality of their relationship with their mental health and substance abuse professional, except when laws or ethics dictate otherwise. Any disclosure to another party will be time limited and made with the full written, informed consent of the individuals. Individuals shall not be required to disclose confidential, privileged or other information other than: diagnosis, prognosis, type of treatment, time and length of treatment, and cost.

Entities receiving information for the purposes of benefits determination, public agencies receiving information for health care planning, or any other organization with legitimate right to information will maintain clinical information in confidence with the same rigor and be subject to the same penalties for violation as is the direct provider of care.

Information technology will be used for transmission, storage, or data management only with methodologies that remove individual identifying information and assure the protection of the individual's privacy. Information should not be transferred, sold, or otherwise utilized.

Choice

Individuals have the right to choose any duly licensed/certified professional for mental health and substance abuse services. Individuals have the right to receive full information regarding the education and training of professionals, treatment options (including risks and benefits), and cost implications to make an informed choice regarding the selection of care deemed appropriate by individual and professional.

Determination of Treatment

Recommendations regarding mental health and substance abuse treatment shall be made only by a duly licensed/certified professional in conjunction with the individual and his or her family as appropriate. Treatment decisions should not be made by third party payers. The individual has the right to make final decisions regarding treatment.

Parity

Individuals have the right to receive benefits for mental health and substance abuse treatment on the same basis as they do for any other illnesses, with the same provisions, co-payments, lifetime benefits, and catastrophic coverage in both insurance and self-funded/self-insured health plans.

Discrimination

Individuals who use mental health and substance abuse benefits shall not be penalized when seeking other health insurance or disability, life or any other insurance benefit.

Benefit Usage

The individual is entitled to the entire scope of the benefits within the benefit plan that will address his or her clinical needs.

Benefit Design

Whenever both federal and state law and/or regulations are applicable, the professional and all payers shall use whichever affords the individual the greatest level of protection and access.

Treatment Review

To assure that treatment review processes are fair and valid, individuals have the right to be guaranteed that any review of their mental health and substance abuse treatment shall involve a professional having the training, credentials, and licensure required to provide the treatment in the jurisdiction in which it will be provided. The reviewer should have no financial interest in the decision and is subject to the section on confidentiality.

Accountability

Treating professionals may be held accountable and liable to individuals for any injury caused by gross incompetence or negligence on the part of the professional. The treating professional has the obligation to advocate for and document necessity of care and to advise the individual of options if payment authorization is denied.

Payers and other third parties may be held accountable and liable to individuals for any injury caused by gross incompetence or negligence or by their clinically unjustified decisions.

Source: National Association of Social Workers, http://www.naswdc.org/Prac/mental.html, November 21, 1999. Used with permission.

Patients in mental institutions have the same rights to visitation and telephone communication as patients in other hospitals, as well as the right to send sealed mail. They also have the right to freedom from excessive medication or physical restraint and experiments and the right to wear their own clothes and worship within the dictates of their own religion. Patients also have the right to receive needed treatment outside a hospital environment (Mechanic, 1999).

Most states make it difficult to commit a person to an institution involuntarily. In many states, however, law enforcement agencies can order that persons be detained in state institutions for a limited time without a court hearing. At the end of that time, a court hearing must be held, and involuntary commitments can be ordered only if persons are found to be dangerous to themselves or others. Often individuals who are not really capable of functioning on their own but who are not found to be dangerous to themselves or others are released to be on their own. Because of this system, many individuals receive what some mental health professionals have termed "the revolving door approach to treatment." Individuals too incapacitated to function on their own are picked up on the streets; admitted to the hospital; given medication, food, and rest; and then released quickly because they legally cannot be held any longer against their wishes.

Children's right to refuse or to demand mental health treatment is an issue that has received even less attention. In many instances, parents commit children to institutions because they do not want to or are unable to care for them. In other instances, the child's problems are the result of family problems that the parents do not want to accept. Currently, both the rights of individuals to avoid treat-ment and the rights of individuals to receive treatment are unclear and need to be clarified further by the Supreme Court.

Consumers of services and their families, like social work professionals, are becoming increasingly concerned about these issues. Advocacy groups for persons with mental health problems have stepped up their efforts to include individuals with mental health problems and their family members in treatment planning (Lin, 1995). The consumer movement emphasizes empowerment, independence, and recovery. Many social workers work closely with consumer groups and have become strong allies of the consumer movement and the changes they advocate.

AVAILABILITY OF RESOURCES AND RESPONSIBILITY FOR CARE

Perhaps the most overriding issue in the mental health, substance abuse, and developmental disabilities arenas is how to manage limited resources to best address the needs of those who require services. Approximately 10% of national health care resources are spent for public and private mental health care (NASW, 1995). Medicaid is the largest funding source of seriously ill people, and mental health costs continue to increase. Mental health delivery systems are also changing with the trend toward community-based programs. Many state mental hospitals have either closed or also offer nonhospital care as part of their services. Although the 1970s and 1980s witnessed a dramatic growth in private psychiatric hospitals and residential treatment centers for emotionally disturbed children and youth, this trend was curtailed by the emergence of managed care, an overriding theme in the delivery of mental health services today. When inpatient hospitalization does occur, stays are much shorter than in the past. The predominant pattern of mental health care today is short hospital stays for stabilization of symptoms and often initial monitoring of prescribed medication, followed by outpatient care at a community facility (Mechanic, 1999). Many individuals, like Joanna in the opening vignette, are caught in a lifelong cycle of numerous short-term hospitalizations, discharge to the community, escalation of symptoms, and rehospitalizations.

Persons who are mentally ill and developmentally disabled, often unable to advocate well for themselves, do not always receive their just share of funding. Public attitudes that still persist in viewing alcoholism and substance abuse as moral issues also have limited funding for substance abuse programs. Many of the gains in mental health and developmental disabilities programs established in the 1960s have been eroded as governments battle over who should have the responsibility for the care of individuals who are mentally ill or developmentally disabled and what constitutes appropriate levels of service for these groups. Although attitudes have changed significantly since colonial times, additional change is required if normalization of these populations is to be achieved. In the following sections, we discuss a number of issues relating to current resources.

Deinstitutionalization

The mental health field has been subjected to considerable shock since the movement toward deinstitutionalization. Some individuals have argued that deinstitutionalization has resulted in the "ghettoization" of persons who are mentally ill and disabled. In many instances, communities have neither the funding nor the commitment to provide care for individuals released from institutions, forcing them to subsist in subhuman conditions in poverty areas.

In 1976, two social workers from the Mental Health Law Project visited Mr. Dixon, who had won his right to freedom in a class action suit several months after being transferred from the hospital to a boarding care facility. The workers described their observations in testimony before a Senate subcommittee:

> The conditions in which we found Mr. Dixon were unconscionable. Mr. Dixon's sleeping room was about halfway below ground level. The only windows in the room were closed and a plate in front of them made it impossible for Mr. Dixon to open them. There was no fan or air conditioner in the room. The room had no phone or buzzer. There would be no capacity for Mr. Dixon to contact someone in case of fire or emergency and this is significant in the face of the fact that Mr. Dixon is physically incapacitated. Mr. Dixon had not been served breakfast by 10 a.m. He stated that meals were highly irregular and he would sometimes get so hungry waiting for lunch that he would ask a roomer to buy him sandwiches. He can remember having only one glass of milk during his entire stay at his new home. (U.S. Senate Subcommittee on Long-Term Care, 1976, p. 715)

Shortly after this testimony, Mr. Dixon returned to St. Elizabeth Hospital and was placed in a more suitable home. Twenty years later, in 1996, a series of articles by an investigative reporter for an urban newspaper in a large southwestern state found similar or worse conditions existing among persons throughout the state who had been released from state hospitals. In one setting, a large number of men were found living in an unheated, un-air-conditioned metal building with no indoor plumbing facilities. They were malnourished and stayed indoors most of the time, watching a small television. Although states have moved to establish regulations, including licensing or certification systems for group and boarding homes for clients of the mental health system, monitoring and sanctioning are difficult. Even if facilities are forced to close, there are often no other facilities to move the residents.

Many states and local communities have successfully reduced the number of individuals who are developmentally disabled or mentally ill living in institutions, but some are reluctant to do so because of inadequate local resources and the economic disruption caused by shutting down institutions in areas where they are the major source of employment.

Deinstitutionalization has also resulted in some unintended consequences. Many people who could function well within an institutional setting do not do as well in a community setting, particularly with little day-to-day supervision. Deinstitutionalization also carries with it the potential for failure to meet established standards of care, as well as the failure to provide follow-up services to clients. Decentralization of care requires a case management system in which social workers or other mental health professionals are responsible for a specific number of clients, ensuring that their living conditions are appropriate, that they are maintaining health care and taking medication, and that their other needs are met.

Some community-based mental health programs, however, have been extremely successful. For example, George Fairweather, a noted mental health professional, has established a series of community programs for individuals who were previously institutionalized. Called Fairweather Lodges, these facilities provide supervised living for individuals in small groups, with residents sharing housekeeping chores. Residents also work in the community, with a lodge coordinator who ensures that residents are successful in the workplace. The coordinator also facilitates support group meetings for residents' families, as well as for lodge members. The rate of reinstitutionalization for this program has been extremely low. Some communities initially reluctant to establish lodge programs now view the lodges and their residents as important parts of the community.

Much remains to be done to develop adequate community-based mental health programs for individuals of all ages. Many previously deinstitutionalized individuals have difficulty adjusting to community living, particularly when adequate support programs are not available. As one former state hospital resident stated:

> At the hospital, I had hot coffee every morning, three meals a day and a warm bed every night, and people to talk to if I wanted to talk. Here, I have the street and that's about it. No food on a regular basis, no bed, and no one to talk to. I didn't have a bad life at the hospital. (Iscoe, 1990, personal communication)

To date, the most significant problem with deinstitutionalization has been the inability of communities to develop the necessary infrastructure to support these individuals in a community setting.

Wide-Ranging Program Alternatives

Other beneficial community programs that have been established for people with mental illness, substance abuse problems, or developmental disabilities include

- partial hospitalization, through which persons attend hospital day programs and receive treatment, return to their homes at night or to work in the community, and return to the hospital for treatment and monitoring the next day;

- day programs for persons who are developmentally disabled that provide education, supervision, and in some instances employment opportunities; and
- halfway houses and refurbished apartment complexes, with resident supervisors who oversee and lend support to residents who are mentally ill, developmentally disabled, and recovering substance abusers.

Many people have been able to return to their own homes. Some go to adult or special children's day care centers during the day while parents work, returning home at night. Respite care programs established in some communities, using trained volunteers, make it possible for family members to find substitute caregivers so they can have some time away from the person on occasion to regain their energies.

Community-based alternatives for the elderly have also received increased attention as the general population continues to age. Prior to the emphasis on deinstitutionalization, many residents of both state mental hospitals and state schools for the developmentally disabled were, in fact, elderly persons who could function in a less restrictive environment if they had someone to care for them. A number of elderly individuals have been successfully placed in nursing homes, often in integrated facilities that accept residents without mental health or disability problems. Other alternatives such as those mentioned in the preceding paragraph have also been developed for older people. However, with our increasingly aging population, mental health advocates are concerned about the availability of mental health services for the elderly. A recent report indicates that almost 20% of persons over 55 experience mental disorders that are not a normal part of

aging, such as depression, substance abuse, Alzheimer's disease, anxiety disorders, and late-onset schizophrenia (Holyrd & Duryee, 1997).

Caring for Children with Disabilities and Developmental Delays

Recent legislation has also provided funding for children with developmental delays, with an increased focus on early childhood intervention. The **Individuals with Disabilities Education Act (IDEA)** replaced previous legislation regarding the provision of special education resources for children and youth with disabilities and included funding for early intervention programs for infants and toddlers with disabilities and their families. The legislation stresses the development of comprehensive, coordinated, multidisciplinary, interagency programs that include public school systems, health agencies, and social services agencies.

This law mandates that public school systems provide educational and social services for children with a range of disabilities, including emotional disturbances; mental retardation; and speech, vision, hearing, and learning disabilities. Parents and educators are required to develop jointly an individualized educational plan (IEP) for each child. The law also requires each child to be placed in the least restrictive setting possible, with the intent that children with disabilities and emotional problems be placed in regular classrooms to the extent possible and in special education classes as a last alternative.

Preschool early intervention programs must also develop an individualized family intervention plan to ensure that families receive the services they need. Services usually include special help for parents, including counseling, since parents often experience significant feelings of denial, belief that there is a "cure" somewhere for whatever disability their child has and they must seek it, self-blame, anger, and grief and loss. Parents also need help in dealing with the myriad of services available that are often confusing and difficult to access and respite care so they can take time for themselves and other children if they have them.

Many communities have preschool programs, funded with state and federal monies to assist children with disabilities, that combine early childhood education with physical and speech therapy and other needed services. Both working and nonworking parents can bring their children to the centers, where trained staff work with the children individually and in small groups to help them progress developmentally. Some preschool programs include children with and without disabilities so that both groups of children can learn to value each other and discover and grow together.

Large numbers of children, however, still have disabilities that prohibit them from remaining in their own homes, and others have parents who are overwhelmed by their own needs and the added stress from having a child with a disability and being unable to provide adequate care. Advances in technology to keep children alive who are born with serious disabilities have resulted in issues about how best to care for those children if they cannot remain at home. The costs to keep such children in hospitals are extensive, and a hospital setting does not provide the kind of nurturing a child needs to develop to his or her maximum potential. As many states have closed their state schools for the mentally retarded/developmentally disabled, attention has been focused on how to care for children previously housed there. In many instances, children have been placed in nursing homes with elderly residents. Although sometimes these experiences have been posi-

tive, they are often the only child, or one of only several, in the facility, which is likely to be ill equipped to meet the special needs of children.

Prevention versus Treatment

The issue of prevention versus treatment, especially within the confines of scarce resources, is a final consideration in responding to the needs of those who are mentally ill, are substance abusers, or have developmental disabilities. Mental health professionals address prevention issues at three levels:

- **Primary prevention,** or prevention targeted at an entire population (for example, prenatal care for all women to avoid developmental disabilities in their infants; parenting classes for all individuals to decrease mental health problems among children)
- **Secondary prevention,** or prevention targeted toward at-risk populations, those groups more likely to develop mental health problems than others (such as individual and group counseling for family members of schizophrenics or alcoholics)
- **Tertiary prevention,** or prevention targeted at those individuals who have already experienced problems to prevent the problems from recurring (for example, treatment groups for alcoholics or mental health programs for individuals who have attempted suicide)

Numerous studies show that prevention programs are cost-effective ways to reduce developmental disabilities and mental health problems. Still, policymakers often focus on short-term solutions to these problems. For example, although substance abuse prevention programs can be expensive, the costs are far less than those to provide residential or other more extensive treatment programs or to pay the costs for imprisonment and services to victims if the substance abuse leads to crime.

Other mental health problems, such as homelessness and family and youth violence, also are currently in the limelight. These problems, while not new, are being recognized as having significant negative impacts not only on the individuals experiencing these problems but on the entire family. This emphasis on intergenerational, cyclical problems has focused attention on the need to provide resources not only to children and their families experiencing these problems but also to adults who grew up in such families (see Chapters 11 and 12).

Cultural and gender differences must also be taken into account when discussing mental health, mental illness, substance abuse, and developmental disabilities. The importance of gender and cultural differences, including both strengths and the impact of oppression and social injustice, on individuals must be considered in relation to theories used to understand human behavior and to identify "normal" and pathological behavior. These differences also must be considered when using diagnostic classification systems such as the *DSM-IV*, identifying the ways that practitioners view and relate to individuals with whom they interact, and determining the ways that mental health and developmental disabilities services are organized and delivered (Goldstein, 1987).

Managed Care

Managed care is at the core of the current debate surrounding mental health services, with many of the arguments about its pros and cons similar to those discussed in the next chapter on health care. With insurance company personnel increasingly making treatment decisions instead of mental health treatment providers, concern has been raised about whether adequate services are being provided. **Managed care,** or the emphasis on accountability and ensuring that services are not provided if they are not needed, has raised a number of ethical dilemmas for social workers and other mental health professionals. These dilemmas include dangers of giving prescription drugs without appropriate monitoring and accompanying therapy if advised, seeing clients for a limited number of visits when their diagnosis clearly warrants more extensive treatment, and treating clients on an outpatient basis when inpatient treatment is warranted.

Insurance coverage for mental health and substance abuse is generally much more restricted than for other types of health care. In 1996, Congress passed the Domenici-Wellstone Amendment to require parity for lifetime and annual dollar limits between mental health services and services for other medical conditions. While this legislation is seen as beneficial by mental health consumers and their advocates, it still has some important restrictions. For example, employers can completely drop coverage for mental health services if they wish. In addition, the legislation only requires parity for employers with more than 50 employees. Despite opposition from many who claimed that mental health parity would bankrupt employers, studies show that full parity costs less than 1% of annual health care costs, or approximately $1 per employee per year, and, that when used in conjunction with managed care, can reduce costs by 30% to 50% (National Alliance for the Mentally Ill, 1999). When the related health problems that are the result of untreated mental health problems are considered, not only for the individual with the mental health problem but also for family members, it is expected that parity legislation will reduce costs by even more in the long run.

Another current managed care issue relates to the costs of prescription drugs. Medication for a number of mental health problems, such as schizophrenia, is expensive. While costs for medication are clearly much less than inpatient hospitalization, Medicare does not pay for prescription drugs, and other sources of funding are often unavailable to persons with disabilities and the elderly.

In spite of its difficulties, managed care is being used as a viable way to limit health and mental health expenditures, and social workers need to be at the forefront to ensure that client rights are considered and the managed care system is held accountable to the clients it serves.

THE ROLES OF SOCIAL WORKERS IN THE DELIVERY OF MENTAL HEALTH SERVICES

Social workers today are involved in the total continuum of mental health and developmental disabilities services. They provide these services in a variety of settings, including traditional social services agencies—such as community mental health centers, child guidance centers, and public social services departments—as well as nontraditional settings—such as the courts, public schools and colleges and universities, hospitals and health clinics, child care centers, workplaces, and the military. While they fulfill a variety of roles, social workers presently form the largest group of psychotherapists in the United States.

The History of Social Workers in Mental Health

The first social workers credited with providing mental health services were the psychiatric social workers hired in New York and Boston mental hospitals in the early 1900s. They were responsible primarily for providing individual therapy to hospitalized mental patients and overseeing the care of discharged patients in foster homes. The mental health field expanded during the 1920s with the establishment of child guidance centers.

With the influence of psychoanalysis and the child guidance movement, social workers in mental health increasingly moved into the role of psychotherapist, with the individual as the unit of attention. Social work's unique perspective on the person-in-environment and intervention at other levels of the environment beyond the individual waned during the 1930s, 1940s, and 1950s. But the civil rights movement and Vietnam War in the 1960s increased activism among the social work profession as a whole, and emphasis was again placed on community organization, advocacy, and a return to the roots of the profession.

The focus on the systems/ecological perspective since the late 1960s has broadened the roles of social workers in all fields, including mental health. Although psychiatrists have traditionally played a more technical role in the mental health system, with an emphasis on medication and biopsychological perspectives, social workers have tried to maintain leadership in the mental health arena: "As the largest group of mental health care providers in the country, . . . social workers are in a unique position to address the social context of clients' problems" (NASW, 1995, p. 4). They are also in a unique position to advocate for the need to look at interventions beyond the individual to other levels of the environment. For instance, social workers might also consider the following questions: Why do some communities and geographic areas have higher incidences of mental illness, substance abuse, people with disabilities, and homelessness than others? What factors constitute a healthy community—or society—that promotes mental health and values diversity? Eliminating environmental racism, oppression, and discrimination; creating adequate housing and employment; and maintaining an environment that values diversity and difference, children and families, and the elderly all can improve the quality of life for individuals and families. Social workers, regardless of their field or the environment in which they practice, need to play a more active role in advocating for social change at all levels of the environment to promote positive mental health.

Career Opportunities in Mental Health

Clinical Social Workers   Many social workers in mental health settings still provide individual counseling, including psychotherapy, to clients. But instead of being referred to as psychiatric social workers, most are called **clinical social workers.** The majority of agencies who hire clinical social workers require that they meet the qualifications of the National Association of Social Workers Academy of Certified Social Workers (ACSW) certification or obtain appropriate state certification or licensing. ACSW certification requires a master's of social work (MSW) degree from an accredited graduate school of social work, 2 years of social work experience under the direct supervision of an ACSW social worker, and a satisfactory score on a competency examination administered by the NASW. State licensing and certification programs have similar requirements but vary by state.

Crisis Intervention and Child and Family Services   Many social work jobs also are available in the field of mental health and developmental disabilities for social workers

with bachelor's of social work (BSW) degrees. BSW social workers provide such services as crisis intervention for women and their children at battered women's centers, and they operate suicide, runaway youth, child abuse, and other types of crisis hotlines (see Chapter 2). They also counsel adolescents and their families at youth-serving agencies and work as social workers in state hospitals and community living programs for the mentally ill and state schools for the developmentally disabled. In these settings, they counsel residents and serve as the primary professional involved with the individual's family.

School-Based Services and Drug Treatment Programs   Social workers also work in schools with troubled students and their families, providing individual counseling, family counseling, and family outreach and leading groups for children and their families in areas such as divorce, child maltreatment, anger management, techniques for getting along with adults, and substance abuse. Legislation establishing services for children with disabilities includes social workers among the professionals authorized to provide services. Social workers are also employed as counselors in alcohol and drug treatment programs. In fact, wherever mental health services are provided, social workers are likely to be employed. Social workers currently compose the largest professional group in public mental health services. Over half of the labor force employed in mental health–related jobs are social workers, and over one-third of the federally funded community mental health centers have social workers as their executive directors.

Social Workers in Multidisciplinary Teams   Social workers in the field of mental health provide a variety of functions. Many work in direct practice, clinical settings, providing therapy to individuals, groups, and families. Many mental health programs use a multidisciplinary team approach, hiring social workers, psychiatrists, physicians, psychologists, psychiatric nurses, child development specialists, and community aides, who work together to provide a multitude of services. While social workers on multidisciplinary teams are involved in all aspects of treatment, most often they are given the responsibility of working with the client's family and the community in which the client resides. Because of their training from a systems/ecological perspective, they help other team members understand the many competing factors that can support or impede a client intervention plan. If resources from another agency are needed, usually the social worker obtains them and ensures that they are provided.

Social Workers as Case Managers   Many social workers in mental health settings provide case management services even if they are not employed in agencies that use multidisciplinary teams. Case managers are responsible for monitoring cases to ensure that clients receive needed services. A case manager does not necessarily provide all services directly but manages the case, coordinating others who provide the services.

BSW social workers who work with persons who are mentally ill, disabled, or homeless often serve as case managers. Assigned a group of clients, they fill a number of roles to ensure that their clients are following intervention plans and functioning adequately. Case managers empower clients to become as self-sufficient as they can by focusing on their strengths and providing support and affirmation. They also serve as the liaison with the client and other service providers when necessary, monitoring the provision of services and advocating for changes in services or additional

services when necessary. Many individuals can function fairly well with a case manager to lend support, ensure that they are taking medication if needed, advocate with an employer if there is a problem, help them access health care if they get sick, and keep them from becoming isolated from their environment.

Many states are employing case managers at community mental health centers to oversee clients who are living in the local community, including those previously in institutions, who can function fairly independently with supervision and support. The case manager meets with the client and contacts her or his family members, employers, and other appropriate individuals on a regular basis to ensure that the client is functioning adequately.

Social Workers as Advocates   Still other social workers involved in the mental health field function as advocates. Organizations such as The Arc (formerly ARC—the Association for Retarded Citizens) advocate for persons with disabilities on an individual basis, ensuring that they receive needed services. For example, a 14-year-old girl with mental disabilities in a junior high school in an urban area was not receiving special education services and had been suspended several times for behavior problems. An advocate assigned to her arranged for the school district to provide the needed testing, saw that she was placed in a special education program that reduced her anxiety level and allowed her to function in a setting where she felt better about herself, and arranged for her to receive counseling. Advocates also work to ensure that groups of citizens are provided for, such as working within a community to ensure that housing is available to individuals with mental health problems and developmental disabilities. Advocates work within an empowerment framework, empowering the population that they work with to advocate for themselves for individual and social change.

Social Workers as Policymakers   Social workers also function in the mental health arena as administrators and policymakers. Many direct mental health programs, and others work for government bodies at the local, state, and federal levels. They develop and advocate for legislation, develop policies and procedures to ensure that the needs of individuals with mental health problems and disabilities are met, and oversee governing bodies that monitor programs to ensure that services are provided. Increasingly, social workers are also being elected to local, state, and national office. Social workers at all governmental levels have played key roles in getting legislation passed that improves services for persons who are mentally ill, chemically dependent, and/or have developmental disabilities or in trying to thwart the passage of legislation deemed detrimental to these groups.

New Trends in Services and Social Work Roles

Although the intent of the Community Mental Health Act was to provide services to individuals within specific geographic areas with the greatest need, particularly in poverty areas with diverse populations, studies have shown that in many instances persons receiving services largely have been middle class and white. The Commission on Mental Health, established by President Jimmy Carter in 1978, found that people of color, children, adolescents, and the elderly were underserved, as were residents of rural and poor urban areas. The commission also found that many services provided were inappropriate, particularly for those people with differing cultural backgrounds and

lifestyles. In many instances when mental health centers were first established, they were directed by psychiatrists trained in psychotherapy or influenced by educational psychologists accustomed to providing testing and working with students. As a result, the staff members often were inexperienced at dealing with nonvoluntary clients, who did not want to be seen, failed to keep appointments, and were unfamiliar with the concept of 1-hour therapy sessions. Staff members often were also unequipped to deal with problems such as family violence, child abuse, and sexual abuse.

As programs developed, many centers became skilled at reaching special populations and developing more effective ways of addressing client needs. In the 1970s, centers were required to establish special children's mental health programs. Currently, many centers provide programs that address special populations such as abused children, individuals with substance abuse problems, and Vietnam veterans. Mental health professionals also assist in the establishment of self-help groups, such as Alcoholics Anonymous, Adult Children of Alcoholics, Alateen, Parents without Partners, and Parents Anonymous (a child abuse self-help and mutual assistance program).

Today, social workers in mental health settings provide crisis intervention, operate telephone hotlines, conduct suicide prevention programs, and provide alcoholism and drug abuse services. Mental health services increasingly are provided in settings other than mental health centers, including churches, nursing homes, police departments, schools, child care centers, the workplace, and health and medical settings. Problems addressed by mental health professionals have expanded to include loneliness and isolation, finances, spouse and child abuse, male-female relationships, housing, drugs, and alcohol. Mental health staff members have become more multidisciplinary, using teams of professionals as well as volunteers.

One of the major issues facing the mental health profession today relates to who pays for services clients receive and how long those services should be provided. Many mental health services are paid for by third-party insurers and, if the client meets eligibility requirements, Medicaid (see Chapter 10). Because of the costs of services and the large numbers of individuals needing them, mental health services are also significantly influenced by managed care. Most insurance companies limit the numbers of sessions for which an individual can be reimbursed for mental health counseling and the number of hospital days for mental health reasons. They also restrict the choice of service providers available, often to a list of professionals and specific hospitals who have agreed to the managed care terms and conditions for that insurance company. Hospital stays, particularly for substance abuse, have been limited, and more insurance providers are mandating outpatient treatment first to determine whether that approach is successful.

Managed care initiatives have also changed the types of outpatient services provided. More agencies are seeing clients in groups and limiting the numbers of group and individual counseling sessions in which a client can participate. The trend is also toward case management, with a case manager, sometimes from the insurance company, sometimes from the agency, monitoring the services received to ensure that they are appropriate. Intervention approaches that focus on "brief" or "short-term" therapy, often using a cognitive-behavioral approach, are being used to attempt to stabilize clients and help them cope more quickly. One short-term intervention approach used by social workers is solution-focused therapy (de Shazer, 1985). This approach focuses on the strengths of clients, empowering them to come up with effective solutions for addressing their problems. Questions such as "What worked before for you?" and comments such as "How have you managed to do as well as you have with all this going on?" use the clients' own ideas and affirm their abilities to cope. While these intervention approaches are effective for some types of mental health problems, they are not as effective for others, such as sexual abuse or substance abuse.

Another trend relates to recent breakthroughs in neuroscience and the discovery of new relationships between biological makeup and mental illness, developmental disabilities, and substance abuse. Specific genes have been identified, for example, that cause diseases associated with developmental disabilities such as cystic fibrosis. Although it was previously believed that schizophrenia was more environmentally than biologically related, new research is showing that factors associated with this serious illness are more likely related to genetic makeup or chemical functioning within the brain. Research suggests similar factors are associated with Alzheimer's disease, and early detection of both diseases, as well as others, is likely. These discoveries represent tremendous breakthroughs, because it is likely that interventions such as gene therapy or medication can be developed to change the course of, or even prevent, these illnesses. A new drug is also being tested that alters an individuals' craving for alcohol and has the potential to significantly reduce problems associated with alcoholism. While exciting advances, these discoveries raise new issues for social workers. First, what are the ethical implications of such knowledge? If early detection is possible—for example, before birth—what are the choices, and who should make them? No matter when problems are identified in individuals, should all individuals have affordable access to such interventions, even if they are expensive? Who should pay for such interventions? And finally, what if an individual decides not to take advantage of such interventions? The issues of right to treatment and client empowerment will surface in new areas and are important ones for social workers.

Although research and the current direction of many mental health professionals supports a systems/ecological approach to dealing with mental health, substance abuse, and developmental disabilities issues, particularly a family systems perspective, limited resources do not always make this possible. It may be more expensive to adopt treatment interventions that involve the entire family; however, such an approach is more likely to reduce recidivism (reoccurrence of the problem) or prevent the problem from getting worse. Researchers and practitioners, for example, have found a psychoeducational approach—whereby individuals and their families receive education that helps them understand the problem their family member is experiencing, the roles they have played in trying to cope with the problem, and possibly more effective ways of coping, as well as family therapy to address the dynamics within their own families—to be highly successful in many situations. But with limited resources, many agencies see only the individual and do not provide additional resources to family members.

With people with mental illness and developmental disabilities and in recovery from substance abuse becoming increasingly empowered to advocate for themselves, including the filing of class action suits, states that find it difficult to provide needed services may be forced to do so by court order. Social workers will continue to play major roles in these arenas at all levels—working directly with clients and their families individually and in groups, empowering them to advocate for themselves, advocating with them,

administering agencies and policies, establishing new programs, and lobbying for the passage of new or continuing legislation.

In the future, more focus is expected on the provision of services at the community level, with local communities determining the level and type of services needed. Pressure from the federal government for community mental health centers to become financially independent will continue. Although some individuals with mental health or substance abuse problems will still need to be hospitalized in state or private psychiatric hospitals, more and more individuals will be treated in community-based programs. One study found that 80% of people in psychiatric hospitals could be treated in local communities if services were available, at half the cost and with more effective outcomes than hospitalization (Ray, 1994).

Community-based treatment models in the future will include "one-stop mental health centers" that incorporate individual and group counseling services, expanded day and partial-day treatment programs, social skills training, and recreation programs, as well as assistance with housing and employment. Increased attention will also be given to sending social workers in therapist or case management positions into clients' homes to provide services there, further reducing the need for outpatient and inpatient care. Intensive case management and therapy services provided in the home on a short-term basis can often stabilize situations and get the entire family working together with the client before problems escalate and hospitalization or other out-of-home services are required.

The NASW adopted a policy statement on mental health in 1994, which states that mental health is a national priority for both the public and private sectors in the United States. The statement suggests political action by the professional organization and social workers to increase funding for prevention, treatment, and research in mental health and for the passage of legislation that requires adequate mental health benefits for all citizens as part of any health reform. The policy also calls for social workers to be included as providers of mental health services under such legislation. Additionally, the policy recommends that clients be placed in least restrictive environments and a mental health service delivery system that allows for a continuum of care, including community-based prevention programs; both short- and long-term inpatient hospitalization; partial hospitalization; and outpatient, outreach, and emergency services, with all services involving families and including case management (Lin, 1995).

SUMMARY

Services for individuals with mental health needs and developmental disabilities have changed significantly since colonial times. Four major revolutions have occurred in the area of mental health since that time: the shift from inhumane to moral treatment, the introduction of psychoanalytic therapy, the move from institutions to community programs and the development of psychotropic drugs that effectively treat many types of mental health problems, and a new emphasis on the rights of clients and patients. Current issues in the mental health field encompass the legal rights of clients and whether they should be able to refuse or demand treatment; scarce resources and conflict over the roles of federal, state, and local governments in providing services; attention to substance abuse and the expansion of substance abuse treatment facilities; the need for more effective services for women, people of color, the homeless, and individuals in rural

settings; additional services that address problems such as child maltreatment and alcohol and drug abuse, particularly for low-income groups; and the special needs of rural and ethnic populations.

Social workers currently play a critical role in providing mental health services, serving as therapists, advocates, case managers, administrators, and policymakers. These roles are expected to continue and expand in the future. Rapid changes in society brought about by technology and globalization are expected to continue and intensify. These changes will bring increased feelings of stress, isolation, and alienation among many individuals in our society. The mental health needs of all individuals will become an even more important area of focus as social change is shaped by these factors.

KEY TERMS

addiction
Alcoholics Anonymous (AA)
alcohol
alcoholism
Americans with Disabilities Act (ADA)
clinical social workers
deinstitutionalization
depressants
developmental delay
developmental disability
Diagnostic and Statistical Manual (DSM or DSM-IV)
dual diagnosis
hallucinogens
Individuals with Disabilities Education Act (IDEA)

least restrictive environment
managed care
medical model
moral treatment
narcotics
National Association of Mental Health (NAMH)
National Institute of Mental Health (NIMH)
primary prevention
psychoanalysis
psychotropic drugs
secondary prevention
substance abuse
tertiary prevention

DISCUSSION QUESTIONS

1. Discuss the problems in defining mental illness.

2. Identify and briefly describe at least four frameworks that can be used in understanding mental health problems.

3. Do you agree with Szasz's concept of mental health? Discuss your rationale for either agreeing or disagreeing.

4. Identify the four major revolutions in the field of mental health.

5. Identify at least three different ways that substance abuse may be conceptualized.

6. Identify at least four ways that substance abuse is costly to society.

7. What is your definition of a substance abuser? Identify at least three factors at each level of the environment that can place an individual at risk to become an alcoholic.

8. Discuss the meaning of the term *developmental disabilities*. How does this term contrast with previously used terminology to identify persons within this category?

9. Discuss the advantages and disadvantages of current efforts at deinstitutionalization.

10. How have the media portrayed persons with emotional problems, substance abuse, and developmental disabilities? Compare the portrayals in two recent popular films. What messages do these portrayals give to individuals with similar characteristics? To the general public about individuals with these characteristics?

11. Identify at least five areas in which social workers employed in mental health settings might work. What are some of the roles in which they might function?

12. What are the advantages and disadvantages of managed care in addressing mental health issues? From a client perspective? From a social worker employed in a mental health agency perspective?

INFOTRAC COLLEGE EDITION

To learn more about topics included in this chapter, enter the following search terms:

ADA

alcohol abuse

community mental health

depressive disorders

drug abuse

managed care

mental health advocates

mental health costs

mental health laws

mental health policy

mental health services

mentally ill

suicide statistics

ON THE INTERNET

http://www.nami.org/

http://www.hcfa.org/

http://www.apa.org/

http://www.mentalhealth.gov/

http://samhsa.gov/

http://www.naswdc.org/

http://www.ddrcco.com/

REFERENCES

American Association of Suicidology. (1999). *Suicide statistics*. Available: www.suicidology.org.

ARC. (2000). *Developmental disabilities*. Available: www.thearc.org.

Barhydt, Adrienne Rubin. (April 10, 1996). *The disability rights activist: Why disability rights?* Available: http://www.disrights.org/dr-whydr.html.

Barrera, M. (1995). *Implementing the Americans with Disabilities Act: Issues for social workers*. Unpublished paper, School of Social Work, University of Texas, Austin.

Black, C. (1987). *It will never happen here*. New York: Ballantine.

Burman, S., & Allen-Meares, P. (1991). Criteria for selecting practice theories: Working with alcoholic women. *Families in Society: Journal of Contemporary Human Services, 72*(7), 387–393.

Burt, M. (1992). *Over the edge: The growth of homelessness in the 1980s*. Washington, DC: Urban Institute.

de Shazer, S. (1985). *Keys to solution in brief therapy*. New York: Norton.

Deutsch, A. (1949). *Shame of the states*. New York: Columbia University Press.

Developmental Disabilities Center. (2000). What is a developmental disability? Available: http://www.dbcboulder.com/whatsdd.htm.

Felix, R. (1967). *Mental illness: Progress and prospects*. New York: Columbia University Press.

Finkelstein, N. (1994). Treatment issues for alcohol- and-drug-dependent pregnant and parenting women. *Health and Social Work, 19*(1), 7–15.

Goldstein, E. (1987). Mental health and illness. In *Encyclopedia of social work* (18th ed., Vol. 2, pp. 102–109). Silver Springs, MD: NASW Press.

Holyrd, S., & Duryee, J. J. (1997). Differences in geriatric outpatients with early- vs. late-onset depression. *International Journal of Geriatric Psychiatry, 12*, 1100–1106.

Ivanoff, A., & Reidel, M. (1995). Suicide. In *Encyclopedia of social work* (Vol. 3, pp. 2358–2372). Washington, DC: NASW Press.

Johnson, A. (1995). Homelessness. In *Encyclopedia of social work* (Vol. 2, pp. 1338–1346). Washington, DC: NASW Press.

Karls, J. M., & Wandrei, K. E. (1994). *Person-in-environment system: The PIE classification system for social functioning problems*. Washington, DC: NASW Press.

Kesey, K. (1962). *One flew over the cuckoo's nest*. New York: Basic Books.

Koroloff, N., & Anderson, S. C. (1989). Alcohol-free living centers: Hope for homeless alcoholics. *Social Work, 34*, 497–504.

Kutchins, H., & Kirk, S. (1997). *Making us crazy: DSM: The psychiatric bible and the creation of mental disorders*. New York: Free Press.

Lex, B. (1994). Women and substance abuse: A general review. In R. Watson (Ed.), *Addictive behaviors in women* (pp. 279–327). Totowa, NJ: Humana.

Liebow, E. (1993). *Tell them who I am: The lives of homeless women*. New York: Free Press.

Lin, A. (1995). Mental health overview. In *Encyclopedia of social work* (19th ed., Vol. 2: 1705–1711). Silver Springs, MD: NASW Press.

Mechanic, D. (1999). *Mental health and social policy: The emergence of managed care* (4th ed.). Boston: Allyn & Bacon.

National Alliance for the Mentally Ill. (1999). *Facts about mental illness*. Available: http://nami.org/fact.htm.

National Association of Social Workers. (1995, January). Community mental health centers grow. *NASW News*, p. 4. Silver Springs, MD: Author.

National Association of Social Workers. (1999). *Mental health bill of rights project: Principles for the provision of mental health and substance abuse treatment services*. Available: http://www.naswdc.org/prac/mental.htm.

National Institute of Mental Health. (1999). *Research fact sheets*. Available: http://www.nimh.nih.gov/publicat/resfacts.cfm.

National Institute of Mental Health. (2000). *Depression*. Available: http://www.nimh.nih.gov/.

Nelson-Zlupko, L., Kaufman, E., & Morrison Dove, M. (1995). Gender differences in drug addiction and treatment. *Social Work, 40*(1), 45–95.

New York State Office on Alcoholism and Substance Abuse. (1999). *Services*. Available: http://www.oasis.state.ny.us/.

Orlin, M. (1995). The Americans with Disabilities Act: Implications for social services. *Social Work, 40*(2), 233–239.

Parkside Medical Services Corporation. (1988). *Participant handbook*. Park Ridge, IL: Author.

Phoenix House. (1999). *News and research*. Available: http://www.phoenixhouse.org.

Presidential Commission on Mental Health. (1978). *Report of the Presidential Commission on Mental Health.* Washington, DC: Government Printing Office.

Rapp, C., Shera, W., & Kisthardt, W. (1993). Research strategies for consumer empowerment of people with severe mental illness. *Social Work, 38*(6), 727–733.

Ray, C. (1994). *Managed care workshop notes.* Adelphi, MD: Vesta.

Reid, J., Macchetto, P., & Foster, S. (1999). *No safe haven: Children of substance abusing parents.* New York: Columbia University National Center on Addiction and Substance Abuse.

Rosenhan, D. (1973). On being sane in insane places. *Science, 179,* 250–257.

Royce, J., & Scratchley, D. (1996). *Alcohol problems and alcoholism: A comprehensive survey.* New York: Free Press.

Sosin, M. (1989). Homelessness in Chicago. *Public Welfare, 47*(1), 22–27.

Szasz, T. (1998). Myth of mental illness. In *Encyclopedia of mental health* (Vol. 2). New York: Academic Press.

U.S. Department of Health and Human Services. (1994a). Addictive and mental disorders found together. *SAMHSA News, 2*(2).

U.S. Department of Health and Human Services. (1994b). Perception of drug risk drops. *SAMHSA News, 2*(2).

U.S. Senate Subcommittee on Long-Term Care. (1976). *Hearings on long term care.* Washington, DC: U.S. Department of Health, Education, and Welfare.

Williams, J. (1995). Diagnostic and statistical manual of mental disorders. In *Encyclopedia of social work* (Vol. 1, pp. 729–739). Washington, DC: NASW Press.

Williams, J., & Spitzer, R. (1995). Should *DSM* be the basis for teaching social work practice in mental health? Yes! *Social Work Education, 31*(2), 148–153.

SUGGESTED FURTHER READINGS

Allen, S., & Mor, V. (1998). *Living in the community with disability: Service needs, use and systems.* New York: Springer.

Bentley, K. J., & Walsh, J. M. (2000). *The social worker and psychotropic medication: Toward effective collaboration with mental health clients, families, and providers.* (2nd ed.). Pacific Grove: Brooks/Cole.

Bickenbach, J. (1993). *Physical disability and social policy.* Buffalo, NY: University of Toronto Press.

Brink, T. L. (Ed.). (1994). *The forgotten aged: Ethnic, psychiatric and societal minorities.* Binghamton, NY: Haworth.

Farber, S., & Szasz, T. (1993). *Madness, heresy, and the rumor of angels: The revolt against the mental health system.* Chicago: Open Court.

Goffman, E. (1961). *Asylums: Essays on the social situation of mental patients and other inmates.* Garden City, NY: Doubleday.

Green, H. (1964). *I never promised you a rose garden.* New York: Holt, Rinehart, & Winston.

North, C., & Smith, E. (1994). Comparison of white and non-white homeless men and women. *Social Work, 39*(6), 639–647.

Perlin, M. (2000). *The hidden prejudice: Mental disability on trial.* Washington, DC: American Psychological Association.

Rapp, C. (1997). *The strengths model: Case management with people suffering from severe and persistent mental illness.* New York: Oxford University Press.

Sands, R. (1991). *Clinical social work practice in community mental health.* Upper Saddle River, NJ: Prentice Hall.

Scheff, T. (1966). *Being mentally ill.* Chicago: Aldine.

Schwartz, D. (1994). *Crossing the river: Creating a conceptual revolution in a community and disability.* Cambridge, MA: Brookline.

Select Committee on Children, Youth and Families. (1990). *Women, addiction, and perinatal substance abuse fact sheet.* Washington, DC: U.S. House of Representatives Select Committee.

Sproul, B. (Ed.). (1996). *Children's mental health: Creating systems of care in a changing society.* Baltimore: Brookes.

Szasz, T. (1997). *Insanity: The idea and its consequences.* Syracuse, NY: Syracuse University Press.

Townsend, E. (1998). *Good intentions overruled: A critique of empowerment in the routine organization of mental health services.* Toronto: University of Toronto Press.

Turner, F., & Golan, F. (1992). *Mental health and the elderly: A social work perspective.* New York: Free Press.

HEALTH CARE

Alice and Ruben Mendoza and their 2-year-old daughter, Carmen, live in a rural community in the Southwest. Until 2 years ago, Alice and Ruben owned a family restaurant; however, because of a downturn in the economy, they were forced to declare bankruptcy. Since then, Ruben has worked seasonally as a farm worker and as a construction worker, and Alice has worked as a waitress in a neighboring town. Three years ago, Alice became pregnant. Because she and Ruben did not have health insurance, Alice waited until she was 5 months pregnant to see a doctor. Two months later, she gave birth prematurely to a daughter. Shortly after the birth, the baby began experiencing severe respiratory and cardiac problems, and the doctors decided to fly her to the regional neonatal center 300 miles away. The baby remained at the neonatal center for 3 months, requiring heart and lung surgery, as well as an extended period of intensive care.

When Carmen finally was allowed to return home, she required extensive care, and Alice was unable to return to work. Already financially strapped, the Mendozas were now faced with a $75,000 medical bill for Carmen's delivery and care. A visit to the local human services department to seek Medicaid was unsuccessful. Although Alice and Ruben's income was less than $10,000 per year, they earned too much to qualify for the medical assistance. Alice's boss and other friends held a dance to raise money for the family, which netted $4,000.

At this point, Alice and Ruben are overwhelmed with medical bills and are unsure whether they will ever be able to pay them all. Doctors say that Carmen is developmentally delayed and is likely to need extensive physical therapy and possibly more surgery later on. Although Ruben and Alice had hoped to have a larger family, they have decided they cannot afford to have any more children. Over the last 6 months, Ruben has developed kidney problems and has already missed 5 days of work. But he feels that he can't afford to see a doctor with the already extensive medical bills and so is hoping that whatever is wrong will clear up by itself.

At the present time, **health care,** care provided to individuals to prevent or promote recovery from illness or disease, in America is in a crisis state. On one hand, many of America's citizens, like Ruben and Alice Mendoza, are faced with the payment of mammoth medical bills as a result of life-threatening situations. Nearly 39 million Americans under the age of 65, or about 16%, do not have any health insurance at all (U.S. National Center for Health Statistics, 2000). On the other hand, national expenses for health care have increased at incredibly high rates—from $73.2 billion in 1970 to

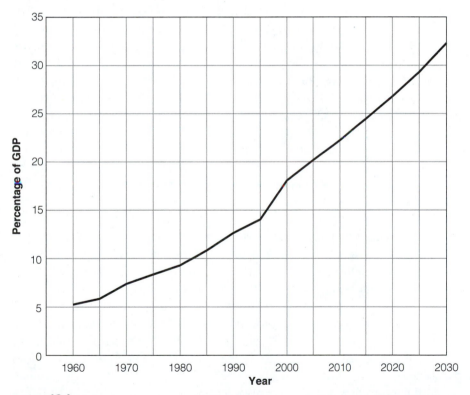

FIGURE **10.1**

U.S. HEALTH CARE COSTS AS PERCENTAGE OF GROSS DOMESTIC PRODUCT

Sources: Statistical Abstract (1995, p. 109); Rice (1995, p. 1169) (Copyright 1995, National Association of Social Workers, Inc.); and Lenkefeld and Welsh (1995, p. 1207).

an estimated $1,228.5 billion in 1999. Health care expenses currently make up about 14% of the U.S. gross domestic product, or a per capita cost (cost per person) of $4,340; see Figure 10.1 (Health Care Financing Administration, 1999). Health care expenditures in this country are projected to total $2.2 trillion (16.2% of the gross national product) by 2008. The health care industry is the third largest in the United States, preceded only by agriculture and construction.

Debates over national health care issues focus on two primary concerns: First, how much of our country's resources should be allocated to health care? Second, how should those resources be allocated? As our knowledge and technology in the health care arena continue to expand, decisions in the area of health care increasingly will become moral and ethical. Given scarce resources, for example, should an infant who requires tens of thousands of dollars to be kept alive be given maximum treatment to save its life, particularly when the child may live a life continually fraught with health problems and possibly retardation? And what about organ transplants and kidney dialysis—should these be made available to everyone? If not, who should get them? Given the growing numbers of persons with AIDS, how many dollars should be allocated to research, education, and treatment, and who should pay what costs? Does the government have the right to mandate good health practices for women drug users who are pregnant or to impose penalties on persons with AIDS who do not practice safe sex? With more U.S. citizens living longer, to what extent should resources be allocated toward health care for older persons? And to what extent should attention be given to environmental concerns, such as nuclear power, sanitation, and pollution and their impact on personal health? Finally, given the high costs of health care, who should pay for health care for the indigent—the federal government, states, local communities, or individuals and their families themselves? If individuals cannot afford health care, should it be denied to them?

Increasingly, social workers are playing a central role in helping policymakers, medical practitioners, and family members make these critical decisions. Social workers provide services in a variety of health-related settings, ranging from traditional hospitals to family planning clinics, rape crisis centers, home health care programs, and hospice programs for dying individuals and their families. Studies project that the area of health care, particularly as it relates to the elderly, is the fastest-growing area of employment for social workers today.

In this chapter, we give an overview of our country's current health care system, the problems it faces, and the types of health care policies and programs currently available. We also discuss the roles social workers play in making those policies and programs possible.

A Systems/Ecological Approach to Health Care

Because the systems/ecological perspective was first introduced as a mechanism to explain the functioning of the human body, this perspective has a longer history within the health care arena than other arenas in which social workers function. As early as the Greek and Roman eras of civilization, it was observed that many health problems were precipitated by changes in the environment. An ancient Greek medical text entitled *Airs, Waters, and Places,* said to be authored by Hippocrates, explained health problems in terms of person-environment relationships. This work attributed human functioning to four body fluids: blood, phlegm, and black and yellow bile. As long as these body fluids were in equilibrium, an individual was healthy. But Hippocrates attributed changes in the balance of these fluids to ecological variations in temperature, ventilation, and an individual's lifestyle in relation to eating, drinking, and working. Negative influences in the environment caused these fluids to become unbalanced, which in turn resulted in illness.

Other early works subscribed to germ theory, which is based on the premise that illness is a function of the interactions among an organism's adaptive capacities in an environment full of infectious agents, toxins, and safety hazards. The Greeks and Romans also were cognizant of the relationship between sanitation and illness. Early Roman writings suggested that people could predict and control their health through the environment and prevent epidemic diseases by avoiding marshes, standing water, winds, and high temperatures. Public baths, sewers, and free medical care were all ways that early civilizations used to promote health and reduce disease (Catalano, 1979).

The focus on the relationship between individual health and the environment continued during later centuries. Frank's medical treatise, *System of a Complete Medical Policy* (written in 1774–1821), advocated education of midwives and new mothers, a healthy school environment, personal hygiene, nutrition, sewers and sanitation, accident prevention, collection of vital statistics such as births and deaths, and efficient administration of hospitals to care for the sick.

Numerous studies throughout the years have attributed incidence of infant mortality, heart disease, and cancer to environmental influences. A number of studies, such as Dohrenwend and Dohrenwend's (1974) well-known research, show strong relationships between stressful life events and the subsequent development of physical disorders, supporting Hippocrates' earlier theories of the ways that a negative lifestyle can affect health. Brenner (1973) demonstrated the relationships between health problems such as heart disease, infant and adult mortality rates, and other health indicators and national employment rates between 1915 and 1967. He found that when employment rates were high, health problems were low and that low employment rates were associated with higher incidences of health problems.

The interactions between environmental factors, such as unemployment, and mental health significantly affect individual health. Increased attention began to be paid to the relationship between health problems and mental health problems in the late 1970s with the release of the surgeon general's national health report, *Healthy People,* which emphasized the important link between physical and mental health, noting the significance of strong family ties, supportive friends, and use of informal and formal support systems in promoting healthy individuals (U.S. Surgeon General, 1979).

Lazarus (1991) takes a somewhat different systems perspective, presenting research findings that show that people who perceive their environments as stressful, such as those living in highly urban or highly rural areas, place their psychological systems in jeopardy and develop ways to cope that are tied to their perception of the situation. For example, an elderly man living in a rural area who perceives himself as being extremely isolated and without the resources to get him to a hospital quickly if he becomes ill is more likely to experience health problems than an elderly man

who perceives that he is living in an area where health care is more readily available to him. As can be seen in Table 10.1, the greatest contributions to premature death are not individual hereditary factors but environmental and lifestyle factors. Studies show that the following factors affect health status significantly.

Income

The higher your income, the more likely you are to be in good health. The poor are much more likely to have health problems. This can be attributed to the fact that individuals with higher incomes are more likely to have health

---

TABLE 10.1   **MAJOR FACTORS CONTRIBUTING TO PREMATURE DEATH; ESTIMATED PERCENTAGE CONTRIBUTION TO CAUSE OF DEATH**

Leading Causes of Death	Age-Adjusted Death Rate*	Lifestyle (%)	Environment (%)	Inadequacy of Health Care Services (%)	Genetic/ Hereditary Factors (%)
Cardiovascular disease	281.4	54	9	12	25
Cancer	204.1	37	24	10	29
Strokes	56.1	50	20	10	22
Pulmonary diseases	36.0	50	22	7	21
Nonmotor vehicle accidents	34.0	51	31	4	4
Motor vehicle accidents	16.1	69	18	12	1
Influenza/pneumonia	29.7	23	20	18	2
Diabetes	19.6	34	0	6	60
HIV	13.2	NA	NA	NA	NA
Suicide	12.0	60	35	3	18
Homicide	10.0	63	35	0	2
Total All 11 causes together	852.9	51	19	10	20

*Per 100,000 population

NA = Data not available.

Source: Data compiled from National Center for Health Statistics (1995) and U.S. Department of Health and Human Services (1995).

insurance, seek medical care earlier and more often, buy and eat more nutritious foods, and experience less mental stress. The poor also are more likely to live in areas that are environmentally unhealthy, such as areas with poor sanitation or close to hazardous wastes.

According to the U.S. National Center for Health Statistics (2000), most Americans report themselves to be in good health. However, nearly twice as many African American persons than whites report that they are in fair or poor health. Twenty-one percent of people who earn less than $15,000 report being in fair or poor health, while only 4% of people earning $50,000 or more report they are in fair or poor health. Chronic disease has a devastating impact on minority populations. For example, the prevalence of diabetes among African Americans is about 70% higher than among white Americans, and the prevalence among Latinos is nearly double that for white Americans (Centers for Disease Control and Prevention, 1999).

Studies show that the impact of low income on health is especially damaging to infants and children. Newborns' chances of death or serious illness at birth can be linked directly to whether their mothers have health insurance. Uninsured babies are 30% more likely to die or to experience serious medical problems at birth than insured babies. Nearly 40% of all poor children in the United States are not covered by Medicaid, the federal medical care plan for the poor, or private health insurance (*Statistical Abstract of the United States,* 1999).

Ethnicity

Primarily because of income, whites as a group enjoy better health than people of color. **Infant mortality rates,** the number of infant deaths compared to total infants' births during a given time period, are twice as high for people of color as for whites. Infants born to uninsured African American mothers are twice as likely to die or to experience serious medical problems than babies born to insured mothers. People of color are less likely to seek health care for themselves and their children. Half of all African American preschoolers, for example, are not fully immunized, and 40% of all African American women, compared to 20% of white women, do not receive any prenatal care during their first trimester of pregnancy (Edwards, 1990).

People of color are also more at risk to develop heart disease, diabetes, and cancer. African American males are 85% more likely to experience strokes than white males, and African American females are 80% more likely to experience strokes than white females. High blood pressure, a major cause of kidney failure, strokes, and heart disease, affects African Americans one-third more than whites. New research indicates that the link between high blood pressure and ethnicity is low socioeconomic status. Researchers suggest that the high blood pressure could be due to environmental stress caused by oppression and limited access to social and economic resources (Astrachan, 1991). African Americans are twice as likely as whites to become disabled, often because of high blood pressure and related problems.

Health problems that should not be major problems in a wealthy industrialized country such as the United States are increasing among all groups but particularly among people of color. Studies of health care along the United States–Mexico border, for example, show high rates of tuberculosis, hepatitis, and malaria. Life expectancies for people of color are also much shorter than for whites: 73.9

years for white men compared to 68.9 years for nonwhite men and 79.7 years for white women compared to 76.1 for nonwhite women (U.S. National Center for Health Statistics, 2000).

Gender

The average life expectancy for both men and women has increased since 1950—7 years for men and 8 years for women. Although the fact that the average life expectancy for women is greater than for men can be viewed as an advantage for women, it is also a disadvantage for them. Because of the difference in life expectancy and the fact that women have less built up in Social Security due to staying at home and raising children, increasing numbers of elderly women who become widowed have little or no health insurance coverage and limited Social Security benefits. Thus, they are more likely to spend their last years living in poverty, which in turn places them at even more risk to experience poor health.

Age

Our country's oldest and youngest citizens are at the highest risk to experience poor health. The elderly are at risk as a result of both the aging process and because many live in poverty—one-third of today's elderly are poor and do not seek health care as needed due to the high costs. Eighty to 90% of the more than 1.5 million persons in the United States with Alzheimer's disease, for example, are 65 and older. The aging factor will be of even greater significance as the U.S. population continues to age: nearly 13% of the population is over 65, and by 2040, one of every five persons in the United States will be over 65 (*Statistical Abstract*, 1999). Current estimates indicate that the nursing home population will grow

four times faster than the population of all other Americans during the next 50 years (Rice, 1995).

Although the United States is one of the wealthiest countries in the world, it continues to have the highest infant mortality rate (7.2 deaths per 1,000 live births) than any Western country (U.S. National Center for Health Statistics, 2000). As the number of children growing up in poverty continues to increase, U.S. children will be at a greater risk to experience serious health problems.

The major causes of death vary significantly by age. Although tremendous gains in preventing some major causes of death have taken place, many deaths are not related to major physical illness, particularly in youth. Accidents are still the leading cause of death for people under 25 years of age (see Table 10.2). Increased violence in our society has also affected causes of death, with homicide one of the three leading causes of death for persons 5 to 25. HIV/AIDS was the eighth leading cause of death in the United States in 1997 (U.S. National Center for Health Statistics, 1999).

Disability

Individuals with both permanent and temporary disability are much more at risk to have serious health problems than nondisabled people. The fact that they may be less resilient because of their disability is often compounded by the lack of affordable, accessible, appropriate health care that allows them to maintain good preventive health practices.

Rural and Urban Areas

Individuals living in extremely rural or highly populated urban areas are more at risk to have health problems. This can be attributed to the

TABLE 10.2	TOP CAUSES OF DEATH IN THE UNITED STATES BY AGE IN 1997		
Age	Number 1 Cause	Number 2 Cause	Number 3 Cause
Infants	Congenital anomalies	Premature birth	SIDS
1–4	Accidents	Congenital anomalies	Cancer
5–9	Accidents	Cancer	Congenital anomalies
10–14	Accidents	Cancer	Suicide
15–24	Accidents	Homicide	Suicide
25–34	Accidents	Suicide	Homicide
35–44	Cancer	Accidents	Heart disease
45–54	Cancer	Heart disease	Accidents
55–64	Cancer	Heart disease	Respiratory diseases
65+	Heart disease	Cancer	Strokes

Source: U.S. National Center for Health Statistics (2000).

increasing environmental hazards such as pollution and increased stress from living in a highly populated urban area and to the lack of medical facilities for prevention and early medical care found in extremely rural areas. Over half of all people at the poverty level live in rural areas, and individuals in rural areas are more likely to suffer from emotional disorders than people in urban areas (see Chapter 15).

Applying a Systems/Ecological Perspective

It is vital that a systems/ecological perspective that focuses on the interaction and interdependence between person and environment be used in understanding **health risk factors,** or those factors that affect individuals' health

and place them at risk for serious health problems and health conditions (see Table 10.2).

The current emphasis on holistic health care stems from a systems/ecological approach to health care. This perspective views all aspects of an individual's health in relation not only to how that individual interacts with family members, the workplace, and the community but also to how the environment, including community quality of life as well as legislation and funding available to support quality of life, affects a person's health. This perspective slowly is replacing the more traditional medical model used by health practitioners, which often focuses on symptoms and malfunctions of only one part of the body without focusing on other body systems or the environment within which the individual interacts. The World Health Organization defines **health** as "a state of complete physical, mental, and social well-being and not merely the absence of disease or infirmity" (Schlesinger, 1985). This definition reflects the systems/ecological perspective in viewing health as clearly dependent on a combination of environmental, physiological, sociological, and psychological factors.

THE EVOLUTION OF HEALTH CARE IN AMERICA

Early emphasis for health care in the United States focused on keeping people alive. Persons born in the United States 200 years ago had only a 50% chance of surviving long enough to celebrate their 21st birthday. One-third of all deaths were of children less than 5 years old. Even then, people of color had higher death rates. In the late 18th century, the death rate was 30 per thousand for whites and 70 per thousand for slaves (U.S. Public Health

Service, 1977). Health practitioners at that time were limited in number and training and faced great difficulties in keeping their patients alive because of environmental constraints, such as poor sanitation and extreme poverty. Many illnesses resulted in catastrophic epidemics, which claimed the lives of entire families. In 1793 during a yellow fever epidemic in Philadelphia, three physicians were available to care for 6,000 patients stricken with the disease. Thus, early attempts to improve health care in the United States included national and state legislation relating to control of communicable diseases, sanitation measures such as pasteurization of milk, and education for midwives, physicians, and young mothers (U.S. Public Health Service, 1977).

Although more recent legislation and programs have focused on control of chronic, degenerative diseases such as heart disease and cancer, on self-inflicted illnesses such as cirrhosis of the liver, and on other health problems such as accidents and violence, most efforts are still directed to restoring health after illness has occurred. The health care system in the United States still allows large numbers of U.S. citizens to remain unserved or underserved, and mortality rates remain higher than in many developed countries (Rice, 1995).

CRITICAL ISSUES IN CURRENT HEALTH CARE DELIVERY

Many domestic policy professionals believe that the United States is experiencing a crisis in health care. While health care costs are increasing significantly, greater numbers of Americans are finding health care inaccessible to them. Health care statistics show that more infants are dying at birth, and other people are experiencing serious health problems that are often treatable.

Funding and Costs of Health Care

The rapidly increasing cost of health care at all levels in the United States—for consumers, local health care practitioners, community hospitals, local governments, and state and federal programs—is considered one of the most critical issues facing our country today. The United States spends over $3 billion a day on health care alone, with present predictions that this amount will increase to almost $6 billion a day by 2008, or $2.2 trillion per year and 16.2% of the gross domestic product; see Table 10.3 (Rice, 1995).

Individuals like the Mendozas, whom we introduced at the beginning of this chapter, are not the only ones experiencing financial bankruptcy because of health care costs. Physicians are leaving independently owned practices, particularly in rural and poverty areas; hospitals are closing; insurance companies are going out of business; communities and states are in the red due to increased costs of indigent health care; and the federal government's Medicaid and Medicare systems are in danger of not having enough money to meet the need. Medicaid is being cut significantly by the U.S. Congress, and proposals are being considered to cut Medicare funding as well. In spite of the costs, services are increasingly fragmented, inaccessible, and unattainable for many U.S. residents and not well matched to the needs of those receiving them when they are provided. In fact, the health care system in the United States unfortunately is an excellent example of how lack of planning and funding

| TABLE 10.3 | GROSS DOMESTIC PRODUCT (GDP) AND NATIONAL HEALTH EXPENDITURES BY SOURCE OF FUNDS (1929–2030) |

	PUBLIC FUNDS		PRIVATE FUNDS		TOTAL			
YEAR	Amount (billion $)	Percentage of Total	Amount (billion $)	Percentage of Total	GDP (billion $)	Amount (billion $)	$ per Capita	Percentage of GDP
1929	3.2	86.4	0.5	13.6	103.1	3.6	29	3.5
1950	9.2	72.8	3.4	27.2	284.8	12.7	80	4.5
1955	13.2	74.3	4.6	25.7	398.0	17.7	101	4.4
1960	20.5	75.5	6.7	24.5	513.4	27.1	143	5.3
1965	31.3	75.3	10.3	24.7	702.7	41.6	204	5.9
1970	46.7	62.8	27.7	37.2	1,010.7	74.4	346	7.4
1975	77.8	58.5	55.1	41.5	1,585.9	132.9	592	8.4
1980	145.0	58.0	105.2	42.0	2,708.0	250.1	1,064	9.2
1985	248.0	58.7	174.6	41.3	4,038.7	422.6	1,711	10.5
1990	390.0	57.8	285.1	42.2	5,522.2	675.0	2,601	12.2
2000	859.9	49.4	879.9	50.6	9,637.0	1,739.8	6,148	18.1
2010	1,819.2	48.0	1,968.8	52.0	17,238.0	3,787.8	12,522	22.0
2020	3,776.1	48.2	4,063.2	51.8	29,594.0	7,839.4	24,278	26.5
2030	7,753.0	48.5	8,216.7	51.5	49,936.0	15,969.6	47,891	32.0

Sources: Bruner, Waldo, and McKusick (1992); U.S. National Center for Health Statistics (1992, Table 112; 1993, Tables 114 and 122); and Rice (1995, p. 1169). Copyright 1995, National Association of Social Workers, Inc. *Encyclopedia of Social Work.*

has created an ineffective, narrowly focused, fragmented, and expensive approach to a major social welfare problem.

Emphasis during the 1950s and 1960s was on providing the best possible health care to all Americans and improving health personnel, services, and research. But as costs for health care have skyrocketed, attention has shifted to ways to control costs and to determine who should pay for what expenditures. In 1997, the U.S. health care system provided nearly 800 million examinations in physicians' offices; treated over 30 million persons in over 6,000 hospitals; provided care to over 1.3 million persons, mostly elderly, in over 16,000 nursing homes; provided over 500 million outpatient visits to hospitals; and offered home health and hospice care to over 8 million people (*Statistical Abstract,* 1999).

Health Insurance Plans and Managed Care

In 1996, nearly 16% of the total U.S. population did not have some form of private health insurance (purchased by individuals or employers from companies such as Blue Cross/ Blue Shield) or government health insurance (Medicare, Medicaid, and military plans). Medicare costs in 1996 totaled $203.1 billion, while Medicaid costs totaled $121.7 billion (*Statistical Abstract,* 1999).

One factor that has contributed to the increased costs for both private and public health care has been the shift from retrospective to prospective payment systems. In the past, with the exception of insurance for hospitalization, most health care was paid for after you used it—you went to the doctor, and you paid the full amount after your visit. Today most health care is paid for in advance through premiums to private insurance companies or federal programs such as Medicaid, because the health care industry is trying to contain costs and promote preventive health care.

Most current health care plans are based on a **managed care system,** a system of health care delivery that limits the use and cost of services and measures performance through a program of careful monitoring and control. Under managed care, health care professionals hired by health insurance companies and large employers systematically review specific health care needs and determine the most cost-effective ways to provide for them. After review, limited options are presented to consumers. Some plans include preferred provider organizations (PPOs) that offer health care through a network of specific providers. An individual who chooses other providers than those in the preapproved network usually must get specific permission from the health care plan to do so, pay additional costs to use other providers, or not have those health care costs covered by the plan at all.

Another important group in the health care industry is **health maintenance organizations (HMOs),** which consist of prepaid medical group practices to which individuals pay monthly fees and receive specific types of health care at no cost or minimum costs per visit. At least 76.6 million Americans are enrolled in HMOs (U.S. National Center for Health Statistics, 1999). Payment of a monthly amount to a health insurance company or HMO entitles a person—and, if insured, the person's family—to needed health care on demand at either no additional cost or a limited cost—for example, 15% of the cost, with the insurance or health care company paying the additional 85%.

Such managed care plans try to stress more preventive services, reduce hospital stays, and allow fewer expensive medical tests. But concern has been expressed about some managed care efforts. For example, what happens when managed care organizations override the recommendations of physicians and limit or deny coverage for medical care or treatment? State and federal policymakers have responded to these issues by filing legislation and enacting laws. Virtually all states have adopted one or more laws addressing specific consumer concerns. These laws focus on increasing consumer access to services (for example, emergency care, prescription drugs, specialists), prohibiting the use of incentives that encourage physicians to deny care, and assuring consumer rights in the case of disputes.

To varying degrees, these laws provide health care consumers some measure of reassurance. However, managed care consumers still cannot count on basic protections. There is little consistency across the states in managed care consumer protections. Some states have enacted only one or two protections (for example, the prohibition of so-called provider "gag rules" (see p. 287) or the guarantee for women that they have direct access to obstetricians and gynecologists). Few states have established comprehensive protections for managed care enrollees.

The Families USA Foundation (1998) provided a representative sampling of managed health care protections in its report *Hit and Miss: State Managed Care Laws.* These protections include

- the right to go to an emergency room and have the managed care plan pay for resulting care, if a person reasonably believes he or she is experiencing an emergency;
- the right to receive health care from an out-of-network provider when the health plan's network of providers is inadequate;
- the right of a person with a serious illness or disability to use a specialist as a primary care provider;
- a seriously ill person's right to receive standing referrals to health specialists;
- a woman's right to gain direct access to an obstetrician or gynecologist;
- the right of a seriously ill patient or a pregnant woman to continue receiving health care for a specified period of time from a physician who has been dropped by the health plan;
- the establishment of a procedure that enables a patient to obtain specific prescription drugs that are not on a health plan's drug formulary;
- the right to appeal denials of care through a review process that is external to, and independent of, health plans;
- the establishment of consumer assistance, or ombudsman, programs;
- prohibitions against plans' use of so-called "gag rules"—rules that prevent physicians and health providers from fully disclosing treatment options to patients;
- prohibitions against plans' reliance on inappropriate financial incentives to deny or reduce necessary health care;
- the establishment of state laws that prevent plans from prohibiting participation in clinical trials; and
- the creation of state laws enabling enrollees to sue their health plans when they improperly deny care.

A survey of state consumer protection laws as of June 1998 revealed the following findings (Families USA Foundation, 1998):

- No state has passed a series of laws addressing all of the protections listed earlier.
- Vermont has enacted the greatest number of those protections (11 in total), South Dakota the fewest (none).
- Sixteen states have enacted between five and nine of these protections.
- Thirty-three states have enacted from one to four of these protections.
- Approximately one-third of Americans with employer-provided health care (approximately 51 million persons) are in "self-insured" plans and are preempted from patient protections established by state laws.
- Of those who have health insurance provided by their employer, 83% (approximately 124 million Americans) are preempted under the Employee Retirement Income Security Act (ERISA) of 1974 from seeking state-prescribed remedies for wrongful denials of care, and federal remedies for these individuals are unavailable as well.

As can be seen, the unevenness in state consumer protection legislation is compounded by ERISA, which exempts many millions of Americans from the state protections that do exist. As a result, even within the same state, protections vary. There is one set of rules for those who purchase their own insurance, another for those in employer-paid self-insured plans, and yet another for those in employer-paid plans that are not self-insured. This variability is an enormous source of confusion for consumers, leaving them uncertain about their health care coverage and concerned about whether they will get the care they need.

A recent survey by the Kaiser Family Foundation and Harvard University's School of Public Health found that 61% of Americans believe managed care plans decrease the amount of time doctors spend with patients. Nearly 60% believe managed care plans make it harder for sick people to see medical specialists. Over half of those surveyed say managed care has hurt the quality of care for people who are sick. In one of the most troublesome findings, 55% of survey respondents are at least "somewhat worried" that, if they are sick, their "health plan would be more concerned about saving money than about what is the best medical treatment" (Kaiser Family Foundation, 1998).

Although prospective health care has been an attempt to promote early preventive use of care to create a nation that is physically healthier and to reduce costs, it has not been highly successful at either task. Administrative costs alone to manage such a complex system have escalated over the years.

Health care costs continue to rise rapidly in spite of efforts of cost containment. Increases can be seen at every level: the average cost of health care per person per year in the United States is now $4,340, the highest rate of any industrialized country. Between 1983 and 1993, employees' share of health insurance premiums increased 330%! Despite this increase, the cost of health care benefits borne by employers remains at a high level, and these costs are passed on to consumers through higher prices for products and services. For example, when someone buys a domestic automobile, upwards of $700 of the cost represents health care expenses for employees and their families (Edwards, 1990).

Comparing Health Care Costs to Outcomes

Although the United States currently spends more on health care than any other country, its health care system does not produce superior outcomes in comparison to other countries (see Table 10.4). In 1998 the United States ranked 17th in life expectancy and 14th in infant mortality among 20 industrialized countries with populations of 6 million or more (*Statistical Abstract*, 1999).

In 1998, infant mortality rates in countries with 6 million or more people ranged from 3.9 per 1,000 live births in Sweden to 143.6 per 1,000 in Afghanistan. The U.S. rate was 6.4. Thirteen countries had infant mortality rates lower than that of the United States. The life expectancy in 1998 ranged from 80.0 in Japan to 40.9 in Ethiopia. The U.S. average life expectancy was 76.1, or a ranking of 17th among the countries cited. It is understandable that Afghanistan's infant mortality rate would be so high and Ethiopia's life expectancy so low, since life in these countries is so challenging. However, it is more difficult to understand why the United States' infant mortality rate is higher than most Western countries and why its life expectancy for both males and females is much lower, since the United States spends more than any other country per capita on health care (*Statistical Abstract*, 1999).

When comparing significant health care indicators, the U.S. investment in health care has failed to achieve its intended outcomes. One in five of all children in the United States are born to mothers who received no prenatal care in the first 3 months of pregnancy (Children's Defense Fund, 2000). Although studies show that as much as $14 a day can be saved for every dollar invested in immunizations,

TABLE 10.4 COMPARISONS OF HEALTH CARE COSTS, LIFE EXPECTANCY, AND INFANT MORTALITY RATES

Country	Percentage of GDP Allocated to Health Care (1993)/Rank	Health Care Costs per Capita (1993)/Rank	Infant Mortality Rate* (1995)/Rank	Average Life Expectancy (1995)/Rank
United States	14.1/1	$3,299/1	7.9/17	76.0/20
Canada	10.2/2	1,971/3	6.8/10	78.3/6
Switzerland	9.9/3	2,283/2	6.3/6	78.4/3
France	9.8/4	1,835/4	6.5/8	78.4/3
Austria	9.2/5	1,777/6	6.9/12	77.8/10
Finland	8.8/6	1,363/12	5.2/2	76.2/18
Netherlands	8.7/7	1,532/8	6.0/5	78.0/8
Germany	8.6/8	1,814/5	6.3/6	76.6/17
Australia	8.5/9	1,494/11	7.1/15	77.8/10
Italy	8.5/9	1,523/9	7.4/16	77.4/13
Belgium	8.3/11	1,601/7	7.0/13	77.2/14
Sweden	7.5/12	1,266/14	5.6/3	78.4/3
Japan	7.3/13	1,495/10	4.3/1	79.4/2
Spain	7.3/13	972/16	6.7/9	77.9/9
United Kingdom	7.1/15	1,213/15	7.0/13	77.0/16
Denmark	6.7/16	1,296/13	6.8/10	76.1/19
Greece	5.7/17	500/17	8.3/19	77.8/10
Cuba	NA	NA	8.1/18	77.1/15
Hong Kong	NA	NA	5.8/4	80.2/1
Israel	NA	NA	8.4/20	78.1/7
†Turkey	2.7	146	45.6	71.5

*Per 1,000 births

†Turkey is included for comparison purposes only; it is not ranked in the top 20 of any category

NA = Data not available.

Source: Data compiled from U.S. National Center for Health Statistics (2000).

large numbers of children in the United States remain unimmunized: 60% of infants do not receive the immunizations they need by the age of 7 months (National Association of Social Workers [NASW], 1995). In 1990, many children died because of a large measles outbreak in the United States, and increasing numbers of children are getting whooping cough and other illnesses that had declined significantly in recent years.

Although costs of health care, like costs in other areas, have increased because of inflation, other reasons for rising health expenditures also must be considered. Some attribute increased costs to more extensive use of medical resources by a more educated population interested in preventive health care. They argue that accessibility to group insurance plans through the workplace and the increase in HMOs and other health programs aimed at reducing health costs actually increase costs because of more extensive use. Statistics show, however, that many Americans, particularly poor individuals—people of color, single-parent females, and the elderly—work for employers who do not offer health insurance or are paid such low wages that they cannot afford the health insurance offered. Thus, they are less apt to use health care resources; but when they do, they are more likely to need more costly services because they have not sought preventive care.

Even with today's emphasis on wellness and public awareness about the potential damages of smoking, alcohol and other drug consumption, and lack of exercise, few dollars are spent on prevention by private citizens and all levels of U.S. government. This trend continues even though studies show that dollars spent for prevention pay for themselves as much as eight times over in the long run (Van Den Bergh, 1995).

An Increasing Elderly Population

Other trends may also explain the rising costs of health care in the United States. Because of increased access to health care, improved knowledge and technology, and a better quality of life, people are living longer, resulting in increased need for medical care for those 65 and older. Composing approximately 13% of the population and more likely to be poor and unable to pay for health care than other groups, persons over 65 have three times more health problems and needs than persons in other age groups. Between 1998 and 2050, the population of people over 65 will increase from 34 million to 56 million in the United States, or a nearly 61% increase (*Statistical Abstract*, 1999).

As this population continues to increase, costs will also increase. Few insurance premiums cover the costs of nursing home care, and those that do are rapidly increasing the premiums they charge for such coverage. The insurance system, particularly in care for the elderly, is also fragmented, with separate systems paying for home health care, medical equipment, nursing homes, and medical transportation to and from health care facilities (Ford Foundation, 1989). It is estimated that by the year 2040, people 65 and older will account for more than half of the total personal health care expenditures in the United States.

Medicare and Medicaid costs are also expected to increase significantly. Medicare costs in 1996 were $200.3 billion; they are expected to increase at an annual growth rate of 10%. Medicaid costs, which were $121.7 billion in 1996, are also expected to increase significantly as the elderly population increases. Although only 12% of the Medicaid population in 1996 was 65 years and older, this group accounted for over 30% of Medicaid expenditures. In contrast, Aid to Families with Dependent Children (AFDC) recipients and their families made up 66% of the Medicaid population but accounted for only 24.5% of expenditures, while persons with disabilities made up 17% of the population and accounted for 42% of expenditures (*Statistical Abstract*, 1999).

Increased Knowledge and Availability of Technology

A second explanation for the increased costs of health care is the greater availability of knowledge and technology for saving lives: neonatal procedures for infants born prematurely; heart, lung, and other organ transplants; and heart surgery to restore circulation and reduce incidence of heart attacks and other cardiac problems. Currently, the extent of and knowledge about technology exceed the dollars necessary to support such sophisticated systems and make them available to everyone in need. In many instances, heroic procedures are covered by health care policies, whereas preventive care, such as long-term care, rehabilitative services, and health education, are not (Ford Foundation, 1989). Although values issues are inherent when discussing health care, our current health technologies have become very costly. Current studies suggest, for example, that persons who receive heart transplants live an average of 4 years longer than persons who do not receive transplants, at a cost of $100,000 per transplant, or $25,000 for every additional year of life.

Additionally, with greater numbers of private hospitals and the difficulties public medical facilities face in remaining solvent, health care has become increasingly competitive. Many private hospitals are now owned by large corporations with real estate subsidiaries and their own insurance divisions. In many instances, the heightened competition has resulted in duplicative purchases of expensive equipment by hospitals in close proximity. While hospitals struggle to compete with each other for paying clients, the number of people who are unable to pay hospital bills continues to increase. The limits on **public health insurance** (that is, Medicare and Medicaid) reimbursements to hospitals also have created serious financial problems for many hospitals that are unable to provide services at reimbursement levels. The number of hospitals in the United States has been steadily declining in recent years, from a total of 6,965 in 1980 to 6,201 in 1996. In addition, hospitals are increasingly losing large sums of money as a result of uncompensated care. Today, nearly 1 in 10 patients is indigent and unable to pay for medical costs at all.

Emphasis on Third-Party Payments

A third reason that has been suggested for escalated health care costs is the use of third-party billing by many medical practitioners (billing an insurance company directly rather than billing the patient). Many physicians and hospitals charge the maximum amount allowable under an insurance system, whereas they might otherwise be reluctant to charge individual clients the same amount if they knew the clients would be paying for the services directly.

Faced with rapidly increasing costs, the 1,500 private insurance companies in the United States that cover about half of the population are now minimizing their risks by reducing benefits covered, requiring second opinions in many instances, and excluding the chronically ill. At the same time, insurance premiums continue to increase, with high costs to employers who pay portions of employees' premiums as well as to employees themselves. As a result, many employers, particularly smaller ones, are now either no longer covering employees or their families or are covering a smaller percentage of premiums, so that employees are paying much larger shares. More and more people who carry health insurance on an individual rather than an employee policy are being forced to cancel their policies because they cannot afford them, requiring local communities to pick up the rising costs of their health care when they become ill and cannot pay their bills.

Increased Costs of Health Care for the Poor

A fourth reason for the increased costs of health care is the number of poor individuals who need health care and cannot afford to pay for it. As this number continues to increase, federal and state governments are struggling with the high costs of health care. But efforts to reduce Medicaid and Medicare expenditures by setting ceilings for reimbursable costs have led some physicians and nursing homes to refuse to accept clients under these health care assistance plans, claiming they lose too much money because the actual costs are much higher than the ceilings allowed.

Even though there are problems with the Medicaid system of health care for the poor and with group insurance programs, of greater concern are the large numbers of persons who have no health coverage at all. Over half of the poor in the United States are either not covered by Medicaid or do not use the system. Those who have neither Medicaid nor other health insurance coverage often become destitute immediately when they or members of their family suffer health problems. Few families can afford even several thousand dollars in health care costs, and many health problems can easily cost a family over $10,000. Unfortunately, when individuals and other available health care programs cannot pay for health care, local communities and taxpayers must bear the costs. Kingston and others (1988) studied the health care needs of poor persons aged 50 to 64 who received services at a New York City shelter for the homeless and did not qualify for federal health care programs. They found that 75% of this group had had some type of medical treatment during the past year, 30% had been hospitalized, and 76% had received emergency room services. The city had to pay for the health care.

Many local public hospitals that are obligated to accept medically indigent patients are operating in the red; one local hospital spent over $2 million on a young child with serious health problems, because the girl was not covered by any type of private or public health care plan. Thus, the hospital—and the local taxpayers—absorbed the costs of her care. The story had a happy ending; the child was adopted and moved to a home with parents equipped to provide for her special needs at a cost much, much less than the $1,500 per day cost for her hospital care.

But the costs of indigent health care to local communities are increasing. Many state legislators and citizens do not understand the complicated reimbursement system for government programs such as Medicare and Medicaid. For every dollar of Medicaid money spent, for example, the state contribution is about 40 cents and the federal contribution is about 60 cents. But conservative legislatures limit dollars allocated for state health care, not always understanding that limiting state costs reduces the number of federal dollars available to the state and ultimately results in more money, not less, paid by that state's citizens.

One large state, for example, consistently limits its legislative authorization of state dollars for health care coverage for the poor. As a result, less federal money comes into that state and more goes to other states. In one recent year, for example, for every $3.00 that a citizen of the state paid in federal income taxes, only $1.89 was returned to the state. The other $1.11 went to other states for their programs. Yet because the state authorized only a limited Medicaid program, large numbers of women and children were not eligible to receive Medicaid benefits. When they became ill, they went to public hospitals, funded by local tax dollars, with the hospitals having to absorb the costs of their unpaid care.

Increased Numbers of Malpractice Suits

U.S. society's encouragement of lawsuits is another cost-raising factor. All medical practitioners fear the increasing number of malpractice suits being filed. One study found that all practitioners face at least one suit during their careers, no matter how competent they are. This development has resulted in extremely high costs for malpractice insurance and practitioners who feel compelled to order numerous tests, exploratory surgery, and other medical procedures when they are not sure what is wrong with an individual, to eliminate the risk of a lawsuit for a wrong decision.

CURRENT MAJOR HEALTH PROBLEMS

Although many health problems that faced Americans in the past have been all but eliminated, new ones arise on which attention must be focused. Current major health problems facing the United States and its citizens include heart disease, cancer, stroke, pulmonary disease, diabetes, kidney disease, and liver disease (U.S. National Center for Health Statistics, 1999).

Heart disease, strokes, and cancer remain the three leading causes of death in the United States. Nearly one-third of the total deaths in the United States in 1997 were due to diseases of the heart. Cancer rates continue to rise and are increasingly associated with environmental factors. Cancer will eventually be the cause of death of one out of every three persons in the United States. Breast disease is the leading cause of death for women, and rates of breast cancer are increasing in the United States. While new technology and medications have made treatment of these diseases more effective, they remain major causes of death.

AIDS

Acquired immunodeficiency syndrome (AIDS) has affected all of our social institutions and most communities in the United States. Although with recently discovered medication regimes, the life spans of many people diagnosed with HIV (human immunodeficiency virus) infection have increased considerably after the diagnosis, the disease has a high fatality rate and continues to spread to all segments of the population. Because the method of transmission of the virus is tied to culturally sensitive topics, including the use of illegal drugs, sex, and sexual orientation, AIDS is often viewed by society in political and moral contexts rather than as a serious public health issue (Lloyd, 1995).

AIDS first came to the attention of health authorities in the early 1980s. Through December 1998, a total of 688,200 cases of AIDS had been identified in the United States, including more than 8,461 children. According to the U.S. National Center for Health Statistics (2000), 410,800 people have died from the disease or related causes, including 4,984 children. Worldwide, 33.4 million people are estimated to be living with HIV/AIDS. Of these, 32.2 million are adults and 1.2 million are children under 15. Women are becoming increasingly affected by HIV. Approximately 43%, or 13.8 million, of the 32.2 million adults living with HIV or AIDS worldwide are women. "More than 95% of all

HIV-infected people now live in the developing world, which has likewise experienced 95% of all deaths from AIDS. One out of every three children orphaned by HIV/AIDS is under age 5" (*U.S. National Center for Health Statistics Fact Sheet*, 2000, p. 2).

A new definition adopted by the national Centers for Disease Control and Prevention broadened conditions from those previously associated with the virus. It is expected that this new definition will allow for earlier detection of persons infected with the virus, double the numbers of persons known to have it, and lengthen their survival time (Lloyd, 1995).

When a person is referred to as being **HIV-positive,** it means that the person has tested positively for AIDS, is infected with the virus, and has HIV antibodies present in his or her blood. HIV is an intracellular parasite that binds to molecules in the body, causing the destruction of cells that help maintain the immune system and leading to a gradual but progressive destruction of the entire immune system (McGrath, 1990). During the primary HIV infection period, 50% to 90% of individuals develop a mononucleosis-like infection that begins 1 to 3 weeks after infection and continues for 1 to 2 weeks (Lloyd, 1995). But most individuals will not recognize HIV-related symptoms at this point, and test results are usually not accurate until approximately 6 months after getting the virus. Although persons who test positive for AIDS may not show symptoms of AIDS for many years, they are carriers of the virus and can infect others with it.

Previously, AIDS-related conditions were viewed in three stages: infection with the virus, AIDS-related complex (ARC), and clinical AIDS. But these conditions are now seen on a continuum from the point of infection to clinical AIDS. Conditions related to AIDS include fever, weight loss, swollen lymph nodes, diar-rhea, fatigue, and night sweats. In addition, laboratory tests show a low white blood cell count, low red blood cell count, low platelet count, or elevated levels of serum globulins. Other conditions include a low number of T-helper cells and a low ratio of T-helper to T-suppressor cells. This condition moderately damages the body's immune system.

As the disease progresses, the body's immune system begins to collapse. This results in the recurrent development of otherwise treatable infections, which continue to break down the body's resistance and stress the entire system. Kaposi's sarcoma, a rare skin cancer, is a common disease associated with AIDS. As more women are diagnosed with AIDS, cervical cancer and chronic yeast infections have been added to the list of conditions associated with the disease. Many persons with AIDS die from a rare form of pneumonia caused by the organism *Pneumocystis carinii* (U.S. National Center for Health Statistics, 2000).

More and more is becoming known about how the disease can be treated, and with new medications and medical treatment, the death rate for HIV infection declined by almost one-half from 1996 to 1997 (U.S. National Center for Health Statistics, 2000). However, the virus has already become resistant to some of the newest treatments identified such as so-called "cocktail drugs" that combine several powerful drugs into a single treatment regimen. Current research efforts have yet to find a cure or vaccine to prevent its spread. AIDS is transmitted by exchange of body fluids, primarily blood and semen. To date, there is no evidence that AIDS is transmitted by casual contact such as shaking hands, sharing drinks from the same glass, getting an insect bite, sneezing, or living or working with a person infected with the virus. Persons at the highest risk to be exposed to AIDS are homosexual and bisexual men, intravenous drug users who share needles, persons who are exposed to the virus through blood transfusions, and babies born to mothers who are infected with the AIDS virus.

Although AIDS originally hit the populations of gay men and substance abusers hardest, the highest rates for newly infected individuals are among women through heterosexual transmission of the virus. Nearly 40% of the cases reported to the Centers for Disease Control and Prevention through December 1998 were men and women 20 to 39 years of age. AIDS specialists have suggested that because it takes several years for AIDS symptoms to show up, instead of looking at data relating to the numbers of persons with full-blown AIDS, we should focus on the numbers of persons who have the HIV virus in their blood. Results of blood testing of persons with AIDS reported to the Centers for Disease Control and Prevention confirm that whereas rates among homosexual and bisexual men have stabilized, rates among the heterosexual population, particularly intravenous drug users, women, and children, are increasing. Nearly 40% of all AIDS cases reported to the Centers for Disease Control through December 1998 represented persons of African American descent (not Hispanic). An additional 18% represented persons of Hispanic descent. In 1998, more African Americans were reported with AIDS than any other racial/ethnic group. The 1998 rate of reported AIDS cases among African Americans was 66.4 per 100,000 population, more than two times greater than the rate for Hispanics and eight times greater than the rate for whites. Almost two-thirds of all women reported with AIDS were African American. African American children also represented almost two-thirds of all reported pediatric AIDS cases (U.S. National Center for Health Statistics, 2000).

The AIDS epidemic, which began in the United States among urban middle-class adults, has now spread to rural communities and to poorer and younger population groups (Pan American Health Organization, 1999). The brunt of the epidemic is being felt most by groups whose access to services and information is limited by low income. Young adults (under age 25) are quickly becoming the most at-risk group, now accounting for an estimated 50% of all new HIV infections in the United States (NASW, 1999). Pediatric AIDS cases make up 1.2% of all cases, with the average age of diagnosis 6 months and the average life span 2 years. Many of these children never leave the hospital after birth, and their care is expensive in both financial and emotional costs to hospital employees who work with the children and their families.

Once the AIDS antibody is discovered, estimates are that it costs $80,000 to cover all health care costs of a person with AIDS. Most people with AIDS eventually have to quit their jobs if they are employed and often lose their health insurance. Persons with AIDS and their families face serious financial problems as well as discrimination in both communities and the workplace and problems in obtaining health care, housing, employment, social services, and emotional support. Although the Americans for Disabilities Act (see Chapter 9) specifically mentions persons with AIDS in its listing of groups of people with disabilities covered under the act, oppression and discrimination still are major issues faced by individuals with AIDS and their families (see Box 10.1 for the NASW policy statement on AIDS). Additionally, approximately 100,000 children have lost one or both of their parents to AIDS. Developing permanent plans for their children is another difficult issue that parents with AIDS are forced to address.

BOX
10.1

Humane Treatment for Persons with AIDS: The National Association of Social

Because of the complex biopsychosocial issues presented by AIDS, ARC, and HIV infection, social workers, with their special knowledge, skills, and sensitivity, can make a unique contribution to the management of this crisis by pursuing action in eight areas:

1. **Research:** Basic research, including epidemiological, clinical, and psychosocial studies, is imperative. Social workers, particularly in the area of psychosocial research, have a special contribution to make. They have been at the forefront of issues relating to AIDS and have demonstrated significant leadership in identifying critical issues and needs and have a responsibility to continue in these research efforts.

2. **Public Education and Dissemination of Information:** Accurate information about AIDS; HIV infection control measures; prevention; treatment; and medical, financial, and psychosocial resources available should be widely distributed. The fears of caregivers and the general public must be addressed with appropriate education and interventions. Adequate public funds must be authorized for educational efforts among the general public to reduce the fear of AIDS, ARC, and HIV infection and the stigmatization of persons assumed to be at risk for infection. Adequately funded public education programs should encourage

prevention, early treatment, and formulation of new behaviors to reduce the risks of HIV infection. Professional health care organizations, training programs, and continuing education programs should incorporate the latest information and address especially the needs of minority groups, adolescents, women, infants and children, the developmentally and physically disabled, and the chronically mentally ill. Education and training programs must accommodate differences in culture and ethnicity among people. Program materials must be clear and explicit and targeted to individuals of all sexual orientations. Social workers should work cooperatively with existing AIDS-related educational, treatment, and research organizations. Especially important, social workers should be educated and updated on all AIDS-related issues, including prevention strategies, and should play major roles in reducing public hysteria and prejudice.

3. **Psychological and Social Support:** Comprehensive psychological and social support is necessary to help persons with AIDS, ARC, and HIV infection and all individuals close to them. Extended families, including domestic partners and significant others, represent rich resources of emotional and social support, just as they represent a

Workers Policy Statement on AIDS

network of persons likely to be affected by the disease-related changes, including death, of persons with AIDS and HIV infections. All care providers should respect the individuality of people with AIDS, ARC, and HIV infection and the importance of the individual's relationships with family, domestic partners, and close friends.

The diversity of interpersonal relationships and support systems should be recognized, nurtured, and strengthened. Supplemental services, including support groups, counseling, and therapy, should be made available to people with AIDS and AIDS-related conditions and their loved ones as well as to others who feel vulnerable. In addition, all providers of care should have access to support groups and related services to alleviate the stress inherent in assisting persons with AIDS-related conditions. All AIDS-related service organizations should provide for support, supervision, respite, and recognition of social workers engaged in the emotionally demanding work of serving people with AIDS.

4. **Service Delivery and Resource Development:** A comprehensive service delivery system to respond to AIDS based on a case management model must include suitable housing, adult-child foster care, home health and hospice care, appropriate, affordable health care, access to legal services, and transportation services. Children needing foster care should be provided care at the least restrictive level in nonsegregated settings. Traditional health and social welfare agencies including income maintenance programs must become responsive; eligibility requirements and coverage by health insurance and income maintenance should be adapted to meet the rapid onset and catastrophic effects of AIDS. The health status of people with AIDS-related disorders may vary daily. Currently, service delivery systems do not take health care needs and work requirements into consideration. Systems should be more flexible in providing services for individuals with AIDS-related disorders.

Adequate funding both from public and private sources should be provided to assist alternative health and social services that deal with AIDS and AIDS-related conditions in various communities. Such services, many of which are complementary to and cooperative with mainstream services, help broaden and strengthen the range of traditional supports available to persons with AIDS and AIDS-related conditions. Social workers should be encouraged to be involved in the initiation of—and serve as membership on—local, statewide, regional, and national AIDS task forces.

5. **Civil Rights:** No person should be deprived of civil rights or rights to confidentiality because he or she has been diagnosed as having contracted AIDS, is infected with HIV, or is assumed to be at risk for infection. Nondiscrimination laws should be extended and existing legal protection should be vigorously enforced to protect individuals with AIDS, ARC, and HIV infections from being presumptively deprived of health care, employment, housing, and immigration rights.

6. **HIV Testing:** Social workers should be concerned particularly with the violation of human rights and the psychosocial consequences to people taking HIV antibody tests. Given the potential for serious discrimination, all testing should be voluntary, anonymous, and conducted with informed consent. Social workers should make certain that the limits of the predictive value of such testing are known in advance by clients. Appropriate pre- and post-test counseling must be offered by social workers or other skilled professionals. Social workers are mandated to protect client confidentiality.

7. **Professional Accountability:** The helping professions and appropriate licensing authorities should use their full range of persuasive and regulatory powers to assure that people with AIDS, ARC, and HIV infection and their significant others are not discriminated against in their eligibility for or receipt of services because of their illness or lack of financial or social resources.

8. **Political Action:** Social workers, individually and organizationally, should participate with other groups to lobby actively at local, state, and federal levels on behalf of people with AIDS in order to improve their quality of life; protect their civil liberties; and to advocate for increased funding for appropriate education, prevention, interventions, treatment, services, and research.

The National Association of Social Workers (NASW), as the organizational arm of the profession, must help coordinate a response to AIDS, ARC, and HIV infection by pursuing the multi-faceted strategy outlined in this policy statement.

Source: National Association of Social Workers (1994), *Social work speaks: NASW policy statements* (3rd ed.) (Washington, DC: NASW Press). Copyright 1994, National Association of Social Workers, Inc.

While many of these children go to live with relatives, increasing numbers of children need foster care and adoption placement (Conover, 1994).

In contrast to the other major life-threatening diseases that strike most U.S. citizens, federal expenditures for AIDS are much less, totaling about $6 billion annually (Seelye, 1995).

Other Illnesses and Health Problems

Other illnesses receiving increased attention are diabetes, musculoskeletal diseases such as arthritis and osteoporosis, and respiratory diseases. These problems are much more likely to be experienced by the poor, people of color, and the elderly, who are less likely to be able to afford both preventive and rehabilitative health care.

Recent research is finding that some life-threatening diseases, such as Huntington's disease and cystic fibrosis, are genetically linked. Researchers indicate that within the next several decades, prenatal genetic screening will most likely be able to indicate the presence of hypertension, dyslexia, cancer, sickle-cell anemia, manic depression, schizophrenia, type 1 diabetes, familial Alzheimer's disease, multiple sclerosis, and myotonic muscular dystrophy (Rothstein, 1989). Others predict that genetic screening will also show a predisposition for addictions to alcohol and other drugs.

These discoveries will increase the level of debate regarding moral and ethical choices in relation to birth, fetal and parental rights, abortion, and emotional and dollar costs to individuals and society. If it is certain that a child will be born with multiple sclerosis, AIDS antibodies, or cancer, who should decide the outcome? If the child is born, who should pay the costs for care? Present preg-nancy termination rates for women who decide to have genetic screening are nearly 100% for muscular dystrophy and cystic fibrosis, 60% for hemophilia, and 50% for sickle-cell anemia. But what if the disease is one that occurs much later in life, such as Huntington's disease; is not fatal, such as Down syndrome; or reveals a "predisposition" to a disease, such as cancer, heart disease, or schizophrenia? The field of **bioethics** is a fast-growing one in which social workers can play a major role.

Another health concern is the increased numbers of persons with serious head or spinal injuries who are brain injured, multiply disabled, or both. Many require years of rehabilitation, and some require institutional care for the remainder of their lives. As technology enables many more persons who experience such injuries to remain alive more often than in the past, costs for their care also increase. Because large numbers of persons have received head and spinal injuries due to motorcycle accidents when they were not wearing helmets or had alcohol- or drug-related accidents or car accidents when they were not wearing seat belts, additional concerns are raised about who should pay for health costs and how much should be paid.

Catastrophic Illness

Increased national attention is also being given to the problems encountered by families when a catastrophic illness occurs. A **catastrophic illness** is a chronic and severely debilitating condition that results in high medical costs and long-term dependence on the health care system. Although many families can provide health care for themselves during typical, less serious bouts of illness, a catastrophic illness most often can wipe out the savings of even a fairly wealthy family.

To date, proposals have failed for national legislation to provide national health insurance for individuals and families who experience a catastrophic illness when their available health insurance is exhausted and the costs for the care have reached a certain limit. The Catastrophic Health Care bill, passed by both the House and the Senate in 1988, provided coverage for families and the elderly who experienced catastrophic illness or disability. But it was repealed in 1989 after a strong lobby by middle- and upper-middle-class elderly persons, who protested against increased Medicare premiums included in the legislation (Clift & Hager, 1989). The bill provided Medicare benefits at full coverage after 1 year of hospitalization but increased the deductible for benefits as well as the costs for premiums. The bill also did not cover long-term nursing home care. Although many national groups and health care lobbyists continue to advocate for a national health insurance program that provides some type of health care coverage for all individuals in the United States, coverage limited only to catastrophic health care is a compromise measure more likely to be approved. Thus, it is likely that some sort of catastrophic health care bill will pass in the near future.

Teenage Pregnancy

Attention has been directed toward at-risk groups that generate additional health problems. Recently, the group most publicized has been teenage parents. In 1997, the teen birthrate in the United States was 52.9 live births per 1,000 population (U.S. National Center for Health Statistics, 2000). Studies show that pregnant teens receive little or no prenatal care, poor nutrition during pregnancy, and limited services (U.S. Department of Agriculture [USDA], 1990). As a result, they are at more risk of having miscarriages and of giving birth to premature and low-birth-weight infants and ones with congenital problems.

Prenatal services and nutritional assistance such as the Supplemental Nutrition Program for Women, Infants, and Children (WIC) are not only cost-effective but result in healthy infants better able to grow up to become healthy adults. A 1-year study by the USDA found, for example, that low-income pregnant women who participated in the food and nutrition education program saved an estimated $573 for every newborn. Birth weights increased and the number of premature births declined among program participants.

Environmental Factors

Increased attention also is being paid to environmental factors and their impact on the health of individuals. These include hazardous household substances and other poisons, as well as the quality of household building materials, such as lead-based paints and formaldehyde in insulation. Workplaces also present risks to health, and increased attention is being given to environmental protections for employees from dangerous chemicals, pollutants in the air, and hazardous jobs. Nineteen percent of fatal work injuries in 1996 represented exposure to harmful substances or environments (*Statistical Abstract*, 1999). An estimated one-fifth of all cancer deaths are associated with occupational hazards.

A recently publicized environmental hazard, associated with increased incidence of cancer and respiratory diseases, has been the discovery of harmful asbestos in many older buildings. Yet in spite of the known health risk, workers hired to remove asbestos in many instances have not been given needed protection to avoid exposure to the substance. Fifty percent of persons who have long-term exposure to asbestos die; the remainder suffer long-term debilitation from respiratory complications such as asbestosis.

Other occupational risks receive little attention. For example, 30% of uranium miners develop lung cancer (U.S. Senate Committee on Labor and Human Resources, 1994).

For all persons living in the United States, regardless of occupation, the environment is an increasing health hazard. The rising amount of ozone in the air and other pollutants in the air and in food products has resulted in significant increases in heart disease, cancer, and respiratory diseases in the United States in comparison to other countries. Other environmental risks are receiving increased attention, such as road and traffic safety; unsafe housing; contaminated food, meat, and dairy products; pest and animal control; biomedical and consumer product safety; inappropriate disposal of chemical and human wastes; storage and treatment of water; and control of nuclear energy plants.

Smoking is increasingly being seen as an environmental hazard. New studies suggest that smoking poses a health threat not only to smokers but to those who inhale their smoke. Cigarette smoking is the single most preventable cause of premature death in the United States; each year, more than 400,000 Americans die from cigarette smoking (Centers for Disease Control and Prevention, 1993). Recent federal and state legislation, local community ordinances, and workplace policies limit smoking to specially designated areas or prohibit it completely. For example, smoking is not allowed on airline flights. The $206 billion settlement with more than 40 states, reached in November 1998, will pour billions of dollars into state treasuries over the next 25 years and provide about $1.5 billion for research and advertising against underage tobacco use. All of this money is coming from an industry that has not paid any damages previously despite decades of litigation ("Big Tobacco Fights Legal Battles," 1998). This settlement is far narrower than either the unsuccessful tobacco agreement proposed in Congress in 1997 or the tobacco bill championed in 1998 by Senator John McCain (Republican-Arizona) but defeated by the Senate's Republican leadership. Those measures would have forced large price increases on cigarettes, granted the Food and Drug Administration broad authority over tobacco, and imposed financial sanctions if smoking rates failed to decline. None of those provisions are included in the agreement with the states referenced here. The tobacco fight is likely to persist as additional lawsuits are being lodged against the industry and the U.S. Justice Department is continuing its wide-ranging investigation of the industry.

Prevention and Wellness Programs

Increased attention is also being given to preventive aspects of health care, although prevention is still secondary to intervention after a health problem has occurred. Some businesses have established wellness programs, with exercise and fitness programs, nutrition and weight control programs, smoking cessation workshops, and other health prevention efforts. A number of employers are working with insurance companies to offer incentives to employees who are low health risks, such as salary bonuses or reduced insurance rates. Problems in the workplace and the broader society due to substance abuse have also led employers and insurance companies to establish substance abuse prevention programs in the workplace.

Ethical Issues

As health care costs continue to increase, more people need health care, and new technology and knowledge make it possible to keep people alive who previously could not have been helped. For these reasons, ethical dilemmas in the area of health care continue to increase. Many of these issues are already before our courts. When infants born 3 and 4 months premature can be saved, at what point, if at all, should abortion be prohibited? When infants require extensive neonatal care to survive, should such care be made available, even if the parents cannot afford the costs? Should the circumstances change to provide such care if the infant can survive but with serious mental and/or physical disabilities? If technology for heart and lung transplants is available, should everyone of all ages and income groups have equal access to these procedures? If genetics testing reveals that a fetus has a serious illness or disability, what choices should be considered, and who should be involved in the considerations? If people can survive with medical care or special procedures, should they have a right to decide whether to receive the care or to be allowed to die? Do people have the right to choose unsafe behaviors, such as riding motorcycles without helmets, not using seat belts, or using drugs or alcohol heavily, when injuries or other health problems may result in high costs to others—taxpayers, state, and local governments and other individuals in the same insurance group? Does a pregnant woman have the right to drink alcoholic beverages, use other drugs, or smoke if it can compromise the survival of her child? Who makes such decisions? What are the rights of the individual? Of the parents if the person is a child? Of the state or local governments if they are to pay for the care?

Several recent court cases have attempted to address some of these issues. In the early 1980s, the so-called Baby Doe case received national attention. This case involved an infant born with serious health problems who would have been seriously disabled—physically and mentally—with surgery and who would have died immediately without surgery. The parents did not want the child to have surgery or to suffer but instead to die a peaceful death. Some members of the hospital staff wanted the child to have the surgery; others wanted the child to die. Concern has been raised in similar situations throughout the country. In some instances, it was reported that infants had been starved to death or had experienced great pain when life supports were removed from them before they died. Special legislation was introduced that would have required local child welfare agencies to handle all such situations as child protective services cases and conduct investigations before medical decisions were made to ensure that children were being protected. The legislation was changed before it passed so that this did not happen, but it did mandate that hospitals establish special review boards to deal with such cases.

Some states have also made legislative decisions that have addressed serious ethical issues. In 1987, the state of Oregon voted to stop using its Medicaid funds to pay for liver, heart, bone marrow, and pancreas transplants and to use the $2.3 million saved to provide prenatal care for women in poverty. Other states, including Alabama, Arizona, Texas, and Virginia, have set limits on what they will pay for organ transplants. Illinois passed transplant legislation allowing funding for transplants but appropriated only a limited amount to pay for them. The California legislature decided to pay for transplants but then reduced its Med-

Preventive health care is far more cost-effective than medical problems that arise when preventive services are not provided. This young infant's mother, for example, received no prenatal care, and he was born prematurely, requiring intensive care and a hospital stay of several months.

Daniel Nichols/Liaison Agency

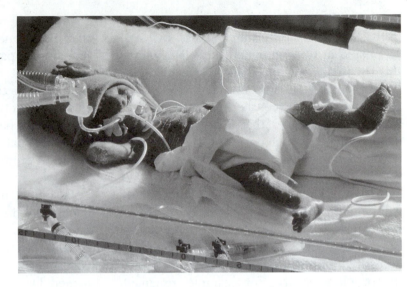

icaid funding shortly thereafter, cutting health care benefits to 270,000 Californians. Citizens groups throughout the United States are forming to address such ethical decisions. One of the first, Oregon Health Decisions, formed in 1983, has held meetings throughout the state to determine and then advocate for priorities for health funding.

Another major ethical issue relates to decisions surrounding the right to die. The Karen Quinlan case (and other similar cases involving people who are kept alive only because of life support systems but are in a coma or not in touch at all with their surroundings) generated increased debate over the issue. Other situations involving persons who have serious health problems and decide themselves that they wish to die are also receiving attention. Ethical issues are also raised regarding the role of others in aiding those who decide they want to die.

Opponents of assisted death object that physician participation in assisting people to die violates the basic moral obligations of physicians to do no harm. The debate about legalizing euthanasia (painless termination of life to end a terminally ill patient's suffering) raises a host of ethical and legal questions. How does one assess the competency of those requesting death? Is physician or nurse involvement necessary and, if so, to what extent, for those seeking to end their lives? In 1997, the U.S. Supreme Court unanimously upheld Washington and New York state laws banning assisted suicide (*Compassion in Dying v. Washington* and *Quill, Klagsbrun, and Grossman v. New York*). The Court ruled that the Constitution does not guarantee citizens the right to end their lives with a doctor's help, but it left individual states the option of legalizing the practice. Oregon is the only state that has passed a law in favor of assisted suicide. In 1994 and again in 1997, Oregon voters approved a measure allowing physicians to prescribe lethal medications when requested by a mentally competent adult who is suffering in the final stages of terminal illness. In 1998, 15 people in Oregon ended their lives under this law (University of Pennsylvania, 1999).

Although those situations obviously involve some degree of choice, the American Medical Association estimates that 70% of the 6,000 deaths that occur each day involve some sort of negotiation regarding life or death. A U.S. survey found that 80% of persons interviewed approved of laws allowing medical procedures withheld if the patient wishes (Malcolm, 1990). In many instances, such ethical dilemmas can be avoided, and dollars saved, by providing accessible and affordable health care before the problem occurs. For example, pregnant women who do not receive care during the first 3 months of pregnancy are 30% more likely to deliver infants with low birth weights. Costs for providing such infants with neonatal intensive care range from $20,000 to $400,000 per child. Not only is over $1,000 saved for each day that an infant remains in its mother's uterus between the 29th and 34th week of pregnancy, but the ethical dilemmas that often occur with such cases are also avoided (Lamon & King, 1994).

New genetic technologies promise to make medical ethics an even more central part of social decision making. For example, the Human Genome Project, a 15-year, federally funded $3 billion effort to code the entire human genetic map, has already resulted in the discovery of a number of genes that may lead to particular diseases or traits. This project will also give individuals more information about their own genetic makeup. Medical ethicists are debating whether this genetic information is the exclusive property of patients or is properly the concern of insurers, employers, and society at large.

Gene therapies are also being developed that use genetically engineered viruses to manipulate patients' cells. Some have wondered about whether the manipulation of human cells through genetic engineering is somehow contrary to the laws of nature or religion; others have proposed that it will lead to the manipulation of human sperm or eggs for purposes of improving the hereditary qualities of a race.

Cloning, or the production of organisms genetically identical to a parent, has also become a controversial topic in medical ethics. In 1997, Scottish scientist Ian Wilmut and his colleagues announced the birth of a sheep named Dolly that was produced from a cell of an adult female sheep. The following year scientists in South Korea announced that they had created an embryo from the cells of an adult woman, although they halted the embryo's growth when it consisted of only four cells. These events, and several other successful attempts at cloning mammals, made many people think that cloning humans may one day be possible. This possibility has touched off a debate about the ethics of creating human clones, the circumstances under which human cloning might be used, and the possibility of using the technique to manipulate the traits of children. This issue remains unresolved and will continue to challenge medical ethicists well into the 21st century.

Finally, recent debate and advertising have focused attention on the role of alternative medicine in health care, and bioethicists debate the rights of patients to insurance reimbursement for alternative therapies and the need for standards for their use. Several studies examine psychoactive alternative medicines, including St. John's wort and gingko biloba, and their potential use in treating depression, memory loss, and Alzheimer's disease. The lack of standards for their use has prompted worry that healthy Americans will engage in unsafe experiments with enhancement drugs. Several other alternative therapies, including acupuncture and crystal healing, were formally included in managed care plans around the United States.

HEALTH PLANNING

To eliminate problems in costs of health care, duplication of care in some areas and gaps in others, and interface of public and private sector health care delivery, several important pieces of legislation have been passed.

Hill-Burton Act

Passed in 1946, the Hill-Burton Act funded construction of a number of rural hospitals. Amendments in 1964 authorized the development of areawide hospital planning councils and the concept of areawide hospital planning. The act also specifies that hospitals that receive funding through this legislation cannot refuse to serve clients if they are unable to pay for services.

Medicare and Medicaid

National legislation has also established Medicare and Medicaid programs, which provide the majority of federal financing for health care. Medicare is a special health care program for the elderly, to be used as a supplement to their other insurance programs (see Chapter 13), whereas Medicaid is available only to low-income individuals and families (see Chapter 8). The growth of both programs has been extensive.

In 1996, Medicare was funded at a cost of $203.1 billion and served 38.1 million elderly and disabled persons. It is now experiencing a serious financial crisis. Current estimates predict that the Medicare trust fund will not be able to pay for services shortly after 2000. Although Medicare pays many costs, it does not provide long-term care for chronic needs, particularly nursing home care, or for other costs such as special wheelchairs that might enable more elderly to be cared for in their own homes. Because of increases in premiums for Medicare, in 1996 it paid for less than 50% of the total costs of health care for senior citizens. Analysts predict that significant reductions in federal spending of Medicare programs will occur during the next 5 years.

In 1996, Medicaid was funded at a level of $121.6 billion and served 36.1 million elderly, disabled, and indigent persons. Approximately 57%, or $69.3 billion, of this funding came from the federal government. Nearly 25% of the Medicaid expenditures in 1996 were associated with the AFDC program. Some 30% of the expenditures went to support the medical costs of persons age 65 and older. About 12% of total health care costs in the United States are reflected by Medicaid expenditures (*Statistical Abstract,* 1999).

Although costs for Medicaid have increased, many of the poor do not qualify for coverage; in 1996, for example, only 45.5% of our nation's poor were covered by Medicaid. The Omnibus Budget Reconciliation Act of 1989 mandated states to increase the number of pregnant women and children covered under Medicaid from those at or below 130% of the poverty level to those at or below 133%. In 1992, federal legislation extended Medicaid coverage to families who are at or below 185%. The 1988 Family Support Act also extended

Medicaid coverage to AFDC (now TANF) recipients for up to 1 year after they become employed. Although more expensive initially, it was hoped that this plan would actually reduce government health care costs, since large numbers of recipients who leave the TANF rolls have been forced to return when they or their children experience health problems and they have not been able to become financially stable enough to afford health insurance.

It was hoped that the extension of Medicaid as a transitional benefit would help recipients remain off TANF once they obtained employment. However, with the passage of the 1996 welfare reform legislation, the poor have not always accessed Medicaid benefits for which they are eligible. Many individuals are leaving the TANF rolls because they have obtained jobs, but they are often low-level jobs that do not pay health insurance or offer opportunities for promotion into jobs that do. State agencies that oversee TANF and Medicaid programs, sometimes because they are overworked and sometimes as a conscious effort to save money, do not always inform clients that they are still eligible for Medicaid when clients leave the TANF rolls. Other individuals who do not qualify for TANF are also not always informed about Medicaid eligibility when they come into public assistance offices seeking help. In some states, individuals are told they need to find a job and are given information on seeking employment without receiving information on other critical services they may need and qualify for, such as health care. Since many people living in poverty are reluctant to ask additional questions because they are afraid they will be denied any services at all, some advocacy organizations are publicizing the fact that Medicaid and other benefits are available to the groups they advocate for.

Although Medicare was intended to provide the bulk of health care for the elderly, with Medicaid intended to serve children and families, increasing amounts of Medicaid dollars are being used to pay for nursing home care that is not provided under Medicare. In 1996, for example, two-thirds of all nursing home residents in the United States were covered by Medicaid (*Statistical Abstract*, 1999). State and federal budget crises in Medicaid result not from increased costs to serve families but from the need to cover nursing home and other extensive health care costs for the increased numbers of elderly persons who cannot afford to pay for health care not provided by Medicare.

Like Medicare, Medicaid is also likely to be cut significantly by the federal government in the near future. But because Medicaid is viewed as health care for poor people rather than for the elderly, the program lacks a powerful constituency to advocate on its behalf and may be more vulnerable to significant cuts (NASW, 1995).

Maternal and Child Health Act

Title V of the Maternal and Child Health Act, through the Supplemental Food Program for Women, Infants, and Children (WIC), provides screening, counseling, and food supplements for pregnant women and children up to 5 years old who are at nutritional risk because of low income. Studies show that WIC reduces infant deaths, low birth weight, and premature births and increases good health and cognitive development among preschoolers. Since the Reagan administration significantly reduced funding for the program, some states have been able to document that infant deaths, low birth weight, and premature births are on the increase and can be tied to the reduction in WIC programs. Additionally, because states have the option of offering the program, only half of eligible women and children in the United States typically receive WIC services.

Healthy Steps for Young Children Program

Healthy Steps is a new, across-the-board approach to pediatric health care for all children from birth to age 3 that focuses on their physical, psychological, emotional, and intellectual growth and development. It is dedicated to encouraging strong relationships between pediatric practices and parents. By focusing on families with very young children, the Healthy Steps approach will ensure that children are nurtured at an important time in their development, with the expected outcomes that they will grow and develop into well-adapted, healthy children who are confident young learners. Several agencies and organizations are involved in the Healthy Steps initiative: the Commonwealth Fund, community and regional foundations and local health care providers, the American Academy of Pediatrics, Boston University School of Medicine, the Department of Population and Family Health Sciences, and the Johns Hopkins University School of Public Health. Fifteen national evaluation sites and 9 affiliate sites are currently implementing the Healthy Steps approach in 14 states across the country (Healthy Steps, 1999).

Children's Health Insurance Program (CHIP)

In August 1997, Congress enacted the Children's Health Insurance Program to expand health insurance coverage for low-income chil-

dren up to age 19. Established as Title XXI of the Social Security Act, CHIP is a voluntary program that entitles states to approximately $40 billion through 2007 ($20.3 billion over the first 5 years of the program and an additional $19.4 billion over the second 4 years of the budget period). States must supply matching funds, but the required matching rates are lower than Medicaid rates. As of August 1, 1999, all 50 states and the District of Columbia had developed plans for children's health insurance expansions under CHIP; all but three had received federal approval (Ullman, Hill, & Almeida, 1999).

The Balanced Budget Act of 1997 provides states with three options for increasing coverage under CHIP: expand Medicaid, establish a new insurance program separate from Medicaid, or implement a combination of both. Of the 51 CHIP plans set forth by each state and the District of Columbia, 18 expand Medicaid, 17 create programs separate from Medicaid, and 16 do both. At least 10 of the states that have created "new" programs have actually developed Medicaid look-alikes (Ullman et al., 1999)

States will receive federal block grant payments on a matching basis, up to a limit established for each state based on the allocation formula in the law. The law limits the extent to which states can impose premiums or cost sharing (that is, deductibles, coinsurance, and copayments) for health care provided to children enrolled in separate state programs financed with child health block grant funds. In general, states cannot adopt cost-sharing or premium policies that favor higher-income families over lower-income families. States are also prohibited from imposing cost sharing for well-baby and well-child care, including immunizations. Finally, states cannot count money raised through premiums or cost

More than 37 million individuals in the United States do not have health insurance. Although this mother and father work full-time, their workplaces do not provide health insurance and they cannot afford the high cost of private health insurance premiums. They are constantly worried that their children will get sick and they will not be able to pay for their health care.

© Annie Griffiths Belt/Corbis

sharing as state dollars for purposes of meeting the block grant's matching requirements.

Other Child Health Provisions under the Balanced Budget Act of 1997

In addition to the child health block grant, the Balanced Budget Act of 1997 includes a number of provisions designed to increase children's health care coverage through the Medicaid program. These provisions are largely independent of the new child health block grant and apply regardless of whether a state elects to use its block grant funds to expand Medicaid or establish a separate state program. Despite the large amount of new federal funds invested in the CHIP initiative, only about 1.6 million of the 11.9 million uninsured children in the United States will actually receive health care coverage each year under the programs the states develop with the block grant funds.

Comprehensive Health Planning Act

Passed in 1966, the Comprehensive Health Planning Act expands on the concept of local health planning districts to coordinate services and also requires review of other factors affecting the health of area residents, such as life-style and environmental conditions. The National Health Planning and Resources Development Act of 1974 further mandates the establishment of health systems agencies and statewide health coordinating councils to prevent the overbuilding of medical facilities such as obstetric and neonatal special care units and to monitor the availability of pediatric beds, open heart surgery, and expensive technological equipment such as megavoltage radiation equipment. The focus of this legislation is to increase availability of services in rural or other underserved areas and eliminate duplication in other areas, as well as to provide high-quality care at reduced costs by requiring rate review panels and professional standards of care.

Health Maintenance Organization Legislation

The Health Maintenance Organization Act of 1972 allows the development of health maintenance organizations (HMOs) to reduce health care costs for individuals. Most HMOs require a monthly fee, which allows free or low-cost visits to a special facility or group of facilities for health care. HMOs are intended to reduce health costs and encourage preventive health care. However, because of increased concerns raised by HMO clients and physicians about limited access to needed health care, a number of states have passed legislation specifying the rights of clients served by HMOs.

CARE Act

The Ryan White Comprehensive AIDS Resources Emergency (CARE) Act of 1989, named in honor of 18-year-old Ryan White (who died of AIDS in 1989) authorizes emergency funds to metropolitan areas hardest hit by AIDS, grants to states for comprehensive planning and service delivery, early intervention with HIV-infected infants, and the development of individual pilot projects to serve children with AIDS and to provide AIDS services in rural areas. This act was reauthorized by Congress in 1996.

Future Legislation: Health Care Reform

The absence of universal access to health care is creating a dual system of health care in the United States. Health care is readily available for those persons who are employed in organizations that offer adequate health care coverage who can afford to pay health care premiums and are healthy enough to be covered. Others are either receiving government health care benefits, most likely Medicaid and/or Medicare, or have no options for health care because they are unemployed, underemployed, or employed by employers that do not offer adequate benefits or offer benefits that are too expensive to purchase. Many individuals are caught in the middle as health care providers and employers grapple with ways to reduce quickly escalating health care costs. For example, some health care plans restrict benefits that cover previous health problems, often denying benefits to those who need them most. Thus, if an individual changes jobs or an employer changes benefit plans, new rules may force reduced coverage or no coverage at all. These individuals then may not obtain preventive health care or may end up with health care problems so serious they are forced to leave the workforce, possibly becoming eligible for Medicaid or other government health care.

Efforts continue to be made through legislation and other policy arenas to balance health care costs with quality of care. It appears likely that some sort of mandated universal health care program will be established at some point. Currently, the United States and South Africa are the only two industrialized countries that do not have some type of government-funded universal health care system.

Because of the complexity of reasons for increased health care costs and the many groups concerned about health care in the United States, tackling health care reform is difficult. President Bill Clinton made health care reform the single most important issue when he first took office. But his administration's efforts to oversee the overhaul of the health care system met with resistance from a wide range of sources. While most individuals and constituency groups agree that reform is needed, a great deal of diversity persists in suggestions about the types of reforms that should be adopted.

Many advocates for a universal health care system in the United States are calling for a national health insurance program for all types of health care, not just catastrophic illness. Those in favor of such a program base their support on the following arguments:

- Costs for health insurance are too high for large numbers of individuals to afford.
- Many local hospitals are going into debt because they are having to pay health care costs for the increasing numbers of indigent persons.
- Health costs are higher because persons are not seeking preventive health care, which would be more likely were there a national health insurance program with such an emphasis.

Those against such a program pose the following arguments:

- Such a program would mean going to a system of socialized medicine.
- The costs would be too high.
- Individuals would lose their freedom of choice regarding which health care provider they want.
- People would clog the health care delivery system with trivial health problems that do not require medical attention.

Proponents of government-funded health care programs have proposed a variety of alternatives. Many, including NASW, call for a universal access, single-payer system with national standards. They want to eliminate the relationship between health care and employment so that those who are jobless, employed by employers without available or affordable health care, or not covered because of previous health conditions can still receive health coverage. Some plans call for the federal government to collect funds for a national health care program from various taxes, with the program administered by private insurance companies instead of by a single government system. Others advocate for a "pay or play" proposal, with employers providing health care to their employees contributing to a public fund to pay for those without insurance or underinsured. Critics of this plan say that it is a punitive system that does not guarantee universal coverage and still creates a dual health care system. Other plans call for having persons claim a tax credit on their income tax form if they use health care and providing health coverage only for catastrophic illnesses.

Changes in the congressional makeup in the fall 1994 elections seem to have put health care reform on the back burner. The Republicans' Contract with America in 1995 did not mention health care reform at all. Current plans call for eliminating federal bureaucracy and channeling health funds to the states to administer directly. Many state leaders, including a number of governors, are concerned that such efforts merely pass the burden of complex issues and astronomical costs to them.

Some states have already begun to implement health care reforms. Minnesota, for example, funds a program to provide health care to all children who fall below a certain income level and are not covered by other programs. Oregon, realizing that most health care dollars are spent on long-term care for the elderly and persons with disabilities, has shifted its focus on long-term care from institutions to less expensive home and community-based options. Termed "aging in place," with services delivered to the individual rather than requiring the individual to go to the services, the number of nursing home beds per 1,000 population has been reduced by 25%, with 27 beds per 1,000 senior citizens compared to 42 nationally; the per capita cost for long-term care is $448 compared to $693 nationally; and the state has saved $400 million from 1981 to 1994; see Box 10.2 (Concannon, 1995).

BOX 10.2

Living in Their Own Homes

Ella Nelson, of Eugene, Oregon, was 105 years old January 19 and still lives in her own home. She is surrounded by familiar furniture and knickknacks. Photographs of family and friends—from her childhood in turn-of-the-century Sweden to the latest great-grandchild—cover walls and shelves.

She is able to live at home and maintain her independence because of Oregon's home- and community-based care program. She employs a live-in provider, who is paid by the state, and also has a lift chair and a quad cane, both purchased by the state. Mrs. Nelson's family provides respite care on the weekends. SDSD estimates that the cost of her in-home care is about half of what it would be in a nursing facility.

Of course, Ella Nelson is one of only eight Medicaid-eligible centenarians living at home in Oregon. More typical are Herb and Martha Sweeny (not their real names), who live in Woodburn in Oregon's mid-Willamette Valley. He is 73, and she is 62 and has a heart condition that prevents her from performing household chores such as vacuuming or scrubbing. They are nevertheless able to live in their own home because the state pays for 2 hours of housekeeping a week.

"It's better to be here in our own home together," she says, "than to have to be put into a home that would take care of us."

That has been Oregon's thinking for a dozen years. Caring for older citizens in their homes saves money, keeps them healthier, and is responsible for Oregon's being the only state with fewer Medicaid-eligible seniors living in nursing homes today than 10 years ago.

These seniors are among more than 25,000 statewide whom the state helps—about two-thirds of them with nursing, housekeeping, cooking, laundry, and other services in home- and community-based care. They have in common that they are poor. Three-fourths are women. But by keeping people in community-based care—in their own homes, in adult foster care, or in assisted-living facilities—nearly three people can receive services for every one living in a nursing facility.

Note: Ella Nelson died at home of natural causes February 26, 1995—*Ed.*

Source: Concannon (1995, p. 13). Reprinted with permission of the American Public Human Services Association. Copyright © 1995. All rights reserved.

States also are passing other health care legislation that includes limiting the amounts that can be collected in malpractice suits in an attempt to keep medical costs down, mandating the availability of health care for indigent persons and reducing the burden on local hospitals in poor areas of states, and establishing procedures for decision making about organ transplants and life-threatening situations. Proposals will continue to be made and debated at all levels of government.

Scuka (1994, p. 582) suggests the following criteria for evaluating proposals for health care reform:

- Does the proposal provide universal coverage so no U.S. citizen or legal resident is deprived of access?
- Does it eliminate the link between employment status and health insurance coverage?
- Does it eliminate cost sharing such as copayments and deductibles that could impede access because of out-of-pocket costs?
- Are preexisting medical conditions prohibited as a condition for restricting or excluding individuals from coverage?
- Is universal access given priority over specialty care services for a limited population so that no one gets extraordinary care until everyone gets minimal care?
- Are there controls on purchase of expensive technology to limit duplication?
- Is there a nationwide system of standard fees to control rising costs?

Legislation, planning, and service delivery at all levels will need to focus on reducing the costs of health care while expanding its accessibility. Other critical issues in the next decades include reducing the fragmentation of care, developing private and/or government insurance for long-term health care for the elderly, and increasing the availability of funding for home health and respite care. More resources will be devoted to outpatient community-based care and case management. Greater attention will also be given to prevention, including teen pregnancy and violence as well as AIDS education, and to the promotion of lifestyle changes such as improved diet and the elimination of substance abuse and smoking.

SOCIAL WORK ROLES IN THE DELIVERY OF HEALTH SERVICES

Today, social workers play many roles in the provision of health care in a variety of settings. In fact, social work in health care, particularly in working with the elderly, is one of the fastest-growing occupational areas today. Health care is the third largest field of social work practice, with 14% of social workers employed in health care settings. Recent developments have expanded the social work profession's involvement in the health care arena. Federal legislation relating to nursing homes requires that all nursing homes in the United States with 120 or more beds must have a social worker with a BSW or MSW degree. Changes in legislation relating to Medicare also now mandate that social workers with an MSW degree who also have professional social work certification should be reimbursed for providing outpatient mental health services to the elderly. Previously, only psychiatrists or psychologists could be reimbursed under Medicare for these services. As the number of home health care agencies expands, the role of social workers in assessing mental health needs and providing intervention and case management services will also expand. Social workers will also need to pay increased attention to the strengths of the family members of persons with health needs as greater demands are placed on natural caregivers (Poole, 1995). As individuals with serious physical and mental injuries continue to live longer due to increased technology, the role of social workers in rehabilitation hospitals will also increase. Additionally, for the first time, federal legislation providing training monies for people interested in health care includes social workers as well as nurses and physicians.

Both roles and settings have increased significantly since social workers became involved in health care issues. As early as 1888, social workers were advocating for some sort of insurance coverage for all U.S. citizens. Jane Addams and other social workers focused on health care prevention and community action relating to concerns such as poor sanitation, malnutrition, unsafe housing, and poverty (Poole, 1995).

The first known hospital social worker was employed at Massachusetts General Hospital in Boston in 1905. At that time, hospitals and general physicians were the major sources of health care. The social worker worked with the physician, other hospital staff, and the patient's family to ensure that high-quality care and attention continued after the patient returned home. Although responsibility for care after a patient leaves the hospital is still a major one for many social workers in health care settings, today social workers in these settings provide a variety of other tasks as well. Social workers often serve as a liaison between the patient's family and health care staff. They help the staff understand family concerns and how family constraints and other environmental factors may affect a patient's ability to recover. They also help patients and their families understand the implications of illness and issues re-

lating to recovery and care. In many instances, the social worker provides support to the family when a death occurs or a patient's condition worsens.

Social workers in health care settings provide a number of other functions:

- Conducting screening and assessments to determine health risk factors, particularly those involving the family and the broader environment
- Offering social services to patients and their families, such as individual counseling to help a patient deal with a major illness or loss of previous capabilities due to accident or illness, helping family members grieve over a dying individual, or helping a teenage mother accept her decision to place her child for adoption
- Providing case management services, including working with other social and health services agencies regarding patient needs, such as helping arrange for financial assistance to pay hospital bills, nursing home or home health care for patients when they leave the hospital, or emergency child care for a single parent who is hospitalized
- Serving as a member of a health care team and helping others understand a patient's emotional needs and home or family situation
- Advocating for the patient's needs at all levels of the environment, including the patient's family, hospital and other health care settings, social services agencies, school, workplace, and community
- Representing the hospital and providing consultation to other community agencies, such as child protective services agencies in child abuse cases

- Providing preventive education and counseling to individuals relating to family planning, nutrition, prenatal care, and human growth and development
- Making health planning and policy recommendations to local communities, states, and the federal government in areas such as hospital care, community health care, environmental protection, and control of contagious diseases

Whereas many social workers function in agencies administered by and hiring primarily social workers (called **primary settings**), health care settings are considered **secondary settings** because they are administered and staffed largely by health care professionals who are not social workers. Social workers in health care settings must be comfortable with their roles and be able to articulate their roles and functions clearly to other health care professionals. A strong professional identity is important for medical social workers. Additionally, social workers in health care settings must be able to work comfortably within a medical model. Knowledge and understanding of the medical profession and health care are important for social workers, as is the ability to function as a team member with representatives from a variety of disciplines. Social workers in health care settings, particularly hospital settings, must be able to handle crisis intervention, and they most often prefer short-term social work services rather than long-term client relationships. They must be able to work well under pressure and high stress and be comfortable with death and dying.

Hospital Settings

The American Hospital Association requires that a hospital maintain a social services department as a condition of accreditation. Social workers in hospitals may provide services to all patients who need them, or they may provide specialized services. Larger hospitals employ emergency room social workers, pediatric social workers, intensive care social workers, and social workers who work primarily on cardiac, cancer, or other specialized wards. A number of large hospitals have added social workers who provide social services primarily to AIDS patients. Other hospitals use social workers in preventive efforts, providing outreach services, including home visits to mothers identified during their hospital stay as potentially at risk to abuse or neglect their children. Still others use social workers to coordinate rehabilitative services, serving as a case manager to ensure that occupational, physical, recreational, speech, and vocational therapy services are provided. Social workers work in both public and private hospitals, providing both inpatient and outpatient care. Many are employed by Veterans Administration (VA) hospitals, which have a long-standing tradition of using social workers to work with persons who have served in the armed forces. Many VA social workers provide specialized counseling relating to physical disabilities and alcohol and drug abuse. A number of VA social workers now specialize in post-Vietnam stress syndrome and provide services to Vietnam veterans and their families.

Because of accreditation standards, most medical social workers must have master's degrees in social work. Many graduate schools of social work offer specializations in medical or health care.

Long-Term Care Facilities and Nursing Homes

Many persons who suffer from illness or disability do not need the intensive services of a hospital, but they cannot care for themselves in their own homes without assistance. For some individuals, particularly the frail elderly, **long-term care facilities,** programs that provide medical care and other services to individuals including the elderly and the disabled, such as nursing homes, are most appropriate. There are various levels of care facilities, with licensing and accreditation requirements for each. From 1965 to 1972, social work services were mandated for all nursing homes that cared for residents covered by Medicare. Beginning in 1990, all nursing homes with 120 or more beds must employ a social worker. Social workers in these settings help residents adjust to the nursing home environment, help families deal with their guilt and feelings of loss after such placements, serve as liaisons to other social services and health care agencies, provide individual and group counseling and other social services for nursing home residents and their families, network with others interested in services for the elderly at the local and state levels, and advocate for improved services for the clients they serve.

Provision of social work services to the elderly in health care settings is probably the fastest-growing area of social work, and many schools of social work are offering specializations at the master's-degree level in health and gerontology and special courses at the BSW level in these areas to meet the demand.

Community-Based Health Care Programs

Many social workers, at both the BSW and MSW levels, are employed in local community-based health care programs. Most state health departments operate local health clinics, which provide a variety of health services available to low-income residents as well as community education programs for all residents. Such programs include immunizations, family planning services, prenatal care, well-baby and pediatric services, nutrition and other types of education programs, and basic health care. Many health clinics employ social workers to work with patients and their families as other health care services are provided. For example, some clinics operate high-risk infant programs, which include social services for parents of infants at risk for abuse, neglect, or other serious health problems or those who already have serious health problems and whose parents need monitoring and support. Social workers also work with local community groups and schools, providing outreach programs to publicize and prevent such problems as sexually transmitted diseases and teen pregnancy.

Social workers are also employed in family planning clinics, such as Planned Parenthood, providing counseling and help in decision making regarding pregnancy prevention or intervention, such as planning for adoptive services in an unwanted pregnancy. With new technology that can diagnose problems in embryos in the uterus, many health providers also are employing social workers to offer genetic counseling, helping clients understand possibilities of giving birth to infants with potential problems and make appropriate decisions regarding whether to become pregnant or to terminate a pregnancy.

Many social workers are employed in community health care settings that provide services to persons with AIDS and their families. Social workers perform individual, family, and group counseling; serve as case managers assisting clients and their families in accessing community resources; provide advocacy for clients and their families; and offer community education programs.

Increasingly, other health care settings are recognizing the impact of environmental factors, such as unemployment, on mental and physical health. To help address the relationship, previously traditional health care settings increasingly are employing social workers. In many areas, for example, local physicians' clinics, usually operated by a small group of physicians who share a practice, are hiring social workers to provide counseling to patients in an effort to improve mental health and reduce stress. HMOs are also hiring social workers to perform similar functions.

Home Health Care

Many states and communities are recognizing the need for **home health care,** or services that enable persons with health problems to remain in their own homes. In 1995, the United States had 14,000 home health care establishments, with 749,000 employees. Total expenditures for home health care services for that year amounted to $13.2 billion (*Statistical Abstract,* 1999). Home health care services most often preserve self-esteem and longevity for the individual and are far less costly than hospital or nursing home care. Trained nurses and home health aides, as well as social workers, make home visits to perform health care in a person's home. Social workers provide counseling to both the client and family, help clients cope emotionally, and serve as case managers, ensuring that appropriate resources are provided to deal with client needs. Home health care allows the elderly, persons with AIDS, and other people who do not need to be hospitalized the right to have greater control over their lives. Such care also offers them dignity and emotional support they might not receive in a hospital or other institutional setting. Because home health care programs are more cost-effective than hospitalization or other institutional care, these programs will be expanded during the next several decades, and more social workers will be needed to work in them.

State Department of Health and Health Planning Agencies

Many social workers at both the BSW and MSW levels are employed in health care policy and planning jobs. They help make critical decisions regarding funding, policies, and programs for state legislatures, federal officials, and state and local health departments and planning agencies. A social worker might determine how many more elderly could be served if Medicaid income eligibility requirements were changed from 130% to 150% above the poverty line. A social worker also might develop plans to implement a community-wide AIDS education program, or suggest ways that a local hospital can be more responsive to the needs of the primarily African American and Latino population it serves. In one state, for example, planners in the state health department recommended that the agency solicit bids for infant formula for infants served by the WIC program instead of contracting with the same company the agency had always used. The bids received were much lower than the amount the department was paying for the formula, enabling the department to serve many more clients while still saving money.

The impact of environmental changes on individuals, disease prevention and control, monitoring of solid waste and water facilities, and emergency and disaster planning are other areas in which social workers in these programs become involved. Many social workers have become heavily involved in policies and studies relating to the impact of AIDS in the United States, for example. State health departments provide services relating to dental health, family planning, nutrition, and teenage pregnancy; nutrition programs for pregnant women and young children; periodic health screening programs for infants and young children; substance abuse programs; and teenage parent services. Health departments and other federal, state, and local agencies also develop policies and implement plans for the provision of emergency and disaster services. Social workers from a number of federal, state, and local public and private agencies, for example, were involved in planning and overseeing emergency services after the hurricane and subsequent flooding in California in 1994 and the bombing of the federal building in Oklahoma City in 1995.

The national Public Health Service provides health and health-related services to indigent populations in areas with few medical practitioners, such as Native American reservations and migrant areas. The service also monitors communicable diseases and provides research in a variety of health areas. Many students who receive federal funds to attend college or professional schools in health-related areas, including social work, are required to devote a set number of years of service to the Public Health Service after graduation. Other federal programs such as the National Institutes of Health (NIH) also provide research and policy alternatives. Both the Public Health Service and the NIH employ social workers at the BSW and MSW levels. The NIH, for example, employs social workers in direct-care settings established to develop new techniques in health care, such as its pediatric AIDS program in Washington, DC.

Other Health Care Settings

Social workers are involved in numerous other health-related programs. Many work for the American Red Cross, for example, providing emergency services to families when disaster strikes. Recently developed health programs that often employ social workers include women's health clinics, which currently number over 1,000 and provide gynecological and primary care using a holistic health approach; genetic counseling centers; and rape crisis centers. Many emergency medical service (EMS) programs in large cities are employing social workers to assist in crisis intervention during family violence, child maltreatment, rape, and homicide.

Hospices are multiplying throughout the country and employing social workers in their agencies. Originally begun in England, hospice programs allow terminally ill persons to die at home or in a homelike setting surrounded by family members rather than in an often alien hospital environment. Using the stages of grief described by Elizabeth Kübler-Ross (1969/1997) as a framework, many hospices employ social workers to work with families and the dying person or to supervise a cadre of volunteers who provide similar services. As more elderly persons and persons with AIDS continue to live longer, the need for hospice programs will increase. Similarly, as critical issues in health care continue to be identified, the functions of social workers in health care settings will continue to expand.

SUMMARY

The state of health care in the United States has been declared a national crisis by many policymakers and health care experts. Issues relating to health care continue to be controversial and complex. As health care costs continue to rise, new technology and medical discoveries continue to be made. Ethical issues in health care—such as who should receive services at what cost, who should be allowed to make decisions about the right to refuse medical care, and who should be held accountable when a person's health is jeopardized by that person or another individual—are becoming increasingly complex and arising more often than in the past.

Addressing issues of diversity in health care is also critical. Understanding how individuals' cultures shape their views about health and wellness, illness, health care providers and interventions, birth and death, and their own roles in preventing and dealing with health-related concerns and helping empower persons to communicate those views to others involved in their care are essential and important roles for social workers in health care settings.

The AIDS epidemic has focused additional attention on the health care system. With more persons living longer, concerns about health care will become increasingly evident. The relationships between environmental factors and health need additional exploration. Finally, the large numbers of Americans, particularly children and the poor, who receive inadequate health care, if any, and the long-term implications for these individuals in all areas of their lives and for our country as a whole must be addressed.

Finding a balance of health care that is available, accessible, acceptable, and affordable, yet accountable to funding sources, is the highest priority for the United States in this decade. Whatever the balance established, social workers will play an ever-increasing role in both the planning and the delivery of health care services. Social work in health care settings is one of the fastest-growing areas of social work today.

KEY TERMS

acquired immunodeficiency syndrome (AIDS)
bioethics
catastrophic illness
health
health care
health maintenance organizations (HMOs)
health risk factors
HIV-positive

home health care
hospices
infant mortality rates
long-term care facilities
managed care system
primary settings
private health insurance
public health insurance
secondary settings

DISCUSSION QUESTIONS

1. Discuss some changes in the focus of health care that have taken place in the United States since colonial times.

2. Identify at least three reasons why health care costs have increased over the last decade.

3. Which groups of persons in the United States are most at risk to experience problems with their health? Why?

4. What are some of the ethical issues faced by health care providers and policymakers? Who do you think should receive priority in access to health care if costs prevent it being available to everyone?

5. Select one of the recent proposals for health care reform. Using Scuka's criteria, evaluate the proposals. Which proposals do you think have the most merit, and why?

6. What are some preventive programs social workers can implement to reduce the need for health care in the United States?

7. Identify at least three roles social workers might play at various levels of the environment in dealing with the AIDS epidemic. Why is AIDS such an important issue for the world today?

8. Identify at least five roles social workers can play in the delivery of health care services. How do careers for social workers in health care compare to careers in other areas in terms of availability and opportunity? Why?

INFOTRAC COLLEGE EDITION

To learn more about topics included in this chapter, enter the following search terms:

children's health

health care costs

health care financing

health care insurance

indigent health care

medical social work

rural health care

uninsured

wellness

ON THE INTERNET

http://www.hcfa.org/

http://www.wnet.org/archive/mhc.overview/essay.html

http://www.cdc.gov/nchstp/hiv_aids/dhap.htm

http://www.nga/Pubs/IssueBriefs/1996/96102/RuralHealth.asp

REFERENCES

Astrachan, A. (1991, February 6). Research links hypertension, racial stress. *New York Times Service.*

Big tobacco fights legal battles. (1998). Available: http://washingtonpost.com/wp-s...onal/longterm/tobacco/overview.htm.

Brenner, M. H. (1973). Fetal, infant and maternal mortality during periods of economic stress. *International Journal of Health Sciences, 3,* 145–159.

Bruner, S. T., Waldo, D. R., & McKusick, D. (1992). National health expenditures projections through 2030. *Health Care Financing Review, 14*(1), 1–29.

Catalano, R. (1979). *Health behavior and the community: An ecological perspective.* New York: Pergamon.

Centers for Disease Control and Prevention. (1993). Smoking-attributable mortality and years of potential life lost—United States, 1990. *Morbidity and Mortality Weekly Report 1993, 42*(33), 645–648.

Centers for Disease Control and Prevention. (1999). Available: http://www.cdc.gov/.

Children's Defense Fund. (2000). *The state of America's children yearbook, 2000.* Available: http://www.childrensdefense.org/.

Clift, E., & Hager, M. (1989, October). A victory for the haves? *Newsweek, 144*(16), 38.

Concannon, K. (1995). Home and community care in Oregon. *Public Welfare, 15*(2), 10–16. Washington, DC: American Public Welfare Association.

Conover, T. (1994, May 8). Finding a new mother. *New York Times Sunday Magazine,* pp. 27–36, 58–63.

Dohrenwend, B. S., & Dohrenwend, B. P. (Eds.). (1974). *Stressful life events: Their nature and effects.* New York: Wiley.

Edwards, R. (1990). Health system's crisis calls for a cure. *NASW News, 35*(6), 2, 4.

Families USA Foundation. (1998). *Hit and miss: State managed care laws.* Washington, DC: Author.

Ford Foundation. (1989). *The common good: Social welfare and the American future.* New York: Author.

Health Care Financing Administration. (1999). *National health expenditures projections.* Available: http://www.hcfa/gov/stats/NHE-Proj/proj1998/tables/table1.htm.

Healthy Steps. (1999). *Healthy Steps for children: A national initiative to foster healthy growth and development.* Available: http://www.healthysteps.org/.

Kaiser Family Foundation. (1998). *Kaiser/Harvard national survey of Americans' views on consumer protection in managed care.* Menlo Park, CA: Author.

Kingston, E., Petersen, C. S., Magaziner, J., Lopez, E. D., Joyce, C., Kassner, E., & Sowers, S. (1988). Health, employment and welfare histories of Maryland's older general assistance recipients. *Social Work, 33*(2), 105–109.

Kosterlitz, J. (1989, December). States bracing for "medigap" abuses. *National Journal, 21*(50), 3056–3057.

Kübler-Ross, E. (1997). *On death and dying.* New York: Simon & Schuster. (Original published 1969.)

Laman, J., & King, M. (1994). Promoting healthy babies. *NCSL Legisbrief.* Washington, DC: National Conference of State Legislators.

Lazarus, R. S. (1991). *Emotions and adaptation.* New York: Oxford University Press.

Lenkenfeld, C., & Welsh, R. (1995). Health systems policy. In R. Edwards (Ed.), *Encyclopedia of social work.* Washington, DC: NASW Press.

Lloyd, G. (1995). HIV/AIDS overview. In R. Edwards (Ed.), *Encyclopedia of social work* (Vol. 2, pp. 1257–1290). Washington, DC: NASW Press.

Malcolm, A. (1990, June 10). Whose right to die? *Austin American Statesman,* pp. D1, D4.

McGrath, M. (1990). HIV: Overview and general description. In P. Cohen, M. Sande, & P. Volberding (Eds.), *The AIDS knowledge base.* Waltham, MA: Medical Publishing Group.

Metropolitan Council/Metropolitan Health Planning Board. (1985). *Prescription for health.* St. Paul, MN: Metropolitan Council.

National Association of Social Workers. (1994). *Social work speaks: NASW policy statements* (3rd ed.). Washington, DC: NASW Press.

National Association of Social Workers. (1995). *Health and mental health care in the 104th Congress.* Washington, DC: NASW Press.

National Association of Social Workers. (1999). *HIV/AIDS: A fact sheet for practitioners.* Available: http://www.naswdc.org/PiecesNASW/aidsday.htm.

Pan American Health Organization. (1999). AIDS epidemic continues to grow, spread to rural poor, PAHO says. Available: http://www.paho.org/.

Poole, D. (1995). Health care: Direct practice. In R. Edwards (Ed.), *Encyclopedia of social work* (Vol. 2, pp. 1156–1165). Washington, DC: NASW Press.

Rice, D. (1995). Health care: Financing. In R. Edwards (Ed.), *Encyclopedia of social work* (Vol. 2, pp. 1168–1175). Washington, DC: NASW Press.

Rothstein, M. (1989, Fall). AIDS rights and health care costs. *National Forum, Phi Kappa Phi Journal,* 7–10. Baton Rouge: Louisiana State University.

Schlesinger, E. (1985). *Health care social work practice: Concepts and strategies.* St. Louis, MO: Times Mirror-Mosby.

Scuka, R. (1994). Health care reform in the 1990s: An analysis of the problems in three proposals. *Social Work, 39*(5), 580–587.

Seelye, K. (1995, July 5). Reduction urged in AIDS funding. *Austin American Statesman,* p. A-7.

Statistical abstract of the United States. (1995). Washington, DC: U.S. Government Printing Office.

Statistical abstract of the United States. (1999). Washington, DC: U.S. Government Printing Office.

Ullman, F., Hill, I., & Almeida, R. (1999). *CHIP: A look at emerging state programs.* Series A, No. A-35. Washington, DC: Urban Institute.

University of Pennsylvania. (1999). *Bioethics: An introduction.* Available: http://www.med.upenn.edu/~bioethic/outreach/bioforbegin/beginners.html.

U.S. Department of Agriculture. (1990). *Five state study of women, infants and children program.* Washington, DC: U.S. Government Printing Office.

U.S. Department of Health and Human Services, Centers for Disease Control. (1995). *Ten leading causes of death in the United States.* Washington, DC: U.S. Government Printing Office.

U.S. National Center for Health Statistics. (1992). *Health: United States, 1991.* DHHS Publication No. PHS 92-1232. Hyattsville, MD: U.S. Public Health Service.

U.S. National Center for Health Statistics. (1993). *Health: United States, 1992.* DHHS Publication No. PHS 93-1232. Hyattsville, MD: U.S. Public Health Service.

U.S. National Center for Health Statistics. (1995). *Statistical reports.* Hyattsville, MD: Author.

U.S. National Center for Health Statistics. (1999). *Health: United States, 1999.* Available: http://www.cdc.gov/nchs/.

U.S. National Center for Health Statistics. (2000). *Fastats.* Available: http://www.cdc.gov/nchswww/fastats.htm.

U.S. Public Health Service. (1977). 200 years of child health. In E. Grotberg (Ed.), *200 years of children.* Washington, DC: U.S. Department of Health, Education, and Welfare.

U.S. Senate Committee on Labor and Human Resources. (1994). *Oversight of the Radiation Exposure Compensation Act: Hearing of the U.S. Senate Committee on Labor and Human Resources.* Washington, DC: U.S. Government Printing Office.

U.S. Surgeon General. (1979). *Healthy people: The surgeon general's report on health promotion and disease prevention.* Washington, DC: U.S. Department of Health, Education, and Welfare, Public Health Service.

Van Den Bergh, N. (1995). Employee assistance programs. In R. Edwards (Ed.), *Encyclopedia of social work* (Vol. 1, pp. 842–849). Washington, DC: NASW Press.

SUGGESTED FURTHER READINGS

Aday, L. (1993). *The health and health care needs of vulnerable populations in the United States.* San Francisco: Jossey-Bass.

Aronstein, D., & Thompson, B. (1998). *HIV and social work: A practitioner's guide.* Binghamton, New York: Haworth.

Bayer, R. (1989). *Private acts, social consequences: AIDS and the politics of public health.* New York: Free Press.

Biomedical ethics and the bill of rights. (1989). Special issue. *National Forum: Phi Kappa Phi Journal.* Baton Rouge: Louisiana State University.

Cowles, L. (1999). *Social work in the health field: A care perspective.* Binghamton, NY: Haworth.

De Vita, V. T., Jr., Hellman, S, & Rosenberg, S. A. (Eds.). (1992). *AIDS: Etiology, diagnosis, treatment and prevention* (3rd ed.). Philadelphia: Lippincott.

Edwards, R. (Ed.). (1997). *Encyclopedia of social work, 1997 Supplement.* Washington, DC: NASW Press.

Fitzgerald, H., Lester, B., & Zuckerman, B. (Eds.). *Children of color: Research, health, and policy issues.* New York: Garland.

Germain, C. (1984). *Social work practice in health care: An ecological perspective.* New York: Free Press.

Goode, R. (1999). *Social work practice in home health care.* Binghamton, NY: Haworth.

Health & Social Work journal. Washington, DC: NASW Press.

Holosko, M., & Taylor, P. (1992). *Social work practice in health care settings.* Washington, DC: NASW Press.

Kiefer, C. (2000). *Health work with the poor: A health worker's primer on serving low-income clients.* Rutgers, NJ: Rutgers University Press.

Loxley, A. (1996). *Collaboration in health and welfare: Working with difference.* London: Kingsley.

Lynch, V. J., Lloyd, G. A., & Fimbres, M. F. (1993). *The expanding faces of AIDS: Implications for social work practice.* Westport, CT: Auburn House.

McLoed, E., & Bywaters, P. (2000). *Social work, health and equality.* New York: Routledge.

O'Brian, M. (1992). *Living with HIV: An experiment in courage.* New York: Auburn House.

Rosengarten, L. (1999). *Social work in geriatric home health care: The blending of traditional practice with cooperative strategies.* Binghamton, NY: Haworth.

Safford, F., & Krell, G. (1997). *Gerontology for health professionals: A practice guide* (2nd ed.). Washington, DC: NASW Press.

Shamess, G., & Lightburn, A. (Eds.). (1998). *Humane managed care?* Washington, DC: NASW Press.

Shilts, R. (1987). *And the band played on: Politics, people and the AIDS epidemic.* New York: St. Martin's.

Social Work in Health Care journal. Binghamton, NY: Haworth Press.

Wernet, S. (Ed.). (1999). *Managed care in the human services.* Chicago: Lyceum.

THE NEEDS OF CHILDREN, YOUTH, AND FAMILIES

Divorced for 2 years, Ernestine Moore is struggling to survive. Her five children are in a foster home while she tries to stabilize her life. Ernestine is looking forward to the day when she and her children can live together as a family again.

Ernestine came from a large family. Her father drank often and beat her mother, her siblings, and her. Pregnant at age 16 and afraid of what her father would do, she eloped with the father of her child, a 19-year-old high school graduate named James Moore who worked at a fast-food restaurant. The first year was fairly peaceful for the new family, although money was a continual problem. Lacking health insurance, they took several years to pay the bills for the birth of the baby. But both James and Ernestine were excited about the baby, and Ernestine worked hard to provide a good home for her husband and baby. She wanted desperately to have the kind of home and family she had not had as a child.

Ernestine and James had three more children during the next 6 years. Because one of the children had multiple health problems, financial pressures continued to mount, and life became increasingly stressful. James began to drink heavily and beat Ernestine often. He also physically and verbally abused one of their sons, who was diagnosed as developmentally disabled. When Ernestine became pregnant with her fifth child, her husband left her. Since that time, he has only paid child support for 6 months.

After James left, Ernestine moved in with a sister, who had three children of her own. To support her children and help contribute to the rent her sister was paying, she got two jobs, one in a fast-food restaurant and one at night cleaning a bank. Shortly after her new baby was born, this arrangement ended because of continual arguments between the two sisters over money, space, and child rearing.

At that point, Ernestine applied for food stamps and medical assistance and moved into a two-room apartment. She applied for low-income housing, and although she was eligible, she was told there was a 2-year waiting list. Ernestine hired a young teenage girl to care for her children while she worked. Tired and overwhelmed, Ernestine had little time to spend taking care of the children or the apartment. She became increasingly abusive toward the children. The older children did poorly in school and were continually fighting, stealing, and vandalizing. Neighbors in the apartment complex saw the younger children outside at all hours, unsupervised, often wearing only diapers. They often heard screaming and the baby crying throughout the night.

The baby-sitter quit because Ernestine was behind in paying her. When she missed 2 days of work while she tried desperately to find another sitter, Ernestine was fired from her fast-food job. Afraid that she would also lose her cleaning job, she began putting the younger children to bed at six o'clock and leaving the oldest child (age 8) in charge until she returned home. Finally, Ernestine and her children were evicted from the apartment because of failure to pay the rent. For 2 weeks the whole family slept in a friend's car. Finally, when the oldest child came to school with multiple bruises and complaining of a sore arm and revealed the family's living situation to her teacher, the local child protective services agency was called. The social worker discovered all of the children badly bruised and malnourished, and the oldest girl had a broken arm. Ernestine was overwhelmed and angry, and she felt extremely guilty about what had happened to her children.

The children were placed in foster care with an older, nurturing couple. With more structure and a stable living situation, the children began doing better in school and were able to develop some positive relationships with others. Ernestine visited the children often and began to see the foster parents as caring individuals who seemed almost like parents to her.

Ernestine enrolled in a job-training program and was hired as a health care aide for a local nursing home. She enjoys her job and is talking about getting her high school equivalency certificate and going to nursing school. Her social worker encouraged her to join Parents Anonymous, a support group for abusive parents. For the first time, Ernestine Moore has developed positive, trusting relationships with others. She has located an affordable duplex, and she and her social worker are making plans to have the children return home on a permanent basis.

The family is probably the most significant social system within which all individuals function. Within the family we first develop trusting relationships, a special identity, and a sense of self-worth. Traditionally, the family has been looked upon as a safe, protective haven where individuals can receive nurturing, love, and support. However, it is increasingly difficult for children and their families to grow up in today's complex and rapidly changing world. Daily, children are confronted with family financial pressures, the need for one or both parents to work long hours, or the physical or mental illness or loss of a family member.

Unable to cope with these pressures, family members often turn to alcohol or drugs, resort to violence, or withdraw from other family members and do not respond to their needs. Sometimes, because they did not receive love and nurturing when they were children, the parents are unable to provide this for their own children. Sometimes, they do not know how to provide for their own children because they have never learned what children need at certain ages or what to expect from them. Many parents are unable to meet the needs of family members adequately during a crisis, such as death or a serious illness.

How well a family is able to meet the needs of its members also depends on other systems within the family's environment. The workplace, neighborhood, community, and society with which that family interacts have a tremendous impact on the family's well-being. Bronfenbrenner (1979) and Garbarino (1992) suggest that more attention should be given to intervention in these broader systems than in the past, rather than just providing services to individual family members. A family that functions within an unsupportive environment is much more susceptible to family problems than one functioning within a supportive environment. If the family lives in a community that has no programs available to family members, that also may threaten the family's well-being.

Consider Ernestine Moore's situation. Abused as a child, she learned to distrust others and failed to have her emotional needs met during her childhood. This left Ernestine feeling worthless and inadequate. Individuals with low self-esteem are more likely to get pregnant at an early age. They also are more likely to abuse their children than other parents. Ernestine also learned from her own parents that anger is dealt with by hitting. Life with an alcoholic father taught Ernestine many dysfunctional behavior patterns she carried into her own life.

In this chapter, we discuss general issues and trends to consider when focusing on the needs of children, youth, and families; the types and extent of problems that can have an impact on children and their families; and factors that place families more at risk to experience those problems. In

Chapter 12, we focus on services and policies that prevent or alleviate problems experienced by children, youth, and families, as well as the roles that social workers play in providing these services and developing and implementing policies.

ISSUES TO CONSIDER WHEN ADDRESSING CHILD AND FAMILY NEEDS

All families have strengths and many diverse ways of coping to survive and stay together. However, no matter how many strengths a family has, past and present impacts from the broader environment may make it difficult, if not impossible, for families to meet their own needs without additional support. In fact, all families need support beyond the family to survive and to reinforce their internal strengths. The African saying "It takes a village to raise a child" is perhaps more true in today's modern world than ever before.

What Is a Family?

The typical American family in the 1950s, 1960s, and 1970s included a husband, a wife, and 2.6 children. Today, fewer than 10% of American families are of this type. Thirty-two percent of all families are headed by only one parent, usually a woman. That figure increases to 36% for Latino households and 64% for African American households. About 5% of single-parent households are headed by men who have assumed responsibility for raising children following a divorce, separation, or death of a spouse (*Statistical Abstract,* 1999). Many families have extended family members such as grandparents, aunts, uncles, or cousins living with them. Oth-

ers are gay or lesbian couples with children. Still others have adopted or foster children either informally or by legal agreements with the court system. It is also becoming more and more common for individuals to live together who are not related by blood or marriage.

Some would argue that it is impossible to come up with a standard definition of a **family.** Others provide a broad definition of a family exemplified by the following: any group of individuals who are bonded together through marriage, kinship, adoption, or mutual agreement (Goode, 1964). When discussing the needs of children and families, a family is referred to within the context of a parent figure or figures and at least one child. Perhaps the most important issue in relation to what constitutes a family is that although all children and families have similar needs—to be loved, wanted, accepted, fed, clothed, given shelter, and protected—no two families are alike. Each family may be viewed as its own unique system.

How Are Families of Today Viewed?

Two of the most relevant frameworks for considering the family in the context of the social welfare system are the systems/ecological framework and the life-span development framework. The systems/ecological framework focuses on the exploration of the interactions between family members and other levels of the environment, such as extended family members, the neighborhood, the school, places of worship, the workplace, the community, the state, and other larger systems such as the economic system and the political system.

A second framework for considering the family in the context of the social welfare system is the life-span development framework discussed in Chapter 3. The family as a social system has more impact on the individual throughout the life cycle than any other system. Even before birth, the physical and emotional health of the family in which the child will be born and the environment in which the family functions significantly affect the child's future. How well individuals learn to trust others, develop autonomy, take initiative, be industrious, have a positive identity, be intimate with others, give something of themselves back to others, and face death with integrity are all shaped extensively by relationships within the family.

Families also go through distinct stages of development. Carter and McGoldrick (1998) discuss stages in the family life cycle: the unattached young adult, courtship and early marriage, the transition to parenthood and care of young children, raising adolescents, launching children and moving on, and later life, which includes involvement in the next generation of marriage and parenting. Every family will experience changes as its members grow and change, and the family's needs and interactions with the social welfare system will differ according to the particular stage of development the family is in. Carter and McGoldrick have also identified specific changes that are characteristic of divorced families and families who experience the remarriage of a parent.

What Is a Healthy Family?

Much of the literature about families focuses on family problems without considering what constitutes a healthy family. All families experience some type of problem at some point during their family life cycle, but some families are better able to cope with family problems because of the availability of financial resources and social support systems, and the physical and mental health of family members. A major crisis—no matter how healthy the family is—will have a serious impact on the family and is likely to result in at least temporary need for assistance from the social welfare system in some way.

Studies show that a number of factors are associated with healthy families. These include the opportunity to express all ideas and feelings, no family secrets, a valuing of everyone's opinions and feelings, rules that are flexible yet enforced with consistency, positive energy, and opportunities for growth and change. Persons are more likely to grow up to be successful adults if they experience the following as a child: a positive, nurturing relationship with at least one caregiver; consistent parenting, particularly during their 1st year of life; well-balanced discipline; at least a 2-year separation in age from any siblings; and access to others who can provide emotional support if their immediate families cannot do so (Werner & Smith, 1992).

How Are Family Problems Defined?

What constitutes a family problem depends on the perspective of the individual defining the problem. It also depends on such factors as the social and historical context within which the problem takes place; the attitudes, values, and norms of the community and the society in which the family lives; previous life experiences and professional background of the person defining the problem; legal definitions of the problem; and the availability of resources to address the problem.

Cultural Attitudes   Cultural attitudes, values, and practices shape how family problems are defined. For cultures in which women become sexually active as soon as they reach menses, teenage pregnancy is not likely to be considered a problem. Some cultures think it abusive that we make young children sit in a dental chair and force them to open their mouths and have their teeth pulled out. Some family policy experts suggest that the United States as a society is less supportive of children and families than other countries. In many Scandinavian countries, for example, the government provides free health care to children, subsidies for working parents to stay home when their children are young, and free child care. It has also been suggested that our country's fascination with violence as exemplified through the media and sports events has a strong impact on the high incidence of violence within the family and that the emphasis placed on sex in the media contributes to the high incidence of teenage pregnancy.

Community Norms and Values   The norms and values of the community also shape the way family problems are defined. If everyone within a community is unemployed and lives in substandard housing and all children are poorly fed and clothed, the families in that community living under those circumstances are not likely to be seen as neglecting their children. But children living in a family like that in a wealthy community most likely would be considered neglected. Whipping a child with a belt is not as likely to be considered child maltreatment in some communities or parts of the country as it is in others.

Attitudes and Values   The attitudes, values, personal life experiences, and professional background of the person defining the problem also influence how a problem is defined. A person raised in a conservative family, for which drinking of any alcoholic beverages was considered taboo, might define alcoholism differently than a person raised in a family for which drinking alcoholic beverages was commonplace. A physician may be more likely to define child abuse only in terms of physical characteristics, whereas a social worker may be more likely to consider emotional or educational neglect as an important form of child maltreatment.

Legal Definitions   Legal statutes also provide definitions of some types of family problems. These definitions vary by country and state and often leave a great deal of room for interpretation. For example, the Child Abuse Prevention and Treatment Act of 1974 defines child maltreatment as "the physical or mental injury, sexual abuse or exploitation, negligent treatment, or maltreatment of a child by a person who is responsible for the child's welfare, under circumstances which indicate that the child's health or welfare is harmed or threatened" (42 Section 5016g).

Terms such as *mental injury, threatened,* and *negligent treatment* often are difficult to interpret. At the same time, they allow leeway for additional protection of children. For example, a child who is constantly threatened with a knife or gun, even though never actually hurt physically, is likely to suffer serious emotional problems.

Availability of Resources   The availability of resources to address the problem may be the most important factor in how a problem is defined. The broader the definition, the more children and families will be identified as having the problem and needing assistance; the narrower the definition, the fewer identified as having the problem and needing assistance. The legal definition just given, for example, allows for the inclusion of neglected and emotionally maltreated children. In fact, when a similar state definition was first implemented, three times as many cases of child neglect were reported as cases of child abuse. More than 25 years later, because of scarce resources and significantly more cases reported, physical abuse and neglect cases are investigated and substantiated about equally, and only the most serious cases are defined as such. Resources are so stretched to their limits in many states that more narrow definitions of child maltreatment are being used. During the Kennedy and Johnson administrations, when resources to address domestic social problems were abundant, the emphasis was on developing programs "to achieve the maximum potential of all children." The emphasis shifted under the Nixon, Reagan, and Bush administrations to "meeting minimum levels of care for children and their families," thus significantly narrowing the numbers of families and children who fit within the definition of needed services. The debate between the Clinton administration and the more conservative congressional majority in the mid-1990s exemplifies the debate relating to the role of government and how social problems are defined. As the debate continues, children in the United States are faring less well than they did in the 1980s (see Table 11.1).

TABLE 11.1   HOW AMERICAN CHILDREN ARE DOING

Millions of children thrive in America. However, a profile of U.S. children developed by KIDS COUNT, a project of the Annie E. Casey Foundation, reveals a nation failing to keep pace with the needs of its youngest citizens. From 1985 to 1996, we made little progress or slipped backwards in 7 of 10 measures of child well-being. Child poverty expanded. Births to unmarried teens climbed. More children are living in families with only one parent. More babies are being born at-risk because they are underweight. We made little progress in graduating young people from high school on time. Our only advance has been in reducing the death of infants and young children, though that progress has not been shared equally by all children. The 21st century offers us a choice—to do nothing and consign our children to rising risk and in so doing be complicit in their eclipsed futures, or to rise to the occasion and reverse these results.

	TREND DATA	
Indicators of Child Well-Being	**1985**	**1996**
Percent low-birth-weight babies	6.8	7.4
Infant mortality rate (deaths per 1,000 live births)	10.6	7.3
Child death rate (deaths per 100,000 children ages 1–14)	34	26
Rate of teen deaths rate by accident, homicide, and suicide (deaths per 100,000 teens ages 15–19)	63	62
Teen birth rate (births per 1,000 females ages 15–17)	31	34
Percent of teens who are high school dropouts (ages 16–19)	11	10
Percent of teens not attending school and not working (ages 16–19)	11	9
Percent of children living with parents who do not have full-time, year-round employment	33	30
Percent of children in poverty	21	20
Percent of families with children headed by a single parent	22	27

Source: Kids Count Data Book (1999, p. 7). Reprinted with permission.

What Causes Families to Have Problems?

Families have problems for many reasons, and some families experience similar problems but for different reasons. There is no single cause for a given problem, which is why it is important to use a systems/ecological perspective in addressing family problems. It is also more appropriate to say that certain factors are associated with specific family problems, rather than saying that factors cause those problems. This means that a family experiencing a problem may have other problems as well, but it is often difficult to determine which problem caused the other.

We know that problems often go together. You are likely to find child abuse, spouse abuse, alcoholism, and teenage pregnancy within the same family. Individuals with these problems are more likely to be under stress, be worried about financial pressures, have low self-esteem, and come from families in which similar problems existed than are individuals in families without these problems.

Services for children and families often are provided by problem area—for example, alcoholism, child abuse and neglect, and spouse abuse—rather than as services that focus on the family as a system. This is due largely to the categorical basis on which state and federal funding generally is allocated. This categorical funding system has resulted in fragmented and duplicated services, as well as gaps in services in which client groups "fall through the cracks."

How Do Cultural and Gender Differences Affect Family Problems?

While statistics show that more children and families who experience family problems in the United States are white and headed by two parents, that statement is true only because there are more white, two-parent families than other types of families (Children's Defense Fund, 2000). Thus, it is important to consider not only raw counts but rates—that is, numbers of individuals of a certain group experiencing problems compared to the total population of that group. Such comparisons show that some groups are more vulnerable, or at risk, to experience certain problems than other groups.

Single women and people of color with children are more at risk to experience family problems in the United States than men and whites. Several reasons explain why women and people of color are more vulnerable in this way. In 1996, 26.1% of African American families lived below the federal poverty level, over three times the rate for whites. The rate for Latinos was 26.4%. In that same year, the poverty rate for female-headed African American households was 35.7%. Half of children in America will live in a single-parent family at some point in their childhood, one in three will be poor at some point in their childhood, and one in five is poor today (Children's Defense Fund, 2000).

Because individuals who experience poverty are far more likely to experience stress, they are far more at risk of experiencing other family problems. Thus, women and people of color, by the very nature of their positions within the socioeconomic hierarchy, are more likely to experience family problems. Additionally, these groups traditionally have had less power than other groups and not only are more vulnerable to being ignored or blamed for causing problems but also are unable to advocate for solutions and resources to address the problems they face. Women, for example, are often paid less and hired into lower-level jobs than men. Those who reenter the workplace after or while in more traditional marriages where they have not been employed outside the home ("displaced homemakers") are at a disadvantage in getting jobs that allow them to support their families adequately. They also are forced to bear the brunt of child care and other child-related needs. Traditional attitudes about women and people of color are changing, but because of a scarcity of resources available to address their needs, they continue to be at the bottom of the social structure in our country.

Children growing up in families in which social support is not available are more likely to experience problems in development, have low self-esteem, drop out of school, become pregnant at an early age, and have difficulty in finding adequate employment. Because they often lack appropriate role models and have been raised in an environment of hopelessness and despair, having children is often the only way they feel competent as people. With few skills and even fewer resources and opportunities, the cycle of the at-risk family often is repeated with their own children.

Although some attention is being given to the special needs of women and people of color and their families, this attention does not always address the problems from a broad context. For example, with the increased divorce rate and the growing number of people having children out of marriage, women have been targeted as "America's new poor," and much attention has been given to the **feminization of poverty** (DiNitto, 1999). However, in addition to providing more social supports to women and their families, the problem needs to be addressed from a systems/ecological perspective—women alone are not responsible for pregnancy or divorce; men's responsibility in such situations also must be addressed.

Additional factors must be taken into account when considering the relationship between family problems and people of color and women. While such families also are more likely to experience poverty and stress and thus are more likely to experience alcoholism or spouse or child abuse or be too overwhelmed by these pressures to parent their children adequately, they are also more likely to be labeled as having such problems. An African American or Latino parent who abuses a child, for example, is much more likely to take the child to a public hospital or clinic for treatment, where the case is likely to be reported to authorities. A white parent, however, is much more likely to take the child to a private physician and perhaps to a different private physician if the child is abused again.

Families of color and single-parent women also are more likely to seek help for family problems at public services agencies, such as local mental health centers, than at private psychological counseling programs. White parents having problems with children are far more likely to be able to afford to send them to private residential treatment facilities for therapy, whereas children of color are much more likely to be sent to juvenile detention centers, where such treatment usually is not available.

Individuals studying social welfare systems need to be aware that children who grow up in families headed by people of color and women are more vulnerable than children growing up in other families. Family problems must be considered within the context of the broader environment, including the impacts of oppression and discrimination, and these considerations are important as we work to shape the environment to make it more supportive for children and their families.

CHANGING FAMILY SITUATIONS

Issues of diversity need to be considered when working with children and their families. Many families today experience changes in composition due to divorce and separation, often requiring difficult transitions for all family members. An increasing number of children are being raised in single-parent families, necessitating additional effort from these parents to provide for their children. Many single parents who marry or remarry already have children, creating additional transitions and the development of new relationships for children as well as adults. Increasingly, children are being reared by gay or lesbian parents, often in the face of oppression from the community and society in which they live. While each of these situations often strengthens the family, family members may face specific issues that are helpful to understand when working with them.

Divorce and Separation

The divorce rate in the United States has increased from 3.5 per 1,000 population in 1970 to 4.3 per 1,000 population in 1996 (*Statistical Abstract,* 1999). One of every three marriages ends in divorce, with each marriage involving an estimated two children. Current projections suggest that over half of today's children will spend at least some time in a single-parent household (Children's Defense Fund, 2000). Divorce and separation often result in crises for family members. For adults, the separation or divorce signifies the loss of an intimate relationship that also brought security and support. Separation or divorce also signifies a loss of hopes and dreams as well as feelings of failure. Although there may be relief over the divorce, being alone also brings fear, anxiety, loneliness, and guilt, especially if there are children involved. Initially, parents are usually so caught up in dealing with their own emotions that they have little energy left to help their children cope with their feelings. Thus, at a time when their children need them most, many adults find themselves unable to reach out and help them.

For children, the divorce almost always is traumatic. If a great deal of fighting existed in the family, children may feel a sense of relief. But they, too, experience anger, guilt, fear, and sadness. Often, children blame themselves for their parents' divorce. They will frequently change their behavior, either acting overly good or overly bad, in the hope that this will bring their parents back together. Parents often fail to say anything to their children about an impending divorce, because of their own grieving and the belief that their children will cope better if they are not burdened with adult problems.

Studies suggest that the most important factor that helps children get through a divorce is having someone to listen and provide support to them. Parents need to explain that they are divorcing each other and not the child and that both of them will continue to love and spend time with the child. Some children may not react visibly when they are informed that their parents are separating or divorcing. However, if children do not react immediately after the divorce, they are likely to hold their feelings inside and express them at a later age (Wallerstein & Blakeslee, 1996).

Talking about the divorce and giving them a chance to express their feelings are important aspects in helping children cope with divorce. Children experiencing a divorce in their family usually regress at the time of the divorce. They may exhibit such behaviors as nightmares and bed wetting, thumb sucking, behavioral problems at school and at home, a drop in academic performance at school, list-lessness and daydreaming, changes in eating habits, increases in illness, and, if preadoles-cents or adolescents, experimentation with alcohol, drugs, sexual activity, and other risk-taking behaviors. If one parent has much less contact than in the past, children may develop extreme fears that they will be abandoned by the other parent or worry about what will hap-pen to them if the parent they are living with dies (Wallerstein & Kelly, 1996).

Although children are likely to cope better with divorce if the adults cope well, it usually takes children longer to recover, primarily because they have no control over the situa-tion. Various studies (Wallerstein & Blakeslee, 1996; Wallerstein & Kelly, 1996) show that it takes children at least 3.5 years to work through a divorce. In some cases, individuals may still be struggling with the situation 10 to 20 years later. Children fare better after a divorce if they maintain a positive relationship with both parents and if the parents do not speak negatively about each other or use the children to fight their battles with each other.

Custody and visitation problems often have a negative impact on a child following a divorce (see Figure 11.1). Although the situa-tion is changing, mothers are much more likely to obtain custody in a divorce. Courts have em-phasized a long-held doctrine that, in a child's "tender years," the mother is more important in the child's life, and unless totally unfit, she should receive custody of children in a divorce. Although in many instances today fathers want custody and are equally and often more capa-ble of caring for their children, less than 10% of divorces result in children living with their fathers. Because the average woman's income decreases significantly following a divorce and the average man's income increases, children of divorce often view their fathers as "Santa Clauses" or "Disney dads." Their fathers may buy them presents and take them special places, let them stay up later, and let them have fewer rules than their mothers, who are buying the necessities and maintaining the daily rou-tine, which usually requires more discipline. Mothers may resent that they cannot give their children the same fun aspects of life, whereas fathers often find visitation time with their chil-dren artificial and awkward and don't know what else to do with them.

Parents also often expect the child to decide where to live and where to spend holi-days, creating undue pressure on the child, who knows he or she will be forced to hurt one parent no matter what the decision. Child wel-fare professionals recommend that children be allowed to give input in such decisions, but final decisions should be made either by the parents or, if they cannot agree, by a trained mediator skilled in divorce conflicts or by the court (Wallerstein & Blakeslee, 1996).

Increasingly, parents are opting for joint custody, in which both parents equally share custody and, often, time spent living with the child. Some parents alternate the child's living with them every 3 or 4 days, whereas others have the child with them for 6 months and then switch the living arrangements. In some instances, to maintain stability for the child, the parents move in with the child, who remains in the same home, one at a time for a specified period of time. The research is inconclusive, however, as to the benefits of dif-ferent types of custody. Many experts suggest joint custody if the parents have a positive rela-tionship with each other, since this provides the child with two strong role models who love

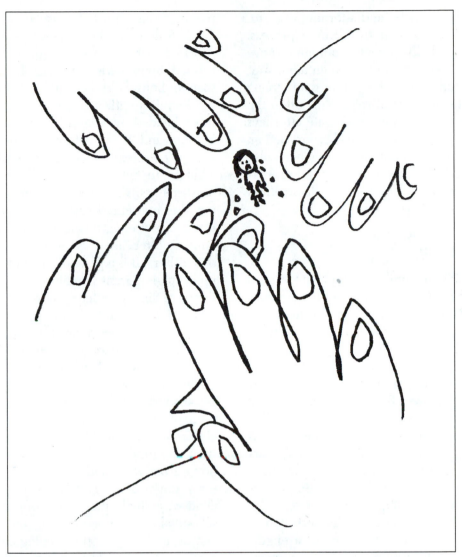

FIGURE 11.1

A 9-YEAR-OLD GIRL WHOSE PARENTS ARE INVOLVED IN A CUSTODY BATTLE DEPICTS HER FEELINGS IN A DRAWING

and pay attention to the child and communicates that the child is wanted and loved by both parents equally. Other experts suggest that joint custody, particularly if it involves a great deal of moving back and forth on the child's part, creates instability and a lack of permanence and that the child has no place to truly call his or her own.

The need for support to families experiencing divorce, particularly for children, is receiving increased attention. Many cities have established family **mediation** centers, where a team of social workers and attorneys work together with families in the divorce process. This approach helps parents maintain positive relationships with each other in an adult way, resolving conflicts together rather than forcing them to take adversarial roles, as is often the case when individuals have separate attorneys and pursue the divorce through court action. Public schools and family service agencies also have established special programs and support groups for children experiencing divorce and their parents.

Single Parenting

Currently, 25% of families in the United States are headed by a single parent, either because of divorce or separation or, increasingly, because of unmarried women giving birth to children (Children's Defense Fund, 2000). There is no evidence that suggests that growing up in a single-parent family is inherently positive or negative. Researchers have found that when socioeconomic status is controlled for, children in single-parent families fare as well as those in two-parent families. Factors that have a greater impact on how children fare are poverty and conflict between parents (Quinn & Allen, 1989; Wallerstein & Kelly, 1996). Single-parent families, like other families, need to be viewed from a strengths perspective, with attempts to eliminate environmental barriers that place such families at risk and to build on family strengths (see Table 11.1).

There are, however, a number of barriers that affect the well-being of single-parent families. The major barrier for most is income; a single-parent woman is more likely to be poor and, if not within the poverty definition of poor, experiencing financial stress. The median income for married households and single-

parent, female-headed households in 1996 was $49,858 and $16,398, respectively (*Statistical Abstract,* 1999). Incomes for white female-headed households were significantly higher than for households headed by women of color.

Families with a single income, especially those headed by a woman, are more likely to be poor and, if not within the poverty definition of poor, experiencing financial stress. In addition to financial pressure, single parents must maintain sole responsibility for overseeing the household and child rearing. As a result, children growing up in single-parent families often are used to different lifestyles than others. It is a paradox of children growing up in single-parent families that, on one hand, they are likely to have more freedom than other children and, on the other hand, they must take on much more responsibility. Children of single parents often have increased freedom because they must spend more time by themselves while their parents are working. Because child care is so expensive, many children of single parents, especially school-age children, become "latch-key" children, responsible for themselves until their parents get home from work. Others must be responsible for younger siblings. It is not unusual for a child of a single parent to come home from school alone, do homework and household chores, and prepare the evening meal. Single-parent children also must assume more responsibility for themselves because of the unavailability of supervision.

Single-parent children who are the same gender as the parent who has left the home also may assume many of the roles of the absent parent—for example, mowing the lawn and doing household repairs. They also may serve as companions to their parents, who may be lonely or too busy or hurt to establish adult relationships. Parents may confide in children about money, relationships with their ex-spouse, and other adult matters and expect children to accompany them on activities such as shopping trips, meetings, or parties. They also may place children in a situation of role reversal, expecting children to comfort them. Other parents become overly protective, worrying that since they have lost a significant relationship with an ex-spouse, they also may lose the relationship with the child.

Children in single-parent families may experience inconsistent discipline. A parent may be too tired to discipline at some times or too stressed and likely to overdiscipline at others. Parents' dating and development of opposite-sex relationships also can be stressful to children in single-parent families. Many children, particularly if they feel abandoned by the absent parent or do not have a positive relationship with that parent, may be anxious for the parent with whom they reside to remarry. Older children who have been in a single-parent family for a longer period of time may see any dating by their parent as a threat to their own relationship and may do everything possible to destroy such relationships. Such issues as how much to tell children about dating, how involved they should be in decision making about serious relationships or remarriage, whether to have "overnight" guests and live-in partners, and how to help children handle a relationship that has ended are of concern to single parents and their families.

Children growing up in single-parent families also may have fewer options regarding long-range plans for their future. Income and time limitations of such families may preclude college or other post–high school education. Other issues these children may face include the fear of being kidnapped by the noncustodial parent, one or more forms of child abuse by the parent or parent's friends, alcoholism or drug abuse by one or both parents, and concerns about the child's own sexuality and ability to establish long-term opposite-sex relationships.

Increasingly, schools, child guidance centers, and community mental health centers are offering special programs for children growing up in single-parent families. Programs include individual and group counseling, family counseling, and the development of self-help groups for children. Big Brother and Big Sister programs, which match adult role models in one-to-one relationships with children, also help children in single-parent families develop healthy relationships with adults of the opposite sex of the custodial parent figure to ensure that children experience positive relationships with both male and female adults. A number of books and other materials are also available to help both children with single parents and their families. Longitudinal studies of children growing up in single-parent families are also helping identify strengths of such families, as well as problem areas, to be better able to help children growing up in this type of family constellation.

Gay and Lesbian Parenting

Studies show that many gays and lesbians have been married before declaring their homosexuality (Laird, 1995). In addition, many gays and lesbians may decide to have children while they are in same-sex relationships or as single parents. Difficulties may arise, however, when gay and lesbian parents seek custody of children through the courts; both men and women in recent years have had difficulty gaining custody if they are gay or lesbian in spite of research that shows that there are few differences between gay or lesbian families and non-gay or lesbian families. Children born and/or raised in families in which one or more parents is gay or lesbian are no more likely to be gay or lesbian themselves than children born and/or raised in families in which both parents are heterosexual. Studies also have found that gay and lesbian parents do not influence their children to become gay or lesbian and that children raised by homosexual parents are not emotionally impaired. Although a number of individuals suggest that children are at risk to be molested by gay or lesbian parents, researchers have found that a child is more at risk to be molested in a heterosexual household than in a homosexual one (Laird, 1995; Moses & Hawkins, 1982).

Families with gay and lesbian parents must address some specific issues, however. For example, homosexual parents may not want their employers to know that they are gay or lesbian because they fear being fired. Thus, children may have to keep the homosexuality a secret from others. Many gay and lesbian parents also worry about how their children's friends and their parents will react to their being homosexual, and, as children grow older and more aware, they may fear this as well. Gay and lesbian parents may also fear that their children will be ridiculed or discriminated against. As in any family, children who are dealt with honestly and have open communication with their homosexual parents usually are better adjusted than children who find out about the homosexuality from others or sense the homosexuality but are not allowed to discuss it with their parents.

Stepparenting and Blended Families

With increased numbers of single-parent families, second marriages are also on the rise. Eighty percent of divorced adults remarry, and 60% involve at least one child. Half of all children who spend some portion of their childhood with a single parent mother will eventually live for some period with a stepfather (Arnold, 1998). The U.S. Bureau of the Census predicts that within the next few years, more Americans will be living in stepparent families than nuclear families (Stepfamily Foundation, 2000). A number of these families involve marriages between partners who each have children from previous marriages. Such families are often referred to as **blended families.**

Because remarriage typically generates a number of strong feelings among both children and adults involved that are often difficult to resolve, over 60% of second marriages with children fail (Arnold, 1998). Whereas adults may feel a sense of joyousness and security, children are likely to feel a sense of loss in relation to the parent, who must now be shared with the spouse, as well as anxiety over what the addition of another adult will mean to their own well-being. They also may experience concern about balancing the stepparent relationship with that of the absent birth parent. If the new marriage brings other children, relationships between stepsiblings may bring forth feelings of competition and jealousy.

The development of stepfamily relationships can be a difficult process, and time and effort are required on the part of all family members to make the new family constellation work. Children frequently feel distant from their new stepparent and may see that parent as a replacement for their absent parent. Even if they like the stepparent, conflicts over loyalty to their birth parent may prevent them from establishing a positive relationship with that person. If the child functioned as more of a "partner" in the family than a child prior to the new marriage, feelings of displacement and jealousy toward the stepparent can occur. Additionally, many children, no matter how old, still have fantasies of their birth parents reuniting, and the remarriage represents a threat to these fantasies. Stepsiblings also may mean less attention for birth children, as well as possible competition outside the family boundaries regarding friends, sports, and school.

In addition to the development of emotional bonds among family members, adjustments to changing family roles, responsibilities, and family identity must be made in a blended family. Rules often are readjusted, and many times are more strict than they were in the single-parent household. If children are still in contact regularly with their own birth parent, they are now essentially members of two households, each with its own distinct culture and rules. Problems regarding multiple role models and parental figures can create confusion for children. Some experts in stepparent family relationships suggest that the stepparent should not in any way undermine the absent birth parent relationship but should establish him- or herself as a parental figure in the family and take an active role in immediate family issues such as rules and discipline. Other experts argue that the parenting should be left completely to the child's parents, with the stepparent working to establish a positive bond with the child but as an adult friend rather than a parental figure, staying out of decisions regarding rules and discipline.

Although remarriage can increase the stability, security, and financial resources for children, working through the implications of such changes takes a great deal of time before there is acceptance. Special parent education classes for stepparents; support groups for stepparents, spouses, and children in stepparent families; and family counseling programs are available in many communities to help focus on the strengths of such families and provide support in working through problem areas.

FAMILY PROBLEMS AFFECTING CHILDREN

Families today face increasing pressures from the broader environment. They often live in communities that have limited support for families. Because today's families are more diverse, the issues to consider when addressing their needs are more complex than in the past. More and more children and families need social support beyond the family because of problems such as substance abuse, spouse abuse, and child maltreatment. Additionally, as increasing numbers of children grow up in communities rife with poverty and violence and do not receive the nurturance and guidance they need for healthy development, they are more likely to enter adolescence angry, depressed, and searching for attention and acceptance wherever they can find it. Thus, problems associated with youth crime, membership in gangs, violence, and teenage pregnancy and parenthood are on the rise. Suicide not only is a serious problem for adolescents but is also on the rise among younger children.

Substance Abuse

Current evidence indicates that almost half of U.S. adults have been exposed to alcoholism in the family (U.S. National Center for Health Statistics, 1999). Until recently, substance abuse has been viewed as an individual disease rather than a family problem. But recent studies have found that individuals raised in such families are five times as likely to become substance abusers themselves. Twenty percent of juvenile delinquents and children seen in child guidance and mental health clinics come from families where alcohol abuse is a problem. Other studies show a high degree of relationship between substance abuse and family violence. The National Center on Addiction and Substance Abuse (1999) found that children of substance-abusing parents were almost three times more likely to be abused and more than four times more likely to be neglected than children of parents who are not substance abusers. Other studies suggest that an estimated 50% to 80% of all child abuse cases substantiated by state child protection agencies involve some degree of substance abuse by the child's parents. Seventy percent of infants abandoned in hospitals have parents who are addicts; many of these children are born addicted to drugs as well.

Children who manage to "survive" in substance-abusive families seldom escape unscathed. Adult children of alcoholics manifest coping characteristics they developed as children within their own families, including a compulsion to control, a need to overachieve, and a need to please others continually (Black, 1987). They also have many fears—they worry about being abandoned, physical and emotional harm, and personal violence to themselves or other family members. They also experience feelings of loneliness, guilt, anger, shame, and sadness. Because of messages they receive in their families and the resulting feelings of guilt and shame, they maintain as secrets not only what is going on in the family but their own feelings as well.

In looking at a substance-abusive family from a systems/ecological perspective, one can see how substance-abusive families develop a way of functioning with the abuser as the central family member that, although dysfunctional to outsiders, is functional to the family in that it facilitates survival. Family members or others who facilitate continuation of substance abuse are called **enablers.** For example, a spouse may make excuses for the substance abuser's behavior to other family members, friends, or employers. An older child may take on a "hero" role, believing that by being a "perfect" child, the substance abuse will stop or be less likely to disrupt the family. This child is likely to get excellent grades in school, take care of younger children, nurture both parents, and work toward keeping family members happy no matter what the costs to the child. Another child in the family may take on a "scapegoat" role, subconsciously believing that negative attention directed at him or her will take the attention away from the substance-abusing parent. Conflict between the parents over the substance abuse may instead be directed at the child, who is always getting in trouble at home, at school, and in the neighborhood. Yet another child may assume the role of the "lost child," believing that the family is better able to cope if he or she is out of sight. These children are always in their rooms, under the table or in the corner, or at friends' homes. They seek little attention and, in fact, go out of their way not to call any attention to themselves at all. A final role a child in such families may assume is the "mascot" role. These children, often the youngest, become the pets or clowns of the family, always available to be cuddled when cuddling is demanded or to entertain when entertainment can alleviate some of the family's pain (Ackerman, 1983).

Some experts in the substance abuse field take issue with the term *enabler,* because although it describes many characteristics typical of individuals in families with a substance abuser, it still places the focus of attention on the abuser. Instead, they prefer to use the term **codependent,** or a person who relies extensively on others for self-worth and self-definition, focusing more on pleasing or controlling others than creating a healthy sense of self (Beattie, 1987). These individuals argue that the term *codependence* defines the problem more clearly as belonging to the codependent person and indicates a need for individual recovery for that person separate from the substance abuser (Schaef, 1986). All definitions and models of codependence focus on the impact of the behavior on the codependent individual and the long-term consequences, regardless of whether the person remains in a relationship with the substance abuser.

Researchers who have studied relationships in substance-abusive families point out the enormous costs these roles have played on the individual family members throughout their lives, as well as on the total family. Such roles actually promote the substance abuse, and family members are seen as unknowingly encouraging the substance abuse. This is why current substance abuse intervention strategies view the abuse as a family systems problem; if communication patterns and roles within families are not changed concurrently with treatment for the substance abuser, the substance-abusive behavior is likely to return quickly, reinforced by the behaviors of other family members.

The ways that families typically cope with substance abuse can be divided into four phases. The first phase is the *reactive phase*, in which family members deny that the substance abuse exists and develop their own coping strategies around the substance-abusive parent, usually—sometimes intentionally— enabling the abuse to continue. These strategies range from nagging to making excuses or covering up the abuse, to staying at home and trying to prevent the substance abuse, to denying emotional feelings. Children in such families may suffer from birth defects as a result of the substance abuse. They may be torn

between parents who demonstrate conflicting and often confusing behavior. They may avoid activities with peers because of fear and shame. They may not trust others, or they may learn destructive and negative ways to get attention (Ackerman, 1983).

The second phase in a substance-abusive family is the *active phase,* in which family members become aware that there is a substance abuse problem, that they do not live in a normally functioning family, and that help is available. Family members begin to realize that the abuser does not control the family, that they have the power to make changes in their own behaviors, and that they cannot assume responsibility for the substance abuser. At this point, members may join self-help groups such as Al-Anon or Alateen, in which others going through similar experiences within their own families can lend support.

The third phase in a substance-abusive family is the *disequilibrium phase*. This phase, while painful and difficult for all family members, must be experienced if the problem is to be alleviated. It occurs after family members are aware that a problem exists, but all efforts to change the abuser or the family dynamics have been unsuccessful. During this phase, family members consider openly whether disruption is the only alternative. This often leads to polarization among family members. This phase often ends in divorce, with subsequent separation of family members if the abuser still will not seek help. Although usually the family fares better in the long run, at the time the experience is often doubly traumatic for children, who then have to cope with the problems of both alcoholism and divorce. It is estimated that divorce occurs in approximately 40% of family situations that reach this phase (Ackerman, 1983). For those families that do not choose separation, the traditional family communication patterns may be shaken enough that the family begins to change actively. Whether disruption occurs or the substance-abusing family member agrees to make a concerted effort to change, the family is forced to reorganize. This requires new and different roles for family members (Ackerman, 1983).

The final phase in a substance-abusive family is the *family unity phase*. Many families with substance abuse problems never reach this phase. Being free of substance abuse is central to this phase; however, it is not enough. Acceptance of the family member as a non-substance abuser and lasting changes in family communication patterns must take place if the family is to remain free of recurring substance abuse problems.

Spouse Abuse

Although definitions of **family violence** differ across state lines, a general definition often used is an act carried out by one family member against another family member that causes or is intended to cause physical or emotional pain or injury to that person. Family violence typically has been separated into two major categories: spouse abuse (also referred to as "domestic violence," "battering," or "relationship abuse") and child abuse. Recent attention also has focused on elder abuse or children abusing their parents.

Although spouse abuse received national attention during the well-publicized O. J. Simpson trial, most attention up until that time focused on the abuse of children. Child abuse first received attention as a major national issue in the 1960s, with impetus from the medical profession and other professionals and concerned child advocates, but spouse abuse did not gain attention until a number of years later. Attempts to combine forces by

women's advocates were met with resistance from child abuse advocates. Early attempts to develop programs and secure legislation for spouse abuse were spin-offs from rape crisis centers, which often were run by feminists at the grass-roots level.

Professionals, particularly those from the medical profession, were concerned that joining forces with feminists might place child abuse programming in jeopardy. Thus, currently there is only limited legislation and centralized programs to deal with spouse abuse, although significant efforts in both legislation and federal programs exist for child abuse. More important, very limited federal dollars have been appropriated for spouse abuse programs. Some states have earmarked funding for spouse abuse programs, but these programs often are either small adjuncts to child welfare/child abuse departments or under the auspices of special women's commissions, implying that spouse abuse is a woman- or child-related problem rather than a family problem of concern to everyone. Some child abuse programs have funded spouse abuse programs only by suggesting that children raised in a home in which spouse abuse is present are emotionally abused.

Although men are sometimes abused in partner relationships, the majority of spouse abuse is perpetrated by men. Studies indicate that women are the individuals abused in 92% of spouse abuse situations (U.S. Department of Justice, 1998a). An additional reason that attention to spouse abuse was late in developing relates to ways men and women are viewed in our society: men are regarded in power positions both within and outside the home. Although men are seen as having power over children as well, it is much easier for the general public to become concerned about abused children than abused women. Many individuals still subscribe to the myth that women who are beaten somehow deserve it or that they must enjoy it or they would not put up with it.

Estimates are that 1 to 4 million women in the United States are physically abused by their partners annually (U.S. Department of Justice, 1998b, cited by National Violence Against Women Office, 2000). Domestic violence is found across ethnic, racial, and socioeconomic lines. Violence by a partner accounts for about 20% of violent crime experienced by women (U.S. Department of Justice, 1998b, cited by National Violence Against Women Office, 2000). Women are up to six times as likely to suffer violence at the hands of a partner or ex-partner than from a stranger and are more likely to suffer injury when the assailant is an intimate (Bachman & Saltzman, 1995; Koss, Woodruff, & Koss, 1994). Twenty-two to 35% of emergency room visits by women are in response to partner violence (Abbot, Johnson, Koziol-McLain, & Lowenstein, 1995; McLeer & Anwar, 1989; Randall, 1990). Thirty-three to 50% of women who are physically assaulted by their partners also suffer sexual assault at their hands (Frieze & Browne, 1989). Three-fourths of women over age 18 who report being raped and/or physically assaulted were abused by a current or former partner, date, or boyfriend (U.S. Department of Justice, 1998a, cited by National Violence Against Women Office, 2000). Violence between heterosexual couples extends beyond the marital relationship. Approximately one-third of college students report experiencing relationship aggression (White & Koss, 1991), and 40% of teenage girls report knowing someone who has been hit or beaten by a boyfriend (Kaiser Permanante, 1995, cited by National Violence Against Women Office, 2000).

While the majority of attention in the media has focused on physical violence, there are other types of spouse abuse. Susan Schecter, a researcher and expert in the field of spouse abuse, classifies emotional spouse abuse in five major categories (cited in Davis 1995, p. 782):

- Isolation, which includes behaviors such as not allowing a partner to go anywhere without the partner, monitoring and questioning telephone calls, and trying to keep the partner from being involved with anyone else other than the abuser
- Economic abuse, which denies access to resources, such as education, clothing, medical care, and the ability to work for pay
- Humiliation and degradation
- "Crazy-making" abuse, which includes placing responsibility for the abuse on the person who is being abused, changing interpretations of the person's reality, and other erratic behavior that leads the abused person to begin to believe that she is crazy
- Suicidal and homicidal threats

A number of factors commonly are associated with spouse abuse. Men who assault their wives generally have low self-esteem and feel inferior. Feeling powerless outside the family, they exert their power within the domain of their homes. Male perpetrators of domestic violence are more likely to be younger and to abuse alcohol or drugs (Barnett & Fagan, 1993; Hotaling & Sugarman, 1990; Pan, Neidig, & O'Leary, 1994). It is more difficult to interpret factors associated with women who are abused. Lenore Walker (1999) has identified "learned helplessness" as a common trait among abused women. She suggests that women have learned to act passive and helpless as a way of coping with their violent spouses and have been conditioned to believe that they are powerless to get out of the violent situation. Others (Frieze & Browne, 1989) suggest that battered women exhibit symptoms consistent with posttraumatic stress syndrome, a diagnosis commonly given to persons who have suffered severe trauma. Frieze and Browne (1989) suggest that women in violent domestic situations react emotionally to their experiences and are often paralyzed and unable to act to defend themselves or their children. They exhibit the characteristics of learned helplessness, blaming themselves for their abuse, or they redefine the event, rationalizing that it wasn't that serious or that it was a rare occurrence.

Many times, abused women are reluctant to leave violent situations because they have no employable skills and are concerned about being able to survive, particularly if they have children. Other studies show that battered women are not always passive—they often seek help in dealing with the abuse, but they love their husbands in spite of the violence and believe they will reform. In many violent situations among spouses, the period following the violence is almost like a honeymoon period, with the abusive spouse often crying, being extremely sorry for the violence, threatening suicide if he is deserted, promising never to be violent again, and being extremely loving and supportive. It is difficult for a woman who loves her husband not to be taken in by this repentant behavior, at least initially.

Other studies show that women with low self-esteem, particularly those who were physically or sexually abused as children, feel so worthless that they believe they deserve the violent treatment. Such women are more at risk to be abused than other women. While in most situations the woman is passive and the man abusive, in other situations both spouses are violent. But because of size differences, it is most often the woman who is hurt. Other factors that place couples more at risk for spouse abuse include substance abuse, financial stress and poverty, and the male's unemployment or underemployment.

The lack of policies and programs that address spouse abuse are tied to the oppression of women in our society. Working toward eliminating the oppression of all groups will reduce spouse abuse. Several federal policies have been passed that support spouse abuse programs. The Family Violence Prevention and Services Act of 1984 provides funding for shelters for abused persons, but the funding is limited and does not come close to meeting the demand for shelter. The Victims of Crime Act, also passed in 1984, gives priority to abused spouses in receiving compensation for crime-related costs. Landmark legislation in the area of domestic violence was passed in 1994 as part of the federal Crime Act. The Violence against Women Act makes it a crime to cross state lines to abuse a partner, prohibits individuals who have restraining orders filed against them for domestic violence from possessing firearms, creates tougher penalties for sex offenders, requires sex offenders to pay restitution to their victims, requires states to pay for rape examinations, and creates protections for survivors of rape from inappropriate inquiries about their personal lives. The act also commits more than $1.6 billion over a 6-year period for domestic violence programs, including the hiring of police, prosecutors, and victim-witness counselors and the establishment of prevention programs (Violence against Women Office, 2000).

In spite of recent state and federal initiatives, programs that address spouse abuse are extremely limited. Many communities have established safe houses and battered women's shelters, where battered spouses and their children can seek refuge. These programs also provide counseling for both women and children and assist them in legal issues, locating housing and employment, and developing support networks. Sadly, many women seeking shelter at such programs are turned away because of lack of space. While community outreach programs have been established that provide counseling and other services to survivors and perpetrators of spouse abuse, most programs usually begin to treat the violence after it has reached an intolerable point and change is difficult, particularly for the male abuser.

Child Maltreatment

Reported cases of child abuse continue to increase at epidemic rates, and current resources are unable to serve the many abused and neglected children and their families who come to the attention of available programs. In 1997, child protective services (CPS) agencies in the United States investigated an estimated 2 million reports alleging the maltreatment of almost 3 million children, more than double the number of reported cases in 1980 (U.S. Department of Health and Human Services, 1999). Several studies suggest that even more children suffer from abuse and neglect than are seen through official statistics from state CPS agencies (see Figure 11.2). Exact figures on numbers of abused and neglected children do not exist because most maltreatment happens within the confines of family privacy; even when cases are known to others, they are often not reported.

Child maltreatment falls into four main categories: physical abuse, sexual abuse, child neglect, and psychological maltreatment. Neglect is the most frequently reported type of maltreatment, with over half of all reports of this type. Reports of sexual abuse, however, have increased most in recent years. This is probably

because of increased awareness about sexual abuse, which has eliminated some of the secrecy that previously surrounded the problem.

Children of all ages are maltreated. While infants are most at risk to be severely abused or neglected, most maltreated children are school age. Among children confirmed as maltreated by CPS agencies in 1997, more than half were 7 years of age or younger, with almost 26% younger than 4 years old. About 27% of confirmed reports were children ages 8 to 12; another 23% were youth ages 13 to 18. The distribution across both genders is fairly equal; in 1997, about 52% were female and 48% were male. In 1996, just under 55% of those children were white; 30.8% were African American, 12.2% were Latino, 1.3% were American Indian/Alaska Native, and 1% were Asian/Pacific Islander (U.S. Department of Health and Human Services, 1999).

Physical Abuse

Using the Harm Standard developed for the National Incidence Study of Child Abuse and Neglect, the estimated number of physically abused children in the United States increased by 97% between the second national incidence study conducted in 1986 and the third such study conducted in 1993. When these children were classified according to the injury or harm they suffered from maltreatment that fit the Harm Standard, there was a significant increase in the incidence of children who were seriously injured between the two studies. The estimated number of seriously injured children quadrupled in the intervening 7 years (U.S. Department of Health and Human Services, 1999).

Most children who are **physically abused** receive bruises, welts, or abrasions. These injuries are caused by parents whipping or spanking children with objects such as belts,

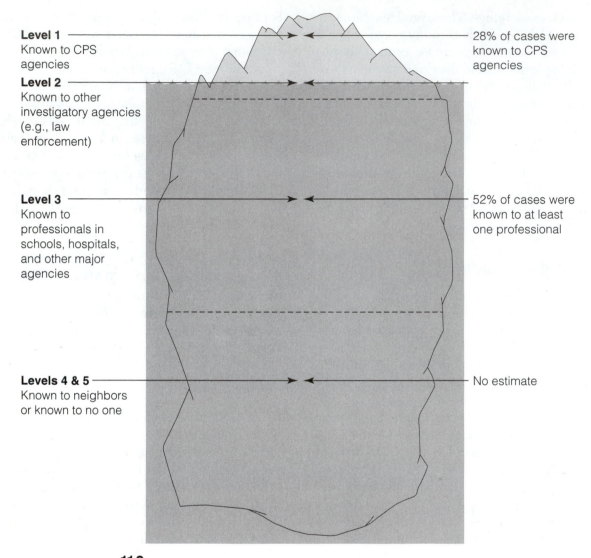

Level 1
Known to CPS
agencies

Level 2
Known to other
investigatory agencies
(e.g., law
enforcement)

Level 3
Known to
professionals in
schools, hospitals,
and other major
agencies

Levels 4 & 5
Known to neighbors
or known to no one

28% of cases were
known to CPS
agencies

52% of cases were
known to at least
one professional

No estimate

FIGURE **11.2**

KNOWLEDGE ABOUT MALTREATED CHILDREN: THE TIP OF THE ICEBERG

This figure depicts the estimated incidence of actual cases of child maltreatment and who
in the community knows about these cases. As the figure shows, the child protective services (CPS) agencies that are mandated to provide services in such cases actually know
about only 28% of cases that other professionals know about. This percentage does not
even include those cases that only neighbors or immediate family members know about,
suggesting that known cases of maltreatment are only the tip of the iceberg when it
comes to how much child maltreatment actually exists. This study was conducted for the
third time in 1993. Since the time of the second study in 1986, the number of abused and
neglected children increased by two-thirds.

Source: Figure adapted from National Center on Child Abuse and Neglect (1996).

extension cords, hair brushes, or coat hangers. Often, imprints of the objects can be seen on the child's body. When these types of injuries occur on the face, head, or more than one plane of a child's body (such as the back and arms) and are in various stages of healing (for example, bruises in varying colors), child abuse is suspected.

Children also receive broken bones and burns, as well as internal injuries, as a result of physical child abuse. Physicians can use X rays to determine the types of breaks and when they occurred. Children with spiral fractures, for example, may have experienced the break when a caretaker became angry and twisted one of their limbs. Children who are physically abused with one suspected broken bone or other serious injury will often have fractures or other injuries in various stages of healing in several areas of the body. This condition, termed **battered child syndrome** by C. Henry Kempe, a physician instrumental in advocating for child abuse legislation, is a diagnosis now recognized by medical professionals. One of the most serious types of child maltreatment is an internal injury to the head, which usually results in internal bleeding, brain damage, and death. Shaking a child severely can also result in serious injury, including blindness (due to detached retinas), brain injury, and death. Children may be burned on their hands, feet, and other parts of their bodies with cigarettes or lighters. Parents with unrealistic expectations about toilet training often burn children by placing them in extremely hot water when they have soiled themselves.

Many factors are associated with families who physically abuse children: financial problems such as unemployment and poverty, isolation, unrealistic parental expectations about child development or children's abilities to meet parental needs for love and attention,

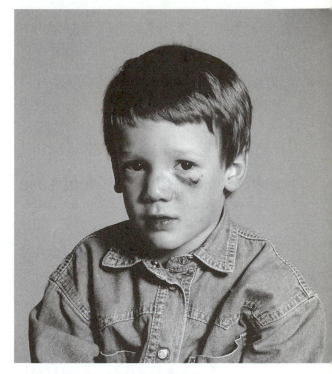

Physical child abuse occurs most often among school-age children. This young boy just brought home his report card; studies show that reports of abuse increase when report cards are distributed.

H. Schmidimayr/Liaison Agency

alcoholism and drug abuse, abuse or maltreatment of the parent during childhood, lack of education about nonphysical alternatives to discipline, low impulse control, and inability to cope well with stress. Studies show that only about 10% of parents who maltreat their children are seriously psychologically disturbed.

Studies also show that some children are more at risk of physical abuse than others. Children who are born prematurely or with congenital problems, children who somehow do not meet parental expectations or are perceived as different by their parents, and children who are the result of unwanted pregnancies are more at risk to be abused physically than other children. Many parents who abuse children begin with role reversal within the family system, expecting the child, even as an infant or toddler, to meet their emotional needs. When the child resists or is unable to do so because she or he is too young,

the parent may feel rejected, become angry and frustrated, and abuse the child.

Children who grow up in communities with few economic resources and few support systems available to families also are more at risk to be abused (see Box 11.1). Cultural con-

---

BOX 11.1

Indicators of Risk for Child Abuse and Neglect

1. **Child previously reported:** There have been previous founded or unfounded reports of abuse or neglect of the child or his or her siblings in the family system.
2. **Parent abused as a child:** The parent remembers having been abused as a child, or this fact is documented in the parent's history.
3. **Age of the parent:** The parent was under age 18 at the time of the reported child's or the first child's birth.
4. **Age of the child:** There are differences in the occurrence and type of abuse of infants, young children, or adolescents.
5. **Family composition:** This factor generally refers to a single parent raising children alone, including a never-married, separated, or divorced parent and children living in an extended family household.
6. **Domestic violence in the home:** In a home where violence frequently occurs, a child may be injured accidentally or purposely; emotional abuse is a factor.

7. **Separation of a parent or child for a long period:** The child may have been raised by a grandmother or other family member or have been in foster care.
8. **Parent or caretaker's abuse of substances:** The parent or the caretaker may be abusing drugs or alcohol to the extent that parenting is affected or distributing drugs, both of which affect the child's safety and healthy development.
9. **Physical, mental, or emotional impairment of the child:** The child has been diagnosed or observed to be mentally retarded, cognitively limited, physically or emotionally disabled, or chronically ill.
10. **Physical, mental, or emotional impairment of the parent:** The parent or other caretaker has been diagnosed and treated for mental illness or has a physical or emotional disability or a chronic physical or mental illness.
11. **Low socioeconomic status:** The family is dependent on or eligible for public assistance.

Source: Brissett-Chapman (1995). Copyright 1995, National Association of Social Workers, Inc.

ditions also have an impact on physical abuse. Studies show that cultures that value children and share parenting with others beyond the nuclear family have less child abuse than other cultures (Korbin, 1982).

Sexual Abuse

Sexual abuse, more than any other type of child maltreatment, has received increased attention in recent years. The estimated number of sexually abused children under the Harm Standard increased by 125% between the second and third national incidence study of child abuse and neglect conducted in 1986 and 1993, respectively (U.S. Department of Health and Human Services, 1999). Reported cases of sexual abuse have increased significantly, for two reasons: (1) increased public awareness of the problem and (2) children's greater exposure to more adults than in the past, including child care providers, stepparents, and other adults, thereby increasing the likelihood of sexual abuse.

Child **sexual abuse** can be defined as "any childhood sexual experience that interferes with or has the potential for interfering with a child's healthy development" (National Center on Child Abuse and Neglect, 1993, p. 9). Thus, child sexual abuse can include acts such as fondling in addition to sexual intercourse. Legislation also mandates that state child abuse laws include child pornography and sexual exploitation in definitions of sexual abuse. This expands the definition to include acts such as taking pictures of children in sexual poses or for purposes of sexual gratification.

Many individuals are unaware until later in life that they have been sexually abused, either because they repress the act or because they have no idea of what constitutes healthy adult-child interactions, assuming all children experience such treatment. Others are reluctant to report the abuse because they are ashamed or embarrassed, have been threatened, or are worried about possible repercussions for themselves and their families. Some studies suggest that 27% of women and 16% of men were sexually abused before reaching the age of 18 (Finkelhor, Hotaling, Lewis, & Smith, 1990). It is estimated that only 6% to 12% of cases are reported to law enforcement agencies at the time that they occur (Berliner, 1995).

While most individuals think of sexual abusers as strangers who accost children in the park, the majority are known and trusted by the children they abuse. The first category of abusers consists of parents. Sexual abuse by birth parents, commonly referred to as **incest,** is considered by many to have the most serious personal and social consequences. Abusers also may be other parent figures, such as stepparents. The second category of abusers consists of family members other than parent figures. This includes siblings, grandparents, and uncles or aunts. Sexual relationships between siblings are reported to be the most common. The broadest definition of incest includes sexual relationships between any family members. The third category of sexual abusers includes trusted adults. These may be teachers, baby-sitters, neighbors, coaches, leaders of children's groups, or other adults. The last, and least frequent, types of sexual abusers are strangers or remote acquaintances. It is estimated that only about 12% of reported child maltreatment is perpetrated by someone outside the child's family (U.S. Department of Health and Human Services, 1999).

Although all children are at risk to be sexually abused, those who are seen as most vulnerable are often singled out by perpetrators. Children living without their birth fathers, living in stepparent families, having mothers employed outside the home, having a mother who is ill, observing violence between parents, or having a poor relationship with parents are characteristics that make children more likely to be sexually abused (Finkelhor, 1986). Boys are most likely to be abused by nonfamily members and girls by family members, and 95% of girls and 80% of boys who report being sexually abused indicate that their abuser was a male. Ethnicity is not clearly associated with differences in rates of sexual abuse, but it is associated with differences in related factors such as age of child and type of perpetrator (Berliner, 1995).

The reasons that adults sexually abuse children are complex and vary according to the individual abuser. Characteristics of perpetrators of sexual abuse include poor impulse control, low frustration tolerance, low self-esteem, denial, manipulation, social and emotional immaturity, abuse of alcohol and other drugs, and isolation (Tower, 1996). About one-fourth of male offenders report being sexually abused as children, and about half began sexually abusing others during adolescence (Berliner, 1995).

Most abusers engage in a seductive, power role with children with whom they become involved. Children, wanting affection and too young to know how to draw boundaries themselves between positive affection and sexual abuse, initially may become involved and then be too afraid to tell anyone what is going on. Although the sexual abuse acts themselves may not involve physical force on the adult's part, the child is trapped in the situation because adults are in power positions with children. Some abusers tell children that the relationship is the only thing keeping the family together, or the abuser is the only one who really loves and understands them. Other abusers threaten physical harm to the child or to other family members if the child refuses to cooperate or tells anyone what is going on. For example, they say that their mother will "go crazy," the child will be taken out of the home, or the adult will sexually abuse a younger sibling.

Studies on the effects of sexual abuse on children show that it is extremely harmful emotionally and that many individuals who have been sexually abused suffer long-term effects. The impact of sexual abuse on children depends on factors such as the following (Sgroi, 1982): the child's age when the abuse occurred; the type of sexual abuse that took place; the relationship of the abuser to the child; the length of time the abuse occurred; how long it was between the time the abuse occurred and someone found out that it was going on; other characteristics of the child's family and available positive support to the child; and reactions from family members and professionals when the sexual abuse finally is discovered.

Issues faced by survivors of sexual abuse include lack of trust and feelings of betrayal, powerlessness, isolation, blame, and a sense of loss (Conte, 1995). Others experience problems such as depression, anxiety or panic disorder, and posttraumatic stress disorder. Many persons who have been sexually abused see themselves as victims due to the trauma of the abuse and have extremely low self-esteem; difficulty in establishing intimate, trusting relationships with others; and problems with their own families and marriages when they become adults. Without intervention, persons who have been sexually abused are more at risk than others to turn to alcohol, drugs, or suicide to ease their pain. Many communities have established programs that promote public awareness of sexual abuse and early intervention with families once cases are reported to attempt to address such long-term effects.

Child Neglect

Neglect is characterized by acts of omission; this usually means that something that should have been done to or for a child was not done. **Child neglect** can be defined as "a condition in which a caretaker responsible for the child either deliberately or by extraordinary inattentiveness permits the child to experience available present suffering and/or fails to provide one or more of the ingredients generally deemed essential for developing a person's physical, intellectual and emotional capacities" (National Center on Child Abuse and Neglect, 1980, p. 3).

Many states include specific categories in their definitions of child neglect, such as failing to provide adequate food, clothing, or shelter for a child (physical neglect); leaving a child unattended for inappropriate periods of time (lack of supervision); leaving a child alone or not returning when expected to care for a child (abandonment); not providing medical care for a child (medical neglect); failing to provide an education for a child (educational neglect); and not tending to a child's emotional needs (emotional neglect). The National Center on Child Abuse and Neglect's national reporting system determined that 149,425 children were deprived of necessities for survival in 1996 (U.S. Department of Health and Human Services, 1999).

Although some individuals view neglect as less dangerous to a child than abuse, this is not the case. Studies have shown that as many children die each year from neglect as from abuse. Many are burned in fires or drown in bathtubs while left alone or with inadequate supervision; others die because their parents did not obtain medical care for them soon enough when they became ill. Neglected children may suffer from more long-term consequences of their maltreatment than abused children. Adults who did not have their physical or emotional needs met as children are much more likely to have problems in finding and maintaining jobs, developing positive relationships with other individuals and remaining in marriages, and parenting their own children adequately.

Failure to Thrive

One type of neglect that is receiving increased attention is **nonorganic failure to thrive,** a form of parental deprivation. Failure to thrive has been medically defined as describing a child who is three percentiles or more below the normal weight for his or her particular age. The child seems to be being fed on a regular basis by its caretakers, and nothing organically wrong can be found with the child, yet it does not gain weight and literally fails to thrive. When placed in a hospital and given nothing more than regular feedings of its normal diet, coupled with love and attention (for example, holding and cuddling), the child begins to gain weight immediately. Bowlby's (1951) classic studies of maternal deprivation and children raised in orphanages in Europe without love and attention found a high death rate and significant differences in intelligence quotient (IQ) and physical and emotional development when compared to children raised in environments where they received love and attention. Similar findings are evident among children diagnosed with failure to thrive syndrome.

Neglectful Parents

Parents who neglect their children differ from other parents at the same socioeconomic level. While there is a strong relationship between poverty and neglect, not all parents who are poor neglect their children. The typical neglectful parent, as compared with nonneglectful parents also living in poverty, is more isolated, has fewer relationships with others, is less able to plan and to control impulses, is less confident about the future, and is more plagued with physical and psychological problems. Neglectful parents also are more likely to say that they have never received love and were unwanted by their parents. Many have been raised by relatives or in foster care. Neglectful parents often began life lonely, and continue to live in isolation. Polansky, Ammons, and Gaudin (1985) found that neglectful parents had difficulty identifying neighbors or friends with whom they could leave their children if they needed emergency child care or from whom they could borrow five dollars in an emergency. They are extremely isolated from both formal and informal support networks; many neglecting parents describe their social workers as being their best or only friends.

Polansky, Chalmers, Buttenweiser, and Williams (1991) classify five types of neglecting parents:

- *Apathy-futility syndrome*—These neglecting parents have all but given up on life. They see little hope for the future and view all efforts to try to relate to either their children or others as futile. They convey an attitude of hopelessness and despair. Usually neglected themselves as children and in many instances in the past beaten down whenever they tried to make a go of life, they lack the physical or emotional energy to relate to their children. A neglectful parent with apathy-futility syndrome is likely to be found lying on the couch in a chaotic household that hasn't been cleaned or cared for, with children unkempt and uncared for, left largely to fend for themselves. Children raised by this type of neglectful parent suffer from physical, medical, educational, and/or emotional neglect, as well as lack of supervision.

- *Impulse-ridden behavior*—This type of parent may be loving and caring and may provide adequate food, clothing, and medical care most of the time. But this parent has trouble making appropriate decisions and often behaves impulsively. Such parents suddenly may decide to go to a party and leave their children alone, or they may answer the telephone and become so engrossed in the telephone conversation that they forget that their child is unattended in the bathtub. They often get in trouble with employers over impulsive behavior at work, with creditors because of impulsive spending habits, and with friends because they make commitments and then impulsively change their minds and go off with others instead. Neglectful parents with impulse-ridden behavior are restless, intolerant of stress, and lacking in consistency. Their children never know exactly what to expect and, in fact, may be abandoned for long periods by an impulsive parent who suddenly decides to go off somewhere on a trip. Children of neglecting parents of this type are likely to suffer from abandonment, lack of supervision, and emotional neglect. Additionally, because of the inconsistency they experience, they are likely to have difficulty trusting others, developing positive relationships, and being consistent themselves.

- *Mental retardation*—Although only a small percentage of neglectful parents are mentally retarded, neglect can occur if parents do not receive, or cannot comprehend, parenting information or adequate supervision to help them care for the child.

- *Reactive-depressive behavior*—These parents are so depressed they cannot parent adequately. They may be depressed because of the death or loss of a significant person in their lives, the birth of a child, or the end of a love relationship.
- *Psychotic behavior*—These parents may be in such a delusional state that they cannot adequately parent the child.

Neglectful parents often are more difficult to help than abusive parents, particularly those who are apathetic and feel hopeless. Unlike abusive parents, who still have enough spirit to be angry, many neglectful parents experience feelings of despair and futility. These feelings are much more difficult to change. By helping neglectful parents develop trust in other individuals and increase their self-esteem, particularly through links with supportive individuals, social workers can help them begin to care adequately for their own children.

Neglect is also more affected by environmental factors than other types of maltreatment. Because of its relationship to poverty, some experts note that it may be more appropriate to talk about the unmet needs of the child rather than the inappropriate actions of the parents (Zuravin, 1992) and focus on the community and societal responses to meeting the needs of children. Most of the attention and resources in the area of child maltreatment have gone to physical and sexual abuse rather than to neglect. Because studies show that neglect is just as detrimental to children as abuse—and in some instances, more so—increased concern needs to be given to this type of child maltreatment.

Psychological Maltreatment

Psychological maltreatment, also often referred to as "emotional maltreatment," is the most difficult to define, the most difficult to substantiate, and the most difficult to obtain resources for. It probably, however, is the most common type of child maltreatment, and like other types of child maltreatment, it can result in serious long-term consequences for the child. Child maltreatment professionals suggest that there are two types of emotional maltreatment: emotional abuse and emotional neglect (Garbarino, Guttman, & Seeley, 1986). Emotional abuse is viewed as acts of commission, or emotional acts against a child. Emotional abuse is often verbal; it includes being told continually how bad the child is, perhaps that parents wish the child had never been born, and being blamed for all the parents' and family's problems.

Almost all parents psychologically abuse their children at one time or another; one child development expert notes that children receive six negative messages about what they do for every one positive message (Ginott, 1965). Continual psychological abuse can lower self-esteem and undermine a child's feelings of competence. Parents also psychologically abuse children in other ways; some parents, for example, give away children's prize possessions to "another child who will appreciate it," telling children that they don't deserve special things because "they are bad." Less often, parents psychologically abuse children by shaving their heads or doing other humiliating things as forms of punishment. Children who are forced to watch parents or others in the family being beaten or otherwise abused also experience psychological abuse. Children forced to experience sexual abuse are

Words hit as hard as a fist.

"You're pathetic. You can't do anything right!"

"You disgust me. Just shut up!"

"Hey stupid! Don't you know how to listen."

"Get outta here! I'm sick of looking at your face."

"You're more trouble than you're worth."

"Why don't you go and find some other place to live!"

"I wish you were never born!"

Children believe what their parents tell them. Next time, stop and listen to what you're saying. You might not believe your ears.

Take time out. Don't take it out on your kid.

Emotional maltreatment is probably the most common type of child maltreatment. The National Committee for the Prevention of Child Abuse and other programs have developed media campaigns to focus attention on this problem.
Courtesy of the National Committee for Prevention of Child Abuse

 Write: National Committee for Prevention of Child Abuse, Box 2866E, Chicago, IL 60690

also psychologically abused; in fact, some experts suggest that the psychological abuse has just as severe, if not more severe, consequences for the sexually abused child than the sexual abuse itself (National Center on Child Abuse and Neglect, 1996).

Psychological neglect relates to acts of omission involving a child and includes the failure to meet the child's emotional needs. Parents who psychologically neglect children may provide for their physical needs, but they usually interact very little with their children.

Common parent-child activities such as cuddling, holding, reading or singing, going places together, or just talking together are nonexistent for children who are emotionally neglected. Children who do not have their emotional needs met are likely to become adults who cannot give emotionally to their own children. Such adults may not only psychologically neglect their own children but also subject them to other types of maltreatment.

Garbarino et al. (1986, p. 8) provide a broader conceptualization, using the term *psychological maltreatment,* which they define as "a concerted attack by an adult on a child's development and social competence, a pattern of psychically destructive behavior." They suggest that psychological maltreatment takes five forms:

- *Rejecting,* in which the adult refuses to acknowledge the child's worth and the legitimacy of the child's needs
- *Isolating,* in which the adult cuts the child off from normal social experiences
- *Terrorizing,* in which the adult verbally assaults the child, creating an environment of fear and terror
- *Ignoring,* in which the adult deprives the child of essential stimulation and responsiveness
- *Corrupting,* in which the adult stimulates the child to engage in destructive antisocial behavior and reinforces deviance

The conceptualization offered by Garbarino and colleagues is based on a systems/ecological perspective, which suggests that emotional deprivation or emotional trauma in one domain of children's lives increases their vulnerability to similar experiences in other domains.

Problems Associated with Adolescents

Until recently, little attention has been given in the literature about children and family problems to the special needs of adolescents. Problems associated with adolescents— including youth crime, gangs, violence, and teenage pregnancy—have currently escalated and drawn extensive media attention. Many family development specialists are quick to point out that prevention and early intervention efforts aimed at young children and families would quite likely have eliminated many of these adolescent problems. They note that adolescents who come through the juvenile justice system as delinquents, gang members, runaways, or due to pregnancy most often come from families who have experienced many of the problems discussed in this chapter but have not received appropriate services and support.

The Juvenile Justice System   Although delinquent adolescents are required by law to be treated differently than adults, the present juvenile justice system does not have the resources to address the numerous family problems and provide the extensive treatment that many juveniles need. Many who are released from the juvenile justice system quickly enter the adult criminal justice system. But as juveniles commit more severe crimes at younger ages, how to address their needs effectively and protect them, as well as those they harm, is becoming a more pressing issue. Many states are changing laws relating to juveniles to make the system tougher on them.

Runaways   In the United States today, because of the scarcity of resources available to address family problems, most resources are targeted toward younger children, who are more vulnerable than adolescents. In one state with few resources, school personnel find themselves agreeing with teenagers when they determine that their only recourse to escape a serious family situation is to run away from home. Because youth shelters and services are limited, a youth advocate in another state suggested that her only alternative to ensure that teens had safe shelter was to suggest that they get arrested so they could be booked into the juvenile detention center.

Adolescents labeled as delinquent often should more appropriately be considered "throwaways" or "push-outs," as more and more families fail to provide for the needs of their children and find themselves with emotionally damaged adolescents (National Coalition for the Homeless, 1999; Children's Defense Fund, 2000). The homeless youth population is estimated to be approximately 300,000 young people each year (Institute for Health Policy Studies, 1995). An estimated 2.8 million youth living in U.S. households reported a runaway experience during the prior year (U.S. Department of Health and Human Services, 1995). Most runaways are running in an attempt to cope with serious problems, including physical and sexual abuse, family alcoholism or drug abuse, divorce or spouse abuse, other family problems, or failure in school. A study of youth agencies found that two-thirds of teens who came to them for help had been abused or neglected and did not feel that they had a home to return to (Bass, 1992). Although the Runaway and Homeless Youth Act of 1974 provided funding for emergency shelters for runaway youth, available resources fall far short of the need. Children served are also increasingly younger: in 1994, 42% of youth served at shelters were age 14 and under, while 54% were 15 to 16 (de Anda, 1995). Runaway youth are also at risk for experiencing other problems such as crime, assault, rape, robbery, prostitution, and participation in the development of pornographic materials, as well as for getting sexually transmitted infections and diseases, including HIV/AIDS.

Academic and Employment Problems

Many adolescents experiencing problems also suffer academically. Family problems often result in learning disabilities and other learning problems. Young persons who do not feel good about themselves and are faced with daily problems at home are not likely to do well in school. Increased concern is being expressed about dropout rates of youth and the high illiteracy rate of both young and older adults. The 1997 high school completion rate for whites was 82.9% for males and 83.2% for females. For African Americans, those figures were 73.5% for males and 76% for females. For Latinos, they were 54.9% for males and 54.6% for females (Statistical Abstract, 1999). Even with a high school education, increasing numbers of persons in the United States are illiterate. A recent study found that 56% of Latino adults, 44% of African American adults, and 16% of white adults in the United States are illiterate.

Youths who do not complete high school suffer in their ability to locate suitable employment. The Children's Defense Fund (2000) reports that a college degree is now the single greatest factor in determining access to better job opportunities and higher earnings, yet two-thirds of U.S. high school graduates lack the college degree that is critical to success. There is a serious lack of employment available for young adults, particularly those who are African American and Latino, even when they do graduate from high school. In 1993, more than half of all African American high school graduates not enrolled in college were unemployed, whereas only approximately 25% of white high school dropouts were unemployed (Children's Defense Fund, 1994). The increasing dropout and illiteracy rates, especially for Latino and African American populations, have raised serious questions about the ability of the United States to maintain an adequate pool of qualified workers, since the demand for employees requires a minimum of a high school education and technological skills. The limited availability of job skills training and adequate employment suggests that poverty rates, particularly for African Americans and Latinos, will continue to increase.

Teen Pregnancy   Another major problem facing our country today is teen pregnancy. While the rates of children born to teen mothers have decreased slightly in recent years, births by members of this age group still present a number of problems. The rates differ significantly by ethnicity: in 1996, births to whites, African Americans, and Latinos amounted to 11.3%, 22.9%, and 17.4% of the total, respectively. In that same year, nearly 39% of the births to teen parents were to mothers 15 years old and younger (*Statistical Abstract,* 1999). There are also ethnic differences in relation to decisions made about what to do when a pregnancy occurs; white females are much more likely to have an abortion, while African American and Latino females are much more likely to give birth and raise the child. Fewer than 10% of these youths give their child up for adoption. Becoming a parent when a teenager interrupts, sometimes permanently, the teen's successful transition into adulthood.

Teens today are faced with a great deal of pressure from many sources—peers, the media, advertising—to see their primary self-worth in terms of their sexuality. With limited opportunities to be successful in other arenas, such as the family, school, and the workplace, many male and female teens feel that using their sexuality, and producing a baby, are the only ways they can feel good about themselves and have someone to love them. Many factors are associated with teen pregnancy, including poverty, low self-esteem, lack of information about reproduction, school failure, lack of appropriate health care and other services, and poor family relationships. Additionally, emphasis on pregnancy prevention and intervention has focused on teenage females, and little has been done in regard to prevention and intervention with teenage males. A survey

regarding the use of condoms by adolescents, for example, found that only 2.1% to 38.0% used them when they had intercourse (de Anda, 1995). Even more important, attention to pregnancy prevention often begins only when teens (females) reach age 13. Developing positive self-esteem, effective decision-making skills, a strong value system, and a sense of responsibility for one's self and others—all major deterrents to teen pregnancy— are characteristics shaped from birth on.

Whereas in the past most teens who became pregnant relinquished their babies for adoption, either formally through agencies or informally through relatives, today the majority of teens are choosing to keep their babies. This places tremendous pressure on both the teen mothers and their children. Infants born to teenagers are much more likely to have low birth weight, be premature babies, or have congenital or other health problems. Their mothers also are more likely to drop out of school, remain unemployed or underemployed, and raise their children in poverty than parents who are not teenagers. The cycle often repeats itself. Teen pregnancy is both a cause and a result of poverty. In 1996, teens of color constituted approximately 40% of the U.S. poverty population for this age group (*Statistical Abstract,* 1999).

Crime   Increased concern is also being raised about youth crime. Key findings of the 1999 national report of juvenile offenders and victims are summarized here (Office of Juvenile Justice and Delinquency Prevention, 1999; see also Table 11.2):

- In 1997, law enforcement agencies made an estimated 2.8 million arrests of persons under the age of 18.
- In 1997, an estimated 2,300 murders (approximately 12% of all murders) in the

TABLE 11.2 INCREASES IN ARREST RATES OF ADOLESCENTS UNDER 18, 1989–1998

Offense	Percent Increase in Arrest Rate
Total	24
Violent crimes (murder, forced rape, robbery, aggravated assault)	15
Property crimes (burglary, larceny/ theft, motor vehicle theft, arson)	−12
Other assaults	68
Weapons violations	15
Drug abuse violations	86

Source: Adapted from Snyder (1999).

United States involved at least one juvenile offender.

- Between 1981 and 1997, the violent crime arrest rate for juvenile males and females increased 20% and 40%, respectively.
- Between 1994 and 1997, the number of murders involving a juvenile offender dropped 39%; this decline was attributable entirely to a decline in homicides by firearms.
- One of every four juveniles who will come to a juvenile court charged with a violent offense will have a court record by their 14th birthday.
- On a typical day in 1997, nearly 106,000 juveniles were being held in a residential facility as a result of a law violation.
- African American juveniles are held in residential custody in the United States at twice the rate for Latinos and five times the rate for whites.
- Allowing one youth to leave high school for a life of crime and drug abuse costs society $2 million (pp. 1–2).

Gangs Increased numbers of youth are also joining gangs. The 1996 National Youth Gang Survey revealed the following key results (U.S. Department of Justice, Office of Justice Programs, 1999):

- There were 4,824 jurisdictions throughout the country with active youth gangs in 1996; some 30,818 gangs and 846,428 gang members were active in these jurisdictions.
- Gang activity was reported in 74% of large cities, 57% of suburban counties, 34% of small cities, and 25% of rural counties.
- The number of gang members nationwide was evenly split between juveniles and adults.
- Over 70% of gang members were reported to be between 15 to 24 years old.
- Males were reported to be substantially more involved in gang activity than their female counterparts (females constituted only 10% of gang members throughout the country).
- Caucasians accounted for 14% of all gang members nationwide.
- Latino and African American gang members continued to constitute the majority of gang members.
- Young gang members were estimated to have been involved in 2,364 homicides in large cities and 561 homicides in suburban counties.
- Youth gang members were more involved in larceny/theft, followed by aggravated assault, burglary, and motor vehicle theft.
- An estimated 43% of drug sales in the surveyed jurisdictions involved gang members (pp. xiii–xiv).

The results of this survey indicate that the youth gang problem in this country is substantial and affects communities of all sizes.

A major reason that many youth join gangs is to belong; many gang members indicate that gangs are "like families to them," and for many youth, gangs replace the nurturing and support and sense of belonging that they find lacking in their own families. Gang members often commit crimes or violent acts as part of initiation rites or other gang-related activities. Peer pressure is considerable for youths who join gangs, and it is difficult for members to say no to their peers when they become involved in inappropriate and/or illegal activities and to leave gangs once they join them (McWhirter, McWhirter, McWhirter, & McWhirter, 1993).

Suicide and Children's Mental Health

Changes in society, communities, and the family have resulted in increased instability of many children and adolescents in the United States. Children are too often the victims of divorce, family and community violence, substance abuse, and other types of family, community, and societal dysfunction. In one recent study, researchers found that 12% of all U.S. children suffer some type of emotional illness, but fewer than 28% of those children receive treatment. Many children and adolescents become involved in substance abuse, becoming alcoholics or addicts, often at young ages, or suffering serious physical and emotional injuries as a result. In 1997, accidents were cited as the number one cause of death among adolescents. Suicide was the third leading cause of death for adolescents and the fifth leading cause of death for children 5 to 14 years old (*Statistical Abstract*, 1999).

There were 30,535 suicides in the United States in 1997 (83.7 suicides per day). Of this number, 4,186 (13.7%), were committed by persons 15 to 24 years old. Males are more successful than females in committing suicide

Depression and suicide are common among youth, particularly those who feel helpless and hopeless about their lives. These youth have all experienced recent losses of family members through violence, illness, and suicide.
© Joseph Sohm; ChromoSohm Inc./Corbis

because their methods are more lethal; in 1997, there were 4.1 male completions for each female completion (American Association of Suicidology, 1999). It is estimated that each suicide intimately affects at least six other people. Suicidal individuals often try other ways to stop their pain first, frequently with drugs and alcohol, before turning to suicide. Children and adolescents who attempt suicide feel helpless, hopeless, and powerless, and they are often experiencing or have experienced a series of losses in their lives. When they are in an environment over which they feel they have no control, sexual experimentation, use of alcohol and drugs, suicide attempts, eating disorders, and other risk-taking behaviors become ways to either gain control over what they perceive as an uncontrollable environment or to escape from it.

Professionals working with adolescents believe that *mattering,* or the degree to which a person believes he or she is important to others, is a significant aspect in the prevention of mental health problems among children and youth. They identify three aspects of mattering that are significant: (1) feeling that you command attention from others, (2) feeling that you are important to others, and (3) feeling that others depend on you (Rosenberg & McCullough, 1992).

Homelessness There is a strong relationship between other problems discussed in this chapter and homelessness (see Chapter 8). As rents and purchase prices of homes throughout the United States continue to escalate, and federal funds to build low-income housing continue to be reduced, more and more families and their children are becoming homeless.

Families with children are the fastest-growing group of homeless in the United States. The average homeless family consists of two parents with an average age of 27 and three children with an average age of 6. Many families are forced to live in welfare hotels in unsafe neighborhoods, tents, or automobiles. Without a permanent address, it is difficult for parents to locate employment and for children to attend school. The psychological consequences of being homeless can be developmentally devastating to children, who may then repeat the same patterns with their own families.

SUMMARY

Children, youth, and families in the United States experience problems for many reasons. From a systems/ecological perspective, factors associated with family problems are complex and interactive. Societal and cultural factors, as well as the level of support available to families from the communities in which they reside, have an impact on the nature and extent of problems experienced by families. However, all families have strengths that can be used to draw from when they do experience problems. Effective intervention and prevention programs can capitalize on these strengths when working with children, youth, and families. But effective intervention and prevention efforts must be undertaken within the broader context of understanding the complexities of the family problems discussed in this chapter. In Chapter 12, we address programs and policies that help families in need and the roles that social workers play in providing these policies and programs.

KEY TERMS

battered child syndrome
blended family
child neglect
codependent
custody
enablers
family
family violence
feminization of poverty

incest
mediation
nonorganic failure to thrive
physical abuse
psychological maltreatment
sexual abuse

DISCUSSION QUESTIONS

1. Identify and discuss at least three of the issues that must be considered when defining a family problem.

2. Discuss briefly at least three issues that often surface in families who experience divorce.

3. Describe at least four roles family members might play where substance abuse is a problem.

4. Describe the dynamics of a violent spousal relationship.

5. Identify and briefly describe the four types of child maltreatment.

6. Identify at least five factors likely to be associated with families who abuse or neglect their children.

7. Briefly discuss at least four reasons that teenagers today are likely to become parents.

8. Why are children, youth, and families of color more likely to be at risk of serious problems than white children, youth, and families?

INFOTRAC COLLEGE EDITION

To learn more about topics included in this chapter, enter the following search terms:

child maltreatment

domestic violence

emotional abuse

family structure

teenage pregnancy

unmarried mothers

youth gangs

ON THE INTERNET

http://www.calib.com/nccanch/

http://www.acf.dhhs.gov/

http://www.americanhumane.org/

http://child.cornell.edu/

http://childhelpusa.org/

http://www.childrensdefense.org/

http://www.cwla.org/

http://www.preventchildabuse.org/

REFERENCES

Abbott, J., Johnson, R., Koziol-McLain, J., & Lowenstein, S. (1995). Domestic violence against women: Incidence and prevalence in an emergency department population. *Journal of the American Medical Association, 273,* 1763–1767.

Ackerman, R. (1983). *Children of alcoholics.* Holmes Beach, CA: Learning Publications.

American Association of Suicidology. (1999). 1997 national suicide statistics and facts. http://www.suicidology.org/suicides_statistics97.htm.

Arnold, C. (1998). *Children and stepfamilies: A snapshot.* Washington, DC: Center for Law and Social Policy.

Bachman, R., & Saltzman, L. E. (1995). *Violence against women: Estimates from the redesigned survey.* U.S. Department of Justice Special Project NCJ-154348. Washington, DC: Office of Justice Programs, Bureau of Justice Statistics.

Barnett, O. W., & Fagan, R. W. (1993). Alcohol use in male spouse abusers and their female partners. *Journal of Family Violence, 8*(1), 1–25.

Bass, D. (1992). *Helping vulnerable youths: Runaway and homeless adolescents in the United States.* Washington, DC: NASW Press.

Beattie, M. (1987). *Codependent no more.* Center City, MN: Hazelden Foundation.

Berliner, L. (1995). Child sexual abuse: Direct practice. In R. Edwards (Ed.), *Encyclopedia of social work* (Vol. 1, 408–417). Washington, DC: NASW Press.

Black, C. (1987). *It will never happen to me.* New York: Ballantine.

Bowlby J. (1951). Maternal care and mental health. *Bulletin of the World Health Organization, 3,* 355–534.

Brissett-Chapman, S. (1995). Child abuse and neglect: Direct practice. In R. Edwards (Ed.), *Encyclopedia of social work* (Vol. 1, pp. 361–362). Washington, DC: NASW Press.

Bronfenbrenner, U. (1979). *The ecology of human development.* Cambridge, MA: Harvard University Press.

Carter, E., & M. McGoldrick. (1998). *The expanded family life cycle: Individual, family, and social perspectives* (3rd ed.). Boston: Allyn & Bacon.

Children's Defense Fund. (1994). *Children's defense budget: An analysis of the FY 1994 federal budget and children.* Washington, DC: Author.

Children's Defense Fund. (2000). *The state of America's children yearbook 2000.* Washington, DC: Author.

Conte, J. (1995). Child sexual abuse: Overview. In R. Edwards (Ed.), *Encyclopedia of social work* (Vol. 1, pp. 402–408). Washington, DC: NASW Press.

Davis, L. (1995). Domestic violence. In R. Edwards (Ed.), *Encyclopedia of social work* (Vol. 1, pp. 780–789). Washington, DC: NASW Press.

de Anda, D. (1995). Adolescent overview. In R. Edwards (Ed.), *Encyclopedia of social work* (Vol. 1). Washington, DC: NASW Press.

DiNitto, D. (1999). *Social welfare: Politics and public policy.* Boston: Allyn & Bacon.

Finkelhor, D. (1986). *A sourcebook on child sexual abuse.* Newbury Park, CA: Sage.

Finkelhor, D., Hotaling, G., Lewis, I., & Smith, C. (1990). Sexual abuse in a national survey of adult men and women: Prevalence, characteristics, and risk factors. *Child Abuse and Neglect, 14,* 19–28.

Frieze, I., & Browne, A. (1989). Violence in marriage. In L. Ohlin & M. Tonry (Eds.), *Family violence.* Chicago: University of Chicago Press.

Garbarino, J. (1992). *Children and families in the social environment* (2nd ed.). New York: Aldine de Gruyter.

Garbarino, J., Guttman, E., & Seeley, J. (1986). *The psychologically battered child.* Lexington, MA: Lexington.

Ginott, H. (1965). *Between parent and child.* New York: Avon.

Goode, W. J. (1964). *The family.* Upper Saddle River, NJ: Prentice Hall.

Hotaling, G. T., & Sugarman, D. B. (1990). A risk marker analysis of assaulted wives. *Journal of Family Violence, 5*(1), 1–13.

Institute for Health Policy Studies. (1995). *Street youth at risk for AIDS.* San Francisco: University of California.

Kaiser Permanente. (1995). *Children now.* Los Angeles: Author.

Kids Count Data Bank. (1999). Greenwich, CT: Annie E. Casey Foundation.

Korbin, J. (1982). *Cross-cultural perspectives on child abuse.* Berkeley: University of California Press.

Koss, M. P., Woodruff, W. J., & Koss, P. G. (1991). Deleterious effects of criminal victimization on women's health and medical utilization. *Archives of Internal Medicine, 151,* 342–347.

Laird, J. (1995). Lesbians: Parenting. In R. Edwards (Ed.), *Encyclopedia of social work* (Vol. 2, pp. 1604–1616). Washington, DC: NASW Press.

McLeer, S. V., & Anwar, R. (1989). A study of battered women in an emergency department. *American Journal of Public Health, 79,* 65–66.

McWhirter, J., McWhirter, B., McWhirter, A., & McWhirter, E. (1993). *At-risk youth: A comprehensive response.* Pacific Grove, CA.: Brooks/Cole.

Moses, A., & Hawkins, R. (1982). *Counseling lesbian women and gay men: A life issues approach.* St. Louis: Mosby.

National Center on Addiction and Substance Abuse. (1999). *No safe haven: Children of substance-abusing parents.* Available: http://www.casacolumbia.org.

National Center on Child Abuse and Neglect. (1980). *Neglect: Mobilizing community resources.* Washington, DC: U.S. Department of Health and Human Services.

National Center on Child Abuse and Neglect. (1993). *Child sexual abuse: Intervention and treatment issues.* Washington, DC: U.S. Department of Health and Human Services.

National Center on Child Abuse and Neglect. (1996). *Third national incidence study of child abuse and neglect.* Available: http://www.calib.com/nccanch/pubs/.

National Coalition for the Homeless. (1999). *Homeless youth: NCH Fact Sheet #11.* Available: http://nch.ari.net/youth.html.

Office of Juvenile Justice and Delinquency Prevention. (1999). *OJJDP statistical briefing book: The national report notebook.* Available: http://www. ojjdp.ncjrs.org.

Pan, H. S., Neidig, P. H., & O'Leary, K. D. (1994). Predicting mild and severe husband-to-wife physical aggression. *Journal of Consulting and Clinical Psychology, 62*(5), 975–981.

Polansky, N., Ammons, P., & Gaudin, J. (1985, January). Loneliness and isolation in child neglect. *Social Casework,* pp. 38–47.

Polansky, N., Chalmers, M., Buttenwieser, M., & Williams, D. (1991). *Damaged parents: An anatomy of child neglect* (2nd ed.). Chicago: University of Chicago Press.

Quinn, P., & Allen, K. (1989). Facing challenges and making compromises: How single mothers endure. *Family Relations, 38,* 300–395.

Randall, T. (1990). Domestic violence intervention calls for more than treating injuries. *Journal of the American Medical Association, 262,* 939–940.

Robertson, M. (1989). *Homeless youth in Hollywood: Patterns of alcohol use, 1989.* Berkeley, CA: Alcohol Research Group.

Rosenberg, M., & McCullough, B. (1992). Mattering: Inferred significance and mental health among adolescents. *Research in Community and Mental Health, 2,* 163–182.

Schaef, A. (1986). *Co-dependence: Misunderstood— mistreated.* San Francisco: Harper & Row.

Sgroi, S. (1982). *Handbook of clinical intervention in child sexual abuse.* Lexington, MA: Lexington.

Snyder, H. (1999). *Juvenile arrests 1998.* Washington, DC: Office of Juvenile Justice and Delinquency Prevention.

Statistical Abstract of the United States. (1999). Washington, DC: Bernan.

Stepfamily Foundation. (2000). *Statistics on stepfamilies.* New York: Author.

Tower, C. (1996). *Understanding child abuse and neglect* (3rd ed.). Boston: Allyn & Bacon.

U.S. Department of Health and Human Services. (1995). *Youth with runaway, throwaway, and homeless experiences: Prevalence of drug use and other at-risk behaviors, 1995.* Silver Spring, MD: National Clearinghouse on Families and Youth.

U.S. Department of Health and Human Services. (1999). *The scope and problem of child maltreatment.* Available: http://www.acf.dhhs.gov/programs/cb/ncanprob.htm.

U.S. Department of Justice. (1998a). *Prevalence, incidence, and consequences of violence against women: Findings from the National Violence against Women Survey.* Washington, DC: Author.

U.S. Department of Justice. (1998b). *Violence by intimates: Analysis of data on crimes by current or former spouses, boyfriends, and girlfriends.* Washington, DC: Author.

U.S. Department of Justice, Office of Justice Programs. (1999). *National Youth Gang Survey, 1999.* Rockville, MD: Juvenile Justice Clearinghouse.

U.S. National Center for Health Statistics. (1999). Fastats. Available: http://www.cdc.gov/nchs/.

Violence against Women Office. (2000). *Summary of criminal provisions of the Violence against Women Act.* Available: http://www.ojp.usdoj.gov/vawo/laws/.

Walker, L. (1999). *The battered woman syndrome* (2nd ed.). New York: Springer.

Wallerstein, J., & Blakeslee, S. (1996). *Second chances: Men, women and children a decade after divorce* (2nd ed.). New York: Houghton Mifflin.

Wallerstein, J., & Kelley, J. (1996). *Surviving the breakup: How children and parents cope with divorce.* New York: Basic Books.

Werner, E., & Smith, R. (1992). *Overcoming the odds: High risk children from birth to adulthood.* Ithaca, NY: Cornell University Press.

White, J. W., & Koss, M. P. (1991). Courtship violence: Incidence in a national sample of higher education students. *Violence and Victims, 6*(4), 247–256.

Zuravin, S. (1992). Child-neglecting adolescent mothers: How do they differ from their nonmaltreating counterparts? *Journal of Interpersonal Violence,* (74), 471–490.

SUGGESTED FURTHER READINGS

Allen-Meares, P. (1995). Children: Mental health. In R. Edwards (Ed.), *Encyclopedia of social work* (Vol. 1). Washington, DC: NASW Press.

Costin, L. B., Karger, H. J., & Stoesz, D. (1996). *The politics of child abuse in America.* New York: Oxford University Press.

Fraser, M. (1997). (Ed.). *Risk and resilience in childhood: An ecological perspective.* Washington, DC: NASW Press.

Gelles, R., & Cornell, C. (1990). *Intimate violence in families* (2nd ed.). Newbury Park, CA: Sage.

Kozol, J. (1995). *Amazing grace: The lives of children and the conscience of a nation.* New York: Crown.

McNeece, C. A., & DiNitto, D. (1994). *Chemical dependency: A systems approach.* Upper Saddle River, NJ: Prentice Hall.

Miringoff, M., & Miringoff, M. (1999). *The social health of the nation: How America is really doing.* New York: Oxford University Press.

Pelzer, D. (1995). *A child called "it": One child's courage to survive.* Dearfield Beach, FL: Health Communications.

Reid, J., Macchetto, P., & Foster, S. (1999). *No safe haven: Children of substance-abusing parents.* New York: National Center on Addiction and Substance Abuse.

Williams, C. (1995). Adolescent pregnancy. In R. Edwards (Ed.), *Encyclopedia of social work* (Vol. 1). Washington, DC: NASW Press.

SERVICES TO CHILDREN, YOUTH, AND FAMILIES

Juanita Kingbird, a social worker with the local family services agency, is involved in a number of activities that prevent families from becoming dysfunctional, as well as ones that help families when they have special needs. Her agency provides a variety of programs, including parenting programs that teach child care to teenage parents; an outreach program that seeks out parents who are under stress or need help parenting their children; and individual, family, and group counseling for children and family members of all ages. Recently, the agency has developed a shelter for adolescents who cannot remain in their own homes and a respite care program for families of children with developmental disabilities. The agency also provides homemaker services, child care, and employment services to help families remain economically self-sufficient and able to stay together.

Juanita begins a typical day by returning a crisis call from a mother whose son ran away from home the night before, after a family argument. She calls the school social worker and arranges for her to try to locate the boy if he is in school and talk with him. She then holds two counseling sessions with adolescents who are staying in the shelter, focusing on their feelings about becoming independent and separating from their families. Juanita then leaves for the local high school, where she leads a support group for teenage parents. After the group, she meets individually with several of the parents and helps one of them obtain an appointment with a specialist for her developmentally delayed infant. She has a quick lunch with the school social worker to coordinate services both are providing to some of her clients, and then she meets with the runaway boy, who did come to school, getting him to agree to meet with her and his mother later on in the day. On the way back to her office, Juanita stops off to make a home visit to one of her clients who has been emotionally abusing her two young children. Juanita interacts with the mother and her children, role-modeling good communication patterns and ways to give feedback and set limits positively.

Juanita returns to the office in time to attend a staffing on another family with social workers from the five other agencies involved. Although the family has many serious problems, the coordinated intervention plan developed by the agencies seems to be effective, as everyone reports the family is making progress. Juanita then meets with the runaway boy and his parents. They negotiate family rules and boundaries and agree to try to live together without major conflicts, returning in a week for another family counseling session. After a long and eventful day, Juanita leaves the agency to go home, glad that she has a supportive family waiting for her so that she does not burn out from getting too emotionally involved with her clients.

Juanita enjoys her job very much. Although she finds it difficult to deal with the many needs of the families with whom she is assigned to work, especially when children are suffering, she has learned to share small successes with family members. "If I can make things better in some small way each day for one child or one parent, my job is more than worthwhile," she stated in a recent newspaper interview.

Programs and policies that address the needs of children, youth, and families are as diverse as the types of needs experienced. Traditionally, the system that has provided programs and policies that address child and family concerns has been called the **child welfare service delivery system.** This system includes the "network of public and voluntary agencies in social work practice that specializes in the prevention, amelioration, or remediation of social problems which are related to the functioning of the parent-child relationship network through the development and provision of specific child welfare services" (Kadushin & Martin, 1988, p. 30).

In this chapter, we focus on services that address the children, youth, and family-related needs discussed in Chapter 11. We also discuss the roles that social workers play in providing services to children, youth, and families.

CURRENT PHILOSOPHICAL ISSUES

All policies and programs that address the needs of children, youth, and their families must consider not only the social and cultural context of the child's family, the community, and the broader environment but also a number of current philosophical issues and assumptions.

The Right to a Permanent, Nurturing Family

The first assumption is that every child has a right to grow up in a permanent, nurturing home and that every attempt must be made to provide such a home whenever possible. This assumes that the child's own home should be seen as the best option for that child whenever possible. Such a philosophical position dictates that services should be provided first to the child's family and that every attempt should be made to keep the child and the family together. This position has led to the development of **family preservation programs,** or services provided to a child and his or her family while they remain together, rather than placing the child in a foster home or other type of substitute care. Increasingly, special attention is being given to those services that will keep families together rather than removing children from their family settings.

In the past, many children receiving services in an overloaded service delivery system became lost in the system, with no chance to return home, be adopted, or become emancipated. There was no way of determining exactly how many children were in substitute care, and in some instances, children were sent to other states because care was less expensive and responsibility for their care could be shifted elsewhere. Although foster care was, and still is, supposed to be temporary, many children placed in foster care at young ages needed extended care and left only because they reached age 18 (the system does not provide care for adults). Children often lived in five or more foster homes and had as many or more social workers. Some children moved around so much they never went to the same school for an entire school year.

Concern among many individuals and advocacy organizations has led to legislation at both the state and federal levels that mandates **permanency planning.** This concept ensures that when a child and family first receive services, a specific plan is developed that states what is planned to help keep that family together if possible and, if not, what will be done to provide a permanent, nurturing home for the child. Specific actions are identified to take place within certain time limits, and these actions are monitored by the court and/or a citizen review panel. If a family receives services without making enough progress to provide for a child's most basic needs, the parents' rights can be terminated and the child placed in an adoptive home, rather than the child remaining in limbo in the foster care system. Such planning allows agencies to make more realistic decisions about helping children and their families and ensures that families know specifically what they need to do to be allowed to continue to parent their children.

The Best Interests of the Child

Decisions about needs of children and families should be based on what is in the **best interests of the child.** Sometimes, even with the most appropriate intervention, it is questionable whether it is best for children to remain with their own families. In such circumstances, should decisions regarding where a child is placed (that is, remain with his or her own family or be placed elsewhere) focus on the child's best interests, the parents' best interests, or the family's best interests? Although experts agree that the rights of both the parents and their children need to be considered, current trends give attention first to the child's best interests. This means that before any decision is made, careful attention must be given to what the most beneficial outcome will be for that particular child. In *Before the Best Interests of the Child* (1979) and *Beyond the Best Interests of the Child* (1973), Goldstein, Freud, and Solnit give careful consideration to this issue. They argue that in determining what is best for a child, the **least detrimental alternative** for that child must be considered. In other words, if it is detrimental for a child to remain with his or her family, one must then ask what the least harmful alternative would be.

Legislation now requires that courts appoint a guardian *ad litem* (one who advocates for the minor on a limited and special basis) in certain child welfare situations, such as hearings when a parent's rights are being terminated. The guardian *ad litem*'s sole purpose is to represent the best interests of the child and to make a recommendation to the court with those interests in mind. This is especially important in situations where the parents have an attorney advocating for the return of a child to the parents, and the state child welfare agency has an attorney advocating for placing the child in substitute care or terminating parental rights.

Goldstein and colleagues (1973) also focus on considering who is the most significant person(s) to be involved in planning changes in a child's life. Until recently, decisions regarding

where a child should be raised usually involved the child's biological mother and then father. But often, the early rearing of many children is by a relative or a foster parent rather than their biological parents. Goldstein, Freud, Solnit, and others stress the importance of considering the child's **psychological parent** rather than biological parent, who might not always be the same individual.

Considerations before State Intervention

Another important philosophical issue is determining under what circumstances the community or state should intervene in family matters. In the past, families were considered sacred, and intervention in family matters seldom took place. Such intervention, when allowed, has been based on the doctrine of *parens patriae*. This doctrine is based on the concept that the state is a parent to all of its children and has the obligation, through regulatory and legislative powers, to protect them and, when necessary, provide them with resources needed to keep them safe.

Now, with increased attention to such family problems as child abuse, child neglect, domestic violence, and substance abuse, many children are growing up in unsafe and nonnurturing environments. Many family advocates argue that early intervention is necessary to keep a family together, as well as to protect the child from growing up with severe emotional damage. Other advocates suggest that intervention in families should take place less often, because there are too many instances when the intervention—especially when limited resources do not allow for the family to be rehabilitated—is more harmful than no intervention at all. These advocates suggest that intervention in families should take place only when requested by a parent, such as in child custody disputes; when a parent chooses to relinquish parental rights and place that child for adoption, or when a parent is seriously mal-treating a child.

The issue of when a government entity has the right or the obligation to intervene is increasingly before the courts. Many child advocacy groups have filed class action suits against state child protective services agencies, charging failure to provide needed services to protect children from serious maltreatment. But in 1990 the Wisconsin State Supreme Court ruled that a state cannot be expected to protect all children in the state who are at risk from serious injury or death. This issue is likely to come to the attention of the U.S. Supreme Court at some point.

Preventing Family Disruption and Dysfunction

Another major issue is whether scarce re-sources should be targeted toward preventing family problems. And, if prevention is chosen, should it be primary, secondary, or tertiary? All three are important in strengthening families. Most intervention with families today occurs after problems have already occurred rather than before, and even those programs are not available to many parents and families in need of such services (see Box 12.1).

Because resources are scarce, little atten-tion is given to any type of prevention at all. Of the few prevention programs available, the focus is tertiary in nature. For example, the current focus is on family preservation; how-ever, in many instances children must be severely abused or families must experience a serious crisis before services are available, and by that time family preservation is not as likely to be a realistic option.

How Accountable Are Parents?

A final issue receiving increased attention today is the extent to which parents should be held accountable in regard to caring for their children and what should be done to parents who do not give children adequate care. A number of specialists in family dynamics sug-gest that punishment is more likely to make parents angry and less likely to teach them how to be better parents. These specialists hold that effective intervention programs and the availability of resources are much more optimal for children than punishment of their parents and likely separation from them. Other experts suggest that a compromise is most effective: that parents whose family problems pose severe consequences for their children be brought before the court and ordered to receive help, with punishment ordered if the help is refused.

The relationships between parents' prob-lems and consequences for a child are also coming before the courts for decisions. For example, should a woman who fears for her own life if she intervenes to protect her child be held accountable for the injury of the child? In two recent child abuse fatality cases, one in New York and one in Texas, a battered woman was charged with failing to protect her child from her violent husband. In the New York case, the mother was found not guilty. In the Texas case, the woman received a prison sen-tence that was longer than the sentence her husband received because she was tried sepa-rately by a different jury. The court also termi-nated her parental rights. The 1995 case of the woman from South Carolina who drowned her two young sons also resulted in extensive debate. Should parents who have experienced severe maltreatment themselves as children and/or who have serious emotional problems

BOX
12.1

Tasha and Family Deserve a Good Chance

Tasha loves her children. This is not in question. Tasha holds Patik and Felicia, ages 2 and 4, close to her, pulling their heads to hers, smiling, singing the Barney song. "I love you . . . you love me . . ."

Her two older children, Robert and Honree ("I was 13 when I had him," says Tasha. "What did I know about spelling a French name?"), are helping women lay out doughnuts, sandwiches and loaves of bread on a table set up on a sidewalk in inner-city Baltimore.

The food is for giving away to hungry people. It has been donated to an organization that does that, and more. For four days, Tasha and her children have stayed in a shelter operated by this organization. While food is being laid out, a taxi pulls up, carrying a woman and a little boy. Both have been beaten by the boy's father. They, too, are looking for shelter. And more.

Honree, at 8, the oldest of Tasha's children, watches the women giving away food, then asks if he, too, may have a pair of the thin, white rubber gloves the women wear to handle food. The next time someone approaches the table, Honree is right there.

"May I help you?" he says. "You can have one sandwich, a doughnut and three loaves of bread, if you want to. May I get it for you? Here, will you sign this?" A man takes a second sandwich. "Please," says Honree, "there isn't enough. You can only have one sandwich." The man faces down this dignified boy and, after a couple of beats, returns the second sandwich.

For several hours, Honree runs the free food table. He is polite and firm. . . . He means to do it right.

Tasha has laid Patik down for his nap. Patik sleeps, curled on a blanket on the sidewalk. His sweet baby face carries in it all the possibilities in the world. He does not yet know how limited his are.

Meanwhile, Tasha answers questions from the white, middle-class women who have come to help distribute food, only to find an 8-year-old boy doing it better.

"My own mother was a junkie," says Tasha. "She's been clean for six years now.

be held accountable for their actions? If so, should those experiences be considered when penalties for their actions are assessed? When the South Carolina woman was a young child, her mother committed suicide, her stepfather molested her when she was a young teenager, and she had a history of psychiatric problems. Although the prosecuting attorney asked that the woman receive the death penalty, the jury recommended that she receive a life sentence. Unless efforts are increased to prevent problems such as domestic violence and child maltreatment from occurring and to intervene quickly and effectively when they do, many more tragic situations such as these are likely to occur.

She made me go to a parenting program for a year. My children's fathers? Two are dead from drugs. The other two, they don't do anything for the kids. Nothing at all. Yea, I did drugs. I'm in the program now. AA, you know?"

Tasha looks at Felicia, who, at 4, already is beautiful. "I got to do what I can to make sure her life is different. I don't want her to be 13 and make the choices I made. Or only have the choices I had. But it's hard. I can't get a good job because I can't get my GED because I can't get child care. Actually, I can't get any kind of job until I can work out the child-care thing. I'm getting a place to live next Monday. The social worker called and said we'd go look at it. I told her I don't have to look at it. If it's got a roof and walls and locks on the door and windows and a toilet that flushes, I'll take it."

Tasha's children play with one another, and with others. Robert and Felicia sing a song about a rabbit and smile at everybody. Their smiles can light a whole day. They hug people, too, probably because they have been hugged. Honree works the food table. It seems clear he's been helping his mother take care of the smaller kids. This is an intelligent boy, alert, interested, quick, kind. One wants to do something. Something that will give Honree his chance. Something that will give Tasha an opportunity to give Honree— and Robert and Felicia and Patik—a chance. Something.

One thinks of politics. But politics is theory and politicians take too long to do anything. Tasha, Patik, Felicia, Robert and Honree are not theory—they are people— and they don't have too long.

Two men, old and wasted, approach the free food table. The sandwiches are all gone, Honree tells them. Tasha looks up and seeing the old men, takes two sandwiches that had been given to her children and says, "Here. Take these. My kids got fed last night. They're not as hungry as you."

And so it goes.

Source: Written by award-winning TV producer and best-selling author, Linda Ellerbee (1995), p. A15. Used by permission of *Austin American Statesman.*

DEFINING SERVICES TO CHILDREN, YOUTH, AND FAMILIES

Traditionally, services to children, youth, and families have been defined as **child welfare services.** Initial definitions of child welfare, promoted by child welfare experts such as Alfred Kadushin, focused on residual services, appropriate when the normal institutional arrangements for meeting social needs of children and youth—primarily the family—break down. In his seminal child welfare book, Kadushin (1980) suggests that the goals of child welfare services are "to reinforce, supplement or substitute the functions that parents have difficulty in performing; and to improve conditions for children and their families by modifying existing social institutions or organizing new ones" (p. 5).

The Social Security Act of 1935, the most significant piece of national legislation ever passed in relation to providing support to children and families, has a specific section (Title IV-B) that mandates states to provide a full range of child welfare services, defined as follows (Section 425):

[P]ublic social services which supplement, or substitute for parental care and supervision for the purpose of:
1. preventing or remedying, or assisting in the solution of problems which may result in the neglect, abuse, exploitation or delinquency of children,
2. protecting and caring for homeless, dependent, or neglected children,
3. protecting and promoting the welfare of children of working mothers and
4. otherwise protecting and promoting the welfare of children, including the strengthening of their own homes where possible or, where needed, the provision of adequate care of children away from their homes in foster family homes or day care or other child care facilities.

Because of negative connotations associated with the term *welfare* and the current emphasis on the importance of strengthening the family to support the child, child welfare services today more often are referred to as services to children, youth, and families (or as child and family services). They also are viewed in a broad sense, not only focusing on the more traditional child welfare services of child protection for maltreated children, foster care, and adoption to keep children safe but also emphasizing family preservation and supportive services to families, such as child care and parenting programs.

THE HISTORY OF SERVICES TO CHILDREN, YOUTH, AND FAMILIES

Some historians argue that societal attitudes toward children and families have improved significantly since the settling of the United States, as have policies and programs that are supportive of children and families. Others argue that little has changed for the better and that history has had a tendency to repeat itself. They suggest that a review of debates about the needs of children and families in the 1880s and early 1900s includes many of the issues discussed today—youth crime, family violence, and substance abuse. Regardless of whether today's children and families are better or worse off than in the past, reviewing the history of services to children, youth, and families shows clearly the historical base of our present child welfare service delivery system.

Colonial Times

In colonial times, children were considered to be the responsibility of their families, and little attention was given to children whose families were available to provide for them, no matter whether the family actually met the child's needs. Children usually came to the attention of authorities only if they were orphaned and relatives were not available to provide for them. Churches and a few private orphanages cared for some dependent children; however, prior to 1800, most orphans were placed in almshouses, or indentured, that is, given to families to function as servants. The focus during this time period was on survival, since death often occurred at early ages; fewer than half of all children born in this country prior to the 1800s lived to the age of 18.

The Nineteenth Century

During the 1800s, increased attention began to be given to the negative effects of placing young children in almshouses along with insane, retarded, and delinquent people and those with disabilities. In 1853, Charles Loring Brace founded the Children's Aid Society of New York, which established orphanages and other programs for children. Brace and others felt that such programs were the most appropriate way to "save" many children from the negative influences of their parents and urban life (Axinn & Levin, 1997). Brace viewed rural Protestant families as ideal parents for such children, and he recruited many foster families from the rural Midwest to serve as foster parents. During the mid-1800s, "orphan trains" carrying hundreds of children stopped at depots throughout the Midwest, leaving behind those children selected by families at each stop (Axinn & Levin, 1997). By 1880, the Children's Aid Society of New York had sent 40,000 children to live with rural farm families (Axinn & Levin, 1997). A number of individuals and organizations strongly criticized this move. Some called attention to the negative effects of separating children from their parents; however, the greatest criticism involved religious conflicts. The majority of children placed in foster homes were from Irish immigrant families who were predominantly Catholic, whereas their foster families were primarily German and Scandinavian Protestants. The outcry led to more emphasis on the development of Catholic orphanages and foster homes.

Still, little attention was focused on children living with their own families or with other families as a result of informal placement arrangements, and no standards or any system of intervention existed to address the needs of abused and neglected children and their families. This changed in the 1870s as the result of a now-famous case involving a young girl in New York named Mary Ellen. Abandoned by her parents at birth, Mary Ellen was living with relatives who beat her severely, tied her to her bed, and fed her very small amounts of food from a bowl—like a dog. A visitor to Mary Ellen's neighborhood was appalled at the abusive treatment she was receiving from her caretakers and reported the situation to a number of agencies in New York City. When none would intervene, the visitor, reasoning that Mary Ellen fell under the broad rubric of "animal," finally got the New York Society for the Prevention of Cruelty to Animals to take the case to court and request that the child be moved from the family immediately. As a result of the Mary Ellen case, New York established the Society for the Prevention of Cruelty to Children, and other northeastern cities followed suit. These organizations, however, focused primarily on prosecuting parents rather than on services to either children or their families. The establishment of Charity Organization Societies (COS) and settlement houses in the late 1800s gave increased attention to children and families, as well as to the environments in which they functioned.

The majority of other efforts in the 1800s and early 1900s focused on children's health needs. Illness was frequent, and the death of children was commonplace during this period. It was also because well-off families saw prevention of disease as a way to keep the diseases of immigrants from spreading to their own children (Axinn & Levin, 1997). Immunization laws, pasteurized milk legislation, and other sanitation laws were passed during this time. Other relevant legislation focused on child labor laws and compulsory school attendance. Increased attention began to be given at both state and national levels to the responsibilities of government to provide for children and families, and many states passed legislation establishing monitoring systems for foster care and separating facilities for dependent, neglected, and delinquent children from those for adults.

The Early Twentieth Century

The most significant effort toward the establishment of a true service delivery system for children, youth, and families during the early 1900s was the creation of the **U.S. Children's Bureau** in 1912. This was a result of the first White House Conference on Children, held in 1910, and the activities of a coalition of child advocates from the settlement houses, COS groups, and state boards of charities and corrections. The legislation establishing the U.S. Children's Bureau was significant, because it was the first national legislation recognizing that the federal government had a responsibility for the welfare of the country's children. Julia Lathrop was appointed the first chief of the bureau, and its first efforts were aimed at birth registration and maternal and child health programs, in an attempt to reduce the high infant mortality rate and improve the health of children. One of the bureau's first publications, *Infant Care,* a booklet for parents, has undergone over 20 revisions and remains the most popular document available from the U.S. Government Printing Office today. In its current form, the Children's Bureau is responsible for a number of federal programs for children, youth, and families and is a part of the U.S. Department of Health and Human Services.

During the first 30 years of the 1900s, states continued to become more involved in services to children, youth, and families, particularly in the South and West, where strong private agencies did not exist. Many states established public departments of welfare that also were responsible for child and family services, including protecting children from abuse and neglect, providing foster homes, and overseeing orphanages and other institutions for children. The establishment of the American Association for Organizing Family Social Work (which later became the Family Service Association of America) in 1919 and the **Child Welfare League of America** in 1920 gave further impetus to the child and family services movement. Both of these organizations stressed the role of the social work profession and established recommended standards for the provision of services. During the 1920s, attention turned to parenting and facilitating the development of healthy parent-child relationships. Child guidance centers were established, and the emphasis on psychoanalysis led to increased attention to child therapy. Establishment of adoption as a formal child welfare service and subsequent adoption legislation also occurred during this period.

The Social Security Act of 1935

Services to children, youth, and families became more formalized with the passage of the **Social Security Act** of 1935. This act established mothers' pensions, which later became the Aid to Families with Dependent Children (AFDC) program, and also mandated states to establish, expand, and strengthen statewide child welfare services, especially in rural areas. The definition of child welfare stated earlier in this chapter incorporated the following trends currently seen in state and federal child welfare services:

- Recognition that poverty is a major factor associated with other child and family problems
- A shift from rescuing children from poor families and placing them in substitute care to keeping children in their own homes and providing supportive services to prevent family breakup
- State intervention in family life to protect children
- Increased professionalization and bureaucratization of child welfare services
- An emphasis at the federal level that it is the federal government's responsibility to oversee the delivery of child welfare services within states to ensure that all children and families in the United States have access to needed services

In spite of the Social Security Act, problems persisted with the delivery of services to children, youth, and families. Access to services remained unequal, and many children continued to grow up in poverty. Some child welfare services, such as adoption, were provided primarily to white middle-class families, and few child welfare services adequately addressed the needs of African American, Latino, and Native American children and their families. Many children, particularly children of color, spent their entire childhood in foster care. What initially was meant to be temporary care until families stabilized enough for their children to return became a permanent way of life for many children.

The 1960s and 1970s

In the 1960s, the Kennedy and Johnson administrations took a strong interest in children, youth, and families. Services during these administrations were broader and tar-

geted at prevention and elimination of poverty. Many of these programs were based on the emerging belief that children's lives were influenced by their environment and that heredity played only a minimal role in individual outcomes. The focus became to "maximize the potential of all individuals" and to help them become productive adults. As a result, infant care centers and **Head Start** (a preschool program focusing on physical, social, emotional, and cognitive development) were established, and increased emphasis was placed on education, as well as on job training and employment programs for youth and their parents. With this broad-based focus, traditional child welfare services received less attention in favor of strengthening families and preventive services.

When President Nixon took office, the focus shifted from providing maximum resources to meeting minimum standards in regard to child and family services. With only a few exceptions that Congress actively advocated, services to children, youth, and families narrowed. In addition, funding, programs, and policies reverted to more traditional child welfare services, including protective services to abused and neglected children and their families, foster care, and adoption.

During the Nixon administration, because of increased concern about the high costs of child care and the number of children left alone because their parents could not afford child care, Congress attempted to pass legislation that would give states funding for child care subsidies for low-income working parents. It was reasoned that this approach not only would keep more children safe but also would reduce the number of women on AFDC and the number of families living in poverty. But it was not until 1990 that child care legislation—the A Better Child Care (ABC) Act—was introduced in Congress with a wide base of support. That legislation, which was not supported by the Bush administration, also failed, as has most other child and family services legislation since the Carter administration.

Other significant legislation that was enacted in the 1970s includes the 1974 Juvenile Justice and Delinquency Prevention Act, which established limited funding for runaway youth programs; the Indian Child Welfare Act (1976), with an emphasis on preventing disruption of Native American families; and the Education for All Handicapped Children Act (1975), which mandated, through public school systems, the provision of educational and social services to children with disabilities.

Child Abuse Legislation   The most significant child welfare legislation of the 1970s provided services in the area of child abuse and neglect. In 1974, Congress passed the Child Abuse Prevention and Treatment Act (Public Law 93-247). This act established the National Center on Child Abuse and Neglect as part of the Department of Health, Education, and Welfare (now the Department of Health and Human Services). It required states receiving federal dollars to strengthen child maltreatment programs in the areas of state definitions and reporting laws regarding child maltreatment. It established research and technical assistance programs to assist states in developing child maltreatment prevention and intervention programs. And it established special demonstration programs that could later be adapted by other states. When the act was renewed 3 years later, a new section was added to strengthen adoption services for children with special needs (children who were waiting to be adopted and considered difficult to find

homes for because of ethnicity, age, or developmental disabilities).

Adoption Assistance and Related Child Welfare Legislation

In 1980, Congress passed the Adoption Assistance and Child Welfare Act. For many years, advocates had been urging that legislation of this type be passed, because they had become increasingly concerned about the large numbers of children "drifting" in the foster care system and about those who were legally free for adoption but for whom homes were not being found. A number of studies (Maas & Engler, 1959; Vasaly, 1976) indicated that the child welfare services delivery system perhaps was doing more harm than good to children. Researchers in one study (Shyne & Schroeder, 1978) found that although foster care philosophically was (and is) intended to be short term (6 months or less) while parents prepare for family reunification through counseling and other types of assistance, this was not the experience of many children.

The 1977 National Study of Social Services to Children and Their Families produced the following key findings:

- Approximately 1.8 million children were served by public child welfare agencies.
- Thirty-eight percent of the children served were children of color.
- More than 500,000 children were in out-of-home placement.
- The average length of placement in foster care was 2.5 years.
- Approximately 200,000 foster care children needed permanent homes, and half were already free for adoption, but only half of those who were legally free were receiving adoption services (U.S. Depart-

ment of Health and Human Services, Children's Bureau, 1997, pp. 4–5).

The Adoption Assistance and Child Welfare Act (Public Law 96-272), passed in 1980, changed the thrust of services to children, youth, and families. By placing ceilings on the amounts that states could receive for foster care, the act encouraged the establishment of own-home services and reductions in the number of children in foster care. It also required the development of comprehensive case plans and 6-month reviews for all children receiving child welfare services so that they do not languish in foster care and provided federal funding to subsidize the adoption of children with special needs.

Although Public Law 96-272 authorized increased expenditures for services to children and families in their own homes, not enough funding was included in the U.S. budget to overcome the imbalance that continued to exist between foster care and child welfare services designed to prevent placement. The *Final Report of the National Study of Protective, Preventive and Reunification Services Delivered to Children and Their Families* released by the U.S. Children's Bureau in 1997 contains five major findings regarding the impact of Public Law 96-272:

1. Between 1977 and 1994 there was a dramatic decline in the number of children receiving child welfare services, from an estimated 1.8 million to 1 million. This decrease reflects a child welfare system that has evolved from a more broad-based child and family services system into a system primarily serving abused and neglected children and their families.
2. The intent of Public Law 96-272 and other federal policies to shift child welfare from a foster care system to an in-home, family-based system has not been realized. There has been little change in the number of children in foster care since 1977. From 1977 to 1994 there has been a 60% decline in the number of children receiving in-home services.
3. Despite provisions in Public Law 96-272 for conducting an inventory of children in foster care longer than 6 months and for holding administrative and dispositional hearings, foster care drift remains a problem. Although the average length of stay in foster care has declined overall, more than one-third of the children placed in foster care remain there for more than 18 months.
4. Children of color, particularly African American children, are more likely than white children to be in foster care placement than to receive in-home services, even when they share the same problems and characteristics.
5. Children of color also remain in foster care longer than white children. Kinship foster care, or placement with relatives, does not explain the dramatically longer stays in foster care for African American and Latino children when compared to white children. For each racial/ethnic group, no statistically significant relationship was found between kinship placement and the mean length of time children spent in foster care (U.S. Department of Health and Human Services, Children's Bureau, 1997, pp. 1–3).

The Mid-1980s and the 1990s

In 1986, Public Law 99-272 established the Independent Living Program, which provided funding for states to develop or strengthen services for youth age 16 and older that either were in or had been in the foster care system. Other legislation passed during the mid-1980s focused on runaway and homeless youth, provisions for one-time payments to adoptive parents for adoption-related costs such as legal fees, grant programs for family preservation and support services, and the Children's Justice Act. In 1990, Public Law 101-239 was enacted, requiring that case plans for children in foster care include health and education records.

One of the most significant pieces of child welfare legislation in the 1990s was the Omnibus Budget Reconciliation Act of 1993 (OBRA 1993), which established a new family preservation and family support services program. This act filled an important piece missing from the earlier 1980 Adoption Assistance and Child Welfare Act by providing $1 billion in new funding over a 5-year period to be used by states to prevent foster care placement. The creation of a separate funding source for family preservation and family support programs was intended to ensure that funds be used to strengthen families and not for child abuse and neglect investigations and foster care placements (U.S. Department of Health and Human Services, Children's Bureau, 1997, p. 7).

In addition, OBRA 1993 and amendments to the legislation passed in 1994 and 1997:

- established funding for state courts to improve handling of foster care and adoption proceedings;
- provided funding for states to develop automated data systems to better track children and families receiving child welfare services and outcomes;
- permanently extended the Independent Living Program for youth 16 and older;
- mandated that judicial hearings for children be held within 12 months after the initial 18-month judicial hearing (U.S. Department of Health and Human Services, Children's Bureau, 1997, p. 7).

This legislation highlighted family services and prevention as national priorities and provided opportunities for states to implement child welfare reforms.

During the 1980s and 1990s debate was also taking place related to the extent to which race and ethnicity should be factors in foster care and adoptive placement. In 1994, Congress passed the Multiethnic Placement Act (Public Law 103-382) to promote the placement of children of color, who remain in foster care much longer than white children and are less likely to be adopted. This act prevents children from being denied placement with a foster or adoptive parent solely on the basis of the race, color, or national origin of either the prospective parent or the child involved. The act also requires states to "recruit and retain foster and adoptive families that reflect the racial and ethnic diversity of the children for whom homes are needed" (*Adoption 2002*, 1997, p. 3). Congress amended the Multiethnic Placement Act in 1996, repealing some of the language in the earlier legislation that could have been used to circumvent the intent of the law and providing strict penalties for agencies receiving federal funding if they violate the act.

Although child welfare advocates heralded the increased emphasis on supportive services to families and decreasing foster care placements, increased concern began to be raised about the balance between foster care and in-home services. In many geographic areas, foster care numbers decreased and children and families remained together and improved their functioning. However, in some geographic areas, large numbers of children continued to remain in foster care even when assessments showed they most likely would have done well in their own homes with appropriate supportive services. In still other geographic areas, increased funding received for reduced numbers of children in foster care was coupled with an increase in severe injuries and child deaths of children remaining in their own homes. To address these concerns regarding the balance between safety and permanency, Congress passed the Adoption and Safe Families Act of 1997 (Public Law 105-89) as an amendment to the child welfare section of the Social Security Act. Funding and services provided under this act are based on the following principles:

- Safety is the paramount concern that must guide all child welfare services.
- Foster care is temporary.
- Permanency planning efforts should begin as soon as a child enters care.
- The child welfare system must focus on results and accountability.
- Innovative approaches are needed to achieve the goals of safety, permanency, and well-being (*Adoption 2002*, 1997, pp. 4–5).

Congress passed legislation in other areas of health and human services during the late 1980s and early 1990s that had the potential to affect the child welfare system. These programs include the following:

- Public Law 99-457 (Special Education for Infants and Toddlers), which provides services, including case management services, to children from birth to age 2
- Omnibus Budget Reconciliation Act (OBRA) of 1984, which made limited funding available to provide grants to states to develop services for children

with emotional disturbances
- The Developmentally Disabled Assistance and Bill of Rights Act (1990), requiring states to establish services in the least restrictive settings possible
- The Adolescent Family Life demonstration program, which provides support for pregnancy prevention as well as services to pregnant and parenting teens

One of the drawbacks to these legislative efforts, in addition to the limited funding authorized to implement the requirements of each act, has been the continued categorization of legislation. Such categorization leads to the establishment of programs limited to narrow populations and reinforces the fragmentation of services. Recent sessions of Congress also have placed additional ceilings on amounts available for child and family services. Thus, even attention to a newly publicized area deemed important, such as legislation establishing programs targeted at gangs and youth crime, has usually not meant increased funding.

Despite the demands of serving a child welfare population of increasing size and complexity, states made significant inroads in the areas of foster care prevention and family-centered services during the 1980s and 1990s. The development of family preservation programs, efforts to reduce the length of stay in foster care, emphasis on culturally appropriate casework practice, and expansion of kinship care are important components of a strong child welfare service delivery system.

Support to Get Families Off Welfare

The federal legislation that had the potential to be the most significant for children and families since the Social Security Act of 1935 was the Family Support Act of 1988 (see Chapter 8).

Proponents of this legislation argued that this comprehensive package of services would reduce some of the problems with previously fragmented services created by categorical legislation. However, funding to provide such services was limited from the very beginning. Moreover, implementation of the act at the state and local levels required extensive coordination and services among human services agencies, school districts, community colleges and universities, employment and job training programs, child care programs, health care providers, transportation programs, and private and public sector employers. Because of the costs of efforts to initiate or strengthen welfare reform programs, many states were unable to provide sufficient resources to address the needs of AFDC recipients wanting to get off welfare. In a number of instances, often-disappointed and otherwise motivated clients were placed on waiting lists for education, job training, and child care programs. Other clients were placed in jobs that paid the minimum wage so that states could meet federal requirements to maintain funding for their programs; however, these jobs did not pay enough or provide benefits that allowed clients to become self-sufficient.

The mood of Congress and the rest of the country took a dramatic shift in the mid-1990s with regard to public welfare programs. Hailing the legislation as "the end of welfare as we know it," President Clinton signed the Personal Responsibility and Work Opportunity Budget Reconciliation Act of 1996 (HR 3734) into law in August 1996. This law, which eliminated the AFDC program as an entitlement program and replaced it with the Temporary Assistance to Needy Families (TANF) block grant, has serious implications for children. Under TANF, rigid time limits have been imposed as to how long and under what conditions clients can continue to receive assistance for themselves and their children. The legislation also consolidates separate child care programs created during the 1980s. In addition, it mandates changes in the Food Stamp Program, SSI for children, benefits for legal immigrants, the Child Support and Enforcement Program, and child nutrition programs (U.S. Department of Health and Human Services, Children's Bureau, 1997). Evaluations of the early impact of the Personal Responsibility Act on families and their children have produced mixed results. The long-term impact of this legislation on the health and well-being of children, youth, and families in the United States remains to be seen.

Moving into the 21st Century

In an executive memorandum dated December 14, 1996, President Clinton said:

> I am committed to giving the children waiting in our Nation's foster care system what every child in America deserves—loving parents and a healthy, stable home. The goal for every child in our Nation's public welfare system is permanence in a safe and stable home, whether it be returning home, adoption, legal guardianship, or another permanent placement. While the great majority of children in foster care will return home, for about one in five, returning home is not an option, and they will need another home, one that is caring and safe. These children wait far too long, typically over 3 years, but many children wait much longer to be placed in permanent homes. Each year state child welfare agencies secure homes for less than one-third of the children whose goal is adoption or an alternate permanent plan. I know we can do better (*Adoption 2002*, 1997, p. 1).

President Clinton directed the secretary of health and human services to make recommendations for strategies to move children more quickly into permanent homes and to double the number of children adopted or permanently placed during the next 5 years.

In February of 1997, Shalala issued *Adoption 2002: A Response to the Presidential Executive Memorandum on Adoption* as a "blueprint for bipartisan federal leadership in adoption and other permanent placements for children in the public welfare system" (p. 1). The report is based on the following premises:

- Every child deserves a safe and permanent family.
- Children's health and safety is a paramount concern that must guide all child welfare services.
- Children deserve prompt and timely decision-making as to who their permanent caregivers will be.
- Permanency planning begins when a child enters foster care; foster care is a temporary setting.

- Adoption is one of the pathways to a permanent family.
- Adoptive families require supports after a child's adoption is legalized.
- The diversity and strengths of all communities must be tapped.
- Quality services must be provided as quickly as possible to enable families in crisis to address problems. (*Adoption 2002*, 1997, pp. 1–2).

The report calls for the development of model state legislation to advance the goal of giving every child in the U.S. child welfare system a safe, permanent home.

The *Adoption 2002* report concludes, "that all the nation's leaders collectively share equal levels of responsibility for America's children, whether their sphere of operation is in local communities or in business, the professions, science, education, social services, or any other type of work" (*Adoption 2002*, 1997, p. 8). The

A newspaper cartoonist captures the essence of the systems/ecological framework and the need for giving attention to children at all levels of the environment.

Ben Sargent, Editorial Cartoonist/ *Austin American Statesman.* Reprinted by permission.

report argues that child welfare reform must be broad-based and interdisciplinary. The years ahead will bear witness to how well the country responds to this challenge.

PREVENTIVE SERVICES TO CHILDREN IN THEIR OWN HOMES

Although preventive services receive less attention than other types of services, many programs strengthen families and reduce chances for family dysfunction.

Natural Support Systems

Given the scarcity of resources, increased attention is being given to the strengthening of **natural support systems** to assist families. Many families develop social networks of friends, relatives, neighbors, or coworkers who provide emotional support; share child care, transportation, clothing, toys, and other resources; offer the opportunity to observe other children, parents, and family constellations and how they interact; and provide education about child rearing and other family life situations. But studies show that many families who experience problems are isolated and lack such support systems. Many social services agencies, churches and synogogues, and other community organizations are assisting communities in the establishment of support systems for new families and other families who lack natural support systems to help them meet their needs. Some communities have established telephone support programs for various groups, in which individuals can receive support and information about appropriate resources.

Home-Based Services

Recently in the United States increased emphasis has been on the provision of **home-based family-centered services,** or services delivered to children and families in their own homes, with a focus on preserving the family system and strengthening the family to bring about needed change. Comprehensive services, which are usually overseen by a single case manager assigned to the family, include homemaker services, respite care, child care, crisis intervention, financial assistance, substance abuse treatment, vocational counseling, and help with various concrete services, such as locating housing or transportation. Most home-based service programs include the following features:

- a primary worker or case manager who establishes and maintains a supportive, nurturing relationship with the family;
- small caseloads of two to six families, with a variety of service options used for each family;
- a team approach, with team members providing some services and serving as a backup to the primary worker/case manager;
- a support system available 24 hours a day for crisis calls or emergencies;
- the home as the natural setting, with maximum use of natural support systems, including the family, extended family, neighborhood, and community;
- parents remaining in charge of and responsible for their families as educators, nurturers, and primary caregivers; and
- a willingness to invest at least as much in providing home-based services to a family as society is willing to pay for out-of-home care for their children (Lloyd & Bryce, 1980).

Most families receiving home-based family-centered services are families with multiple needs who have received fragmented services for long periods of time from a number of agencies. Many children from these families have also spent time in substitute care. But because of the chronic and severe problems experienced by such families and the repeated crises they often experience, past efforts have been largely ineffective.

Home-based family-centered services are based on a systems/ecological approach to family intervention, viewing the entire family as the focus of help. Intervention is short term and goal oriented, focusing on behavioral change. Intensive services are usually provided to families for 60 to 90 days, which averages out to the same number of families a worker providing traditional child welfare services serves during a 1-year period. But the ability to focus on a limited number of families intensively has important benefits. First, it gives workers a chance to stabilize the family so that it can function either independently or with fewer services while allowing children in the family to remain in the home. Second, it allows workers to make a determination more quickly and with more documentation if the family cannot be stabilized, allowing children to be placed more quickly in adoptive homes rather than remaining in limbo in either a dysfunctional life-threatening family situation or the instability of foster care.

Studies comparing home-based family-centered service programs to more traditional child welfare services show that when 18% to 20% of children who would otherwise enter substitute care can be maintained safely in their own homes, the home-based services pay for themselves. Evaluations of home-based family-centered programs vary, but some programs show that 75% to 90% of children are able to remain in their own homes when such services are provided (Lloyd & Bryce, 1980; WESTAT, 1995).

Parent Education

While most people are required to learn math and English in school, little attention is given to one of the most important roles they are likely to play as adults—that of being a parent. Many communities offer parenting classes aimed at a wide range of parents: prenatal classes for parents before the birth or adoption of their first infant, classes for parents of toddlers and preschoolers, classes for parents of school-age children, and classes for parents of adolescents. Such programs offer education about basic developmental stages of children and adolescents and alternative methods of child rearing and discipline. They also encourage the development of mutual support systems among participants, who often relax about their roles as parents when they realize that other parents have similar concerns and struggles.

One successful parent education prevention effort is Healthy Families in America, launched by the National Committee for the Prevention of Child Abuse in partnership with Ronald McDonald Children's Charities in 1992. The goal of the program is to provide early intervention and home visits to new parents during pregnancy and after birth to provide parenting information, information about community resources, and opportunities for parents to talk with staff about their hopes, concerns, and stresses. The program has been effective in Hawaii, and over 100 programs have now been established in 22 states (National Committee for the Prevention of Child Abuse, 1995).

Child Development and Child Care Programs

Accessible and high-quality child care programs that are affordable for working parents, particularly single parents, also can assist in preventing family breakdown. Such programs help parents ensure that their children are happy and safe in a comfortable, nurturing environment while their parents work, thus reducing parental stress. Many child care programs offer additional opportunities for parents, including parenting education classes, baby-sitting cooperatives, social programs, and the opportunity to develop support systems with other parents and children. But affordable, high-quality child care programs often

Quality child care programs that provide care for children and support and modeling for their parents facilitate healthy child development and positive training.

Le Goy/Liaison Agency

are unavailable to working parents, particularly in inner city or rural areas. Child care for infants, children with disabilities or other special needs, school-age children during vacations and holidays, and children who are sick also is not widely available in the United States. An additional gap in services relates to evening and night child care for parents who must work two jobs or late shifts.

Special programs are available for low-income parents, but they are often limited in the hours and in the number of children they can serve. Head Start, perhaps the most successful program established under the Office of Economic Opportunity in the 1960s, provides a developmental learning program for preschool children as well as health care, social services, and parent education. Infant-parent centers, which allow parents the opportunity to learn how to interact and play with their children in order to stimulate their development, also are available to some parents on a limited basis.

Recreational, Religious, and Social Programs

Often when services for children, youth, and families are discussed, no attention is given to the major roles that community resources other than social service agencies play in meeting family needs. The broader social, recreational, and religious programs must also be included when discussing programs that strengthen the welfare of children and their families. Faith-based organizations such as churches and synagogues meet the spiritual, emotional, social, and recreational needs of many children, youth, and families. They often play a major role in establishing special preventive services, such as child care programs, outreach centers, and parent education programs. Increasingly, the business community is providing preventive services through the workplace, including informational programs held during the lunch hour for working parents, recreational facilities and programs for employees and their families, and the facilitation of coworker support systems. Many communities offer substantial recreational programs for families that are free and provide family entertainment. Serious gaps exist in most communities, however, in providing appropriate recreational programs for adolescents. Some experts attribute increases in adolescent problems, including teenage pregnancy and delinquency, to the lack of available programs for this age group.

Health and Family Planning Programs

Early screening of health problems also reduces child and family problems. Health problems place increased stress on families, and access to affordable health care from prenatal care to adulthood is an important aspect of preventing family breakdown. Additionally, access to programs that provide help in responsible decision making about becoming a parent, through family planning clinics, faith-based organizations, and other community resources, reduces the risk of unwanted children and assists families in exploring options when pregnancy occurs.

A number of programs have successfully reduced infant mortality and developmental disabilities through the provision of comprehensive prenatal care. In California, for example, state-funded health programs that had not previously paid for health education, nutrition, counseling, or vitamins for pregnant women began to do so in the early 1980s. Such efforts cut the percentage of very low-birth-weight babies more than half when compared to a similar group that did not have access to the program; they also saved an estimated $1.70 to $2.60 in neonatal care costs for every dollar spent on the program. Other successful programs include storefront operations located in accessible areas and "resource mothers" who provide mentoring and support for pregnant teens (Schorr, 1989).

Education about Family Problems

Finally, education about the various types of family problems—and, should they occur, about resources available—is a significant form of prevention. Many communities provide programs that focus on preventing sexual abuse of children by teaching children about types of touch and what to do when they find themselves in an uncomfortable situation with an adult or older child. Other communities offer alcohol and drug awareness programs.

Appropriate Educational Opportunities

Most studies identify strong relationships between difficulties in school and individual and family problems. Programs that give children an opportunity to learn in ways that help them feel good about themselves and develop a sense of competence help to prevent family- and child-related problems. Such children are less likely to have children while in school, drop out of school, or live their lives in poverty. School-based social services allow for close cooperation among children and adolescents, teachers and school administrators, parents, and the community.

SCHOOL SOCIAL WORK

One specialized field that focuses on services to children, youth, and families is school social work. **School social work,** or social services offered in a school-based setting, provides the opportunity to identify needs of children and their families early and to facilitate early intervention before problems become more serious. Social workers in school settings offer parenting education, and facilitate the development of positive mental health for children through special outreach programs in the school.

School social work includes individual, family, and group counseling, as well as crisis intervention services. School social workers deal with suicidal students; students and their families and friends after a serious injury or death has occurred; and students in conflict with fam-

---

A Day in the Life of a School Social Worker

- 8 A.M.: A student is in my office waiting to talk. He is 7 years old and is crying. Last night his 16-year-old brother took his gun, drove to the park, and shot himself dead. The little boy knew his brother was upset and had tried to talk to him. The family had hidden the gun. The little boy thought he could have stopped it from happening.

- As I was talking with this student, a frantic call came in from the school office. A 7-year-old girl is bruised and battered. The secretary says the little girl is shaking like a leaf. I ask a social work intern to help the little boy find a quiet place to try to rest as he had not slept the night before. The girl got in the middle of a domestic violence episode the night before. Her drunk stepfather came over in the middle of the night, beat her mother, trashed the place, tore out the phone, battered the child, and vowed to return. After comforting the child I asked her to draw pictures of her feelings while I

report the abuse to CPS* and check on the boy.

- Another call from the office. An 8-year-old's father had overdosed the previous weekend. He is dead. The little girl had just returned to school.

- The 7-year-old girl had drawn a 6-page "story" of the night's events. She expressed terror about her stepfather returning. Together we came up with a plan for her, pending investigation of the abuse and a home visit to her mother:
  1. Ask to stay at her grandmother's place temporarily. If that can't be arranged, follow the next steps.
  2. Crawl out of her bedroom window.
  3. Wake the neighbors by screaming "HELP! HELP!!! CALL 911!!"
  4. Pound on their door.

- A regular student in the CIS Program† dropped by. She is 7 years old and is very sad. She and her mother and sister have been homeless for months. She has not seen her older sister since spring break. Her mother is using ily members, peers, or school authorities (see Box 12.2 for an account of a school social worker in an inner-city elementary school). School social workers serve as members of intervention teams who work with children with developmental disabilities or other special needs, often serving as the liaison to parents and the community when special services are needed. The Education for All Handicapped Children Act has been updated to specify that schools may hire social workers to provide social services to special-needs children, and dropout prevention legislation in some states also suggests the hiring of social workers.

School-based social work services are advantageous for many reasons:

---

again. They are staying at a man's apartment. His name is "Killer."

- A Child Protective Services worker arrived to interview the 5-year-old boy who had been found "having sex" with a 7-year-old boy at the baby-sitter's place over the weekend. I talk with the CPS worker about the 7-year-old girl. She will see the child today!
- The 4-year-old girl I had just begun to work with was not at school. The day before I made a CPS report for medical neglect. She has open sores all over her head. She is developmentally delayed; her height, weight, and head circumference are all below the 10th percentile. She comes to school dirty and in inappropriate clothing. She has never seen a doctor. Mom refuses to come to any appointments, even for immunizations provided at the school. The other six children appear to be healthy and well fed.
- And finally I made time to talk with the 10-year-old CIS student who the

afternoon before had picked up her little brother out of a pool of blood and called 911. She had been watching him outside; he was hit in the crossfire by two bullets. As of this writing he is in a coma. The 10-year old is in two of our "pre-employment" groups: the "child care club" and the "nurse assistants."

- 7 P.M.: I end the day by writing this to process these events so that I might be able to sleep tonight. I also remind myself of all the children in similar circumstances who have been helped by our program and hope that we can improve the situations for the children I saw today as well.

*CPS—Child Protective Services

†CIS Program—the Communities in Schools Program directed by the school social worker

Source: Written by Deborah Selbin, a school social worker and program manager of an inner-city, social services program at the elementary level. The program is part of Communities in Schools–Central Texas, a dropout prevention program that works with at-risk children and their families. Reprinted with permission.

- The social worker gets to see the child or adolescent in a natural setting, interacting with peers, teachers, and school administrators, which gives the social worker a different perspective than seeing a client in an office or agency.
- The social worker has access to large numbers of children and families in need of services; most children age 5 to 18 attend school.
- The social worker can help parents and school personnel use a systems/ecological approach to better address the child's needs, focusing on the relationships among the child, home, school, and broader community.
- The social worker can help school personnel understand the importance of family and community variables in relation to the child's capacity to function in the school setting.

SERVICES TO CHILDREN AND FAMILIES AT RISK

Although it is sometimes easier to locate community resources for children and families already at risk than to find preventive services, such services are also limited and fragmented. Many studies of child and family services find that lack of coordination among service providers is a problem identified by both service providers and recipients. Some communities have made special efforts to increase coordination, avoid duplication, and reduce gaps in services available to at-risk children and families, such as the following:

- "First-stop" resource centers where families can receive thorough assessments so that they can be referred to appropriate agencies rather than going from agency to agency only to learn that services are not available to them or do not meet their needs
- Computerized databases that contain critical information on the services available to the target population
- Centralized information and referral systems
- Colocation of offices and programs
- Coordinated multiagency service networks

Through such efforts, at-risk families, often reluctant to trust service providers and without transportation to access services, can receive individual and family counseling, complete forms to receive public assistance, get help in finding employment and housing, and attend parenting classes and parent support groups— all at the same location.

Health and Hospital Outreach Programs

Many health clinics and hospitals have established special programs to address the needs of children and families who are at risk of family disruption or dysfunction. (These and other services to families at risk are shown in Box 12.3.) Some clinics have high-risk infant programs, for example, that provide intensive services to teenage parents, parents of low-birth-weight or premature infants or infants with disabilities, parents with substance abuse problems, and parents who never seem to have established appropriate relationships with their children. Clinics offer a variety of services, such as weekly outreach programs conducted by a public health nurse, individual counseling, play groups for children and support groups for parents, role modeling of appropriate child care, and assistance in obtaining other resources as needed.

Support Service Options for Families at Risk

Family Relationships Support Services: Casework with individual parents or couples; family groups; family life education discussions; marriage seminars; pastoral counseling; AA or special counseling.

Housing: Tenant advocacy linkage; maintenance and repairs planning; landlord-neighbor tension resolution; housing relocation for improved space and environmental supports; mortgage financing; other.

Parenting Assistance: Respite provisions; homemaker services; foster grandparent role modeling and support; increased possibilities for extended family involvement; other, such as family day care.

Socialization Matrix of Parents: Adult and family recreational and social opportunities enhancement; direct services or linkage; adult education and advancement groups; programs that support and enhance the parent's and family's culture and ethnicity.

Socialization of Children: School-, agency-, or community-based programs such as recreation, camping, trips, interest and hobby building, shared homework, part-time work experiences; programs that support and enhance the child's culture and ethnicity.

Income and Economics: Advocacy and/or job-finding; training stipend; on-the-job training program linkage; help with income supports such as TANF, food stamps, Medicaid, SSI; budget management assistance; other advocacy.

Health: Child and adolescent health clinic services; family physician, outpatient or inpatient resources; public health nursing or other in-home consultation; adaptive equipment and prosthetic devices.

Remediation of Behavioral Problems: Individual or group approaches to problem modification by direct involvement of social worker with child; linkage with special school; tutoring; activity group.

Source: Adapted and reproduced by permission of the publisher, F. E. Peacock Publishers, Inc., Itasca, Illinois. From B. McGowan and W. Meezan, *Child Welfare: Current Dilemmas, Future Directions,* 1993 Copyright, p. 179. Originally appeared in Sr. Mary Paul Janchill, *Guidelines for Decision-Making in Child Welfare* (New York: Human Services Workshops, 1981), p. 13.

Hospitals offer similar programs. In some hospitals, specially trained nurses identify at-risk mothers in the delivery room and work with hospital social workers to give those mothers intensive care and support during their hospitalization, in addition to outreach services for both parents after the hospital stay. In a number of instances, such programs help parents realize they do not wish to be parents and help them relinquish children for adoption or place them in foster care while they receive additional help. More often, such programs prevent child abuse or neglect and help parents establish positive relationships with their children. Pediatric AIDS programs have also been established in many major metropolitan area hospitals. Such programs attempt to stabilize the health of infants and older children infected with the HIV virus. Because many parents do not want to or cannot care for children with AIDS and it is difficult to locate foster families willing to do so, many children with AIDS remain in the hospital for extended periods of time.

In some areas, special health clinics have been established to provide services for adolescents. Clinics offer basic health care; information on adolescent development and puberty and sexually transmitted infections and diseases; and, in some instances, pregnancy tests, contraceptive information, and prenatal care. Some clinics are located in public high schools. Although this setup has caused some controversy, studies show that physical and emotional problems, sexually transmitted infections and diseases, and pregnancies have decreased significantly in these schools.

One successful family planning approach began with a health clinic connected to a St. Paul, Minnesota, high school, which paved the way for health clinics attached to other city high schools. Thirty-five percent of female students came to the clinic for family planning services, reducing the numbers of children born to students by more than half and the number of second pregnancies to less than 2%. Other health clinics established in high schools have found that rather than increased sexual activity, girls became sexually active later instead of earlier when they could talk honestly about sex with a trusted adult. Additional opportunities for teens, such as school success and job training and employment opportuni-

ties, also must be provided so that self-esteem and adulthood can be tied to factors other than having a child (Schorr, 1989).

Child Care

Although attention usually is given to child care for working parents, child care also is used as a service for at-risk parents to enable children to remain in their own homes. Many parents need respite from their children and cannot attend to their needs 24 hours a day. Child care gives parents time to meet their own needs and gives children the emotional support they may not be getting at home. It allows families to stay together and is less costly than foster care and less traumatic for the child. In many states, some child care providers receive special training to enable them to work more effectively with at-risk parents and children. In some instances, child care providers develop surrogate parent or positive role relationships with parents, giving them and their children much-needed emotional support.

Many times, parents under stress reach a point where they need a break from their child, or they will abuse or neglect the child. Other times, parents lack natural support systems to help them during a crisis. Families with children with severe developmental disabilities need time to attend to their own needs but must cope with their children's needs 24 hours a day. Many communities have established various forms of crisis or respite care programs for such families. Some agencies have respite care programs for parents of children with developmental disabilities, in which specially trained adults care for children evenings or weekends so parents can have time to themselves. Other communities have established crisis nurseries or shelters, where parents under severe stress or in a serious emergency can leave their children for a limited amount of time. Some programs even provide emergency transportation for the children; most require counseling for parents under extreme stress while their children are in crisis care.

Some communities offer respite care for adolescents who need time away from their parents. Most emergency shelter facilities for teens also provide crisis and family counseling to help stabilize the situation so the teen can return home. But special services for teens are lacking in many areas. In some communities, the only resource available for children as young as 12 or 13 is the Salvation Army's general shelter.

Increased attention is also being given to child care for working parents, particularly for the working poor. The inability to find affordable child care can often be the last straw that creates an additional crisis for families who are already at risk and under severe stress. Many single parents lose their jobs or are forced to quit them because of a lack of child care.

Homemaker Services

Many agencies provide homemaker services to families who are at risk or who have abused or neglected their children. Homemakers are specially trained individuals, often indigenous to the community, who have been parents themselves and can serve as a nurturing, supportive role model for other parents. Homemakers offer practical suggestions and education about housekeeping, child care, nutrition and cooking, health and safety, shopping, budgeting, and access to community resources. Additionally, they may serve as surrogate parents to both parents and children in the family and often develop positive, trusting relationships with family members who may have been previously isolated. Homemaker services are far more cost-effective than out-

of-home care and often prevent the necessity to separate children from their parents.

Crisis Intervention Programs

Various community agencies provide **crisis intervention** services to families in crisis, which deescalate the crisis and often result in a subsequent referral for additional help, such as counseling. Law enforcement agencies in many communities have crisis intervention teams that handle domestic disputes, including situations of spouse and child abuse. Some youth shelters have crisis intervention for adolescents and their parents. Hospitals also provide crisis intervention services in emergency rooms, dealing with child maltreatment, family violence, and other serious family problems. Intervention often can be more effective in a crisis situation than in a noncrisis situation, because the crisis throws the family into a state of disequilibrium. Studies show that families are more receptive to change and to agreement to services such as counseling during a period of disruption, because regular defenses and the family balance are no longer intact.

Counseling

Individual, marital, and family counseling services are available in many communities for families experiencing problems. Mental health centers, social service agencies, child and family service agencies, child guidance clinics, employee assistance programs, churches, schools, youth services programs, and hospital outreach programs often provide various types of counseling services (see Box 12.4 for a young woman's experience with her school district's teen parent program). Such services often are available only on a limited basis, due to scarce resources and the large number of persons

BOX
12.4

Impact of Social Work Intervention

Elena Vasquez grew up in an inner-city area with her mother and five brothers and sisters. Her father left the family when Elena was a toddler, and her mother worked long hours to try to keep the family fed and clothed until her diabetic condition prevented her from keeping a job. Forced to go on welfare, Elena's mother became depressed and was constantly in and out of the hospital as her diabetes created other health problems. As the oldest girl living at home, Elena took care of her brothers and sisters and tried to maintain the household. Increasingly behind in school and lacking attention from adults and peers her own age, she fell in love with a neighbor boy at 13 and became pregnant at 14. Although she tried to stay in school, after the baby was born she found it increasingly difficult to care for her newborn infant, her siblings, and her mother. Leaving her baby with her boyfriend's mother in the afternoons, Elena got a part-time job at a fast-food restaurant

so her family could have some additional income. Overwhelmed with life, Elena's boyfriend and his family provided her with emotional support, and 6 months after the birth of her first baby, Elena found herself pregnant again. However, a short time later, her boyfriend found another girlfriend, leaving Elena alone and discouraged.

Desperate, she went to her junior high school counselor, who sent her to the school district's special program for teen parents. There she was assigned to meet regularly with a social work intern from a neighboring university. The social work intern referred Elena's mother to a nearby health clinic that was better able to meet her health care needs and got her siblings involved with the school social workers at their schools. Seeing an incredible resiliency in Elena, the intern slowly gained Elena's trust and helped her realize the potential she had to create a viable life for herself, her baby, and her soon-to-be-born child. Elena met with

needing services, and may not always be available at no cost or on a sliding scale. Specialized counseling to address family problems such as family violence or sexual abuse often is unavailable in many communities.

Studies show that for many problems, group counseling is more effective than individual counseling, or a combination of both is more effective than individual counseling alone. For example, children who have been

sexually abused need to hear from other children that they are not the only ones who have had such an experience. Sexual and physical abusers, as well as others with family problems, often deny that there is a problem, and group therapy sessions with others in similar situations typically break down their defenses more quickly than individual counseling.

Increased attention by helping professionals is being given to family counseling as an the intern weekly for the remainder of the year. Her attendance was almost perfect, and she was soon getting excellent grades. It was then, when Elena was 15, that she vowed she wanted to be a social worker just like the intern and work with teenagers who became pregnant.

Although life wasn't easy for her, Elena graduated from high school and, because of her experiences with her mother's health, got a job at a local health clinic. A hard worker who was highly motivated, Elena quickly moved up through the support staff ranks and became a clinic supervisor. When her children started school, Elena began taking classes at the local community college. Slowly she progressed through school while working full-time, volunteering at the local battered women's shelter and a nursing home, and providing exceptional care for her children, attending their sports events and prodding them to do well academically. When her children were in junior high school, her oldest child the same age Elena had been when she first became pregnant, Elena transferred to the social work program at the state university. In her senior year she asked to do her internship at the same agency where she had been a client 15 years ago. After determining that Elena was mature enough to work with pregnant teens without her own personal experiences influencing her work with clients, the university placed Elena in one of the agency's teen parent programs. While Elena was an intern, the funding for the agency was being reviewed by the state legislature, and she asked to testify on behalf of the program and share with legislators the impact the program had had on her life. As you can imagine, Elena's testimony was extremely powerful and well received. At this point, Elena has graduated and is working with teen parents as a case manager at the agency. Her children are doing well in school and making plans for their own careers.

effective way to strengthen individual functioning and address needs. Family counseling is effective in helping families understand behavior and coping patterns, establish more productive communication patterns, identify needs and resolve problems, and support each other as family members. In almost all situations in which a family member is experiencing a problem or undergoing a stressful change, family counseling can help the entire family reinforce positive changes, address negative patterns appropriately, and also serve as a source of support to each other.

Some agencies have initiated multifamily groups, or groups of families that receive therapy jointly. Many times individuals can see their own issues and family dynamics more clearly while watching other families interact, because they are too involved when such interactions occur within their own families.

Teenagers, for example, may be more likely to listen to another parent who offers feedback than to their own parents, and parents are often more likely to listen to other teens or parents than to family members.

Social workers have played an important role in this shift in focus from individual to family counseling. Social workers in particular focus on the strengths of family members and of the family as a total system, building on those strengths to make the system more supportive of its individual members.

Support and Self-Help Groups

Support groups and **self-help groups** also are effective ways of helping children, youth, and families cope with family problems. Such groups help individuals realize that they are not the only ones coping with a given problem. They also assist members in developing new ways to cope as they learn from each other. Perhaps most important, persons who may see themselves as being inadequate have a chance to reach out and give something to someone else. Self-help groups include the following:

- 12-step programs such as Alcoholics Anonymous for alcoholics, Al-Anon for family members of alcoholics, Alateen for teen family members of alcoholics, Narcotics Anonymous, and Adult Children of Alcoholics
- Parents Anonymous for abusive or potentially abusive parents
- Parents United for sexually abusive parents
- Tough Love for parents of out-of-control adolescents
- Parents without Partners for single parents

Many communities have established support groups for adults, children, or teens dealing with divorce, stepparenting, the death of a loved one or other type of loss, or those living with a family member with a physical or emotional disability. Schools have established support groups for students experiencing difficulty functioning within the school setting, coping with family problems such as divorce or abuse, and recovering from substance abuse, as well as for students who are teen parents. As resources become constrained, social service agencies are realizing that in many instances more individuals and families can be served effectively through support and self-help groups.

Volunteer and Outreach Programs

Many traditional social services agencies are overloaded with cases and can provide only limited services—and those only to families with the most severe problems. A number of agencies have established volunteer components, whereas other agencies have been established that use only volunteers. In many instances, because they can spend more time with families, volunteers can be highly successful in intervention and prevent family disruption. Most volunteer programs have established effective screening mechanisms for recruiting volunteers with good nurturing skills who can relate well to clients. Many have been parents themselves, some are grandparents, and others are students or already involved in human services. Volunteers usually receive extensive training and are supervised by a social work case manager.

Several communities and states have successful volunteer programs. Suspected Child Abuse and Neglect (SCAN) of Arkansas and Family Outreach Centers (established by the National Council of Jewish Women) both use highly trained volunteers to work on a one-to-one basis with abusive and neglecting families. The SCAN model is based on a reparenting framework, which focuses on developing trust, followed by working through the stages of psychosocial development that the parents missed during childhood. Volunteers in such programs visit often and converse with parents and children, assist in problem solving and gaining access to community resources, and serve as a surrogate parent/role model/friend to the parent and family members. Similar programs have been developed in which volunteers work with teenage parents and abused and neglected children. The national Big Brothers/Big Sisters program uses volunteers as friends and role models to children from single-parent families. Studies show that volunteer programs can keep families together. Given the continuing increase in the number of families needing services and declining resources, volunteer programs are likely to increase.

Programs for at-risk families are funded by federal, state, and local governments as well as the private sector. The United Way provides funds for numerous programs for families at risk in many communities. Faith-based organizations, foundations, and private contributions fund other programs. Increasingly, public-private partnerships are being developed with funding from a variety of sources. In many instances, state and local governments contract with private agencies to provide services, and many private agencies receive funding from multiple sources, both public and private. Which entity should pay for what type of services is an increasingly complex issue at all levels in the United States. As the number of at-risk families continues to increase and as federal and state funding continues to be limited, more emphasis is being placed on local communities to fund such programs. But local governments, employers, and private

Many social services programs work with families in their homes.

Pete Souza/Liaison Agency

contributors are not always able or willing to provide the needed assistance. New ways of providing services, as well as the development of new and more effective cost sharing, are issues that will have to be explored in more depth during the first decade of the 21st century.

CHILD PROTECTIVE SERVICES

The federal Child Abuse and Neglect Prevention and Treatment Act mandates that all states designate a single agency that is in turn mandated to oversee services to abused and neglected children and their families. Such services are usually termed **child protective services.** Families reported to that agency as being abusive or neglectful must be investigated by the agency to ascertain whether the maltreatment report can be substantiated. All states have statutes that establish a minimum standard of care that caretakers are expected to provide to their children. If the worker investigating the case determines that this standard is not being met by the parents, the family is slated to receive protective services. This is an involuntary program—that is, the parents did not request or volunteer to receive the services.

Investigations of Child Maltreatment

In implementing the mandated services, child protective services workers cooperate closely with other professionals, including law enforcement officers, attorneys, health care providers, and educators. Child protective services workers assume a variety of roles in providing protective services, in cooperation or jointly with other agencies. They may offer intake services, in which they screen reports of child maltreatment, interviewing persons

reporting cases over the telephone to obtain information needed to make a preliminary determination about how serious the report is and if it needs to be investigated immediately. Most states require life-threatening situations to be investigated immediately or within 24 to 48 hours and less serious cases to be investigated within 10 days.

Child protective services workers, by themselves or jointly with law enforcement officers, also conduct investigations of child maltreatment, interviewing children, parents, other family members, and collateral contacts such as teachers and neighbors to determine the nature and extent of the reported maltreatment. Investigations involve examining and interviewing the child, attending to the child's immediate emotional needs during the investigation, and making a preliminary assessment about whether maltreatment is occurring. If a positive finding is confirmed, investigators determine whether the maltreatment is causing or could cause permanent damage to the child's body or mind, how severe the maltreatment has been, and whether the situation is life-threatening and warrants immediate removal of the child to a safer environment. In some instances other resources, such as physicians, may be used to assist in gathering needed information. Investigations of child maltreatment require knowledge and skill in the identification of various types of maltreatment, interviewing techniques appropriate with children and adults who may be apprehensive and reluctant to cooperate, and a balance of compassion and firmness. Striking a balance between use of authority and the use of compassion, or between the ability to confront and the ability to be empathic, is one of the challenges of being a child protective services worker (Crosson-Tower, 1998).

Determination of Intervention Approach

The outcome of an investigation of child maltreatment is an assessment of the situation and the most appropriate actions to take. Child protective services workers are not expected to prove that the maltreatment is a criminal offense or to determine who perpetrated the maltreatment—those actions are within the domain of the courts. Their role is to determine whether the child needs to be protected and what is needed to provide that protection. Workers have four options when assessing a possible situation of child maltreatment:

1. to determine that the child is not being maltreated and withdraw from the case;
2. to offer help to the family;
3. to determine that the child is at serious risk and/or that the parents are uncooperative and make arrangements to take the family to court; and
4. with the court's permission, to remove the child from the home immediately and place the child in emergency care and later, usually foster care.

Child protective services workers most often determine that, although services are required, it is safe to leave the child in the home while the services are being provided. Children are most often removed from the home for the following reasons:

• The child or a sibling has been seriously injured or abandoned.
• The parent/caretaker states that he or she is going to kill or injure the child.
• Evidence suggests that the child has experienced sexual abuse, and the perpetrator is still in the home or has easy access to the child.

• A current crisis exists, such as a psychotic parent or a parent in jail because of substance abuse.
• There is little or no cooperation from parents, and the child is at serious risk for substantial harm.

Child protective services workers, like other helping professionals, are most effective if they identify strengths in their clients and the clients' environment and work to empower clients to make choices that keep the children safe. But if, after trying to provide mandated services to a family, the protective services workers believes that the family is resistant to the services and is making choices that fail to keep the child(ren) safe, they may take such cases to court and request that the court order services. This way, if the family does not comply, the worker can bring the case back into court and request more serious options, such as placing the child in foster care. Some states mandate court involvement with all families receiving child protective services.

The issue of when to involve the court in child protective services cases is not always universally agreed on. Advocates for early involvement argue that it gives workers leverage in dealing with families because the authority of the courts is present immediately. Advocates for limited involvement believe that most families are more receptive to services without court action because they feel more empowered and thus can maintain a less adversarial relationship with their worker. A number of states are developing two-track child protective services programs, with those clients who can be charged with criminal charges under the auspices of an investigative unit and the majority of other clients under the auspices of an assessment/intervention unit. Proponents of this approach think that it will remove the adversarial relationship that occurs when a law enforcement investigation is done for those families who need family preservation or other supportive services (American Public Welfare Association, 1995).

Typical Services Provided

Child protective services workers provide a variety of services to the families with whom they work:

- Their primary goal is to keep children safe, and they make every effort to ensure that children can be safe in their own homes.
- They often serve as case managers, arranging for community resources such as housing, employment, transportation, counseling, health services, child care, homemaker services, or financial assistance.
- They provide counseling, parent education, and support.
- They may assist a client in getting involved in a faith-based organization or support group, or they may suggest (or require) that the client attend Parents Anonymous or be assigned a volunteer.
- Often, they develop a contract with a parent delineating specific goals the family must accomplish to be removed from the child protective services caseload.

Child protective services is challenging work because of the emotional aspects of working with abused and neglected children and the multiple roles that child protective services workers must play. A number of national organizations, including the Child Welfare League of America, the American Association for Protecting Children, and the American Public Human Services Association, have established specialized training programs for staff, as well as worked with states to explore new ways to provide protective services. Many states have developed computerized risk management systems that help workers assess family situations and needs and the safety of children involved.

Child protection agencies are also increasing collaboration efforts with other systems that come into contact with abused and neglected children. Increased attention is being given to the need to develop collaboration between child welfare and domestic violence programs. Domestic violence and child abuse often occur within the same families, and programs targeted at each serve overlapping populations. Collaborative training, shared use of resources, and coordinated case management efforts can remove many barriers that may prevent women from being harmed when their children are under protection or vice versa. Such programs strengthen the concept of family preservation. Some battered women's shelters, for example, have a family preservation worker assigned to the shelter to work onsite with the program's clients and their children (Schecter & Edleson, 1995).

As reports of child maltreatment continue to increase and often involve children more severely injured than in the past, the role of child protective services as part of the child and family service delivery system is undergoing extensive debate. Because of the scarcity of resources, child protective services is the dominating child welfare service in many communities. Although child protective services agencies once publicized their role as providing services to children and families to prevent child maltreatment from occurring or recurring, their current message is that they protect children. Because of staff shortages, many agencies can barely respond to all reports received and are unable to investigate all but the most serious reports. With increases in child maltreatment due to more extensive crack and cocaine use, poverty, and homelessness, the emphasis of child protective services is more often one of "damage control" rather than intensive services. This shift in philosophy places other community organizations in the role of preventing child maltreatment, as well as providing the extensive services needed to keep it from recurring.

FAMILY PRESERVATION SERVICES

Keeping families together is also being emphasized for families who in the past would have been separated. Such families usually have complex needs, with family members experiencing (in various combinations) child abuse, child neglect, sexual abuse, and substance abuse or exhibiting oppositional behavior in the home, school, and community, often including delinquency (Tracy, 1995). Goals of family preservation programs are

- to allow children to remain safely in their own homes,
- to maintain and strengthen family bonds,
- to stabilize the crisis situation that precipitated the need for placement,
- to increase the family's coping skills and competencies, and
- to facilitate the family's use of appropriate and informal helping resources.

Efforts geared toward family preservation have built on the earlier permanency planning emphasis of the late 1970s, after several studies found that many children were remaining in foster care with little attention given to other alternatives.

As increasing numbers of children, particularly children of color and those living in poverty, were removed from their own homes and placed in foster care, more attention began to be given to finding ways to keep families together or to reunite them, rather than having children languish in foster care. In most instances, because of scarce resources and negative beliefs about biological families, only limited efforts were made to work with them, since they were often viewed as a large part of the problem rather than the solution.

The Adoption Assistance and Child Welfare Act of 1980 (Public Law 96-272) required that efforts be made to avoid family disruption, reunify families after separation, and place children in permanent settings if they could not be reunited. The number of family preservation programs increased rapidly in the 1980s. These programs are based on traditional social work practice, which includes home visits and intensive approaches with high-risk families. Currently there are more than 400 family preservation programs in the United States.

The Child Welfare League of America delineates three types of family preservation programs (Tracy, 1995):

- *Family resource programs,* which are usually community based and provide support and education services
- *Family-centered services,* which provide case management, counseling, and education for families with problems that threaten their stability
- *Intensive family crisis services,* which are designed for families in crisis when removal of the child is imminent or reunification with the family is taking place.

Although programs vary, they offer crisis intervention; staff members available to provide around-the-clock services if needed; low caseloads; and highly intensive, time-limited services, similar to other own-home services previously described.

Family preservation programs incorporate a family systems perspective in working with families, viewing the family as a dynamic system with equilibrium out of balance due to the unmet needs of various family members. Emphasis in family preservation programs is on empowering family members to get needs met and to develop new skills in problem solving and communication to stabilize the family system. Family preservation social workers do not blame families for failure. The model is based on the assumption that the family is an important influence on children and that separation has detrimental effects on both parents and children. Through role modeling, counseling, and interactions with family members, the program focuses on values, respect, listening rather than giving advice, and help with goal setting, coping, and problem-solving skills. Social workers try to connect with and get to know all family members in a nonjudgmental way. The first stage of services is often spent addressing concrete needs such as housing or food. As the social worker develops a relationship with the family, emphasis is consistent with good social work practice—not on diagnosis and labeling but on understanding the day-to-day reality of the family and how it functions. Interventions often include contracts, encouragement, and reframing of issues (Tracy, 1995).

Evaluation of family preservation programs is difficult because families' needs and how they are addressed vary, as do interventions used. Programs are also finding that while the original program goal was to prevent out-of-home placement of a child or adolescent, the program may not be able to prevent such a placement from occurring, and that in fact some placements are necessary (Barth,

Courtney, Duerr Berrick, & Albert, 1994). Other outcome measures, such as an increase in positive communication among family members, need to be studied.

SUBSTITUTE CARE

Although every attempt is made to keep children in their own homes, sometimes this is not possible. Parents may have too many unmet needs of their own, experience serious health or emotional problems, or be too uninterested in parenting to care for their children adequately. In such situations, **substitute care** is located for the children involved. Unless the situation is an emergency—which many state laws define as a life-threatening situation—a child protective services worker cannot remove a child from a family without a court order. Even with emergency removals, court orders must be obtained, usually within 24 hours, and hearings held with parents present.

Types of Substitute Care

There are a number of different types of substitute care. Many communities have established crisis shelters, available to take children 24 hours a day until a family situation can be stabilized or other care that best meets a child's needs can be located. Although attempts are made to place children with relatives or neighbors so that they can remain in their immediate environment, this is not always possible. Other types of substitute care include foster homes, group homes, residential treatment facilities, and psychiatric treatment facilities. Once a child is placed in substitute care, the worker (in collaboration with the family, if possible, and with the child, depending on the child's age) must develop a plan either to return the child home or to terminate parental rights, placing the child in an adoptive family. Under federal law, the court must review the case every 6 months to ensure that the child is not in limbo in the child welfare system.

If a child does need to be placed in substitute care, every effort should be made to ensure that the placement is the least restrictive option, although this is not always done. Thus, relatives, neighbors, and others with whom the child is familiar should be considered first if they meet criteria to be positive substitute parents for the child. Consideration also should be given to finding care for the child consistent with his or her cultural background, preferably in the same neighborhood or school area. Since it is important that the birth parents visit the child, if this is in the best interests of the child, attention also needs to be given to accessibility of the parents as well.

Foster Care

If appropriate relative or kinship placements or other suitable arrangements cannot be made, the child most often is placed in foster care with a foster family. **Foster care** means that children live in homes with families other than their birth parents until they can return to their birth parents or be adopted. Foster parents are recruited and trained to relate to children and their birth parents. They are often parents already and may take in more than one foster child. Many foster parents keep in touch with their foster children after they leave, and some adopt the children if they become available for adoption.

All states have strict standards regarding foster care, including training that individuals must complete before becoming foster parents and to continue as foster parents, the number of children foster parents can take, appropriate discipline and treatment of children, and supervision of foster parents. A number of states train foster parents to parent certain types of children—for example, adolescents, children with AIDS, or children who have been sexually abused. Foster parents also develop support systems, and many belong to local and national foster parent organizations. Although foster parents are paid each month to care for each child, they often spend more than they receive and in almost all instances give large amounts of love and attention to the children they parent.

Currently, almost all children who require foster care have been abused or neglected. Because more children whose safety is threatened are being removed from their homes, there is a growing need for additional foster parents nationwide. Many localities are having difficulty finding foster parents willing to parent adolescents and younger children with serious emotional problems that often have resulted from child maltreatment.

Some children have difficulty handling the intimacy of a foster family, particularly if they have been seriously abused or neglected. In other instances, a foster family may not be found for a particular child—it is difficult to find foster homes for adolescents, for example. Group homes, which usually have a set of house parents to care for 5 to 10 children or adolescents, are an alternative to foster care. Such homes attempt to maintain a homelike atmosphere and provide rules and structure to children and adolescents. They also may include regular group counseling sessions for residents.

A major problem with the foster care system is the shortage of adequate foster homes. As a result, children often remain for long periods of time in emergency shelters and institutions, and many foster homes have more children than they can adequately handle. The shortage of adequate foster homes causes children to be moved from home to home frequently. A 1990 study conducted by the American Public Human Services Association revealed that more than half of children in substitute care had been moved at least once. Almost 28% of the children studied had had two foster care placements, 23.6% had had three to five placements, and 6.1% had had six or more placements (Center for Law and Social Policy, 1994).

Residential Treatment

Children and adolescents who need more structure than foster care or group homes can provide may be placed in **residential treatment** programs. More expensive to maintain than foster care and group homes, these programs provide consistent structure for children and adolescents, as well as intensive individual and group counseling. Most residential treatment programs help the child establish the boundaries that may be missing from home, focus on building self-esteem and competence, and help the child resolve anger and other issues from his or her family experience.

The goal of residential treatment is to develop enough coping skills that the child can return home better able to deal with the family situation. Ideally, the family also has undergone counseling, so they do not enter into old roles that may force the child back into previous behaviors to survive. Family counseling does not always occur, however, and it is often up to the child to cope on returning to the family and community. In situations where returning home or living with a nonparent relative is not possible, a child may be placed in a less restrictive setting, such as a group home or foster care. Children and adolescents with more serious problems may be hospitalized. In hospital settings, more restrictions are usually placed on the child, more intensive therapy is usually provided, and it is more likely that medication will be used. In other instances, children or adolescents, primarily delinquent adolescents, are placed in juvenile detention facilities. Studies suggest that white, middle-class children are more likely to be placed in residential treatment or hospital programs, while poor children and children of color are more likely to be placed in juvenile detention facilities.

Although recent attempts have been made to strengthen the substitute care system, problems remain. Perhaps the greatest problem is the lack of resources available to birth parents to enable them to reunite with their children. Overloaded service delivery systems often thwart social workers from providing needed services to parents. As a result, social workers are reluctant to terminate parental rights and free children for adoption. On the other hand, because they cannot provide needed services, they are also reluctant to return children to unsafe homes. Thus, children languish in the foster care system. Studies show, however, that when intensive services are provided to parents, even those who have multiple problems and have been separated from their children for long periods of time can be reunited successfully with them (Emlen, 1977; U.S. Department of Health and Human Services, Children's Bureau, 1997).

ADOPTION

When parents choose not to or cannot provide for their children, the court terminates their parental rights and the child becomes legally free for **adoption.** But many children in the United States, particularly African American children, are adopted informally by relatives without a formal court hearing ever taking place. The focus of adoption has changed significantly in recent years. In the past, the emphasis was on finding a perfect child for a couple who biologically could not have children, with an attempt to match the child to the parents according to physical features such as hair and eye color. Today, the emphasis is on finding an appropriate parent for a child—that is, one who can best meet the child's needs.

Adoption Issues

The types of adoption that are taking place in the United States have also changed. Until the 1970s, most formal adoptions in the United States involved couples who adopted healthy infants. But most adoptions that take place today are adoptions by stepparents, which is a result of the increasing rates of divorce and remarriage. Today there are also fewer infant adoptions. This is because many young women of all ethnic groups are choosing to keep their babies rather than place them for adoption. But traditional maternity homes/adoption agencies still provide residential and health care and counseling services before birth and, in some instances, postadoption counseling as well.

A major issue relating to adoption is the length of time it takes to move children through the child welfare services system once they are removed from their homes. Because of the priority given to family preservation, efforts are made first to ensure that parents are given the opportunities and resources to provide safe, supportive homes for their children. If children are in substitute care, the initial plan whenever possible is to return them to their birth parents. Making the decision to terminate parental rights and sever the parent-child relationship is one of the most difficult decisions anyone has to make. Even though parents may not be able to provide for their children's needs, most children have to deal with separation and loss issues throughout their lives if they are not raised by their parents. The extent that they have to address these issues depends on many factors, but all children, no matter how exceptional their adoptive and foster parents are, still have to struggle with the impact of not being raised by their birth parents. There is no perfect way to predict whether and when parents will be able to change enough to provide for their children or the best type of placements for children if their parents are unable to care for them.

Most children who become legally free for adoption because their parents' rights have been terminated spend a number of years in foster care. Sometimes they go back and forth between their birth parents and foster parents before they move into an adoptive family. Social workers in child-placing agencies work with children before placement, preparing them for what adoption is like and helping them address grief and loss issues surrounding their birth parents so they can begin to attach more readily to their adoptive parents. Many children in foster care have parents whose legal rights have not been terminated and have to wait for that legal process to occur. In 1995, there were 483,629 children in foster care in the United States. Approximately 74,931 had a goal of adoption but were not yet legally free for adoption. An additional 32,236 were legally free and awaiting adoption. Half of the children legally free and awaiting adoptive families in 1995 were African American, and 97% were older than 1 year of age (Child Welfare League of America [CWLA], 1997).

Adoption of Children with Special Needs

The majority of children legally free and available for adoption in the United States are considered **children with special needs.** Such children, while traditionally considered by many to be unadoptable, have been placed successfully in a variety of family settings. Children with special needs are those who are children of color, are older, have physical or emotional disabilities, or are members of sibling groups. In 1995, 47 public child welfare agencies reported that 27,115 children were adopted from foster care; 93% of these children were considered to have one or more special needs (CWLA, 1997).

Adoption agencies also have focused on parents they had not previously considered. In the 1960s and 1970s, emphasis was on transracial adoption; currently most agencies focus on finding parents who are of the same ethnic or cultural background as the child, if possible. Advocacy by groups such as the Association of Black Social Workers has given impetus to the emphasis on ethnicity when placing children for adoption. A number of agencies have established special outreach programs to African American and Latino communities to recruit adoptive parents. In the 1980s Father George Clements, an African American priest in Chicago, worked to establish the "One Church, One Child" campaign. This effort was based on the premise that if each church in the United States, particularly churches with primarily minority congregations, could work to have one child adopted by a member of its congregation, the adoption of children with special needs would no longer be so critical. This campaign has spread throughout the United States and has been one of many successful efforts to place such children in adoptive families.

Concern about waiting children of color has raised a number of issues about how and when ethnicity should be considered in child placement. Several states have passed or considered legislation relating to this issue. Minnesota, for example, passed legislation mandating that children be placed in settings that reflect their heritage whenever possible. Other states, criticized by white parents who want to adopt children of color, developed laws and policies stating that race and ethnicity are important factors in child placement but not the only factors. The Howard M. Metzenbaum Multiethnic Placement Act enacted by Congress in 1994 prohibits any federally funded program from denying the opportunity to become a foster or adoptive parent based solely on the ethnicity, race, or national origin of either the foster or adoptive parent or the child involved. The act also prohibits any federally funded program from engaging in discrimination in a placement decision on the basis of ethnicity. This act further states that race, ethnicity, or national heritage can be used as one of a number of factors in making placement decisions but not as the only factor (Barth, 1995). The act does specify that states need to expand efforts at recruiting families of color as adoptive and foster parents.

Many children have become caught in the middle of arguments about the importance of ethnicity in regard to placement, with psychological damage done to them no matter what the decision has been. In several situations that have received national attention, children of color have been placed with white foster parents, remaining with them for extensive periods of time. Later, when the foster parents have tried to adopt the child, the children have been placed in adoptive homes with parents of the same heritage as the child. Any very young child, regardless of ethnicity, experiences separation trauma when removed from a psychological parent who has been the primary caretaker for that child. One key aspect in avoiding such conflicts is to use the same criteria, including ethnicity, when placing children in temporary settings that are used when placing children in permanent homes.

In addition to trying to recruit more families of color, adoption agencies are recruiting single parents, working parents, foster parents, and parents with large families already. Experience is showing that all of these families can successfully parent. An additional emphasis is on placing siblings together in the same adoptive family. Previously, many siblings were separated, often forever.

The Adoption Assistance Act, previously discussed, allows monthly living allowances and medical expenses for families who could not otherwise afford to adopt children with special needs. More assertive and creative outreach efforts have resulted in children being adopted who were previously considered unadoptable, including many who in the past would have been relegated to a life in a state institution.

Other current adoption trends include foreign-born adoptions and open adoptions. In 1996, 11,340 children were adopted by U.S. families from other countries. The largest numbers of children were adopted from China, Russia, and Korea (U.S. State Department, 1996). *Open adoptions* allow the birth parent(s) to be involved in the selection of the adoptive parents and, in some instances, to be able to maintain contact with the child as the child grows up. While adoption services have been strengthened, there are still barriers to successful placements, particularly of children with special needs. Agencies and individuals still consider some children unadoptable, and some agencies are reluctant to work on placing children across state lines, even when parents (or children) in other states can be located.

As the number of adoptions of children with special needs has increased, agencies and

adoptive parents have also recognized the need for postadoption services for children and their adoptive families. Children who have experienced the loss of their birth parents as well as extensive child maltreatment have special needs that often continue or do not surface until long after the adoption is final. Adoptive parent groups have been instrumental in advocating for legislation, establishing adoption programs, and supporting other adoptive parents. Currently, they provide the primary support after placement in many communities.

An additional issue relating to adoption that has gained recent attention is what should be decided when birth parents want to reclaim their children after they have been placed for adoption. Such incidents are traumatic for everyone involved and, like the conflicts with ethnic placements, can usually be avoided if good child welfare practice is followed and licensed adoption agencies are used. But if the system fails in some way, the courts are required to decide who obtains custody of the child. In many instances, however, Goldstein, Freud, and Solnit's concept of the psychological parent and the extensive research on attachment and the impact of separation on children have not been considered, and children have been moved into new settings with complete strangers.

A number of adoption-related issues will continue to be raised in the next decade:

- Who has priority in gaining custody of children in an adoption dispute after an adoption has taken place?
- How important is ethnicity in determining child placement, and at what point should ethnicity be considered?
- To what extent should adopted children have contact with birth parents and siblings?

- What ethical issues should be considered in paying young pregnant girls large amounts of money for their unborn children without going through an agency?
- What rights should surrogate parents have?

CHILD WELFARE AND CULTURAL DIVERSITY

Whatever the types of child welfare services provided, they must be responsive to the day-to-day realities of diverse populations. Ideally, this means that all aspects of the child welfare service system should be culturally competent. That is, federal, state, and local entities as well as individual social workers who provide child welfare services must

- understand the impact of culture on individuals, families, and communities;
- recognize that while some factors may be more typical of one ethnic group than another in general, there is vast diversity within groups, and they should not assume specific factors just because someone is from a given group;
- value the diversity of individuals and cultural groups, and view the diversity as a strength rather than a deviation; and
- recognize the impact of oppression and social and economic injustice on at-risk populations.

Child welfare workers need to learn as much as possible about the cultures of the diverse populations with which they work, including history, family structure, family dynamics, religion, language, music and art, traditions, communication patterns, and views about seeking help and about social

work and social welfare (Prater, 1992). For example, strengths of African American families identified by various researchers include strong kinship bonds that go beyond the nuclear family, flexibility of family roles, a strong work ethic, and a strong religious orientation (Hill, 1989). These strengths are seen from a child welfare perspective in the informal kinship system regarding children's living situations; many African American children live with relatives other than their birth parents or nonrelatives considered kin without going through a formal foster care or adoption process.

Until recently, child placement agencies did not consider relative or kin placements, which meant that African American children were often placed with nonrelatives when close family members were available who could serve in parental roles for them. The church was also often overlooked by child welfare agencies as a resource in keeping African American families together or helping children when families could not care for them. In one southern city recently, a church was awarded custody of a sibling group.

Many Asian persons, particularly first-generation immigrants, hold traditional Asian values, which emphasize the needs of the family above the needs of the individual. Another value emphasizes the importance of bringing honor to a family. Thus, outsiders knowing about family problems can be viewed as bringing shame to the family. Asian family members may be reluctant to share information with social workers about how children are being cared for or what is needed to help them (Mass & Yap, 1992). They also may hesitate to disagree with individuals they view as authority figures, including social workers. This cultural pattern may be seen when clients

Social workers must help reinforce the rich heritage of each cultural group. Here, teen Ballet Folklorico dancers celebrate Cinco de Mayo.

Stone/Bob Thomason

seem to agree with a social worker but then do not follow through on what was agreed.

Latino cultures also value family as a means of socializing family members about culture as well as sources of social support and coping. Many Latino persons will leave jobs and immediate family members to travel long distances to help other family members in need. Males also play important roles in most Latino cultures and view protecting and supporting their families as critical. Mothers in Latino families are also important and respected. Social support systems in many Latino families include not only parents and extended family members but also godparents, who can often be looked to as a resource. The church is also a viable resource for many Latino families (Delgado, 1992).

Just as there is diversity within the African American, Asian, and Latino cultures, there is vast diversity within Native American cultures.

Some tribes are matrilineal, meaning that the mother's family is looked to first when legal issues such as adoption are addressed, as well as for other types of social support, while other tribes are patrilineal. Native Americans also value the family, with an emphasis on cooperation and respect for the elderly. They may seek out elderly members of the family or the tribe for consultation about child welfare issues and may remain quiet or defer to these persons when interacting with them (Red Horse, 1988).

We have presented just a few examples of ways that culture can shape interactions with social workers and child welfare agencies. These examples must be placed in the context of the rich heritage of each cultural group and not be taken as fact out of that context. The critical issue is to view the client from his or her day-to-day reality and from the way that person's culture shapes that reality, rather than to overlook culture completely, misunderstand it, or assume an "expert" role and stereotype without looking at the uniqueness of each individual. To be culturally competent when dealing with children, youth, and families, social workers must be self-aware and in touch with their own culture and the ways that their culture shapes their beliefs about and interactions with others. They must also be knowledgeable about other cultures and willing to learn from clients and see the clients as the experts in regard to their own lives and needs.

CHILD WELFARE AND THE FUTURE

A major debate in the child welfare field relates to what direction should be taken in providing services to children, youth, and families in the future. Some experts indicate that much more knowledge is needed before significant positive changes can be made. Others indicate that to be effective, wide-scale change will be required. Lisbeth Schorr (1989), in her book *Within Our Reach: Breaking the Cycle of Disadvantage,* holds the premise that we already know enough to prevent many of the "rotten outcomes" facing today's children and youth (p. xvii). In a nationwide review of child welfare programs, she found many programs that were effective. Schorr indicates that for programs to work for children and families in high-risk environments, they must be comprehensive, intensive, and flexible and meet a wide range of needs. Schorr also calls for intervention at macrolevels of the environment as well as at lower levels, advocating for economic and welfare reform. Consistent with the systems/ecological framework, she identifies three themes in relation to reduction of environmental risk factors (p. 29):

- Risk factors leading to later damage occur more frequently among children in families that are poor, especially if they are persistently poor and live in concentrated areas of poverty.
- The needs of at-risk children are not just individual but societal.
- The knowledge to help is available; the problem is a commitment to resources rather than a lack of knowledge.

Programs cited by Schorr (1989) as successful include:

- Vans that provide health care to rural areas, also delivering clean drinking water and lumber to build outdoor bathroom facilities where none exist
- Using high school students in a health professions program to track and work with young parents of high-risk children
- Quality child care programs with well-trained caregivers
- Public school programs that value active learning and parent and community participation

Schorr identifies the following characteristics in those programs she studied that were working:

- They provided a broad spectrum of services, including social and emotional support as well as concrete services such as food, housing, employment, and transportation.
- They were flexible in collaborations with a wide range of social services and other providers in regard to funding, policies, and program structure.
- They used a systems/ecological focus, seeing the child in the context of the family and the family in the context of the broader environment and working with all levels as needed.

- Social workers and other staff members were regarded as caring individuals who could be respected and trusted.
- Services were regarded as coherent and easy to use.

Duncan Lindsey (1994), another well-known child welfare expert, takes a different approach. He takes issue with the more narrow view of child welfare services advocated in the past. In his book *The Welfare of Children,* Lindsey advocates for comprehensive reform of the current child welfare system, suggesting that it abandon its residual focus and instead turn its attention to the economic security of children, youth, and families. Lindsey notes that in the past several decades, the majority of attention to child welfare services has been devoted to child abuse and neglect. He points out that in spite of that attention, child abuse and neglect reports continue to rise and the child welfare system continues to be overloaded with critical cases. Lindsey argues that reporting systems and services dedicated to child abuse and neglect have become a red herring ("a highly charged issue that devotes attention away from the real and more difficult problem"), when the broader issues are economic structure and poverty (p. 157). He cites a report from the U.S. Advisory Board to the National Center on Child Abuse and Neglect (1991), which indicates the following:

> It is not a question of acute failure of a single element of the system. Instead, the child protection system is plagued by "chronic and critical multiple organ failure." No matter which element of the system that the Board examined—prevention, investigation, treatment, training, or research—the Board found a system in disarray, a societal response ill-suited in form or scope to respond to the profound problem facing it. . . . The system the nation

has devised to respond to child abuse and neglect is failing. (p. 123)

Lindsey (1994) calls for a complete overhaul of the child welfare system, transferring all responsibility for investigation and handling of child protective services cases to the criminal justice system and focusing attention on the root causes of problems such as child maltreatment. He believes that the country must abandon its historic focus on dealing with symptoms rather than causes and embrace a preventive system that focuses on economic structure. According to Lindsey, until this is accomplished, the physical and mental health of children, youth, and families will continue to decline, with serious consequences not only for them but for the country as a whole.

As part of his broad-based approach, Lindsey (1994) advocates for a number of innovative but controversial options. He proposes a Universal Child Support Collection system, in which noncustodial parents would be placed under a "child support" tax table with money for child support withheld from their paychecks based on earnings and the number of children they are supporting. Their employer would withhold the determined amount along with other withholding taxes, with the monies going indirectly to the custodial parent through a central collection system (p. 239). Lindsay also advocates for a universal Guaranteed Child Exemption. Similar to the current child exemption allowable under federal law for employed parents, this system would be extended to those individuals who either are unemployed or not in the labor market. All children would be guaranteed a monthly allotment regardless of their parents' employment status. Another idea that Lindsey proposes is the establishment of a "social savings account" for children (p. 309). Like social security, a system would be set up that would provide funding for each child annually from birth until the child reaches age 18. Parents could also contribute to the account, which could be used for approved career program expenditures.

Other advocates for changes in the child welfare service system also call for an even broader approach, including

- an exploration of issues relating to teen pregnancy and parenting, including the role of males and declining economic opportunities for people of color, particularly African American males;
- an examination of the relationship between divorce rates and women on public assistance; and
- establishing a more culturally competent delivery system.

Social workers at all levels of the environment—agency, community, state, nation, and world—are advocating in various other ways for improving services to children, youth, and families.

The Role of Social Workers in Providing Services to Children, Youth, and Families

Social workers play many roles in providing services to children, youth, and families. In fact, this is the most traditional area of social work practice. The "child welfare worker," first a volunteer during the 1800s and then a trained social worker in the 1900s, is most often the stereotype of social workers. But the roles of social workers in this area have expanded significantly, and social workers at the BSW, MSW, and Ph.D. levels all are actively involved in providing services to children, youth, and families. At the BSW level, social workers are involved as

- child care workers in group homes and residential treatment centers;
- women's and children's counselors at battered women's shelters;
- counselors at youth shelters;
- crisis counselors in law enforcement agencies; and
- child protective services and foster care workers in public social services agencies.

An entry-level position in the area of child and family services usually offers broad-based experience that gives social workers a great deal of flexibility to move to other jobs in working with children and families (in either direct services or supervisory positions) or in other areas of social work. Some states require a minimum of a BSW degree for certain child and family positions, such as child protective services and foster care staff.

A growing number of social workers specialize in child protective services, investigating reported cases of abuse and neglect and intervening when necessary. They work closely with the courts, law enforcement agencies, and community-based family intervention, self-help, and volunteer programs. Foster care staff recruit foster families and oversee their training, and they often work with the child and foster family while the child is in foster care, helping the child adjust (see Box 12.5).

Many BSW graduates work as child care workers in residential treatment and psychiatric care facilities, serving as members of treatment teams and working directly with children and adolescents to implement the team's plan. Such experience is valuable in learning skills in working with emotionally disturbed children and their families. Other social workers are employed in agencies such as Big Brothers and Big Sisters of America, assessing

---

BOX
12.5

Do You Have the Characteristics to Be a Competent Social Worker?

The Child Protective Services Training Institute at the University of Texas at Austin recently reviewed client satisfaction research to understand what constitutes an effective client-worker relationship. According to the research, child protective services clients want social workers who show they are

- Willing to listen and help
- Accurately empathic
- Genuine and warm
- Respectful and nonjudgmental

- Fair
- Accessible
- Supportive and practical
- Experienced and competent

Child protective services programs, like most other social service programs, provide training after hiring. But many of these characteristics relate to social work values and skills learned in BSW social work programs.

Source: Urwin (1994).

---

children and potential volunteers and monitoring the matches after they are made.

Increasingly, BSW graduates are being hired as social workers in family preservation programs, family support programs that assist families in getting off public assistance, and programs that provide services to children with developmental disabilities and their families. Social workers at the BSW level are also hired to work as substance abuse counselors in inpatient and community-based adult and adolescent treatment programs. Special certification in the area of substance abuse is often required for such jobs.

School social workers also often require special state certification, which varies from state to state. In some states, BSW graduates can be hired as school social workers, whereas other states require teaching experience and graduate-level courses or an MSW degree. With increased attention to school dropouts and increases in such problems as school violence and teenage pregnancy, school social work is a rapidly growing area. School social workers

- provide individual, parent, and family counseling;
- lead groups of students who are teen parents, on probation, recovering from substance abuse, experiencing family problems such as divorce or abuse, or having problems relating to teachers and peers;
- provide crisis intervention services such as suicide intervention;
- organize parent education and parent support groups;
- advocate for the needs of children and families within the school system and the community; and
- network with other social services agencies in the community to assist parents

and their children in accessing appropriate services.

The National Association of Social Workers has a school social work division, and two school social work journals are published nationally.

Some BSW graduates also become employed in advocacy or policy-related positions, as legislative assistants or staff members of state or federal child and family services organizations or agencies, such as the Children's Defense Fund. An MSW degree may be required for some of these positions, particularly those related to policy analysis.

A number of other social work jobs in the child and family services arena require an MSW degree. This is due partly to the standards established by the CWLA, which many agencies follow, and partly to the fact that some child and family services are highly specialized. In almost all instances, an MSW is required of an adoption worker. Most child guidance centers and child and family service agencies also require MSW degrees. Many social work or therapist positions in residential treatment centers require an MSW, as do clinical social work positions in adolescent and child psychiatric treatment programs. Most schools of social work have child and family or child welfare concentrations at the graduate level, which provide special course work in this area, as well as field placements in child and family services settings. With the implementation of the Ph.D. degree in social work, some child guidance or child and family services agencies are attempting to hire agency directors at this level. Additionally, persons who want more highly specialized clinical experience are earning Ph.D. degrees, enabling them to do more intensive therapy with children, youth, and families.

If students are interested in a social work career in the area of child and family services, a number of child welfare and child and family journals, as well as numerous books on all areas discussed in this chapter, are readily available. In addition, many child and family services programs have volunteer programs. Volunteer experience is highly recommended as it helps students determine whether they are interested in this area and also provides sound social work experience.

SUMMARY

Policies and programs that focus on the needs of children, youth, and families are developed and implemented within the context of society and community attitudes and values, awareness about needs, and the availability of resources. The presently preferred focus is prevention and early intervention, keeping families together, and making decisions based on the best interests of children. But the lack of resources places large numbers of children, youth, and families in jeopardy of disruption and serious dysfunction. Because individual and family needs are diverse, as are available programs to address them, many opportunities exist for social workers interested in children, youth, and family services.

KEY TERMS

adoption
best interests of the child
child protective services
Child Welfare League of
   America
child welfare service
   delivery system
child welfare services
children with special
   needs
crisis intervention

family preservation
   programs
foster care
Head Start
home-based family-
   centered services
least detrimental
   alternative
natural support systems
permanency planning
psychological parent

residential treatment
self-help groups
school social work

Social Security Act
substitute care
U.S. Children's Bureau

DISCUSSION QUESTIONS

1. What is meant by the concepts the best interests of the child, least detrimental alternative, and psychological parent?

2. Describe briefly at least three prevention programs used with children and their families.

3. Compare home-based family-centered services with substitute care and adoption. What are the advantages and disadvantages of each?

4. Identify at least two areas in which social workers at the BSW and MSW levels might be employed in a child and family services position.

5. What is meant by special-needs adoption?

6. Select one of the "family problem areas" discussed in this chapter. Identify at least one prevention and one intervention program you would suggest to address that problem area.

7. Identify at least three problems with the current children, youth, and families service delivery system. What are some possible solutions?

8. Debate the following arguments, giving a rationale for both pro and con positions:
   a. Child abuse is a "red herring" that has directed attention away from the more critical child welfare issue of poverty.
   b. The knowledge to make things better for children and families is within our reach; we just have to begin to put the tools in place to do so.

INFOTRAC COLLEGE EDITION

To learn more about topics included in this chapter, enter the following search terms:

adoption assistance

adoptive parents

child abuse laws

child welfare agencies

family foster care

foster parents

kinship care

prenatal care

school-based social services

Title IV-E

transracial adoption

ON THE INTERNET

http://www.acf.dhhs.gov/

http://www.cwla.org/

http://www.childrensdefense.org/

http://guthrie.hunter.cuny.edu/socwork/nrcfcpp/

http://spaulding.org/adoption/NRC-adoption.html/

http://www.nicwa.org/

REFERENCES

Adoption 2002. (1997). Washington, DC: U.S. Department of Health and Human Services, Children's Bureau.

American Public Welfare Association. (1995). *W Memo,* 7(5).

Axinn, J., & Levin, H. (1997). *Social welfare: A history of the American response to need* (4th ed.). New York: Longman.

Barth, R. (1995). Adoption. In R. Edwards (Ed.), *Encyclopedia of social work* (19th ed., pp. 48–59). Washington, DC: NASW Press.

Barth, R., Courtney, M., Duerr Berrick, J., & Albert, V. (1994). *From child abuse to permanency planning.* New York: Aldine de Gruyter.

Center for Law and Social Policy. (1994). Child welfare: A system in crisis. *Family Matters, 6*(1).

Child Welfare League of America. (1997). *Child welfare stat book, 1997.* New York: Author.

Crosson-Tower, C. (1998). *Exploring child welfare: A practice perspective.* Boston: Allyn & Bacon.

Delgado, R. (1992). Generalist child welfare and Hispanic families. In N. Cohen (Ed.), *Child welfare: A multicultural focus.* Boston: Allyn & Bacon.

Ellerbee, L. (1995, June 23). Tasha and family deserve a good chance. *Austin American Statesman,* p. A15.

Emlen, A. (1977). *Overcoming barriers to planning for children in foster care.* Portland, OR: Portland State University.

Goldstein, J., Freud, A., & Solnit, A. (1973). *Beyond the best interests of the child.* New York: Free Press.

Goldstein, J., Freud, A., & Solnit, A. (1979). *Before the best interests of the child.* New York: Free Press.

Hill, R. (1989). *Research on the African-American family: A holistic perspective.* Boston: University of Massachusetts Press.

Kadushin, A. (1980). *Child welfare services* (3rd ed.). New York: Macmillan.

Kadushin, A., & Martin, J. (1988). *Child welfare services* (4th ed.). New York: Macmillan.

Lindsey, D. (1994). *The welfare of children.* New York: Oxford University Press.

Lloyd, J., & Bryce, M. (1980). *Placement prevention and family unification: Planning and supervising the home-based family-centered programs.* Oakdale: National Clearinghouse for Home-based Services, School of Social Work, University of Iowa.

McGowan, B., & Meezan, W. (1993). *Child welfare: Current dilemmas, future directions.* Itasca, IL: F. E. Peacock.

Maas, H., & Engler, R. (1959). *Children in need of parents.* New York: Columbia University Press.

Mass, A., & Yap, J. (1992). Child welfare: Asian and Pacific Islander families. In N. Cohen (Ed.), *Child welfare: A multicultural focus.* Boston: Allyn & Bacon.

National Committee for the Prevention of Child Abuse. (1995). Healthy Families America: Stopping child abuse before it starts. *Memorandum, 2*(6).

National Study of Social Services to Children and Their Families. (1977). Washington, DC: Author.

Prater, G. (1992). Child welfare and African-American families. In N. Cohen (Ed.), *Child welfare: A multicultural focus.* Boston: Allyn & Bacon.

Red Horse, J. G. (1988). Cultural evolution of American Indian families. In C. Jacobs & D. D. Bowles (Eds.), *Ethnicity and race: Critical concepts in social work* (pp. 86–102). Silver Springs, MD: National Association of Social Workers.

Schecter, S., & Edleson, B. (1995, Spring). In the best interests of women and children: A chance for collaboration between child welfare and domestic violence. *Prevention Report,* pp. 3–4. Iowa City: National Resource Center on Family Based Services, University of Iowa School of Social Work.

Schorr, L. (1989). *Within our reach: Breaking the cycle of disadvantage.* New York: Anchor.

Shyne, A., & Schroeder, A. (1978). *National study of services to children and their families.* Washington, DC: U.S. Children's Bureau, Department of Health, Education, and Welfare.

Tracy, E. (1995). Family preservation and home-based services. In R. Edwards (Ed.), *Encyclopedia of social work,* (19th ed., pp. 973–982). Washington, DC: NASW Press.

Urwin, C. A. (Ed.). (1994). What clients want from workers. *Child Protection Connection, 2*(1). Austin, TX: CPS Training Institute, University of Texas.

U.S. Advisory Board on Child Abuse and Neglect. (1991). *A caring community: Blueprint to an effective federal policy on child abuse and neglect.* Washington, DC: Author.

U.S. Children's Bureau. (1999). *The President's Initiative on Adoption and Foster Care.* Available: http://www.acf.dhhs.gov/program/cb/special/02adptl.htm.

U.S. Department of Health and Human Services, Children's Bureau. (1997). *National study of protective, preventive and reunification services delivered to children and their families.* Washington, DC: U.S. Government Printing Office.

U.S. State Department. (1996). Available: http://www.usimmigration.com.

Vasaly, S. (1976). *Foster care in five states.* Washington, DC: US Department of Health, Education, and Welfare.

Westat, Inc. (1995). *A review of family preservation and family reunification programs.* Available: http://aspe.hhs.gov/hsp/cyp/fpprogs.htm

SUGGESTED FURTHER READINGS

Algate, J., Malucio, A., & Reeves, C. (1990). *Adolescents in foster families: Child care policy and practice.* Chicago: Nelson-Hall.

Billingsley, A. (1992). *Climbing Jacob's ladder: The enduring legacy of African-American families.* New York: Simon & Schuster.

Child Welfare. A bimonthly journal published by the Child Welfare League of America, New York.

Children's Defense Fund. (Annual). *Children's defense budget: Analysis of the federal budget and children.* Washington, DC: Author.

Cohen, N. (Ed.). (1992). *Child welfare: A multicultural focus.* Boston: Allyn & Bacon.

Costin, L. B., Karger, H. J., & Stoesz, D. (1996). *The politics of child abuse in America.* New York: Oxford University Press.

Dolgoff, R., Feldstein, D. D., & Skolnik, L. (1997). *Understanding social welfare* (4th ed.). New York: Longman.

Gambril, E., & Stein, T. (Eds.). (1994). *Controversial issues in child welfare.* Boston: Allyn & Bacon.

Garbarino, J. (1992). *Children and families in the social environment.* New York: Aldine de Gruyter.

Gustavsson, N., & Segal, E. (1994). *Critical issues in child welfare.* Thousand Oaks, CA: Sage.

Kamerman, S., & Kahn, A. (1990). Social services for children, youth and families in the United States. Special issue, *Children and Youth Services Review* (Vol. 12, Nos. 1–2). New York: Pergamon.

Mason, M., Skolnick, A., & Sugarman, S. (1998). *All our families: New policies for a new century.* New York: Oxford University Press.

Petr, C. G. (1998). *Social work with children and their families.* New York: Oxford University Press.

OLDER ADULTS

Needs and Services

Eighty-one-year-old Clara lives in a residence in South Carolina that she and her husband Bill bought in 1955. At that time, the home was located in a nice lower-middle-class neighborhood. During the early years of their marriage, Clara and Bill raised two children. Bill worked as a carpenter until his retirement 11 years ago. Bill and Clara were doing pretty well until Bill died 6 years ago. They had little in the way of savings; however, they received Supplemental Security Income (SSI; public assistance for the aged) payments. When Bill died, Clara's benefits were cut by approximately one-third, making it difficult for her to meet budgetary needs now. Clara is in pretty good health, although she is in the early stage of Parkinson's disease and has high blood pressure and osteoporosis. Clara's medications cost her quite a bit each month. Although the house is paid for, she also has to contend with yearly taxes and tries to keep the place insured. The house is badly in need of roof repairs, but Clara does not have the funds to make them.

Clara's two children both live in Georgia and have children of their own. Neither of these children is able to provide any financial assistance to Clara since they work at semi-skilled jobs and have very limited incomes. Clara has recently become concerned over the "rundown" shape of the neighborhood. Many of her neighbors over the years have died, and younger lower-income people have moved in. Drugs and drug transactions are common nowadays. Clara is afraid to go outside by herself and has to depend on volunteers from the church to take her to get groceries. She is becoming more and more isolated and continues to live in fear that someone will break into her house and take what little she has.

The experience that Clara is undergoing is not typical of the majority of older adults, although far too many share similar experiences. In general, most older adults experience high levels of life satisfaction, purpose in life, good health, and contentment. For persons who experience problems similar to those of Clara, however, the struggle to survive often limits their ability to enjoy life. Unfortunately, the myth that all older persons are alike tends to obscure the reality that there is as much variation among the older population as there is between the young and the old.

The number and percentage of people reaching old age are greater than they have ever been throughout recorded history. This is in part because life expectancy has increased dramatically since 1900. For example, in 1900, life expectancy for individuals was approximately 47 years; by 1995, it was slightly over 82 years. Viewing this phenomenon from the perspective of age distribution, in 1900 only 3 of 100 Americans were over age 65; in 1997, nearly 13 of each 100 were 65 or over. Not only are more individuals reaching age 65, but they are also living longer (see Table 13.1). The data also indicate that in 1997, 34% of all persons 65 or over were between ages 75 to 84, and an additional 11% were over age 85. Overall, 45% of the over-65 population was over age 75 (*Statistical Abstract,* 1998). To many experts, this suggests that there are really two groups of older adults—the old and the old-old (elderly). One unanticipated consequence of extended longevity is that many adults in their 60s are caring for their parents who are in their 80s and 90s.

While living a long life is a goal to which most of us aspire, the consequences to society have the potential of being catastrophic. Assuring that essential resources are available to meet the needs of the older population places a heavy burden on government and private resources, including families. More and more, middle-aged Americans are becoming the

TABLE 13.1	POPULATION PROJECTIONS BY AGE: 2000–2050 (IN THOUSANDS)	
Year	**65 and Over**	**85 and Over**
2000	34,710	4,259
2010	39,408	5,671
2020	51,400	6,460
2030	69,378	8,455
2040	75,233	13,552
2050	78,859	18,223

Source: Statistical Abstract (1998).

"sandwich generation," having to provide for their children while they also are providing for their elderly parents. But many families cannot offer such support, especially when major health problems occur, and many elderly people do not have families available to give even emotional support. Thus, there is an increasing reliance on federal and state government to provide for such needs. For example, it is estimated that one-fourth of the federal government's expenditures are allocated to meeting the needs of the older population. With continually increasing numbers of older adults in our society, even larger government allocations will be necessary in the future (see Figure 13.1).

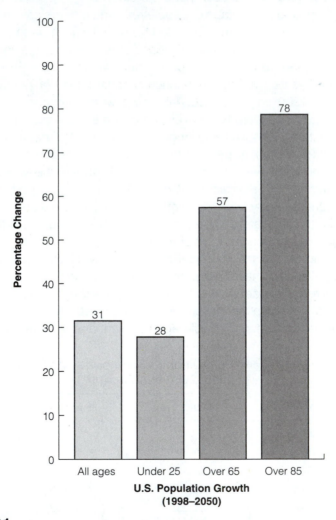

FIGURE **13.1**

THE U.S. POPULATION IS GROWING OLDER

Source: Statistical Abstract (1998).

In this chapter, we examine the more salient issues and problems an older population creates for society, review their problems of adaptation, and identify resources that have been developed to create physical and social support systems designed to meet their needs.

PHYSIOLOGICAL AGING

Most people are very much aware of physical changes they have experienced in their lives. The process of change through growth and physical maturation is not fixed but continues throughout the life cycle. During midlife (around the age of 45), we go through a stage of physical change that is called *senescence.* Senescence is generally defined as the onset of the degenerative process. It is at this stage that adults develop an awareness of significant bodily changes—the graying or loss of hair, wrinkling of the skin, a slowing down of the pace, and an awareness that old age will eventually be a reality.

Old age may be accompanied by sensory losses. Visual acuity may decrease, and bifocals may become necessary. Hearing problems may increase, and many older adults need hearing aids. In very late life, tactile (touch) and olfactory (taste) senses may lose their fine-tuning. These changes do not, of course, happen at any particular age, nor do they affect the aged to the same degree. Losses may be minor and hardly detectable in some but be major dysfunctions in others. Unless sensory losses are profound, they seldom limit the older adult's ability for social interaction and maintenance of a normal and fulfilling lifestyle. Even when more serious sensory debilities exist, proper prosthetic supports often allow the older person to maintain a normal life.

Although sensory losses are noticeable, even more significant changes occur internally. Changes in the cardiovascular system are often reflected in elevated blood pressure and loss of elasticity in the lungs. Renal capacity is reduced, and the bladder loses approximately one-third of its capacity. There is a loss of brain weight as well as muscular strength. Estrogen and testosterone levels are reduced, and other hormonal changes occur. With the exception of disease factors, however, none of these changes reduces older adults' ability to maintain an active, well-balanced life.

As incredible as it may seem, scientists have not yet determined why we age. A number of theories—including those regarding wear and tear (external stress causes organisms to wear out), autoimmune responses (the organism's immune system becomes less effective in throwing off challenges to the system), cellular (cells are reduced in number, and the organism's ability to replicate lost cells decreases) and cross-linkage (changes in collagen occur, with a subsequent loss of elasticity in body tissue)—have been put forward as viable theories of aging (Hooyman & Kiyak, 1993). Students who hope to work with older adults should familiarize themselves with these theoretical perspectives.

Social workers who specialize in working with older adults should be sensitive to physiological changes that are normal processes of growing old. When placed in the proper perspective, these changes should not be viewed negatively but rather as part of the normal life development continuum.

BEHAVIOR AND ADAPTATION TO OLD AGE

Although in this chapter we do not discuss in detail the developmental processes of later life, we do offer a few observations to dispel some of the myths that many individuals believe regarding the aging process. First, be aware that aging is a normative process and not a fixed dimension of the life cycle. Young children age, as do older adults. All societies attach significance to various stages of the life cycle. Aging is not only a chronological process; it has symbolic meaning as well. Cultures determine, for example, the age at which their members should enter school, marry, begin careers, enter the military, have children, become grandparents, and retire. Norms for behavior are prescribed at various developmental stages of the life cycle. Old age has been viewed too often as a period of dramatic decline. Thus, older adults are expected to be less active, need fewer resources, contribute less to society, and become more content and serene.

Scientific data buttress many of the symbolic definitions assigned to old age. Physiological changes, including the loss of muscular strength, sensory losses, and reduced lung elasticity, are but a few of the measurable differences between older adults and the young. On the other hand, many of the presumed losses associated with cognitive functioning have been demonstrated to have little substance in fact. Intelligence and intellectual functioning, once thought to decline appreciably in old age, are not measurably affected by the process. Behavior in old age is an individual matter and not attributable to the aging process alone. Any accurate assessment of adaptation in late life must consider the effects of the environment on behavior, as well as the physiological and cognitive characteristics present within the behavioral context.

In recent years, several theories of aging have emerged that seek to explain or describe adaptation in late life. Among the more prominent ones are **disengagement theory, activity theory, exchange theory,** and **developmental theory** (Bengston & Schaie, 1998; Berger, 1993; Kail & Cavanaugh, 1999; Newman & Newman, 1997; Rice, 1995; Santrock, 1999).

Disengagement theory assumes that biological degeneration and social withdrawal are coterminous and functional for the individual and society. It contends that as older adults decline physically, they have less need and desire for social interaction and progressively become "disengaged" from social roles. But more penetrating analysis reveals that it is societal discrimination against older adults that limits the social contexts (and thus opportunities) for social interaction. Social barriers, such as mandatory retirement, constrain the opportunities for participation in society. For some this means limited income resources and fewer friendship networks.

Activity theory "implies that social activity is the essence of life for all people of all ages," who must maintain adequate levels of activity if they are to age successfully (Barrow, 1996, p. 69). Presumably, more active older adults will achieve greater satisfactions and thus age more adaptively. Activity theory has provided the basis for a number of programs developed for older adults, such as the Retired Seniors Volunteer program (RSVP), Senior Luncheon programs, the Foster Grandparents program, the Green Thumb program, and activity programs in nursing homes.

Developmental theory emphasizes positive adaptation and life satisfactions based on mastering new tasks as the individual moves through the life cycle, including old age. Life-span development is viewed as a normal process that encompasses new challenges, new tasks, and flexibility in incorporating changes into the repertoire of behaviors. Older adults must accept the physiological changes they experience, reconstruct their physical and psychological life accordingly, and integrate values that validate their worth as older adults (Bengston & Schaie, 1998).

Developmental theory postulates that the psychological crises of late life are "integrity versus despair" and "immortality versus extinction" (Newman & Newman, 1997). Integrity, according to Newman and Newman, is "not so much a quality of honesty and trustworthiness . . . as it is an ability to integrate one's sense of past history with one's present circumstances and to feel content with the outcome" (p. 551). Despair suggests that the opposite of integrity will occur—that is, the inability to integrate past history with the present or to achieve contentment with the outcome. Confrontation with the psychosocial crisis of immortality versus extinction occurs in very late life. *Immortality* refers to the extension of one's life through one's children, contributions to social institutions, spirituality, and positive influences one has had on others. *Extinction* suggests the lack of connectedness and attachment and the fear that death brings nothingness (Newman & Newman, 1997).

Exchange theory attributes social withdrawal of the aged to a loss of power. Having once exchanged their expertise for wages, the aged must comply with mandatory retirement in exchange for pensions, Social Security pay-

ments, and Medicare. Thus, the power advantage has shifted from them as individuals to society. The effect of this power loss results in withdrawal from meaningful social interaction and greater dependence on those holding power over them.

Society's role in creating the behavioral and value context for older adults must be examined to gain insights into the problems and issues implicit in understanding adaptation in later life. Our society, for example, stresses productivity and distributes varying degrees of rewards and power in relation to it. Retirement serves to disengage older adults from socially recognized productive efforts. Instead of being consumers of products from their own current productive efforts, older adults are forced to be consumers of the products from the efforts of others. As we now turn our attention to the problems and issues confronting older adults, you should keep in mind that there are no simple solutions to problems. Social work with older adults who have problems may bring some relief to those individuals helped, but it does not address the causes of those problems. Changing the social systems that produce the problems is a more tenable solution, albeit more difficult.

ATTITUDES TOWARD GROWING OLD

Negative attitudes toward the aged are among many of the harsh realities people face in old age. Although a pronounced positive shift has occurred in attitudes toward aging in recent years, negative attitudes persist. Our society often has been characterized by its emphasis on youth and productivity. Independence is stressed and is enabled by financial supports gained through employment. Retirement often drastically reduces available income and may contribute to dependency. As a result, older adults are often viewed as being of less value to society.

Negative attitudes also are expressed through the process of exclusion. Media, for example, have avoided the use of older adults in television commercials, while advertisements in newspapers and magazines use younger persons to convey messages. Until recently, older adults, when used in film or advertising, were portrayed as dependent, irascible, or sickly. Fortunately, there is evidence that the media are beginning to present a more accurate portrayal of older adults.

Collectively, many societal practices have reinforced negativism toward old age. Many of these practices, such as mandatory retirement, have supported the idea that older adults are less capable of making contributions through work and to society. Various rules and regulations governing employment limit the opportunity for them to make such contributions. The discrimination or differential treatment based on age alone is called **ageism.** Like other forms of discrimination, ageism is institutionalized and, as a result, often subtle. Individuals are often unaware that they reinforce it through their attitudes and practices. Unfortunately, negative attitudes toward older adults may be expressed by professional practitioners as well as the general public. In a classic study, Riley (1968) identifies nurses, medical doctors, attorneys, the clergy, and social workers, among others, as giving preference to younger individuals as clientele. There is little evidence that this situation has changed.

Negative attitudes toward older adults often result in the loss of social status, with the accompanying diminished self-concept. Also, real-life issues further compound the problem. For example, as adults grow older, they invariably lose significant others through death, and they must deal with their own physical decline, which may limit activities and opportunities for mobility. Although the majority of older adults are independent and experience high levels of life satisfaction, these changes (or losses) invariably affect their quality of life.

As we review other problem areas experienced by older adults, keep in mind that attitudes, although not always directly linked with behavior, tend to shape our priorities and practices. Viewing the older population as "excess baggage" is not the bedrock on which positive responses to the needs of older adults will be achieved.

RETIREMENT

The impact of **retirement** on human behavior continues to be a topic of major interest. Although retirement often has been viewed as synonymous with old age, that scarcely is the case in our society today. Data indicate that more and more Americans are electing to retire at earlier ages, while, on the other hand, many older citizens continue to work either full- or part-time in the labor force. This mixture of age and work (either full- or part-time) clouds our ability to arrive at a precise definition, or line of demarcation, that clearly separates those among us who are retired from those who are not. When, for example, is an individual considered to be retired? Is the military "retiree" receiving a full retirement pension from the military, yet working full-time in a civil service position, considered retired? Or the 72-year-old receiving full Social Security benefits from the federal government who works full-time as a court bailiff? And what about the 69-year-old homemaker receiving SSI? Certainly, many other examples would further muddy the already murky waters of the definitional dilemma.

As a result, researchers use operational definitions that seldom are accepted universally. Some view individuals as retired if they receive a pension from their employer for past work performed, regardless of their present work status. Others identify retirees as those individuals who receive retirement pension benefits that exceed any monies earned through present work, and many identify a person in retired status who receives a pension and works half-time or less. Obviously, the retiree living on a pension and not working presents us with far fewer definitional problems. There is agreement that the retired status is achieved only in relation to benefits earned through employment of one type or another.

Although it is difficult, primarily because of the definitional problems just described, to ascertain how many individuals are added to the retirement pool each year, it must be large, although 53% of those age 65 and over continue to participate in the labor force (*Statistical Abstract*, 1998). Table 13.2 indicates the percentage of those in the labor force by age, gender, and ethnic status. For many retirees, income resources often are reduced drastically upon retirement. Few would disagree that the quality of life is related to available spendable income and that for many retired individuals, meeting basic survival needs is often difficult. Luxurious lifestyles and world cruises often portrayed in magazines targeted for the retired "over-50" population and sponsored by associations such as the American Association of Retired Persons are options available only to a relatively small percentage of retirees. Understandably, many retirees remain concerned about the stability of the Social Security system, which, incidentally, has been the catalyst for retirement on a grand scale.

Income, of course, is not the only factor affecting positive adjustment to retirement.

TABLE 13.2	**PERCENTAGE OF THOSE 65 AND OLDER IN THE LABOR FORCE BY GENDER AND ETHNIC STATUS, 1997**	
	Male	**Female**
White	12.8	5.1
African American	11.6	5.2
Latino	13.4	4.6

Source: Statistical Abstract (1998).

Health is a matter of great importance and concern. As the retired population grows older, good health becomes more problematic. Few survive beyond their seventies without some debilitating health problem, such as arthritis, high blood pressure, poor digestion, or related problems. For most, such problems do not severely restrict mobility or daily activities. For others with more severe conditions, the role of patient tends to eclipse preferred retirement activities. Concerns over meeting medical expenses, or anticipated expenses, may lead to conservative spending patterns that, in turn, reduce options and activities. Most older adults rely primarily on Medicare, a federal health insurance program available to individuals 65 and older. For the retiree in poor health, health-related problems may diminish satisfactions in the world away from work. Future-oriented retirees who have developed interests and activities also seem to achieve greater gratification.

The need for research on retirement continues to be crucial. Although social scientists have made great strides in the last several decades, the potential value of retirement-related research becomes more manifest as the number of retirees in this country grows. From past efforts, we have developed an emerging body of knowledge and understanding of the effects of retirement on individuals.

Obviously, there is much more to learn. Appropriate and valid social policies must be undergirded with a sound knowledge base.

In the past decade considerable emphasis has been given to preparation for retirement. So-called preretirement planning is based on the notion that people who prepare adequately for retirement adjust better to the lifestyle changes that accompany it. Many major corporations as well as public agencies have developed preretirement training programs for their employees. These programs usually emphasize estate planning; forecasting of income; identification of federal, state, and private resources for older adults; and strategies for dealing with such issues as relocating, living alone, and planning for leisure-time activities. Although no compelling evidence indicates that participation in preretirement planning positively affects adaptation to retirement, there is a mounting consensus that it does. Logic alone would suggest that life changes can best be successfully managed when adequate preparation has been made.

Retirement is emerging as a desirable goal for more Americans as it becomes more commonplace and publicly accepted. Our attention will now be directed in more detail toward the social and adaptive issues related to growing old in our society.

OLDER ADULTS AND THEIR FAMILIES

Facts refute the myth that older adults are abandoned by their families, because family members continue to be the primary source of emotional support and, in times of illness, care for their elderly members (Administration on Aging, 2000). Less than 5% of the older population is without family members. As Table 13.3 illustrates, the majority of older men are mar-

ried, but the majority of older women are widowed. As women grow older (75 and up), the likelihood increases that they will become widows and must rely more on family members other than their spouse. Most older married couples express general satisfaction with their marriage and the mutual emotional support that it brings. The majority have adult children with whom they maintain contact. Few older adults live with their children—and most do not want to, preferring instead to remain as independent as possible. Grandchildren also play important roles such as offering companionship and emotionally gratifying interaction, reducing loneliness, and often accepting caretaking responsibilities.

If older adults become debilitated with health problems, they often turn to their adult children for support. As a consequence, adult children may find the situation stressful, particularly because of the increased time demands. Middle-aged children of older adults have the responsibility of providing physical and emotional support to their own children while also giving support to their parents. Because of this dilemma, middle-aged people have been called the "sandwich generation." This strain may push these middle-aged children to their emotional and physical limits. As older adults live longer, they may need familial support for a number of years.

TABLE 13.3	MARITAL STATUS OF OLDER ADULTS AGE 65 AND OVER	
Marital Status	Male (%)	Female (%)
Single (never married)	4	5
Married	75	43
Widowed	15	45
Divorced	6	7

Source: U.S. Bureau of the Census, (2000), *Current Population Survey,* March 1998 update (P20–514)

Although most families manage the demands adequately, the potential for intergenerational conflict is ever present.

Families continue to be a viable resource for older adults, giving them both comfort and identity. Although research continues to provide inconclusive findings about the overall quality of intergenerational relationships, it does suggest that most older people maintain regular contact with their family members, who are the primary source of assistance when needed.

DYING AND DEATH

Death can occur at any point in the life cycle; however, death rates increase dramatically among those age 50 or over. Occurrences of death in later life tend to be the product of disease rather than accidents (see Table 13.8, later in this chapter).

Every culture shapes attitudes toward death as well as life. Our society tends to overemphasize a rational view of death as being a natural yet highly individualized event. Most of us are not engaged with the dying and consequently have little experience that prepares us for coping with either the death of others or our own death. Consequently, most people are uncomfortable when confronted with dying individuals, and we are apprehensive about our own death.

In a classic work, Elisabeth Kübler-Ross (1975/1997) laid the groundwork for helping dying persons come to grips with the remaining part of their lives. Her contribution, along with others, created a framework for social workers and other professionals to provide assistance for the dying as well as their families, often through the aid of a hospice. **Hospices** are "dedicated to helping individuals who are beyond the curative power of medicine to remain in familiar environments that minimize pain, and to maintain personal dignity and control over the dying process" (Hooyman & Kiyak, 1993, p. 389).

The hospice movement originated in England, and the first U.S. hospice was established in Connecticut in the 1970s. This movement has grown rapidly since that time, and now hospices are located in major cities as well as in some rural areas. Be aware, however, that the vast majority of dying persons are not served by a hospice because of the lack of resources or knowledge that such services are available.

In recent years, controversy has been introduced into the dying process in the form of "voluntary" or "involuntary" euthanasia. The medical community has long embraced the philosophical tenet that life should be preserved as long as medically possible, even through the technique of artificial means such as respirators. Taking a contrary position, supporters of the "right to die" movement feel that the individual should have the right of choice in governing the time and circumstance under which death should occur. Proponents of the right-to-die position emphasize the importance of the **living will,** a legal device that enables an individual to delineate the conditions under which he or she would refuse artificial means to maintain life. Organizations such as the Hemlock Society support not only the concept of the living will but also the right of individuals to induce their own death under circumstances in which they are experiencing great pain and suffering without hope of recovery.

Social workers who work with older adults will invariably work with the dying. Through the application of their skills, social workers can assist individuals and families in handling interpersonal losses and protect the dying person's dignity, integrity, and right to choices.

AGING AND MENTAL HEALTH

The state of mental health among older adults is not appreciably different from that of the population in general. Unfortunately, adaptive problems such as disorientation, memory loss, excessive dependency, and senility are assumed to be inherent to the aging process. The pervasiveness of these myths results in the view that older adults, in general, experience mental

---

The elderly face discrimination and often lack support when dealing with health and other problems. Here, a social work intern visits with an elderly man who has just been admitted to the hospital from a nursing home.

Daniel Nichols/Liaison Agency

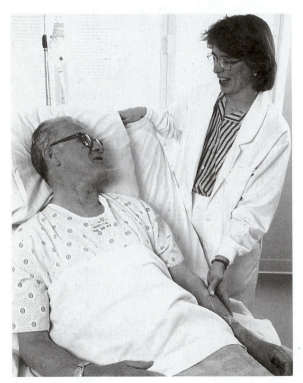

health problems. Like individuals in other stages of the life cycle, older adults may experience problems of a mental nature that result in dysfunction. And, as with younger people, these problems generally are responsive to treatment. In some instances, these adaptive problems have been present throughout the life cycle. Other individuals have managed to function adequately and do not develop mental health problems until late in life, often as a result of interpersonal loss, organic deterioration, or some traumatic event. On the other hand, activity and future orientation appear to be associated with good mental health. Maintaining enthusiasm and working toward goals are antithetical to the development of dysfunctional behavior.

Problems experienced in old age may be analyzed using a systems/ecological perspective. The way that an individual interacts within the environment strongly influences that individual's mental health. Many of the symptoms of dysfunctional behavior that appear in old age may be attributable to environmental factors. Social isolation and loneliness often appear to produce maladaptive behaviors. Overmedication often results in memory loss, disorientation, loss of vigor, or loss of appetite. Depression, one of the more common mental health problems in late life, may be caused by bereavement, anxiety related to income security, a limited social friendship network, health concerns, relocation, and related factors. Ageism and lack of attention to problems of the elderly have led to increased concern about this group's high suicide rate. In 1997, for example, the suicide rate for the population in general was 11.4 per 100,000 people. For adults 65 and over, the rate was 16.9 per 100,000 people—considerably higher. While older adults constitute only 12.7% of the population, 18.8% of all suicides occur in the older population (American Association of Suicidology, 2000).

Alzheimer's disease has emerged as one of the more publicized types of organic brain syndromes in later life. Given the nature of the disease, it is difficult to ascertain precisely the extent to which it occurs in the older population; however, it is estimated that 5% of adults over 65 suffer from this disease (American Psychiatric Association, 2000). Alzheimer's is typically an insidious progressive disease that results in increasing maladaptation. Disorientation, memory loss, wandering, and inappropriate behavior are among the symptoms. In the later stages the person requires total care, including feeding, bathing, and all routine maintenance activities. Alzheimer's disease imposes heavy demands on family members, who are the primary caretakers in the initial stages. Both physical and emotional demands related to caring for a loved one with a disability increase as the disease progresses. Alzheimer's support groups have been formed in many communities to provide emotional support for caregivers as well as an opportunity to share ideas related to effective techniques in caring for the person.

Dramatic changes in the mental health of individuals are seldom caused by the aging process alone. Individuals possessing well-integrated personalities who prepare themselves for changes related to retirement, develop leisure-time interests, and plan for the future are less vulnerable to age-related stress factors.

INCOME SECURITY

One of the more persistent anxieties experienced by older adults relates to income security. As one grows older, the ability to secure income through employment tends to become more problematic, and the reliance on pensions, savings, investments, and Social Security increases. For the majority of older adults, income available after retirement is generally below what they received while working full-time. For some, it may be less than half. Few of our present-day older adults earned sufficient income to allow them to "put away" money for retirement. Also, retirement incentive plans such as IRAs, tax-deferred annuities, and Keogh plans were nonexistent during the time of their employment. As a result, many retirees are forced to live on Social Security payments alone. Table 13.4 illustrates the sources of income for retirees in 1999.

As Table 13.4 reflects, only 18% of retirees' income is derived from pensions. This suggests that the majority of older Americans are not covered by pension plans. This, coupled with the fact that Social Security was not designed to be a "complete" retirement system, serves to create a financial dilemma for many retirees. Fortunately, the overall financial picture is improving. The average household income for adults over 65 has risen, although it is dramatically lower for African Americans and Latinos than for whites (see Table 13.5).

TABLE 13.4   RETIREMENT INCOME SOURCES

Source	Percentage of Total Income
Social Security	90
Assets	63
Pensions	45
Earnings	21
Public assistance	5

Source: Social Security Administration, (2000), *Income of the Population 55 and Older: 1998.*

TABLE 13.5	MEDIAN INCOME OF HOUSEHOLDS CONTAINING FAMILIES HEADED BY PERSONS OVER 65 YEARS OF AGE	
Ethnicity		**Median Income**
White		$32,398
African American		22,102
Latino		21,935

Source: U.S. Bureau of the Census (1999).

Along with the slight increase in overall income, there has been a corresponding decrease in the poverty level for older adults. For example, the poverty rate for people 65 and over in 1970 was approximately 25%. In 1996, it was near 10.8%—a dramatic decrease. However, the plight of the older poor and near-poor should not be minimized. As Table 13.6 shows, elderly Latinos and African Americans are much more likely to be poor than whites.

For many Social Security recipients who fall in the lower to lower-middle income brackets, working to supplement their income is often not an option. (See Table 13.7 for 2000 benefits and changes to Social Security and Medicare.) The Social Security Act serves as a clear disincentive to work. For example, recipients who are between the ages of 62 and 65 find that earnings over $10,080 are taxed at the rate of $1 for every $2 earned—a 50% tax rate. For those aged 65 to 69, the rate of taxation is

TABLE 13.6	PERCENTAGE OF THE AGED BELOW THE POVERTY LINE, 1996	
Ethnicity		**Percentage**
White		9.4
Black		25.3
Latino		24.4

Source: U.S. Bureau of the Census (1999).

33% (or $1 for every $3 earned over $17,000). This "tax" comes through a reduction in their Social Security check. Although federal regulations clearly prohibit discrimination based on age, the Social Security system clearly does so, as evidenced here. Fortunately, in 2000 Congress passed legislation eliminating the "earnings" penalty for Social Security recipients, thereby reducing work disincentives.

Recent debates concerning the future of Social Security benefits have raised the concern of many older citizens. The Social Security "trust" fund has long been tapped by Congress to assuage general budget expenditures. Recent congressional debates over privatizing all or part of Social Security has left many older adults fearing that their benefit levels will be reduced. Other proposals such as raising the age at which one would become eligible for Social Security benefits, as well as discussion over means-testing benefits eligibility, have resulted in considerable skepticism as to whether Social Security guarantees will be available in the future. Nothing that the Congress has done to this point has allayed those fears.

While money does not always produce happiness, it is related to satisfaction in later life. The common myth that older adults need less income to meet their living needs is hardly buttressed by fact. The need for food, clothing, shelter, recreation, transportation, and the ability to buy gifts for family members does not decline with age, while the cost of health care usually increases, often significantly. Lowered standards of living, unmet needs, and the inability to adequately meet those needs may result in feelings of inadequacy, despair, loss of self-esteem, and poor health. Income is an enabling resource that affects the options available in life. As income declines, so do those options with the resulting loss of independence.

TABLE 13.7	SOCIAL SECURITY AND MEDICARE CHANGES: HOW 2000 BENEFITS AND CHANGES STACK UP

Benefit Category	Benefit
2000 cost-of living adjustment (COLA)	2.40%
Tax rate for employees (unchanged)	7.65%
Social Security portion	6.20%
Medicare portion	1.65%
Tax rate for self-employed (unchanged)	15.30%
Maximum taxable payroll earnings	
Social Security	$72,600
Medicare	No Limit
Retirement earnings tax exemption	
Under age 65	$10,080
Age 65–69	$17,000
Maximum Social Security monthly benefit for worker retiring at 65 in January 2000	$1,433
Maximum monthly Social Security benefits	
All retired workers (after COLA)	$804
Couple, both receiving benefits	$1,348
Widow(er)	$775
Maximum SSI monthly payments	
Individual	$512/month
Couple	$769/month
Medicare Part B monthly premium	$45.50/month
Part A deductible for hospital stay—1st 60 days	$776
Copayment for days 61–90	$194/day
Copayment for lifetime reserve days	$388/day
Copayment for skilled nursing facility—days 21–100	$ 97/day
Hospital Insurance Premium	$301
Reduced Hospital Insurance Premium	$166

Sources: U.S. Department of Health and Human Services (2000); Social Security Administration (2000).

Many of the support and social services designed to assist older adults with their unmet needs might not be necessary if retirement income were sufficient to enable the nonworking aged to meet those needs at the marketplace. Unfortunately, the United States continues to lag behind other industrialized nations in replacement (retirement) income for its aged, ranking fourth in payments to couples and eighth in income benefits for the single older adult.

HEALTH AND HEALTH CARE SERVICES

In later life, the probability of developing health problems becomes more pronounced. Unfortunately, this condition has led many observers to conclude that aging and poor health are synonymous. Such is not the case, if you consider that health problems in old age are treatable and correctable, just as they are at earlier stages in the life cycle. Older adults

Many elderly are becoming more vocal about their rights and are advocating for their needs at all levels of government.

© Robert Maass/Corbis

are more prone to develop illnesses such as pneumonia, influenza, and gastrointestinal complaints than the population in general. Also more common in old age are chronic diseases, including heart disease, hypertension, cancer, arthritis, diabetes, emphysema, osteoporosis, and visual impairments (Barrow, 1996). Table 13.8 shows the health problems that are the leading causes of death for older adults.

Only 5% of the older adult population is affected by health problems so severe that their mobility is limited. The majority are able to move about the community even though they may have one or more disease symptoms.

Health care resources are provided primarily through Medicare and Medicaid. **Medicare** is a government health insurance program designed to pay for hospital care and related medical expenses for persons over 65. Because of the costs of medical care, the amount of benefits paid by Medicare has decreased to approximately 50% of the total cost of the care. The inability of older adults to pay the portion of medical fees not covered by Medicare has resulted in large numbers not seeking necessary medical attention.

Both Medicare and **Medicaid** (health insurance for the poor) have made it possible

TABLE 13.8	LEADING CAUSES OF DEATH FOR PERSONS AGE 65 AND OLDER BY GENDER, 1996 (DEATHS PER 100,000 POPULATION)		
Cause of Death		Male	Female
Heart diseases		2,022	1,707
Malignant neoplasms		1,458	915
Cerebrovascular diseases		373	442
Pulmonary diseases		339	212

Source: Statistical Abstract (1998).

for many older adults to obtain needed medical treatment. Due to personal cost-related factors, however, many older adults often are forced to delay seeking treatment until health conditions become severe or life-threatening. Neither of these health insurance programs is designed to provide funding for preventive health care. Doubtless, many serious health problems could be averted or become less problematic if attention were given to preventive health measures.

As with other government-funded benefit programs, Medicare and Medicaid funds are rapidly approaching deficit spending levels. Various solutions to the financing of health care have been proposed. These include a reduction of benefits, more stringent eligibility requirements, and an expansion of government coverage for catastrophic cases. Solutions to financing must be found if the health needs of our older population are to be met.

ABUSE AND NEGLECT

Because of limited research, little is known about the form and pervasiveness of abuse and neglect of the elderly. *Neglect* is the failure to perform the needed activities or tasks essential for meeting one's daily needs. *Abuse* is a physical or psychological act intended to inflict harm. As is the case with battered children or spouses, the knowledge that older persons are abused and neglected is antithetical to our social morality.

Self-neglect is perhaps the most common. Many older adults lack the necessary resources or skills to provide adequate nutrition or maintain daily household living tasks, such as washing dishes, cleaning the house, and securing proper health services. Self-neglect is more frequent when older persons are socially isolated and have little involvement with family or friends. Caretakers, usually family members, also may be involved in the neglect of elderly people's physical and emotional needs. Neglect often occurs when an older adult lives with a son or daughter and is dependent. Ignoring daily and special needs, denying transportation, failing to include aged persons as members of family households, ignoring their desires to contribute, and providing improper clothing and diet are among the more common forms of neglect of the aged.

Like neglect, abuse usually occurs when the older adult is living with a relative. Abusers often are overtaxed mentally and emotionally and lash out when demands are made on them by older family members. Physical abuse takes the form of slapping, shoving, punching, or placing the older adults in restraints. Psychological or emotional abuse results from threats (of sending the older adults to nursing homes and so forth), ignoring, ridiculing, taking their Social Security or other income and giving them no spending money, cursing, and reminding them that they are a burden.

Recent statistics compiled by the federal government estimate that some 450,000 elderly persons age 60 and over experienced abuse and/or neglect in domestic settings in 1996 (Administration on Aging, 2000). Of this total, only 16% were reported to and substantiated by adult protective services (APS) agencies. Thus, over five times as many new incidents of abuse and neglect were unreported than those that were reported to and substantiated by APS agencies in 1996. Many states have enacted legislation to protect older adults from abuse and neglect. Family violence is an unfortunate and dehumanizing product of our society that generally is directed toward those dependent on others for some aspect of their care. Adult protective services are designed to shield older adults from further harm. Unfortunately, such services do little to alleviate the causes of the problem.

LONG-TERM CARE

Most older Americans enjoy reasonably good health, with only 5% experiencing health problems so debilitating that they require long-term care (often thought of as nursing home care). The contemporary long-term care industry has emerged primarily as a result of Medicare and Medicaid legislation, which allows third-party payments to the providers of health care services. Nursing homes and other long-term care facilities typically are licensed by state health departments, which have the responsibility of periodically reviewing such facilities to ensure that minimal standards of care are maintained. In addition, all states require that administrators of long-term care facilities be licensed, although considerable variation exists in administrator-licensing requirements among the states.

The media quite often portray nursing homes as dehumanizing warehouses where residents are neglected and abuse is common. Staff are often characterized as being incompetent, uncaring, and disinterested in providing high quality of care for the residents. Unfortunately, for some nursing homes and other types of long-term care facilities, these allegations are valid. Even though the majority of these facilities make every effort to provide quality care, caring for debilitated, aging residents is both physically and emotionally demanding. High rates of staff turnover are common, placing further stress on facilities in the selection and training of nursing care staff. In recent years, however, more stringent state standards and skillful investigation and evaluation techniques by state regulatory agencies have resulted in a higher level and quality of services. The **Omnibus Budget Reconciliation Act of 1987 (OBRA)** introduced major nursing home reforms, including strengthening residents' rights, establishing written care plans, providing required staff training, and requiring that certified social workers be employed. These efforts were designed to create a safe and secure environment for residents in which appropriate medical and nursing care would be administered by a caring staff.

The majority of nursing homes and other long-term care facilities in this country are proprietary; that is, they are private, profit-making businesses. Some facilities are non-profit and are usually operated through the auspices of religious organizations or units of state or local governments. There appears to be little difference in the quality of care between the private profit-making facilities and nonprofit ones. Privately owned facilities are more vulnerable to "shaving" services to maximize profit. Strict enforcement of standards, however, minimizes any significant differences in the services provided for residents.

Long-term care facilities will continue to be the most viable resource for the debilitated elderly. Many facilities, particularly those affordable by more wealthy elderly, offer a range of living options. An individual or couple can move into a private apartment that is part of the facility and maintain independence if they desire, although meals in a central dining area, educational and recreational activities, and some health care may be available to them, often for increased cost. As health deteriorates and independence is diminished, nursing care, meals, and other services are readily available without the individual having to move. If the person's health deteriorates to the point he or she cannot be alone in an apartment, usually a facility more like the traditional nursing home on the same property is available to which the individual can be moved. This option is preferable to many elderly because they can make plans to live in one location with a minimum of disruption if their health deteriorates.

Alternatives such as home health care, visiting nurses, and personal care homes enable the older adult to reside in the community for a longer period of time, but they tend to defer, not replace, the need for nursing home care (see Figure 13.2). As the need for additional nursing home/long-term care beds increases, financing the needed care will become more critical. Government financing plans are strained already, and should forecasted budget reductions become a reality, alternative financing or other more cost-effective plans must be developed to assure that the debilitated elderly receive essential health care services. In a number of communities, faith-based organizations, unions, and private profit-making organizations are developing residential facilities for the elderly.

HOUSING

Although the majority of older adults are homeowners, housing often is a major concern for them. The rate of substandard homes

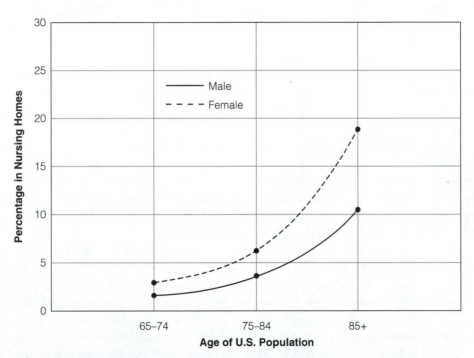

FIGURE **13.2**

PERCENTAGE OF RESIDENTS IN NURSING HOMES AMONG THE U.S. POPULATION AGE 65 AND OVER, 1995

Source: Statistical Abstract (1998).

among the elderly exceeds those for other age groups. Many of their houses become dilapidated over the years, and in later life the ability of older adults to maintain or repair them is often limited by low incomes. In addition, older adults find it very difficult to secure home repair loans. They must be content with progressively deteriorating housing, which often results in inadequate protection from the heat, cold, and other threatening climatic conditions.

Government housing for the aged typically is difficult to secure because of the high demand for low-cost housing units. Even when available, low-cost housing often appears unattractive, impersonal, and lacking in privacy; often has high crime rates; and is too noisy. The advantages include low rent and adequate protection from weather extremes. More units are needed for older adults but are not likely to be forthcoming due to government budgetary limits.

Housing alternatives for the more economically secure aged have recently expanded. High-rise, self-contained apartment complexes have been developed through the auspices of both religious organizations and private sponsorship. These facilities are typically attractive, provide all the amenities for comfortable living, and assure peer interaction and essential social supports. Many of these facilities, as discussed in the section on long-term care, also provide differing levels of medical care, nursing services, and meals, should individuals become unable to care for themselves in their own apartments. Such facilities, however, are much more costly, and many require substantial down payments before an individual is accepted as a resident. Although housing communes are not abundant, they are growing in popularity and provide a family-type living experience for older participants. This type of housing arrangement develops when several older adults pool their resources to rent or purchase a dwelling and share in its upkeep. Basic living costs for such things as food and utilities are shared, thus enabling each participant to spend less on basic living needs.

TRANSPORTATION

Transportation is essential for grocery shopping, attending church services, keeping appointments with doctors and dentists, visiting friends, and maintaining contact with families. Most older adults must travel some distance to procure the necessities for daily living, but it often is very difficult for them to do so. Many who once owned an automobile find the hazards of driving and the cost of vehicle maintenance and insurance beyond their capacity to manage. As a result, they depend on alternate sources of travel. Public transit systems usually are not satisfactory. Bus routes typically are developed for employed workers who regularly use this type of conveyance. Scheduling often results in long walks to bus stops, transfers, and prolonged riding time. In addition, it is extremely difficult for older adults to carry grocery bags onto the bus and walk several blocks from the stop to their residences.

A few transit systems have developed specialized services for the aged and people with disabilities, operating on a door-to-door basis by appointment. Few are available to serve the elderly on an on-call basis. Users must anticipate needs (often as long as 2 weeks in advance), make the appointment, and hope that they are not forgotten.

Volunteers have been engaged in providing transportation services for the elderly in some communities. Although only a small minority who need such services are able to get them, this option has enabled many older adults to gain mobility for securing needed goods and services. Nutrition programs also have provided transportation to luncheon programs, and some have been able to extend their transportation services to include shopping and social visits. This type of transportation alternative is available only to a comparatively few older adults in need.

The absence of transportation has resulted in many older adults becoming home-bound. Often the result is social isolation, which leads to the loss of incentive, decreased activity, self-deprecation, and eventually psychological and physical deterioration, thus confirming the stereotype that older adults elect not to participate in the mainstream of life.

Unfortunately, little has been accomplished in addressing transportation needs of the aged. Indeed, government budget cuts have significantly reduced transportation programs designed for the elderly in many communities. How do we expect older adults to be independent, shop for themselves, attend meetings, and remain engaged with societal institutions if they lack the transportation resources to do so? Such is the case for many of our aged today.

PEOPLE OF COLOR AS OLDER ADULTS

The problems of adaptation discussed earlier in this chapter are also experienced by older people of color, but to a much greater extent. Life expectancy for African Americans is appreciably less than for whites for persons 65 and over (see Table 13.9). Since neither genetics nor heredity has been a factor contributing to a shorter life expectancy for these groups, social and cultural factors are more likely to account for this differential in longevity. As a result of social discrimination, larger proportions of nonwhite populations experience lower incomes, more physically menial and demanding work, and fewer opportunities to achieve essential life support services. This has resulted in more severe and unattended health problems, inadequate nutrition, fewer opportunities for social advancement, near-poverty wages, and an oppressive cultural environment. Growing old under these adverse conditions has to be difficult.

While the figures have been dropping in recent years, the percentage of the elderly in the United States is still high, especially for persons of color. For example, in 1998, the percentage of aged white persons living below

TABLE 13.9 LIFE EXPECTANCIES OF WHITE AND AFRICAN AMERICAN POPULATIONS, AGE 65 AND OVER, 1995

Age	Mean of White and African American	White	African American
65	16.4	17.4	15.4
70	13.2	14.0	12.4
75	10.4	10.8	10.0
80	7.8	8.0	7.6
85+	5.7	5.8	5.6

Source: Statistical Abstract (1998).

the poverty level was 8.9%, compared to 26.4% for aged African Americans and 21.0% for aged Latinos (U.S. Bureau of the Census, 2000). Without regard to age, these figures are dramatically higher for households headed by women: 27.6%, 42.8%, and 46.7% for whites, African Americans, and Latinos, respectively.

Many of the necessary support services often are not available to aged people of color because of discrimination, language differences, lack of information concerning eligibility requirements, limited entitlement, pride, and less than vigorous outreach services. Unfortunately, for many elderly people of color, poverty, limited options, and discrimination mean that they cannot attain the security, contentment, and life satisfaction that most other older Americans do.

SERVICES FOR OLDER ADULTS

In recent years, a wide array of social, health, and related support services have either been developed or extended to provide for the needs of the aged. On the federal level, the majority of these programs have their legislative base in either the Social Security Act or the Older Americans Act. Social Security Act programs cover both income maintenance through social insurance and SSI and health services through either Medicare or Medicaid. The Older Americans Act provides supplementary services through funding of nutrition programs, transportation, social services, and the coordination of services for the aged.

Through both governmentally and privately sponsored sources, such older-citizen participation programs as Foster Grandparents, Green Thumb, and the Retired Seniors Volunteer Program, as well as a variety of self-help programs, have been developed within the past decade.

Older adults in the Foster Grandparents program, for example, are employed part-time to work with children in state schools, hospitals, and child care centers, as well as with pregnant teenagers and abusive and neglectful parents. Senior centers provide a site in many communities where older adults can interact, eat nutritious meals, participate in recreational activities, and pursue hobbies or crafts. Through the auspices of the Older Americans Act, areawide agencies on aging (AAAs) have been established throughout the country that coordinate services to the aged. Among their many functions are such activities as assessing the needs of the older population, providing or contracting for congregate meals programs, developing transportation services, serving as information and referral resources, and acting as advocates for the aged in assuring that communities will be attentive to their needs.

Meals-on-wheels programs provide hot meals for the home-bound aged and attempt to provide essential social contact with older adults who find it difficult to leave their homes because of limited mobility related to a variety of physical debilities. Adult day care centers enable older adults to remain in the community. Often participants live with a working son or daughter who cannot provide the required daily monitoring for the older person; day care centers assume caretaking responsibilities during the periods when their children are away at work. These centers usually have a variety of activities and provide health checkups and supervision for participants. Mental health services are provided through mental health/ mental retardation outreach centers, and counseling services usually are available to the aged and their families through many local social services agencies. Older adults living in rural areas often are disadvantaged in that many of these services are not readily available to them, although nutritional and transportation resources usually are offered.

Although community services are helpful in meeting many older adults' needs, they are not widely available in proportion to the numbers in the community that could potentially benefit from them. Outreach efforts have been reasonably successful in securing participation; however, resources are limited, and funding levels limit the number that can be served. Often, agencies are not located strategically, and therefore the participation of many older adults is limited. Also, outreach efforts would be more effective if older adults could be employed as care providers.

The need for support services for the aged will continue to grow with the expansion of our older population. New funding sources must be developed to accommodate this growing need. Social, health, and related services are essential in promoting the well-being of the older population.

SOCIAL WORK WITH OLDER ADULTS

The U.S. Bureau of Labor Statistics (2000) projects a 37.6% increase in social workers, a 73.4% increase in human service workers and assistants, and a 46% increase in home health and personal care aides between 1998 and 2008. This projection amounts to some 165,000 new jobs during this time frame. Due to the aging of the American population, it is expected that a growing proportion of these jobs will involve providing services to persons 65 and over.

Many schools of social work have developed specializations in **gerontology** (the scientific study of aging, the aging process, and the aged), and social work research has focused on problems of adaptation and life satisfactions in old age. As a result, research and

literature on this topic have developed rapidly, and a knowledge base for intervention is being established. It is now recognized that older adults experience many of the same problems evident at other stages of the life cycle: personal adjustment problems, marital problems, relocation, family conflict, adjustment to separation and loneliness, anxiety over limited income, mental illness, and interpersonal loss, among others. Growing along with this recognition is the acknowledgment that the aged are responsive to social work change efforts.

Generalist practice at the microlevel is the most common form of social work intervention with the aged. This type of practice includes working with older adults and their families on specific problems, such as enhancing personal adjustment, securing resources to meet their needs, providing emotional support in decision making, dealing with death and dying, and managing family conflict. Intervention often employs a counseling and guidance approach, stresses problem clarification and the development of options and priorities, and provides an opportunity for the client to express anxiety and emotion.

Community-based practice focuses on exolevel community systems as targets for creating a more responsive opportunity structure for the aged. Using an advocacy approach, social workers identify issues such as poor housing and lack of transportation and health care and mobilize community resources to help bring about change through the development of resources to meet these needs (Kirst-Ashman & Hull, 1997).

Social workers with an older adult clientele must be aware of the special problems they encounter. Many of the aged have been self-sustaining members of society and have developed problems of adaptation only after reaching old age. Accumulated, interpersonal losses (such as the loss of a spouse, friends, familiar environment, job, income, physical health) often produce behavior patterns that inhibit the achievement of life satisfactions and the fulfillment of daily living needs.

Social workers are employed currently in a variety of agencies that serve the elderly, including mental health centers, family service agencies, nursing homes, nutrition programs, recreational centers, hospitals, health and nutrition centers, volunteer programs, transportation and housing programs, protective services programs, and community planning agencies. Social work activity with older adults will continue to be intensified and interventive techniques refined as the theoretical knowledge base expands, resulting in more effective services to the ever-increasing older population in need of them.

SUMMARY

In this chapter, we have described some of the more salient characteristics of the older adult population, along with many of the issues and problems that are of particular concern to individuals who are age 65 or over. Social workers who work with older adults must be aware of the physiological, psychological, and social changes that occur through the process of aging to form effective interventive efforts. Of particular concern are problems that relate to income inadequacies, health care costs, housing and transportation, abuse and neglect, family support, and the availability and efficiency of various community programs that assist older adults with their living needs and that are culturally sensitive, recognizing the diversity that exists among the elderly.

While the majority of older adults experience few problems of sufficient magnitude to deprive them of life satisfactions, far too many suffer from deprivation that relates to limited resources and unattended health problems. Social workers can assist in meeting this challenge by developing their understanding, knowledge, and skill in working with older individuals. They can also work with the community in developing and using resources that will enrich the quality of life for vulnerable elderly people.

KEY TERMS

activity theory
ageism
aging
developmental theory
disengagement theory
exchange theory
gerontology
hospices

living will
Medicaid
Medicare
Omnibus Budget
    Reconciliation Act
    of 1987 (OBRA)
retirement

DISCUSSION QUESTIONS

1. Discuss some of the factors associated with physiological aging. How do these factors affect adaptation?

2. Review the theories of aging. Which of these theories seems most useful in social work intervention?

3. Why is the definition of retirement such a problem? Examine your own notion about what constitutes the most relevant definition.

4. Describe some of the more salient problems experienced by older adults. How would you see a generalist social worker providing assistance to persons experiencing those problems?

5. As the population continues to grow older in terms of both real numbers as well as percentages, what effect do you think this will have on our society? On social work practice?

INFOTRAC COLLEGE EDITION

To learn more about topics included in this chapter, enter the following search terms:

Alzheimer's disease

America's aging

elder abuse

elder care

geriatric care

hospice care

managed care

mandatory retirement

retirement community

social security

ON THE INTERNET

http://www.aoa.dhhs.gov/

http://www.aarp.org/

http://www.ssa.gov/

http://www.alzforum.org/

http://ninds.nih.gov/

http://www.alzheimers.com/

REFERENCES

Administration on Aging. (2000). Caregiver support. Available: http://www.aoa.dhhs.gov/factsheets/default.htm.

American Association of Retired Persons. (1999). *A profile of older Americans, 1999.* Washington, DC: Author.

American Association of Suicidology. (2000). Suicide statistics. Available: http://www.suicidology.org/suicide_statistics97.html.

American Psychiatric Association. (2000). *What is Alzheimer's disease?* Available: http://www.psych.org/public_info/alzheim.html.

Barrow, G. M. (1996). *Aging, the individual, and society* (6th ed.). St. Paul, MN: West.

Bengston, V., & Schaie, W. (Eds.). (1999). *Handbook of theories of aging.* New York: Springer.

Berger, K. S. (1993). *Developing person through the life span.* New York: Worth.

Hooyman, N. R., & Kiyak, H. A. (1993). *Social gerontology: A multidisciplinary perspective* (3rd ed.). Boston: Allyn & Bacon.

Kail, R., & Cavanugh, J. (1999). *Human development: A life span view.* Pacific Grove, CA: Brooks/Cole.

Kirst-Ashman, K., & Hull, G. (1997). *Generalist practice with organizations and communities.* Chicago: Nelson-Hall.

Kübler-Ross, E. (1997). *Death: The final stage of growth.* Upper Saddle River, NJ: Prentice Hall. (Originally published 1975.)

Newman, B. M., & Newman, P. R. (1997). *Development through life: A psychosocial approach* (7th ed.). Chicago: Dorsey.

Rice, F. P. (1995). *Human development: A life-span approach.* New York: Macmillan.

Riley, M. W. (1968). *Aging and society.* New York: Russell Sage Foundation.

Santrock, J. (1999). *Life span development.* New York: McGraw-Hill.

Social Security Administration. (2000). *2000 Social Security changes.* Available: http://www.ssa.gov/pressoffice/2000colafact.htm.

Statistical abstract of the United States, 1998. (1998). 118th ed. Washington, DC: U.S. Government Printing Office.

U.S. Bureau of the Census. (1999). *Current population reports.* Washington, DC: Government Printing Office.

U.S. Bureau of the Census. (2000). *Current population reports.* Washington, DC: Government Printing Office.

U.S. Bureau of Labor Statistics. (2000). *Career guide to industries.* Available: http://stats.bls.gov/oco/cg/cgs040.htm.

U.S. Department of Health and Human Services. (2000). *Medicare deductible, coinsurance and premium amounts, 2000.* Available: http://www.hcfa.gov.stats/mdedco00.htm.

SUGGESTED FURTHER READINGS

Allen, J., & Pifer, A. (Eds.). (1993). *Women on the front lines: Meeting the challenge of an aging America.* Washington, DC: Urban Institute Press.

Browne, C. (1995). Empowerment in social work practice with older women. *Social Work, 40,* 358–364.

DeCalmer, P., & Denning, G. (1993). *The mistreatment of elderly people.* Thousand Oaks, CA: Sage.

Estes, C. L., & Swan, J. H. (1993). *The long term care crisis.* Thousand Oaks, CA: Sage.

Greene, R. R., & Watkins, M. (Eds.). (1998). *Serving diverse constituencies: Applying the ecological perspective.* New York: Aldine de Gruyter.

Kelly, J. R. (Ed.). (1993). *Activity and aging.* Thousand Oaks, CA: Sage.

Margolis, R. J. (1990). *Risking old age in America.* Boulder, CO: Westview.

Miringoff, M., & Miringoff, M. L. (1995). *The social health of the nation: How America is really doing.* New York: Oxford University Press.

Moody, H. R. (1998). *Worlds of difference: Inequality in the aging experience.* Thousand Oaks, CA: Pine Forge.

Turner, B. F., & Troll, L. E. (1993). *Women growing older: Psychological perspectives.* Thousand Oaks, CA: Sage.

Van Den Bergh, N. (Ed.). (1995). *Feminist practice in the 21st century.* Washington, DC: NASW Press.

CRIMINAL AND JUVENILE JUSTICE

Joe is a 32-year-old man whose current address is Huntsville State Prison. He is serving a 20-year sentence for armed robbery. This is not Joe's first term in prison, but he hopes that it will be his last.

Joe first came to the attention of the criminal justice system at age 14, when he was arrested for stealing a car. The third child in a family of six children, Joe grew up with his mother and siblings in a poverty-stricken area of a large eastern city. He was abused physically by his mother during his childhood and received little positive attention from her. From first grade on, Joe had difficulty in school. He had a short attention span, regularly disrupted the classroom, and rarely completed his schoolwork.

At the time of his first arrest, Joe was in the seventh grade for the second time. He was placed on probation, and his family was referred for counseling. However, because his mother worked long hours, she was never able to arrange the counseling sessions. Joe became more of a problem in school as well as in the neighborhood in which he lived. He began skipping school, experimenting with drugs, and committing a series of burglaries. His mother could not handle his frequent bursts of anger or get Joe to respond to limits she set for him.

When Joe was 16, he spent 3 months in a juvenile detention facility, where he responded well to the structure provided by the program. When he left the program, he was assigned a probation officer and returned to live with his family. The conditions of his probation stipulated that he attend school on a regular basis, maintain a strict curfew, and report to his probation officer monthly. Joe followed these conditions for several months; however, he continued to experience difficulty in school and dropped out 4 months after he returned home. He held a series of jobs at fast-food restaurants but had difficulty coming to work regularly and became frustrated because he was not earning very much money. Increasingly, he gravitated toward older young adults who hung out on the street and seemed to have the freedom and the money for which he yearned. Joe's new friends liked him, and he felt accepted by them and enjoyed being with them. Joe soon became involved with them in selling drugs and committing burglaries.

Joe then experienced a series of arrests for drug dealing, burglary, and assault, which resulted in several stays in various detention facilities. Just before his last arrest, Joe married a 19-year-old, who recently had their baby. He is anxious to get out of prison and begin to get to know his son and support his family. He is frustrated by the lack of educational opportunities and counseling at the prison. He has enrolled in a prison program to try to earn his high school equivalency certificate and hopes to be released to a community halfway house and enroll in a job-training program. He knows that he will need job skills and help in dealing with his anger and frustration if he is to maintain a successful marriage, keep a job, and stay out of prison.

In this chapter, we look at the four components of the criminal justice system: legislative, law enforcement, judicial, and corrections. Although social workers play some role in all of these, the focus of our attention will be on the corrections component and social work roles involved in rehabilitation. Consistent with the overall focus of this text, we will look at the rehabilitation strategies in light of the competing views of criminal behavior.

THE CRIMINAL JUSTICE SYSTEM

Public social problems are specific conditions in the society that are perceived as sufficiently bothersome to merit intervention by government. Crime is clearly such a condition. Citizens have a right to expect government protection from crime. Society has a need to apprehend suspended offenders, to convict the guilty and free the innocent, and to punish and rehabilitate the convicted appropriately.

These steps constitute the ordered processes of the criminal justice system. The criminal justice system is expected to act as both a specific and a general deterrent to crime.

The **criminal justice system** in its broadest sense refers to the means used to enforce those standards of conduct required to protect individuals and property and to maintain a sense of justice in the community. A system of criminal justice creates the laws governing social behavior, attempts to prevent violations of these laws, and apprehends, judges, punishes, and makes efforts to rehabilitate those who violate the laws. Crime is a legal concept with political origins. Crimes are acts that are seen as a threat to individual or community well-being. Some acts are more serious than others.

No modern society allows citizens to roam about completely unrestricted. Two principal restraints curb criminal behavior: (1) morality, enforced by an individual's social conscience; and (2) law, enforced by the police and the courts. Any decline in the former is usually matched by a rise in the latter. That is, if traditional restraints on behavior are eroded (for example, disapproval of family, friends, and others we love and respect; informal discipline within social institutions such as schools and places of employment; and private lawsuits), it becomes necessary to increase legal restraints on that behavior (Samaha, 2000).

The criminal justice system consists of four components:

- the *legislative component,* which deems certain acts to be criminal;
- the *law enforcement component*, which seeks to deter crime and to apprehend and prosecute lawbreakers;
- the *judicial component,* which determines whether the laws are valid under the U.S. Constitution and prescribes penalties for illegal behavior; and
- a *corrections component,* which administers penalties and performs rehabilitative functions.

Each of these components is discussed in further detail in the following sections.

Legislative Component

Criminal codes define the types of conduct that are criminal and establish a range of penalties for such behavior. Three basic kinds

of crime are measured by the major criminal statistics in the United States (Samaha, 2000): (1) violent or personal crime or actions that hurt or threaten to hurt people; (2) property crime or actions that take, damage, or destroy or threaten to take, damage, or destroy people's property; and (3) other crimes or behavior such as disorderly conduct, public drunkenness, drug use, and prostitution (p. 28).

In the United States, each state is allowed to enact its own criminal statutes, within the restrictions dictated by the U.S. Constitution. Crime definitions are specific to legislative acts. Since social change is a constant, the U.S. Congress, state legislatures, and local bodies such as city councils are continually defining or redefining criminal behavior.

Social workers are likely to engage in political action to persuade legislative bodies to classify certain behaviors as criminal, such as abusing or neglecting a child, or to declassify certain prohibited behaviors as noncriminal, such as homeless people sleeping on the streets. It should not come as a surprise that others might oppose social workers' intentions or actions. Social workers' commitment to social and economic justice might be at odds with individuals who have little tolerance for those who do not adhere to mainstream ways of thinking and acting. The ideal legislative system attempts to define and enact a consensus criminal code—one that forbids, or extracts penalties for, behavior that most of us find threatening to the community—while protecting the rights of individuals to express their own lifestyles within the boundaries of the code.

Law Enforcement Component

Law enforcement includes four main functions: preventing crime, investigating crime, apprehending criminal suspects, and assisting in criminal prosecution (Samaha, 2000, p. 133). Law enforcement officers are bound to enforce all criminal statutes with equal emphasis (that is, full enforcement). Rarely, however, do law enforcement efforts attempt to enforce every criminal statute all of the time. Instead, they enforce some laws sometimes against some people **(selective enforcement).** This discretion tends to increase as crimes decrease in severity. The kinds of behavior that most people agree are not compatible with civilized standards include (Samaha, 2000)

- public drinking and drunkenness;
- begging and aggressive panhandling;
- threatening behavior and harassment;
- obstruction of streets and public places;
- vandalism and graffiti;
- street prostitution;
- public urination and defecation; and
- unlicensed vending of most kinds, including the more aggressive forms such as washing windshields of stopped cars and demanding money for the service (p. 135).

When a law enforcement officer has probable cause to believe that a certain individual has violated a law, the officer is legally "empowered" to make an arrest. Arrested persons are generally taken into police custody until arraignment. Then a trial judge or a grand jury determines whether there is probable cause for the arrested person to stand trial. As shown in Figure 14.1, there are many "stops" in the system from suspicion to trial. The officer often turns away or gives a warning; cases are pleaded away at arraignment, and so forth.

Social workers play significant roles and have strong beliefs about how the enforcement component should proceed. For example, should law enforcement officers'

discretion in domestic disturbance cases be eliminated? Domestic disturbances are especially challenging to law enforcement officers. Police also believe that intervention in domestic cases is the most dangerous part of their job. Does this belief influence law enforcement's position on making arrests in such situations? Are more women harmed or killed as a result? Law enforcement officers also have a dual responsibility when dealing with the mentally ill: to find mentally ill people and take them to a hospital and to confine a person who officers believe is mentally ill and likely to injure him- or herself or others if not immediately hospitalized. How much discretion, if any, should law enforcement officers exercise when dealing with the mentally ill? Who makes that decision? How do we ensure that law enforcement officers are adequately trained to deal with mentally ill individuals? Both of these examples constitute fertile areas for the involvement of social workers in law enforcement.

Judicial Component

Following arrest, individuals charged with a crime become defendants, and decision making regarding their future shifts from law enforcement officers to the criminal courts. Formally, courts are legal institutions where lawyers play the leading roles and make most of the decisions. Informally, most decision making takes place behind closed doors and in the corridors of the courthouse. Courts are political and social institutions as much as they are legal institutions. That is, they are sensitive and respond to the needs and demands of the public, special interest groups, and individuals. Courts use discretionary decision making to balance the law and extralegal, professional, organizational, and societal goals. In essence,

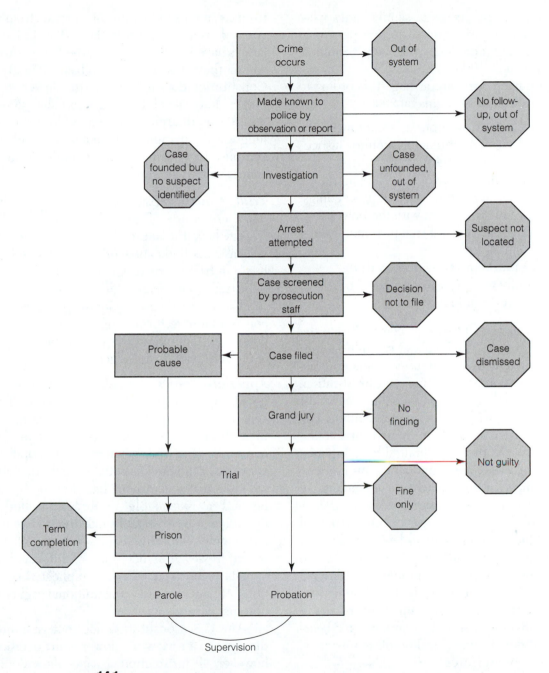

FIGURE 14.1

THE PATH THROUGH THE CRIMINAL JUSTICE SYSTEM

Note: The stop signs show how a crime drops out of the system. Rectangles represent stages in the system.

formal court proceedings simply ratify what lawyers and other criminal justice personnel have already decided informally (Samaha, 2000; Zemans, 1995).

Criminal courts are arranged according to three levels or tiers (Samaha, 2000):

- **Lower criminal courts** (sometimes called superior, municipal, county, justice of the peace, and magistrate courts)— courts with the power to decide minor cases and to conduct pretrial proceedings
- **Trial courts**—courts with the power to conduct pretrial and trial proceedings in all criminal cases
- **Appellate courts**—courts with the authority to review the decisions of trial and lower criminal courts (p. 253)

Lower Courts   The lower courts decide the majority of criminal cases, typically minor crimes such as traffic offenses, drunk and disorderly conduct, shoplifting, and prostitution. As such, they are the only contact that most people have with the criminal courts. The lower courts are courts of limited jurisdiction in that their authority is limited to trying misdemeanor cases and conducting preliminary proceedings in felony cases. Defendants in lower courts have the same rights as defendants in trial courts; however, as a practical matter, judges try most cases less formally than trial courts and without juries. Finally, the lower courts perform a number of additional tasks, including deciding bail; assigning lawyers to defendants who cannot afford them; and conducting pretrial or preliminary hearings to decide the legality of confessions, searches, and seizures.

It is important to note that in about two-thirds of lower court systems, judges are not required to be members of the state bar. While some states require lower court judges

to pass an examination or attend training courses, as a general rule the judges in lower courts have less training than the lawyers with whom they deal on a daily basis. The U.S. Constitution does not require that lower court judges have legal training (Samaha, 2000). Some would argue that many lower court judges are only minimally qualified to rule on complex legal issues, decide guilt or innocence, or pass sentence.

Trial Courts   Trial courts, on the other hand, are courts of general jurisdiction. That is, they have the authority to decide all criminal cases. Adjudication or court proceedings begin in trial courts (original jurisdiction), and only trial courts can adjudicate felony cases (exclusive jurisdiction). Not surprisingly, trial courts adhere to formal rules more than lower courts do. Only members of the state bar are allowed to preside as judges.

Appellate Courts   Appellate courts hear and decide appeals of trial court decisions. Proceedings in appellate courts are more formal than those of lower criminal courts or trial courts. In most states, intermediate appellate courts hear the bulk of initial appeals, deciding whether the government has proved its case beyond a reasonable doubt and whether defendants have established their defenses adequately. Supreme courts (courts of last resort) review the decisions of intermediate appellate courts as well as complicated questions of law and the constitutional rights of criminal defendants.

The U.S. Constitution does not guarantee the right to a review of a lower court decision; however, all jurisdictions by law allow defendants to have the decisions of lower courts reviewed by courts of appeals. It is worth noting that the overturning of a decision of a lower court does not automatically close the case. In many cases in which a lower court decision is overturned by an appellate court, the government proceeds with retrying the defendant.

More than 90% of all criminal cases never reach the formal trial stage. They are adjudicated by way of guilty pleas in a process known as plea bargaining. **Plea bargaining** involves negotiations among the prosecutor, the defendant, and the defendant's counsel that lead to the defendant's entering a guilty plea in exchange for a reduction in charges or the prosecutor's promise to recommend a more lenient sentence. The process may take place at the arraignment, at the preliminary hearing (if there is one), or during the trial itself. A defendant who agrees to a plea bargain may not receive the trial to which he or she has a constitutional right. Guilty pleas, however, do relieve the courts, which could not possibly handle the trials of all accused persons. Prosecutors are often willing to accept plea bargaining, particularly when the case against a defendant rests on weak evidence or questionable witnesses, and a trial could result in an acquittal.

It is important for social workers to have a working knowledge of the judicial system in the United States since many of their clients are involved at some level with that system. Social workers may also be called as expert witnesses in trial court proceedings, for either the prosecution or the defense. Finally, social workers must have a clear understanding of their obligations under the NASW Social Work Code of Ethics when it comes to criminal behavior on the part of their clients (Kirst-Ashman & Hull, 1997).

Corrections Component

Once convicted, criminals are sentenced and passed on to the next component of the crim-inal justice system—corrections. The term *corrections* is based on the idea that the state can reform or correct criminals. Corrections agencies in the United States supervise convicted criminals while they are in state custody in one of three settings: the community, jails and prisons, and a combination of incarceration and community supervision (Samaha, 2000, p. 366).

Most people convicted of crimes in the United States are not in prison. According to the Bureau of Justice Statistics (1999c), about 3.4 million men and women were on probation in this country at the end of 1998, a 3.7% increase from the previous year.

Probation   **Probation** should not be confused with the term *parole;* the principal difference between the two is that probation replaces incarceration and parole follows incarceration. In addition, counties typically administer probation, whereas states are responsible for the administration of parole. Essentially, probation substitutes community supervision for incarceration. Formally, it is a criminal sentence. Those who receive probated sentences are in the custody of the state, legally accountable to the state, and have limited freedom and privacy.

About half of those on probation in 1997 had committed minor offenses such as driving while intoxicated, or DWI (Bureau of Justice Statistics, 1998). The remainder were felons who had committed violent and serious property offenses. Most minor offenders receive probation because they are not considered a high risk to public safety. It should be noted that probation was not set up for or intended to deal with repeat felony offenders.

Typical conditions of probation require those on probation to obey the law; possess no weapons or explosives; work, go to school, or get vocational training; pay child support; obtain written permission from the probation officer to change their residence, change employment, or travel outside the community; notify the probation officer of any arrests or criminal investigations; and refrain from the use or selling of illegal drugs. Felony probationers are usually required to fulfill the following special conditions: drug testing, drug or alcohol treatment, community service work, mental health counseling, residence in a community facility, daytime reporting to their correctional officer, house arrest, and paying probation fees to help pay the cost of probation (Samaha, 2000, p. 370).

Probation ends when one of two events occurs: the probationer successfully completes the term of probation or the court cancels or revokes the probation. Revocation of probation can occur when the probationer is either arrested for or convicted of a new crime **(recidivism)** or when a technical probation violation takes place such as failure by the probationer to notify the probation officer of a change of address. While half of all probationers commit technical probation violations, only about 20% of these violations actually result in revocation of the probation.

Intermediate Punishment

Intermediate punishments (offenders remain in the community under strict supervision) have replaced both probation and parole because of a rapidly expanding prison population, shrinking government budgets, the shifting of penal policies from rehabilitation to retribution and incapacitation, and the desire to have a middle ground between either/or choices of probation or parole.

So-called community corrections are geared to punish offenders, protect the community, save money, prevent prison crowding, rehabilitate offenders, reintegrate offenders into the community, and provide humane treatment of offenders (Samaha, 2000, p. 367).

Intermediate sanctions programs, popularized in the U.S. during the 1980s and 1990s, include intensive supervised probation (probationers must contact their probation officer more often; enjoy less freedom and privacy; work, get treatment, or go to school); home confinement (also referred to as house arrest or home detention); shock incarceration (correctional boot camps); community service; day reporting centers; and fines (Samaha, 2000, p. 378).

Incarceration

The number of inmates confined in federal and state prisons or in local jails in the United States has increased from 1,148,702 in 1990 to 1,825,400 in 1998, an average annual increase of 6% (Bureau of Justice Statistics, 1999b). At the end of 1998, state prisons were operating at between 13% and 22% above capacity, while federal prisons were operating at 27% above capacity. California, Texas, and the federal system held one-third of the prisoners in the nation. This increase has produced a serious shortage in prison and jail capacity. In some states, prisons and jails have become the primary industries in many rural areas, creating a strong lobby to keep corrections facilities full so they can remain a source of employment for area residents. In fiscal 1995, federal, state, and local governments spent more than $112 billion for civil and criminal justice, a 73% increase over 1985. For every resident, the three levels of government together spent $430. From 1982 to 1995, increases in expenditures for civil and criminal justice for states, counties, municipalities, and the federal government amounted to 251%, 224%, 151%, and 292%, respectively. States

Although services for incarcerated persons are usually limited, innovative programs such as anger management and substance abuse treatment groups help reduce recidivism.

Stone/Jon Bradley

now spend more on criminal justice than municipalities, counties, or the federal government (Bureau of Justice Statistics, 1999a).

Longer sentences and more frequent **incarceration** were expected to reduce crime. A study of time served in prison by federal offenders, from 1986 to 1997 (Bureau of Justice Statistics, 1999d), revealed quite the opposite. Prison sentences imposed increased from 39 months, on average, to 54 months. The proportion of the sentence imposed that offenders entering federal prison actually serve increased from 58% in 1986 to 87% in 1997. Overall, time served increased from 21 to 47 months for those entering federal prison in 1986 and 1997, respectively. Time to be served increased from 23 to 75 months for weapons offenders, from 30 to 66 months for drug offenders, and from 74 to 83 months for bank robbery offenders. For those released from federal prison, time served increased from 15 months, on average, during 1986 to 29 months during 1997.

Little research evidence suggests that longer terms reduce recidivism. Violence in crime is often linked to participation in other criminal activities such as drug use. Thus, the incarcerated offenders are replaced quickly on the streets by others. Incapacitation of the one offender does not necessarily reduce the propensity of others to commit the same offense. It appears that prison time has been used as an expression of public outrage with little thought to its deterrent or incapacitation effect on other criminals.

THE JUVENILE JUSTICE SYSTEM

Extensive debate has taken place in the U.S. regarding whether juvenile offenders should be treated differently than adult offenders. There is considerable variation among states in their definitions of juveniles. Most states exclude children under 8 from juvenile justice jurisdiction, but differ about the upper age, with some using 16 and others 18 for determining juvenile or criminal justice jurisdiction (Samaha, 2000).

Delinquency includes actions that would be criminal if an adult engaged in them. Status offenses such as truancy, underage drinking, curfew violations, running away, and incorrigibility are illegal only if children engage in them. Thus, the term *juvenile delinquency* can refer to a youth who has committed a crime, a status offense, or both. Notwithstanding these definitional difficulties, several facts stand out regarding juvenile delinquency. Youths are substantially more crime-prone than adults. The juvenile arrest rate for serious property crimes is 6 times the adult rate and twice the adult rate for violent crimes. The majority of youth arrests are for property crimes such as theft and burglary and youth-only offenses such as truancy, runaway, and curfew. Younger offenders commit crimes in groups of four or more five times more often than adults. Serious juvenile crime is concentrated in urban areas, with higher arrest and conviction rates among youth of color. Youths are frequently armed (Samaha, 2000, pp. 495–496).

How to handle youthful offenders has been an issue debated throughout the history of the United States. Until the late 1800s, youthful offenders were treated in the same way as adult offenders, for example, imprisoned with adults and even sentenced to death. **Juvenile courts** in the U.S. were first established in Cook County, Illinois, in 1899. The philosophy of the juvenile courts has been that they should act in the child's best interest. Juvenile courts thus have had a treatment and rehabilitation orientation. Instead of a focus on a specific crime, as in adult criminal proceedings, the focus of juvenile courts is on the psychological, physical, emotional, and educational needs of the child, rather than the child's guilt. However, the in-

crease in youth crimes, particularly violent crimes committed by very young offenders, has put pressure on the juvenile justice system to rethink the efficacy of the treatment and rehabilitation focus that has been the hallmark of the system for so long.

In the 1960s, Gerald Gault, age 15, was tried in the Arizona juvenile court for allegedly making an obscene phone call to a neighbor. Neither the accused nor his parents were given advance notice of the charges against him. He was not informed of his legal rights and, if found guilty, could have been held within the criminal justice system until he reached the age of majority. The procedures used by the Arizona officials in the Gault proceeding were not unreasonable. They were in accord with the thinking of the times—namely, that advance notice and formal trial are likely to stigmatize a child and violate many confidentialities. The focus of concern was on the state as a parent rather than the state as the embodiment of a social conscience. Thus, Gault was brought before the juvenile court and tried without proper safeguards.

In 1967 the case went to the Supreme Court. The majority opinion, written by Justice Abe Fortas, vehemently criticized the juvenile correctional establishment and made it clear that regardless of intent, juveniles should not be deprived of their liberty without the full set of due process rights available to an adult. This case restored to juvenile procedures safeguards that often had been ignored, including notification of charges, protection from self-incrimination, confrontation, cross-examination, and the like (Niger, 1967).

The wisdom of the *Gault* decision is still disputed today. It undoubtedly gives minors the same basic constitutional rights enjoyed by adults. However, the return to a focus on whether a young person has committed a crime often masks the need for help exhibited by young persons caught up in court processes. The *Gault* case has brought about a critical reassessment of juvenile procedures and has suggested that the treatment and rehabilitative role of the juvenile correctional system must be secondary to the process of protecting the rights of the juvenile before the criminal justice system.

Juvenile Justice Agencies

The main agencies that deal with juvenile delinquency are legislatures, police, prosecutors, defense attorneys, correctional facilities, treatment centers, halfway houses, and social service agencies. Legislatures define the scope of legal authority of these agencies. They also determine when older juveniles can be transferred to the criminal justice system as adults in a process called *certification*. Finally, legislatures determine the budgets that support agencies administering juvenile justice programs and services (Samaha, 2000, p. 497).

Juvenile Courts

Juvenile courts in the U.S. have several often competing goals: helping children in need, treating and/or punishing juveniles who commit crimes, and protecting society from juvenile crime. The juvenile court process typically involves intake, adjudication, and disposition. **Intake** follows police referrals to juvenile court and usually involves the following actions: detaining juveniles during case investigation, filing a petition for a formal court hearing, and dismissing cases altogether. Status and property offenses account for most referrals to juvenile court. Only a small proportion of referrals involves crimes against persons, and most of these referrals involve minor assaults (Office of Juvenile Justice and Delinquency Prevention,

1998). **Adjudication** follows intake and is the legal process that judges conduct in juvenile court with assistance from probation officers. If the judge determines that the allegations in a particular petition are proven, then the juvenile for which the petition was filed is considered to be formally delinquent. **Disposition** follows adjudication and is the legal process by which judges decide how best to resolve delinquency cases. Juvenile court judges choose from a wide array of dispositions, from dismissal of the case to commitment to a secure juvenile correctional facility (Samaha, 2000).

Juvenile Corrections

Juvenile corrections can be divided into community corrections and institutional corrections. The Task Force on Corrections, National Advisory Commission on Criminal Justice Standards and Goals (1973), defines *community corrections* as "All correctional activities that take place in the community. The community base must be an alternative to confinement of an offender at any point in the correctional system" (p. 222).

Probation is the most widely used form of community juvenile corrections. Juvenile probation is an informal probation supervised by the police. Under this type of probation, juveniles are usually required to report periodically to police departments and to follow police-established conditions for behavior.

Juvenile Correctional Institutions

Juvenile correctional institutions (foster homes, shelters, group homes, halfway houses, ranches and camps, detention centers, and training schools) range from short-term, nonsecure facilities serving a limited geographic area to long-term, highly secure facilities serving large geographic areas. Foster homes are used at all stages in the juvenile justice process. Shelters (nonsecure residential facilities) hold juveniles following arrest or adjudication while awaiting more permanent placement.

Group homes (nonsecure, relatively open community-based facilities) mainly hold juveniles who have been adjudicated delinquent. Larger and less family-like than foster homes, group homes allow more independent living in a more permanent setting. Residents of group homes usually attend school—in the home or in the community—or work. Group homes provide support and structure in nonrestrictive settings that facilitate the goal of reintegration into the community.

Halfway houses (large, nonsecure residential centers) provide both a place to live and personal and social services that emphasize experiencing normal group living, attending school, securing employment, working with parents to resolve problems, and generally participating in the community. Ranches and camps (nonsecure facilities, almost always located in rural and remote areas) emphasize outside activity, self-discipline, and the development of vocational and interpersonal skills. Juveniles adjudicated delinquent are usually placed in camps and ranches instead of more secure facilities such as training schools.

Detention centers (temporary custodial facilities) are secure institutions that hold juveniles who have committed more serious offenses. Training schools contain the most serious delinquents, those who are security risks, those who have substantial prior records, and those who have exhausted other juvenile court dispositions (Samaha, 2000).

Dual System of Justice

Every jurisdiction in the United States operates separate systems for responding to juvenile and adult criminal behavior. Each system is governed by a different set of laws and procedures. Juvenile courts typically handle cases for persons under 18; adult criminal courts handle the others. This dual system of justice has received considerable scrutiny recently as the proportion of serious youthful offenders has increased. For example, juveniles were involved in 17% of all violent crime arrests in 1997 (Office of Juvenile Justice and Delinquency Prevention, 1998).

A variety of reforms that would change the way that serious youthful offenders are treated are being considered currently (Samaha, 2000):

- Reducing the juvenile court's maximum age limit from 18 to 16
- Increasing the use of juvenile records, particularly in adult courts, to help identify high-risk offenders and treat them accordingly
- Replacing the juvenile court's rehabilitation philosophy with a get-tough policy in which the sentencing objective becomes punishment that fits the crime
- Making sentencing of juveniles charged with specific, violent crimes mandatory
- Prosecuting juvenile career criminals
- Replacing the two-track system with a three-track system: a family court for neglected and dependent youths under 14 years of age, a juvenile court for 14- to 18-year-olds whose crimes are not particularly serious, and a criminal court to handle offenders over 18 and juveniles whose crimes are serious.

These reforms, however, only serve to treat the symptoms and not the causes of juvenile delinquency. While appealing to many who support a get-tough approach to dealing with youth crime, such approaches serve little purpose in preventing the crime from occurring in the first place.

Alternatives to Get-Tough Policies

Several alternatives to get-tough policies aimed at reducing youth crime have been identified. At the 1994 American Society of Criminology (ASC) annual meeting, Attorney General Janet Reno appealed to the assembled scholars of criminology for their assistance in dealing with some of the major crime and criminal justice issues facing the nation. The ASC formed 12 task forces to respond to Reno's plea. The Early Prevention and Intervention for Delinquency and Related Problem Behaviors Task Force (American Society of Criminology, 1994) concluded:

> Many children in the United States are lacking fundamental elements essential for human development. While these children are legally entitled to safe shelter, adequate food, basic health care, and sufficient preparation for adult economic viability, the actual lack of access to these resources has been linked to a failure to develop normally, to economically and socially marginal lives, and to persistent criminality. (p. 8)

The task force lists as promising approaches the following: (1) better accountability and quality assurance in public and private agencies mandated to provide essential resources for infants, toddlers, and school-age children; (2) advocates who are able to help caregivers and adolescents circumvent bureaucratic barriers in agencies mandated to provide essential resources; (3) neighborhood-based youth development organizations that provide sustained and comprehensive support and opportunities needed for wholesome development from early childhood through the teen years; (4) parental counseling, perinatal care for pregnant offenders, and hands-on parenting classes for offenders with babies and young children; (5) therapeutic communities (TCs) or similar residential programs for prison or jail inmates who are within a year of release and who have just been released—in particular, TCs in which inmates receive professional help in assessing and improving their interactions with children and spouses; (6) family focus/parenting programs with active door-to-door outreach in communities in which many children have fathers in jail or prison; (7) referral and advocacy for health, nutrition, and related services for children of parents under juvenile/criminal justice system supervision or conditional release; (8) accessible educational services/employment skills training for young mothers, especially in tandem with Head Start–type child care for their infants and toddlers and more traditional Head Start child care for their preschool-age children; (9) recruitment of more stable extended family members to care for the children of offenders, especially in cultural groups in which the extended family has traditionally played a key role in child rearing; (10) neighborhood-based collaborative community and youth development programs that emphasize provision of basic needs for infants and preschool children and actively recruit and sustain participation of older children during nonschool hours; (11) referrals of 10-, 11-, and 12-year-olds detained by the police to neighborhood organizations providing sustained activities during the nonschool hours, under the guidance of adults trained to provide the types of support and opportunities young adolescents and their families benefit from and enjoy; (12) provision of support services to the families of such youths, particularly parent training and home visitation programs to assist in family organization, social skills, and problem solving; (13) for older teens who have persistently been engaging in delinquent behavior, placement in communal detention settings where youths gradually

Many community-based treatment programs for juveniles include community service projects. Here, a group of youth on probation participate in the cleanup of a river.
© Jim West/Impact Visuals

earn status and privileges through vocational achievement and contributions to the welfare of all in the community, followed by supervised participation in similar activities after they earn their way out of detention.

Implementation of these strategies will take the sustained political will of Congress, as well as individual state legislatures. It will also take an unwavering commitment by society at large to ensure that each child born in this country has the opportunity to grow and thrive. This is indeed a tall order and one that needs the full resources of the social work profession to be filled.

REHABILITATION

Rehabilitation programs for criminal offenders cover a wide range and serve many purposes. In addition to reducing an offender's further criminal activity, prison rehabilitation programs con-

tribute to improved prison management, help accomplish the mission of meting out humane punishment, and give prisoners something to do. Programs aimed at the rehabilitation of offenders include vocational training, work release, financial assistance, prison industries, and treatment (Samaha, 2000).

Vocational Training

Vocational training is usually viewed as central to rehabilitation because most prisoners have limited, if any, skills qualifying them for legitimate work. However, the results of actual vocational rehabilitation programs have been disappointing. Vocational training has failed as an effective rehabilitative tool for several reasons: Prison budgets cannot support purchasing sufficient quantities of the equipment used in the training; many unions do not accept workers whose apprenticeship credentials were obtained while in prison; and most prisoners do not serve long enough sentences to fulfill apprenticeship requirements, or their training is interrupted (Samaha, 2000). Notwithstanding these problems, vocational training enjoys more public support than academic education programs—the public believes that vocational training is more practical and useful than academic learning.

Work Release

Work release programs are viewed as more effective than vocational training in decreasing criminal activity among participants. Work release has numerous positive rehabilitative effects. It provides the offender with a stable work record and job experience. It allows an offender to support his or her dependents while in prison. It has the potential to provide new job skills. It provides the offender with money at the time of release and often with a job. It allows the offender to maintain contact with the free community and limits at least somewhat the offender's immersion in the prison community. It may also change an offender's attitude toward him- or herself as well as toward society (Witte, 1975, p. 99).

Financial Assistance

Some rehabilitation programs provide offenders released from prison with financial assistance through employment. Such programs have found that released prisoners who received the aid were arrested less frequently and were able to find better jobs than those who did not receive assistance.

Prison Industries

Prison industries were considered a major element in the rehabilitation of prisoners in the U.S. during the early 1900s. Prison reformers of the time argued that work was not only useful but also therapeutic. However, despite their popularity, prison industries were scaled back because of the following factors: ethical questions about using prison labor, competition with private industry, the belief that prisoners are supposed to suffer and not make as much money as people working outside, and the opposition of labor unions and small businesses.

Prison industries appeared on the scene again beginning in the 1980s. The major justification for their return was the idea that prisoners should pay for their imprisonment. Prison industries were believed to support the three-pronged goal of creating work, reducing idleness, and helping manage prisons. In 1997, nearly 80,000 prisoners were working in prison industries, generating $1.62 billion in sales (Samaha, 2000, pp. 446–447).

Treatment

Treatment programs in prisons most often include either counseling or some type of behavior modification system. Counseling programs assume that the cause of criminal behavior is an underlying emotional problem. On the other hand, behavior modification treatment programs focus on how people behave in social situations that get them in trouble and on changing that behavior.

Issues in Rehabilitation

Prison rehabilitation programs have been controversial from their inception. Two primary questions fuel this controversy: Should we rehabilitate prisoners? And can we rehabilitate prisoners? Often, strongly held ideological beliefs regarding the rehabilitation of prisoners have confounded major prison rehabilitation evaluation efforts. Results of studies evaluating rehabilitation are decidedly mixed if one considers whether the programs actually rehabilitate the offender. As noted earlier, however, rehabilitation programs serve purposes other than preparing offenders to work hard and play by the rules when they leave prison. They also keep prisoners busy, and keeping them busy keeps them out of trouble. Rehabilitation programs are also viewed as consistent with orderly, safe, and humane confinement (Logan & Gaes, 1993).

CRIME PREVENTION

In response to a mandate from Congress in 1998, the National Institute of Justice (1998) conducted a systematic review of more than 500 scientific evaluations of crime prevention practices in the United States. The study found that most crime prevention programs have not yet been evaluated with enough scientific evidence to draw defensible conclusions. The study concludes, however, that enough evidence is available to create provisional lists of what works, what doesn't, and what's promising. Key promising prevention initiatives included the following:

IN COMMUNITIES

- Gang offender monitoring by community and probation and police officers
- Community-based mentoring by Big Brothers/Big Sisters of America
- Community-based after school recreation programs
- Dispersing inner-city public housing residents to scattered-site suburban public housing

IN SCHOOLS

- Schools within schools that group students into smaller units
- Training or coaching in thinking skills for high-risk youth
- Teaching of social competency skills
- Communication and reinforcement of clear, consistent norms
- Building school capacity to initiate and sustain innovation through organizational development strategies
- Improved classroom management and instructional techniques

IN FAMILIES

- Battered women's shelters aimed at reducing the rate of repeated harm to women who take other steps to seek help beyond staying in the shelter

IN LABOR MARKETS

- Job Corps (intensive residential training programs for at-risk youth)
- Prison-based vocation programs for adult inmates
- Enterprise zones with tax-break incentives in areas of extremely high unemployment

BY CRIMINAL JUSTICE AGENCIES AFTER ARREST

- Drug courts that order and monitor a combination of rehabilitation and drug treatment
- Intensive supervision and aftercare of minor and serious juvenile offenders
- Fines for criminal acts in combination with other penalties
- Drug treatment in jails followed by urine testing in the community

IN PLACES

- Adding a second clerk to reduce robberies in already-robbed convenience stores;
- Redesigning the layout of retail stores to reduce shoplifting

- Improving training and management of bar and tavern staff
- Metal detectors to reduce weapon carrying in schools
- Street closures, barricades, and rerouting

BY POLICE

- Proactive arrests for carrying concealed weapons
- Proactive drunk driving arrests
- Community policing with meetings to set priorities
- Policing with greater respect for offenders
- Field interrogations of suspicious persons
- Mailing arrest warrants to suspected perpetrators of domestic violence who leave the scene before police arrive
- Higher numbers of police officers in cities (pp. 6–12)

The Office of Justice Programs of the U.S. Department of Justice (1999) emphasizes the following elements as building blocks for successful community crime prevention initiatives: (1) collaborative, community-based partnerships that draw on the knowledge of all stakeholders; (2) programs that build community capacity to identify and understand local problems; (3) a broad range of coordinated, integrated programs that nurture families and communities, (4) comprehensive efforts that support parenting, child abuse and domestic violence prevention, victim assistance, child support enforcement, truancy, conflict resolution, youth mentoring, teen pregnancy prevention, and other child development and supervision programs; (5) giving communities the tools they need to build capacity (strategic planning; leadership training for residents; risk assessment; use of data analysis tools for decision making; and identification of local, state, and federal resources); (6) a knowledge base

of best practices to share across disciplines and communities; and (7) evaluation of both the process and impact of community-based crime prevention efforts (Chapter 2, pp. 1–2).

The reader is also referred to the discussion of viable alternatives to get-tough policies aimed at reducing youth crime discussed earlier. Many of these strategies are focused on strengthening family systems as a means of preventing crime.

The U.S. criminal justice system is evaluated not only by its capacity to prevent and contain crime but also by the justice meted out by the system. The system's dual responsibility to protect the citizenship rights of criminals as well as their victims constitutes the core of the criminal justice system. Law-abiding citizens want to be protected from criminal behavior but also from unwarranted intrusion of the criminal justice system into their private lives. The duality of these demands imposes costs and constraints on police, court officers, and prison and parole officials. Since in the final analysis "law and order" exponents and "civil libertarians" want the same things, where does the policy problem lie? It lies in the question of emphasis and balance, and the latter seldom seems to exist.

VIEWS OF CRIMINAL BEHAVIOR

A number of views of criminal behavior compete to explain why people commit crimes. Crime can be viewed as psychologically aberrant behavior, socially induced behavior, a consequence of rational thought in which criminals simply see crime as just another way to make a living, or a complex interactive process of an individual's personal characteristics and the many factors that constitute his or her environment. The explanation accepted by various citizens constitutes the structure on which they wish the criminal justice system to be built.

PSYCHOLOGICAL VIEWS OF THE CRIMINAL PERSONALITY

One school of thought suggests that criminals differ from noncriminals in some fundamental way, other than the obvious one of having been convicted. The distinguishing trait has been thought over the years to be reflected in body or head shape, skull size, chromosome structure, specific patterns of response to projective tests, or the complex labeling process of psychiatric diagnosis. Of course, a circular reasoning process is evident in all of the psychological-physiological attempts to establish a criminal type. There also is a kind of satisfaction in the notion of a criminal type, because crime policy then becomes, simply, segregation of the criminals from the rest of society.

A second psychological interpretation of the **etiology of crime** is only slightly more sophisticated. Crime is seen simply as a manifestation of a compulsion derived from unresolved conflicts between the superego (the personality component that serves as one's conscience, according to Freud) and the id (the personality component that serves as one's free spirit). Someone with a criminal personality—by definition a defective ego—is unable to overcome the desire to defy social taboos, yet the conflict reflects itself in an unconscious desire to be caught.

Anecdotal evidence suggests that criminals do operate this way—they may deliberately, albeit unconsciously, leave the clues that lead to their arrests. Were it not for the seriousness of the incidents, this behavior often would be truly comic. One young criminal brought a pair of pants to the cleaners and, after being presented with the claim check, he pulled a gun and robbed the attendant. He returned 3 days later with the stub of the claim check to pick up his pants and was patient enough to wait when the same attendant said the pants were on the way. The young man waited calmly while the police came and arrested him. Another pair of criminals left the motor running in the getaway car, but because they had failed to check the fuel gauge before the robbery, their car ran out of gas while they were holding up the bank.

A more sophisticated psychological theory of the etiology of crime also contains in its assumptions the prescription for a proper anti-crime policy. The following is a summation of what can be classed as a psychosocial theory of crime. Criminal behavior is learned. There is a relationship between the type of criminal behavior learned by individuals and their socioeconomic status in society; that is, certain classes of persons will learn different ways of crime. The processes involved in learning criminal behavior are the same as those in learning other behavior that entails learning a technique as well as values.

This view of criminality is less encompassing than the more simple etiological-psychological views of crime. It does not attempt to explain which people will commit crimes—an impossible task—but rather why and how those who have committed crimes are systematically different from those who do not.

Social Views of Criminal Behavior

Another perspective suggests that crime is not caused by individual physical or mental deficiencies but by societal breakdown. Proponents of this perspective focus on industrialization, racism, poverty, and family breakdown as major factors that create social disorganization and, in turn, increases in crime. Sociological inquiries into crime frequently are based on statistical correlates, such as the increasing breakdown of the traditional family or variations in unemployment and crime rates. The more sophisticated inquiries fall short of establishing a direct path of causation. Crime is seen as a result of many factors within the context of the offender's society. Street crime and white-collar crime are seen as very different expressions of social maladjustment. Regardless of specifics, the essence of the sociological perspective is that general **deterrence factors** (or those things that are likely to stop people from committing crimes), rehabilitation, and reeducation of offenders constitute the best safeguards against repeated crimes.

The social view of crime advocates a criminal justice system that offers a variety of social intervention strategies. One such strategy of importance to social work practitioners is collaboration between social workers and police officers at the earliest intervention point. When the suspected offender is first in police custody, social workers and police officers are expected to concur on the case disposition. The argument is made that, despite their disparate professional orientations, both social workers and police officers are experienced in dealing with troubled people at crisis points in their lives. Individualization of response is seen as critical.

No one sociological perspective is seen as dominant. Consider, for example, the following typology of crime:

- Violent personal crimes (for example, murder)
- Sexual offenses
- Occupational/white-collar crimes
- Political crimes
- Organized crimes
- Professional crimes
- Crimes without victims

Each of these types of crime has its own sociological pattern, and each crime type places a unique set of demands on the criminal justice system.

Economic Rationale of Crime

A final perspective is that crime is simply another form of entrepreneurship that happens to be illegal. Proponents of this view see the criminal as an amoral person who calculates the costs and benefits of a particular crime, much as a businessperson calculates the costs and benefits of opening a new store. In the economic formulation, potential criminals assess the costs of getting caught and sentenced against the probable benefits of successful completion of the crime. They decide to be criminal or not, depending on the outcomes of their calculations. People who are not poor commit fewer crimes because the costs of going to prison (in lost wages, deprivation of status, amenities of life, and so forth) are higher for them than for others. If we subscribe to this theoretical perspective, then to contain crime all we need to do is increase the probable chances of being caught, sentenced, and sent to jail. Little or no empirical evidence suggests a valid basis for this theory (Hillman, 1980).

Each of these views of crime—and we have listed only three—provides a policy paradigm for the criminal justice system, from the role of the arresting officer to the responsibilities of the parole and probation workers. One's beliefs about why some people commit crimes are the obvious source of ideas about how to contain crime.

PROGRAM ALTERNATIVES

For every 36 crimes committed, one person is sentenced to prison. Only one crime in every four reported results in an arrest of a suspected offender. There is roughly one arraignment for every three arrests, and although nearly 95% of all criminal arraignments result in criminal conviction or guilty pleas, only one in three results in a prison term (Samaha, 2000). These numbers mislead as much as they reveal, for tracking a particular crime (acknowledging that crimes are greatly underreported) to a particular sentence is a Herculean statistical task. One thing that is unambiguous in these numbers is the enormous amount of discretion that operates within the criminal justice system. Figure 14.1, presented earlier, portrays the complex pathways in the criminal justice system. At each new stage (represented by the rectangles) an opportunity exists for diversion out of the criminal justice system. Only a small percentage of all crimes result in criminal convictions.

The U.S. criminal justice system is largely an English invention, but it includes some important innovations that are the peculiar products of the United States. These innovations are the elements of the system in which social work is most explicitly and importantly involved; these are the programs of probation, parole, and juvenile procedures. The U.S. system is perhaps more fragmented than the criminal justice system in most countries. The criminal justice system can be seen first as composed of three parts: police, courts, and correctional arrangements. With federal, state, and local involvement at each level and a separation into adult and juvenile divisions, a multipartite system emerges. More dramatic is the fact that no subsystem views the criminal problem from a total perspective. Each entity is busily resolving its own problems. The result is a highly fractured system that is difficult to describe, evaluate, or control.

Despite the lack of cohesion and the internal tensions, actions within one subsystem clearly have reverberations throughout the entire system. "Success" or "failure" in one part may generate significant problems for another part. Should state and local police, by virtue of more personnel or better investigation, apprehend 25% more offenders, both the courts and the correctional system would have to absorb more defendants and prisoners. If the prison system released a higher proportion of recidivists, police and the courts would have to deal with a larger population of criminals. On the other hand, overcrowded prisons generate backups in local jails. All elements of the criminal justice system must respond to the factors in the larger society that accelerate criminal behavior. Because the criminal justice system is not examined or funded as an entity, each component accepts and adopts its own strategies. The fundamental adaptation for one part often produces particular problems for another entity within the system.

THE ROLE OF SOCIAL WORK IN THE CRIMINAL JUSTICE SYSTEM

The role played by the social work community in the criminal justice system has been relegated almost exclusively to the correctional components of the system. Police agencies only recently have begun to use social workers; these social work functions usually have low priority in law enforcement budgets and often fall quickly to budget cuts. Adult courts have made relatively little use of professional social workers. Social workers most frequently work in the criminal justice system in the juvenile courts, rehabilitation centers, prisons, and parole programs. Such uses of social workers, however, need to be assessed in a systemwide context.

Some law enforcement experts suggest that the majority of police calls are family or crisis oriented rather than crime related. When crimes occur, they often are the result of family problems; many homicides, for example, occur among family members rather than outside the family. Increasingly, crime is associated with other social problems, such as alcohol or drug abuse.

Social workers play various roles in law enforcement agencies. Many agencies have crisis intervention teams, consisting of both police officers and social workers, that respond to domestic violence calls or calls to assist victims of rape or other violent crimes. Some law enforcement agencies have established special victim assistance programs. Often staffed by social workers, these programs provide follow-up services to victims of crime, helping them work through their feelings. They also help victims locate emergency funding, shelter, employment, counseling, and other needed services.

Many police departments also have special child abuse or sex crimes units, which sometimes include social workers on their staffs. The social workers assist in investigating reported cases, interviewing children and other individuals involved, contacting other agencies such as child welfare departments and hospitals, and arranging for emergency services when needed. A number of police departments also hire social workers to work in

youth programs. In Pittsburgh, for example, social workers operate inner-city recreation programs. In Austin, Texas, the police department has had a social worker managing a dropout prevention program in the public schools. Such social workers provide counseling and drug and alcohol education and serve as positive law enforcement role models to youth at risk of becoming involved in crime.

The social worker's role in prison and prison life is usually peripheral. The social worker usually is involved only when convicts enter or leave prison. The classification and assignment process at entry point and pardon and parole recommendations are influenced by social workers in some correctional settings. Many BSW graduates become probation or parole officers, helping youth and adults learn new skills and behaviors that will deter them from committing additional crimes and recommending stricter penalties to the court if they violate probation or parole. Others work in youth correction facilities, including halfway houses and community-based programs. Although social services in prisons for problems such as substance abuse are limited, some BSW graduates work within prisons as well.

SUMMARY

In the sad history of crime and punishment, reform is always just beyond the horizon. As this chapter shows, a dreary picture is drawn from practice and current procedures. Police practices do not deter crime, the courts do not dispense justice, the corrections system does not correct, and the parole system does not facilitate ex-prisoners' reentry into society as law-abiding citizens. Part of the problem is that while large sums of money are spent, the emphasis is on building more prisons and jails to house criminals rather than spending that money on crime prevention efforts.

Funds alone are not the problem. Despite a considerable and growing body of knowledge of what works and what does not work in police, court, and correctional settings, insufficient attention is paid to integration within the system. Each unit of the system seeks to improve its operation and to clarify its mission, but at the expense of other components within the system. A more effective integration of police, court, and prison practices is required.

The failure of the criminal justice system also is due to uncertainty about what it is expected to deliver: Is it safe streets, a just system, effective rehabilitation, or simple containment? Effective policies require clarity, choice, commitment, and closure. The segmented structure of the criminal justice system precludes all of these. As a consequence, during some periods, society throws money at certain aspects of the overall problem; during other periods, other aspects are funded. Clearly, more careful assessment and interventions are needed.

KEY TERMS

adjudication
appellate courts
courts
criminal codes
criminal justice system
delinquency
deterrence factors
disposition
etiology of crime
incarceration
intake
intermediate
    punishments

juvenile correctional
    institutions
juvenile courts
lower criminal courts
plea bargaining
probation
recidivism
rehabilitation
selective enforcement
trial courts

DISCUSSION QUESTIONS

1. To what extent is the policy dilemma of the criminal justice system reflected in the juvenile justice system? What are your views about how youth who commit serious crimes should be dealt with in the juvenile justice system?

2. Which of the three views of crime, if any, is most consistent with social work practice theory?

3. If systems integration is the central problem of the criminal justice system, how can the contemporary social worker enhance the probability of that integration?

INFOTRAC COLLEGE EDITION

To learn more about topics included in this chapter, enter the following search terms:

community policing

criminal law

crime prevention

crime rehabilitation

juvenile delinquency

youth crime

youth crimes

youth gangs

youthful offenders

ON THE INTERNET

http://www.ojp.usdoj.gov/bjs/

http://fjsrc.urban.org/index.shtml

http://www.fbi/ucr/ucreports.htm/

http://www.crime.org/links_nat.html/

http://ojjdp.ncjrs.org/

http://juvenilejustice.com/

http://abanet.org/crimjust/juvjus/home.html/

References

American Society of Criminology. (1999). *Early prevention and intervention for delinquency and related problem behaviors.* Columbus, OH: Author.

Bureau of Justice Statistics. (1998). *Probation and parole in the United States, 1997.* Available: http://www.ojp.usdoj.gov/bjs/.

Bureau of Justice Statistics. (1999a). *Direct expenditures by level of government, 1985–95.* Available: http://www.ojp.usdoj.gov/bjs/.

Bureau of Justice Statistics. (1999b). *Prisoners in 1998.* Available: http://www.ojp.usdoj.gov/bjs/.

Bureau of Justice Statistics. (1999c). *Probation and parole in the United States.* Available: http://www.ojp.usdoj.gov/bjs/.

Bureau of Justice Statistics. (1999d). *Time served in prison by federal offenders, 1986–97.* Available: http://www.ojp.usdoj.gov/bjs/.

Hillman, D. (1980). *The economics of crime.* New York: Routine.

Kirst-Ashman, K., & Hull, G. (1997). *Generalist practice with organizations and communities.* Chicago: Nelson-Hall.

Logan, C. H., & Gaes, G. G. (1993). Meta-analysis and the rehabilitation of punishment. *Justice Quarterly, 10,* 247.

National Advisory Commission on Criminal Justice Standards and Goals. (1973). *Corrections.* Washington, DC: U.S. Government Printing Office.

National Institute of Justice. (1998). *Preventing crime: What works, what doesn't, what's promising.* Available: http://www.ojp.usdoj.gov/nij/.

Niger, A. (1967). The *Gault* decision, due process and the juvenile court. *Federal Register, 31*(4), 8–18.

Office of Juvenile Justice and Delinquency Prevention. (1998). *Estimated number of juvenile arrests, 1997.* Available: http://ojjdp.ncjrs.org/ojstatbb/qa001.html.

Samaha, J. (2000). *Criminal justice* (2nd ed.). Belmont, CA: Wadsworth/Thomson Learning.

U.S. Department of Justice. (1999). *Empowering communities to address crime in Office of Justice programs fiscal year 1999 program plan.* Available: http://ojp.usdoj.gov/99progplan/chap2.htm.

Witte, A. D. (1975). *Work release in North Carolina: An evaluation of its post-release effects.* Chapel Hill, NC: University of North Carolina.

Zemans, F. (1995). "In the eye of the beholder: The relationship between the public and the courts." In G. L. Mays & P. R. Gregware (Eds.), *Courts and justice.* Prospect Heights, IL: Waveland.

Suggested Further Readings

Brake, M. (1992). *Public order and private lives: The politics of law and order.* London: Routledge.

Friedman, L. (1993). *Crime and punishment in American history.* New York: Basic Books.

Klein, M. (1997). *The American street gang: Its nature, prevalence, and control.* New York: Oxford University Press.

Masters, R. (1993). *Counseling criminal justice offenders.* Lewiston, NY: Mellen.

Morrison, B. (1997). *As if: A crime, a trial, a question of childhood.* New York: Picador.

Neely, R. (1994). *Tragedies of our own making.* Urbana: University of Illinois Press.

Zimring, F. E. (1998). *American youth violence.* New York: Oxford University Press.

15 SOCIAL WORK IN RURAL SETTINGS

Joe and Hilda McDowell live on a 160-acre farm in southern Missouri. Joe inherited this farm from his father; his grandfather originally obtained the farm in the early 1900s. Three generations of McDowells have eked out their living on this farm and raised their families there. Joe and Hilda both dropped out of high school in the 10th grade and were married on Hilda's 18th birthday. They now have four children: Tommy, 9; Grace, 7; Hortense, 6; and Jimmy, 4.

Over the past few years, it has become increasingly difficult for the McDowells to produce sufficient farm products to meet the family's basic needs. They are heavily in debt for farm equipment loans and owe back taxes on the farm since 1992. They have found it virtually impossible to compete with large farm operations. The children attend school sporadically. None have proper clothing (a luxury the McDowells cannot afford). Tommy has severe dental problems, and Hilda's health problems have limited her ability to assist with crops. Living 85 miles away from a small city has made it impossible for Joe to try to supplement the family's income through gainful employment, and, even if he could locate a job, he would only be able to earn minimum wages because of his limited skills.

Joe and Hilda are deeply invested emotionally in their farm, its family tradition, and the rural way of life. Considering their indebtedness, the back taxes they owe, and almost no opportunity to make their farming operations a productive one, it is likely that they will lose the farm through foreclosure. Joe and Hilda worry about their future and that of their children.

Today, approximately 27% of the nation's population live in rural areas. Although the majority of our citizens reside and work in urban areas, the population of small towns and outlying areas has increased over the past decades. According to Offner, Seekins, and Clark (1992), rural America is a "mix of elderly people, children, miners, timber workers, veterans, service providers, industrial workers, self-employed workers, urban escapees, the persistently poor, federal land managers, people with disabilities, and an array of many others" (p. 6). Strikingly, only 12% of the rural population is directly engaged in agriculture. In addition, as more individuals and families become disenchanted with the high crime rates, fast pace, and overcrowded conditions of cities, it is likely that rural populations will continue to expand.

Rural areas, with their characteristic small towns, farms, and ranches of varying sizes, offer an appreciably different environment and lifestyle than that found in metropolitan areas. Although automobiles and airplanes have given many rural residents access to the resources of major cities, isolation and long distances to the cities' resources continue to pose problems for others. On the average, people living in rural areas have more limited resources than do urban residents. For example, it is estimated that over half of America's substandard houses, half of America's poor, a high percentage of the unemployed, and the majority of the untreated ill live in rural areas.

In this chapter, we will review some of the more salient characteristics of rural America and identify social welfare and social work resources available in rural communities.

RURAL: AN OPERATIONAL DEFINITION

Arriving at a universally agreed-on definition of *rural* is more difficult than you might think. Generally, such definitions are based on population counts (the census) of a specified area rather than on the behavioral traits and customs of people. For example, the "hillbillies" from Tennessee, Arkansas, and West Virginia who migrated into many northern cities brought with them their customs, values, and traits. Disadvantaged and unsophisticated in the ways of urban life, they had a great deal of difficulty adapting to the demands of urban life. Uneducated and unskilled, they were relegated to poverty and a continual struggle for survival. Although their customs and habits positioned them clearly as rural transplants, once in the urban environment, they were no longer considered rural. Urban dwellers moving into rural areas have experienced similar **culture shock.** The point is that definitions of *urban* or *rural* are not subject to the behavioral attributes of population groups but to population size. Seemingly, such definitions should constitute a rather simple task, yet it is complex.

The U.S. Bureau of the Census classifies as **rural** communities those that are composed of 2,500 or fewer people. This classification has limited utility in that it only enables us to separate those communities statistically identified as rural from those that are not. For example, in terms of access to resources, is a small, isolated rural community of 2,500 in Utah the equivalent of a similarly sized, incorporated, "bedroom" community 25 miles from Houston? Probably not.

In addition, millions of Americans live on farms or ranches that are some distance from villages, towns, or cities. In many of these areas, small farms are close together, whereas in others, miles may separate families from each other. Rural inhabitants often are identified as *rural-farm* or *rural-nonfarm* to further clarify and differentiate the nature of rural residency. Clearly, there are differences and distinctions in the daily living requirements and patterns of the small-town resident and those of the farm dweller.

Farley, Griffiths, Skidmore, and Thackery (1982) have suggested that rural life might be conceptualized as ecological, occupational, and sociocultural. Each conceptual aspect provides a basis for differentiating among rural towns and outlying areas. Many of these characteristics are reflected in the section that follow. As you read these discussions, be aware that the life of a small farmer in Georgia may be appreciably different from that of a goat rancher in western Texas.

CHARACTERISTICS OF RURAL POPULATIONS

Data are available that provide an overview of rural life. Approximately 55 million Americans are living in rural areas, and that number is increasing. Many of the areas in which rural residents live are predominantly agricultural, with crops, poultry, cattle, sheep, or goats as the main sources of livelihood. Inhabitants may live on small acreages and be self-sufficient or work for large commercial farms. Many attempt to do both. Increasingly, major industrial developments are seeking out rural areas to establish plants or factories, thus providing opportunities for employment. Jennings (1990) has further described rural communities as characterized by the following:

- Basic trust
- Basic friendliness
- Isolation
- Resistance to change
- Suspicion toward newcomers or outsiders
- Tendency for children to take on the identity of their parents
- Independence of spirit, yet vulnerable
- Similarity to a family system, especially regarding roles
- Financial and experiential poverty
- Reliance on informal and/or natural helping systems first for assistance
- Concrete thinking and more reserved behaviors
- Traditional values and conservatism
- More holistic, less compartmentalized lives

The strength and intensity of any (or all) of these characteristics may vary, depending on the organization and density of the population of the rural area as well.

Table 15.1 presents a comparison of metro (urban) and nonmetro (rural) areas of the United States for selected socioeconomic variables. When compared to their urban counterparts, rural residents are more likely to be older, make less money, live in poverty, make do with an inadequate or functionally deficient trans-

| TABLE 15.1 | SELECTED COMPARISONS OF RURAL AND URBAN COMMUNITIES IN THE UNITED STATES |

Characteristic	Value
Per capita income (1997) dollars	
Urban areas	$26,861
Rural areas	$19,090
Percentage persons living at or below poverty level	
Urban areas	12.3%
Rural areas	14.4%
Unemployment rate	
Urban areas	4.4%
Rural areas	4.8%
Share of total population age 60 and over	
Urban areas	15.0%
Rural areas	18.4%
Share of population with Medicare coverage	
Urban areas	12.7%
Rural areas	16.2%
Share of hospitals with negative total margins	
Urban areas	19.5%
Rural areas	25.1%
Percentage of county roads that are inadequate for current travel patterns	38%
Percentage of rural bridges that are structurally or functionally deficient	50%

Sources: Brown (1996, 1997); Capalbo and Heggem (1999); U.S. Department of Agriculture (1997, 1999, 2000).

portation infrastructure, and face challenges in locating and accessing health care services. In short, despite America's love affair with moving out of the cities and into the country, the rural infrastructure is not well prepared to support such a change. Major efforts will have to take place within rural communities to ensure that population migration to these communities is accompanied by the appropriate level of planning regarding the housing, educational, medical care, transportation, and commerce infrastructures in these communities. Failure to do so will jeopardize the overall quality of life in these communities—the main reason people wanted to move there in the first place.

SOCIAL ORGANIZATIONS OF RURAL COMMUNITIES

Unlike major metropolitan areas, rural communities have social networks that are more personalized and informal. Many of the prominent and powerful community leaders are descendants of early settlers, often large landowners, and leaders in community affairs. Residents, both affluent and poor, tend to be known by many people in the community. Privacy and anonymity are seldom achieved. Good, as well as bad, news travels through the informal community network with amazing speed. Reputations are routinely established for residents and are changed only with great effort. Newcomers often find themselves in an out-group category and, regardless of their interest or endeavor, discover it difficult to be accepted fully into the inner circles of community life. Judgments concerning the character, ability, and competency of individuals tend to be based on subjective assessments. The success or failure of community residents usually is considered to be the result of personal effort and motivation. Hence, the poor, unemployed, or downtrodden are viewed as individuals who lack the determination to achieve. Divorce and poverty typically are classified as personal failures, and strong negative sanctions serve as constant reminders that deviation from the norm is accompanied by increasing social distance and exclusion from free and full participation in community life.

On the other hand, responses to people in need are often quick and personal. A death in the family or a farm failure stimulates neighbors to respond with goods and services designed to assist the needy through the crisis situation. Droughts, floods, tornadoes, and other natural disasters create a bond among farmers and ranchers and a unity of purpose with shared concern. People often show reciprocity by sharing labor for the harvesting of crops, assisting others in times of need, and organizing to counteract threats to community life. Often politically conservative, rural communities are characterized by resistance to innovation and skepticism concerning modern technological innovations. "City slickers" are viewed with disdain and not to be trusted until proven worthy of trust. They are considered to be uninformed as to rural residents' needs. Honesty and strong character are valued as desirable traits.

The action hub of rural communities centers around the church, the local bank, the county extension office, small businesses, the feed store, and the local school system. As a consequence, the local banker, ministers, the county agent, store owners, and school administrators usually hold powerful influence over community life. County government is typically relegated to the county judge and county commissioners. The sheriff's office handles law enforcement, although many small towns also have a police force. Violations of the law are considered to be a personal offense against the community, and mitigating circumstances are usually downplayed or viewed as irrelevant. The social organization of rural communities is as varied as the locations in which they occur. Although there are common threads of roles and relationships that knit the community together in any setting, each locale has its own character.

SUPPORT SERVICES IN THE RURAL COMMUNITY

Many of the **support services** that urban residents take for granted are often scarce or nonexistent in rural communities. An absence of doctors, nurses, social workers, dentists, or attorneys is not uncommon in small rural towns. Adequately staffed hospitals with up-to-date equipment are expensive to develop and maintain, and small communities lack the resources to finance them. As a consequence, many health-related problems go unattended, or people rely on traditional cures or folk medicine. Resources for the treatment of mental illness are particularly lacking. But individuals exhibiting "peculiar" behavior often find acceptance in rural areas, and their families may experience considerable understanding and social support from neighbors. Social work and social services are distributed sparsely in rural areas, often because of the community's mores or limited financial support capabilities.

As noted earlier, the church is a significant institution in rural life. Congregations are quick to respond to those in need and set the pace for community action in time of crisis. The church also is the center for community activities, sponsoring various social get-togethers and recreational opportunities. Religion typically plays a vital role in setting the moral tone and in meeting the spiritual needs of rural residents. Ministers are viewed not only as spiritual advisers but also as community leaders.

In agricultural areas, the county extension office, funded by the **U.S. Department of Agriculture,** provides many services valued by the farm community to assist rural areas, and the county liaison office provides a variety of community and family services. Technical assistance is made available for crop planting and harvesting, ranch management, disease control, care of livestock, food preparation, home canning, and other activities related to farm, ranch, and home management. Informally, the **county agent** often becomes aware of personal problems and serves as counselor, case manager, and resource finder. He or she also often functions as an advocate or broker (with the local banker or other lending agencies) for farmers experiencing financial disaster.

Recreational activities are often limited in rural areas. The absence of a local movie house, skating rink, park, library, and other outlets for children and teenagers severely restricts opportunities for leisure-time activities. Many small communities literally "roll up the sidewalks" at dark. As a consequence, the local school often is a prominent source for recreational get-togethers and sponsors dances and holiday programs. Athletic events are usually well attended and serve as the central focus for young people and adults to meet and socialize. The school, along with the church, is among the primary institutions for social organization in the rural community.

The importance of **natural helping networks,** many of which have been mentioned in the preceding paragraphs, should not be minimized in **rural social work.** Historically, those networks of friends, relatives, congregations, clubs, civic groups, and related entities have constituted the backbone of assistance to those in need. The rural culture of values and mores that gave rise to assisting each other in times of crisis and need to a large extent remains intact today—particularly in the more isolated areas. Social service workers who understand this phenomenon and are skillful at identifying relevant natural groups often find that their efforts to provide assistance are enhanced by incorporating natural helping networks into the helping process.

SOCIAL PROBLEMS IN RURAL AREAS

The romantic view that rural areas are peaceful, serene, and devoid of the types of problems found in large cities and metropolitan areas fails to portray the reality of rural life. Unfortunately, rural areas are not devoid of social problems, and the impact of those problems is often far greater on rural residents than those living in cities because of the distance or absence of support services. In the following sections, we examine a few of the more prominent problems.

Mental Health in Rural Areas

Although mental health problems have always existed in rural environments, considerable concern has been expressed over what appears to be an increase in dysfunctional mental health problems since the 1980s. J. Dennis Murray (1990), past president of the National Association of Rural Mental Health (NARMH), has pointed out that (1) the prevalence of mental illness in rural America at least equals, if not exceeds, that in cities, and (2) rural areas have higher rates of emotional disorder (especially depression). Murray has expressed concern over the limited resources to address these problem areas. It is also commonly known that the suicide rate in rural areas is similar to that found in cities.

In addition to these more severe and traumatic problems, the psychological and emotional anguish associated with marital discord and parent-child conflicts has intensified as a result of the frustration and insecurity related to the unsettled farm economy. Child abuse, for example, once thought to be a primarily urban problem, is also found in rural areas in ever-increasing numbers. Many view such problems as a reflection of the ecological instability of rural life as it exists today. The abuse of alcohol and other drugs and local youth gangs, often viewed as symptoms of economic and social unrest, have also become more significant problems in many rural areas.

The availability of mental health resources to meet the needs of the rural constituency varies with population density but is generally considered woefully inadequate. Some reasons for the lack of service availability and the limited use of available resources are described in the *Rural Health Reporter* ("Mental Health Services," 1989) as follows:

- Artificially configured service areas
- Very large service areas
- Stigma and the lack of privacy
- Staff shortages
- Inadequate facilities
- Absence of support services
- Few treatment alternatives

In addition to these problems, inadequate financial resources and community resistance present barriers that must be overcome if individuals and families in need of mental health services are to receive them. As discussed later in this chapter, resources necessary to assist rural families are very limited.

Health Care Problems

Problems associated with health care are also of concern to rural Americans. Health indicators, for example, reflect that infant mortality and chronic disease rates are higher in rural areas than in urban ones. The rural aged generally suffer from chronic illness and poor health in far greater numbers than their urban counterparts. Resources such as hospitals are being curtailed with increasing frequency, leaving the rural residents with little access to health care treatment centers that are nearby. This situation results in either postponing necessary care or traveling great distances to secure it—often beyond the means of the patients or their families to manage.

Although most rural areas have emergency medical services (EMS), these services often are not prepared to handle life-threatening diseases or severe traumatic injuries. In addition, the recruitment of doctors, nurses, and other health care professionals for practice in rural areas has been relatively unsuccessful. For instance, as of 1998 one Texas county consisting of over 960 square miles with a rural population of over 6,000 had only two medical doctors, with the closest hospital 40 miles away.

Solutions to rural health problems are difficult to achieve, but the health needs of rural residents must become a priority for policymakers. The **1989 Omnibus Health Care Rescue Act (HB 18)** was designed to provide some relief in the form of additional health care resources, although even with its implementation, major gaps in service continue to exist. Some of the more recent health care concerns such as AIDS create even more demand on rural health resources. The demands on rural health providers will continue to escalate while resources to meet the needs are limited.

The shortage of medical doctors and specialists also imposes limited choices and available resources from which to select treatment options for disease and illness in many rural areas. Patients requiring kidney dialysis or other complicated health problems often must travel long distances for treatment or, in some cases, move to a location where treatment facilities are easily accessed. Furthermore, turnover rates among medical practitioners tend to be higher in rural areas, and attracting and retaining qualified medical personnel are difficult (Winslow, 1990).

In recent years, one innovative approach to improving the quality of care for rural residents is the product of our high-tech society. Through the vehicle of **telecommunications,** rural practitioners have immediate access to large medical centers where consultation is available for both diagnostic and treatment regimens. "Telemedicine" has rapidly expanded throughout rural areas of the United States and has the capacity to enhance the quality of care for those clients who lack the capacity to receive care in a major medical center (Capalbo & Heggem, 1999).

Poverty

Lower incomes and erratic employment opportunities contribute to higher rates of poverty and disease in rural areas. Among the rural population, which makes up about 27% of the total U.S. population, almost 16% live below the poverty level (Institute for Research on Poverty, 2000). Gore (1995) points out that poverty rates are higher than those found in urban areas, while income is 27% lower for rural residents than that of their urban counterparts. Persons of color living in rural areas are more likely to be poor than their white counterparts: about 35% of all rural African Americans and 34% of all rural Latinos live in poverty, compared to 13.5% of whites (Institute for Research on Poverty, 2000). The rural poor tend to work primarily at menial jobs; however, their ability to achieve higher-paying jobs is affected by the fact that they are often less well educated than their urban counterparts. Their income-earning capacity is also affected by seasonal employment, illness, and injury.

The majority of the rural poor are engaged in crop harvesting, which is often unpredictable, pays poor wages, and frequently requires that families move from place to place to secure employment. Although many of these families no longer travel great distances to harvest crops, they are generally referred to as *migrant workers*.

Other types of employment such as working in a feed store, being a nurse's aide, clerking at a hardware or department store, or performing similar types of jobs generally pay only minimum or near minimum wages—hardly sufficient income to enable one to meet family financial needs, as the wages are often at, or slightly above, the poverty level. Career mobility is severely limited, and it is common to find workers who, with 20 or 30 years of experience, continue to earn only a minimum wage.

As mentioned earlier, the children of these workers, like their parents, receive less education than their counterparts who live in urban

Poverty is found frequently in rural areas. For example, *colonias* located on the U.S.-Mexico border have received little attention from state and federal governments and lack critical necessities such as safe drinking water and shelter.

Paul S. Howell/Liaison Agency

areas. Disease rates and higher infant mortality rates reflect the substandard conditions under which many live. Small-town school systems, already strained for financial resources, are often not diligent in enforcing mandatory school attendance laws. School personnel also find it hard to convince youth and their families that school attendance is important in the long run when efforts of as many family members as possible are needed just for the family to survive. As a result, many children are not encouraged to pursue an education and, instead, work alongside their parents to help the family make enough income to survive. Consequently, a vicious cycle is set in motion, perpetuating intergenerational patterns of farm laborers who are poor and lack the necessary resources to break out of poverty.

Rural communities are also more segregated than urban areas. Racial segregation, limited political participation, and impoverish-ment continue to characterize the plight of people of color in rural communities. Attempts to organize farm labor and implement civil rights legislation have met with only limited success due, primarily, to the resistance of large landowners and commercial farmers who seek to maintain the status quo and exert sufficient power to assure that reform does not occur. In states that border Mexico, such as Texas, New Mexico, Arizona, and California, many people view undocumented persons negatively, believing that they compound problems in the farm labor market through their willingness to work for lower wages. However, experience has shown that they do jobs that otherwise would not be filled. Since most undocumented persons are concerned with being detected by federal immigration officials (and returned to Mexico), they are vulnerable to exploitation by landowners who seek cheap labor. The recent decline in the value of the peso has further exacerbated the problem, prompting large numbers of undocumented persons to cross the border to seek work and better living conditions in the United States.

Poor white farm workers experience many of the same problems. Typically less educated than urban whites, they are viewed stereotypically as people with less incentive and motivation to succeed. Limited resources and skill levels keep them on the farm. Illiteracy rates are higher and poverty is more pervasive among rural whites than urban whites. When rural whites do migrate to cities, they often are relegated to low-paying jobs and experience considerable difficulty in becoming assimilated into the urban environment.

Perhaps the conditions of the poor are best described in an article by Colby (1987), who cites an anonymous poor rural resident:

> Poverty is dirt. You say in your clean clothes coming from a clean house, "Anybody can be clean." Let me explain housekeeping with no money. For breakfast I give my children grits with oleo, or cornbread with no eggs or oleo. . . .What dishes there are, I wash in cold water with no soap. . . . Look at my hands, so cracked and red. . . . Why not hot water? Hot water is a luxury. Fuel costs money. . . . Poverty is . . . remembering quitting school in junior high because "nice" children had been so cruel about my clothes and my smell. . . . Poverty is a chisel that chips on honor until honor is worn away. (pp. 9–10)

The problems of the rural poor are compounded by the lack of community support services—public water and sewage, fire and police protection, transportation, employment opportunities, and related services.

The Rural Family

The notion that rural families experience a high degree of harmony, are problem-free, and enjoy high levels of life satisfaction is not necessarily borne out by fact. This idyllic view, while desirable, is an illusion that may serve to filter out the reality of existing conditions. Just as in urban areas, negatives related to strained relationships, substance abuse, divorce, child abuse and neglect, sexual exploitation, and a myriad of related problems are not uncommon in rural areas. Certainly the rural environment has much to offer its residents, and the majority of them find contentment and satisfaction within the context of family solidarity. Unlike urban families, however, for rural families when problems do emerge, finding solutions may become more problematic. Many rural children with special problems such as physical, mental, or learning disabilities often find that needed support programs are lacking. Marital discord and related interpersonal relationship issues may go unattended. Teenage pregnancy has become more prevalent, as have single-parent families. Among the poorest (although not limited to them), early marriage, coupled with limited education, serves to lock younger couples into a life with low wages and insurmountable barriers to career mobility.

Even where limited support services are available, rural families tend to be reticent about using them. For example, one small Southwest town of 3,500 people seldom used a mental health service except for court-ordered substance abuse cases. Careful community analysis reflected strong value ties to self-help and self-management of problems. Anonymity was also treasured and served to deter residents from using available mental health assistance. Only after an innovative plan was implemented in which a social worker was housed in the local medical clinic did matters change. Prospective clients first visited the medical center, where they were referred by the doctor to the social worker when mental health or family-related problems were detected. Within a relatively short period after the plan was implemented, the social worker had a full caseload including marital conflict problems, spousal alcoholism, family violence, depression, and related dysfunctional behaviors (Shuttlesworth, 1993).

This brief discussion suggests that regardless of the environment in which human beings live, problems can and do emerge. How these problems are managed, however, is a function of values, skills, community support systems, and opportunity structures for finding satisfactory solutions.

THE CRISIS OF THE SMALL FARMER

Remember the McDowells from the start of the chapter? Like them, many small farmers are facing a similar crisis. Low farm prices, high production costs, imports, and a convergence of related factors have created a crisis for the small landowner farmer. Reemerging in the 1990s, farm and ranch foreclosures have again skyrocketed, which has resulted in the displacement of large numbers of farmers and ranchers who depended on agricultural production for their livelihood. Like the McDowells' experience, it is not uncommon for intergenerational farms and ranches to be lost through foreclosure. Displaced farmers and ranchers often lack the skills required to become absorbed readily into other aspects of the labor market, particularly in the instance of older farmers and ranchers. Major commercial farm operations have contributed to the demise of small farm operations through volume production, which lowers unit prices for products. The small operator, even under optimum conditions, has great difficulty competing.

Currently, few resources are available to assist the small farmer and rancher in main-taining property and purchasing the equipment essential for successful competition. The federal government's priority of reducing deficit spending has taken its toll on farm supports. Along with these problems, the stress and tension associated with the loss (or probable loss) of one's farm or ranch create havoc for these families. Problems such as increased family conflict—including spouse and child abuse—alcoholism, and depression are not uncommon in rural areas populated by ranchers and farmers operating as a single family business. The increase in stress and problems that often accompany it serve as disincentives for prospective new farmers to engage in agricultural operations. Many jobs are lost, and a way of life is destroyed. Some individuals, once productive and self-sustaining, must turn to public assistance as a means of survival. Urbanites must always be reminded that their survival also depends on a healthy agricultural industry.

SOCIAL WELFARE IN RURAL COMMUNITIES

The United States has many more small communities and towns than cities or major metropolitan areas. These communities vary in size and in their proximity to major metropolitan areas. For example, Tilden, Texas, a county-seat town of approximately 350 residents, is situated in a county that covers approximately 1,400 square miles. It is the largest town in the county. What type of organized social welfare programs would one find in this community? What is needed? To what extent could the community support social welfare services?

You should be wary about generalizations concerning the nature and extent of organized social welfare programs in small towns and rural areas, because they vary greatly in size, nature, and ability to finance needed services. Many rural areas have very few services, and those available tend to be basic ones. Typically, public welfare services, mental health and developmental disabilities outreach centers, and public health services are available, although they usually are minimally staffed, offer only limited assistance, and often may be reached only by a drive of several hundred miles. It is not unusual for counties to offer a limited welfare assistance program and for county administrative officials (usually the county judge) to administer benefits, along with their other duties. A few rural communities have Community Action Agencies (a residual of the War on Poverty programs), although attempts to organize rural areas, in general, have been unsuccessful. Senior citizens' luncheon programs may be provided by a branch of an areawide agency on aging. Employment agencies, family planning services, and family counseling agencies and related services are not typically found in rural areas. Ginsberg (1976) suggests some innovative changes that would increase the service capacity to meet the needs of rural populations:

1. Public social services must often expand their efforts to include services that they might not provide in cities. For example, a public welfare office might be charged with much more responsibility for family counseling, community development, and social welfare planning simply because the office exists, is staffed with knowledgeable people, and needs to help meet problems that occur, despite the absence of agencies. Similarly, a community mental health program may be required to provide some youth services activities that its urban counterparts would leave to other agencies.

2. Many activities are voluntary and depend, therefore, on the good will and interest of their supporters rather than upon full-time professional staff. This is particularly true of social welfare planning efforts, which are often the result of social welfare professionals working together without additional compensation to create and sustain a structure for coordination and planning. Some direct service and community development activities are conducted in a similar manner.

3. Although formal structures may not exist, many informal services are offered in rural communities. In fact, it is the nature of communities, both rural and urban, to develop services to address human problems. For example, the functions carried out by mental health agencies in large cities may be performed in rural communities by the police or the sheriff's office. A single individual may carry out a program serving children. Churches may assume responsibility for everything from food baskets to family counseling. It is important for social workers in all communities to understand the nature of the service delivery system. In rural America that structure may be hard to identify because of its informal nature.

4. A single formal agency in a rural area may provide functions that are often handled by multiple agencies in an urban area. Youth-serving programs such as 4-H, the Boy Scouts, Girl Scouts, and Campfire Girls may be the only resource for activities that in a larger area would be handled by the YMCA, YWCA, settlement houses, recreation centers, Boys and Girls Clubs, and other programs.

5. The importance of individuals and families in providing for the social welfare

needs of others in rural areas should not be overlooked. As has already been suggested, one public-spirited woman may function almost as effectively as an agency or office. Knowing about such people and gaining their assistance is crucial for the rural social worker.

6. Perhaps most important is the fact that some formal organizations exist in rural areas that are important but different from those one finds in urban settings. The best example is probably the cooperative extension services, which are overseen by each state (along with U.S. Department of Agriculture administration and funds), usually under the supervision of state land-grant universities. The traditional function of such programs is to provide consultation on agricultural activities to farmers and ranchers as well as homemaking information to rural women. However, they have expanded their functions dramatically, with many cooperative extension programs now heavily committed to community improvement and development programs in areas as diverse as housing, drug abuse treatment, and social welfare planning. Working with such organizations, which are most prominent in rural areas, is essential for the rural worker.

As suggested earlier, public social services are generally extended to rural areas through the auspices of state agencies. For example, state mental health programs generally have satellite offices in rural areas that are implemented through regional offices, as do state departments of human services that offer public assistance programs. Regional Education Service Centers provide resource assistance for rural schools. Ironically, "per capita spending for rural human services programs is substantially lower (than in urban areas) despite the fact that rural areas have a significantly larger proportion of poor people" (Offner et al., 1992, p. 6; see also Cordes, 1989). In general, however, organized social welfare services in rural areas are not as well developed, well organized, or efficiently staffed as those that serve urban populations. Additional resources must be developed in rural areas if services equivalent to those in urban areas are to exist. In the past decade, efforts have been made to update and improve rural social services. Projects such as the Great Plains Staff Training and Development for Rural Mental Health in Nebraska, the information and advocacy efforts of the National Association of Rural Mental Health, and the caucus of national rural social workers and rural human service workers are all active in promoting higher levels and quality of service in rural areas.

SOCIAL WORK IN RURAL SETTINGS

The practice of social work in rural communities is both similar and different from that practiced in urban areas. The core of knowledge, methods, and skills of social work practice undergirds practice in both environments. The nature of rural settings, the problems experienced, and the lack of resources converge to confront the social worker with a unique set of challenges. Creativity and the ability to innovate and influence community members to mobilize in meeting needs are crucial skills for successful practice in rural settings. No other type of social work compares with rural social work practice in intervening within the "total environment." The rural social worker by her- or himself must often provide the rural dweller with services, support, and hope while simultaneously helping to change the environment in order to provide better transportation, increased medical care, and a more responsive community. Unlike urban social workers, the social worker in a rural area may feel frustrated by the absence of fellow professionals and a social service network. Opportunities for consultation and feedback are limited, so decision making is often difficult and problematic.

Social workers who both live and practice in rural areas find that they are seen as neighbors as well as professional practitioners. Almost everyone in the community knows who they are, and they may be called on at home as well as the office to provide a wide range of services. Their service constituency may consist of children, adults, the mentally ill, the incarcerated, the bedridden, the distressed, and the abandoned. At any one time, the social worker may be assisting a family in locating a nursing home placement for an older parent, securing resources for a child with a disability, counseling with a pregnant teenager and her family, collaborating with local ministers in developing leisure-time activities for youth, assisting school personnel in developing management techniques for a hyperactive child, or working with the court in securing rehabilitation resources for a delinquent child. These varied demands require that the social worker be flexible, have good communication skills, engage both private and public resources, and have a basic understanding of community values and practices.

Practicing social work in a rural setting subjects the social worker to a "life in a fish bowl." Everyone tends to know the social worker both professionally and personally. His or her private life is closely scrutinized. Since social workers, like other community people, have problems, the way they are managed becomes a matter of community concern. Like ministers, their work is expected to meet high personal and moral standards, and any devia-

tion may lower community esteem. In rural communities, the ability to separate personal life from professional competence is difficult. Often, the social worker's credibility is at stake should personal problems go unresolved.

Maintaining client confidentiality is difficult. Neighbors may become clients. Community residents typically know when problems are being experienced and when professional assistance has been sought. A casual encounter at the grocery store may prompt a resident to inquire as to how a client is progressing. As Fenby (1978) indicates:

> At times a client will be open about his or her knowledge. "I hear you had oil burner problems this morning and Art sent his truck out." At times there is a subtle change in the therapy hour, and the therapist cannot discount the fact that information from the "outside" is affecting the interaction "inside." For example, a client who had been working well in therapy became evasive and distant, although nothing discernible had caused the change. Probing uncovered that the woman had discovered that my husband was on a yearly contract at the college, and had surmised that therefore I would not be staying in the area. She thought that therapy would end in failure, uncompleted.
>
> In a small world it is essential to be aware of contamination from outside information in the process of therapy. (p. 162)

Social workers who have periodic assignments in the rural area but do not reside there encounter other problems. Typically, they are regarded as outsiders. In some instances, they have not had the opportunity to become aware of community priorities and values. Often, they are viewed as having little vested interest in the community and, as a result, respond to special client problems out of context. Community resistance may become an additional barrier to problem solving. Sensitivity to the

BOX
15.1

Some Characteristics of Effective Rural Social Workers

1. They are especially skillful in working with a variety of helping persons who are not social workers or who may not be related to the profession of social work, as well as with peers and colleagues.
2. They are able to carry out careful study, analysis, and other methods of inquiry in order to understand the community in which they find themselves.
3. They utilize their knowledge of the customs, traditions, heritage and contemporary culture of the rural people with whom they are working to provide services to the people with special awareness and sensitivity.
4. They are able to identify and mobilize a broad range of resources which are applicable to problem resolution in

rural areas. These include existing and potential resources on the local, state, regional and federal levels.

5. They are able to assist communities in developing new resources or ways in which already existing resources may be better or more fully utilized to benefit the rural community.
6. They are able to identify with and practice in accordance with the values of the profession and grow in their ability and effectiveness as professional social workers in situations and settings where they may be the only professional social worker.
7. They are able to identify and analyze the strengths and/or gaps and shortcomings in governmental and nongovernmental social policies as they affect the needs of people in rural areas.

importance of interpersonal relationships with community leaders is essential in gaining support for change efforts.

An old social work axiom suggests that "change comes slow." While this premise is open to debate, it is valid in rural social work practice. Timetables and the pace of life tend to be slower. Urgency is offset by practicality and patience. Waiting matters out may be given more credence than intervention. Social workers must learn to stifle their frustration and impatience yet retain their persistent efforts in the helping process. As their credibil-

ity and competence become more established, community resistance will turn into support, and the contribution made to the community as a problem solver will become enhanced.

By now you should be aware of some of the more salient differences between social work practice in rural areas and that in urban areas. The models of intervention used in urban areas are generally not effectively transportable to rural areas because of the nature, culture, diversity, and resource limitations of rural areas. Urban areas—due to their characteristic population density, opportunity struc-

8. They accept their professional responsibility to develop appropriate measures to promote more responsiveness to the needs of people in rural areas from governmental and nongovernmental organizations.

9. They are able to help identify and create new and different helping roles in order to respond to the needs and problems of rural communities.

10. They initiate and provide technical assistance to rural governing bodies and other organized groups in rural communities.

11. They are able to practice as generalists, carrying out a wide range of roles, to solve a wide range of problems of individuals and groups as well as of the larger community.

12. They are able to communicate and interact appropriately with people in the rural community, and adapt their personal life-style to the professional tasks to be done.

13. They are able to evaluate their own professional performance.

14. They are able to work within an agency or organization and plan for and initiate change in agency policy and practice when such change is indicated.

15. On the basis of continuous careful observation, they contribute knowledge about effective practice in rural areas.

Source: Statement on "Educational Assumptions for Rural Social Work" by Southern Regional Education Board, Manpower Education and Training Project Rural Task Force, Atlanta, Georgia.

tures, and resource bases—serve to challenge social planners in a manner quite different from the models needed for effective application in rural environments.

RURAL SOCIAL WORK AS GENERALIST PRACTICE

It should be apparent to you at this point that the variety and diversity of the tasks inherent in rural social work practice can best be accom-

plished by the generalist practitioner. Social workers in rural communities are called on to work with individuals, families, and groups and in community organization. Administrative and management skills are essential in rendering needed services (see Box 15.1). The abilities to define problems operationally, collect and analyze data, and translate findings into practical solutions are requisites for enriched practice. The rural practitioner is a multimethod worker who appropriately facilitates in the problem-solving process. Knowledge of resources, resource development, methods of linking clients with resources, and case management is required of the rural social worker. We discuss other essential requirements for generalist social work practice in Chapter 2.

THE BACCALAUREATE SOCIAL WORKER AND RURAL SOCIAL WORK PRACTICE

Social work in rural communities is both challenging and rewarding. Self-reliance and the ability to work apart from social work support systems are attributes that rural social workers must have to function effectively. Many undergraduate social work programs are located in small cities or large towns adjacent to rural areas and specialize in rural social work practice. Field placements typically use rural agencies to familiarize students with skills essential for practice in those settings.

The BSW social worker's generalist practice perspective will prove invaluable in working with rural populations. The opportunity to engage existing formal and informal organizations in extending or developing resources to meet community needs is a continuing challenge the BSW social worker can address competently. The social worker also will find that individuals and families in rural areas often have problems and need assistance in problem solving. Knowledge and expertise in problem identification, outreach, linking of target systems with resources, resource development, education, and problem solving help enrich the lives of rural inhabitants as well as strengthen community support systems. The abilities to understand community value systems and to experiment with innovative techniques in working with community residents are essential assets for productive practice.

Until recently, social workers have not been inclined to engage in rural social work practice. Fortunately, this attitude is changing. Job opportunities in rural communities are increasing, and the potential for a satisfying and rewarding career in rural social work practice is greater now than ever before.

SUMMARY

Rural environments are both like and unlike urban ones. In this chapter, we have identified characteristics that tend to differentiate between rural and urban areas in social organization, lifestyles, informal and formal helping networks, and the types of problems that are more likely to be experienced by rural residents. We also reviewed the unique issues related to rural social welfare delivery systems as they related to diversity and availability in meeting human need. Of particular importance, we examined the role of natural help-ing networks within the context of their viability as a resource in problem solving. We identified the methods and functions of social work practice in terms of the varied demands placed on the rural social worker, highlighting the relevance of generalist practice to addressing rural problems along with the ideal fit for the BSW. Job opportunities are increasing, and the challenges of a successful social work career in providing needed services for rural communities are attracting social workers in greater numbers into rural communities.

KEY TERMS

county agent	rural
culture shock	rural social work
natural helping networks	support services

telecommunications
U.S. Department of
   Agriculture

1989 Omnibus Health
   Care Rescue Act
   (H.B. 18)

http://www.rurdev.gov/Nrdp/

http://www.rurdev.usda.gov/

http://nch.ari.net/

DISCUSSION QUESTIONS

1. Review the case study presented at the beginning of this chapter. How might a generalist social worker help the McDowell family?

2. How are social problems found in rural areas different from those in urban areas?

3. To what extent is generalist social work practice viable in working with individuals and families in rural communities? Why?

4. With fewer formal social welfare programs available in rural areas, how are natural helping networks useful to the social worker?

5. Should the social worker who works in a rural area also live there? What are the advantages of doing so? The disadvantages?

INFOTRAC COLLEGE EDITION

To learn more about topics included in this chapter, enter the following search terms:

rural elderly

rural family

rural poor

rural social services

rural welfare

telemedicine

ON THE INTERNET

http://www.nalusda.gov/ric/richs/elderpg.htm/

http://www.kumc.edu/instruction/medicine/NRPC/

REFERENCES

Bedics, B. (1987). The history and context of rural poverty. *Human Services in the Rural Environment, 11*(1), 12–14.

Brown, D. (1996). Rural America's transportation network: Issues for the 1990's. *Rural Development Perspectives, 11*(2), 10–17.

Brown, D. (1997). When rural communities lose passenger rail service. *Rural Development Perspectives, 12*(2), 13–18.

Capalbo, S. M., & Heggem, C. N. (1999). Innovations in the delivery of health care services to rural communities: Telemedicine and limited-service hospitals. *Rural Development Perspectives, 14*(3), 8–13.

Colby, I. (1987). The bottom line: A personal account of poverty (anonymous author). *Human Services in the Rural Environment, 11*(1), 9–11.

Cordes, S. M. (1989). The changing rural environment and the relationship between health services and rural development. *Health Services Research, 23*(6), 757–784.

Farley, O. W., Griffiths, K. A., Skidmore, R., & Thackery, M. G. (1982). *Rural social work practice.* New York: Free Press.

Fenby, B. L. (1978). Social work in a rural setting. *Social Work, 23*(2), 162–163.

Ginsberg, L. H. (1976). An overview of social work education for rural areas. In L. H. Ginsberg (Ed.), *Social work in rural communities: A book of readings* (pp. 6–8). New York: Council on Social Work Education.

Gore, A. (1995). Issues in rural life. Presentation made to the National Rural Conference, Washington, DC.

Institute for Research on Poverty. (2000). *Who is poor?* Madison: University of Wisconsin.

Jennings, M. (1990). Community mobilization. Presentation made to the National Association of Rural Mental Health Workers, Lubbock, TX.

Mental health services not meeting needs of rural residents. (1989, Fall). *Rural Health Reporter.* Austin: Texas Rural Communities.

Murray, J. D. (1990, April 12). Written testimony submitted to the Regional Field Hearing on Mental Illness in Rural America.

Offner, R., Seekins, T., & Clark, F. (1992). Disability and rural independent living: Setting an agenda for rural rehabilitation. *Human Services in the Rural Environment, 15*(3), 6–8.

Shuttlesworth, G. (1993). The rural medical social worker: A pilot project. *Human Services in the Rural Environment, 15*(4), 26–29.

U.S. Department of Agriculture. (1997). *Issues in rural health: How will measures to control Medicare spending affect rural communities?* Economic Research Service Information Bulletin No. 734. Washington, DC: Author.

U.S. Department of Agriculture. (1999). *Changes in the population age 60 and older, by age and residence.* Economic Research Service Report RDRR-90. Washington, DC: Author.

U.S. Department of Agriculture. (2000). *United States fact sheet.* Available: http://www.econ.ag.gov/epubs/other/usfact/US.htm.

Winslow, W. (1990). Reducing turnover among rural mental health specialists. Presentation made to the National Association of Rural Mental Health Workers, Lubbock, TX.

Wooten, D. B. (1989). AIDS in rural California. *Human Services in the Rural Environment, 13*(1), 30–33.

SUGGESTED FURTHER READINGS

Beale, C. (1993, September). Poverty is persistent in some rural areas. *Agricultural Outlook,* Report No. AO-200, pp. 22–27.

Coward, R. T., & Cutler, S. (1989). Informal and formal health care systems for the rural elderly. *Health Services Research, 23*(6), 785–806.

Cromartie, J. B. (1993). Higher immigration, lower out-migration contribute to nonmetro population growth. *Rural Conditions and Trends, 7*(3), 13–17.

Dwyer, J. W., Lee, G. R., & Coward, R. T. (1990). The health status, health services utilization, and support networks of the rural elderly: A decade review. *Journal of Rural Health, 6*(4), 379–398.

Fuigitte, G. V., & Beale, C. L. (1993). The changing concentration of older nonmetropolitan population, 1960–90. *Journal of Gerontology, 48*(6), 278–288.

Glasgow, N. (1993). Poverty among rural elders: Trends, context, and directions for policy. *Journal of Applied Gerontology, 12*(3), 302–319.

Moore, M., & Davis, K. (1995, Winter). Preserving and strengthening Medicare. *Health Affairs, 14*(4), 31–46.

Poole, D. L., & Daily, J. M. (1985). Problems of innovation in rural social services. *Social Work, 30,* 338–344.

Pratt, D. S. (1990). Rural occupations and health. *Journal of Rural Health, 6*(4), 399–418.

Shreffler, J., Capalbo, S., Flaherty, R., & Heggem, C. (1999). Community decision-making about critical access hospitals: Lessons learned from Montana's medical assistance facility program. *Journal of Rural Health, 15*(2), 180–188.

U.S. General Accounting Office. (1995). *Intercity and passenger rail: Financial and operating conditions threaten Amtrak's long-term viability.* Report No. GAO/RCED-95-71. Washington, DC: Author.

Summers, A., Schriver, J. M., Sundet, P., & Meinert, R. (Eds.). (1987). *Social work in rural areas.* Batesville: Arkansas College.

York, R., Denton, R., & Moran, J. R. (1989). Rural and urban social work practice: Is there a difference? *Social Casework, 70,* 201–209.

SOCIAL WORK IN THE WORKPLACE

Bill and Meredith Hunt, both 32 years old, live in a small house in a rapidly deteriorating part of the city with their three children, ages 2, 4, and 8. Bill works at a large manufacturing plant as one of several workers who monitor a largely automated assembly line. Meredith works as a computer programmer for a large company. The Hunts' two youngest children attend a child care center, and their oldest child attends school.

Until recently, Bill's job has been the most important aspect of his life. He is well liked as an employee, and in the neighborhood, his job is viewed as desirable. But Bill is finding that his job is a lot less meaningful to him than it has been in the past. His raises are less frequent and are not enough to pay even for necessities. Last year, Bill and the other assembly-line workers were laid off for 2 months because of a production slowdown. Most manufacturing companies in the area are buying their parts from abroad, and Bill's company increasingly is automating its operations, reducing the need for employees. There is even talk of shutting down the plant and moving it to Mexico. Bill is frustrated about the recent layoff and the lack of pay and concerned about how long his job will last. Although he knows that his wife has to work to make ends meet, Bill resents the fact that she has less time for him and feels bad because he can't provide for his family on his own.

Within the last 2 years, Bill has begun drinking heavily. He has beaten Meredith several times, and he yells at the children and spanks them more often. Bill's supervisor has noticed a change in his job performance and is ready to give him formal notification that he needs to improve or risks being fired. Bill feels tired, financially pressured, and emotionally defeated.

Meredith also finds herself emotionally drained. In addition to her job, she maintains primary responsibility for taking care of the house and the children. She gets up at 5:30 A.M., and it is always after midnight before she has everything done and collapses into bed. Because the child care for the Hunts' two children costs over half of Meredith's take-home pay, they can't afford child care for their oldest son before and after school. Meredith worries about him being at home alone and makes several telephone calls to him each afternoon. Additionally, neither of the companies the Hunts work for allows employees to take leave when the children are sick, and all three children have been sick a lot lately. Meredith has missed 6 days of work in the last 2 months to care for her sick children. On three other occasions, she has kept her oldest son home from school to take care of the younger children.

Meredith's mother, who lives in a neighboring city, recently was diagnosed with cancer and is scheduled to have major surgery. Meredith would like to spend several days with her mother during and after the surgery since her other siblings live out of state. But she has used all of her vacation days for her children's illnesses, and her company has no policies that provide for leave in such situations.

Recently, Meredith has been having difficulty sleeping and stomach problems. Her doctor prescribed tranquilizers, which she takes more often than called for by the prescription. Meredith's coworkers are worried about her, but they resent having to do extra work when she is absent or not able to work as quickly as she usually does. Her boss has commented on the decline in her job performance. Meredith likes her job very much but also is very worried about her husband, her children, and her mother. She feels guilty because her working places extra pressures on her family. Her oldest son is not doing well in school, and Meredith is too tired to help him. All of the children vie constantly for her attention. Both Meredith and Bill feel caught between the pressures of work and their family, and they are becoming increasingly overwhelmed by the demands of both.

Most individuals over the age of 18 have two major domains in which they interact: the family and the workplace. While attention to social problems and individual needs usually includes an emphasis on the family, rarely is there any focus on the relationship between the individual and the workplace. This omission has caused us to help individuals and their families less often and not as effectively as we could.

Consider again the systems/ecological perspective to understanding problems discussed in Chapter 3, particularly the way systems overlap and interact with each other and the individuals who function within those systems. Think about this perspective in relation to the Hunt family. Though until recently the Hunts have been a close-knit family, work is a primary focus in their lives. It produces the economic resources needed to provide food, clothing, shelter, and the recreational activities affordable to them. When we meet someone, frequently our first question is not "To what family do you belong?" but rather "Where do you work?" In U.S. society, a person's status in life is defined largely by occupation. The type of work that we do defines much of our self-respect, self-fulfillment, identity, and status. Until recently, both Bill and Meredith received positive fulfillment from their workplaces. They got along well with coworkers and received raises, recognition for jobs well done.

At first, their two jobs allowed the Hunts to support their family adequately. The positive aspects of work spilled over into the family, and they also maintained positive support within the family. But the overlaps between the two domains began to create additional pressures for both Bill and Meredith. Conflicts began about which came first—home or work—when there didn't seem to be enough energy for both. What should be done when children or relatives get sick? How much money should be spent on child care? Who is going to prepare the meals when both parents are tired? What types of jobs and career paths should be pursued when the type of work available seems to be changing? All these issues had an impact on Bill and Meredith's relationships and ability to function, both at home and at work.

For both Bill and Meredith, work currently has many negative implications. Ideally, they will seek help from some type of social service program before either their family or their jobs become jeopardized further. A social worker or other helping professional that becomes involved with the Hunts' problems cannot help them effectively if work issues are not taken into consideration.

In this chapter we explore current and projected workforce demographics, the changing nature and meaning of work, problems created by work and family tensions, and the roles the workplace and social workers can play in attempting to prevent such problems from occurring or recurring.

A Historical Perspective on Work and Family Relationships

In most Western countries, particularly in the United States, much of the basis of society can be traced to the Protestant work ethic, which stems from the Protestant Reformation of the 17th century. This ethic suggests that work is an expectation of God and laziness is sinful. Attitudes toward paupers during the early colonization of the United States and toward welfare recipients today stem from the impact of the work ethic on our society.

For women, however, the emphasis was different; the primary role of women was to maintain the family and to support the ability of men in the family to work outside the home. Until the 1970s, this pattern changed only during wartime, when women were needed in the factories because men were away at war. But as soon as peace returned, women returned to the home and men to the workplace. Those women who did work outside the home—because of necessity, interest, or both—often were considered to be outside their appropriate role. It is interesting to note, for example, that until the 1970s most studies regarding work focused on the negative impact of the *unemployed* male on his family or on the negative impact of the *employed* female on her family (Bronfenbrenner & Crouter, 1982).

In recent years, much has changed in regard to the relationship between the individual and the workplace. Probably the biggest change has been due to the large number of women who are working, including those with children. Other changes have taken place as well. Workplaces are more diverse, in regard not only to gender but also ethnicity. Increasing numbers of African Americans, Latinos, and other people of color are joining the workforce. Between 1998 and 2008, the U.S. civilian labor force is expected to change in the following ways (U.S. Bureau of Labor Statistics, 2000a):

- 8.5% increase in men age 16 and over;
- 14.2% increase in women 16 years old and over;
- 54.4% growth in persons age 55 to 64;
- 13.8% increase in African Americans age 16 and over;
- 40.3% increase in Asians and Pacific Islanders, American Indians, and Alaska Natives 16 years old and over; and

- 36.8% growth in Latinos 16 years old and over.

Employees' expectations about work have also changed. Individuals today expect more from the workplace than just a paycheck: recognition, a voice in decision making, benefits, and flexible working hours. Numerous studies have focused on the fact that many workers today put other priorities ahead of their jobs. Additional problems receiving increased attention from the workplace include substance abuse; increased costs of health care and other benefits; maternity, paternity, and sick leave; and the overall increase in employees' stress. Because work for pay is such an important aspect of our society, fluctuations in the U.S. economy in recent years have raised added concern about the unemployment and the underemployment of many individuals. The unemployed and underemployed are much more likely to be women and people of color, most often with children. Unemployment and underemployment—and the fear of both—cause added stress not only to individual employees but to their families as well.

A growing number of experts view the relationship between work and family life as one of the most critical policy issues to be addressed during the next decade. In many instances, special social services and other programs have been established in the workplace to assist employees and their families to maintain or increase productivity. Increasingly as well, social services programs in the workplace are helping workers deal with layoffs and business closings.

Occupational social work (sometimes called "industrial social work") has emerged as a growing field for social workers. Occupational social workers generally work in a corporation's human resources department or health unit. They help workers cope with job-related pressures or personal problems that affect the quality of their work. They provide counseling to employees whose performance is hindered by emotional or family problems or substance abuse. They also develop education programs on a variety of quality-of-life issues and refer workers to community programs for assistance (U.S. Bureau of Labor Statistics, 1999b). By applying a systems/ecological perspective, social workers have the potential to play a major role in strengthening relationships between the individual, the family, and the workplace.

THE CHANGING NATURE OF THE WORKFORCE

Today's workforce is considerably different from what it was even a decade ago. In the past, most employees were white males who were employed in business and industry and who often stayed with one company until retirement. The current workforce is much more diverse. Employees today are much more likely to be women and people of color employed in often low-paying service-related jobs. The median annual earnings of service workers in the United States in 1998 were $15,647 (U.S. Bureau of the Census, 2000). Additionally, because of technological and economic changes, many workplaces have closed, **downsized** their operations, or changed the nature of their work and the type of resources needed, including personnel. Employees today are more likely to change jobs frequently and experience several career shifts before they retire. Being terminated from a job for reasons

other than job performance will also become much more common as global changes that affect the workplace continue to occur.

More Women in the Workforce

Many of today's work-related programs and policies are based on work and family demographics as they existed during the 1950s: an almost exclusively male workforce and a male breadwinner supporting his stay-at-home wife and 2.6 children (an average figure). But currently, fewer than 10% of American families can be classified this way. In 1996, nearly 70% of two-parent families had both parents employed full time. In 1997, over 70% of all working women had children under 18, and over 60% had children under 6 years of age. More than half of all women with children under 1 year of age are employed outside the home. (U.S. Bureau of Labor Statistics, 1997a).

The increase in the number of women employed outside the family has been fairly sudden, leaving both employers and families unprepared to deal adequately with the resulting implications. Many individuals argue that the reason for this phenomenon has been primarily economic—that the majority of women work as an economic necessity rather than by choice. Others argue that the women's movement and the realization that women have choices open to them other than remaining at home have created this shift. Still others believe that the women's movement occurred because women were forced by economics to enter the workforce, and once there, they faced unfair conditions and began lobbying for changes and more options. Still others counter that more women are working because of the increased emphasis on self-fulfillment and consumption among both genders. Although studies indicate that some women work because of choice, most women who are mothers want to work less than they do now.

Whatever the reason or reasons for the increased number of women in the labor force, this factor more than any other has focused attention on the relationship between work and family. When only one family member left the home each day and operated within the work system, there was less necessity for overlap or interaction between the work and family systems, and it was fairly easy to keep them separate. But when two family members become involved in the work system, it is impossible to keep the two systems separate.

Single-Parent Families

Other demographic shifts require special attention as well. In 1997, the percentage of family households in the United States headed by white, African American, and Latino women was 14%, 47%, and 24%, respectively (U.S. Bureau of the Census, 1997). Nationally, women in general earn nearly 27% less than their male counterparts in the workforce (U.S. Women's Bureau, 1999). The percentage of all workers paid hourly wages at or below the federal minimum wage of $5.15 per hour was 10.8% for women and 6.7% for men in 1997. Some 21% of part-time workers were paid at or below this rate. Latinos and African Americans were paid at this rate more often than whites (*Statistical Abstract*, 1998). Low wages make survival for individuals, particularly those with families, extremely difficult. While experts recommend that no more than 30% of take-home pay be spent on housing, many poor families spend as much as 70%. Many also cannot afford health insurance, even if it is available through their place of work. Two-thirds of the nearly 42 million persons in the United States

without health insurance have full-time jobs (U.S. Bureau of the Census, 1998).

The median income in 1998 for all married households was $54,276. For all single-parent, male-headed families, it was $39,414, compared to $41,384 for white male-headed families, $30,360 for African American male-headed families, and $32,239 for Latino male-headed families. For all single-parent, female-headed families, median income was $24,393, compared to $27,542 for white female-headed families, $17,737 for African American female-headed families, and $18,452 for Latino female-headed families (U.S. Bureau of the Census, 1999). When both ethnicity and gender are accounted for, white males earn the highest wages and African American women, the lowest (see Figure 16.1).

Emerging Issues

For women and their families, issues such as patterns of child rearing and affordable child care, flexible working hours, transportation to and from work, and job training, in addition to salary, benefits, pensions, and compensation, are crucial. For their employers, absenteeism and tardiness, sick leave, and employee stress are critical factors. Increased numbers of women in the workforce are expected to lead to the following results:

- More heavily subsidized and regulated child care
- Readjustments to tax systems such as the "marriage penalty," which penalizes families in which both spouses are employed outside the home, and child care deductions
- Decreased flexibility of the workforce as two-career families become less willing to relocate

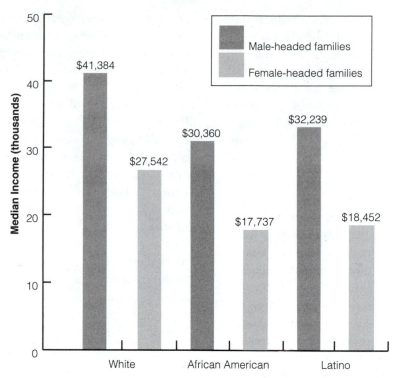

FIGURE 16.1

SINGLE-PARENT FAMILIES' MEDIAN INCOME BY ETHNICITY AND GENDER

Source: U.S. Bureau of the Census (1999).

- Fewer distinctions between males' and females' jobs and wage rates
- An increase in part-time, flexible, and stay-at-home jobs and a decrease in total work hours per employee
- A restructuring of private benefit policies to reflect the needs of two-income families and single workers
- More stringent public programs, with access to benefits more segregated between those available to wage earners and those available through government to low-income earners and the unemployed

A Smaller, Aging Workforce

As a result of the decrease in the number of babies being born, the workforce is expected to decrease in size and will also grow older. Between 1996 and 2006 the labor force is projected to grow by about 11%. This increase is less than the 14% increase over the previous 10-year period ("Labor Force 2006," 1997), a slower gain than at any time since the 1930s. This in turn will decrease the national rate of economic growth. Economic growth also will depend more heavily on the increased demand for products such as travel and tourism, restaurant meals, luxury goods, and health care.

Whereas the overall population between 2000 and 2025 is projected to grow by only 22%, the number of persons age 55 to 64 will increase by 65% and the number of persons age 65 to 74, by 95%. The increased aging of the workforce and of society is likely to have the following impacts:

- The workforce will be more experienced, stable, and reliable.
- A continuing decrease in the number of workers available to assume responsibility for those not in the workforce will have long-term implications for areas such as Social Security.
- Jobs in areas such as fast-food service may be plentiful due to the decreasing number of younger workers; however, the labor market for younger workers may actually tighten as companies initially forced to raise wages to attract young workers develop other strategies such as increased automation.
- If workplaces continue to reduce middle-management positions and develop less hierarchical work organizations, competition will rise among workers to move up within organizations, and those workers who leave or lose jobs will have a difficult time seeking new jobs at their previous levels.

Greater Ethnic Diversity within the Workforce

During the next decade, African Americans, Latinos, and other people of color will continue to enter the workforce in greater numbers than their white counterparts. Non-whites will make up over 38% of new work entrants and more than 25% of the workforce in the year 2006. African Americans will make up 10.7% of the workplace; Latinos, 11.7%; and Asians, 4.9% ("Labor Force 2006," 1997).

The number of immigrants entering the United States is also expected to increase. Estimates suggest that if immigration patterns continue, even under the most conservative estimates Latino and Asian populations in the United States will grow by 30% to 35% between the years 2000 and 2010 (*Statistical Abstract,* 1998). This shift in population will be most significant in the South and the West, particularly Texas, Arizona, and California. Given the changing nature of work in this country (strong backs and nimble fingers are no longer primary assets), immigrants will have a difficult time finding work that pays enough to make ends meet, particularly if they are unable to gain access to education and job-training programs.

The increase in ethnic diversity in the workforce is likely to have a number of implications:

- People of color will continue to be discriminated against, work in lower-paying jobs, and be promoted to management positions less often than whites.
- People of color will continue to earn less than whites, and unemployment rates and earnings may actually worsen for them. In 1996, the median household income for African Americans was 63% of the median household income for whites, while the median household income for Latinos was 67% of that for a white household (*Statistical Abstract,* 1998).
- Unemployment rates will continue to be higher for people of color in comparison to whites. The unemployment rate for

African Americans was 2.38 times higher than for whites in 1997, while the rate for Latinos was 1.83 times higher during that same time period; see Figure 16.2 (*Statistical Abstract,* 1998).

- African Americans and Latinos will continue to be overrepresented in dead-end jobs and in declining occupations.
- African Americans and Latinos will continue to live in inner-city areas with

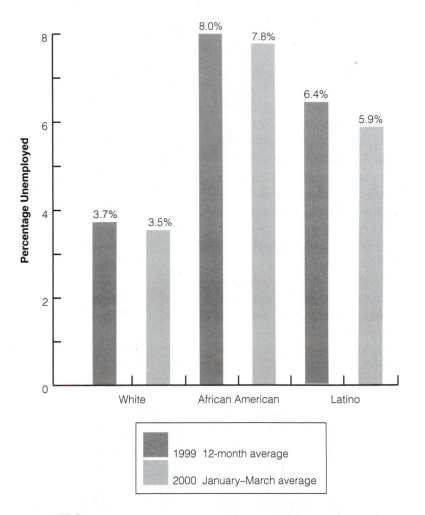

FIGURE **16.2**

SEASONALLY ADJUSTED UNEMPLOYMENT RATES BY ETHNICITY: 1999 (12-MONTH AVERAGE) AND 2000 (JANUARY–MARCH AVERAGE)

Source: U.S. Bureau of Labor Statistics (2000b).

severe problems that place their residents more at risk for unemployment.

• Immigrants will represent the largest share of the increase in both the population and the workforce since World War I and will also often experience barriers due to language and lack of education (Johnston & Packer, 1987).

Employment experts are concerned that unemployment and low wages will worsen for people of color, because they also have disproportionately high school dropout rates and more problems with literacy than whites. These issues indicate that the changing nature of the workforce will have significant implications for employers and employees alike, particularly for those companies that have previously hired primarily young white males.

National debates about affirmative action will also have implications for workplaces. If affirmative action legislation is changed, some work sites may not feel compelled to hire as many women and people of color. Those who are hired may find less support available because employers and employees may be less inclined to provide fair treatment when some policies emphasizing such treatment are eliminated.

Types of Jobs Available

The types of jobs in which workers are employed also have changed. Through the 1960s, the majority of workers were employed in blue-collar jobs. But as the United States has shifted from a manufacturing-based economy to a service-based economy, fewer and fewer workers are employed in blue-collar positions. In 1997, over half of the workforce was in white-collar jobs (*Statistical Abstract,* 1998). Jobs in the least-skilled job classifications will continue to grow at a slower pace, while the number of white-collar and skilled professional jobs will experience the greatest growth. Between 1996 and 2006, employment in service-providing industries will grow by approximately 30%. Business, health, and education services will account for 70% of the growth within the service industry. Computer and data-processing services will add over 1.3 million jobs from 1996 to 2006 as a result of technological advancements and the need for higher-skilled workers. Little or no change is expected in employment in agriculture, forestry, fishing, and related occupations. Computer engineers' and system analysts' jobs are expected to grow rapidly to satisfy expanding needs of scientific research and applications of computer technology (U.S. Bureau of Labor Statistics, 1999b). New jobs will require higher levels of education and greater skills in mathematics and language. Of the 25 occupations with the largest and fastest employment growth, high pay, and low unemployment between 1996 and 2006, 18 will require at least a bachelor's degree. Education will be essential in getting and keeping a high-paying job. Labor force groups with lower than average educational attainment in 1996, including Latinos and African Americans, will continue to have difficulty obtaining a share of the high-paying jobs unless they raise their educational attainment (U.S. Bureau of Labor Statistics, 1999b).

Shifts in the types of jobs available are likely to lead to a dual workforce—more jobs available in the white-collar and skilled areas, primarily in services, requiring high levels of education, and a limited number of jobs available in manufacturing and low-level service jobs, requiring less education and skill. Such changes are likely to make the workforce even more segregated, with more people of color, immigrants, and women in the less-skilled, lower-paying jobs and more white males in the higher-paying jobs requiring greater education and skill.

The shift in jobs away from major industrial centers in the North and East to the Sunbelt and West Coast, as well as the move away from small agricultural production, also has had a significant impact on workers and their families. Many individuals and families who have remained in industrial centers or farm areas have been forced to move or to take lower-paying jobs or seek financial assistance for the first time in their lives. They often have lost their homes, farms, and businesses and face an unpredictable future.

THE CHANGING NATURE OF WORK

During the 1990s, workplaces of all types continued to shift their emphasis to remain competitive in a global marketplace that is changing rapidly. Workplaces that have been able to survive have had to be increasingly innovative and flexible. As a result, many workers have lost jobs, have been shifted to new roles within the organization, or have had to become contract workers of the organization with which they were previously employed. Increasingly, in an effort to remain competitive, organizations have streamlined their operations by eliminating hierarchy and the positions associated with it. Instead, organizations are seeking to be leaner and more agile to take advantage of changing market opportunities. Cross-functional work teams are becoming more common in today's workplaces. These teams are formed to meet a specific organizational goal, then dismantled once that goal has been achieved. In some organizations, salaries and raises are based on the entire team's performance rather than on individual performance.

These shifts have significantly affected employees in all sectors of business and commerce. The key to being a successful employee is to be flexible and willing to work at multiple tasks, changing to new tasks quickly. Interpersonal skills are more important than in the past, as is knowledge of new technology. Today's workers have to find new ways to measure their job performance, since salary increases often occur less frequently due to the need of organizations to remain economically competitive. Promotions are now based on how well an employee can add value to his or her organization as well as its customers.

Additionally, because the costs of employee benefits have increased at such a rapid rate, many workplaces are eliminating benefits or requiring workers to pay a greater share of the benefits. The trend to add new benefits to keep employees on the job has also stopped in most workplaces as more and more qualified applicants are applying for positions when they become vacant. These changes have created additional stress for employees at all levels of work organizations, including top-level managers, as job security becomes increasingly a thing of the past.

Such issues have important implications when addressing employee concerns and the roles social workers and others can play in dealing with them. Because so many changes have occurred in the workplace and the nature of work, it is difficult to predict accurately the future needs of employees and their families, how those needs will surface in the workplace, and which strategies are most likely to meet them (see Box 16.1).

Unemployment and Underemployment

Although being employed often creates numerous problems for employees and their

BOX
16.1

The Changing Work Paradigm

What It Used to Be (Pre-1970s)

- The workforce is predominantly white and male—few women and people of color
- Companies are paternalistic, yet don't always act in the best interests of employees
- Companies meet the most basic needs of employees
- Employees have little say in the workings of the organization
- Benefit programs are traditional and limited
- Most employees work for the same organization for their whole work lives. In many instances, generations of families work for the same organization
- Employees do what they are told to get ahead—the company comes first
- Organizations are highly structured with a rigid chain of command
- The only talk about families is to ensure that top executives have one (marriage is assumed to be a virtue)
- Big is definitely better
- The only economy is the U.S. economy

What It Became (1970s, 1980s, and 1990s)

- The "new breed worker" replaces the "organization man"; quality of worklife becomes more important than simply getting ahead
- Women and people of color enter the workforce in increasing numbers
- Employees begin to demand more say in what happens at work
- The dual wage-earning family is common
- Employee loyalty to the company is no longer unquestioned
- The global economy emerges—companies can no longer be concerned only with what goes on at home
- New "perks" are created to retain highly sought after employees
- Leveraged buyouts become popular
- Average employee tenure drops significantly
- Many companies falter because they do not adapt to the global economy or can not change quickly enough to meet new and different markets

families, and vice versa, the ramifications of unemployment are far more serious. Layoffs and unemployment are expected to increase as the nature of work continues to change. A total of 3.6 million workers were displaced between January 1995 and December 1997 from jobs they had held for at least 3 years (U.S. Bureau of Labor Statistics, 1998). **Displaced workers** are defined as persons age 20 and older who lost or left jobs because their plant or company closed or moved, there was insufficient work for them to do, or their position or

- The information age explodes
- Increasingly, companies merge, down-size, or do both to become more competitive
- The service industry grows by leaps and bounds
- Workers with limited skills and little education are increasingly displaced
- Companies start to realize that past success guarantees nothing

What It Is Now (2000 and Beyond)

- Women and people of color constitute more than 50 percent of the workforce, although their presence in executive and management positions is still disproportionate
- Successful organizations are flexible and able to change focus quickly
- Advances in information technology make the global marketplace the only marketplace
- Traditional employee benefits are replaced with a menu of benefits, many of which require significant employee contributions

- Organizations are flatter and leaner
- Even current success guarantees nothing
- Only those organizations that can adapt to constantly changing market conditions are able to survive
- Having satisfied customers is not enough—organizations must provide additional value to their customers to retain them
- Increased use of contract labor and outsourcing displaces many traditional employees
- Strategic planning is redefined
- Outside of legal protections, employee entitlements no longer exist
- There are no job guarantees
- Employees are asked to "give at the office" in new ways
- Faster is better
- Product development cycles decline significantly
- What makes sense today may have no relevance tomorrow

Source: R. J. Ambrosino, *The Changing Work Paradigm* (Austin: University of Texas at Austin, 2000). Reprinted with permission.

shift was eliminated. Of these 3.6 million workers, 47% lost their jobs because their plant closed or their company shut down or moved. An additional 21% lost their jobs owing to insufficient work for them to do, and 32% lost their jobs because their position or shift had been abolished. Displacement from manufacturing accounted for a much smaller share of the total, while displacement from nonmanufacturing industries such as services, trade, and finance, insurance and real estate accounted for the larger share.

Because work not only provides economic support to families but also is a basic definition of an individual's self-worth, increased unemployment is an issue of national concern. Studies show that unemployment and low economic status are associated with poor family cohesion and family deterioration (Rubin, 1994).

Although official unemployment rates have remained at 6% or below for the past few years, some employment experts suggest that they have actually increased as much as 25%, because the rates do not reflect those individuals who are not actively seeking employment. Unemployment rates for African Americans are double those for whites (*Statistical Abstract*, 1998).

Underemployment, or persons placed in jobs that are at a lower level than they are qualified for, is also an increasing problem. A recent study found that one-third of Americans reported that they were underemployed in their present jobs.

When faced with unemployment or underemployment, many individuals and their families relocate to a supposedly more opportune area. Such areas, however, usually are largely unprepared to address the many needs created by a rapidly expanding population. Housing and other necessities are either unavailable or more expensive than anticipated; the availability of work for certain types of workers is inflated or exaggerated; and transportation, utilities, and education are often lacking or underdeveloped. The absence of support from family and friends also faces those relocating to new areas to find work; and social services agencies, overwhelmed by the population influx, are unable to provide resources to meet many employee and family needs.

For employees and their families who remain in unproductive areas, as well as for those who relocate to new areas, stress rises significantly. Social services agencies in these areas report significant increases in family financial problems, suicides, family violence, substance abuse, marital problems, juvenile delinquency, and other mental health–related problems.

THE CHANGING WORKFORCE: ATTITUDES AND VALUES

Demographic changes in the workforce have had a considerable impact on changing attitudes and values toward work. Although most employees continue to be fairly satisfied with their jobs, discontent is growing among certain segments of the labor force over the nature and meaning of work. Employers today are experiencing a new type of worker, first described by policy analyst Daniel Yankelovich (1979) as the "new breed worker." Yankelovich contrasts today's worker with the "organization man" of the 1950s (Whyte, 1956). This term would be considered sexist today, but it was appropriate at that time since the workforce was primarily male. Whyte's organization man was one who put the needs of the organization for which he worked above all else. He came to the company intending to remain there for his entire career, worked long hours, willingly traveled and relocated for the company, and viewed his paycheck as his primary reward for his loyalty and hard work.

Today's worker is much different. Concerns about quality of life and a willingness to express such concerns to employers have forced employers to place an emphasis on additional incentives beyond the paycheck. An insistence on individual accomplishment and self-fulfillment, priorities given to interests outside the workplace, and personal recognition on the job suggest that employees expect work to have additional meaning beyond the extrinsic rewards of a paycheck.

Less support from family members and lack of time to develop supportive relationships with others outside the workplace have resulted in a growing number of individuals who maintain a strong identity with the workplace and expect the majority of their needs to be met by their work. It is not uncommon, for example, for employees to seek help when dealing with problems, including marital and other family problems, from coworkers rather than from neighbors or friends with whom they have little or no affiliation. In addition, a growing number of younger, more educated workers, especially in the high-tech field, expect high salaries, rapid promotions, and challenging jobs. Because of increased acceptance of alternate lifestyles and the large number of families in which more than one individual is employed, the traditional work ethic has diminished significantly.

The changes in the types of workers in today's workforce and their attitudes toward work have occurred so rapidly that the workplace, for the most part, has been unable to adjust at a comparable pace. Many workplaces still expect the loyalty of Whyte's organization man, to which they were accustomed, yet they are increasingly faced with employees for whom loyalty to one's workplace is not always a high priority.

IMPLICATIONS FOR EMPLOYEES AND THEIR FAMILIES

Most of the attention relating to changes in the types of individuals now in the workplace has been directed toward the impact on the family rather than on the workplace. The majority of this attention has been focused on two-parent families, although these conflicts are also experienced, perhaps more so, by employees who are single parents. As suggested earlier, when work and family domains begin to overlap, in many instances this overlapping creates conflicts such as the following (Rubin, 1994):

- Lack of time for individuals for themselves and family members
- Stress caused by balancing work and family schedules and priorities
- Problems in obtaining adequate child care and other parenting issues
- Feelings of isolation due to lack of time and energy to develop friends and support systems
- Financial difficulties

Several studies focusing on the impact of work on family life have stemmed from Wilensky's (1960) early work in this area suggesting that people experience a **spillover effect,** in which feelings, attitudes, and behaviors from the workplace spill over into leisure life and vice versa. Five possible work-family relationships emerged from these studies:

- *Spillover effect*, in which one domain affects the other in either a positive or negative way—for example, if you really like your job, this will add satisfaction to your family life.
- *Independent*, in which work and family life exist side by side but are independent from each other, making it possible to be satisfied and successful with your job but not your family, for example.
- *Conflict*, in which work and family are in conflict with each other and cannot be reconciled. In a conflict relationship, sacrifices are required in one area to be satisfied and successful in the other—for example,

spending less time at home with family members to be successful at your job.

- *Instrumental,* in which one domain is primarily a means to obtain something for the other; for example, a job is seen only as a way to earn money to maintain a satisfying family life.
- *Compensation,* in which one domain is a way of making up for what is missing in another; for example, a recently divorced man puts all of his energies into his job, works long hours, and socializes only with coworkers.

In helping both employees and their family members understand how they can better balance work and family life, it is useful for social workers and other helping professionals to get them to look at how they view their work-family relationships.

A recent study by Bond, Galinsky, and Swanberg (1998) found that the quality of employees' jobs and the supportiveness of their workplaces are better predictors of job satisfaction, commitment, performance, and retention. *Job quality* is defined as "autonomy on the job, learning opportunities, meaningfulness of work, opportunities for advancement, and job security." *Workplace support* is defined as "flexibility in work arrangements, supervisor support, supportive workplace culture, positive coworker relations, absence of discrimination, respect in the workplace, and equal opportunity for workers of all backgrounds" (p. 12). The authors argue that if employers want to maximize satisfaction, commitment, performance, and retention, they must provide high-quality jobs in a supportive environment, regardless of the industry involved.

When examining the impact of work on the individual and family, one additional perspective that deserves attention is the importance of life events. Rapoport and Rapoport (1980) advocate the use of a **life-span model,** in which the meaning of work and family changes as individuals move through childhood, adolescence, youth, adulthood, midlife, and old age. Individuals often are pressured to give full attention to both work and family life at the same period of life—for example, learning and beginning a successful career at the same time that they have recently married and are beginning to have children. Some policy analysts suggest that companies should consider not focusing on promotions and moves up the career ladder for their employees until they are middle-aged and have already dealt with the child-rearing years. The importance of looking at life span can also be seen when focusing on the large number of individuals who make midlife career changes, not because they are necessarily unhappy with their jobs but because they are dealing with personal developmental issues that are age related.

The majority of attention given to the impact of work on the family has been devoted to working wives and mothers. For all families in which mothers work, the impact on the family, particularly the children, is an issue that has been well researched. Current findings indicate that, taken by itself, a mother's employment outside the home has no negative effects on the child. Factors that may affect children of working mothers include the following (Bronfenbrenner & Crouter, 1982):

- The quality of child care that the child receives while the mother is working
- The overall stability of the family itself
- The type of employment
- The family's socioeconomic status
- The quality and quantity of time that either parent spends with the child

Increased Stress

Not surprisingly, the majority of studies focusing on work and family issues find that increased stress on the employed family member and the family itself is the issue most often identified by those individuals studied. Some mental health experts suggest that the tremendous growth in the number of individuals seeking mental health services can be attributed to heightened pressures faced by individuals trying to balance the demands of job and family. Recent studies have also focused on **dual-career families,** or families that have both spouses pursuing their own careers, particularly in relation to the changes in family roles and responsibilities when both parents work. Although most studies find that both parents in dual-career families experience stress and less time for themselves and family members, it is the wives and mothers who feel these pressures the most. Although in many dual-career families husbands share more in child-rearing responsibilities, the majority of child-rearing responsibility still falls on the wife. Studies also show that although husbands take on more of the parenting tasks, housekeeping responsibilities fall almost totally on the wives, even among families in which both husbands and wives view themselves as being less traditional in the division of household tasks than other couples.

Both men and women from dual-career families list advantages as being additional income, greater opportunities for meaningful communication and growth because both individuals are stimulated by jobs, and more sharing in parenting roles. But women in such families face numerous role conflicts, citing lack of time to accomplish tasks both at home and at work, lack of time for self, lack of time for spouse, and lack of time for children. Furthermore, some studies find that partners in dual-career families are not having as many children as in the past. When families do have children, childbearing occurs within a shorter span of years so that the parents can continue working (Gilbert, 1993).

Relocation

Increases in the numbers of dual-career families have also resulted in problems when one spouse has a job opportunity in another geographic location. Which spouse's job should prevail and under what conditions presents conflicts in many marriages when such opportunities arise. These dilemmas have resulted in more employers providing relocation services that include help in finding employment for spouses, as well as an increase in the number of **commuter families,** or families in which spouses are employed in different locations, often in different parts of the country. Many more workers are also refusing promotions that require relocation.

Financial Problems

In many families, both parents are employed outside the home, but their incomes are still below or barely above the poverty level. Financial pressures are especially great for women, people of color, and other workers less likely to be well educated or trained—and, as a result, more likely to be employed in low-paying jobs. Those individuals who are single parents (also most likely to be women and people of color) are especially vulnerable to financial pressures. Increasingly, the majority of poor in the United States are working. In 1996, almost 20% of families whose incomes were below the poverty level had at least one family member working full-time or more on a year-round basis (*Statistical Abstract,* 1998). Even those persons who work full time at minimum wage (currently $5.15 per hour) find it difficult to support themselves and their families. A full-time worker earning the minimum wage in 1999 and supporting a household of three persons earned a salary that fell nearly $6,000 below the poverty level. Advocates for the **working poor** suggest that continuing to ignore this population will result in substantial costs to families as well as to the U.S. economy. Options for assisting the working poor to improve their situation include the following (Lindsey, 1994; Shapiro & Greenstein, 1987):

- Increasing the minimum wage to a living wage
- Expanding allowable income tax credits for working parents
- Establishing future security accounts for all children that can be used for education or job training once they reach age 18

Additionally, 29% of the U.S. workforce is not covered by employee health insurance. These employees, more likely to be women and people of color, have eight times as many dependents as individuals who are covered by insurance. When these families do have health crises, they are likely to face severe financial problems. Many employers continue to hire workers as temporary or part-time workers so that they will not have to pay part of their health insurance and other benefits (*Statistical Abstract,* 1998).

One of the most important pieces of legislation in regard to work and family issues, the **Family and Medical Leave Act,** was passed by Congress in 1993 after several previously unsuccessful attempts. The act requires employers with more than 50 employees to provide up to 12 weeks of unpaid leave to eligible employees for certain medical or family reasons, such as the birth or adoption of a child or the serious illness of a child, spouse, or parent. The act also specifies that most employees must be able to return to their original jobs or equivalent positions with equivalent pay, benefits, and other conditions of employment (U.S. Department of Labor, 1993).

Accidents and Other Occupational Hazards

Accidents and other on-the-job health hazards create additional stresses for employees and their families. Coal miners whose daily contact with coal dust results in black lung disease, workers in chemical plants who contract cancer and miscarry or produce children born with congenital deformities, and construction workers who may be hurt by heavy equipment place themselves and their families in jeopardy. A number of individuals have successfully sued employers for mental anguish that they or their family members experienced as a result of such situations.

The United States continues to have a much higher rate of industrial health and safety accidents than other countries. In 1970 the federal **Occupational Safety and Health Act** was passed to address this problem. The act sets health and safety standards in industrial workplaces through onsite inspections and citations for violations. The regulatory function is through the Department of Labor, while research and technology are addressed through the **National Institute of Occupational Safety and Health (NIOSH),** housed within the Department of Health and Human Services. NIOSH also sets standards that relate to hazardous materials. But cutbacks in staff and the fact that anonymous reports from workers are less likely to be investigated than those that are from companies and relate to immediate danger have jeopardized the effect of the act.

Approximately 25 deaths each workday, or 6,000 each year, result from industrial accidents. African Americans and Latinos are most likely to be employed in the most dangerous jobs and occupations and are most at risk to suffer accidental injury or death while on the job. Although increased publicity has been given to occupational hazards such as exposure to asbestos and other dangerous chemicals, efforts to deal effectively with such concerns have been limited at both state and federal levels.

Violence in the Workplace

Workplace violence is an increasing problem identified by employers and their employees. Some employees are bringing their family problems to work or are harassed by others, often family members, while at work. In 1994 the U.S. Justice Department conducted a survey relating to workplace violence. It reported that nearly 1 million employees are victims of violent crimes at work each year and that an estimated 8% of rapes, 7% of robberies, and 16% of assaults occurred at work. Over 30% of the situations involved armed perpetrators; 30% of them were armed with handguns. The total number of violent workplace crimes cost about half a million employees an average of 3.5 days of missed work per crime and more than $55 million in lost wages ("Justice Department Reports," 1995).

Sexual Harassment

Sexual harassment is another concern in the workplace, to both employers and their em-

ployees. The costs of sexual harassment can be extremely damaging both emotionally and from a cost perspective to employees, and employers are legally responsible to ensure that sexual harassment does not occur. It is difficult to obtain accurate figures about the actual incidence of sexual harassment in the workplace, because half of all people who are harassed never report it. They may fear that they will lose their jobs or experience other retribution, that they will not be taken seriously, or that they have somehow contributed to the harassment. Title VII of the Civil Rights Act of 1964 specifies that discrimination that violates individual rights occurs if:

- Individuals are offered rewards in return for sexual favors or threatened with punishment if they do not provide them
- A hostile environment is created that interferes with employees' ability to concentrate on their job tasks because of behaviors such as making lewd comments and telling inappropriate sexual jokes, displaying inappropriate artwork and other materials, and touching or threatening to touch individuals in inappropriate ways
- An employee's job or job opportunities are jeopardized because of another person who is responding positively to requests for sexual favors (Petrocelli & Repa, 1992)

Social workers in the workplace often provide employee training regarding what constitutes sexual harassment and how to handle it if it does occur, assessment and conflict resolution if such incidents are reported, and counseling to those who have been sexually harassed. They also advocate and encourage employee empowerment to ensure that the workplace culture does not support such behavior.

Dependent Care for Working Parents

In 1998, of the 70.2 million families in the United States, 34.1 million, or 48.5%, had children under the age of 18. Of these families, the following can be considered likely to have work-related child care requirements: 15.9 million married couple families with both wife and husband in the labor force and 5.2 million female-headed families with the woman in the labor force (U.S. Bureau of Labor Statistics, 1999a). In 2000, half of all preschoolers had mothers in the labor force (Children's Defense Fund, 2000).

In 1995, 88% of mothers with children age 6 and under who were employed 35 hours or more per week used some type of non-parental arrangement to care for their child. Organized child care facilities such as day care centers or nursery schools were used 39% of the time. Relatives other than the mother were used 33% of the time, and non-relatives such as in home baby-sitters and family day care providers were used 32% of the time. Families with employed mothers are spending more on child care than they did in the past: child care costs for these families averaged $79 per week in 1993 compared with $64 per week in 1986 (*Statistical Abstract,* 1998).

Care of elderly parents is another problem increasingly affecting employees. More than 7 million Americans, mostly women, care for dependent adults, usually aging parents. Forty-two percent of these women have full-time jobs. Women caring for dependent adults report health problems, emotional disorders, and problems with absenteeism and tardiness (Pritikin & Reece, 1995).

Elder care services can vary tremendously. Types of elder care include the following (National Institutes of Health, 1997):

- Adult day care provided in a home or center-based setting
- Home health care, which allows the elderly person to remain in a familiar environment and to maintain a certain level of independence
- Group homes, which offer a residential setting for elders who need very limited assistance (nursing care and other arrangements are available from outside agencies)
- Skilled nursing facilities, which offer 24-hour residential services in a nursing home setting

Changing Expectations about Balancing Work and Family Life

Changing expectations regarding what is important in life also have implications for both families and the workplace. Increasing numbers of individuals are reassessing trade-offs between work and family life. Assuming no financial hardship exists, many people today are willing to reduce their salaries to have more personal or family time. Others are willing to turn down a promotion if it seriously jeopardized the amount of time they could spend with their families. The term **downshifting** refers to the voluntary limiting of job demands so employees can devote increased time to their families or to themselves.

Implications for the Mental Health of Employees and Their Families

Increasingly, employees and their families, lacking a support system and unable to cope with life's pressures, succumb to divorce, family violence, substance abuse, suicide, or other health or emotional problems. For workers and their families facing such pressures, however, options are often limited. Many individuals work because they must support their families, often as the sole source of support for those families. For those who earn low wages and cannot rely on other family members to offer emotional support or assistance in family needs such as child care, the toll on them and their families can be extensive (for example, the Hunts, the family described at the beginning of the chapter). Even for those who have more options, such as being able to afford child care or rely on relatives, or who work different hours than other family members, balancing work and family pressures is still difficult.

IMPLICATIONS FOR THE WORKPLACE

The problems that have an impact on the individual employee and his or her family also have a significant effect on the workplace. The United States is currently ranked eighth in productivity among Western countries. Job turnover, absenteeism, and other costs created by employee and family problems are expensive to both the workplace and the consumer, who ultimately is forced to absorb these costs.

Costs of Substance Abuse

Alcoholism and drug abuse cost the United States nearly $276 billion in productivity impacts, health care costs, and other impacts (crashes, social welfare, criminal justice, costs of drug treatment, and so forth) in 1995. Table 16.1 gives the workplace outcomes by current drug and heavy alcohol use in 1997 reported by the 1997 National Household Survey on Drug Abuse. In addition, the money spent on drugs saps the country's economic power. U.S. users are estimated to spend $57

TABLE 16.1 WORKPLACE OUTCOMES BY DRUG AND HEAVY ALCOHOL USE

Outcome	Current Illicit Drug User (%)	Heavy Alcohol User (%)
Worked for three or more employers in the past year	4.3	4.4
Missed 2 or more days of work in the past month due to illness or injury	8.5	8.5
Skipped 1 or more days of work in the past month	5.0	5.1
Voluntarily left an employer in the past year	15.4	15.8
Fired by an employer in the past year	1.2	1.4
Had a workplace accident in the past year	5.5	5.3

Source: Substance Abuse and Mental Health Services Administration (SMHSA), 1999.

billion annually on cocaine, heroin, marijuana, and other drugs (Office of National Drug Control Policy, 1999).

Other Problems That Cost Employers

Other health and mental health problems also are expensive, particularly if they are not addressed early. National health care expenditures in the United States in 1999 were projected to reach $1,228.5 billion, or $3.6 billion per day (Health Care Financing Administration, 1999). Mental illness results in $17 billion in lost productivity each year. Eighty-five percent of industrial accidents and 32% of worker-related accidents and heart attacks are attributed to employee stress each year (Van den Bergh, 1995). A study conducted by the Massachusetts Institute of Technology found that untreated depression, a common but serious emotional illness, cost $23.8 billion in absenteeism and lost productivity, with direct costs for treatment and rehabilitation costing $12.4 billion and lost earnings due to depression-induced suicides costing $7.5 billion ("Simple Math," 1995).

Increased Demands on Employers

Many studies suggest that emotionally based individual and family problems exact a heavy toll on both the individual and the workplace in relation to health care costs. In March 1999, employer costs for employee compensation for civilian workers (private industry and state and local government) in the United States averaged $20.29 per hour worked (U.S. Bureau of Labor Statistics, 1999b). Wages and salaries accounted for 72.5% of these costs; benefits accounted for the remaining 27.5%. In 1997, labor unions covered 15.6% of the U.S. workforce, and their collective bargaining powers also obtain additional benefits that support workers and their families (*Statistical Abstract,* 1998). The high cost of health care is a major issue for employers. Many are not only increasing employee-paid costs of health care but also reducing the extent of benefits available.

As more and more workers are looking to the workplace to meet affiliational needs, additional problems arise on the job. Coworkers and supervisors find themselves spending increased amounts of work time listening to employees' problems, ranging from marital disputes to more serious problems such as substance abuse and family violence. A supervisor who oversees 15 employees recently noted that in 1 day she had helped find temporary shelter for a woman employee who had been beaten the previous night by her spouse, listened to another employee whose son was in jail for cocaine abuse and theft and referred him to a counseling center, confronted an employee regarding a job error and learned that he was in the midst of a divorce from a 25-year marriage, and covered for another worker who had to leave early because she had a sick child.

ADDRESSING WORK AND FAMILY PROBLEMS: WHOSE RESPONSIBILITY?

Given the serious costs to workers of employee- and family-related problems, their families, and the workplace, many groups have become involved in developing strategies to address these problems. Social services counselors are much more likely to address factors related to the job when working with individuals and family members than they have in the past. Many communities have developed task forces and programs to provide affordable child care and transportation for employees. A number of public schools have established before- and after-school child care programs, and some schools schedule parent-teacher conferences and other events during evening hours so that most working parents can attend. Social services agencies in some communities have come into the workplace to provide noontime seminars and other programs relating to topics such as coping with divorce, substance abuse, and parenting.

A growing number of employers have also realized that they have a social responsibility to address such problems. Today, many employers have replaced their personnel departments with human resources departments that have expanded roles, including a more holistic approach to employee needs. Human resources departments oversee personnel, social services, and health and wellness, along with other employee-related programs. Some employers have used social workers as consultants to assist managers in determining how they can better meet their employees' needs. Using a systems/ecological approach, appropriate interventions can be directed at all levels of the workplace, from the total corporate environment to the individual employee.

Some companies have established **employee assistance programs (EAPs),** which provide counseling and other social services to employees, and often their families, through the company (EAPs are discussed in detail in the next section). Fifty-eight percent of all employees in medium and large firms were covered by EAP programs in 1995 (*Statistical Abstract*, 1998). Others have expanded health coverage to cover treatment for substance abuse, mental health counseling, and dental care. A number of both public and private employers have established flexible working hours for their employees, also called **flextime,** which allows employees to work hours that vary from a typical 8 A.M. to 5 P.M. workday. For example, a worker could work four 10-hour days each week or work a different set of hours from other employees, perhaps 6 A.M. to 3 P.M.

Other employers allow **job sharing,** a system that allows two people to share the same job, which means each person usually works half-time. Another alternative for employers is to create permanent part-time positions. Some employers also allow employees to work in their homes. For example, workers with disabilities and those with children can access employers' computer networks to complete word processing and other tasks without leaving their homes. This practice is sometimes referred to as **flexiplace.**

Still other employers have stress reduction and health promotion programs, including on-site fitness centers where employees and their families can exercise. Thirty-four percent of all employees in medium and large firms were covered by wellness programs in 1995 (U.S. Bureau of Labor Statistics, 1997a). Some employers also provide on-site child care for employees or other child care programs; several companies have even established special programs that provide care for school-age children during the summer or when the children are sick.

EMPLOYEE ASSISTANCE PROGRAMS

A number of organizations have established formal EAPs to provide counseling to their employees. A survey conducted by the American Society for Personnel Administration found that 79% of organizations that responded had EAPs; of those who did not have them, 55% planned to establish them shortly. EAPs are mandated in federal government agencies, including the military, and in most state, county, and city governments as well. A related group of programs known as membership assistance programs (MAPS), under the auspices of labor unions, offer similar social services to union members (Van den Bergh, 1995).

Originally, EAPs were established to provide counseling and treatment for employees with alcohol problems; a recovering alcoholic, often one of the company's own employees, usually worked as the program coordinator. Today, a wide variety of EAPs are available. Although many are still primarily alcohol related, others are "broad-brush" programs, addressing a wide range of employee issues, including divorce, child rearing, family violence, and financial problems. Many innovative programs have been developed for employees and their families through EAPs. An increasing number of EAPs are offering services relating to the care of elderly parents. EAPs are also called on when workers are relocated or laid off or when companies close. Social workers employed in EAPs become involved in a wide range of situations involving employees—discrimination, including unfair treatment of people of color, women, new immigrants, and persons with AIDS; the needs of workers with disabilities; the effects of toxic chemicals and pollutants on employees; and the effects of the physical and emotional demands of the workplace on employees.

There are four major types of EAPs (Van den Bergh, 1995):

- *Internal programs,* or those provided in-house by professional staff who are employees of the organization;
- *External programs,* those provided through referral to an outside contractor that actually provides the services, usually off the workplace site (this model has seen the most growth in recent years);

- *Consortium programs,* in which several employers pool resources together to provide "group coverage" (this model is less expensive for its members, who can share the costs of operating an EAP with other consortium members, and also may work better for smaller organizations); and
- *Association programs,* whereby an occupational association (such as the Association of Airline Pilots) or professional organization (such as state bar associations or NASW) provides EAP services. Advantages of this model are the EAP's sensitivity to the unique aspects of the profession/occupation served and possible reduced stigma because the EAP is not directly connected with the employee's workplace.

Most workplaces that use models other than the internal model have a full- or part-time coordinator (employed by the company) who trains supervisors in how to recognize troubled employees and make referrals and who publicizes the program within the com-

Many workplaces have employee assistance programs, which provide individual counseling as well as workplace prevention programs. Here, a group of employees meets with a social worker to discuss how to handle workplace and family conflicts.

Stone/Bruce Ayres

pany. This coordinator provides the initial screening of employees to ensure that the EAP services are appropriate; however, a referral is then made to a contracting social services agency or trained professional outside the company that provides the services.

EAPs have a proven track record in reducing employee absenteeism, decreasing health care costs, and increasing employee productivity. Kennecott Copper Company, for example, estimated that it saved $6 for every dollar spent on its EAP. Equitable Life Insurance found that absenteeism due to alcoholism was cut in half after EAP referral to and treatment by alcohol programs. Data from the 3M Company suggest that 80% of employees who used the EAP showed improved attendance, greater productivity, and improved family relations. Finally, Illinois Telephone saved $1.2 million over 9 years as a result of its EAP (Van den Bergh, 1995). Moreover, the American Society for Personnel Administrators surveyed 409 employers that had EAPs and found that 98% of respondents said the benefits of their EAPs outweighed the costs; 46% said that having an EAP had improved their employees' morale (Van den Bergh, 1995).

EAPs also oversee managed health and mental health care for employees, attempting to reduce inadequate and ineffective services. In this role, EAP staff conduct assessments of employee needs, determine the most appropriate type of care needed, and refer the employee or family member to the most appropriate resource. EAP personnel also often serve as case managers in such situations, ensuring that the services are received and monitoring the case until it is terminated. Employees receive an incentive in reduced copayments for using these services. This role has raised ethical issues for social workers in some instances if the emphasis is on saving costs for the employer at the expense of providing the most appropriate services for the client.

Another critical issue that EAP workers confront is confidentiality, with increasing numbers of EAPs adopting clear guidelines about the circumstances under which information about employees is given to management. Most programs advocate total confidentiality between the EAP and employees unless a crime has been committed or the employee is dangerous to him- or herself or others.

DEPENDENT CARE PROGRAMS

Companies are responding to the needs of employees in other ways. Many organizations have helped to establish a variety of child care programs. The Families and Work Institute in New York City has developed the following list of child care options for employers ("Child Care Options for Employers," 1995):

- Sponsor near or on-site child care center(s)
- Support a local child care center
- Create or support a family child care network
- Establish or support after-school care
- Set up or support a vacation/holiday program
- Create or support backup or emergency care
- Establish or support a sick child care program
- Offer resource and referral services
- Organize parenting seminars
- Sponsor caregiver fairs
- Offer vouchers and discounts
- Implement dependent care assistance plans

- Make grants to local organizations that agree to provide access to employees
- Make grants to local organizations to generally improve the supply or quality of child care
- Provide in-kind contributions such as supplies or expertise from the company
- Promote public education and awareness about child care issues

A growing number of corporations have responded. For example, NationsBank (now Bank of America) invested $25 million to provide child care benefits to 65,000 employees. In a survey conducted by Work/Family Directions, 62% of the respondents indicated that the child care program affected their decision to remain at the bank. GTE Corporation offers emergency care on snow days and school holidays, allows employees to bring their children to work, and has private nursing rooms for new mothers. Twenty-one member businesses of the American Business Collaboration for Quality Dependent Care announced their joint commitment to a $100 million initiative to develop and strengthen school-age child care projects in communities throughout the United States. The focus of this effort is on supporting programs that are innovative and replicable. In an example of the growing child care partnerships across the country, the state of Washington formed Child Care Advantages (CCA), a state-level connection between the Office of Child Care Policy and the Office of Business Assistance. The CCA provides businesses with financial and technical assistance in developing on-site and near-site child care facilities. Qualified businesses receive direct loans, loan guarantees, or grants to start or expand child care facilities through a Child Care Facility Fund ("Child Care Options for Employers," 1995).

Other companies have worked with communities in establishing child care referral systems, helping employees locate appropriate child care that best meets individual needs, or they offer flexible spending packages in which employee benefits can be designed for the care of elderly dependents. Some companies provide vouchers for child care, allowing parents to contribute a portion of their employee benefits for child care of their choice. Others provide a variety of after-school and summer child care programs and programs for sick children. Some companies, realizing the amount of money lost every time a child is sick, provide nurses to go to parents' homes and care for children, paying a portion of the cost for this service (Vinet, 1995).

While not yet well documented, child care programs appear to be cost-effective to employers. The turnover rate for one company was 1.8% for those employees with children in its child care program, compared to 6.4% for employees who did not enroll children in the program. One company in Houston, Texas, reported saving 3,700 hours in absenteeism in 1 year after its child care program was established. The company had a waiting list of potential job applicants, whereas a similar company without child care was having difficulty recruiting workers (Center for Social Work Research, 1983).

Because so many employers were finding that their employees were having problems with dependent care for both children and the elderly, a number have expanded their efforts to include this population as well. For example, the IBM Corporation, a founding member of the American Business Collaboration for Quality Dependent Care noted earlier, has provided funding to improve the quality and availability of dependent care for the elderly since the early 1990s (Vinet, 1995).

Although a limited number of work sites have special provisions for sick children, most organizations do not allow employees to take personal leave time when children are sick. In 1995, only 22% of U.S. companies (medium-sized and large firms) provided personal leave time when children were sick (U.S. Bureau of Labor Statistics, 1997b).

Some firms have implemented other programs to increase productivity, including flexible work schedules, health and wellness programs, transportation systems, recreation teams, and employee work groups that work together to improve the workplace and its environment. Coworkers also play an important role in lending support to other employees and their families. Many coworkers are turning to their fellow employees for support during times of crisis. Help with child care and transportation and advice about coping with teenagers or divorce are all types of assistance increasingly provided by coworkers rather than neighbors, friends, or relatives.

In spite of this assistance, the need for affordable, accessible child care for working parents was recently identified as the most critical need for families in the United States. Twenty-nine million children currently need child care, but many parents—particularly those at or near the poverty level—cannot afford the costs of good care. Child care costs are less than 10% of total expenditures for the average family but often over one-third of total expenditures for the working poor (Lindsey, 1995).

SOCIAL WORK IN THE WORKPLACE

One area in which the profession of social work is expanding is in providing social services in the workplace. As mentioned earlier, this area is known as *industrial* or *occupational social work*. Many view this specialization as relatively new, but this is not the case. In fact, it is interesting to note that the profession of social work owes its name to industry. The term *social work,* introduced in the United States in the early 1890s apparently as a direct translation of the German phrase *Arbeiten sozial,* was used to refer to housing, canteens, health care, and other resources provided to employees by Krupp munitions plants to support the industrial workforce (Carter, 1977). Although in many other countries industry is the largest field in which social workers practice, in the United States industrial social work developed and was practiced between 1890 and 1920, then was largely dormant until the 1970s.

Historical Developments

The development of welfare and social work programs in industry began with mutual aid societies and volunteer programs established as a result of many of the progressive reform movements during the late 1800s and early 1900s. Positions of "social secretary," "welfare manager," or "welfare secretary" existed in many American industries, including textile mills in the south, Kimberly Clark, and International Harvester. Welfare secretaries had backgrounds primarily in religious or humanitarian work, with little previous experience in either social work or industry. In general, they were responsible for overseeing the physical welfare (safety, health, sanitation, and housing), cultural welfare (recreation, libraries, and education programs), economic welfare (loans, pensions, rehabilitation, hiring, and firing), and personal welfare, which included social work (then called *case work*), of employees and their families (Carter, 1977).

According to a U.S. Bureau of Labor Statistics survey, by the mid-1920s, most of the largest companies in the United States had at least one type of welfare program, and about half had comprehensive programs (Axinn & Levin, 1997). Sociologist Teresa Haveren reviewed old records and conducted a historical study of work and family relationships at the Amoskeag Textile Mill in New Hampshire in the late 1800s and early 1900s. The company, like many other industries during that time, provided the following for employees:

- Corporate housing close to the mill for working parents
- Boarding houses for young single employees
- English, sewing, cooking, and gardening classes
- Nurses who provided instruction in housekeeping, health care, and medical aid and visited the sick and elderly regularly to provide food and assistance
- A charity department to provide needy families with clothing, food, and coal and assistance to widows with large families if their husbands died or were injured on the job or were former employees
- A hospital ward for employees injured on the job
- A dentist for employees' families
- A child care program and kindergarten
- A children's playground with attendants to supervise the children
- A swimming pool and ice skating rink
- An Americanization program
- An athletic field and showers
- Lectures, concerts, and fairs
- A Boy Scouts program (Haveren, 1982)

Although many companies were generous with assistance, services were denied if an individual refused to work. Thus, the system was designed to encourage loyalty to the organization, not simply to provide benefits to employees. Since many industries employed entire families, often in the same work unit, it can also be argued that this system made it less difficult for workers to make the transition from family to factory, with many family members seeing little difference between work life and family life.

During the late 1920s, opposition to these programs came from a number of fronts, including employees themselves. Many employees were immigrants, including women. As they became more acculturated within the United States, they saw such welfare programs as paternalistic. The rise of the labor movement also increased negativism toward corporate welfare programs. Labor leaders considered such programs antiunion, believing that the welfare secretary diffused employee unrest without bringing about changes that would improve working conditions for employees. The emergence of scientific management of the workplace turned the focus to improving workers' efficiency. Later, scientific management and welfare work merged into a new field, personnel management. At the same time, public and private social services agencies became more prevalent, decreasing the need for businesses to offer the many services they had previously. Thus, corporate welfare programs declined.

During World War II, the National Maritime Union and United Seaman's Service operated an extensive industrial social work program, providing assistance to the families of the more than 5,000 union members who had been killed during the war. Because unions feared social workers hired by companies would not be sympathetic to unions, other unions initiated industrial social work programs. Until recently, unions were responsible for the majority of industrial social work programs in the United States (Carter, 1977).

Social Workers' Roles

With the decline in manufacturing and other heavy industries and the shift to a service economy, the term *industrial social work* has been replaced by *occupational social work* in the United States. Historically, occupational social work has served a variety of functions in business and industry. Profit often has been a major motivation of employers who provide social work services, in hopes that these services would increase productivity and morale.

But social workers have affected the workplace in ways other than providing social services to employees and their families. Social workers have also played a role in

- Integrating new groups of inexperienced workers (such as women, people of color, and immigrants) into the work world
- Consulting with businesses on how to increase diversity in the workplace and to be sensitive to the needs of diverse groups
- Strengthening relationships between the corporate world and the community; and in organizational development through redesign of work to make the workplace more humane for employees

In addition to expertise in working with troubled individuals and families, social workers also are trained in the art of effective communication and negotiation, skills that lend themselves well to advocating for employee needs or working to improve conditions within a workplace and increase the understanding between employees and employers.

It seems logical that social workers should become more actively involved in the workplace. Occupational social work lends itself to the provision of services within a natural setting; the majority of adults, after all, are employed. The opportunity for a universal service delivery system that goes beyond services to the poor, the elderly, and the sick also is ideal for the provision of preventive services, an area that is almost negligible from the broader perspective of total services provided.

While individuals with specializations in fields other than social work, such as human resources management and industrial psychology, also are employed in human relations capacities in business, such as in human resources or employee counseling positions, social work as a profession is strengthening its interests and capabilities in the area of occupational social work (see Box 16.2). The two major professional bodies that guide the profession, the National Association of Social Workers and the Council on Social Work Education, have established task forces, developed publications, and held conferences that focus on occupational social work. In some instances, university social work programs offer courses in occupational social work and related areas, sometimes in collaboration with other departments such as business administration. All programs provide future occupational social workers with knowledge and skill in dealing with substance abuse, marriage and family problems, and other individual and family problems. They also offer courses relevant to working in organizations and the corporate world. To be successful in the workplace, social workers need additional knowledge and skill in business principles, planning and management, marketing, financial management, human resources administration, family counseling, and organizational behavior. Students in

---

BOX
16.2

The Occupational Social Worker

A job description for an occupational social worker might include the following:

- Linking individuals and family members to entitlements and other public and private resources
- Conducting short-term counseling involving a full range of job-related and non-job-related psychosocial and health/disability concerns
- Providing specialized emergency services in areas such as substance abuse, disability management, and mental health
- Identifying and addressing the needs of special populations within the workplace such as older workers and retirees, workers with disabilities, chemically dependent workers, relo-

cated workers, unemployed individuals, dislocated and underemployed workers, ethnic and racial groups, workers exposed to hazardous conditions, and workers with mental health problems
- Addressing issues such as violence in the workplace
- Collaborating with others to identify and address issues of workplace health and safety
- Working with management to minimize problems encountered by part-time and temporary employees
- Assisting workers in accessing vocational and educational opportunities

Source: Reisch, *Social Work in the 21st Century,* pp. 226–238, copyright © 1997 by Pine Forge Press. Reprinted with permission.

---

occupational social work programs also are placed in field internships in corporations and unions, where they work directly with troubled employees and their families or are involved in administration and planning activities.

Much of the focus of occupational social work to date has been on the client as a worker. Although it is important that social work as a profession recognize the importance of work within the individual's life, the emphasis of occupational social work has been primarily at the individual casework level through EAPs and other forms of one-to-one counseling or information and referral ser-

vices. The central focus appears to be on the relationships of work to emotional problems. Social workers have also played a role in addressing work-related social policy issues such as the appropriate division between corporate and social welfare sectors in the provision of social services; the relationships between work and family roles for men and women; the impact of affirmative action programs on women, people of color, and individuals with disabilities; and unemployment. But little attention has been given to the role social work might play from an organizational change perspective.

Social Workers and the Changing Workplace in the Decade Ahead

Many workplaces in the 1990s reflected changes that are not new to social workers. An emphasis on empowering employees to take responsibility for initiative and product design and completion, for example, is consistent with the social work focus of client empowerment. The use of task groups to make decisions and complete projects is also not new to social workers. Social workers are skilled at understanding group dynamics, leadership styles, and the use of a systems/ecological perspective in achieving synergy among systems, including groups. The need for occupational social work continues to be supported by legislation relating to the civil rights and equal opportunities of employees, safe work conditions, and the financial and legal protection of at-risk populations through programs such as workers' compensation, unemployment insurance, and income support programs (Akabas, 1995).

Social workers can play key roles at all levels of the workplace in incorporating these new directions into the workplace culture to ensure that they are effective from both employer and employee perspectives, and that they balance both individual and organizational interests.

Applying a Systems/Ecological Perspective

Because social workers focus on the interactions between the individual and his or her environment, they are well equipped to develop strategies of intervention at various levels of the systems within which the individual functions (see Box 16.3). Consider again, for example, the Hunt family discussed at the beginning of this chapter. Social work intervention could include individual counseling for Bill and Meredith relating to their respective jobs. But because the problems that the Hunts face are associated with their relationship to each other, a social worker might propose marital counseling for the couple, seeing both of them together. Remember, though, that the Hunt children also were having difficulties in the family. It also might be appropriate for a social worker to provide counseling for the entire Hunt family.

Other individuals within the systems in which the Hunts operate may need to be involved, too. Coworkers and supervisors with whom they interact may be exacerbating their problems. The oldest son's teacher also might be helpful in offering insight into the boy's problems. A social worker might wish to work with these individuals in addition to the Hunts, helping others with whom they interact to be more supportive of the Hunt family's needs. There may also be other resources within the community that the social worker might refer the Hunts to, such as a low-cost after-school child care or recreational program for the son, parenting classes, Alcoholics Anonymous, or a family violence program.

The role of a social worker can go beyond the individual and family intervention level. The social worker might realize that numerous individuals at the workplace are experiencing the same kinds of problems as the Hunts, so he or she might establish support groups for employees with similar concerns and needs. An additional role could be to advocate with management for company policies that better support the needs of employees like the Hunts.

BOX
16.3

Assessment of Problem(s)

A comprehensive social worker's assessment of a worker's problem(s) should include the following:

I. Worker
   a. Work History
   b. Current Position—Occupation, Hours, Salary, Fringe Benefits
   c. Job Duties and Responsibilities
   d. Adequacy of Job Performance
   e. Degree and Type of Autonomy and Control in Work Role
   f. Relationships with Colleagues, Supervisors, Subordinates
   g. Specific Work Strains and Satisfactions
   h. Career Goals
   i. Self-Concept as a Worker
II. Work Organization
   a. Size, Location, Function, Physical Setting
   b. General Ambiance
   c. Organizational Structure
   d. Opportunities Provided to Worker for Advancement

   e. Expectations Regarding Loyalty, Performance, etc.
III. Interface between Work and Family
   a. Mesh between Worker's Time and Family Time
   b. Adequacy of Income to Meet Personal and Family Needs
   c. Degree to which Work Role and Responsibilities Intrude on Family Life
   d. Degree to which Family Roles and Responsibilities Intrude on Work Life
   e. Degree to which Work Role Meets Expectations of Significant Others, e.g., Spouse, Children, Family of Origin, Friends
   f. Overlap between Worker and Leisure Activities

Source: J. Cohen and B. McGowan, "What Do You Do?" An Inquiry into the Potential of Work-Related Research. In *Work, Workers and Work Organizations: A View from Social Work,* ed. S. Akabas and P. Kurzman. © 1982, pp. 126–127. Reprinted by permission of Prentice Hall, Upper Saddle River, NJ.

Social workers might work with others within the workplace to implement child care programs, flexible work hours, and adequate sick leave policies. Finally, they might also stretch beyond the workplace in developing state and federal legislation to mandate policies that are more supportive of employees and their families, such as expanding family leave and sick leave policies that allow leave for family-related issues beyond the employee's illness to include all workplaces.

Service Models

The University of Pittsburgh School of Social Work has developed three models of service for occupational social workers that incorporate a variety of roles inherent to the profession of social work:

1. *Employee service model*—focuses primarily on the microlevel of the systems within which employees and their families function. In this model, social work functions include counseling employees and their families, providing educational programs to employees, referring employees to other agencies, implementing recreational programs, consulting with management regarding individual employee problems, and training supervisors in recognizing and dealing appropriately with employee problems.
2. *Consumer service model*—emphasizes intervention at a broader level within the same systems. This model views employees as consumers and assists them in identifying needs and advocating to get those needs met. Social workers work with consumers-employees in assessing their needs, developing strategies to best meet the needs identified, locating and providing community resources to meet the needs, serving as a liaison between consumer-employee groups and social services agencies, and developing outreach programs to meet employee needs.
3. *Corporate social responsibility model*—focuses on intervention at the exo- and macrolevels within the various systems in which employees and their families function. Social workers operating within the realm of this model work with the workplace, community, and society in general in developing and strengthening programs that support individual employees and their families. They provide consultation about human resources, policy, and

donations to tax-exempt activities within the workplace and to community organizations such as the United Way; analyze relevant legislation and make recommendations for additional legislation; administer health and welfare benefits; conduct research to document needs and evaluate programs and policies; and serve as community developers, providing a link among social service, social policy, and corporate interests (Akabas & Kurzman, 1982).

These models often overlap, with social workers in workplace settings providing tasks that fall within more than one model. The majority of social work activity in the workplace to date has been with the employee service model. It is anticipated that as a growing number of social workers practice in an occupational setting, more of their activity will fall within the other two models.

SUMMARY

A systems/ecological approach to social problems focuses on the interactions between individuals and their environments. Until recently, little attention has been given to the interactions among the individual, the individual's place of employment, and the individual's family. But as more women, both with and without children, enter the workplace, and as rapid social change continues to affect many individuals negatively, the relationship between the workplace and the family can no longer be ignored. Individuals experiencing stresses at the workplace invariably bring those stresses home, and vice versa. The costs of employee and family substance abuse, marital discord, parenting problems, and other mental health problems are extensive to both the family and the workplace.

A number of communities and workplaces have developed programs that assist individual employees and their families to better balance work and family pressures. These include employee assistance programs as well as child care, transportation, and health and wellness programs. Studies show that these programs are effective in preventing family and workplace dysfunction. The field of occupational social work is emerging as an area where some impact can be made through intervention in the workplace to improve family functioning as well as increase profitability and productivity for the work organization. Social work as a profession will begin to play a more major role in developing programs within the workplace, as well as advocating for appropriate policies and legislation that provide increased support to employees and their families.

KEY TERMS

commuter families
displaced workers
downshifting
downsizing
dual-career families
employee assistance
   programs (EAPs)
Family and Medical
   Leave Act
flexiplace
flextime
job sharing

life-span model
National Institute of
   Occupational Safety
   and Health
   (NIOSH)
Occupational Safety
   and Health Act
occupational social
   work
spillover effect
underemployment
working poor

DISCUSSION QUESTIONS

1. List four ways that the composition of the workplace has changed over the past 30 years. What effect have these changes had on the workplace?

2. Using a systems/ecological perspective, discuss the relationships among an individual, his or her workplace, and his or her family.

3. Name three types of employee- and family-related problems, and describe how these problems affect the workplace.

4. Name three types of work-related problems that an employee might experience. In what ways might these problems affect the employee's family?

5. Describe five types of programs employers have established to address employee and family needs.

6. Describe the three models on which an industrial social work program might be based. List at least three of the roles an industrial social worker employed in a workplace setting might play.

INFOTRAC COLLEGE EDITION

To learn more about topics included in this chapter, enter the following search terms:

changing workplace

corporate social responsibility

employee assistance programs

employee benefits

global economy

living wage

occupational social work

service economy

work and family life

workforce diversity

workplace violence

 ## On the Internet

http://stats.bls.gov/

http://www.albrecht1.com/

http://crisisprevention.com/

http://www.neas.com/

http://www.naswdc.org/

References

Akabas, S. (1995). Occupational social work. In R. Edwards (Ed.), *Encyclopedia of social work* (Vol. 2, pp. 1779–1786. Washington, DC: NASW Press.

Akabas, S., & Kurzman, P. (1982). The industrial welfare specialist: What's so special? In S. Akabas & P. Kurzman (Eds.), *Work, workers, and work organizations: A view from social work.* Upper Saddle River, NJ: Prentice Hall.

Ambrosino, R. J. (2000). *The changing work paradigm.* Austin: University of Texas Press.

Axinn, J., & Levin, H. (1997). *Social welfare: A history of the American response to need* (4th ed.). New York: Longman.

Bond, J. T., Galinsky, E., & Swanberg, J. E. (1998). *The 1997 national study of the changing workforce.* New York: Work and Families Initiatives.

Bronfenbrenner, U., & Crouter, A. (1982). Work and family through time and space. In S. Kamerman & C. Hayes (Eds.), *Families that work: Children in a changing world.* Washington, DC: National Academy Press.

Carter, L. (1977). Social work in industry: A history and a viewpoint. *Social Thought, 3,* 7–17.

Center for Social Work Research. (1983). *Work and family life issues: A report of a series of corporate forums held with selected work-related organizations in Texas.* Austin: University of Texas Center for Social Work Research.

Child care options for employers. (1995, November/December). *Child Care Bulletin,* p. 6.

Children's Defense Fund. (2000). *Child care now!* Available: http://www.childrensdefense.org/.

Cohen, J., & McGowan, B. (1982). "What do you do?" An inquiry into the potential of work-related research. In S. Akabas & P. Kurzman (Eds.), *Work, workers, and work organizations: A view from social work.* Upper Saddle River, NJ: Prentice Hall.

Foster, B., & Shore, L. (1989). Job loss and the occupational social worker. *Employee Assistance Quarterly, 5*(1), 77–98.

Gilbert, L. (1993). *Two careers, one family: The promise of gender equality.* Newbury Park, CA: Sage.

Haveren, T. (1982). *Family time and industrial time.* Cambridge: Cambridge University Press.

Health Care Financing Administration. (1999). *National health expenditures projections.* Available: http://www.hcfa.gov/stats/.

Justice Department reports on workplace violence. (1995). *EAP Digest, 15*(2), 17.

Johnston, W., & Packer, A. (1987). *Workforce 2000: Work and workers for the 21st century.* Indianapolis: Hudson Institute.

Labor force 2006: Slowing down and changing composition. (1997, November). *Monthly Labor Review, 120*(11), 23–38.

Lewis, B. (1997). Occupational social work practice. In M. Reisch & E. Gambrill (Eds.), *Social work for the 21st century.* Thousand Oaks, CA: Pine Forge.

Lindsey, D. (1994). *The welfare of children.* New York: Oxford University Press.

National Institutes of Health. (1997). *NIH child and elder care.* Available: http://www.nih.gov/.

Office of National Drug Control Policy. (1999). *What America's drug users spend on illegal drugs.* Washington, DC: Author.

Petrocelli, W., & Repa, B. (1992). *Sexual harassment on the job.* Berkeley, CA: Nolo.

Pritikin, E., & Reece, T. (1995). The not-so-golden years: Eldercare issues at work. *EAP Digest, 15*(3), 33–35.

Rapoport, R., & Rapoport, R. (1980). Balancing work, family and leisure: A triple helix model. In C. Derr

(Ed.), *Work, family and career: New frontiers in theory and research.* New York: Praeger.

Rubin, L. (1994). *Families on the fault line: America's working class speaks out about the family, the economy, race, and ethnicity.* New York: Harper-Collins.

Shapiro, S., & Greenstein, R. (1987). *Making work pay: A new agenda for poverty policies.* Washington, DC: Center on Budget and Policy Priorities.

Simple math: Better care leads to better outcomes and lower costs. (1995). *EAP Digest, 15*(3), 16.

Statistical abstract of the United States. (1998). Washington, DC: Bernan.

U.S. Bureau of the Census. (1997). *Current population reports.* Available: http://www.census.gov.

U.S. Bureau of the Census. (1998). *Current population reports.* Available: http://www.census.gov.

U.S. Bureau of the Census. (1999). *Money income in the United States.* Available: http://www.census.gov.

U.S. Bureau of the Census. (2000). *Income 1998.* Available: http://www.census.gov.

U.S. Bureau of Labor Statistics. (1997a, June). *News,* USDL97-195.

U.S. Bureau of Labor Statistics. (1997b, July). *News,* USDL97-246.

U.S. Bureau of Labor Statistics. (1998). *Displaced workers summary.* Available: http://stats.bls.gov/.

U.S. Bureau of Labor Statistics. (1999a). *Labor force statistics from the Current Population Survey.* Available: http://stats.bls.gov/new.release/famee.t04.htm.

U.S. Bureau of Labor Statistics. (1999b). *Occupational outlook handbook.* Available: http://stats.bls.gov/.

U.S. Bureau of Labor Statistics. (2000a). *Employment projections.* Available: http://stats.bls.gov/.

U.S. Bureau of Labor Statistics. (2000b). *Labor force statistics from the current population survey.* Available: http://stats.bls.gov/.

U.S. Department of Labor. (1993). *Family and medical leave act.* Washington, DC: U.S. Government Printing Office.

U.S. Women's Bureau. (1999). *Median and annual earnings for year-round, full-time workers by sex in current and real dollars, 1995–98.* Available: http://www.dol.gov/dol/wb/.

Van den Bergh, N. (1995). Employee assistance programs. In R. Edwards (Ed.), *Encyclopedia of social work* (Vol. 1, pp. 842–849). Washington, DC: NASW Press.

Vinet, M. (1995). Child care services. In R. Edwards (Ed.), *Encyclopedia of social work* (Vol. 1, pp. 367–375). Washington, DC: NASW Press.

Whyte, W. (1956). *The organization man.* New York: Doubleday.

Wilensky, H. (1960). Work, careers and social integration. *International Social Science Journal, 7*(4), 543–560.

Yankelovich, D. (1979). Work, values, and the new breed. In *Work in America: The decade ahead,* C. Kerr & J. Rosow (Eds.). New York: Van Nostrand Reinhold.

Suggested Further Readings

Anastas, J., Gibeau, J., & Larson, P. (1990). Working families and eldercare: A national perspective in an aging America. *Social Work, 35*(5), 405–411.

Ginsberg, L. (1992). *Social work almanac.* Washington, DC: NASW Press.

Hartwell, T., & Steele, P., et al. (1996, June). Aiding troubled employees: The prevalence, cost and characteristics of employee assistance programs in the United States. *American Journal of Public Health, 86*(6), 804–808.

Kurzman, P., & Akabas, S. (Eds.). (1993). *Work and well-being: The occupational social work advantage.* Washington, DC: NASW Press.

Mor-Borak, M., et al. (1993, Winter). A model curriculum for occupational social work. *Journal of Social Work Education, 29*(1), 63–77.

Straussner, S. (Ed.). (1990). *Occupational social work today.* New York: Haworth.

INTERNATIONAL SOCIAL WORK

Sonia is a social worker working in a refugee resettlement camp located in Eastern Europe. Her tasks are many and demanding, and she is forced to work with limited resources in less than optimal conditions. She has been working with a network of social workers from the region and around the world to connect children and families separated from each other as a result of one of the many civil wars in the area. This is a very difficult task as the children and families she seeks to reunite speak many different languages, communications in and out of the camp are limited, and very few people are available to assist her in her work. Many of the children Sonia is working with will never see their parents again—they are either dead or have been forced to settle in another region or country. Others may be reunited with their families but will suffer the emotional scars of war and violence for the rest of their lives. Sonia also works closely with representatives of the International Red Cross, a variety of faith-based organizations, and other refugee resettlement agencies to ensure that the basic health needs of the refugees are met. Together, they are trying desperately to avoid an outbreak of contagious and sometimes deadly diseases caused by the crowded and unsanitary living conditions in the camp. Even though the refugee camp is located in a so-called neutral country, Sonia and her colleagues are constantly exposed to the dangers of war.

Shawn, a social worker and Peace Corps volunteer from Ireland, is hard at work in a small, ill-equipped medical clinic in the heart of a small African country. He works side by side with representatives from a variety of international relief organizations to clothe and feed thousands of individuals suffering from malnutrition. Many face imminent death from starvation. Sean's compassion for his fellow human beings is tested daily in the decisions he must make on behalf of his clients. Some are so weak or sick by the time they reach the clinic that they die shortly thereafter, leaving families and loved ones behind. Shawn is helpless to do anything for them except perhaps to console them or their loved ones who accompanied them on their journey to the clinic. The resources available to Shawn and his colleagues are meager in comparison to the need. He must also wrangle on a daily basis with local authorities who sometimes prevent relief cargo from being unloaded, divert that cargo for some other purpose, or demand bribes in exchange for access to the cargo. Shawn faces time in jail or even summary execution if he pushes too hard for what he believes to be the right thing to do for his clients.

Kristin and Mario, recently married and both social workers from the United States, are working at a rural outpost high in the mountains of the Oaxaca region of Mexico. They are part of a multidisciplinary team of medical personnel and other volunteers who have come to the region to provide basic medical care for the local peasant population, including immunizations. The team also tries to promote preventive health care practices among the population served, but this is difficult because of the severe poverty conditions in which its residents live. Many of the people Mario and Kristin treat have spent days traveling to the outpost, walking over terrain that is barely passable to seek help for themselves and their loved ones. Kristin and Mario have worked hard to establish positive relationships with the members of the community. They are working with a group of women to develop a cooperative to make crafts and clothing from specially dyed and hand-woven cloth. They are also helping establish a school and a child development program for preschoolers. There is no money that changes hands for these services—the local residents are so poor that such an exchange would be out of the question. The payment that Mario and Kristin receive is in the knowledge that they have helped preserve the life of a child, reduced the pain and suffering of a person who would have died without the medical care provided, and helped the residents of the area become more self-sufficient through education and enterprise.

The work of Sonia, Shawn, and Mario and Kristin represent typical examples of international social work, with its focus on achieving social, economic, and political justice throughout the world. Such individuals play a key role in helping improve the quality of life for persons who are victims of persecution, war, famine, dislocation, and political strife. They work side by side with other social work professionals to improve the quality of life for marginalized populations throughout the world. They work in highly volatile political environments, and their physical well-being is often in danger. The conditions under which they must work are far from optimal—they often work in isolated, out-of-the-way places that have little communication with the outside world. They have come together to ensure that basic human rights are honored as well as to do what they can to normalize the lives of individuals who, through no act of their own, have been forced to live a life of abject poverty. Despite language barriers, cultural differences, and the threat of violence and being jailed, these individuals work tirelessly to advance the cause of social work throughout the world.

In this chapter, we will address the mission, goals, and policies of international social work. We will explore how social work transcends geographic boundaries and political ideologies. We will show that the social work profession is thriving in all parts of the world, even in those places in which political restrictions and dangerous living conditions make it difficult to remain actively engaged.

DEFINITIONS AND BASIC CONCEPTS

International social welfare is the field of practice concerned with promoting basic human well-being in a context where cross-national efforts are involved. **Comparative social welfare** is a field of study of how social welfare objectives are obtained in nations other than one's own.

International social work involves the practice of social work to meet social welfare needs from an international perspective. **Comparative social work** entails the comparison of what social workers do in nations other than one's own. What do social workers who engage in international social work do? This is not an easy question to answer, because in the international field many of those who engage in social work do not think of themselves as social workers, and many social workers in the international field do things that we would not normally consider to be social work. Several different terms are used to mean the same thing, and often the same translated term means different things in different nations.

We have defined the term *social welfare* in an earlier chapter. It is useful to deal with how to distinguish between the two concepts of international social work and comparative social work by thinking of them as common social welfare and shared social welfare, respectively. *Common social welfare* refers to those problems, policies, and practices that all nations and states must address (income security, occupational safety, basic health services, and so on). *Shared social welfare* investigations look at these practices by describing and analyzing practice across national borders. The intent is to understand how each nation's social welfare program was developed, how well it works, and perhaps what can be learned from it. *International social welfare* refers to the practice in which many nations work together to respond to a problem that occurs in one nation (for example, a major natural disaster such as flooding, civil strife, or an earthquake).

Comparative Social Welfare

Comparative government and comparative policy are generally considered as parallel areas in the study of political science. Comparative government is a study of the structure, practice, and processes of the public institutions across some sovereign nations. The questions deal with how public decisions are made and how public programs are implemented and enforced. Comparative policy is a study of the inputs and the outputs in particular areas of public programs, such as defense, education, or social welfare. Comparative policy is investigated by political scientists and by specialists in various substantive areas such as social work. The political scientist is interested in building a theory of government; the content specialist is interested in how governments and other institutions carry out specific functions. Some content specialists study comparative policy to obtain new insights and/or ideas for their own country. Others engage in comparative inquiry to build empirical generalizations of how states respond or fail to respond to a particular set of conditions. The generalizations are used to provide empirical support for a broader theory of public choice.

As suggested, there is a difference between shared problems of national governments and common problems of national governments. A common problem is one that faces all states or countries (for example, how to educate its young, redistribute income, or deliver health service to those who are ill and cannot afford private health care). In today's global economy, shared problems arise in the context of common problems—what state A does for its unemployed impacts state B and vice versa. Before common domestic social welfare policy can be turned over to a superordinate body such as the European Union,

we need to know far more about how states solve common social welfare problems.

The first efforts in comparative policy studies were mostly descriptive investigations that examined specific features of the inputs, process, and outcomes in a given set of countries. The "explanations" of the outcomes tended to be state centered. Thus, we might find a historical account of the U.S. adoption of social insurance for the aged or Norway's passage of a mother's allowance. A given policy instrument can be used for a wide variety of purposes. We clearly recognize that Sweden's high welfare guarantee, Germany's high minimum wage policy, the vibrant economy of the United States, or Japan's high capital investment are alternatives to the outcome of increased social protection to all citizens. Comparative welfare helps us learn that basic human needs can be met in many ways.

There is a high level of cynicism in the United States regarding how well the political system allows public policy to reflect public preferences (Dionne, 1991). In recent years, both health and welfare have held a central position in domestic policy debates. The U.S. health care industry decisively rejected a public expansion of the health care system pushed by the Clinton administration (Hacker, 1997; Skocpol, 1996). Just prior to that, the country first adopted and then rescinded a comprehensive program of public catastrophic health care coverage, including long-term care (Holstein & Minkler, 1991). In 1996, the United States adopted a radical reconstruction of its system of income security for single-parent households (Drew, 1996; Weaver, 1998). In all of these choices, a clear preference was made to place a greater reliance on market mechanisms and not the government to deal with the problems at hand. Whatever one's personal preference in these policy choices, most academic and journalistic commentary asserts that all of these public decisions were in accord with overwhelming public preference. The U.S. system of social care is market driven. When you or I become less able to meet our daily activity needs without assistance, to whom should we turn? Should we rely on a spouse, if we have one? Should we rely on our children, if we have them and they are willing to help? Is it reasonable to think that our parish, church, or synagogue will provide such assistance? Perhaps we will be fortunate enough to buy care from some ready and willing open market providers. Or, might we be forced to receive such care through some mechanism of public assistance? The same range of choice applies to finding care for our very young children. Which we would prefer to do and which we are forced to accept are not necessarily the same. It is certainly true that only government could establish a legal right to social care. Because government does it, however, doesn't mean it will do it well, efficiently, effectively, or even equitably. The recent health care debates in the United States reflect the reality that what many people want is not necessarily what they are going to get.

Few would argue that the least privileged citizens in any state would prefer a public system of care because no matter how bad it is, it's probably better than what the market or voluntary or informal system would offer. The same is clearly not true for the more privileged citizen. In *The Three Worlds of Welfare Capitalism,* Gosta Esping-Anderson (1990) points out that to the social democrat, the provision of welfare by market mechanisms is problematic because markets fail to establish rights to welfare, and the market mechanism, to accomplish other ends, is intentionally structured to be inequitable. On the other hand, traditional state welfare arrangements are rejected by

market-oriented liberals because of heavy efficiency costs. They frequently argue these efficiency costs produce the very problems that welfare is structured to combat (Mead, 1997). Such individuals argue that traditional state welfare fails to establish a balance between citizens' rights and obligations. Furthermore, they believe that state constitutions, political institutional structures, and political party function rather than autonomous market forces or citizen preference drive current political choices about relative reliance of sector responsibility for its citizens' social welfare.

In the United States, the social care arrangements at the beginning and the end of life are market-reliant systems. This dominates both our pattern of direct spending and our agency structures. The child day care system in place has really developed since the 1960s. During this time, the number of children in need of any form of substitute care has grown at a fast pace. The share of children in care in market-oriented care centers has grown more than twice as fast as any other system. While there is some outcry for public provision of child day care, it is for the most part a subtitle in how to move single mothers off welfare rather then a debate over how to provide more substantive, adequate, and affordable care for children (Michel, 1999).

Since the early 1960s, the United States has witnessed a near simultaneous shift in political expectations and labor force participation. This has changed the nature and scope of caregiving in substantial ways. The "Great Society" programs of the Kennedy-Johnson years did not survive the loss in faith in government occasioned by the Vietnam War. At the same time, a dramatic change occurred in the patterns of labor force participation that took traditional caregivers (married women) out of the home. These new populations of wage earners were expected to pay for care for their children with their new wages. While this argument makes sense in theory, it does not work well in practice. That is, the cost of child care, particularly infant child care, in the open market far exceeds the capacity to pay for that care for large numbers of women who began entering the workforce at this time. This is especially true for households headed by females or the working poor. The emergence of the service sector as one the largest components of the global economy, coupled with the low salaries paid by jobs in this sector ($7 to $8 per hour on average), makes the argument that women should pay for child care with wages earned even less attractive. If one were to conduct a comparative study of social welfare policies in several countries, including the United States, a reliance on market mechanisms to deal with social problems such as child care would emerge as an important characteristic of U.S. policies, whereas a reliance on the national government would emerge as a major characteristic of policy in Scandinavian countries such as Sweden or Denmark.

International Social Work

Sari (1997) discusses a number of reasons that social workers should have a greater knowledge of international social work practice as well as greater skill in working in other countries or working with international populations within the United States:

- An international cross-cultural social welfare education can broaden one's horizons about alternative economic, political, and social welfare systems.
- A cross-cultural emphasis helps one to understand and appreciate diverse cultures from other countries as well as to gain added insight about one's own values, ideologies, and cultural preferences.

- An international approach exposes one to divergent thinking so that one can view social policies and services more critically and in a comparative perspective because there usually are alternative options.
- Cross-national collaboration between social workers and other human service professionals opens up many possibilities for innovation and change. (pp. 390–391)

This international perspective will allow social workers to practice more effectively in a world that is increasingly interdependent along economic, political, and social lines as well as to contribute in meaningful ways to the reduction of conflict and exploitation in the world.

Social welfare practice in an international context focuses on the study of social problems between nations. Such problems include but are not limited to the following examples:

- Deaths due to war
- Global governance that deals with problems that affect all peoples
- Social justice
- The rights of women and children
- Religious, economic, and political oppression
- Displacement of persons due to war, political strife, and natural disasters
- Marginalization of people through marketplace globalization
- The distribution of wealth
- Poverty
- Human and environmental exploitation (Midgley, 1997; Sari, 1997)

Over 100 million people are estimated to have been killed in wars during the 20th century, including 23 million in the last half of the century. The vast majority of war victims were civilians; indeed, modern warfare is war on civilians. Some would claim that ending the war system is an impossible task, considering

Social workers provide assistance to refugees around the world through a number of international organizations such as the United Nations.

© Howard Davies/Corbis

the often violent history of humankind. Others, including social workers worldwide, would argue that we really have no choice in the matter, that neither civilization nor the environment can long endure the wanton and indiscriminate destruction of modern warfare (Association of World Citizens, 1999).

Global governance through a United Nations that has clearly defined and limited authority and deals with global problems that affect all peoples is also central to achieving a **global village** of social and economic justice, lasting peace, and a sustainable environment (Prigoff, 2000; Stoesz, Guzzetta, & Lusk, 1999). The time must come when people will accept international law to settle global disputes as they now accept their national government in settling disputes between states and provinces. (See Box 17.1 for the United Nations' Universal Declaration of Human Rights, created in 1948.)

Achievement of a global village is also hindered by the inequitable distribution of power and wealth throughout the world. Today, with little more than 10% of the world's population, rich countries and their multinational corporations make virtually 100% of the world's economic decisions, and most of the military ones, without any consultation from the world community. For example, the global arms trade involves billions of dollars of weapons sales every year, with the United States leading this business with over 50% of global sales. World peace cannot be accomplished unless every country is allowed only enough military capability to defend its borders and never enough to wage aggression against its neighbors. Along with this fulfillment of international law is the complete elimination of nuclear, chemical, and other weapons of mass destruction that advocates of a global village of social and economic justice believe serve no valid purpose in maintaining a world community (Association of World Citizens, 1999).

The social work profession has long embraced the notion that justice, particularly social justice, is a critical component in creating

BOX
17.1

Universal Declaration of Human Rights

Preamble

Whereas recognition of the inherent dignity and of the equal and inalienable rights of all members of the human family is the foundation of freedom, justice and peace in the world,

Whereas disregard and contempt for human rights have resulted in barbarous acts which have outraged the conscience of mankind, and the advent of a world in which human beings shall enjoy freedom of speech and belief and freedom from fear and want has been proclaimed as the highest aspiration of the common people,

Whereas it is essential, if man is not to be compelled to have recourse, as a last resort, to rebellion against tyranny and oppression, that human rights should be protected by the rule of law,

Whereas it is essential to promote the development of friendly relations between nations,

Whereas the peoples of the United Nations have in the Charter reaffirmed their faith in fundamental human rights, in the dignity and worth of the human person and in the equal rights of men and women and have determined to promote social progress and better standards of life in larger freedom,

Whereas Member States have pledged themselves to achieve, in cooperation with the United Nations, the promotion of universal respect for and observance of human rights and fundamental freedoms,

Whereas a common understanding of these rights and freedoms is of the greatest importance for the full realization of this pledge,

Now, therefore, The General Assembly, Proclaims this Universal Declaration of Human Rights as a common standard of achievement for all peoples and all nations, to the end that every individual and every organ of society, keeping this Declaration constantly in mind, shall strive by teaching and education to promote respect for these rights and freedoms and by progressive measures, national and international, to secure their universal and effective recognition and observance, both among the peoples of Member States themselves and among the peoples of territories under their jurisdiction.

Article 1 All human beings are born free and equal in dignity and rights. They are endowed with reason and conscience and should act towards one another in a spirit of brotherhood.

Article 2 Everyone is entitled to all the rights and freedoms set forth in this Declaration, without distinction of any kind, such as race, colour, sex, language, religion, political or other opinion, national or social origin, property, birth or other status.

Furthermore, no distinction shall be made on the basis of the political, jurisdictional or international status of the country or territory to which a person belongs, whether it be independent, trust, non-self-governing or under any other limitation of sovereignty.

Article 3 Everyone has the right to life, liberty, and security of person.

Article 4   No one shall be held in slavery or servitude; slavery and the slave trade shall be prohibited in all their forms.

Article 5   No one shall be subjected to torture or to cruel, inhuman or degrading treatment or punishment.

Article 6   Everyone has the right to recognition everywhere as a person before the law.

Article 7   All are equal before the law and are entitled without any discrimination to equal protection of the law. All are entitled to equal protection against any discrimination in violation of this Declaration and against any incitement to such discrimination.

Article 8   Everyone has the right to an effective remedy by the competent national tribunals for acts violating the fundamental rights granted him by the constitution or by law.

Article 9   No one shall be subjected to arbitrary arrest, detention or exile.

Article 10   Everyone is entitled in full equality to a fair and public hearing by an independent and impartial tribunal, in the determination of his rights and obligations and of any criminal charge against him.

Article 11

1. Everyone charged with a penal offence has the right to be presumed innocent until proved guilty according to law in a public trial at which he has had all the guarantees necessary for his defence.
2. No one shall be held guilty of any penal offence on account of any act or omission which did not constitute a penal offence, under national or international law, at the time when it was committed. Nor shall a heavier penalty be imposed than the one that was applicable at the time the penal offence was committed.

Article 12   No one shall be subjected to arbitrary interference with his privacy, family, home or correspondence, nor to attacks upon his honour and reputation. Everyone has the right to the protection of the law against such interference or attacks.

Article 13

1. Everyone has the right to freedom of movement and residence within the borders of each State.
2. Everyone has the right to leave any country, including his own, and to return to his country.

Article 14

1. Everyone has the right to seek and to enjoy in other countries asylum from persecution.
2. This right may not be invoked in the case of prosecutions genuinely arising from non-political crimes or from acts contrary to the purposes and principles of the United Nations.

Article 15

1. Everyone has the right to a nationality.
2. No one shall be arbitrarily deprived of his nationality nor denied the right to change his nationality.

Article 16

1. Men and women of full age, without any limitation due to race, nationality or religion, have the right to marry and to found a family. They are entitled to equal rights as to marriage, during

marriage and at its dissolution.

2. Marriage shall be entered into only with the free and full consent of the intending spouses.

3. The family is the natural and fundamental group unit of society and is entitled to protection by society and the State.

Article 17

1. Everyone has the right to own property alone as well as in association with others.

2. No one shall be arbitrarily deprived of his property.

Article 18 Everyone has the right to freedom of thought, conscience and religion; this right includes freedom to change his religion or belief, and freedom, either alone or in community with others and in public or private, to manifest his religion or belief in teaching, practice, worship and observance.

Article 19 Everyone has the right to freedom of opinion and expression; this right includes freedom to hold opinions without interference and to seek, receive and impart information and ideas through any media and regardless of frontiers.

Article 20

1. Everyone has the right to freedom of peaceful assembly and association.

2. No one may be compelled to belong to an association.

Article 21

1. Everyone has the right to take part in the government of his country, directly or through freely chosen representatives.

2. Everyone has the right to equal access

to public service in his country.

3. The will of the people shall be the basis of the authority of government; this will shall be expressed in periodic and genuine elections which shall be by universal and equal suffrage and shall be held by secret vote or by equivalent free voting procedures.

Article 22 Everyone, as a member of society, has the right to social security and is entitled to realization, through national effort and international co-operation and in accordance with the organization and resources of each State, of the economic, social and cultural rights indispensable for his dignity and the free development of his personality.

Article 23

1. Everyone has the right to work, to free choice of employment, to just and favourable conditions of work and to protection against unemployment.

2. Everyone, without any discrimination, has the right to equal pay for equal work.

3. Everyone who works has the right to just and favourable remuneration ensuring for himself and his family an existence worthy of human dignity, and supplemented, if necessary, by other means of social protection.

4. Everyone has the right to form and to join trade unions for the protection of his interests.

Article 24 Everyone has the right to rest and leisure, including reasonable limitation of working hours and periodic holidays with pay.

Article 25

1. Everyone has the right to a standard of

living adequate for the health and well-being of himself and of his family, including food, clothing, housing and medical care and necessary social services, and the right to security in the event of unemployment, sickness, disability, widowhood, old age or other lack of livelihood in circumstances beyond his control.

2. Motherhood and childhood are entitled to special care and assistance. All children, whether born in or out of wedlock, shall enjoy the same social protection.

Article 26

1. Everyone has the right to education. Education shall be free, at least in the elementary and fundamental stages. Elementary education shall be compulsory. Technical and professional education shall be made generally available and higher education shall be equally accessible to all on the basis of merit.

2. Education shall be directed to the full development of the human personality and to the strengthening of respect for human rights and fundamental freedoms. It shall promote understanding, tolerance and friendship among all nations, racial or religious groups, and shall further the activities of the United Nations for the maintenance of peace.

3. Parents have a prior right to choose the kind of education that shall be given to their children.

Article 27

1. Everyone has the right to participate freely in the cultural life of the community, to enjoy the arts and to share in scientific advancement and its benefits.

2. Everyone has the right to the protection of the moral and material interests resulting from any scientific, literary or artistic production of which he is the author.

Article 28
Everyone is entitled to a social and international order in which the rights and freedoms set forth in this Declaration can be fully realized.

Article 29

1. Everyone has duties to the community in which alone the free and full development of his personality is possible.

2. In the exercise of his rights and freedoms, everyone shall be subject only to such limitations as are determined by law solely for the purpose of securing due recognition and respect for the rights and freedoms of others and of meeting the just requirements of morality, public order and the general welfare in a democratic society.

3. These rights and freedoms may in no case be exercised contrary to the purposes and principles of the United Nations.

Article 30
Nothing in this Declaration may be interpreted as implying for any State, group or person any right to engage in any activity or to perform any act aimed at the destruction of any of the rights and freedoms set forth herein.

Source: United Nations, 1948.

the global village. The global village cannot be achieved without overcoming the many historic prejudices and fears that divide the peoples of the world. Nor can there be peace and lasting stability in the world without achieving a reasonable degree of economic justice. Today only 20% of the world's people own 83% of the world's wealth. The same 20% consume 80% of the world's resources. A 1996 UN Development Program report claimed that fewer than 400 individuals, all billionaires, have as much collective wealth as 45% of humanity. The gap between the rich and the poor continues to widen every year (Rose, 1997). It is estimated that some *1.3 billion people* live in abject poverty in the world. Moreover, thousands die daily from easily preventable disease and malnutrition (Association of World Citizens, 1999).

The concept of **world citizenship** is also central to achieving the global village. Technologically, we have achieved a world community, as evidenced by modern communications, travel, and international trade. However, the world remains a place that is dramatically divided into political, social, religious, and ethnic tribes. While a number of proposals have been advanced to overcome such divisions, the only concept that comes close to conquering them is the idea of world citizenship, or people accepting their responsibility in this interdependent world by thinking and acting as citizens of that world (Association of World Citizens, 1999).

Responding to the Challenge of Globalization

Is the social work profession prepared to respond to the challenges and opportunities of globalization? James Midgley (1997), author of eight books on international and comparative social welfare, would argue no to this question. He identifies the following problems that cur-

rently inhibit the profession's readiness for these challenges and opportunities:

- Lack of international content in social work courses
- Failure to emphasize the importance of an international outlook
- Absence of international exchanges of scholars, practitioners, and other individuals
- Low level of participation of social workers in the activities and programs of international agencies
- Lack of international influence of professional social work organizations
- Lack of authentic commitment to internationalism as a value system
- Low level of understanding of the role of international events in social work practice
- Need to make international exchanges of ideas, staff, and other resources truly reciprocal

Midgley remains optimistic, however, about the social work profession's ability to increase its efforts in the areas of professional education and practice that will enhance its commitment to internationalism. Midgley (1997) concludes, ". . . a stronger commitment by the profession as a whole is urgently needed. Only in this way can social work successfully cope with the demands of the new international order of the future" (p. 66).

Children and Human Rights

According to Amnesty International (1999), children suffer many of the same human rights abuses as adults but also may be targeted simply because they are dependent and vulnerable. Examples of this mistreatment include:

- Torture by state officials

- Unlawful or arbitrary detainment, often in appalling conditions
- Death, maiming, or being forced to flee their homes due to armed conflicts
- Death or abuse in the name of social or ethnic cleansing
- Work at exploitative or hazardous jobs
- Exploitation as combatants by armed forces and armed opposition groups
- Child trafficking and forced prostitution
- Threats or abuse to punish family members who are not so accessible

Often the rights of children are disregarded by the very institutions responsible for their protection: "Children often suffer abuse, neglect, and violence in the administration of juvenile justice. They are frequently beaten and humiliated. Their legal rights are frequently ignored, and their parents are not informed of their whereabouts. They are held in degrading conditions and often are incarcerated with adults. Some are denied their right to fair trial and are given sentences that disregard the key objectives of juvenile justice—the child's rehabilitation and reintegration into society" (Amnesty International, 1999, p. 4).

Millions of children experience war every day of their lives. For some, this is the only existence they have ever known. Others are forced to flee as refugees or displaced persons, often separated from their families. Thousands of children throughout the world have been killed, disabled, or orphaned as a result of armed conflicts. Countless others have died or suffered from starvation, malnutrition, lack of clean water, poor sanitation, or inaccessible medical care. Still others are traumatized for life by being forced to witness brutal deaths. Worse yet, thousands of children around the world are forced to participate in the killing.

Children all over the world are forced to work in fields, sweatshop factories, mines, and brothels. They often work in dangerous and unhealthy environments and are accorded few or no rights. Many are sold or forced into labor. In some countries, children are forced by the government into dangerous or inappropriate work. Most of the 250 million child workers are engaged in domestic labor. Child domestics are often forced to work long hours for little or no salary, often endure permanent or long-term isolation from their families and friends, and rarely have the chance to attend school (Amnesty International, 1999).

The illegal transport and sale of human beings for their labor is a serious violation of human rights. Every year, thousands of women and girls around the world are lured, abducted, or sold into forced labor, prostitution, domestic service, and involuntary marriage. Trafficked children often end up detained by authorities because they have no money for bail or the return home (Amnesty International, 1999).

An estimated 100 million children live and work on the streets throughout the world, begging; peddling fruit, cigarettes, or trinkets; shining shoes; or engaging in petty theft or prostitution. Many have been abandoned, rejected, or orphaned, or have run away from home. Many are addicted to drugs. Street children are often victims of "social cleansing" campaigns, in which local business owners pay to have them chased away or even killed (Amnesty International, 1999).

The International Federation of Social Workers

Problems such as these transcend the efforts of any one nation. To the contrary, they demand the attention and active collaboration of *all* nations if they are to be resolved in a satisfactory manner. Such is the focus of the **International Federation of Social Workers** (IFSW), founded in 1956. The aims of IFSW (2000) are to:

- Promote social work as a profession through cooperation and action on an international basis, especially in regard to professional values, standards, ethics, human rights, recognition, training, and working conditions, and to promote the establishment of national associations of social workers where they do not yet exist
- Support national associations in promoting the participation of social workers in social planning, and the formulation of social policies, nationally and internationally, and the recognition of social work training as well as the values and standards of social work
- Encourage and facilitate contacts between social workers of all countries and to provide media for discussion and the exchange of ideas and experience, through meetings, study visits, research projects, exchange of publications, and other means of communication
- Present the profession on an international level by establishing relations with international organizations, governmental or voluntary, operating in, or interested in, the social development and welfare field, and to assist in the carrying out of social planning, social development, social action, and welfare programs (p. 2)

IFSW is divided into five geographical regions: Africa; Asia and the Pacific; Europe; Latin America and the Caribbean; and North America. Regions arrange their own meetings and conferences and elect representatives to regional organizations and the IFSW Human Rights Commission and Permanent Committee on Ethical Issues. Only one national professional organization in each country may become a member of the federation. Such an organization may be a national association or a coordinating body representing two or more national associations. Each member association or coordinating body must observe the IFSW Constitution.

IFSW partnerships include the following organizations (IFSW, 2000b):

- *Amnesty International,* an international organization working to support human rights globally, both in general and for individuals
- *European Union,* an organization focused on political, social and economic cooperation between its 15 European member states
- *International Association of Schools of Social Work* (IASSW), an international community of schools and educators in social work promoting quality education, training, and research for the theory and practice of social work, administration of social services, and formulation of social policies
- *International Council on Social Welfare* (ICSW), an international and nongovernmental organization operating throughout the world for the cause of social welfare, social justice, and social development
- *United Nations Children's Fund* (UNICEF), an organization dedicated to giving assistance, particularly to the developing countries of the world, in the development of permanent child health and welfare services
- *United Nations,* an international organization formed to promote peace, security, and cooperation throughout the world (p. 1)

One of the purposes of the IFSW is to provide social workers throughout the world with practical as well as philosophical guidelines on a number of key issues. The IFSW has developed a series of 10 policy papers that represent a consensus of professionals from different geographic and professional backgrounds. Topics covered in these policy papers include health, HIV-AIDS, human rights, migration, older persons, the protection of personal information, refugees, conditions in rural communities, women, and children.

Acknowledging that ethical awareness is a necessary part of the professional practice of any social worker, the IFSW adopted a two-part document, *The Ethics of Social Work— Principles and Standards,* at its July 1994 general meeting in Colombo, Sri Lanka. Part II of this document contains the International Declaration of Ethical Principles of Social Work, which has as its purposes to:

- Formulate a set of basic principles for social work, which can be adapted to different cultural and social settings
- Identify ethical problem areas in the practice of social work
- Provide guidance as to the choice of methods for dealing with ethical issues and problems (p. 2)

Today, IFSW represents over half a million social workers in 55 different countries. Its affiliate in the United States is the National Association of Social Workers (NASW).

CAREER OPPORTUNITIES IN INTERNATIONAL SOCIAL WORK

Career opportunities in international social work are extremely diverse, with schools of social work giving increased attention to this important area as we move toward a more global perspective. Opportunities are avail-

able that involve direct work in refugee programs, relief efforts, community development, intercountry and international adoption, education, and health care. Numerous opportunities are also available working with national government organizations, international government organizations, and voluntary organizations to provide technical assistance in implementing new programs and strengthening already-existing efforts and developing and enhancing social welfare policy (NASW, 1999).

Listed here are categories of organizations and agencies that employ social workers in an international social work capacity (Glusker, 1999):

- *International intergovernmental organizations* (IGOs). The best known IGO is the United Nations and its 12 specialized agencies (e.g., UN Development Program, World Health Organization, UN High Commissioner for Refugees, and International Labour Office). Often employees of these organizations come from the ranks of senior members of national governments. Positions in these organizations require extensive experience, linguistic abilities, and political contacts. Entry-level positions are available, but they are difficult to obtain and often require a 2-year application period.
- *International nongovernmental organizations* (NGOs). Like their IGO counterparts, NGOs are international in their membership and scope; however, they tend to be relatively free of governmental restrictions and bureaucracy. NGOs are more likely than IGOs to focus on specialized issues or take particular political or philosophical stances. Examples of

NGOs include Amnesty International, International Planned Parenthood Federation, International Red Cross, International Salvation Army, and the Women's International League for Peace and Freedom. NGOs are a good place for less experienced social workers to look for international positions. Prior experience living abroad and language skills are highly preferred by NGOs for persons desiring professional positions. Prospective applicants may want to consider serving in a volunteer capacity to build their credibility and increase their chances of securing a paid position with this type of organization.

- *United States government agencies.* These agencies perform services to Americans visiting abroad, as well as to the local populace. Obtaining positions in these agencies requires careful planning, as well as the right combination of skills and experience. Persons assuming these positions must also be comfortable with being an official representative of U.S. government foreign and domestic policies. Examples of agencies in this category of international social work employment include the U.S. Agency for International Development, the U.S. Information Agency, the Peace Corps, and the U.S. State Department.

- *U.S.-based nongovernmental organizations.* These organizations may offer some of the most fruitful opportunities for international careers for social workers either as a volunteer or in an entry-level position with little or no prior experience. Examples of agencies in this category of international social work employment include American Friends Service Committee, Direct Relief International, Save the Children, and World Vision.

- *Professional organizations and associations with major international commitments.* These organizations are generally located in the United States but have a substantial commitment to international problems and issues. Positions at all levels are available within these entities, and often individuals will begin their careers in such organizations and work themselves up over time to the highest levels within them. Examples of organizations and associations in this category of international social work employment include the Council for the International Exchange of Scholars, the National Association of Social Workers, and the Society for International Development.

- *University-based programs.* Universities in many countries have active research and service connections to their surrounding communities, especially if they offer social work degrees. Social workers who are considering pursuing doctoral study, or those who already hold doctoral degrees, may also wish to consider applying for either short- or long-term faculty or research positions in universities and research centers located in other countries.

- *Foundation programs.* Foundations engaged in international projects of a human service nature employ social workers as consultants, field representatives, and country directors for programs that the foundation supports. The best way to obtain an entry-level position in a major international grant-giving foundation is to work either as part of a project implementation team or as a member of the core professional staff. Examples of large foundations included in this category of international social work employment include the Carnegie Foundation, the Ford Foundation, and the Rockefeller Foundation.

- *Religious groups and organizations.* Religious groups and organizations sponsor thousands of human service programs around the world. The majority of these programs are located in the developing countries of Africa, Asia, and Latin America. Most are targeted toward the poor, women, or children. Rarely is religious preference of the professional considering working for a religious organization's human service program considered in the employment process.

- *Social work in international corporate settings.* Social work positions within these contexts are numerous, especially for the social worker with the right mix of qualifications and interests. As a general rule, these positions involve providing support services to local personnel or to a company's national personnel assigned abroad for various lengths of time. Most multinational corporations prefer to base their personnel in their home country for extended time periods before considering them for international assignments. Work experience, language skills, and good interpersonal skills are important qualifications for these jobs (pp. 5–7).

Finally, social workers are increasingly taking lead roles in speaking out about violations of human rights and acting to ensure that rights of individuals throughout the world are protected.

SUMMARY

The preceding discussion has highlighted the fact that global issues affect social work clients, individually and collectively, on a daily basis. It should also be clear that the basic mission and role of social workers are being challenged as never before. Two primary questions face the social work community as it enters the 21st century: What role will the social work profession play in this new world? What should social work do to promote equitable societies? The social work profession is in a pivotal position to articulate and develop alternatives to the new social order.

Social workers around the world are actively engaged in a wide variety of community development activities and national movements and organizations as people everywhere struggle to survive. However, it is time that social workers come together internationally to develop a global village or world community that supports the right of all individuals to grow and develop to their fullest potential.

If we as social workers are committed to promoting equitable societies, we must promote inclusion and the empowerment of people. We must strengthen links among education, technology, the environment, and progressive change in a global economy. We must strive to maintain individual cultures and cultural identity in the face of global pressures to become homogeneous. We must actively exchange information and experiences about innovative projects. We must be willing to share lessons learned so that successful ideas and programs can be applied across communities. Finally, we must build on the promise of information technology that made the "global village" a reality that touches everyone and make the world a truly better place to live for everyone.

KEY TERMS

comparative social welfare

comparative social work

global village

International Federation of Social Workers (IFSW)

international social welfare

international social work

world citizenship

DISCUSSION QUESTIONS

1. Contrast the difference between international social work and comparative social work, giving an example of each.

2. Choose one of the problems/social issues discussed in an earlier chapter in the text. How might this problem/issue be addressed differently if you were a social worker in another country?

3. Give some examples of ways an international social worker might intervene from a generalist practice standpoint: working with individuals; with families; with groups; with organizations; with communities; as an administrator; as a social policy expert; as a researcher.

4. What attributes of a social worker do you think are most important in providing international social services?

5. If you were a social worker working in a country that operated under a different values base than your own, what perspective would you take in working with clients from that country? Where, if anywhere, would you draw the line between respecting cultural difference and advocating for basic human rights?

INFOTRAC COLLEGE EDITION

To learn more about topics included in this chapter, enter the following search terms:

child labor

ethnic cleansing

global governance

global village

international social work

marketplace globalization

political refugees

social justice

world community

world poverty

ON THE INTERNET

http://www.undp.org/

http://www.ifsw.org/

http://www.geocities.com/heartland/4862/

http://www.1gc.org/1gc/gateway/about.html/

http://iisd1.iisd.ca/

http://www.index.org/

http://www.interaction.org/

http://www.nisw.org/

REFERENCES

Amnesty International. (1999). *Children's rights: The future starts here.* Available: http://www.amnesty.org/.

Association of World Citizens. (1999). *As citizens of the world.* Available: http://www.worldcitizen.org/.

Dionne, E. J.(1991). *Why Americans hate politics.* New York: Simon & Schuster.

Drew, E. (1996). *Showdown: The struggle between the Gingrich congress and the Clinton white house.* New York: Simon & Schuster.

Esping-Anderson, G. (1990). *The three worlds of welfare capitalism.* Princeton, NJ: Princeton University Press.

Glusker, A. (1999). *A student's guide to planning a career in international social work.* Philadelphia: University of Pennsylvania School of Social Work. Available: http://ssw.upenn.edu/.

Hacker, J. (1997). *The road to nowhere: The genesis of President Clinton's plan for health security.* Princeton, NJ: Princeton University Press.

Holstein, H., & Minkler, M. (1991). The short and painful death of the Medicare Catastrophic Coverage Act. In M. Minkler & C. Estes (Eds.), *Critical perspectives on aging: The political and moral economy of growing old.* Amityville, NY: Baywood.

International Federation of Social Workers. (2000a). *IFSW general information.* Available: http://www.ifsw.org/.

International Federation of Social Workers. (2000b). *IFSW partnerships.* Available: http://www.ifsw.org/.

International Federation of Social Workers. (2000c). *Policy statements and other documents.* Available: http://www.ifsw.org/.

International Federation of Social Workers. (2000d). *The ethics of social work—principles and standards.* Available: http://www.ifsw.org/.

Johnson, H., & Broder, D. (1997). *The system: The American way of politics at the breaking point.* Boston: Little, Brown.

Mead, L. (1997). *The new paternalism.* Washington, DC: Brookings Institute.

Michel, S. (1999). *Children's interests/Mother's rights: The shaping of America's child care policy.* New Haven, CT: Yale University Press.

Midgley, J. (1997). Social work in international context: Challenges and opportunities for the 21st century. In M. Reisch & E. Gambrill (Eds.), *Social work in the 21st century* (pp. 59–67). Thousand Oaks, CA: Pine Forge.

National Association of Social Workers. (1999). *Careers in social work.* Washington, DC: NASW Press.

Prigoff, A. (2000). *Economic for social workers: Social outcomes of economic globalization with strategies for community action.* Belmont, CA: Brooks/Cole.

Rose, N. (1997). The future economic landscape: Implications for social work practice and education. In M. Reisch & E. Gambrill (Eds.), *Social work in the 21st century* (pp. 28–38). Thousand Oaks, CA: Pine Forge.

Sari, R. (1997). International social work at the millenium. In M. Reisch & E. Gambrill (Eds.), *Social work in the 21st century* (pp. 387–395). Thousand Oaks, CA: Pine Forge.

Skocpol, T. (1996). *Boomerang: Clinton's health security effort and the turn against government in U.S. politics.* New York: Norton.

Stoesz, D., Guzzetta, C., & Lusk, M. *International development.* Boston: Allyn & Bacon.

Weaver, K. (1998). Ending welfare as we know it. In M. Weir (Ed.), *The social divide.* Washington, DC: Brookings Institute.

SUGGESTED FURTHER READINGS

Healy, L. (1995). International social work: Organizations and activities. In R. Edwards (Ed.), *Encyclopedia of social work* (pp. 1499–1510). Washington, DC: NASW Press.

Midgley, J. (1990). International social work: Learning from the third world. *Social Work, 35,* 295–301.

Midgley, J. (1993). The challenge of international social work. In M. C. Hokenstad, S. K. Khinduka, & J. Midgley (Eds.), *Profiles in international social work* (pp. 13–28). Washington, DC: NASW Press.

Midgeley, J. (1994). Transitional strategies for social work: Towards effective reciprocal exchanges. In R. G. Meinert, J. T. Pardeck, & W. P. Sullivan (Eds.), *Issues in social work: A critical analysis* (pp. 165–180). Westport, CT: Auburn House.

Midgley, J. (1995). *Social development: The development perspective in social work.* Thousand Oaks, CA: Sage.

Reich, R. B. (1991). *The work of nations.* New York: Knopf.

Renner, M. (1997). Transforming society. In L. R. Brown, C. Flavin, & H. French (Eds.), *State of the world 1997: Worldwatch Institute report on progress toward a sustainable society.* New York: Norton.

United Nations. (1993). *Report on the world social situation 1993.* New York: Author.

Van Soest, D. (1997). *The global crisis of violence: Common problems, universal causes, shared solutions.* Washington, DC: NASW Press.

World Resources Institute. (1994). *World resources: A guide in the global environment.* New York: Oxford University Press.

WHAT DOES THE FUTURE HOLD?

In this last section, we review the history of changes that characterize the social work profession and the field of social welfare, emphasizing the impact of technological and economic changes on the individual, the family, and the community. We also attempt to forecast the probable nature of the social work profession and of social welfare as they are influenced by future changes at the broader societal level. As you read this final chapter, we hope that you will reflect on what you have learned about our social welfare system, the profession of social work, the diversity of our society, and the many challenging issues we face at all levels of our environment.

In this book, we show the need for social services for individuals from birth through death in a variety of settings. We suggest that some individuals, by the nature of their age, gender, ethnicity, social class, and sexual orientation, are more likely to need social services than others. We also illustrate the many settings in which social workers are employed—government poverty programs, mental health clinics, hospitals, prisons, schools, faith-based organizations, long-term care facilities for the elderly—and suggest that opportunities for social work practitioners in different settings and with diverse populations are almost limitless. As you reflect on the chapters you have read and the issues we have raised, we hope that you will develop your own sense of vision about the future and the social work profession, and your role in making our world a better and more humane place.

THE FUTURE OF SOCIAL WORK AND SOCIAL WELFARE

George Swain recently retired after 45 years as a social worker. His first job was as a caseworker in a settlement house, where he earned a yearly salary of $2,000. An active member of the state and local chapters of the National Association of Social Workers, George has been involved in many changes in the social work profession over the years. "In those early years, we did everything for our clients, since there were very few social service agencies," George stated in a recent interview. "In my first job, I led groups of teenagers, ran programs for senior citizens, set up a child care center, started a rat control program in the neighborhood, transported people's belongings when they moved, and took kids into my house when they had nowhere else to go. When I retired as the director of a family services agency, there were 47 other social service agencies in the community, and most of my time and my staff's time were spent coordinating and linking resources for our clients with those other agencies."

"Today," George continued, "services are much more specialized, and we are more aware of human problems. I'm sure, for example, when I look back, that lots of kids I worked with when I was younger were sexually abused, but social workers in those days were relatively unaware of how extensive a problem that was."

George is especially excited because his granddaughter Jessica is a senior in the bachelor of social work program at the state university and will graduate as a social worker this year. Jessica is completing her field internship at a rape crisis center. When she graduates, she hopes to work for the state human services agency, providing services to help families on public assistance become self-sufficient. Both grandfather and grand-daughter agree that social work has grown as a profession and that many challenging opportunities lie ahead for Jessica.

As we begin the 21st century, the United States faces a serious domestic crisis. As more attention is given nationally to our social welfare system—and the roles various segments of society should play in meeting ever-increasing unmet human needs—increased recognition is being given to the importance of the social work profession. The future of social work is a challenging one with numerous opportunities for the profession.

Social work has a historical commitment to help people cope with change, and if the last 10 to 15 years are any indicator, change will become a way of life in this new century. The ambiguity and strain that have existed in the United States since its founding regarding how the unmet needs of our society should be addressed have intensified during recent years. Many Americans are content with the way things are and do not relish the thought of change. As a nation, we tend to be generous and compassionate when it comes to helping one or two individuals in need, but limiting and suspicious when it comes to helping large groups of individuals in a systematic way. How our country balances individual freedom versus collective responsibility is a theme that has been around since early colonial times and has continued into the new century.

Any attempt to forecast future trends must be tentative, at best. History has shown us that change does not always progress at an even rate, nor is its direction always predictable. Nevertheless, it is possible to identify certain trends that suggest what factors will have an impact on the profession of social work and the social welfare system at least in the near future. In this chapter, we briefly identify the major issues relating to the future of social welfare in the United States and probable directions that the profession of social work will take in addressing them.

The Relationship between Past and Present

For us to comprehend the difficulty of predicting the effects of social change on social work and social welfare, it is helpful to review the earlier chapters of this book. The history of the social work profession is related integrally to the unpredictable nature of the world in which we live. The social work profession is called to respond as social change alters the economic base of society, as well as other basic social institutions such as the family, education, religion, and political and social organizations. The rapid growth of the social work profession in the latter part of the 19th century was related directly to the emergence of large urban communities and the accompanying problems associated with them. Problems such as increased numbers of displaced persons, high rates of unemployment, large-scale migration from rural areas into the cities, slums, the rise in poverty, and increasing health-related problems were commonplace during those times. To reduce or eliminate the sources of these problems and to provide support for these displaced people and their families, "trained" helpers had to become an integral part of the solution. The social work profession emerged in response to the need for a cadre of professionals armed with an understanding of human behavior, awareness of how social organizations function, and sensitivity to the effects of the environment as a determinant to individual growth and development.

As the American industrial revolution erupted, the stability inherent in a primarily agrarian society began to disintegrate rapidly. Change intensified as new ways of manufacturing things advanced at increasingly rapid rates. Over the years new ways of manufacturing gave way to new ways of thinking, leading us into what has been termed the information age. Moreover, the structure and function of the family, once stable and secure, have been affected by the stresses and tensions produced by the economic marketplace, which calls for greater mobility, division of labor outside of the home, and a consequent restructuring of family priorities. As a result, families have become less stable, the divorce rate has increased dramatically, multiple marriages are more common, and child abuse, spouse abuse, and various forms of neglect at all levels of society have emerged as more visible problems.

As the nature of work has become more unpredictable, the long-sought goal of financial security has become more difficult to achieve for many people. The poor have continued to be victimized by the lack of opportunity and are often blamed for their condition. Increasingly, individuals' health and mental health needs have not been met. The spread of the HIV infection and the large number of AIDS-related deaths have had far-reaching effects on all segments of society. As the U.S. population has grown older, greater numbers of individuals have become detached from means of production, and they often lack sufficient supports to provide for their maintenance and health-related needs. In addition, violence, crime, delinquency, substance abuse, homelessness, and a variety of related problems have become sources of constant societal concern.

The organization of social welfare services is far different today from that of early colonial times. Gone are the almshouses, the poor houses, and "indoor" relief. Since passage of the Social Security Act of 1935, the social welfare system in the United States has expanded to meet the proliferation and magnitude of new needs, and it now requires substantial societal resources to maintain.

Social workers have stepped up to this challenge, actively assisting a wide variety of individuals whose personal resources cannot provide an adequate level of social functioning and life satisfaction. Today, social workers are skilled in working with the homeless or the displaced, the poor, substance abusers, single parents, and criminal offenders. They are also actively involved with helping persons experiencing marital conflict, family violence, mental illness, problems associated with later life, and a myriad of other related personal and social problems. In addition, the roles of social workers as promoters of social and economic justice and as advocates for disenfranchised populations—the poor, women, people of color, gays and lesbians, people with disabilities—have become increasingly important, as society tends more and more to overlook or reject these groups. As new problems have emerged, the capacity of the social work profession to incorporate the knowledge and skills essential to providing assistance always has been forthcoming.

Social Welfare and the Future

A number of factors have conspired to make it difficult for increasing numbers of individuals to care for themselves without assistance. Chief among them is the globalization of the world's economic resources and a changing political landscape in this country. The impact of these factors is heightened by changing family roles and structure, an aging population, gaps in health insurance, changing needs of the workplace, and the increasing need for long-term care. Unfortunately, our present social welfare system is not well equipped to handle these changes but, rather, fragmented and ill prepared to meet the demand for services. One could say that in its current state, the American social welfare system is fast approaching a crisis state and needs serious refinement and rethinking.

Passage of the Work Opportunity and Personal Responsibility Budget Reconciliation Act of 1996 has reinforced the belief of many Americans that poverty and associated problems are related more to individual failure than to structural problems with the economy. It seems that now, more than ever, many people in the United States have a great deal of ambivalence toward poor people, who are more often than not blamed for their predicament. With the decentralization of funding and control of social welfare problems to individual states, social welfare problems do not always receive the attention they deserve. The unprecedented period of growth and economic prosperity experienced by the United States during the waning years of the 21st century has only served to solidify the belief among many members of society that anyone can succeed, regardless of their life history or current situation. Yet, just below the veneer of poverty lies a growing underclass of individuals, particularly persons of color, who, no matter how hard they try, are unable to pull themselves out of a life of poverty. In a country of apparent prosperity, nearly one in four children lives at or below the poverty line. The effects of poverty will reach far into this new century and in many dramatic ways unless the cycle of poverty is broken.

Additional issues relate to immigration and violence. The United States historically has been a bastion of hope to oppressed individuals from other countries seeking a better way of life, yet the needs of current citizens who are oppressed and living marginal lives must also be considered. Violence has become a major issue in U.S. society and one that affects individuals of all ages. The recent incidents of shootings in public schools across the country have heightened awareness about violent youth and the needs of children and adolescents. Children are increasingly victims of family, community, and societal violence; even if they are not victims directly, growing up in a country where violence is a norm is likely to affect their views of the future and of the environment in which they live.

The United States' increased political polarization has also significantly affected social welfare policies and programs that are attempting to address these problems. With more attention being paid to lobbyists for various issues rather than to citizens themselves, it is increasingly difficult for positions that truly advocate for the common good to be heard. The current debate about critical issues often turns into one of "buck passing," with politicians who are concerned about their futures at the national level trying to pass expensive and controversial programs on to the states to administer, and states trying to pass them on to the local level. The increased polarization of the two political parties at the national level has resulted in venomous retaliations against each other rather than careful attention to social welfare issues and needed social change.

Our unwillingness to intervene results in a society of persons increasingly unable to provide for themselves or others, which has serious implications for all of us. We cannot expect people to take responsibility for themselves if they have no opportunities to escape from inadequate living situations that promote failure. The poorly prepared student of today is the unemployed or underemployed worker of tomorrow. The neglected preschoolers of today will be called on to be leaders of tomorrow. If unmet needs are addressed effectively, we all benefit. If unmet needs are not addressed, we all pay.

Our social welfare system must be one that focuses on our individual strengths and diversity. It must be one that encourages self-sufficiency yet provides humane services for those who are unable to be self-sufficient or who need help from the system to function independently. It must be a system that invests in our nation's children, focusing on the preservation of the family but protecting and nurturing children when this is not possible. It must be a system that

- Works with other systems to provide increased opportunities for adolescents and young adults, lowering school dropout rates, increasing literacy, providing employment training, reducing teen pregnancy, and providing comprehensive health and mental health services

- Helps adults achieve and maintain self-sufficiency, reducing poverty, providing adequate housing and employment, and assuring coverage for health and mental health care
- Pays attention to the needs of the elderly, providing housing and health and long-term care

For most individuals in U.S. society, personal needs can no longer be met by the family alone. We must stop blaming individuals for their perceived shortcomings and look instead at what can be done to develop stronger individuals who can become self-sufficient and to help those who can no longer "go it alone." Government participation is essential to assist those in need. Private and citizen participation is also essential. The issue should not be whether the public or the private sector should meet human needs but how they can work together to meet those needs. Both sectors are interconnected and interdependent parts of the social welfare system. The question of the most effective ways to provide social welfare to meet individual unmet needs is at the heart of a national debate. Most Americans agree that our society is a caring one and that the nation's future rests on how well it responds to the needs of its members today. Each of us, private citizens with public responsibility, needs to examine what roles we can play in strengthening our social welfare system and providing a supportive society for our generation and those that come behind us.

CURRENT ISSUES IN SOCIAL WORK PRACTICE

The positions members of society take toward social problems and the resolution of those problems invariably relate to the resources available. Unfortunately, members of society do not always take an unequivocally progressive stance. For example, fiscal concerns are currently paramount in society. Federal indebtedness and the perceived perspective that there isn't enough money to address social welfare issues have resulted in massive reductions in funds available for solving social problems. As a result, monies for social welfare services have been reduced significantly, and populations at risk have not received the assistance they need to become or remain productive citizens.

The reduction of public monies for social welfare services has resulted in a cry for the private sector to "take up the slack" and provide both funds and extend assistance through volunteerism. Although noble, private efforts have fallen far short of their intended goal because of the magnitude of the need. As indicated earlier, a society inevitably must take a position relative to its commitment to those in need. The position taken and the ways it is expressed are influenced by values, morality, and the availability of resources. In a materialistically oriented society like that of the United States, it is paradoxical that the definition of need is invariably related to the "amount" of resources that society is willing to allocate. Thus, in times of monetary scarcity or when demands are made on individuals to share (through the taxing process) more of their earned incomes, the tendency to redefine need levels is inevitable. This redefinition, of course, does not always address the real need. Today, we stand at a crossroads. Do we continue to reduce allocations for resolving the problems of society's members at risk, or do we reorganize our priorities to assure that the needs of all members of society are met, at least on a minimal basis?

Related challenges facing future social work professionals include determining which of the myriad of societal and individual problems properly fall within the domain of the social welfare system. A traditional view of the social welfare institution is that its services should be residual—that is, incorporating those areas that cannot be served by other societal institutions. However, the social welfare system cannot be a panacea that addresses all needs not being met by other systems. The social welfare system simply cannot be all things to all people. There is a need to define and to limit the boundaries that encompass the social welfare system so that its services can be effective and sustained by available resources. Regardless of this argument, social workers are constantly faced with value conflicts over not addressing human needs when no one else is meeting them.

How do you say no, for example, to a woman with four young children with no housing, no food, and a temporary part-time job, who makes $5 more each month than the income eligibility guidelines allow for receiving cash assistance under the Temporary Assistance to Needy Families (TANF) program? If the federal government or states refuse to provide for certain groups (for example, teen parents, mothers whose public assistance time limits have run out but who are still not self-sufficient), who should provide for them and in what ways? Should children be removed from parents who cannot afford to care for them and placed in other settings, in spite of the emotional costs of separating children from their parents? And who should pay for that care if this is the case? How do you determine whether limited funding should be allocated to the elderly, children, or individuals with disabilities? How do you decide who should have first priority for heart and other organ transplants, whether limited dollars should be spent on neonatal care for premature infants whose prognosis is poor, or at what point resources should no longer be provided to families with little potential to be rehabilitated?

If limited resources do not allow for a full range of preventive and remedial/rehabilitative services, which do you choose? Do you try to prevent problems such as child maltreatment, knowing that in the short run this may limit your resources for those already abused, but in the long run may prevent more abuse? We seem to be stuck with a classic "pay me now or pay someone else later" dilemma. That is, if we pay now to implement a wide range of preventive social welfare programs, the expectation is that we will not have to pay someone else later to address the remedial or rehabilitative needs of those who did not benefit from such preventive programs. But one might ask is this issue simply a political issue, or does it reflect mainstream thinking about the value of prevention in the first place? For example, there is an increasing trend in America to lease things rather than buy them outright. The terms of the leases are fixed, and when they expire, most people return the product to the leasing agent and renew the cycle once again. By doing so, the lessee is really absolved of any preventive maintenance on the product being leased. Rapidly changing technology has also affected the way that members of society think about product longevity. For example, the technological gadget you buy today has practically no shelf life at all. In actuality, that product became obsolete the day after it was invented! Thus, a person's political ideology, sense of social consciousness, and perspective on technology and change all have an impact on whether he or she supports social welfare programs with a preventive focus. The main

difference for social workers is that we are talking about people or human capital and not some resource that can be readily renewed when it becomes used.

Also, as technology continues to generate new knowledge, the social work profession increasingly will have to grapple with sometimes thorny ethical issues. Issues such as genetic engineering, surrogate parenting, assisted death, environment and pollution, and technological measures to prolong life are ethical issues of growing concern for social workers in the 21st century.

Leaders of the social work profession point to a number of critical issues that the profession faces in the 21st century. First, the profession needs to value the diversity within the profession while not forgetting its roots. Harry Specht and Michael Courtney, two social work educators, wrote a thought-provoking book shortly before Specht's death. In *Unfaithful Angels: How Social Work Has Abandoned Its Mission* (1994), the authors chastise the profession for its attention to clinical issues that focus on the microlevel of the environment. Specht and Courtney argue that social work as a profession needs to work at all levels of the environment as well as be committed to social and economic justice and the elimination of oppression and discrimination. They believe that social work has abandoned this commitment by ignoring the poor, abused and neglected children, the homeless, and other vulnerable populations. Specht and Courtney also believe the profession has not given enough attention to empowering individuals, families, groups, and communities to improve their own lives. They advocate for the future of the profession to give more attention to community-based programs that educate individuals about how to solve problems, so that they are empowered to address their own needs,

Future social workers face many challenges—and many opportunities for professional and personal growth.
© Morton Beebe, S.F./Corbis

be paid to exolevel (community) and macro-level (societal) interventions.

Many leaders of the social work profession, however, caution that social workers need to play a more significant role in the provision of health and mental health services and in shaping the changes needed to make managed care more responsive to client needs. They point out that just as the profession values diversity in its clients, it must value diversity within its own group. They further argue that while debating the future of the profession is healthy, such argument draws attention away from the need to view social needs from a continuum, with social workers playing critical policy, research, and service roles at all levels.

Social work historian David Austin (1997) provides excellent perspective on the profession of social work in the 21st century:

> In many ways, the early 21st century may be a very uncomfortable time for many citizens of the United States, even while the economy is strong. The organized profession of social work will face expanding opportunities, while individual social workers will share the discomforts of the larger society. The history of social work can serve as a source of inspiration, but to master the events of the future it is essential that strategic planning for the profession be "grounded" in an understanding of the forces that are actually shaping this society and the profession of social work within it. (p. 406)

The social work profession and the issues it faces are challenging at all levels of society—whether the work is with individuals, families, groups, organizations, or the community or at the state, national, or international level. Social work practitioners need to increase their involvement at the legislative and policy levels and become more involved in the political arena, where key social welfare decisions are made. As society becomes increasingly com-

and the community's problem-solving capacity can also be increased.

Others, while perhaps not as dire in their statements as Specht and Courtney, also believe that social work will lose ground as a profession if it abandons its previous perspective and its uniqueness (Hopps & Collins, 1995). They raise similar questions and suggest that because social workers will function in an even more diverse and complex environment in the coming years, more attention must plex, the number of social workers will continue to grow and their roles will broaden at all levels of practice.

TRENDS IN SOCIAL WORK CAREERS

As we indicated in earlier chapters, social workers today function in a variety of job settings and fields of practice and hold degrees at the undergraduate (BSW), master's (MSW), and doctoral (Ph.D. or DSW) levels. In 1998, approximately 42,000 students were enrolled in BSW programs throughout the United States. That same year, almost 32,000 students were enrolled in MSW programs (Council on Social Work Education, 1999). Since the late 1980s, enrollment in schools of social work at both the undergraduate and graduate levels has increased substantially as more young people commit themselves to helping others.

Social workers held approximately 585,000 jobs in 1996 ("Social Workers," 1999). A survey by the National Association of Social Workers of its members in 1995 found that social workers were employed in a variety of roles (see Table 18.1), with 70% in direct service roles working with individuals, families, and groups (Gibelman & Schervish, 1997). The largest number of social workers were employed in social services settings, inpatient and outpatient health facilities, and solo private practice (see Table 18.2). Within those settings, practitioners were most likely to be providing mental health–related services, followed by services to children and families, and medical and mental health services (see Table 18.3).

BSW graduates, who make up approximately 10% of NASW's membership, were most likely to be employed in medical and mental health facilities and working with the elderly and children and families. Conductors of the

TABLE 18.1   TYPES OF SERVICES PROVIDED BY NASW MEMBERS (1995)

Practice Area	Number	Percentage
Administration-management	14,140	15.5
Clinical-direct service	63,858	70.0
Community organizing—advocacy	182	0.2
Policy	730	0.8
Research	456	0.5
Supervision	5,017	5.5
Teaching	3,740	4.1
Training	91	0.1
Other	3,010	3.3
Total	91,226	100.0

Source: M. Gibelman and P. Schervish, *Who We Are: A Second Look* (Washington, DC: NASW Press, 1997), p. 113. Copyright 1997, National Association of Social Workers, Inc.

TABLE 18.2   PRACTICE SETTINGS REPORTED BY NASW MEMBERS (1995)

Setting	Number	Percentage
Business and industry	177	0.2
Colleges and universities	3,630	4.1
Courts and justice system	1,151	1.3
Health (inpatient)	15,938	18.0
Health (outpatient)	14,344	16.2
Managed care	266	0.3
Mental health (inpatient)	620	0.7
Mental health (outpatient)	2,125	2.4
Private practice (group)	4,604	5.2
Private practice (solo)	12,839	14.5
Residential facility	5,932	6.7
School (preschool–grade 12)	6,021	6.8
Social services agency	18,153	20.5
Other	2,745	3.1
Total	88,544	100.0

Source: M. Gibelman and P. Schervish, *Who We Are: A Second Look* (Washington, DC: NASW Press, 1997), p. 84. Copyright 1997, National Association of Social Workers, Inc.

TABLE 18.3	PRACTICE AREAS REPORTED BY NASW MEMBERS (1995)	
Setting	Number	Percentage
Children and families	2,227	24.9
Criminal justice	1,073	1.2
Elderly people	4,114	4.6
Medical health	11,626	13.0
Mental health	34,700	38.8
Occupational social work	715	0.8
Schools	4,650	5.2
Other	10,195	11.4
Total	89,432	99.9

Note: "Other" category includes combined, community organization—planning, group services, other disabilities, public assistance, and substance abuse.

Source: M. Gibelman and P. Schervish, *Who We Are: A Second Look* (Washington, DC: NASW Press, 1997), p. 101. Copyright 1997, National Association of Social Workers, Inc.

survey indicate that a much stronger presence by social workers is needed in public assistance and other public social services, corrections, and working with persons with developmental disabilities (Gibelman & Schervish, 1997).

A valid question asked by social work students is whether the supply of social workers will exceed the demand, particularly during fiscal cutbacks. Even with funding cutbacks, funding for social welfare programs has increased. The U.S. Department of Labor identifies social work as one of the professions that will continue to expand during the coming decade; it projects that by the year 2005, over 575,000 social workers will be employed in the United States. Projections indicate that by that time, 31.3% of all service-related jobs will be in social services, and 29.2% will be physical and mental health services, including inpatient and outpatient services, long-term care facilities, and home health care ("Social Workers," 1999).

As the population continues to age, fewer younger social workers will be available to replace retirees. Additionally, more social work jobs will become available, particularly in the areas of child protective services, criminal justice, substance abuse, health care, mental health, and gerontology. Although the number of social workers employed in the public sector, particularly government agencies, has declined somewhat in recent years, many government programs are contracting out their services to private nonprofit and private for-profit organizations that are employing social workers to provide services and oversee programs. In 1998, approximately 40% of all social workers were employed by state, county, or municipal government agencies. Most in the private sector were in nonprofit services agencies, community and religious organizations, nursing homes or home health programs, and hospitals (U.S. Department of Labor, 2000). As states have passed licensing requirements for social workers and insurance companies include social workers under third-party reimbursement agreements, an increasing number of social workers are establishing private practices and seeing clients for psychotherapy, marriage and family counseling, and other types of clinical services. This trend is likely to continue.

At the same time as social work services in the private sector are increasing, new attention is being given to the need to encourage social workers to seek jobs in public social service settings, particularly state social service agencies. NASW and other organizations such as the American Public Human Services Association are working together to increase awareness about the challenges of public social services and the commitment that social work as a profession has to the indigent, who are most likely to come to the attention of a public agency. Recent changes brought about by the Welfare

Reform Act of 1996 provide a number of challenging opportunities for social workers to develop or strengthen programs that assist families in becoming self-sufficient. The emphasis on family preservation and national attention given to child maltreatment have also resulted in the increased professionalism of child and family services workers employed within public human services agencies. The Education for All Handicapped Children Act also provides for the hiring of social workers in school settings to work with children with disabilities. Many more schools are hiring social workers to work in a variety of school programs, and NASW recently established a special membership division for school social workers.

The social work profession's commitment to social and economic justice also provides opportunities for social workers to play major roles in helping entities at all levels of society become more culturally competent and in empowering diverse groups to advocate for their share of resources to get their needs met. This challenge means that social workers, both individually and collectively, must continue to educate themselves about different cultural groups and to advocate for the hiring of more social workers that reflect the diversity of the populations that the profession serves. In 1992, 88% of all social workers were white, 6% were African American, 3% were Latino, 2% were Asian, 0.5% were Native American, and 1% represented other ethnic groups. Seventy-seven percent were women, indicating a need for the profession to embrace a feminist perspective that values equality while at the same time working to ensure that social work is not seen as a "women's" profession. The profession is also younger and less experienced as many long-term social workers enter retirement (Hopps & Collins, 1995). Currently, schools of social work and social work employers are attempting to recruit more diverse student bodies and workforces.

Whatever the field of practice or the setting, social workers today and in the future face many challenges—and many opportunities for professional and personal growth. We hope that you will consider joining us as members of the social work profession.

SUMMARY

In this book, we address the current state of the art in social work and social welfare. Throughout each chapter, the effects of social problems on various segments of the population are identified and the societal responses through the social welfare system described. We have also explored the many roles social workers play in addressing social welfare problems. The significant and dramatic modifications in both the social welfare system and the social work profession since the early days of organized helping efforts are apparent. Armed with knowledge and understanding of human behavior and complex organizations, and bringing a systems/ecological perspective to bear, the contemporary professional social worker is uniquely capable of skillful intervention in the resolution of problems. The social worker of the future will have many challenging opportunities to make major contributions to society.

DISCUSSION QUESTIONS

1. What do you see as the three major social welfare issues the United States will face in the first decade of the 21st century? What major issues do you feel will have the most impact on the social work profession? What will your role be in addressing these issues?

2. In which settings are social workers employed most often? In which fields of practice are social workers employed most often? Where are most BSW social workers employed?

3. Discuss some of the future employment opportunities for social work professionals. Which career areas interest you most, and why?

4. What can the profession of social work do to promote social and economic justice? What can you do, both individually and as a social work professional?

INFOTRAC COLLEGE EDITION

To learn more about topics included in this chapter, enter the following search terms:

devolution

political polarization

social justice

social work ethic

social work profession

technology and society

vulnerable populations

work standards

ON THE INTERNET

http://www4.nas.edu/pd/cosepup.nsf/

http://www.brook.edu/

http://www.whitehouse.gov/WH/EOP/OSTP/html/OSTP_Home.html/

http://onlineethics.org/

http://www.DigitalDivideNetwork.org/

REFERENCES

Austin, D. (1997). The profession of social work in the second century. In M. Reisch & E. Gambrill (Eds.), *Social work in the 21st century* (pp. 396–407). Thousand Oaks, CA: Pine Forge.

Council on Social Work Education. (1999). *Statistics on social work education in the United States.* Washington, DC: Author.

Gibelman, M., & Schervish, P. H. (1997). *Who we are: A second look.* Washington, DC: NASW Press.

Hopps, J. G., & Collins, P. (1995). Social work profession overview. In R. Edwards (Ed.), *Encyclopedia of social work* (Vol. 3, pp. 2266–2282). Washington, DC: NASW Press.

National Association of Social Workers. (1990). *Strategic plan.* Washington, DC: NASW Press.

National Association of Social Workers. (2000). *NASW professional social work credentials.* Washington, DC: NASW Press.

Social workers. (1999). *Occupational outlook handbook, 1998–1999.* Washington, DC: U.S. Department of Labor, Bureau of Labor Statistics.

Specht, H., & Courtney, M. (1994). *Unfaithful angels: How social work has abandoned its mission.* New York: Free Press.

U.S. Department of Labor. (2000). *Occupational outlook handbook.* Available: http://stats.bls.gov/.

SUGGESTED FURTHER READINGS

Gambrill, E., & Pruger, R. (Eds.). (1992). *Controversial issues in social work.* Boston: Allyn & Bacon.

Ginsberg, L. (1992). *Social work almanac.* Washington, DC: NASW Press.

Hartman, A. (1994). *Reflection and controversy: Essays on social work.* Washington, DC: NASW Press.

Macarov, D. (1991). *Certain change. Social work practice in the future.* Washington, DC: NASW Press.

Martin, E., & Martin, J. (1995). *Social work and the black experience.* Washington, DC: NASW Press.

Reid, N. P., & Popple, P. R. (1992). *The moral purposes of social work: The character and intentions of a profession.* Chicago: Nelson-Hall.

Glossary

Acquired immunodeficiency syndrome (AIDS) A fatal disease that attacks the body's natural immune system

Activity theory Theory relating to aging based on the premise that social activity is the essence of life for all ages and that all people must maintain adequate levels of activity if they are to age successfully

Addiction A physical and/or psychological dependence on mood-altering substances or activities, including but not limited to alcohol, drugs, pills, food, sex, or gambling

Adjudication The legal process that judges conduct in juvenile court with assistance from probation officers

Adoption A process by which a child whose birth parents choose not to or cannot care for him or her is provided with a permanent home and parents who are able to provide for the child; legal adoptions can take place only when the court terminates the parental rights of the birth parents, but many adoptions, particularly in minority communities, are informal and do not involve the court

Affirmative action programs A legally mandated program established within education, business, and industry to improve opportunities for people of color and women

Ageism Discrimination against the elderly because of their age

Aging The process of growing old

Aid to Families with Dependent Children (AFDC) A public assistance program that provides cash assistance to families with children in need because of the loss of financial support as a result of death, disability, or the continued absence of a parent from the home (changed to Temporary Assistance to Needy Families [TANF] in 1996)

Alcohol Oldest and most commonly abused substance in the world, usually functioning as a depressant but for some persons can also serve as a stimulant or hallucinogen

Alcoholics Anonymous (AA) Self-help group for alcoholics based on abstinence and a 12-step philosophy of living; similar programs exist for family members of alcoholics and addicts and for persons with other types of addictions

Alcoholism Use of alcohol that interferes with personal life, including family, friends, school, job, health, spiritual life, or the law

Americans with Disabilities Act (ADA) Federal legislation that provides protections for persons with disabilities, including employment and accessibility of accommodations

Amnesty International International organization that promotes social justice and human rights throughout the world

Apathy futility syndrome Term used to describe a set of behaviors exhibited by a neglecting parent who is severely depressed and apathetic toward her or his immediate environment, including her or his children

Appellate courts Courts with the authority to review the decision of trial and lower and criminal courts

Assessment The process of making tentative judgments about how the information derived from a client system affects the system

Assimilation The expectation that members of nondominant groups in society will adopt the values and behaviors of the dominant group

Association   A relationship between two or more factors that occur together but are not necessarily causative (such as alcoholism and child abuse)

Battered child syndrome   A medical term used to describe a child with physical injuries in various stages of healing, indicating the child has been physically abused on a number of occasions

Behavior modification   An action intervention, based on the assumption that all behaviors are learned and can be changed, that focuses on reinforcing present positive behaviors to eliminate inappropriate behaviors

Best interests of the child   A standard of decision making used by courts and child welfare agencies that emphasizes what is best for a specific child as opposed to what is best for other family members or persons

Bioethics   Moral and ethical decisions associated with advanced technology in the health care field

Blended family   A family formed by marriage or long-term relationship between partners in which at least one partner brings children from a previous relationship into the new family system

Boundary   The limit or extent of a system; the point where one system ends and another begins

Brain-based economy   An economy that is primarily driven by the intellectual capabilities of its workers

Broker   A social worker who assists clients in locating appropriate resources

Casework   Services provided to individuals, families, groups, organizations, and the community to strengthen social functioning, based on assessing the client situation, identifying client needs, determining appropriate interventions to address identified needs, and monitoring and evaluating the process to ensure that outcomes address needs identified

Catastrophic illness   A chronic and severely debilitating illness that results in high medical costs and long-term dependence on the health care system

Categorical assistance   Cash assistance programs given to individuals and families under the provision of the Social Security Act, which established specific categories of persons in need of cash assistance including the aged, blind and permanently disabled (Supplemental Security Income), and children (Aid to Families with Dependent Children, now Temporary Assistance to Needy Families)

Cause-and-effect relationship   A relationship between factors in which one or more factors can be shown to directly cause a change in an additional factor or set of factors

Charity Organization Society (COS)   The first relief organization in the United States that developed a systematic program to help the needy; promoting "scientific philanthropy" that incorporated individual assessment and development of coordinated service plans before providing services

Child neglect   A condition in which a caretaker responsible for a child either deliberately or by extraordinary inattentiveness fails to meet a child's basic needs, including failure to provide adequate food, clothing, shelter, medical assistance, or education and/or to supervise a child appropriately

Child protective services   Mandated services provided by state social services agencies to families who abuse or neglect their children, for the purpose of protecting children whose safety is seriously endangered by the actions or inactions of their caretaker

Child welfare service delivery system   A network of agencies and programs that provides social services to children, youth, and families

Child Welfare League of America (CWLA)   A national organization consisting of agencies, professionals, and citizens interested in the well-being of children and families; CWLA promotes standards for services, advocates for child welfare policies and programs, conducts research, and provides publications related to child welfare issues

Child welfare services   Social services that supplement or substitute for parental care and supervision when parents are unable to fulfill parental responsibilities and that improve conditions for children and their families

Children with special needs   Children of color, who are older, who have physical or emotional disabilities, or who are members of sibling groups; term used in reference to adoption

Civil Rights Act   Federal legislation passed in 1964 and amended in 1965 that prohibits discrimination based on race, gender, religion, color, or ethnicity in public facilities, government programs or those operated or funded by the federal government, and employment

Class   The stratification of individuals and groups according to their social and economic assets

Classism   Discrimination toward members of a group because of their economic status

Client system   Individuals, families, groups, organizations, or communities at whom intervention is directed to enhance social functioning

Client-centered therapy   Intervention based on the perspective that the client knows most about his or her problems and needs; the therapist seeks to provide an acceptable emotional climate where the client can work out solutions with support and reflection from the therapist

Clinical social workers   Persons whose major focus is to provide clinical social work services, usually individual, group, or family counseling; often in a psychiatric, hospital, residential treatment, or mental health facility; usually requires an MSW (also called *psychiatric social worker* in some settings)

Closed system   A system with a boundary that is difficult to permeate; such systems are usually unreceptive to outsiders

Codependent   A person who lets someone else's behaviors control her or his functioning and focuses on meeting that person's needs, controlling that person's behaviors instead of his or her own

Collective perspective   Holds that social problems reflect fundamental socioeconomic circumstances, barriers to access, and lack of opportunity

Community   A group of individuals who usually live near each other; who share a common environment, including public and private resources, and who identify themselves with that community

Community development   A social work approach to working with communities that considers and respects the diversity of a community's population and uses those differences to achieve positive outcomes for all of its citizens

Community organization   A method of social work practice that involves the development of community resources to meet human needs

Commuter families   Families in which spouses are employed in different locations, often in different parts of the country

Comparable worth   The concept that persons should receive measurably equal pay for the same type of work, regardless of their gender

Comparative social work   The comparison of what social workers do in nations other than one's own

Competencies   Skills that are essential to perform certain functions; social workers must have competencies in a number of areas to be effective professionals

Consumer price index (CPI)   A measure of the average change in prices over time for a fixed "market basket" of goods and services purchased by a specified group of consumers

Contracting   A process of formulating a verbal or written agreement with a client system of established goals based on identified needs, usually including the steps that will be taken to meet those goals, the entities involved, and target dates for completion

Council on Social Work Education (CSWE)   The national organization of schools of social work that focuses on social work education and serves as the accrediting body for professional social work undergraduate (BSW) and master's (MSW) programs

County agent   An employee of a county extension office funded by the U.S. Department of Agriculture; provides technical assistance to persons living in rural areas, including agricultural and home management, as well as community and family services

Courts   Legal institutions in which lawyers play the leading roles and make most of the decisions

Criminal codes   Define the types of conduct that are criminal and establish a range of penalties for such behavior

Criminal justice system   The means used to enforce those standards of conduct required to protect individuals and property and to maintain a sense of justice in the community

Crisis intervention   Intervention provided when a crisis exists to the extent that one's usual coping resources threaten individual or family functioning

Cultural pluralism   The existence of two or more diverse cultures within a given society where each maintains its own traditions and special interests within the confines of the total society

Culture shock   Feelings that may occur when moving to an unfamiliar cultural environment; often results in temporary or long-lasting effects such as anxiety or depression

Custody   A legal charge given to a person requiring her or him to provide certain types of care and to exercise certain control in regards to another individual, as in parental child custody

Deinstitutionalization   A philosophy that advocates care of individuals with mental health problems and developmental disabilities in local community outpatient programs, whenever appropriate to the client's needs, as opposed to hospitalization in an institution

Delinquency   Behavior of juveniles that would be criminal in adults

Depressant   An agent that reduces a bodily functional activity such as staying awake or an instinctive desire such as eating

Deterrence factors   Those things that are likely to stop people from committing crimes

Developmental delay   Delay in communication, self-help, social-emotional, motor skills, sensory development, or cognition in comparison to skills typically observed in other individuals within the same age range

Developmental disability   A severe, chronic disability resulting from physical or mental impairment, usually prior to age 21, which results in substantial limitations of the individual's social, emotional, intellectual, and/or physical functioning

Developmental theory   A theory of human development that emphasizes psychological adjustment to the demands from the environment; these demands change as the individual moves through the life cycle

Devolution   The transfer of responsibility for social welfare programs from the federal government to state and local governments

Diagnostic and Statistical Manual of Mental Disorders (DSM)   A classification system of types of mental disorders that incorporates both organic and environmental factors, developed by the American Psychiatric Association for assessment and intervention purposes (now in its fourth edition, referred to as the *DSM-IV*)

Digital divide   The gap between the technological competence of people with ready access to technology compared to those with limited or no access to technology

Direct practice   A method of social work involving face-to-face contact with individuals, families, groups, and organizations and actual provision of services by the social worker for the purpose of addressing unmet needs; also referred to as *casework* or *social casework*

Disability insurance   A government fund established by the U.S. government in 1957 that provides cash benefits to workers who become totally and permanently disabled; note that some employers also now offer private disability insurance

Disciplinary research   Research designed to expand the body of knowledge of a particular discipline; also called *pure* or *basic research*

Disengagement theory   Theory related to aging based on the premise that as adults decline physically, they have less need and desire for social interaction and progressively become disengaged from social roles

Displaced workers   Persons age 20 and older who have lost or left jobs because their place of employment closed, there wasn't sufficient work for them to do, or their position or shift was eliminated

Disposition   The legal process by which judges decide how best to resolve delinquency cases

Diversion   A process by which persons coming to the attention of the criminal justice system are diverted to other programs such as social services, community services, or educational (defensive driving) programs, rather than going through the court process

Downshifting   The voluntary limiting of job demands so employees can devote increased time to their families and to themselves

Downsizing   Reduction in workforce and/or scope of goods and services produced or delivered to remain economically competitive and/or manage decreasing resources

Dual-career family   A family in which both partners/spouses have careers outside the family

Dual diagnosis   A determination that an individual has other diagnosable emotional problems in addition to substance abuse

Dysfunctional   Impaired or abnormal functioning

Earned Income Tax Credit   A provision of the federal income tax system to give a cash supplement to working parents with low incomes; parents file a tax statement, and if their taxable earnings are below a specific amount, they receive a check for a percentage of their earnings regardless of whether they paid that amount or less in taxes

Educational group   A group formed for the purpose of transmitting knowledge and enabling participants to acquire more complex skills, such as parenting

Ego psychology   A theoretical perspective that emphasizes ego growth and development

Elizabethan Poor Law   Legislation passed in England in 1601 that established categories of the poor, including the deserving poor (orphans, widows, and others) and the nondeserving poor (able-bodied males) and the treatment they were to receive from national and local governments; this law established precedents for policies toward the poor in the United States

Employee assistance program (EAP)   A workplace-sponsored program providing mental health and social services to employees and their families; services may be provided directly at the workplace or through a contractual arrangement by a social service agency

Empowerment   A process to help others increase their personal, interpersonal, or political power so they can take action themselves to improve their lives

Enabler   A person whose behavior facilitates another person's behavior to continue; used most often to describe situations in families in which substance abuse is a problem, and other family members enable the substance abuse to continue by their reinforcing behaviors

Encounter group   A group oriented toward assisting individuals in developing more self-awareness and interpersonal skills through in-depth experiential activities and extensive group sharing

Entitlement   A social welfare program that any individual is entitled to if certain eligibility requirements are met; such programs are based on numbers of individuals in need of the services rather than other limitations, such as resources available or caps put on funding government bodies

Entropy   Unavailable energy in a closed system that creates dysfunction within that system and eventually results in the system's inability to function

Equal Rights Amendment (ERA)   A proposed amendment to the U.S. Constitution to assure the complete and equal rights of all citizens without regard to race, color, creed, or gender; the amendment was not ratified by the number of states necessary for its adoption

Equifinality   The idea that the final state of a system can be achieved in many different ways

Ethics   A framework for determining what is right and wrong and how specific situations should be handled; the National Association of Social Workers Code of Ethics relates to the moral principles of social work practice

Etiology of crime   Theories relating to the origins or causes of crime, including physiological, psychological, and sociological perspectives

Evaluation   A method of showing how a client system or a program has achieved or failed to achieve established goals

Evaluative research   Research undertaken to show how a program achieves (or fails to achieve) its goals

Exchange theory   Theory based on the premise that relationships are exchanges of goods and services, with those in power having the goods and services; in relation to aging, this theory attributes the social withdrawal of the elderly to a loss of power as they lose their income and move to pensions and Medicare

Exosystem level   The level of social environment that incorporates community factors in which an individual does not participate directly but that affects the individual's functioning, such as school board and city council actions

Family   A group of individuals bonded together through marriage, kinship, adoption, or mutual agreement

Family and Medical Leave Act   Requires employers with more than 50 employees to provide up to 12 weeks of unpaid leave to eligible employees for certain medical or family reasons such as the birth of a child or the serious illness of a child, spouse, or parent

Family preservation programs   Family intervention programs whose goal is to keep families together by increasing the coping skills and competencies of family members

Family roles   Roles taken on by family members as a way to cope with the behaviors of other family members and maintain the family system's patterns of functioning

Family violence   The use of force by one family member against another, usually by a family member who is more powerful against a member who is less powerful

Feminist therapy   Intervention that empowers individuals who may be members of an oppressed group to find their own voice and view themselves as equals as they make decisions about their lives

Feminization of poverty   A term used to describe the result of the increasing numbers of single-parent women being classified as poor

Flexiplace   A system that allows employees to work at alternate work sites as opposed to a standard workplace (for example, working in their own homes)

Flextime   A system that allows employees to have varied work hours as opposed to standard work hours (for example, working from 6 A.M. to 3 P.M. rather than from 8 A.M. to 5 P.M.)

Food stamps   In-kind assistance program funded by the U.S. Department of Agriculture designed to supplement the food-purchasing power of eligible low-income households to allow families to maintain nutritious diets and to expand the market for agricultural goods

Foster care   A form of temporary substitute care in which children live with a family other than their birth family until they are able to be returned to their birth family, adopted, or placed in a more permanent setting that best meets their needs

General assistance   Public assistance programs that provide financial aid to persons who are in need but do not qualify for federally authorized programs; usually administered by county and local government and also referred to as *relief programs*

Generalist   A social worker who operates from a systems/ecological perspective, using multiple interventions in working with client systems at the individual, family, group, organizational, community, or societal level and using the strengths of those systems to empower them to change their environment

Generalizable   The ability of a theory to use what happens in one situation to explain what happens in other situations

Gerontology   The study of aging and the aging process

Global village   A place where social and economic justice, lasting peace, and a sustainable environment are achieved

Goal setting   A process used by social workers and other helping professionals with client systems to identify ways to meet their needs; usually includes the identification of specific goals, steps to be taken in meeting those goals, resources needed, and a time frame for completion

Great Society   A social reform program proposed by the Johnson administration in the 1960s to improve the quality of life for all Americans, with emphasis on the poor and disenfranchised; the War on Poverty was one of the major Great Society programs

Gross domestic product (GDP)   The total monetary value of a nation's annual output of goods and services

Group   A social unit consisting of individuals who define status and role relationships to one another; it possesses its own set of values and norms and regulates the behavior of its members

Group work   A process that seeks to stimulate and support more adaptive personal functioning and social skills of individuals through structured group interaction

Hallucinogen   A substance that induces hallucinations

Head Start   A comprehensive early childhood education program, initially established as a Great Society program, which provides developmental learning for preschool children with health care, social services, and parent education components

Health   A state of complete physical, mental, and social well-being that is not merely the absence of disease or infirmity

Health and welfare services   Programs providing services that facilitate individual health and welfare, such as maternal health and child care, public health, family planning, and child welfare services

Health care   Services provided to individuals to prevent or promote recovery from illness or disease

Health maintenance organization (HMO)   Prepaid medical group practice for which individuals pay monthly fees and receive specific types of health at no cost or minimum cost per visit

Health risk factors   Factors that affect a person's health and place her or him at risk for serious health problems (for example, smoking)

HIV-positive   The first stage of acquired immunodeficiency syndrome (AIDS), also called the *seropositive state,* which occurs when a person has tested positively for AIDS and has HIV (human immunodeficiency virus) antibodies in his or her blood

Home health care   Health care provided in a person's home as opposed to a hospital or other institutional health care setting; made available through outreach visits by social workers, nurses, physicians, and other health practitioners

Home-based, family-centered services   Services delivered to children and families in their own homes, with a focus on preserving the family system and strengthening the family to bring about needed change in an effort to prevent family breakup

Homeless   Having no fixed, adequate, regular nighttime residence

Homophobia   A fear of homosexuals and homosexuality

Hospices   Programs for terminally ill individuals and their families that enable them to die with dignity and support, often away from a hospital

Hypothesis   A tentative assumption derived from theory that is capable of empirical verification

Implementation strategy   A plan for carrying out steps required to put a program or plan into practice

Impulse-ridden behavior   Behavior exhibited by neglecting parents with low impulse control, including acting inconsistently, leaving a child alone or in an unsafe situation without realizing the consequences to the child, or giving higher priority to a new activity

Incarceration   The placing of someone in prison

Incest   Sexual abuse between family members

Inclusive   The ability of a theory to consistently explain events in the same way each time they occur

Individualist perspective   Holds that individual problems are the result of bad choices, personal dysfunction, and a culture of poverty

Individuals with Disabilities Act (IDEA)   Federal legislation that mandates the provision of special education resources for children and youth with disabilities, including funding for early intervention programs for infants and toddlers and their families

Indoor relief   Assistance given to the poor and the needy through placement in institutions, such as poorhouses, orphanages, and prisons

Infant mortality rate   The number of infants who die at birth or before they reach a certain age compared to the total number of infants, both living and not living, within that age range, within a specified geographic location and a specified time frame

Institutional discrimination   Discrimination that occurs as the result of accepted beliefs and behaviors and is codified in societal roles and policies

Intake   The process that follows police referrals to juvenile court

Intermediate punishments   A middle ground between either/or choices of probation or parole

International Federation of Social Workers (IFSW)   An organization founded in 1956 to promote social work as a profession through cooperation and action on an international basis and to work toward social and economic justice throughout the world

International social welfare   The field of practice concerned with promoting basic human well-being in a context involving cross-national efforts

International social work   The practice of social work to meet social welfare needs from an international perspective

Intervention   Planned activities designed to improve the social functioning of a client or client system

Intrapsychic   Being or occurring within the mind, psyche, or personality

Job sharing   The sharing of one full-time job by two or more individuals; this practice is increasingly being allowed by employers and is advantageous to those women with young children and persons with disabilities who do not want to work outside the home on a full-time basis

Juvenile correctional institutions   Secure and nonsecure facilities used to detain juveniles who have committed status or other offenses

Juvenile courts   Courts structured to act in a child's best interest

Laissez-faire   An economic theory developed by Adam Smith that emphasizes persons taking care of themselves and limits government intervention

Least detrimental alternative   A decision-making premise that places priority on making decisions regarding children based on which decision will be least damaging or upsetting to the child

Least restrictive environment   A living environment for an individual that maintains the greatest degree of freedom, self-determination, autonomy, dignity, and integrity for the individual, often while he or she participates in treatment or receives services

Life span model   A framework that focuses on relationships between individuals and their environments with major emphasis on where persons are developmentally and what transitional life processes they are experiencing (for example, marriage, retirement)

Living wage   Three times the amount of money needed in a given location to rent an apartment of a given size; rental costs (fair market rents) are established by the U.S. Department of Housing and Urban Development (HUD)

Living will   A formal written statement made by an individual specifying the individual's wishes about how her or his death should be handled, including delineation of which medical procedures and life support systems, if any, should be used and under what conditions

Long-term care facility   A program that provides long-term care to individuals, including the elderly and people with disabilities; state and federal regulations have established specific requirements facilities must meet to be classified as long-term care facilities

Lower criminal courts   Courts with the power to decide minor cases and to conduct pretrial proceedings

Macrosystem level   The level of social environment that incorporates societal factors affecting an individual, including cultural ideologies, assumptions, and social policies that define and organize a given society

Managed care   Health care delivery that limits the use and costs of services and measures performance

Managed care system   A system of health care delivery that limits the use and costs of services and measures performance

Market basket concept   A way of measuring the number of people in poverty based on a formula that includes the estimated costs a family spends to provide a minimum nutritional diet, with adjustments for family size, and a set proportion of income families generally spend for food; families spending less than this proportion of their income are considered below the poverty line

Mediation   Intervention between a divorcing or divorced couple to promote settlement of child custody and property issues to reconcile differences and reach compromises; mediation teams usually include an attorney and a social worker

Medicaid   Federally and state-funded public assistance program that provides health care to low-income individuals and families based on a means test using strict eligibility guidelines

Medical model   A model that considers those with emotional problems as sick and thus not responsible for their behavior; focuses on deficits and dysfunction of client and family rather than their strengths, with little attention given to environmental aspects

Medicare   Federal health insurance program for the elderly

Mesosystem level   The level of social environment that incorporates interactions and interrelations among those persons, groups, and settings that comprise an individual's microsystem

Microsystem level   The level of social environment that includes the individual, including intrapsychic characteristics and past life experiences, and all the persons and groups in his or her day-to-day environment

Migrant workers   People engaged in crop harvesting, which requires that families move from place to place to secure employment

Minority group   A category of people distinguished by physical or cultural traits that are used by the majority group to single them out for differential and unequal treatment

Moral treatment   A philosophy among professionals and advocates working with the mentally ill in the late 1700s and early 1800s that advocated a caring, humane approach, as opposed to a punitive, repressive environment

Multidisciplinary team approach   An approach to working with clients that involves the shared expertise of professionals from a variety of disciplines, such as social workers, health professionals, educators, attorneys, and psychologists

Narcotics   Drugs such as opium and its derivatives, morphine, and heroin that dull the senses, relieve pain, and induce profound sleep

National Association of Mental Health (NAMH)   A national association of professionals and organizations concerned about mental health issues and care of persons with mental health problems; provides education, advocacy, and research

National Association of Social Workers (NASW)   The major national professional organization for social workers, which promotes ethics and quality in social work practice; stimulates political participation and social action; and maintains eligibility standards for membership

National Institute of Mental Health (NIMH)   A federal agency created by the U.S. Congress in 1949 to address mental health concerns; now a part of the U.S. Department of Health and Human Services

National Institute of Occupational Safety and Health (NIOSH)   Federal government program housed within the U.S. Department of Health and Human Services that addresses research and technology issues relating to occupational health and safety and sets federal standards for safe storage, use, and disposal of hazardous materials

Natural group   A group in which members participate as a result of common interests, shared experiences, similar backgrounds and values, and personal satisfactions derived from interaction with other group members (for example, a street gang)

Natural helping networks   An informal system of support available to individuals as opposed to a professional service delivery system; includes individuals such as family members, friends, neighbors, coworkers, and members of organizations in which an individual may be involved, such as a church or synagogue; also called *natural support systems*

Natural support systems   Informal systems of support available to individuals in contrast to professional service delivery systems; examples of natural support systems include family members, friends, neighborhoods, coworkers, and members of organizations in which an individual may be involved, such as a church or synagogue; also called *helping networks*

Nonorganic failure to thrive   A medical condition that results when a child is three percentiles or more below the normal range for height and weight and no organic reason can be determined; placing a child in a hospital and providing an adequate diet and nurturing will cause the child to gain height and weight, suggesting a lack of parental care as the cause

Occupational Safety and Health Act   Sets health and safety standards in industrial workplaces through onsite inspections and citations for violations

Occupational social work   Social work services provided through the workplace that focus on the relationships between work stresses and other systems within which individuals function; also called *industrial social work*

Official poverty   A way of measuring poverty that provides a set of income thresholds adjusted for household size, age of household head, and number of children under 18 years old

Old Age Survivors Disability Insurance (OASDI)   A Social Security insurance program established as part of the Social Security Act of 1935 that provides limited payments to those eligible elderly persons and/or their dependents who have been employed and have had taxes deducted from their wages matched by their employer paid into a funding pool

Omnibus Budget Reconciliation Act of 1987 (OBRA)   Federal legislation that mandated major nursing home reforms, including increased rights for residents, written care plans, training for staff, and the employment of certified social workers

Omnibus Health Care Rescue Act of 1989 (HB 18)   Legislation designed to provide additional health care resources with emphasis on rural areas

Open system   A system whose boundaries are permeated easily

Opportunity structure   The accessibility of opportunities for an individual within that individual's environment, including personal and environmental factors such as physical traits, intelligence, family, and availability of employment

Oppression   Unjust use of power against nondominant groups by the dominant group

Outdoor relief   Cash or in-kind assistance given to persons in need, allowing them to remain in their own homes (for example, public assistance payments for food and fuel)

Outsourcing   The practice by U.S. businesses of having portions or all of their production carried out outside of the United States and its territories

Pastoral counselor   A person who provides counseling service under the auspices of a religious organization, which usually includes an emphasis on spiritual well-being; usually a member of the clergy

Permanency planning   An idea stating that all child welfare services provided should be centered around a plan directed toward a permanent, nurturing home for that child

Person-environment fit   The fit between a person's needs, rights, goals, and capacities and the physical and social environment within which the person functions

Physical child abuse   A physical act of harm or threatened harm against a child by a caretaker that results in physical or mental injury to a child, including beating, hitting, slapping, burning, shaking, or throwing

Planned change   An orderly approach to addressing client needs based on assessment, knowledge of the client system's capacity for change, and focused intervention

Plea bargaining   Negotiations among the prosecutor, the defendant, and the defendant's counsel that lead to the defendant entering a guilty plea in exchange for a reduction in charges or the prosecutor's promise to recommend a more lenient sentence

Policy research   Research that focuses on evaluating the effects of proposed or existing social policy on constituent populations

Populations at risk   Groups that experience prejudice, discrimination, and oppression from the dominant group

Poverty   A determination that a household's income is inadequate, judged by a specific standard

Prejudice   An irrational attitude of hostility directed against an individual, a group, a race, or their supposed characteristics

Primary prevention   A program targeted at the total population to prevent a problem from occurring

Primary setting   A setting in which the types of services a professional provides match the primary goals of the setting (e.g., a hospital is a primary setting for a nurse but a secondary setting for a social worker)

Private health insurance   Health insurance available to individuals and families through the workplace or through purchase of policies with private insurance companies

Private nonprofit social agency   Nongovernmental agencies that provide social services, spending all of their funds to meet the goals of the agency with no financial profit earned by agency owners, directors, or employees

Private practice   In social work, the delivery of client services for pay on an independent, autonomous basis rather than under the auspices of an agency; social workers in most states have an MSW degree, supervision by an advanced practitioner, and pass a licensing or certification examination before establishing a private practice

Private sector   Includes programs and agencies funded and operated by nonpublic entities (for instance, voluntary and proprietary agencies and private businesses)

Probation   Replaces incarceration, in which those convicted face supervised release into the community

Problem-solving approach   A common intervention used by social workers, based on client's motivation and capacity for change and opportunities available to the client to facilitate the change. The client and worker assess needs, identify problems and needs to be addressed, develop a plan to address problems and needs, and implement and monitor the plan, revising as needed.

Pro bono   Providing services at no cost; professionals such as lawyers and social workers do pro bono work with low-income clients for the public good

Psychiatry   A branch of medicine that deals with mental, emotional, or behavioral disorders

Psychoanalysis   A method of dealing with emotional problems that focuses on interpsychic functioning (internal conflicts with the individual)

Psychobiology   A term describing the interactions between biological and environmental factors in understanding human behavior

Psychological maltreatment   Acting out against a person emotionally or psychologically, such as verbally belittling or attacking a person constantly, or failing to meet emotional needs through acts of omission, such as not providing love, attention, and/or emotional support to a person

Psychological parent   A person viewed by a child as being his or her parental figure from a psychological or emotional standpoint rather than a birth relationship; for example, if a boy were being raised by his grandparents and rarely saw his mother, they would be his psychological parents. Many court decisions are being made based on the concept of a psychological parent.

Psychology   A science based on the study of mind and behavior; involves many subspecialties

Psychometric instruments   Tests used to measure psychological functioning

Psychotropic drug   A type of drug used in the treatment of mental health problems, including depression and psychoses, that has resulted in major reductions in numbers of individuals with emotional problems needing long-term hospitalization

Public assistance   Programs that provide income, medical care, and social services to individuals and families based on economic need, paid from state and local taxes, to provide a socially established minimum standard usually set by the state; Temporary Assistance to Needy Families (TANF), food stamps, and Medicaid are public assistance programs

Public health insurance   Insurance provided by the public sector to those in need who are not covered by private insurance programs and meet eligibility requirements, such as Medicaid

Public sector   Programs and agencies funded and operated by government entities, including public schools, agencies, and hospitals

Reactive depressive behavior   Behavior resulting from depression, often due to a loss, that can affect the ability to parent and lead to child neglect

Reality therapy   An intervention, based on the assumption that people are responsible for their own behavior, that effects change by confronting individuals about irresponsible behaviors and encouraging them to accept responsibility for their behaviors and to develop positive self-worth through positive behavior

Recidivism   Return to previous behaviors; for example, when persons released from prison commit new crimes

Recreation group   A group of individuals who engage in recreational activities in a monitored environment

Recreation skill group   A group designed to promote development of a skill within a recreational or enjoyment context

Rehabilitation   Philosophy of punishment that aims at preventing future crimes by changing individual offenders

Relative poverty   Poverty measured by comparing the unit being measured (for example, individuals or families) to a set standard for that unit, such as income, with those falling below that standard identified as being in poverty

Residential treatment   Treatment provided in 24-hour care facilities for persons with mental health or substance abuse problems or developmental disabilities; such programs are usually considered less restrictive than psychiatric hospitals

Retirement   Leaving paid employment, usually based on age; retirees may receive pensions or Social Security benefits depending on their work history and eligibility for such programs

Rural   A social, occupational, and cultural way of life for persons living in the country or in rural communities with fewer than 2,500 persons

Rural social work   Social work provided in rural areas usually based on a generalist practice model that involves the actual provision of many services rather than linking individuals with other social service resources

School social work   A social work approach that involves working with children, youth, and their families within a school setting; school social workers deal directly with children, youth, and their families as well as teachers, school administrators, and other community resources

Secondary prevention   Targeted at specified groups within a larger population that are determined to be "at risk" or more likely to experience a specific problem

than the larger population to prevent the problem from occurring

Secondary setting   A setting in which the types of services a professional provides differ from the primary focus of the setting (for example, a social worker in a hospital works in a secondary setting, while a social worker in a social services agency works in a primary setting)

Selective enforcement   The use of discretion to enforce some laws sometimes against some people

Self-concept   The image a person has of herself or himself in relation to appearance, ability, motivation, and capacity to react to the environment; derived primarily through feedback from others

Self-help group   A group of individuals with similar problems that meets for the purpose of providing support and information to each other and for mutual problem solving—for example, Parents Anonymous and Alcoholics Anonymous

Sexism   Discrimination against an individual because of gender

Sexual abuse   The use of a child by an adult for sexual or emotional gratification in a sexual way, such as fondling, exposure, sexual intercourse, and exploitation, including child pornography

Single-subject designs   Research designs that evaluate the impact of interventions or policy changes on a single client or case

Social action   A social work approach to working with communities that stresses organization and group cohesion in confrontational approaches geared to modify or eliminate institutional power bases that negatively impact the community

Social agencies   Organizations whose primary focus is to address social problems

Social casework   A social work method involving face-to-face contact with individuals, families, groups, or organizations, by which the social worker provides services directly to clients for the purpose of addressing unmet needs; also referred to as *direct practice*

Social group work   A social work method involving intervention with groups of individuals that uses structured interaction to promote individual and group functioning and well-being

Social inequality   Unequal treatment of social groups based on factors such as economic and social status, age, ethnicity, sexual preference, or gender

Social insurance   Financial assistance for those whose income has been curtailed because of retirement, death, or long-term disability of the family breadwinner; paid to former working persons or their dependents through a tax on earned income

Social justice   Fairness and equity in the protection of civil and human rights, the treatment of individuals, the distribution of opportunity, and the assurance of personal and economic opportunity

Social planning   A social work approach to working with communities that emphasizes modification of institutional practices through the application of knowledge, values, and theory; a practical, rational approach

Social Security Act   Major social welfare legislation passed by the U.S. Congress in 1935, establishing social insurance programs based on taxes paid by working persons; public assistance programs to provide for those who do not qualify for social insurance programs and cannot provide for themselves or their families financially; and health and welfare services for children, families, the disabled, and the aged such as child welfare services, maternal and child health services, and services for the disabled

Social Security   An insurance program established as part of the Social Security Act that provides limited payments to eligible elderly persons who have been employed and have had taxes deducted from their wages, matched by their employers, and paid into a funding pool, or to their dependents

Social study   The process of obtaining relevant information about the client system and perceived needs

Social welfare   Efforts organized by societies to facilitate the well-being of their members, usually focused on activities that seek to prevent, alleviate, or contribute to the solution of a selected set of social problems

Social welfare policy   A specific course of actions taken to address an identified social problem, with emphasis on the decisions and choices that help determine those actions

Social work   The major profession that implements planned change activities prescribed by social welfare institutions through intervention with individuals, families, and groups or at community, organizational, and societal levels to enhance or restore social functioning

Social worker   A member of the social work profession who works with individuals, families, groups, organizations, communities, or societies to improve social functioning

Socialization group   A group of individuals whose goal is to help participants develop socially acceptable behavior and behavioral competency

Socialization   The process of learning to become a social being; the acquisition of knowledge, values, abilities, and skills that are essential to function as a member of the society within which the individual lives

Sociologist   An expert who studies society, its organization and demographic structure, and patterns of human interaction, including norms, values, and behavior

Solution-focused therapy   Short-term cognitive behavioral intervention that emphasizes the present situation rather than events in the client's past; strategies include focus on very specific situations and tasks that are assigned to clients to work on between sessions

Specialization   Practice of social work focused on a specific population or field of practice requiring specialized knowledge and skill; contrasts with *generalist practice*

Specific deterrent   A program or sentence targeted at an individual to discourage him or her from repeating inappropriate/illegal behavior

Spillover effect   A term describing the situation when feelings, attitudes, and behaviors from one domain in a person's life have a positive or a negative impact on other domains (such as from the workplace to the family)

Steady state   The constant adjustment of a system moving toward its goal while maintaining order and stability within

Stereotype   A standardized mental picture of a group attributed to all group members

Strengths perspective   An approach to social work that focuses on the strengths of the client system and the broader environment within which it functions rather than on the deficiencies

Substance abuse   Improper use of mood-altering substances such as drugs that results in detrimental effects on an individual's personal life, including school, job, family, friends, health, spiritual life, or the law

Substitute care   Out-of-home care provided for children when parents are unwilling or unable to provide care in their own homes; types of substitute care include foster care, group home care, and residential treatment and are determined based on the child's needs

Supplemental Security Income (SSI)   A program administered in conjunction with the Social Security

Program to provide cash assistance to needy aged, blind, and/or people with permanent and total disabilities who meet certain eligibility standards established by state and federal regulations

Support services   Services that provide support to individuals and families such as health care, legal assistance, housing, and social services

Synergy   The combined energy of smaller parts of a larger system that is greater than the sum of the energy of those parts

System   A social unit consisting of interdependent, interacting parts

Systems/ecological framework   A major framework used to understand individual, family, community, organizational, and societal events and behaviors that emphasizes the interactions and interdependence between individuals and their environments

Task-centered method   A short-term therapeutic approach to intervention that stresses the selection of specific tasks to be worked on within a limited time frame to address the needs of a client system

Telecommunications   A way of communicating electronically that allows remote sites to have access to information and consultation

Temporary Assistance to Needy Families (TANF)   A public assistance program that provides cash assistance to families (primarily single-parent women) with children in need because of the loss of financial support as a result of death, disability, or the continued absence of a second parent from the home; assistance is available on a time-limited basis and requires participation in programs that prepare adults in the family for participation in the workforce; TANF replaced the AFDC program

Tertiary prevention   Efforts targeted at individuals who have already experienced a specific problem to prevent that problem from reoccurring

Testable   The ability of a theory to be measured accurately and validly

Theory   A way of organizing facts or sets of facts to describe, explain, or predict events

Therapeutic groups   Groups requiring skilled professional leaders who assist group members in addressing intensive personal and emotional problems

Trial courts   Courts with the power to conduct pretrial and trial proceedings in all criminal cases

U.S. Children's Bureau   The first federal department established by the federal government in 1912 to address the needs of children and families; federal programs addressing problems of abuse and neglect, runaway youth, adoption and foster care, and other child welfare services are currently housed within the U.S. Department of Health and Human Services

U.S. Department of Agriculture   A federal department that oversees the food stamp program and houses the Agricultural Extension Service, which provides services targeted to rural areas

U.S. Department of Health and Human Services   A federal department that oversees the implementation of legislation relating to health and human services, including public assistance programs, child welfare services, and services for the elderly

Underclass   The lowest socioeconomic group in society characterized by chronic poverty and the inability to pull themselves out of their condition

Underemployment   Persons placed in jobs that are at a lower level than those for which they are qualified

Unemployment compensation   A program established by the Social Security Act that is funded by taxes assessed by employers and is available to eligible unemployed workers

Values   Assumptions, convictions, or beliefs about the manner in which people should behave and the principles that should govern behavior

Voluntary sector   A third sector of society, along with the public and for-profit proprietary sectors, that includes private, nonprofit social agencies

Welfare devolution   Transfer of responsibility for public welfare programs from the federal government to individual states and localities

Workers' compensation   An insurance program that is funded by taxes assessed to employers and is available to eligible workers who are injured on the job or experience job-related injuries or illnesses

Working poor   Full-time workers who earn a salary below the federal poverty level

World citizenship   People accepting responsibility in this interdependent world by thinking and acting as citizens of that world

Index

TO THE OWNER OF THIS BOOK:

I hope that you have found *Social Work and Social Welfare: An Introduction,* **Fourth Edition** useful. So that this book can be improved in a future edition, would you take the time to complete this sheet and return it? Thank you.

School and address: _____

_____

Department: _____

Instructor's name: _____

1. What I like most about this book is: _____

_____

_____

2. What I like least about this book is: _____

_____

_____

3. My general reaction to this book is: _____

_____

_____

4. The name of the course in which I used this book is: _____

_____

5. Were all of the chapters of the book assigned for you to read? _____

   If not, which ones weren't? _____

6. In the space below, or on a separate sheet of paper, please write specific suggestions for improving this book and anything else you'd care to share about your experience in using this book.

_____

_____

OPTIONAL:

Your name: _____ Date: _____

May we quote you, either in promotion for *Social Work and Social Welfare: An Introduction,*
Fourth Edition, or in future publishing ventures?

Yes: _____ No: _____

Sincerely yours,

Rosalie Ambrosino, Joseph Heffernan,

Guy Shuttlesworth, and Robert Ambrosino

FOLD HERE

NO POSTAGE
NECESSARY
IF MAILED
IN THE
UNITED STATES

BUSINESS REPLY MAIL
FIRST CLASS   PERMIT NO. 358   PACIFIC GROVE, CA

POSTAGE WILL BE PAID BY ADDRESSEE

ATTN: Social Work Editor: Lisa Gebo

BROOKS/COLE/THOMSON LEARNING
511 FOREST LODGE ROAD
PACIFIC GROVE, CA   93950-9968

FOLD HERE